EXAMPLES & EXPLANATIONS

Agency, Partnerships, and LLCs

Agency, Partnerships, and LLCs

Sixth Edition

Daniel S. Kleinberger
Professor Emeritus—Mitchell Hamline School of Law
Member, American Law Institute
Member, American College of Commercial Finance Lawyers
Lubaroff Award (2019)
Uniform Law Commission
Special award for extraordinary service, 2018
Reporter, Co-Reporter, uniform business organizations
acts, 1997–2021

ASPEN PUBLISHING

To contact Customer Service, e-mail customer.service@aspenpublishing.com, call 1-800-950-5259, or mail correspondence to:

Aspen Publishing
Attn: Order Department
1 Wall Street
Burlington, MA 01803

1 2 3 4 5 6 7 8 9 0

ISBN 979-8-8920-7946-4

Library of Congress Cataloging-in-Publication Data

Names: Kleinberger, Daniel S., 1950- author
Title: Agency, partnerships, and LLCs / Daniel S Kleinberger, Professor Emeritus—Mitchell Hamline School of Law, Member, American Law Institute, Member, American College of Commercial Finance Lawyers, Lubaroff Award (2019), Uniform Law Commission, Special award for extraordinary service, 2018, Reporter, Co-Reporter, uniform business organizations acts, 1997–2021.
Description: Sixth Edition. | Burlington, MA : Aspen Publishing, 2025. | Series: Examples & explanations series | Includes bibliographical references and index. | Summary: "In the seven years between the publication of the first and second editions of this book, the law of unincorporated business associations underwent a revolution. The limited liability company (LLC) became the entity of choice for a myriad of enterprises, and the Revised Uniform Partnership Act (RUPA) revitalized the law of general partnerships. In some states, the annual number of newly formed LLCs grew to exceed the number of newly formed corporations, and RUPA-with its tilt toward entity continuity and its provisions on limited liability partnerships (LLPs)-made the "shielded" general partnership as usable and interesting as an LLC"—Provided by publisher.
Identifiers: LCCN 2025040547 (print) | LCCN 2025040548 (ebook) | ISBN 9798892079464 paperback | ISBN 9798892079488 ebook
Subjects: LCSH: Agency (Law)—United States—Outlines, syllabi, etc. | Partnership—United States—Outlines, syllabi, etc. | Private companies—United States—Outlines, syllabi, etc. | LCGFT: Study guides
Classification: LCC KF1345.Z9 K6 2025 (print) | LCC KF1345.Z9 (ebook)
LC record available at https://lccn.loc.gov/2025040547
LC ebook record available at https://lccn.loc.gov/2025040548

ABOUT ASPEN PUBLISHING

Aspen Publishing is a leading provider of legal education content and digital learning solutions in the United States and globally. Our innovative products and platforms—designed based on best practices in learning science—engage students and enhance outcomes. From textbooks and audiobooks authored by renowned experts to digital platforms and products like LEAF, Connected eBooks, Connected Quizzing, PracticePerfect, and JD-Next, we empower the next generation of legal professionals with innovative, trusted, and accessible resources.

The Aspen Casebook Series, affectionately known as the "red and black" casebooks among law faculty and students, includes hundreds of highly regarded textbooks across more than 80 disciplines. These range from foundational courses like Torts and Contracts to emerging electives such as Sustainability and the Law of Policing. Our study aids, including the popular *Examples & Explanations* series, help law students master complex topics with clarity and confidence.

Aspen's expertise extends to undergraduate education with our Paralegal, Criminal Justice, and Business Law series, offering the same hallmark quality to a broader audience. JD-Next, our groundbreaking online law school prep course and admissions test, provides a realistic preview of law school, equips students with essential skills for academic success, and evaluates their readiness for legal studies.

Aspen Publishing Is Proud to Be a UWorld Company

Since 2003, UWorld has been a global leader in developing high-quality learning tools for students preparing for high-stakes exams. With a commitment to excellence, UWorld has helped millions of students in undergraduate, graduate, and professional programs in fields such as medicine, nursing, finance, and law achieve their academic and career goals.

Founded by Chandra S. Pemmasani, M.D., during his medical residency, UWorld began focusing on medical education and has since expanded into various academic fields, including law. In 2020, UWorld launched its Legal vertical, starting with its comprehensive Multistate Bar Exam (MBE®) Question Bank, followed by the acquisition of Themis Bar Review, which integrated resources to provide a complete bar exam preparation experience. In 2024, UWorld expanded its offerings by acquiring Aspen Publishing, enhancing its suite of legal education products.

Today, UWorld offers an unparalleled range of study materials that blend active learning methods with expert content, ensuring students and educators can access the most effective resources. From bar preparation to law school success, UWorld is committed to supporting the next generation of legal professionals. Learn more at uworld.com.

October 7, 2023
In Memoriam

Summary of Contents

Contents

Abbreviations

The following abbreviations are used throughout this book.

ORGANIZATIONS

ALI = American Law Institute
ULC = the Uniform Law Commission (also known as the National Conference of Commissioners on Uniform State Laws)

RESTATEMENTS

R.2d = Restatement (Second) of Agency
R.3d = Restatement (Third) of Agency
R.EL = Restatement of the Law of Employment

UNIFORM ACTS (BY ENTITY TYPE)

General Partnership Acts

UPA (1914) = the first uniform general partnership act, approved in 1914
UPA (1997) = Revised Uniform Partnership Act, the revised general partnership act approved in 1997 (following a series of earlier-approved revisions that began in 1992)
UPA (2013) = the most recent uniform general partnership act (formally named UPA (1997) (Last Amended 2013)), a product of the ULC Harmonization Project[1]

1. For an explanation of this project, see Note on the ULC Harmonization Project.

Limited Partnership Acts

ULPA (1916) = the first uniform limited partnership act, approved in 1916

RULPA (1976) = the original Revised Uniform Limited Partnership Act, as approved in 1976

RULPA (1976/1985) = the Revised Uniform Limited Partnership Act, first approved in 1976 and substantially revised in 1985

ULPA (2001) = the first stand-alone uniform limited partnership act, approved in 2001, replacing RULPA (1976) and RULPA (1976/1985) entirely

ULPA (2013) = the current uniform limited partnership act (formally named ULPA (2001) (Last Amended 2013)), a product of the ULC Harmonization Project

Limited Liability Company Acts

ULLCA (1996) = the first uniform limited liability company act, approved in 1996

ULLCA (2006) = the Revised Uniform Limited Liability Company Act (often abbreviated as Re-ULLCA), approved in 2006

ULLCA (2013) = the current uniform limited liability company act (formally named ULLCA (2006) (Last Amended 2013)), a product of the ULC Harmonization Project

Treatise Source

Bishop & Kleinberger on LIMITED LIABILITY COMPANIES = BISHOP & KLEINBERGER ON LIMITED LIABILITY COMPANIES (1994; Supp. 2025–2)

Preface to Sixth Edition

In the seven years between the publication of the first and second editions of this book, the law of unincorporated business associations underwent a revolution. The limited liability company (LLC) became the entity of choice for a myriad of enterprises, and the Revised Uniform Partnership Act (RUPA) revitalized the law of general partnerships. In some states, the annual number of newly formed LLCs grew to exceed the number of newly formed corporations, and RUPA—with its tilt toward entity continuity and its provisions on limited liability partnerships (LLPs)—made the "shielded" general partnership as usable and interesting as an LLC.

In 2002, when the second edition was published, the National Conference of Commissioners on Uniform State Laws (NCCUSL) had just promulgated a new uniform limited partnership act—ULPA (2001)—and the American Law Institute (ALI) was hard at work on the Restatement (Third) of Agency.

In 2008, when the third edition was published, the ALI had just given final approval to the Restatement (Third) of Agency (paying particular attention to agency issues *within* business entities and other modern organizations), ULPA (2001) was gaining enactments across the country, NCCUSL had promulgated a Revised Uniform Limited Liability Company Act, and NCCUSL had begun referring to itself as the Uniform Law Commission (ULC).

By 2011, when the fourth edition was published, the prominence of LLCs had become indisputable, and case law—once scant—was legion. For almost all newly formed, closely held businesses, the LLC was the vehicle of choice. The law of partnerships had come to include an alphabet soup of varieties, and the common law of agency continued to significantly influence the analysis of matters ranging from the prosaic to the profound.

In 2017, when the fifth edition was published, business lawyers (unlike most law professors) had come to recognize the LLC as the dominant vehicle for business entities whose ownership interests are not publicly traded. Partnerships continued to be important—especially to house law firms—and agency issues and agency law were as ubiquitous as ever.

In 2025, as this edition is published, LLC law appears to have reached maturity—i.e., few doctrinal holes remain to be filled; seminal cases are accordingly rare.[1] LLC dominance continues, as does the cold shoulder from

1. There is one exception: the "series limited liability company" and "protected series"—an abstruse concept, located at the edge of limited liability company law, and of very restricted usefulness. Section 16.8 discusses the concept.

most law professors. Partnership law remains important; indeed, some of the most important developments in the implied covenant of good faith and fair dealing have involved limited partnerships.[2] As for the venerable common law of agency, it is front and center in key legal disputes arising from the "gig economy."[3]

The matters covered by this book thus continue to have great current importance. However, this "relevance" accounts for only half the benefits of studying these topics. Regardless of how you plan to use your legal training, studying agency law and the law of unincorporated business organizations will help you "think like a lawyer."

That phrase is a cliché and vague, but it is still useful to indicate (i) intellectual discipline and (ii) a specific approach to posing and answering questions. That approach includes a process that I have labeled "categories and consequences"—analyzing situations by defining categories of behavior and then attaching consequences to those categories. This is not the only way in which lawyers understand the world, but it is certainly a fundamental one.

Agency law is an excellent way to learn about categories and consequences. Indeed, the analytic training that comes with understanding agency law's approach to issues rivals the analytic training available in confronting the Rule Against Perpetuities. Fortunately, mastering agency law is less traumatic.

The analytic benefits of studying partnership law come from several sources: applying the categories and consequences approach in more complex settings; seeing how themes from one area of law (i.e., agency) manifest themselves in a related but distinct area of law; developing familiarity with the concept and function of "default rules"; and learning to distinguish between issues within an organization (*inter se* issues) and issues between an organization and third parties.

To this mix of skills and concepts, studying the law of LLCs, LLPs, and limited liability limited partnerships adds further experience in recognizing old themes in new settings (e.g., power to bind the organization, fiduciary duties within an organization), and further refinement of the distinction between *inter se* issues and third-party issues (e.g., direct versus derivative claims, conflicts between an LLC's articles of organization and operating agreement).

I hope you will find this book useful, whether you are taking a course that considers this book's topics in depth or in passing. If you have questions or comments about the book or the doctrines that it discusses, you can reach me through www.danielkleinberger.com, danielkleinberger@mitchellhamline.edu, or 651-341-7246.

Daniel S. Kleinberger
[month TBD] 2025

2. See Section 15.4.8.
3. See Section 3.2.4(e).

Note on the ULC Harmonization Project

In 2009, the ULC began "an intensive effort to harmonize, to the extent possible, all uniform acts pertaining to unincorporated organizations."[1] The Harmonization Project lasted four years, and the then-current uniform general partnership, limited partnership, and limited liability company acts were central to the effort. The official names of the three harmonized acts are UPA (1997) (Last Amended 2013), ULPA (2001) (Last Amended 2013), and ULLCA (2006) (Last Amended 2013). This book uses abbreviated names: UPA (2013), ULPA (2013), and ULLCA (2013).

1. Uniform Partnership Act (1997) (Last Amended 2013), Prefatory Note to 2011 and 2013 Harmonization Amendments.

Agency, Partnerships, and LLCs

CHAPTER 1

Introductory Concepts in the Law of Agency

§1.1 THE AGENCY RELATIONSHIP DEFINED AND EXEMPLIFIED; ITS PLAYERS IDENTIFIED

§1.1.1 The Classic Definition

Agency is the label the law applies to a relationship in which:

- by mutual consent (formal or informal, express or implied)
- one person or entity (called the "agent")
- undertakes to act on behalf of another person or entity (called the "principal")
- subject to the principal's control.

§1.1.2 The Players: Principal and Agent; Their Ubiquity

Agency relationships are everywhere in the commercial world and in non-commercial realms as well. Whenever a person or organization seeks to act through the efforts of others, the legal concept of agency likely applies. For example:

- A student, seeking a place to live while attending law school, submits a rental application to the manager of an apartment building. Acting on behalf of the building owner, the manager checks the application and then accepts the student as a tenant. The manager acts as the owner's agent.

- A corporate shareholder, unable to attend the corporation's annual meeting, signs a "proxy" that authorizes another individual to cast the shareholder's votes at the meeting. By accepting the appointment, the proxy holder becomes the shareholder's agent.
- A landowner, preparing to leave for an around-the-world tour and wishing to sell Greenacre as soon as possible, gives a real estate broker a "power of attorney." This credential authorizes the broker to sell Greenacre on the owner's behalf, to sign all documents necessary to form a binding contract, and to close the deal. The broker is the owner's agent.
- A local supermarket chain plans to purchase an expensive, state-of-the-art software system to connect a store's cash registers with an inventory management function. The supermarket chain does not have relevant expertise "in house" and so retains a consultant to:
  - advise on which package to buy; and
  - once a package is selected, arrange the purchase on the chain's behalf.

  In arranging the purchase, the consultant acts as the chain's agent.[1]
- A bank, knowing that not all customers like dealing with ATMs, hires tellers to handle customer deposits, withdrawals, and similar transactions. The tellers are agents of the bank.

In each of these situations, someone (the "principal") has asked someone else (the "agent") to provide services or accomplish some task on behalf of the principal and subject to the principal's control. In each situation, the agent has agreed to do so. To each situation, the label of "agency" applies.[2]

Agency relationships also appear in literature, as in Longfellow's "Courtship of Miles Standish." Standish, seeking to court "the damsel Priscilla" but too shy to do so directly, entreats his friend John Alden to communicate to Priscilla the depth and direction of Standish's feelings. Alden agrees and becomes Standish's agent.[3] In Dumas's *The Three Musketeers*, Cardinal Richelieu uses the infamous Lady de Winter as his agent to trick the Duke of Buckingham and steal the diamonds secretly given him by the Queen of France.[4]

1. Whether the consulting work is part of the agency relationship is a difficult question. See Section 1.5.2.
2. The law of agency also applies when a party merely appears to be authorized to act for another. Sections 2.3 and 2.5 discuss the law of apparent authority and agency by estoppel.
3. Henry Wadsworth Longfellow, "The Courtship of Miles Standish," in *Hiawatha, the Courtship of Miles Standish, and Other Poems* (Oxford University Press, 1925).
4. Alexandre Dumas, *The Three Musketeers* (Richard Pevear trans., Viking Adult, 2006) (1844).

An agent can be an individual human being or an organization, such as a limited liability company, corporation, not-for-profit corporation, general partnership, or limited partnership. The same is true for a principal. The R.2d mostly contemplates individual actors, while the R.3d gives considerable attention to organizations both as principals and agents. A machine or computer program, in contrast, cannot be an agent, even when serving an intermediary function.[5]

§1.1.3 The Role of Third Parties

The agency relationship may appear at first to involve only the principal and the agent. But principals typically use agents to deal with the rest of the world, or at least some part of it; thus, the agent often functions as the principal's "interface" with others.[6] As a result, third parties figure prominently in the law of agency.

The R.2d reflects this situation with a paradigmatic approach to illustrations that has influenced generations of law school examples: P represents the principal; *A* the agent; and *T* the third party. The R.3d continues the use of P and *A*, but varies the letters designating third parties.

§1.2 CATEGORIES AND CONSEQUENCES: WHY DO THE LABELS MATTER?

Our system of law operates largely through a process of "categories and consequences"; that is, our legal system defines categories of behavior or characteristics and attaches consequences to those categories. This phenomenon is salient in agency law. People concern themselves with agency law labels because people are concerned about the consequences attached to

5. Thus, the Uniform Computer Information Transactions Act, §102(a)(27) uses a label that is oxymoronic from an agency law perspective: "'Electronic agent' means a computer program, or electronic or other automated means, used independently to initiate an action, or to respond to electronic messages or performances, on the person's behalf without review or action by an individual at the time of the action or response to the message or performance." For further discussion of statutory law's use of agency law concepts and terminology, see §1.6.

6. However, agency law also "encompasses the employment relation, even as to employees whom an employer has not designated to . . . interact with parties external to the employer's organization." R.3d, §1.01, comment c. In this context, the key agency issues are the agent's duty of loyalty to the principal and the question of whether the employer is automatically (vicariously) liable for torts committed by the employee within "the scope of employment." Section 4.1.1 discusses an agent's duty of loyalty. Section 3.2 discusses the notion of *respondeat superior*—vicarious liability for the torts of an employee.

those labels. For example, if *A* is an agent of P, then (among other consequences) *A* owes a duty of loyalty to P and P has certain obligations to indemnify *A*.[7]

This "category and consequences" architecture has two major practical implications for those dealing with agency law: The architecture sharpens the questions we ask and drives the agency analysis.

§1.2.1 The First Practical Implication: Sharpening the Questions We Ask

In the practice of agency law, the question "Is X an agent of Y?" is almost always an incomplete question and usually a bad one. The better question is, "For the purposes of [specified consequence], is X an agent of Y?" The latter question is better because the context (the specified consequence) directs the analysis toward the appropriate subcategories and sub-issues.

Example

In *Great Expectations*, Pip receives ongoing support from an unnamed benefactor who acts through Mr. Jaggers. In the following passage, which occurs just after Mr. Jaggers hands Pip a £500 note, Pip is speaking.

> I was beginning to express my gratitude to my benefactor for the great liberality with which I was treated, when Mr. Jaggers stopped me. "I am not paid, Pip," said he, coolly, "to carry your words to any one," and then gathered up his coat-tails, as he had gathered up the subject, and stood frowning at his boots as if he suspected them of designs against him.[8]

In this context, the question "Is Mr. Jaggers the agent of the unnamed benefactor?" would be at best overbroad. Mr. Jaggers seems to be the agent of the unnamed benefactor for the purposes of delivering money and perhaps information, but not for the purposes of receiving information. ◄◄◄

§1.2.2 The Second Practical Implication: Which Drives the Analysis—Categories or Consequences?

If we think of legal rules as "if/then" structures,[9] then categories come before consequences. **If** a set of facts fits within category A, **then** the consequences of A result.

---

7. See Sections 4.1.1 (Duty of Loyalty) and 4.3.1 (Principal's Duty to Indemnify).
8. Charles Dickens, *Great Expectations*, ch. 36.
9. See Introduction.

However, categories are labels for rules, and the rules are tools for achieving particular types of consequences. In most disputes, consequences drive the analysis. Which agency label or category applies depends on which consequence is at issue.

Example

Tort Victim claims that Y should be legally responsible for X's tort (consequence sought). That consequence means that the relevant category will not be "agent" but rather "servant" (or "employee"), a quasi-subcategory of agent.[10]

Example

Tenant claims to have given notice to Landlord by leaving a note with Landlord's custodian (consequence sought). The relevant agency rules for attribute information to a principal are actual authority and apparent authority.[11] ◀◀◀

In contrast, in transactional lawyering, categorization typically drives the analysis, at least initially. In most transactional situations, the relevant facts are not entirely set, and good legal work involves at least the following five steps:

1. Discerning and understanding the client's business objectives and the client's plans for achieving those objectives.
2. Considering the facts that will result from using those plans to pursue those objectives.
3. Identifying relevant legal categories that might apply to those facts, thereby predicting unpalatable legal consequences that might result from such categories (sometimes known as "assessing the legal risk" or "determining exposures").
4. Rethinking the client's objectives and plans in light of the perceived legal risks (sometimes called "exposures").
5. Seeking to reconfigure the client's objectives and plans (and the resulting facts) so as to:
   - avoid the dangerous categorizations and thereby the unpalatable legal consequences while
   - still achieving most (and perhaps all) of the client's objectives.

---

10. See Section 3.2 discussing *respondeat superior*, which makes a "master" (or "employer") vicariously liable for the torts of a "servant" (or "employee").
11. For a discussion of these subcategories, see Sections 2.2 (Actual Authority) and 2.3 (Apparent Authority).

Thus, in the transactional paradigm, while consequences remain all-important, it is mostly categories that drive the analysis.

§1.3 THE TWO ROLES OF AGENCY LAW: AUXILIARY AND CHOATE

Black's Law Dictionary defines "auxiliary" as "[a]iding or supporting," and "choate" as "[c]omplete in and of itself."[12] These two terms reflect the two different roles of agency law.

§1.3.1 Agency Law as the "Main Event"

Sometimes, agency law "in and of itself" provides the rule or rules sufficient to analyze a situation.

Example

X, while undertaking a task on behalf of Y, learns of a business opportunity different from, but related to, the task. Without obtaining Y's consent or even informing Y of the opportunity, X takes the opportunity for herself. Y later claims that X must "disgorge" the profits realized from exploiting the opportunity. Agency law "in and of itself" can resolve this dispute: (i) Was X acting as Y's agent? (ii) If so, the agent's "duty of loyalty" applies and X must indeed disgorge the profits.[13] ◄◄◄

§1.3.2 Agency Law in Its Supporting Role

Often agency law plays only an auxiliary role, and the "main event" occurs in some realm of substantive law, for example, torts or contracts.[14]

Example

Hadley sues Baxendale, alleging breach of an oral contract for services. Hadley acknowledges that Baxendale himself never manifested assent to the alleged contract but asserts that one of Baxendale's clerks did so. Agency law

12. Bryan A. Garner, ed., *Black's Law Dictionary* 8th ed. (West Group, 2004).
13. For a discussion of this aspect of the duty of loyalty, see Section 4.1.1.
14. The phrase substantive law is most commonly used in contradistinction to procedural law. This book uses the phrase in contradistinction to agency law's auxiliary role.

determines whether the clerk's manifestations are attributed to Baxendale.[15] Although this auxiliary question can be dispositive, the "main event" is in the substantive arena of contract law. ◄◄◄

§1.4 CREATION OF THE AGENCY RELATIONSHIP

§1.4.1 The Restatements View of Creation

The first section of the R.3d describes the creation of an agency relationship as follows:

> Agency is the fiduciary relationship that arises when one person (a "principal") manifests assent to another person (an "agent") that the agent shall act on the principal's behalf and subject to the principal's control, and the agent manifests assent or otherwise consents so to act.[16]

Several aspects of this description warrant special attention. Some relate to elements necessary to create an agency relationship. Others relate to the consequences that follow when an agency relationship exists.

§1.4.2 Manifestation of Consent

The creation of an agency relationship necessarily involves two steps: manifestation by the principal and consent by the agent. The manifestation by or attributable to the principal[17] must somehow reach the agent; otherwise, the agent has nothing to which to consent. When the agent then manifests consent, an agency relationship exists—even though the principal may initially be unaware of the manifestation.

Example

Smitten with equal amounts of love and timidity, Miles Standish manages a face-to-face conversation with his friend John Alden, in which Standish asks

15. For a discussion of the relevant theories of agency law, see Sections 2.2 (Actual Authority), 2.3 (Apparent Authority), and 2.5 (Estoppel).
16. R.3d, §1.01. R.2d §1 was to the same effect, but without gender-neutral language and without the embedded defined terms: "Agency is the fiduciary relation which results from the manifestation of consent by one person to another that the other shall act on his behalf and subject to his control, and consent by the other so to act."
17. A manifestation can be "attributable to the principal" under the doctrines of agency law. See Sections 2.2.2 (Modes of Communicating the Principal's Manifestations) and 2.4.8.

Alden to speak to the fair Priscilla on Standish's behalf. Alden agrees, and an agency relationship exists. ◀◀◀

Example

Disappointed to learn that Jane, her favorite guide, will be unavailable when she visits Alaska, Naomi sends her the following email: "Very disappointed. Will you locate and hire for me someone of comparable quality and price range for the dates I sent you?" Jane hits the "reply" button and types, "Sure." She promptly receives an automated "out of the office" response, indicating that Naomi is gone for the weekend. A principal-agent relation now exists. It is irrelevant that the principal is as yet unaware of the agent's manifestation. ◀◀◀

Example

Jane contacts Dennis, explains the situation, and determines that Dennis is willing and available for the time Naomi wants. Jane then emails Naomi a description of Dennis's qualifications and rate. Naomi promptly replies, "Fine. Go ahead." Jane tells Dennis, "The job is yours." Dennis replies, "Great." Naomi and Dennis are now principal and agent; the principal's manifestation of consent was communicated indirectly but nonetheless effectively. ◀◀◀

§1.4.3 Objective Standard for Determining Consent

To determine whether two persons have consented to being principal and agent, the law looks to their outward manifestations rather than to their inner, subjective thoughts.[18] The law's interpretive viewpoint is that of a reasonable person. In particular:

- Has the would-be principal (WBP) done, said, or omitted to do or say something that the would-be agent (WBA) has *reasonably* interpreted as indicating that the WBP requests and authorizes the WBA to act on behalf of the WBP?
- In response, has the WPA done, said, or omitted to do or say something that the WBP has reasonably interpreted as indicating the WBA's consent to act on behalf of the WBP?

Typically, it is the parties' words that evidence their reciprocal consents. However, given the law's objective standard, a party's conduct can also evidence consent. For example, an agent can manifest consent by beginning the requested task.

18. In this respect, agency law parallels the modern approach to contract formation.

Example

Rachael, the owner of Blackacre, writes to Charlotte, "Please act as my broker to sell Blackacre." Charlotte puts a "For Sale" sign on Blackacre. By beginning the requested task, Charlotte has given the necessary manifestation of consent. An agency relationship exists. ◀ ◀ ◀

The objective standard also means that, in the eyes of the law, two parties can be agent and principal even though one of them had no subjective desire to create the legal relationship. Thus, even a reasonable misinterpretation can create an agency relationship.

Example

Frustrated by the recalcitrance of Thomas Becket, the Archbishop of Canterbury, Henry II of England exclaims, "Will nobody rid me of this troublesome cleric?" Four of Henry's barons overhear the remark and proceed to kill Becket, believing that they are acting on behalf of and subject to the control of the king. Although Henry later protests that he never intended for anyone to kill the Archbishop, the barons nonetheless acted as his agents. In these circumstances, Henry's outward manifestation, reasonably interpreted, indicated consent to the barons acting on his behalf. Henry's subjective intent is irrelevant, regardless of whether his protest is genuine. ◀ ◀ ◀

§1.4.4 Consent to the Business or Interpersonal Relationship, Not to the Legal Label

Agency is a legal concept—a label the law attaches to a category of business and interpersonal relationships. If two parties manifest consent to the type of business or interpersonal relationship the law labels "agency," then an agency relationship exists. The legal concept applies and the label attaches regardless of whether the parties had the legal concept in mind and regardless of whether the parties contemplated the consequences of having the label apply.

Sometimes when parties form a relationship, they expressly claim or disclaim the agency label. For instance, franchise agreements[19] often include a statement to the effect that "this agreement does not create an agency

19. In a franchise agreement, one business ("the franchisor") authorizes another business ("the franchisee") to use the franchisor's name and trademark and to sell either a product produced by the franchisor or an array of services developed by the franchisor. In return, the franchisee typically pays an initial franchise fee plus an ongoing royalty, commission, or service fee. Franchise agreements typically obligate franchisees to operate their business in compliance with requirements set by the franchisor. These requirements can be quite detailed and comprehensive.

relationship" or that "the franchisee is not for any purposes the agent of the franchisor." Courts do consider such statements when trying to determine just what relationship the parties actually established. However, the parties' self-selected label is never dispositive and is relevant only as a window on the underlying reality. For example, a disclaimer of agency status may help show that neither party consented to act on the other's behalf and subject to the other's control. However, if the actual relationship between two parties evidences the elements necessary to establish agency, then all the disclaimers in the world will not deflect the agency label.[20] To paraphrase a former president of the United States, "You can hang a sign on a pig and call it a horse, but it's still a pig."[21]

§1.4.5 Formalities Not Ordinarily Necessary to Create an Agency

An agency relationship can exist even though the parties never express their reciprocal consents in any formal fashion. Ordinarily, the parties' consent need not be in writing. Indeed, as Section 1.4.3 indicates, conduct alone can suffice; in the proper circumstances, words are not necessary.

However, in some jurisdictions the "equal dignities" rule applies. The rule: (i) is statutory; (ii) pertains to transactions that must be in writing in order to be enforceable; and (iii) provides that an agent can bind a principal to such transactions only if the agency relationship is documented in a writing signed by the principal. For example, California law provides: "An oral authorization is sufficient for any purpose, except that an authority to enter into a contract required by law to be in writing can only be given by an instrument in writing."[22]

§1.4.6 Consent and Control

a. As an Element Necessary to Create an Agency Relationship

To create an agency, the reciprocal consents of principal and agent must include an understanding that the principal is in control of the relationship. "Since the whole purpose of the relation of agency is that the agent shall

20. The same approach applies to as whether a business relationship constitutes a general partnership. See 7.2.2.
21. "Bush Assails 'Quota Bill' at West Point Graduation," N.Y. *Times*, June 2, 1991, at A32 (George Bush objecting to certain aspects of the 1991 Civil Rights bill: "You can't put a sign on a pig and say it's a horse.").
22. Cal. Civ. Code §2309 (2015).

carry out the will of the principal,"[23] agency cannot exist unless the "acting for" party (the agent) consents to be subject to the will of the "acted for" party (the principal). The control need not be total or continuous and need not extend to the way the agent physically performs, but there must be some sense that the principal is "in charge." At minimum, the principal must have the right to control the goal of the relationship.[24]

Often the manifestations creating a relationship do not expressly address the issue of control. If the issue is in question, courts will examine how the relationship actually operated in order to decide whether the "acting for" party consented to be controlled. The facts of the relationship may imply or negate consent.

Case in Point—*Krom v. Sharp and Dohme, Inc.*

A hospital patient caught hepatitis from contaminated blood and sought to sue the blood supplier for breach of warranty. To succeed, the patient had to show that he was in privity with the blood supplier, but it appeared that the hospital, not the patient, had made the purchase from the supplier. The patient claimed he was nonetheless in privity, asserting that the hospital was acting as his agent when it obtained the blood. The court rejected the patient's claim, noting that there was no indication that the hospital was in any way subject to the patient's control.[25] ◀◀◀

b. Other Roles for "Consent to Control"

While "consent to control" is an element necessary to establish an agency relationship, issues of control also play a major role in at least three other parts of agency law. It is important to keep all four roles distinct from each other. The other three roles:

1. *Control as an element of "servant"/"employee" status.* Whether the principal has a right to control the physical performance of the agent's tasks determines whether the agent is a "servant" or "employee."[26] As discussed in Chapter 3, this issue is crucial to determining the principal's vicarious liability for certain torts committed by the agent.

---

23. R.2d, Chapter 5, topic 1, Introductory Note.
24. If the control characteristic is lacking, the relationship cannot be a true agency. See Chapter 6, and especially Sections 6.1.2, 6.2, and 6.3.2.
25. *Krom v. Sharp and Dohme, Inc.*, 180 N.Y.S.2d 99 (1958). Today, the patient would have a product liability claim directly against the blood supplier, albeit in some states subject to a "blood shield" statute. See, e.g., *Smith v. Cutter Biological, Inc.*, 823 P.2d 717, 722 (Haw. 1991) (discussing the reach of Hawaii's "Blood Shield Law" and quoting Hawaii Revised Statutes (HRS) §327–51 (1985)).
26. "Servant" is R.2d terminology and found extensively in case law. "Employee" is the term of art for the R.3d and also for the R.-EL.

2. *Control as a consequence.* As a consequence of agency status (rather than as an element necessary to create that status), the principal has the power to control the agent. Even though the agent may have consented to give the principal only limited control, once the agency relationship comes into existence, the principal has the power (though not necessarily the right) to control every detail of the agent's performance.[27]
3. *Control as a substitute method or establishing agency status.* When a creditor exercises extensive control over the operations of its debtor, that control can by itself establish an agency relationship. The R.2d and a few cases treat the debtor as the agent and the creditor as the principal. As a consequence, the creditor becomes liable for the debtor's debts to other creditors.[28]

§1.4.7 Consent to Serve the Principal's Interests

To create an agency relationship the agent must manifest consent to act for the principal; that is, the agent must manifest a recognition that serving the *principal's* interests is the primary purpose of the relationship. The facts of the relationship can and often do imply that recognition.

Example

A law student, rushing to prepare for graduation and the fabulous buffet party to follow, gives a friend a list of last-minute additions to the menu and asks the friend to "do me a favor and make sure the caterer includes these on the buffet." The friend agrees. The friend has impliedly recognized that the endeavor's primary purpose is to meet the law student's needs, not to serve any separate agenda the friend may have. ◀◀◀

§1.4.8 All Elements Necessary

Each element discussed above must be present for an agency to exist. For example, although a construction company's foreman may exercise detailed control over a work crew, the crew members are not the foreman's agents. They have consented to work on behalf of the construction company, not

27. An understanding between the principal and the agent may limit the principal's *right* to exercise control. If a principal violates that understanding when exercising the *power* of control, the agent may sue for damages and may also terminate the agency relationship. See Sections 4.1.3 and 4.1.6.

28. See Section 6.3 for an extensive discussion.

the foreman.[29] A physician provides her expertise for the benefit of her patient but has not consented to act on the patient's behalf or subject to the patient's control. A trustee acts on behalf of the trust beneficiary(ies) but is not subject to their control. Section 1.5.2 and Chapter 6 explain in more detail how to distinguish agency from other relationships.

§1.5 THE RELATIONSHIP BETWEEN AGENCY AND CONTRACT

§1.5.1 The Relationship of Agency Law to Contract Law

a. Agency Is Consensual, but Not Necessarily Contractual; Gratuitous Agents

Although agents and principals often superimpose contracts on their agency relationship, the agency relationship itself is not a contract. Therefore, since the doctrine of consideration belongs exclusively to the law of contracts, an agency relationship can exist even though the principal provides no consideration to the agent. Agents who act without receiving any consideration are "gratuitous agents." In most respects, the rights and powers of gratuitous agents are identical to those of paid agents. The major exceptions concern the right of the parties to terminate the agency and the standard of care applicable to the agent.

b. Contract as an Overlay to an Agency Relationship

Although agency itself is not a contractual relationship, the parties to an agency can make contracts regarding their agency relationship. To take the most common example, the parties can agree that the principal will pay the agent for the agent's services. For further example, the parties can by agreement set a definite term to the relationship or limit the principal's right to control the agent with regard to matters connected with the agency.

Example

A manufacturing company plans to build a large plant and retains a "construction management" firm to manage the project on behalf of the manufacturing company. The contract between the manufacturing company and the construction management firm states: "Using reasonable care, FIRM will select

29. R.3d, §1.01, comment *g*. The foreman and crew are "co-agents" of the construction company. R.3d, §1.04(1). The foreman is a superior agent and the crewmembers are each subordinate agents. *Id.*, §1.04(9).

the various contractors to build the plant, who shall then perform their work under contracts with COMPANY." ◄◄◄

Contracts between agent and principal have limited impact. A contract can change the rights and duties that exist between agent and principal, but a contract cannot abrogate the powers that agency status confers on each party to the relationship. Thus, for example, despite any contract provisions to the contrary:

- the principal always has the power to control every detail of the agent's performance;[30]
- the agent may have certain powers to bind the principal;[31] and
- both the principal and the agent have the power to end the agency at any time.[32]

When an agent or principal exercises a power in breach of the other's contract right, the injured party can bring an action for damages. But as a matter of agency law, the exercise of power cannot be undone or enjoined.[33]

§1.5.2 Distinguishing an Agency from a Mere Contractual Relationship

One of the most difficult lines for students (and often lawyers and judges) to draw is between an agent and an "independent contractor"—that is, a person who provides services simply as a party to a contract. "In any relationship created by contract, the parties contemplate a benefit to be realized through the other party's performance. Performing a duty created by contract may well benefit the other party, but the performance is that of an agent only if the elements of agency are present."[34]

Example

Preparing for a daylong "callback" interview, a law student takes her "power suit" to the dry cleaner. For a fee, the dry cleaner provides a valuable service to the student, which benefits her. In ordinary parlance, the dry cleaner might be seen as cleaning the suit "on the student's behalf." ("Hey, Charley. Who is this suit for?" "We're doing that one for Sarafina Student.") In agency

30. See Sections 4.1.3 and 4.1.6.
31. For example, if the principal allows the agent to run the principal's business and to appear as the owner, the agent has the power to bind the principal through "transactions usual in such businesses . . . although contrary to the directions of the principal." R.2d, §195. For further discussion, see Section 2.6.2. See also Section 2.3 (Apparent Authority).
32. See Section 5.2.
33. Statutes may alter the situation. See Section 1.6.
34. R.3d, §1.01, comment *g*.

law terms, however, the relationship is merely contractual. Reciprocal performance causes each party to benefit. However, in the language of R.3d, §1.01, neither party has consented to act "on the [other's] behalf and subject to the [other's] control." ◀◀◀

Example

A manufacturing company enters into a contract with a distributor, under which the distributor agrees to purchase a specified quantity of goods, conduct its marketing and sales efforts within specified requirements, and limit its sales to a specified territory. The contract permits either party to terminate the arrangement on 60 days' notice, but, as a practical matter, the distributor needs the manufacturer's goods far more than the manufacturer needs the distributor's efforts. Also as a practical matter, the manufacturer may be able to exercise significant control over the distributor beyond the terms of the contract. Moreover, executives of the manufacturing company often refer to the distributor (and other companies like the distributor) as "crucial links in our distribution network." The relationship is not an agency. The distributor has "manifested assent" to the contract, not to "the principal's control." R.3d, §1.01. Although practically the manufacturer may be "in the driver's seat," formally—according to the parties' manifestation to each other—there is no driver's seat. Or rather, each party is driving its own separate, self-interested car. ◀◀◀

§1.6 INTERACTION BETWEEN STATUTES AND THE COMMON LAW OF AGENCY

Although agency is a common law rubric, there is considerable interplay between statutory law and agency law. The interplay runs in both directions. That is, statutes now govern key issues formerly left to the common law, and labels and principles from agency law inform both the drafting and the interpretation of statutes.[35]

For example, one of the most important functions of agency law is to determine when information possessed by an agent is attributed to the principal.[36] However, a statutory rule may well displace the common law if

35. "Modern common law [agency] doctrines operate in the context of statutes," and statutes, both as drafted by legislatures and interpreted by courts, "incorporate definitions or doctrines that are drawn from the common law." R.3d, Introduction (2006).
36. See Section 2.4.

the principal is an organization and the transaction at issue is subject to the Uniform Commercial Code or a business entity statute.[37]

Statutes have also displaced much of the common law applicable to employment relations. The National Labor Relations Act (governing unionization) is perhaps the predominant example. In addition:

> Employment legislation has modified common-law doctrine concerning the fellow-servant rule,[38] under which an employer is not liable for injuries inflicted on one employee by the negligent acts of another, unless the act violates an employer's nondelegable duties. Employment legislation such as Title VII expands an employer's nondelegable duties substantially, subjecting the employer under some circumstances to liability for employee conduct, such as sexually harassing behavior, which usually falls outside the scope of the common-law doctrine of *respondeat superior*. Workers' compensation legislation likewise imposes liability on the employer in circumstances under which the common law did not.[39]

The interplay works in the opposite direction as well, as agency concepts make their way into statutory formulations. The "servant" construct has been especially influential,[40] setting the scope for a wide range of statutes designed to regulate or tax the modern employment relationship. For example, the U.S. Supreme Court has held that:

> Where Congress uses terms that have accumulated settled meaning under . . . the common law, a court must infer, unless the statute otherwise dictates, that Congress means to incorporate the established meaning of these terms. . . . In the past, when Congress has used the term "employee" without defining it, we have concluded that Congress intended to describe the conventional master-servant relationship as understood by common-law agency doctrine.[41]

For purposes of federal employment law, this approach "means in essence that the term 'employee' is to be looked up in the dictionary of the common law."[42]

---

37. See, e.g., UPA (1997), §102(e) (stating rules as to when "a person other than an individual knows, has notice, or receives a notification of a fact"), Uniform Limited Partnership Act (2001), §103(g) (same), and UCC §1–201(27) (stating rules for "[n]otice, knowledge or a notice or notification received by an organization"). But see ULLCA (2006), §103, comment (stating that, in contrast to "previous uniform acts pertaining to business organizations . . . [f]or the most part, this Act relies instead on generally applicable principles of agency law"). In 2013, a ULC Harmonization Project conformed the uniform partnership acts to the approach of the uniform LLC act. For an explanation of the Harmonization Project, see Introductory Note—The ULC Harmonization Project.

38. Discussed briefly in Section 4.3.2.

39. R.3d, Introduction.

40. Discussed generally in Section 1.6 and in detail in Section 3.2.2.

41. *Nationwide Mut. Ins. Co. v. Darden*, 503 U.S. 318, 322–23 (1992).

42. Daniel S. Kleinberger, "Magnificent Circularity and the Churkendoose: LLC Members and Federal Employment Law," 22 Okla. City U. L. Rev. 477, 494 (1997).

The interplay between common law and statute can produce confusing results, particularly when a statute uses a label taken from agency law but attaches consequences that are at odds with basic agency law principles. For example, under the common law of agency, an agent always has the power, if not necessarily the right, to terminate the agency.[43] To exercise this power, an agent must communicate with the principal.[44] Yet modern business law statutes typically refer to "an agent for service of process" for specified business entities while stating that the agent's resignation is effective only 31 days after the agent communicates with a specified public official.[45]

§1.7 MAJOR ISSUES IN THE LAW OF AGENCY

By way of an overview, the major issues in the law of agency can be organized according to the relationship among agency's three players: principals, agents, and third parties.

§1.7.1 Between the Principal and the Agent

a. Under What Circumstances Does an Agency Relationship Exist?

As the R.2d explains, "Agency is a legal concept which depends upon the existence of required factual elements."[46] Agency law is therefore fundamentally concerned with whether particular kinds of relationships qualify as agency relationships. For example, must both parties subjectively consent to the relationship? Must they intend to create the legal relationship? Must they even be aware that they are creating the legal relationship? Must the agent be promised contract-like consideration by the principal?[47]

b. What Duties Does the Agent Owe the Principal?

The principal relies on the agent to accomplish tasks. How perfect must the agent's performance be? In dealing with the principal, may the agent follow the rules for "arm's-length" transactions, such as might apply to the parties to an ordinary contract? In carrying out the tasks of the agency, must the agent

43. See Section 5.1.1.
44. See Section 5.1.1.
45. ULLCA §110 (1996); ULPA (2001) §116; ULLCA (2006/2013) §117(b).
46. R.2d, §1, comment *b*.
47. See Section 1.5.1.

think only of the principal's interests, or may the agent consider its own interests as well?[48]

c. What Duties Does the Principal Owe the Agent?

Must the principal compensate the agent for the agent's efforts? Must the principal alert the agent to risks involved in the agent's task? If the agent somehow gets into trouble, must the principal help out (or even bail out) the agent?[49]

§1.7.2 Between the Principal and Third Parties

a. If a Third Party Has Made a Commitment or Received a Promise in Dealing with an Agent, Under What Circumstances Can the Principal or Third Party Enforce the Commitment or Promise?

People and organizations use agents to get things done, and often the agent's task involves making arrangements with third parties on the principal's behalf. For example, you might use a friend to make last-minute arrangements with the caterer you have hired for your graduation party. A bank might use its tellers to accept deposits from customers and give in return a paper evidencing the bank's resulting indebtedness (i.e., a deposit slip).

When an agency relationship involves this "arrangement making" function, it is essential that:

- The principal be able to enforce commitments that are made by third parties to the agent. Otherwise, the agent could not accomplish much for the principal.
- Third parties be able to enforce against the principal commitments made by the agent. Otherwise, agents could not accomplish much for principals; third parties would generally insist on "dealing direct."

The ability to bind the principal to third parties is thus an essential aspect of the agent's role, and questions about that aspect are therefore very important in the law of agency.[50]

48. See Section 4.1.
49. See Section 4.3.
50. Chapter 2 deals with these issues.

b. If the Agent Knows or Otherwise Possesses Certain Information, Under What Circumstances Will the Law Treat the Principal as if the Principal Possessed That Information?

In many situations the law cares whether and when a party has particular kinds of information. Since principals often act through agents, the law of agency must decide when to hold the principal responsible for information possessed by the agent.

EXAMPLE

Example

Andy sells Blackacre to Asha, innocently assuring her that Blackacre contains no toxic waste. Andy uses an agent to consummate the sale, and Andy's agent knows that a former owner of Blackacre buried loads of noxious chemicals on the land. The agent does not disclose this information to either Andy or Asha. In Asha's subsequent fraud suit against Andy, will the law attribute to Andy the knowledge possessed by his agent?[51] ◀◀◀

c. If the Agent Conveys Certain Information, Under What Circumstances Will the Law Treat the Principal as if the Principal Had Conveyed That Information?

In many situations the law cares whether and when a party communicates particular kinds of information. As with information possessed by an agent, the law of agency must decide when to hold the principal responsible for information conveyed by the agent.

EXAMPLE

Example

Charlotte uses an agent to sell Blackacre to Rachael. Without Charlotte's knowledge or consent, the agent tells Rachael that Blackacre contains a lake "full of delicious trout." In fact, the lake contains nothing larger than minnows and the agent knows it. Will the law attribute the agent's statement to Charlotte?[52] ◀◀◀

d. If an Agent's Acts or Omissions Cause Tort Injuries to a Third Party, Under What Circumstances Can the Third Party Proceed Directly Against the Principal?

When an agent commits a tort, the injured party can of course proceed against the agent. The third party may, however, wish to pursue the principal.

51. See Section 2.4.4.

52. See Section 2.4.6. See also Section 3.4.2 (Misrepresentation by an Agent).

(For instance, the principal may have a deeper pocket or may make a less sympathetic defendant.) The law of agency must therefore determine under what circumstances a principal is liable for the tortious acts of its agent. For example, suppose the law student's friend, rushing to make last-minute arrangements with the caterer, drives negligently and runs over a dog. May the dog's owner recover damages from the law student? Or suppose a newscaster defames an innocent person. May the person sue the broadcast company?[53]

§1.7.3 Between the Agent and Third Parties

a. When an Agent Arranges a Commitment Between the Principal and a Third Party, Under What Circumstances May the Third Party Hold the Agent Responsible for the Commitment?

This question is of great importance to both the agent and the third party. From the agent's perspective, the risks differ greatly as between merely arranging a contract for the principal and being personally liable for that contract's performance. From the perspective of the third party, it may well have been the reputation or credit-worthiness of the agent, not the principal, that induced the third party to make the commitment in the first place.[54]

b. When an Agent, Acting on Behalf of a Principal, Tortiously Injures a Third Party, Does Agency Status Affect the Agent's Liability to the Third Party?

This question occasionally confuses lawyers and even courts, although the answer is straightforward—NO. A tort is a tort is a tort.[55]

53. For a discussion of these questions, see Chapter 3.
54. See Section 4.2.
55. See Section 4.2.3.

CHAPTER 2

Binding Principals to Third Parties (and *Vice Versa*) in Contract and Through Information

§2.1 "BINDING THE PRINCIPAL"

§2.1.1 The Importance and Meaning of "Binding the Principal"

Perhaps the most important consequence of the agency label is the agent's power to bind the principal to third parties and to bind third parties to the principal. R.2d defines "power" as "the ability . . . to produce a change in a given legal relation (between the principal and third parties) by doing or not doing a given act,"[1] and, as explained previously, an agent's power to bind is central to an agent's ability to accomplish tasks on the principal's behalf.[2]

The concept of agency power is essentially a concept of attribution (sometimes called "imputation"). To the extent an agent has the power to bind (according to the several specific attribution rules discussed below), the agent's conduct is attributed to the principal. In the words of a venerable agency law maxim, *qui facit per alium facit per se*.[3] Thus, when a third party asserts that an agent's act or omission has "bound the principal," the third

1. R.2d, §6. R.3d does not include this general definition, but does use similar language in defining "power given as security." R.3d, §1.04(6).
2. See Section 1.7.2.
3. This maxim translates as "who acts through another acts himself." *Black's Law Dictionary* 1249 (1990).

party wants the principal treated legally as if the principal itself had acted or failed to act.

Although the attribution rules differ depending on whether the underlying matter sounds in contract, sounds in tort, or concerns the possession or communication of information, the concept of attribution is ubiquitous.

Example

An applicant to a law school is delighted to receive a letter, signed by the director of admissions, stating, "We are pleased to offer you a place in the incoming class." The statement making the offer is legally attributable to the law school, even though the law school (a juridic person distinct from its director of admissions) never made the statement nor signed the letter. ◄ ◄ ◄

Example

A company's delivery van crashes into a parked car. The accident results from the van driver's negligence, but the car owner seeks damages from the company. The car owner's legal theory attempts to impute to the company the tort of the company's driver. ◄ ◄ ◄

Example

A discount warehouse in Iowa contracts with a railroad to transport 150 tractors from Newark, New Jersey, to the railroad's terminal in Iowa City. The contract between the warehouse and the railroad specifies that the warehouse must pick up the tractors "within three days after receiving notice of their arrival at the Iowa City terminal, and WAREHOUSE shall pay storage fees at a rate of $500 per day for any delay in pick up." The railroad gives notice of arrival by telephoning the loading dock at the warehouse after normal business hours and speaking to a janitor. The janitor fails to inform the warehouse, the warehouse fails to make a timely pick up, and the railroad claims storage fees. In assessing the storage fees, the railroad wants the warehouse treated as if the warehouse itself had received the notice. ◄ ◄ ◄

Example

Charlotte sells Blackacre to Rachael, innocently assuring her that Blackacre contains no toxic waste. Charlotte uses an agent to consummate the sale (sign the closing documents, etc.), and that person knows that a former owner of Blackacre buried loads of noxious chemicals on the land. Charlotte's agent does not disclose this information either to Charlotte or to

Rachael. In Rachael's subsequent suit to rescind the purchase, Rachael wants Charlotte treated as if she directly possessed and suppressed the information about the noxious chemicals. ◀ ◀ ◀

CASE IN POINT

Case in Point—*State v. Dalseg*

"In this consolidated appeal, Jeff Dalseg and Timothy Cestnik challenge the trial court's decision to deny them credit for time served in the Nisqually Tribal Jail 'work release' program. After the men had served more than 11 months of a 12-month work release sentence in the Nisqually program, the State learned that the program did not comply with the statutory requirements for work release and asked the court to order Dalseg and Cestnik to begin serving their sentences in one that did. The trial court agreed, denying the men credit for any time served. We reverse and remand, holding that Dalseg and Cestnik are entitled to day-for-day credit for time served in the Nisqually 'work release' program under the equitable doctrine of credit for time served at liberty. . . . The trial court erred when it denied equitable relief on the ground that 'the Nisquallies' were at fault 'for running them into the wrong program.' Dalseg's and Cestnik's judgment and sentences specifically authorize them to serve their sentences in the Nisqually Tribal Jail work release program. This specific authorization cloaked the Nisqually Tribal Jail officials with apparent authority to execute the sentences. Thus, the Nisqually corrections officers acted on behalf of the State when they enrolled Dalseg and Cestnik in a day reporting program rather than a statutorily-compliant work release program. The error made by Nisqually corrections officers in interpreting and executing the judgment and sentences is attributable to the State."[4] ◀ ◀ ◀

Attribution can also work in favor of the principal, as when a person seeks to hold a third party to a contract entered into by an agent or to information received or communicated by an agent.

EXAMPLE

Example

An art dealer's employee attends an auction on the dealer's behalf and makes the winning bid on a painting. Later, the dealer tenders payment and seeks to compel the auction house to deliver the painting. The dealer seeks to be treated as if it itself had made the winning bid. ◀ ◀ ◀

4. *State v. Dalseg*, 132 Wash.App. 854, 857, 865 (2006).

Example

A residential lease allows either party to terminate on 60 days' notice. The landlord's resident manager gives the proper 60-day notice to a tenant, but the tenant fails to vacate the apartment. In the subsequent eviction action, the landlord wishes to be treated as if it itself had given the requisite notice. ◀ ◀ ◀

§2.1.2 "Binding the Principal" and Questions of Agency Power

Agency law uses its concept of power to analyze "binding the principal" questions. The question "Under the law of agency, did X's act or omission bind Y?" thus becomes "Under the law of agency, did X have the power to bind Y through that act or omission?" Agency law approaches questions of power through five attribution rules. An agent can have the power to bind a principal through:

1. actual authority (including express and implied actual authority);
2. apparent authority;
3. estoppel;
4. inherent power;[5] and
5. ratification.

More than one subcategory of agency power may apply in any particular situation. Indeed, in practice parties often argue attribution rules in the alternative. For example:

- When X made this contract on behalf of Y, X had actual authority to do so. Y is therefore bound.
- And, even if X lacked actual authority, X had apparent authority and so Y is bound.
- And, even if X lacked both actual and apparent authority, X had the inherent power to bind Y, and so Y is bound.
- And, even if X lacked both the authority and power to bind Y, estoppel applies and so Y is bound.

5. Inherent power is actually a collection of attribution rules. See Section 2.6. R.3d excludes from its "black letter" the concept of inherent power, relying instead on concepts of apparent authority, estoppel, and restitution. R.3d, Chapter 2, Introductory Note.

- And, even if X lacked both the authority and power to bind Y and estoppel does not apply, Y subsequently ratified X's act and so Y is bound.

This chapter discusses how each of the five attribution rules pertains to binding a principal in contract and also considers how, in contractual and similar matters, a principal can be bound by information that an agent or apparent agent receives, knows, ought to know, or communicates.[6]

§2.1.3 Attribution (Imputation): Transaction Specific and Time Sensitive

Attribution (also called "imputation") is always transaction specific. For instance, the attribution question is not whether "*A* had apparent authority to bind P," but rather whether "*A* had apparent authority to bind P when *A* did X."

Because attribution is transaction specific, attribution is also time sensitive. With the exception of ratification,[7] all attribution rules are applied exclusively as of the time that the relevant transaction occurred.

Example

T claims that P is bound to a contract formed last Friday at 3 P.M., when T and *A* made certain reciprocal manifestations. The attribution analysis focuses on whether *last Friday at 3 P.M.* *A* had the power to bind P to the contract. ◄ ◄ ◄

Example

T rents an apartment from P on a month-to-month lease. T claims to have given notice of termination to *A* on the last day of last month and further claims that the notice is effective against P. The attribution analysis focuses on whether *on the last day of last month* *A* had the power to bind P by receiving notices related to the lease. ◄ ◄ ◄

6. Chapter 3 considers the attribution rules relevant to tort claims. In that context, the most important attribution rule is *respondeat superior*, an aspect of inherent power. Apparent authority can be relevant for some types of torts, either instead of, or in addition to, *respondeat superior*.

7. Ratification occurs when a principal affirms a previously unauthorized act, and, consequently, ratification analysis has a dual temporal focus: the moment at which the unauthorized act occurs and the moment at which the principal affirms. Section 2.7 discusses ratification in detail.

§2.1.4 Distinguishing the Power to Bind from the Right to Bind

As will be discussed throughout this chapter and the next, various circumstances can *empower* an agent to bind the principal. However, an agent has the *right* to bind the principal only to the extent that the principal has authorized the agent to do so. A principal gives this authorization in the same way (and often at the same time) that the principal initiates the agency relationship—namely, by making a manifestation that reaches the agent.[8]

To the extent an agent has the right to bind a principal, the agent automatically has the power to do so. It is possible, however, for an agent to have the *power* to bind while lacking the *right*. In such circumstances, if the agent exercises the power and binds the principal, the agent wrongs the principal. Then, consistent with the right/power distinction:

- the agent is liable to the principal for the wrongful conduct, but
- the principal is nonetheless bound to the third party.

Example

Rachael, the owner of Rachael's Service Station, promotes Sam to the position of general manager and puts him in charge of the station's day-to-day operations. Although service station managers ordinarily place orders for batteries, tires, and other accessories, Rachael instructs Charlotte to leave that ordering to her. Nonetheless, Charlotte orders batteries. Under the doctrines of apparent authority and inherent agency power,[9] Rachael is bound, even though Charlotte had no right (*vis-à-vis* Rachael, her principal) to place the order. ◀ ◀ ◀

For a graphic illustration of the relationship between the right to bind and the power to bind, see Figure 2-1.

8. R.2d, R.3d, and the case law call this *authorized* power "actual authority." For a detailed discussion of actual authority, see Section 2.2.

9. See Sections 2.3 and 2.6.2. R.3d would treat this situation as involving only apparent authority.

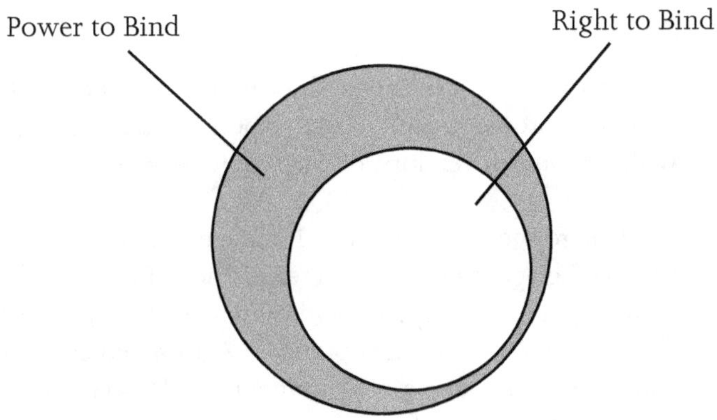

Figure 2-1. The Right to Bind and the Power to Bind

§2.2 ACTUAL AUTHORITY

§2.2.1 The Interface Function and the Agent's Authorized Power to Bind (Actual Authority)

For an agency relationship to come into existence, the principal must manifest consent to have the agent act on the principal's behalf with respect to some goal, task, or set of responsibilities. In many instances, the authorized zone of endeavor involves some "interface" function; that is, some tasks or responsibilities through which the agent connects the principal with third parties.

Example

Rachael hires Charlotte, an attorney, to represent her as vendee in a real estate closing. Part of Charlotte's function is to serve as Rachael's interface with the title insurance company, Rachael's lender, the vendor (through the vendor's attorney, if the vendor has an attorney), the vendor's real estate agent, the "closer," etc. ◄◄◄

Example

Salem is hired as a cashier at UpscaleandPricey Jeans, Inc. His core function is to be the company's interface with its customer at the crucial moment of sale. ◄◄◄

This interface function is ubiquitous in, but not essential to, agency relationships.

Example

A Christmas tree farm hires Al to tend and eventually harvest acres of pine trees. Al's ordinary, authorized responsibilities do not include any contact with customers, vendors, or the public. ◀ ◀ ◀

Where agency involves an interface function, the principal's manifestation to the agent necessarily creates "actual authority" in the agent. Actual authority means an agent's authorized (rightful) power to act on behalf of the principal *vis-à-vis* third parties.[10] Authorized acts can include the negotiation and the making of agreements, and also the receipt, possession, and communication of information.

This section considers the power-to-bind ramifications of actual authority. Chapter 4 considers the ramifications for the obligations between principal and agent.

§2.2.2 Creation of Actual Authority

a. Essential Mechanics (Elements)

Paralleling the creation of the agency relationship itself, creation of actual authority involves:

- an objective manifestation by the principal,
- followed by the agent's reasonable interpretation of that manifestation,
- which leads the agent to believe that it is authorized to act for the principal.

"This standard requires that the agent's belief be reasonable, an objective standard, and that the agent actually hold the belief, a subjective standard."[11]

Example

Two traveling salespeople, Bernice and Joe, are in the hotel bar. As Joe gets up to get another bowl of pretzels, Bernice says, "It's Happy Hour. While you're up, order another round of drinks for us and charge them to me." Joe orders the round and charges the price to Bernice's room. In doing so,

10. As explained by the R.3d., §1.01, comment *c*, "An agent who has actual authority holds power as a result of a voluntary conferral by the principal and is privileged, in relation to the principal, to exercise that power." Some cases refer to actual authority as "true authority."
11. R.3d, §2.02, comment *e*. See also R.2d, §33 ("An agent is authorized to do, and to do only, what it is reasonable for him to infer that the principal desires him to do in the light of the principal's manifestations and the facts as he [i.e., the agent] knows or should know them at the time he acts").

Joe has acted within his actual authority. Bernice's statement constituted the necessary manifestation and Joe's action reflects his interpretation of that manifestation. In the circumstances, Joe's interpretation is certainly reasonable. ◄◄◄

Example

Same situation as above, except that when Joe gets to the bar, he discovers that Happy Hour has ended and that prices have returned to the regular, undiscounted rate. From the bar he conveys that information back to Bernice, who responds by waving her hand in a forward motion. When Joe charges the drinks to Bernice's room, he is acting within his actual authority. Given Bernice's specific reference to Happy Hour, it would initially have been unreasonable for Joe to charge the drinks at the regular rate. However, after checking with Bernice, he received a fresh and different manifestation. ◄◄◄

Restatement on Point—R.3d, §2.02, Ill. 4

"P, a photographer, employs *A* as a business manager. P authorizes *A* to endorse and deposit checks P receives from publishers of photographs taken by P. Based on P's statements to *A*, *A* believes *A's* authority is limited to endorsing and depositing checks and does not include entering into agreements that bind P in other respects. *A* endorses and deposits a check from T, a magazine publisher, made payable to P. Printed on the back of the check is a legend: 'Endorsement constitutes a release of all claims.' It is beyond the scope of *A's* actual authority to release claims that P has against T." The result would be the same even if *A* could *reasonably* have believed that he or she was authorized to endorse the check. Actual authority requires *A's* actual, as well as reasonable, belief. ◄◄◄

b. Scope of Authority

Agency law uses the term "scope of authority" to refer to and delineate the extent of an agent's actual authority.

c. Modes of Communicating the Principal's Manifestation

The principal's manifestation can reach the agent directly or indirectly, and a manifestation that reaches the agent through intermediaries can certainly give rise to actual authority. Indeed, when the principal is an organization (e.g., a corporation, a limited liability company), an agent normally receives communication "from" the principal via the conduct of co-agents.

Example

The board of directors of Scrooge, Inc. ("Scrooge") adopts a resolution allowing a 10 percent Christmas discount for any tenant who pays the January rent before December 25. The secretary to the board writes and distributes throughout the organization a memo based on the resolution. In due course, Robert Cratchit, chief rent clerk for Scrooge in the London area, receives a copy of the memo. He then has actual authority to accept 10 percent discounted rent as full payment for January obligations. ◀◀◀

d. Manifestation Through Inaction

In some circumstances, the principal's manifestation can consist of inaction. When silence, reasonably interpreted, indicates consent, a principal's silence can "speak [or manifest] volumes." For example, when an agent takes particular action, the action comes to the attention of the principal, and the principal makes no objection, the agent may well have actual authority to repeat the action in similar circumstances.

Example

For years, the mechanics at Rachael's Service Station have, on an ad hoc basis, offered a 10 percent discount to regular customers on major service jobs. Rachael, the owner, has never explicitly authorized the practice, but she has been aware of it and has not previously objected to it. As a result of Rachael's silent acquiescence, the mechanics have actual authority to offer the discount. The acquiescence satisfies the "manifestation" requirement. ◀◀◀

e. Assessing the Reasonableness of the Agent's Belief

Agency law determines the reasonableness of the agent's interpretation by considering the same types of information that figure into determinations of reasonableness in other areas of law. In the words of the R.2d: "All . . . matters throwing light upon what a reasonable person in the position of the agent at the time of acting would consider are to be given due weight."[12]

---

12. R.2d, §34, comment *a*. The text of §34 provides the following nonexhaustive list of factors that figure into determining the reasonableness of the agent's interpretation:

> (a) the situation of the parties, their relations to one another, and the business in which they are engaged;
>
> (b) the general usages of business, the usages of trades or employments of the kind to which the authorization [i.e., the principal's manifestation] relates, and the business methods of the principal;
>
> (c) facts of which the agent has notice respecting the objects which the principal desires to accomplish;

In the words of the R.3d: "An agent's understanding of the principal's objectives is reasonable if it accords with the principal's manifestations and the inferences that a reasonable person in the agent's position would draw from the circumstances creating the agency."[13]

The Restatements' references to "reasonable person" reflect an objective standard. In determining the scope of an agent's actual authority, what matters is the principal's objective manifestation and the agent's reasonable interpretation of that manifestation. Any unexpressed, subjective intent of the principal is irrelevant.[14]

f. Fiduciary Duty and the Reasonableness of the Agent's Interpretation

The R.3d makes an interesting connection between the agent's fiduciary duty and the reasonableness of the agent's interpretation. To be reasonable, an agent's interpretation must be made "in light of the context," which includes "the agent's fiduciary duty to the principal."[15] This black letter statement has significant practical implications:

> An agent's fiduciary position requires the agent to interpret the principal's statement of authority, as well as any interim instructions received from the principal, in a reasonable manner to further purposes of the principal that the agent knows or should know, in light of facts that the agent knows or should know at the time of acting. An agent thus is not free to exploit gaps or arguable ambiguities in the principal's instructions to further the agent's self-interest, or the interest of another, when the agent's interpretation does not serve the principal's purposes or interests known to the agent. This rule for interpretation by agents facilitates and simplifies principals' exercise of the right of control because a principal, in granting authority or issuing instructions to an agent, does not bear the risk that the agent will exploit gaps or ambiguities in the principal's instructions. In the absence of the fiduciary benchmark, the principal would be at greater risk in granting authority and stating instructions in a form that gives an agent discretion in determining how to fulfill the principal's direction.[16]

g. Principal's Control of Agent's Interpretation

A principal can protect against ambiguity by being careful to give clear and specific instructions. Moreover, a principal can always cut back or

---

(d) the nature of the subject matter, the circumstances under which the act is to be performed and the legality or illegality of the act; and

(e) the formality or informality, and the care, or lack of it, with which an instrument evidencing the authority is drawn.

13. R.3d, §2.02(3).
14. See Section 1.4.3.
15. R.3d, §2.02(2).
16. R.3d, §1.01, comment *e*.

countermand previously granted authority simply by making an appropriate manifestation and seeing that it reaches the agent. Except in extraordinary circumstances, the later manifestation "trumps" the earlier one. Once the agent knows that the principal wants to remove some or all of the agent's authority, the agent can no longer reasonably believe that it has the authority the principal wants to remove.

Example

Rachael, the owner of Rachael's Service Station, decides that she can no longer afford the 10 percent discount. She calls the mechanics together and says, "Effective right now, no more 10 percent discounts." The next day, one of the mechanics, momentarily forgetting Rachael's instruction, offers the discount to a customer. In doing so, the mechanic has acted without actual authority. After Rachael's instruction, the mechanic cannot *reasonably* believe himself authorized to give 10 percent discounts even though at the relevant moment the mechanic actually thought the 10 percent discount was still okay. ◄◄◄

In some circumstances, the principal's countermanding manifestation can change the agent's actual authority even before the agent learns of the manifestation. If the agent has reason to know of the new instructions, then almost by definition, the agent's interpretation of the principal's prior manifestation is no longer reasonable.

Example

Bligh dispatches Ahab to buy a load of whale blubber and ship it to New York City "ex *Peerless*." After Ahab has bought the blubber but before he has made the shipping contract, Bligh sends the following text message to Ahab: "doubts re Peerless in water use another ship." Text messages are a common means of communication between Bligh and Ahab. Unfortunately, Ahab has let his cell phone battery run down and does not retrieve Bligh's message until after the blubber is loaded on the *Peerless*. Even though Ahab did not actually know of the new instructions when he made the shipping contract for Bligh, Ahab had reason to know—that is, if had he acted reasonably and kept his cell phone in working condition he would have received Bligh's message. Therefore, Ahab's interpretation of his original instructions was no longer reasonable. ◄◄◄

In cutting back or countermanding previously granted authority, the principal may be breaching a contract between the principal and agent.[17]

17. See Sections 1.4.7, 4.1.3, and 4.1.6.

The principal may also be leaving intact the agent's inherent power to bind the principal or an enforceable appearance of authority, or both.[18]

§2.2.3 Irrelevance of Third-Party Knowledge (Unidentified and Undisclosed Principals)

Typically, a third person dealing with an agent knows or has reason to know that the agent is acting as such and also knows or has reason to know who (or what) the principal is. In this situation, agency law characterizes the principal as "disclosed."[19] However, the elements for creating actual authority involve the principal and the agent and have nothing to do with what third parties may or may not know.[20] In determining the existence and extent of an agent's actual authority, the law focuses on the relationship between the principal and the agent (the *inter se* relationship). An agent can thus have actual authority (and therefore power to bind the principal to third parties) even though at the time of the "binding" act or omission, the principal is:

- *unidentified* (i.e., the third party knows or has reason to know that the agent is acting for another, but not who that other is);[21] or even
- totally *undisclosed* (i.e., the third party neither knows nor has reason to know that the agent is acting as an agent and perforce cannot know the principal's identity).

By definition, when the principal is undisclosed or unidentified, the third party can learn of the agent's actual authority only after the agent's exercise of that authority. Nonetheless, if the authority existed at the time of the transaction, the principal is bound.

Example

A power company authorizes a coal broker to buy coal for it. The broker contracts to buy the coal in its own name. When the seller later prepares to deliver the coal to the broker, the seller discovers that the broker has gone out of business. Then the seller discovers that the broker was making the purchase on the power company's behalf and had actual authority to do

18. See Sections 2.6.2 (Inherent Power) and 2.3 (Apparent Authority).
19. R.3d, §1.04(2)(a); R.2d, §4(1).
20. In contrast, the third party's view is pivotal to the existence of apparent authority. See Section 2.3.5.
21. R.3d §1.04(2)(c). In the R.2d, the corresponding term is "partially disclosed," R.2d, §4(2), which, according to R.3d, §1.04, comment *b*, "misleadingly suggests that a portion of the principal's identity is known to the third party."

so. By asserting actual authority, the seller can hold the *undisclosed principal* (the power company) to the contract. Because actual authority is at issue, it is irrelevant that, at the time of contracting, the seller was ignorant of the agency relationship. ◀ ◀ ◀

Example

An attorney contacts an art dealer and contracts to buy a famous Picasso print. The attorney explains that she is acting for a client but declines to identify the client. (The client dislikes notoriety.) If the art dealer later learns the identity of the *unidentified* principal (the client) and can prove that the attorney acted with actual authority, then the art dealer can enforce the contract against the client.[22] ◀ ◀ ◀

§2.2.4 Actual Authority: Express and Implied

In addition to the authority expressly indicated by the principal's words and other conduct, an agent may also have *implied* actual authority. The concept is "black letter" in R.2d, but relegated to the comments in R.3d.[23]

That change does not affect the way the concept operates in practice. R.2d, §35 states: "Unless otherwise agreed, authority to conduct a transaction includes authority to do acts which are incidental to it, usually accompany it, or are reasonably necessary to accomplish it." Sometimes the implication is based on custom or past dealings. Other times, "the principal's objectives and other facts known to the agent" cause an agent to infer that a particular act is authorized.[24] In either case, the agent's inference is reasonable in light of the circumstances.

Comment *b* to R.2d, §35 states the very practical rationale for the concept of implied authority. "In most cases the principal does not think of, far less specifically direct, the series of acts necessary to accomplish his objects." Implied actual authority fills in the gaps.[25]

Example

An insurance broker acted as local agent for an insurance company, with express authority to conduct business for the company in the locality.

22. Whether a principal is disclosed, partially disclosed, or undisclosed matters substantially as to the agent's liability on a contract. See Section 4.2.1.

23. R.2d, §35; R.3d, Ch. 2, Introductory Note, and §2.01, comment *b*.

24. R.3d, §2.01, comment *b*.

25. R.3d, §2.02, Reporter's Notes to comment *d* ("Implied actual authority may also serve as a device to address gaps in the principal's explicit statement of authority.").

Although the insurance company had given no express instructions to the broker on how to handle cancellation notices received from policyholders, the broker had implied authority to receive such notices. Accordingly, notice to the broker was notice to the insurance company. ◄◄◄

Case in Point—*Dweck v. Nasser*

"A minority stockholder, and former president, chief executive officer, and director of a closely held corporation seeks to enforce a settlement agreement terminating the litigation between herself and the defendant [Nasser], the majority stockholder. On November 19, 2007, [Shiboleth] a long-time attorney, business associate, and close personal friend of the defendant agreed to a settlement after protracted negotiations. . . . [Nasser subsequently refused to sign the settlement agreement, asserting that he had never authorized Shiboleth to settle the dispute without Nasser's review of the settlement document. The court disagreed on several grounds, one of which was implied actual authority.]. . . . Nasser directed Shiboleth to settle the action and permitted him to speak 'in his name.' Moreover, he told Shiboleth that he would execute any agreement that Shiboleth and Heyman presented to him. Given this behavior and Shiboleth's long-standing close personal and business relationship with Nasser, it was reasonable for Shiboleth to assume he was authorized to settle the litigation. At his deposition, Shiboleth testified that he had settled many cases for Nasser in the past and that in those circumstances Nasser would instruct him to: '[D]o what you want. That means settle it in our implied terms. That's the way we communicate for twenty years. When he tells me to do what you understand or what you want, in terms of settling a case . . . you are . . . authorized to settle the case.' "[26] ◄◄◄

The express manifestations of the principal can always negate implied authority.

Example

Sartre authorizes Camus to negotiate the sale of a plot of land owned by Sartre.[27] In that locality, land sales are almost always done by warranty deed, a custom that would ordinarily give Camus implied actual authority to sign a warranty deed on Sartre's behalf. However, Sartre tells Camus, "Existence

26. *Dweck v. Nasser*, 959 A.2d 29, 31, 43 (2008) (footnote omitted), vacated and remanded after consideration of the Appellees' Motion to Withdraw Opposition to Appeal, 966 A.2d 348 (Table), 2009 WL 378447 (Del. 2009).

27. In some states, the "equal dignities rule" would require Sartre to put the authorization in a signed writing. See Section 1.4.5.

is uncertain. Use a quit claim deed only." Camus lacks actual authority to adhere to the local custom. ◄◄◄

§2.2.5 Binding the Principal and Third Party in Contract via Actual Authority

If an agent acting with actual authority makes a contract on behalf of a principal, then the principal is bound to the contract as if the principal had directly entered into the contract. In almost all circumstances, the third party is likewise bound on the contract to the principal.

Example

Sam, a research scientist, instructs Irv, his lab manager, "Get me a maintenance contract on the electron microscope. Make sure that we have service 24/7/365. I don't care what it costs." Irv enters into a contract with Selma's Service Company, signing the contract, "Irv, as manager for Sam." Sam, the disclosed principal, is bound to the contract. ◄◄◄

Example

Same situation, except that Irv signs the contract in his own name, without having made any reference to Sam. Sam, the undisclosed principal, is bound to the contract. ◄◄◄

Example

Same situation, except that Irv enters into the contract through a phone conversation with Selma, explaining, "I'm making this agreement for the lab's owner." Sam, the unidentified/partially disclosed principal, is bound to the contract. ◄◄◄

§2.2.6 Binding the Principal via Actual Authority: Special Rules for Contracts Involving Undisclosed Principals

When the principal is undisclosed, the third party is sometimes entitled to: (i) insist on rendering performance to the agent; or (ii) escape the contract entirely.

a. Rendering Performance to the Agent

The third party may insist upon rendering performance to the agent if the contract requires the third party to perform personal services, or if in some other way rendering performance to the undisclosed principal would significantly change the third party's burden. This rule fits the expectations of the third party, who entered into the contract expecting to render performance to the agent, not the principal. Deviating from that expectation is fair only if the deviation does not significantly alter the third party's burdens.[28]

b. Escaping the Contract Entirely

In a narrow range of circumstances, a third party may escape entirely a contract made with an agent for an undisclosed principal. Escape is possible if either:

- the contract so provides; that is, the contract states that it is inoperative if the agent is representing someone; or
- a special (very difficult to establish) kind of fraud exists:
  - — the agent fraudulently represented that the agent was not acting for the principal;
  - — the third party would not have entered into the contract knowing the principal was a party; and
  - — the agent or undisclosed principal knew or should have known that the third party would not have made the contract with the principal.

Misrepresentation of the principal's role is insufficient without the other elements. Mere failure to disclose the principal's existence is always insufficient.

Example

A guitar maker has a guitar for sale. A musician wishes to buy the guitar, but knows that, due to a long-standing feud, the guitar maker will refuse to sell the guitar to him. The would-be buyer therefore asks a friend to make the purchase. The guitar maker says to the friend, "I care about the

28. Agency law here closely parallels contract law. See Restatement (Second) Contracts, §317(2)(a) (stating that a party to a contract may not assign its rights when "the substitution of a right of the assignee for the right of the assignor would materially change the duty of the obligor, or materially increase the burden or risk imposed on him by his contract, or materially impair his chance of obtaining return performance, or materially reduce its value to him").

guitars I make. I want to be sure that they're treated with respect." The friend responds, "Don't worry. I've wanted one of your guitars for a long time. I am looking forward to playing this one for years to come. I'll take good care of it." The guitar maker agrees to a deal, but learns the truth before the friend takes possession of the guitar. The guitar maker is not obligated to go through with the sale. The agent affirmatively misrepresented the principal's role, that misrepresentation induced the seller to make the contract, and both the agent and the principal knew that the guitar maker would not have made a contract with the principal. ◀ ◀ ◀

Example

A railroad company wishes to acquire three parcels of land for a new line. The company fears that the landowners will ask too much money if they learn that the railroad needs the land. It also fears the same result if the landowners are contacted by someone representing an unnamed principal. The company therefore uses three different "straw men." Each of these agents individually approaches one of the landowners. Each of the agents affirmatively states that he or she is acting on his or her own account. Each negotiates for and signs a land purchase contract in his or her own name. Later, before the purchases are closed, the landowners learn that the railroad is the actual purchaser and seek to avoid or renegotiate the deals.

The landowners are bound to the original deals. The agents did actively misrepresent the role of the undisclosed principal, but neither the agents nor their undisclosed principal had reason to know that the third parties would refuse to contract with the principal. To the contrary, both the agents and principal thought the third parties would be delighted to contract with the railroad—but at a substantially higher price. ◀ ◀ ◀

§2.3 APPARENT AUTHORITY

§2.3.1 The Misnomer of "Apparent Authority"

"Apparent authority" is a misnomer. The term refers to the power to bind, not the right. The power derives from the *appearance* of legitimate authority; the doctrine exists to protect third parties who are misled by appearances.[29]

29. For a more extensive explanation of the doctrine's rationale, see Section 2.3.8.

§2.3.2 Creation of Apparent Authority

a. Mechanics

Apparent authority exists when:

- one party ("apparent principal") makes a manifestation, which
- somehow reaches a third party, and
- which alone or (more often) in the context of other circumstances causes the third party to reasonably believe that another party ("apparent agent") is indeed authorized to act for the apparent principal.

In the words of R.3d, §2.03: "Apparent authority is the power held by an agent or other actor to affect a principal's legal relations with third parties when a third party reasonably believes the actor has authority to act on behalf of the principal and that belief is traceable to the principal's manifestations."[30]

b. Relationship to Actual Authority

Apparent authority can coexist and be coextensive with actual authority.

Example

Two traveling salespeople, Bernice and Joe, are in the hotel bar. As Joe gets up to get another bowl of pretzels, Bernice says, "While you're up, order another round of drinks for us and charge them to me." Joe orders the round and charges the price to Bernice's room. If the bartender overheard Bernice's instructions, Joe had apparent as well as actual authority to charge the drinks. ◀◀◀

Apparent authority can also extend an actual agent's power to bind the principal beyond the scope of the agent's actual authority.

Example

An Art Collector arranges for Broker to attend a forthcoming art auction and bid on certain items on Collector's behalf. Collector sends a letter to the Auction House, stating, "At your upcoming auction, Broker will represent me and is authorized to bid on my behalf." In the past Broker has often placed bids for Collector in excess of $50,000. This time Collector tells Broker, "Don't bid more than $25,000 on any item." Collector does not,

30. R.2d, §27 is to the same effect: "Apparent authority to do an act is created as to a third person by written or spoken words or any other conduct of the principal which, reasonably interpreted, causes the third person to believe that the principal consents to have the act done on his behalf by the person purporting to act for him."

however, communicate this limit to the Auction House. Although Broker's actual authority to bid is limited to $25,000 per item, the limit does not apply to Broker's apparent authority. ◀ ◀ ◀

Apparent authority can also exist where no actual agency exists.

Example

The Art Collector arranges for Broker to attend a forthcoming art auction and bid on certain items on Collector's behalf. Collector sends a letter to the Auction House, stating, "At your upcoming auction, Broker will represent me and is authorized to bid on my behalf." Subsequently Collector changes his mind and instructs Broker not to bid for him. Collector neglects, however, to inform Auction House of this change. Although Broker has no actual authority to bind for Collector, Broker does have apparent authority. ◀ ◀ ◀

c. The Question of Reliance

When a third party seeks to bind an apparent principal by claiming apparent authority, must the claimant show detrimental reliance? The question is imprecise (as will be seen), and the answer is somewhat complex.

Under both the R.2d and R.3d, the claimant's inference of authority must be traceable to (and therefore, in some sense, rely on) the principal's manifestation.[31] (First occasion for reliance—Point 1—in the timeline shown in Figure 2-2.)

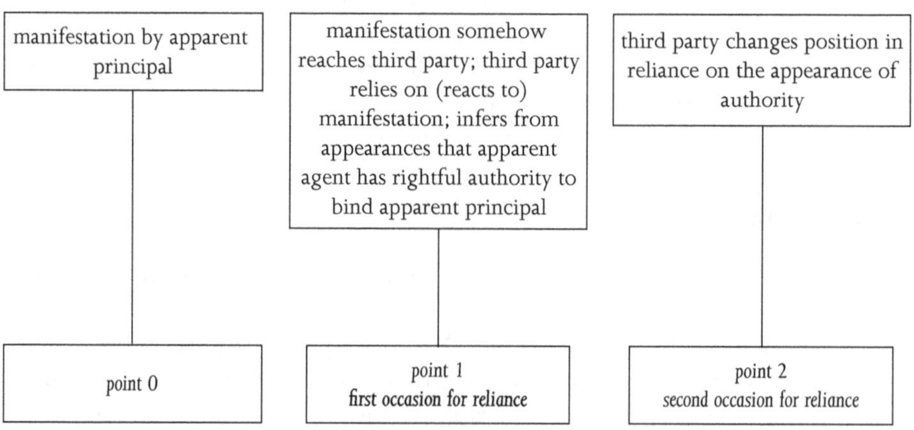

Figure 2-2. The Role of Reliance in Creating Apparent Authority

31. R.3d, §2.03; R.2d §8, comment *d*. The word "traceable" does not appear in R.2d but is part of the black letter of R.3d.

Must there be further reliance? In particular, must a claimant show that the appearance of authority caused the claimant to act to the claimant's detriment? (Second occasion for reliance—Point 2—in Figure 2-2.) Neither Restatement has this requirement, but many jurisdictions do. Indeed, some opinions refer to apparent authority as *agency by estoppel*.[32]

This doctrinal difference may have little practical significance. If a false appearance of authority does not cause a third party to act or omit to act to its detriment, then a claim will rarely be worth pursuing.

§2.3.3 The Necessary Peppercorn of Manifestation

For apparent authority to exist, the third party must be able to point to at least some peppercorn of manifestation attributable to the apparent principal. This peppercorn must form the basis of the third party's reasonable belief that the apparent agent is actually authorized.

The R.3d uses the phrase "traceable to the principal's manifestations" to express this requirement. The "traceable" requirement means that, with one rarely important exception (discussed below), the statements of the apparent agent cannot by themselves give rise to apparent authority.[33]

Example

A silver-tongued salesman, nattily dressed and appearing for all the world to be precisely who he claims to be, rings your doorbell and introduces himself as a representative of the Acme Burial Insurance Company. He shows you an impressive, glossy brochure and a printed contract form. You sign on the dotted line and give the man a $100 down payment. You later discover that the silver-tongued fellow had no connection whatsoever with Acme and that he had created the phony brochures and contract forms as props. Unfortunately, you have no recourse against Acme. Although your belief that the salesman was acting for Acme may have been reasonable, you cannot point to any manifestation by or attributable to Acme, the apparent principal. Consequently, there is no apparent authority. ◀◀◀

---

32. The Restatements also contemplate agency by estoppel, but the Restatement concept of estoppel is subtly different from the doctrine of apparent authority. See Section 2.5 (Authority by Estoppel).

33. Conduct by the apparent agent may be relevant to the reasonableness of the third party's belief, but that belief must ultimately rest on some manifestation attributable to the apparent principal. In contrast, a manifestation by one agent of a principal can give rise to apparent authority for another agent of the principal—if the first agent's manifestation is legally attributable to the principal. For a simple illustration of this phenomenon, see the first Example in Section 2.3.4. See also Section 2.8.

An apparent agent can supply the necessary peppercorn of manifestation only in one very narrow range of circumstances. An actual agent has the implied actual authority to accurately describe the scope of his, her, or its authority.[34] So, if a person with actual authority provides such description to a third party, the description is a manifestation attributable to the principal. As with any other manifestation attributable to a principal, this manifestation can give rise to apparent authority. However, at that moment, by hypothesis the agent has actual authority, so apparent authority *vel non* is a moot point.

The mootness disappears, however, when a person ceases to have actual authority.

Example

You operate a horse ranch. One day a woman approaches you and informs you that she buys horses on behalf of Acme Rodeo Company and that she has the authority to pay up to $2,500 per horse. At that time, her statements are accurate. Two weeks later she returns and purports to commit Acme to purchase a quarter horse for $2,200. Unbeknownst to you, however, three days earlier Acme had expressly restricted her authority to purchases of $1,700 or less. You should be able to hold Acme to the contract through an apparent authority claim. You can certainly show a manifestation attributable to the apparent principal. When the buying agent earlier described her buying authority, she acted within her implied actual authority. That description is therefore a manifestation attributable (and therefore "traceable") to Acme.[35] ◄◄◄

§2.3.4 Noteworthy Modes of Manifestation

a. Through Intermediaries

A manifestation that reaches the third party through intermediaries can still give rise to apparent authority.

---

34. R.2d, §27, comment *c*. The principal can remove this authority by directing the agent not to represent her authority. R.3d does not address this issue, making instead only the more general point that "an agent's own statements about the nature or extent of the agent's authority to act on behalf of the principal do not create apparent authority by themselves." R.3d, §6.11, comment *b*.

35. This Example involves "lingering apparent authority," which is discussed in detail in Section 2.3.7.

Example

Acting on instructions from Art Collector, Art Collector's personal secretary sends a letter to the Auction House stating: "On behalf of Art Collector, I am writing to inform you that, at your upcoming auction, Broker will be representing and bidding for Art Collector." Broker has apparent authority to bid for Art Collector, even though Art Collector herself (the apparent principal) never personally made the relevant manifestation. The secretary's letter constitutes a manifestation *attributable* to Art Collector because the secretary's communication, made within the scope of the secretary's actual authority, binds (i.e., is attributable to) the secretary's principal.[36] ◄◄◄

b. By Position

Sometimes the principal's sole manifestation to the third party may be to put an agent in a particular role. In light of local custom and standard business practices, that role may by itself cause a third party to believe reasonably that the agent has certain authority. This type of apparent authority is sometimes called *authority by position*.

Example

The owner of a dry cleaning store hires Ralph to work at the counter, and expressly authorizes him to accept clothes for cleaning, give receipts, return cleaned clothes to customers, and accept payment from customers. Although the owner expressly forbids Ralph to promise to have any garment cleaned in less than two working days, Ralph promises a law student to have her "interview suit" cleaned "by tomorrow." The doctrine of apparent authority may hold the dry cleaning store to Ralph's promise. Ralph's position (as counter clerk) constitutes the necessary manifestation. The question is whether, based on that bare manifestation, the customer reasonably believed that Ralph had the authority to make the promise. Since it is customary for counter clerks to tell customers when clothes will be ready, and since 24-hour service is not unusual in the dry cleaning business, the answer is probably yes.[37] ◄◄◄

36. For a more detailed discussion of this type of attribution, see Section 2.8.

37. As a "general agent," Ralph may also have bound the owner through inherent agency power. See Section 2.6.2. R.3d relies exclusively on apparent authority. R.3d, ch. 2, Introductory Note, §2.01, comment *b* (explaining that Restatement (Third) does not use the concept of inherent agency power).

Example

After lengthy negotiations with a claims adjuster and without any lawsuit having been filed, an attorney purports to settle her client's insurance claim for $25,000. Unless the client has given the attorney actual authority to settle for that amount, the client is not bound. The mere position of an attorney does not create apparent authority to bind a client to a settlement.[38]

Under the doctrine of "apparent authority by position," the word "position" refers not to physical location but rather to a person's recognized role within an organization and the functions normally performed by a person in that recognized role. In some instances—as in the above Example with Ralph and the dry cleaning—a person's physical position signals that the person has a particular function and role on behalf of the principal. Even then, however, the physical location is merely evidence of the organizational position. ◀◀◀

c. Apparent Authority by Position Within Organizations

Large organizations dominate our economy, and those organizations inevitably distribute responsibilities across many positions. Moreover, even in a small organization employees can have substantially different functions, which may be reflected in job titles.

It is therefore necessary to consider what apparent authority, if any, attaches to positions and titles within an organizational hierarchy. In general:

> [A]n agent is sometimes placed in a position in an industry or setting in which holders of the position customarily have authority of a specific scope. Absent notice to third parties to the contrary, placing the agent in such a position constitutes a manifestation that the principal assents to be bound by actions by the agent that fall within that scope.[39]

Example

Charlotte is employed as a "purchasing agent" by Salem Manufacturing, LLC. Charlotte has the apparent authority to make ordinary and usual purchases on Salem's behalf. ◀◀◀

38. Some courts hold otherwise, but the Example reflects the majority view. The situation is different when a lawsuit is ongoing and a party's attorney of record agrees to a settlement. See, e.g., *Navajo Tribe of Indians v. Hanosh Chevrolet–Buick, Inc.*, 749 P.2d 90, 92 (NM 1988) ("While an attorney's authority to settle must be expressly conferred, it is presumed that an attorney of record who settles his client's claim in open court has authority to do so unless rebutted by affirmative evidence to the contrary.") (citation omitted).
39. R.3d, §1.03, comment *b*.

The particularities of an organization's structure may influence the apparent authority analysis.

> Observing a systematic hierarchy, a third party might reasonably infer that the organization is represented by a particular agent whose acts and statements are compatible with the agent's situation within the organization. Questions of apparent authority in this context often turn on the interplay between general definitions or authority associated [e.g., by custom] with specific positions and observed characteristics of how the organization actually functions.[40]

More particularly:

- *CEO or president*—apparent authority for transactions within the organization's ordinary course of business
- *general manager*—apparent authority for transactions within the organization's ordinary course of business
- *vice president*—no apparent authority, because the title lacks any generalized meaning; however, a "vice president for/of [some specific function]" might have apparent authority to commit the organization to matters normally handled by the person in charge of that function
- *corporate secretary*—apparent authority to certify copies of corporate documents
- *branch manager*—in most jurisdictions, no *per se* apparent authority to bind the principal, but probably apparent authority to communicate decisions on significant matters made by the principal and, in some jurisdictions, apparent authority to make decisions ordinarily made at the branch level

Example

Oz Balloon Tours, Inc. ("Oz") is in the business of selling hot air balloon rides. Oz's sole major asset is its one balloon. Oz's CEO purports to commit the company to sell its sole balloon. The CEO has no apparent authority for this extraordinary transaction. ◀◀◀

40. R.3d, §1.03, comment c.

Example

Same facts, except that the company has 20 balloons, regularly buys new ones, and sells used ones. The CEO has apparent authority to sell one or several used balloons. ◄◄◄

Example

Rachael is the vice president for marketing for Andrew, LLC ("Andrew"), a company that puts on rock concert tours and is known to spend tens of thousands of dollars in advertising. Rachael has apparent authority to enter into a $15,000 radio "buy" in a local media market to advertise a concert sponsored by Andrew. ◄◄◄

An agent's apparent authority can be augmented if the organization provides the agent with standardized form contracts.

Example

Rosencrantz is a branch manager for the First Bank of Polonius, with actual authority to approve loans in amounts less than $50,000. The Bank provides Rosencrantz with copies of a form loan agreement, the first page of which carries the Bank's name and states in bold print: **NOT VALID FOR LOANS IN EXCESS OF $100,000**. Rosencrantz uses a copy of the form agreement to commit the Bank to lend Laertes $75,000. The Bank is probably bound. It is unclear whether Rosencrantz's position as branch manager suffices to create apparent authority for a $75,000 loan. However, Rosencrantz's possession of the form agreements (a manifestation traceable to the Bank), coupled with his position, probably does. ◄◄◄

d. By Acquiescence

Sometimes the principal makes the necessary manifestation by acquiescing in an agent's conduct.

Example

On several occasions, the caretaker of an apartment complex contracts with a roof repair service to fix a leaking roof. Each time, the repair service sends an invoice to the owner of the complex, and each time the owner pays. The repair service has no other contact with the owner. On the next service call, all goes as usual except that the owner refuses to pay. The owner claims that "the caretaker has no authority to order repairs." Even if the owner is correct as to the caretaker's actual authority, the repair service can still collect. By paying the previous invoices without comment, the owner of the complex has made the predicate manifestation to "clothe" the caretaker with apparent authority to order repairs from that particular repair company. ◀ ◀ ◀

Example

After the first two days of trial, attorneys for the two sides negotiate a settlement. With the parties present in open court, the two attorneys read the settlement into the record. Neither party objects. Both parties are bound to the settlement regardless of whether either attorney had actual authority to settle. The clients' acquiescence imparted apparent authority to their respective counsel.[41] ◀ ◀ ◀

e. By Inaction

In limited circumstances, an apparent principal's inaction may constitute a manifestation. For an apparent principal's inaction to give rise to apparent authority, the following criteria must be met:

- Someone (including the apparent agent) must assert that the apparent agent has actual authority.
- The apparent principal must be aware of those assertions and fail to do anything to contradict them.
- The third-party claimant must reasonably believe that the apparent agent is authorized.
- The third-party claimant must be aware of:
  — the assertions themselves,
  — the apparent principal's knowledge of the assertions, and
  — the apparent principal's failure to contradict the assertions.
- The third party's reasonable belief that the apparent agent is authorized must be traceable to the apparent principal's failure to contradict the assertions.[42]

In these circumstances, the apparent principal's silence amounts to acquiescence and is a manifestation that is known to the third party.[43]

---

41. Under the "presumption" rule stated *supra* in note 37, each party's acquiescence would prevent that party from overcoming the presumption, as well as constitute a manifestation creating the appearance of authority for the party's lawyer. In addition, the acquiescence would constitute a manifestation of actual authority from each party to that party's lawyer. See Section 2.2.2 (Manifestation by Principal to Agent via Inaction).

42. If this element is missing, the closely related doctrine of "estoppel" may help the third party. See Section 2.5.

43. Contract law has a comparable rule on "acceptance [of an offer] by silence." Restatement (Second) of Contracts, §69(1)(c).

CASE IN POINT

Case in Point—*Azur v. Chase Bank, USA, Nat. Ass'n.*

"Francis H. Azur filed suit against Chase Bank, USA, alleging [*inter alia*] violations of 15 U.S.C. §§1643 and 1666 of the Truth in Lending Act (TILA) . . . after Azur's personal assistant, Michele Vanek, misappropriated over $1 million from Azur through the fraudulent use of a Chase credit card over the course of seven years. . . . [W]e must evaluate whether Azur's §§1643 and 1666 claims are precluded because Azur vested Vanek with apparent authority to use the Chase credit card. . . . Vanek's responsibilities consisted of picking up Azur's personal bills, including his credit card bills, from a Post Office Box in Coraopolis, Pennsylvania; opening the bills; preparing and presenting checks for Azur to sign; mailing the payments; and balancing Azur's checking and savings accounts at Dollar Bank. According to Azur, it was Vanek's job alone to review Azur's credit card and bank statements and contact the credit card company to discuss any odd charges. Azur also provided Vanek with access to his credit card number to enable her to make purchases at his request. . . . Azur's negligent omissions led Chase to reasonably believe that the fraudulent charges were authorized. Although Azur may not have been aware that Vanek was using the Chase credit card, or even that the Chase credit card account existed, Azur knew that he had a Dollar Bank checking account, and he did not review his Dollar Bank statements or exercise any other oversight over Vanek, his employee. Instead, Azur . . . [failed] to separate the approval and payment functions within [his] cash disbursement process. Had Azur occasionally reviewed his statements, Azur would have likely noticed that checks had been written to Chase. Because Chase reasonably believed that a prudent business person would oversee his employees in such a manner, Chase reasonably relied on the continuous payment of the fraudulent charges."[44] ◄ ◄ ◄

§2.3.5 The Third Party's Interpretation: The Reasonableness Requirement

a. Mere Belief Is Insufficient

For apparent authority to exist, a manifestation attributable to the apparent principal must cause the third party to believe that the apparent agent has authority. Mere belief, however, is not enough. Apparent authority will exist only to the extent that the third party's belief is reasonable.

---

44. *Azur v. Chase Bank, USA, Nat. Ass'n*, 601 F.3d 212, 214, 221 (3d Cir. 2010) (footnotes, internal quotation, and citations omitted). The facts also support a claim of agency by estoppel. See Section 2.5.

In determining whether a third party has reasonably interpreted the apparent principal's manifestations, the law considers the same kinds of information that are relevant to determining whether an *agent* has reasonably interpreted the manifestation of its principal.[45] Apparent authority analysis thus parallels actual authority analysis, except that apparent authority focuses on the interpretations of the third party, not the agent. We can therefore adapt R.2d, §34, comment *a* to read: "All matters throwing light upon what a reasonable person in the position of the [third party] at the time of acting would consider are to be given due weight."[46]

Case in Point—*Streetman v. Benchmark Bank*

The Streetmans' business collapsed when their bank stopped honoring plaintiffs' overdraft checks. Asserting that the bank's loan officer had promised that the bank would honor "all overdrafts," the Streetmans sued. The court first held that the loan officer had no actual authority to make the promise. On the issue of apparent authority, the court stated: "The undisputed evidence clearly shows that the Streetmans knew from dealing with their previous bank that banks have lending limits; consequently, they knew that [the loan officer's] authority was limited and that he could not agree to pay 'all overdrafts' drawn on their account. Moreover, a reasonably prudent person would not believe that Watts was acting within the scope of his authority by promising to pay 'all overdrafts' drawn on the account."[47] ◀◀◀

b. The Third Party's Duty of Inquiry

Sometimes an apparent principal's manifestations create an appearance of authority, but it remains unreasonable for a third party to act upon that appearance without knowing more. The reasonable interpretation requirement thus imposes a duty of inquiry on the third-party claimant.[48] For instance, the manifestation itself may be ambiguous—e.g., a license from a franchisor to a franchisee permitting the latter to use the former's trademark cannot by itself establish a reasonable appearance that the franchisee is an agent of the franchisor.[49] Or the apparent agent's conduct may be

---

45. See Section 2.2.2.
46. R.3d, §2.03, comment c.
47. *Streetman v. Benchmark Bank*, 890 S.W.2d 212, 216 (1994).
48. In this context, the word "duty" is somewhat misleading. Typically, a duty is an obligation the nonperformance of which entitles the obligee to a remedy. In contrast, nonperformance of the duty of inquiry precludes the third party from using apparent authority to support a substantive law claim for a remedy. (This duty of inquiry thus resembles contract law's "duty" to mitigate damages.)
49. *Dinaco, Inc. v. Time Warner, Inc.*, 346 F.3d 64, 69 (2d Cir. 2003) ("If advertising is the stuff of agency [i.e., sufficient by itself to create a reasonable appearance of agency], then every advertisement by a franchisee with the franchisor's mark would confirm an agency.").

sufficiently unusual as to raise doubts. In such circumstances, the third party cannot reasonably interpret the manifestation as an indication of authority without first making some inquiry of the apparent principal.

Case in Point — *Truck Crane Service Co. v. Barr-Nelson*

A supplier of construction services and a general contractor dispute whether the general contractor is liable to the supplier for services furnished to a subcontractor. The president of the general contractor writes a letter denying liability. The supplier subsequently telephones the general contractor and talks with a vice president. Without consulting the president and without actual authority, the vice president acknowledges the liability and signs an agreement guaranteeing the subcontractor's payment. When the general contractor repudiates the vice president's action, the supplier claims that the vice president had apparent authority to make the acknowledgement and sign the guarantee. A court holds otherwise, stating: "The fact that the [supplier] had been notified in writing by [the general contractor's] president that [the general contractor] denied liability for these services put the [supplier] on inquiry as to the authority of any other employee to countermand such a position."[50] ◄◄◄

c. The Role of the Apparent Agent's Conduct

With the one exception discussed in Section 2.3.3 (the example about the horse buyer), the apparent agent's conduct alone cannot satisfy the manifestation requirement. That conduct can, however, enter into the reasonableness determination. Plausible behavior by the apparent agent will buttress the third party's claim; implausible behavior will undercut it.

d. Irrelevance of Apparent Agent's Purpose

A person with apparent authority can bind the apparent principal to a contract even if the person does not intend to benefit the apparent principal and even if the person is lying about being authorized.

Example

A bank teller accepts a customer's deposit of $9,000 in cash, deciding at that moment to pocket the cash for himself. The teller prints the customer her receipt and then "goes on break" and never returns (absconding with the $9,000). When the teller accepted the deposit, he lacked the actual

50. *Truck Crane Service Co. v. Barr-Nelson*, 329 N.W. 2d 824, 827 (Minn. 1983).

authority to act for the bank.[51] He continued to have apparent authority by position, however, and the bank must credit the customer's account with $9,000. ◀◀◀

§2.3.6 The Necessity of Situation-by-Situation Analysis

Although an apparent agent may have apparent authority as to a wide range of acts and as to a wide range of third parties, each claim of apparent authority must be analyzed separately—even different claims from the same claimant. The reasons for this approach inhere in the elements necessary to create apparent authority. For any given claim of apparent authority, the third party must satisfy each of the following four elements *as of* the relevant moment:

1. a manifestation had occurred that was attributable to the apparent principal;
2. the manifestation had reached the third party;
3. the manifestation caused the third party to believe that the apparent agent was authorized; and
4. the third party's belief was reasonable.

If the apparent principal has made more than one manifestation, Element 1 may vary from claimant to claimant. Elements 2, 3, and 4 may vary depending on the identity of the third-party claimant and on the specific act claimed to be authorized. For example, two different third parties may draw different conclusions from the same manifestations. Or, two different third parties may draw the same conclusion, but for one—possessing knowledge or expertise lacked by the other—the conclusion may not be reasonable. Similarly, even with regard to the same third party, one act may reasonably appear authorized while another act may not.

§2.3.7 "Lingering" Apparent Authority

The doctrine of "lingering" apparent authority is the agency law's analog to the concept of inertia.[52] "[I]t is reasonable for third parties to assume that an agent's actual authority is a continuing or ongoing condition."[53] Therefore,

51. Having decided to embezzle from the bank, the teller could no longer reasonably believe himself authorized to accept funds on behalf of the bank.
52. Or, for those who majored in the humanities, "The song has ended/but the melody lingers on." (Irving Berlin).
53. R.3d, §3.11, comment c.

a person's apparent authority can continue after the person's actual authority has ended.

Given the necessity of situation-by-situation analysis, efforts to counteract an impression of apparent authority will be effective only to the extent that the counteracting manifestations: (i) timely reach the relevant third party; or (ii) would have timely reached the third party if the third party had acted reasonably.

Example

Rachael, the owner of Rachael's Service Station, decides that she can no longer afford the 10 percent discount she has long offered to regular customers. She calls her mechanics together and says, "Effective right now, no more 10 percent discounts." The next day, one of the mechanics, momentarily forgetting Rachael's instruction, offers the discount to a customer. The customer accepts and leaves the car for servicing. When the customer returns to pick up the car, the mechanic says, "Hey, I'm sorry. I forgot. We don't give 10 percent discounts anymore." The customer is nonetheless entitled to the discount. Based on past dealings, the mechanic had apparent authority by acquiescence. Although the mechanic now lacks actual authority, the apparent authority remains intact because Rachael's counteracting manifestation has not reached the third party. ◄ ◄ ◄

Example

A landlord fires her resident manager, effective immediately, giving the manager 30 days' notice to vacate the apartment designated as the manager's apartment. The landlord then sends a letter to each tenant in the building, explaining the situation and stating that all inquiries, notices, and payments should be made directly to the landlord. The next morning, before the letter has arrived, a tenant delivers his rent to the former resident manager, who accepts the rent as if nothing had happened. Although the former resident manager lacked actual authority to accept the rent, apparent authority still existed and the tenant's payment is effective as against the landlord. ◄ ◄ ◄

Example

Same facts as above concerning the landlord, the firing, and the letter, but involving a different tenant: a student wholly preoccupied with finishing an assigned paper. For a week the student ignores his mail, including the letter from the landlord. Three days after receiving the letter, the student pays his rent to the former resident manager, who again accepts the rent as if nothing had happened. The student still owes the rent to the landlord.

The former resident manager lacked actual authority as well as apparent authority. (If the student had acted reasonably with regard to his mail, the landlord's letter would have come to the student's attention.)

How long apparent authority can linger depends on the circumstances. The more substantial the transaction involved, the more likely it is that the third party has a duty to reconfirm the purported agent's *bona fides*. Likewise, it matters how distant in time the transaction is from the most recent manifestation traceable to the purported principal. The overarching question is whether the third party's belief continues to be reasonable.

§2.3.8 Rationale of the Apparent Authority Doctrine

When a person purports to bind another in an interaction with a third party but lacks the actual authority to do so, the law must decide which of two relatively blameless parties will bear any resulting loss—the apparent principal or the third party.[54] For two different (though compatible) reasons, where apparent authority existed, the law puts the loss on the apparent principal:

1. So long as the third party has not been careless or silly, any loss resulting from the misapprehension of authority should be imposed on the party who could have prevented the misapprehension in the first place.
2. Any loss should be imposed so as not to disrupt normal commercial operations.

The first rationale is reflected in the doctrine's requirement that the third party's belief be reasonable. The second rationale is served because the doctrine permits a commercial entity to rely on the appearance of authority so long as the appearance can be traced back to a manifestation of the apparent principal and the commercial entity acts reasonably in interpreting that manifestation.

54. In a perfect world this question would perhaps be moot, because the apparent agent would "make good" any harm done. For the relevant legal theories, see Sections 4.2.2 (Warranty of Authority) and 4.1.2 (Duty to Act Within Authority). In the real world, however, holding the apparent agent accountable costs time, effort, and money. Moreover, the apparent agent may be judgment-proof, beyond the jurisdiction of the court, or simply nowhere to be found.

§2.3.9 Apparent Authority and Principals That Are Not Fully Disclosed

An agent for an undisclosed principal can never have apparent authority, because by definition the third party is unaware that the agent is acting for any principal at all. It is therefore impossible for the third party to claim that, at the relevant moment, the agent appeared to be acting for the actual principal.[55]

As to an agent for an unidentified (partially disclosed) principal, apparent authority is possible in theory but rare in practice. The third party must be able to point to some manifestation attributable to the principal that supports an inference that the agent has actual authority to act for *some* principal but which does not disclose the identity of the actual principal.

Example

P, an importer, has purchased a shipment of steel from Brazil and retains *A*, a customhouse broker, to clear the steel through customs. That task requires posting security for any custom duties that may be due, and customhouse brokers typically obtain security bonds on behalf of their clients. Without disclosing P's identity, *A* arranges for T, an insurance company, to post a surety bond for the duties on P's steel. *A* has apparent authority to bind P to pay T for the bond. P has provided *A* with the information about the shipment, which *A* needs in order to arrange the bond, and T is aware that *A* has obtained that information for the owner of the steel. P has thus made a manifestation that *A* is authorized to act on P's behalf, even though neither the manifestation nor any other circumstances have disclosed P's identity.[56] ◄◄◄

§2.3.10 Binding the Principal and Third Party in Contract via Apparent Authority

With regard to binding a principal to contracts, apparent authority creates essentially the same results as actual authority as between the apparent principal and the third party.[57] If an apparent agent, acting with apparent

---

55. *A fortiori*, the third party cannot trace that appearance to a manifestation attributable to the principal.

56. This Example is taken from R.3d, §2.03, Illustration 15, which, according to the Reporter's Notes, is in turn based on *Old Republic Ins. Co. v. Hansa World Cargo Serv. Inc.*, 51 F. Supp. 2d 457, 495 (S.D.N.Y. 1999).

57. However, if the apparent agent acted without actual authority, there are different consequences as between the agent and the principal and the agent and the third party. See Sections 4.1.2 and 4.2.2.

authority, makes a contract on behalf of an apparent principal, then the principal is bound just as if the principal had itself entered into the contract. The third party is likewise bound to the contract.

§2.4 ATTRIBUTION OF INFORMATION

§2.4.1 The Attribution Function and Its Connection with Non-Agency Law

One of the most important functions of agency law is to treat the principal as if the principal knows, receives, or communicates information actually known, received, or communicated by an agent. Other law determines the significance of the attributed information.

Example

A contract between Hunter, Inc., and Rabbit, Inc., requires Hunter to provide Rabbit "48 hours advance notice of any deliveries." The shipping clerk of Hunter telephones Rabbit to give notice of a forthcoming delivery and speaks to a night janitor. Agency law determines whether that conversation constitutes notice to Rabbit. From there, the contract and contract law take over and determine the significance of notice given or omitted. ◄ ◄ ◄

Example

Injured by a defective widget, a tort victim claims that the manufacturer should be liable for punitive damages, and alleges that "said Defendant knew that the said widget design was defective and prone to inflict serious injuries, and said Defendant had known of this defect and danger for at least five years before the sale of the widget that injured Plaintiff in that Defendant's chief engineer knew of said defect." Whether the manufacturer "knew" what the chief engineer knew is a question of agency law. Whether knowingly selling a dangerously defective product should result in punitive damages is a question of tort law. ◄ ◄ ◄

§2.4.2 Attribution as of When?

Attribution of information is always time specific, with one party or another asserting that *at some relevant moment* some person knew, received, or communicated some particular piece of information. Like the consequences of attribution,[58] the relevant moment is determined by other law. To borrow a famous comment from the Watergate events that led a U.S. president to resign, agency law determines "what did he know and when did he know it."[59] Other law determines which "when" matters.

Example

In the products liability Example involving the defective widget, tort law determines that the relevant moment is the moment at which the manufacturer sold the widget that injured the plaintiff. (If the jurisdiction recognizes a post-sale duty to warn, a later moment might be relevant as well.) ◀◀◀

§2.4.3 Attribution of Notice and Notification Received by an Agent

Some legal rules and many contracts require or authorize one person to give "notice" of certain facts to another person or to send another person a "notification." Often a person will attempt to give notice or send notification to a principal by giving the notice or sending the notification to an agent. If the agent has actual or apparent authority to receive the notice or notification, then notice or notification to the agent has the same effect as notice made directly to the principal.[60] The attribution occurs regardless of whether the agent informs the principal of the notice or notification, unless when the agent received the notice or notification: (i) the agent was acting adversely to the principal; and (ii) the third party knew or had reason to know that the agent was so acting.

§2.4.4 Attribution of Facts Known by an Agent

a. Basic Rule

If an agent has actual knowledge of a fact concerning a matter within the agent's actual authority, the agent's knowledge is attributed to the principal. As with the attribution of notice or notification, attribution of a fact occurs regardless of whether the agent communicates the fact to the principal,

58. See Section 2.4.1.

59. According to Senator Howard H. Baker, Jr., the pivotal question in the Watergate crisis was, "What did the President know, and when did he know it?" Fred Shapiro, ed., *Oxford Dictionary of American Legal Quotations* (1993) at 13 (citing Sam J. Ervin, Jr., *The Whole Truth: The Watergate Conspiracy* at 174).

60. Other law determines what the effect will be. See Section 2.4.1.

unless at the relevant moment of attribution:[61] (i) the agent was acting adversely to the principal; and (ii) the third party claiming the benefit of the principal's attributed knowledge knew or had reason to know that the agent was so acting.

Example

Caesar wishes to buy an apartment building for investment purposes and retains Brutus as his agent to find and negotiate the purchase of a good property. Brutus comes into contact with Anthony, who offers a seemingly attractive building for sale at an attractive price. However, when Brutus researches the neighborhood, he learns that the city has just approved a permit to open a halfway house across the street. Anthony offers Brutus $1,000 "so that what Caesar doesn't know won't hurt me." Brutus accepts, and Caesar buys the property. When Caesar subsequently claims fraud in the inducement, Anthony cannot successfully defend by claiming that Caesar knew about the halfway house. Beginning when he accepted the bribe and continuing through the closing of the deal, Brutus was acting adversely to Caesar and Anthony knew it. ◀ ◀ ◀

b. The Auditor Cases

Agency law has recently addressed the so-called imputation defense for auditing firms.

Case in Point — *NCP Litigation Trust v. KPMG LLP*

"In the mid-1990s, two officers of a corporation intentionally misrepresented details concerning the corporation's financial status to an independent auditing firm. That firm in turn failed to detect those misrepresentations for several years. After subsequent audits revealed the officers' fraud, the corporation was forced to acknowledge previously unreported losses of tens of millions of dollars and to declare bankruptcy. A litigation trust, acting as the corporation's successor-in-interest and representing the corporation's shareholders, filed suit against the auditor for negligently conducting the audit. The trial court granted the auditor's motion to dismiss based on the imputation doctrine, which holds that knowledge of an agent generally is attributed to its principal. The trial court concluded that the fraud was imputable to the litigation trust, as the corporation's successor, and that the litigation trust cannot sue the auditor unless the auditor intentionally and 'material[ly] participat[ed]' in the fraud. . . . We hold that the imputation

---

61. See Section 2.4.3.

doctrine does not bar corporate shareholders from recovering through a litigation trust against an auditor who was negligent within the scope of its engagement by failing to uncover or report the fraud of corporate officers and directors."[62] ◄◄◄

Case in Point Contra — *Official Comm. of Unsecured Creditors of Allegheny Health Educ. & Research Found. v. PriceWaterhouseCoopers, LLP*

"On balance, we believe the best course is for Pennsylvania common law to continue to recognize the availability of the *in pari delicto* defense (upon appropriate and sufficient pleadings and proffers), via the necessary imputation, in the negligent-auditor context. This gives appropriate recognition to the fact that it is the principal who has empowered the agent and dovetails with other defenses which may be available to a negligent auditor under prevailing Pennsylvania law, in particular, those related to audit interference."[63]

c. Complexities as to Source and Permanence of Agent's Knowledge

Suppose an agent learns a fact "off" the job—either (i) before becoming an agent, or (ii) while an agent but while "off duty." Is the fact attributed to the principal?

Suppose that during the agency relationship an agent knows a fact related to his or her duties, but by the time the fact is relevant to legal relations of the principal, the agent has forgotten the fact. Is the principal still "charged" with knowledge of the fact?

The answer to each of these questions is yes, and the rationale is straightforward. An agent's duties include communicating to the principal any information that the agent has reason to know might be of interest or importance to the principal.[64] The rules for attributing information assume that the agent fulfills the duty and that the principal does not forget.

Case in Point — *Engen v. Mitch's Bar & Grill*

A bartender serves a patron a couple of drinks, after which the patron assaults another patron. The victim sues the bar for negligence, contending

---

62. NCP Litigation Trust v. KPMG LLP, 901 A.2d 871, 873 (NJ 2006).
63. Official Comm. of Unsecured Creditors of Allegheny Health Educ. & Research Found. v. PriceWaterhouseCoopers, LLP, 605 Pa. 269, 305, 989 A.2d 313, 335 (2010).
64. See Section 4.1.5.

that: (i) the bartender knew from her own "off the job" experience as the assailant's girlfriend that the assailant was prone to violence after a couple of drinks; and (ii) the bartender's knowledge was attributable to the bar, since the fact concerned a matter within the bartender's actual authority (making judgments about who could be served). The bartender's knowledge should be attributed to the bar, despite the "off the job" source of the information.[65] ◄◄◄

§2.4.5 Information That an Agent Should Know but Does Not

According to the R.2d and most courts, the unknown information is not attributed to the principal.[66]

Restatement on Point

P employs *A*, who is president of a bank, to purchase notes for him. *A* is a member of the discount committee of the bank and, if he attended to his duties properly, would know that B had obtained a specific negotiable note from T by fraud. Further, had he made the inquiries that his duty to P required, he would have learned this. Not having performed his duties properly, he does not know this fact and purchases the note from B for P. P does not hold the note subject to T's interest because of *A*'s conduct, since there was no duty of care by P to ascertain the fraud in the original transaction.[67] ◄◄◄

R.3d takes a contrary position: "Notice is imputed to a principal of a fact that an agent knows or has reason to know . . . if knowledge of the fact is material to the agent's duties to the principal. . . ."[68]

---

65. This Example is based on *Engen v. Mitch's Bar & Grill*, No. C7-95-78, 1995 WL 387738 (Minn. Ct. App. July 3, 1995), petition for review denied, (Minn. Aug. 30, 1995). The *Engen* court decided *against* attribution. For criticism of *Engen* and a detailed discussion of the issue, see Daniel S. Kleinberger, "Guilty Knowledge," 22 Wm. Mitchell L. Rev. 953 (1996). For the correct rule, see R.3d, §5.03, cmt. e (stating that "notice is imputed to the principal of material facts that an agent learns casually or through experiences in the agent's life separate from work").

66. R.2d, §277 provides:

> The principal is not affected by the knowledge that an agent should have acquired in the performance of the agent's duties to the principal or to others, except where the principal or master has a duty to others that care shall be exercised in obtaining information.

67. This Example comes verbatim from R.2d, §277, Illustration 1.

68. R.3d, §5.03. In support of this position, the Reporter's Notes cite *Southport Little League v. Vaugh*, 734 N.E. 2d 261, 275 (Ind. Ct. App. 2000) as holding that "a principal is charged with the knowledge of that which his agent by ordinary care could have known where the agent has received sufficient information to awaken inquiry."

§2.4.6 Information Communicated by an Agent to Others

If an agent acting with actual or apparent authority

- gives notice to a third party, or
- makes a statement or promise to a third party,[69] or
- makes a misrepresentation to a third party,[70]

the information conveyed has the same legal effect under contract law as if the principal had conveyed the information directly.[71]

§2.4.7 Direction of Attribution

Agency law attribution works in only one direction—upward, from agent to principal. "Notice of facts that a principal knows or has reason to know is not imputed downward to an agent."[72]

Case in Point—*Knox-Tenn Rental Co. v. Home Ins. Co.*

A patient brings a malpractice case against a hospital and several doctors who work as employees of the hospital. The hospital and doctors tender defense of the case to their professional liability insurer, under a policy naming as insureds both the hospital and its employee doctors. The insurance company desires to "reserve its rights"—that is, take up the defense of the case while reserving the right to later assert that the case is not covered by the policy. Under the insurance contract, in order to reserve its rights, the insurance company must give notice to each insured. Assuming that the hospital will pass on the information to the doctors, the insurance

---

69. Not all promises are enforceable, even if made directly by a principal. Agency law only attributes the agent's promise to the principal; contract law determines whether the promise is enforceable.

70. How can an agent have actual authority to make misrepresentations? Having actual authority to make accurate statements, that agent might make a misstatement innocently, reasonably believing the misstatement to be true. According to Restatement §162, comment *b*, that misstatement would come within the agent's actual authority. Other instances are also possible. A nefarious principal might indeed authorize fraud, and an innocent principal might authorize statements that turn out to be misrepresentations. In any event, where actual authority leaves off, inherent agency power takes over. An agent of a disclosed or partially disclosed principal has inherent power to make an inaccurate statement that, if accurate, would have been within the agent's actual authority. For other instances of inherent power, see Section 2.6.

71. The impact under tort law is subtly different. See Section 3.4.2.

72. R.3d, §5.03, comment *g*.

company gives notice to the hospital but not individually to the doctors. The insurer has waived its reservation as to the doctors, because notice received by a principal (the hospital) is not attributed downward to the agents (the employee doctors).[73] ◀ ◀ ◀

Similarly, imputation does not work "sideways"; that is, attribution is to the principal and not to affiliates or owners of the principal.

Case in Point—*Specialized Tours, Inc. v. Hagen*

The sole shareholder of a corporation sold his stock in the corporation, warranting to the buyer that, to the shareholder's knowledge, the corporation was not in violation of any government regulations. In fact, the corporation was in violation, and its general manager knew of the violation. In the buyer's breach of warranty case, the court properly refused to attribute the general manager's knowledge to the shareholder, because: (i) as a matter of agency law, the general manager is an agent of the corporation (not the shareholder); and (ii) as a matter of corporate law, the corporation is a "person" legally separate from its owner (the shareholder).[74] ◀ ◀ ◀

§2.4.8 Information Attribution Within Organizations

Even most small businesses have more than one agent, and large organizations can have thousands. As stated in Section 2.4.4, "If an agent has actual knowledge of a fact concerning a matter within the agent's actual authority, the agent's knowledge is attributed to the principal." When a principal is an organization, especially a large one, this rule can produce untoward effects—especially if "the left hand doesn't know what the right hand is doing." Attribution can occur even when the agent with the attributed knowledge is not the person acting for the principal in the transaction at issue.

Example

Sylvia, the executive vice president of Widget, Inc. ("Widget"), purchases a products liability insurance policy for Widget, and on Widget's behalf signs an application stating that Widget knows of no present facts that would give rise to a claim under the policy. Sylvia has canvassed all top-level Widget

73. *Knox-Tenn Rental Co. v. Home Ins. Co.*, 2 F.3d 678, 682 (6th Cir. 1993), cited in R.3d, §5.02, Reporter's Notes b to comment c.
74. *Specialized Tours, Inc. v. Hagen*, 392 N.W.2d 520, 531 (Minn. 1986).

employees via email and knows of no such facts. Unfortunately, Widget's risk assessment coordinator does know of one potential claim but has neglected to tell Sylvia. The facts as to the claim are relevant to the risk manager's authorized tasks and are therefore attributed to Widget. Widget's application therefore contains a material, false statement, and the insurance company is entitled to an appropriate remedy.[75] ◀ ◀ ◀

§2.5 ESTOPPEL

To establish apparent authority, a third party must show some manifestation of authority attributable to the principal. But what if:

- an asserted principal has made no such manifestation and has merely sat by while someone else has claimed an agency relationship;
- the claims of authority have led third parties to extend credit, incur costs, or otherwise change their position; and
- the asserted principal knew of the claims and of the danger to third parties and yet did nothing?

In such situations, apparent authority is rarely applicable, because only in very narrow circumstances can the asserted principal's inaction serve as a manifestation.[76] To prevent injustice beyond those narrow circumstances, the Restatements and some courts use the concept of *estoppel*. In the words of R.3d:

> A person who has not made a manifestation that an actor has authority as an agent and who is not otherwise liable as a party to a transaction purportedly done by the actor on that person's account is subject to liability to a third party who justifiably is induced to make a detrimental change in position because the transaction is believed to be on the person's account, if
>
> 1. the person intentionally or carelessly caused such belief, or
> 2. having notice of such belief and that it might induce others to change their positions, the person did not take reasonable steps to notify them of the facts.[77]

75. This Example is based on R.3d, §5.03, Illustration 12.
76. See Section 2.3.4 (Manifestation by Inaction).
77. R.3d, §2.05. R.2d, §8B(1) was generally to the same effect. The R.3d makes explicit a point left implicit by R.2d—namely, that to successfully claim estoppel, the third party must show that its reliance was justifiable.

In concept, the distinction between apparent authority and estoppel is clear enough. Unlike apparent authority, estoppel can apply even though the claimant can show no manifestation attributable to the asserted principal.[78] Estoppel liability can arise from the asserted principal's mere negligent failure to protect against a misapprehension.

Unfortunately, the case law often blurs this distinction. Many jurisdictions make detrimental reliance an element of apparent authority and even refer to apparent authority as "agency by estoppel." Moreover, most situations that give rise to apparent authority also give rise to estoppel. If an asserted principal makes a manifestation sufficient to support a reasonable inference of authority (i.e., to create apparent authority), the asserted principal can probably be said to have "intentionally or carelessly caused such belief" (i.e., estoppel).[79] The R.3d attempts to eliminate this latter source of confusion by defining estoppel to apply only in the absence of a manifestation by the asserted principal.

§2.6 INHERENT AGENCY POWER

§2.6.1 A Gap-Filling Doctrine Based on Fairness

In some situations, an agent has neither actual nor apparent authority, and estoppel does not apply. Yet the agent's position creates the potential for mischief with third parties.

EXAMPLE

Example

Noam purchases Eli's Dry Cleaning, does not change the business name, and hires Eli to manage the dry cleaning store. Although dry cleaning stores customarily order cleaning solvent in large quantities, Noam instructs Eli never to buy more than $50 worth of solvent at a time and has no reason to believe that Eli will disregard these instructions.

However, Eli does disregard them and places a phone order for solvent costing $450. The seller of the solvent believes that Eli is still the owner. Eli has acted without actual authority; his principal's manifestations expressly prohibit the order Eli made. Eli has also acted without apparent authority;

78. For jurisdictions that follow the pure Restatement view of apparent authority, there is another distinction: Apparent authority can exist without a showing of detrimental reliance. See Section 2.3.2 for a discussion of the Restatements' view of apparent authority. As noted in that section, many jurisdictions differ with the Restatements on this point.

79. The quoted language is from R.2d, §8B(1)(a).

there can be no apparent authority by position when the principal is undisclosed.[80] ◀ ◀ ◀

To deal with such situations (and others as well),[81] the R.2d and some courts use the doctrine of *inherent agency power*.[82] The doctrine imposes *enterprise liability*; that is, it places the loss on the enterprise that stands to benefit from the agency relationship. As explained by the R.2d:

> It is inevitable that in doing their work, either through negligence or excess of zeal, agents will harm third persons or will deal with them in unauthorized ways. It would be unfair for an enterprise to have the benefit of the work of its agents without making it responsible to some extent for their excesses and failures to act carefully. The answer of the common law has been the creation of special agency powers or, to phrase it otherwise, the imposition of liability upon the principal because of unauthorized or negligent acts of his servants and other agents.[83]

In the dry cleaner Example above, there is no culpable conduct on Noam's part. To the contrary, Eli has caused mischief while acting counter to Noam's wishes. Yet the third party is also without blame, and the policy issue arises: As between the principal and the third party, who should bear the risk of the agent's misconduct? Who should have the burden of pressing claims against the agent or absorbing the harm the agent has caused?[84]

§2.6.2 R.2d Rule of Inherent Power: Unauthorized Acts by a General Agent

When a principal entrusts an agent with ongoing responsibilities, the notion of an enterprise fairly applies. As a result, the agent has the inherent power to take certain actions even though the principal may have forbidden those actions. The R.2d and many cases use the category of "general agent" as the entrance criterion to this type of inherent power.

---

80. For an explanation of this point, see Section 2.3.9.

81. The doctrine of *respondeat superior*, discussed in Chapter 3, is another major example of inherent agency power.

82. Some courts call the doctrine "inherent agency authority." R.3d eschews the concept of inherent power, relying instead on concepts of apparent authority, estoppel, and restitution. R.3d, Chapter 2, Introductory Note, §2.01.

83. R.2d, §8A, comment *a*.

84. In a perfect world, free of transaction costs, both parties could look to the agent. The world, however, is not perfect. See *supra*, note 52. If the principal is at fault (e.g., has negligently hired an agent with a background of misbehavior), other doctrines will place the loss on the principal. For a discussion of a principal's liability for direct negligence, see Sections 4.4.1 and 4.4.2.

a. General and Special Agents Defined

If a principal authorizes an agent "to conduct a series of transactions involving a continuity of service,"[85] the law labels the agent a *general agent*. If, in contrast, a principal authorizes the agent only to conduct a single transaction, or to conduct a series of transactions that do not involve "continuity of service," then the law labels the agent a *special agent*.

Perhaps the simplest example of a general agent is an employee in charge of a store, a factory, or other place of business. It is not necessary, however, to have wide-ranging or important responsibilities in order to be a general agent. A full-time photocopy clerk is a general agent with regard to photocopying duties.

In theory, the "special versus general" distinction is an "either/or" matter. That is, with regard to any particular responsibility, an agent must be either a general agent or a special agent. In practice, however, this either/or categorization encounters many gray situations.

It is possible for an agent to be a general agent with regard to some matters and a special agent with regard to others. The key factor separating general agency status from special agent status is whether the agent has an ongoing responsibility.

Example

A bank employs Larry as a teller. One day, the bank asks Larry to deal with a caterer and arrange refreshments for a retirement party. With regard to his teller duties, Larry is a general agent. With regard to the party arrangement, Larry is a special agent. ◀◀◀

b. Inherent Agency Power of General Agents

Under the R.2d doctrine of inherent agency power:

- IF a general agent with actual authority to conduct certain transactions:
  — acts in the interests of the principal, and
  — does an act usual or necessary with regard to the authorized transactions,
- THEN the act binds the principal regardless of whether the agent had actual authority and even if the principal has expressly forbidden the act.

Although this rule applies in slightly different forms to all principals,[86] it makes the most difference for undisclosed and partially disclosed principals.

85. R.2d, §3(1).
86. R.2d, §§161 (unauthorized acts of general agents); 194 (acts of general agents); and 195 (acts of manager appearing to be owner).

With a disclosed principal, apparent authority by position will typically produce the same result as inherent power. With an undisclosed or partially disclosed principal, however, apparent authority is of no help.

Example

Sylvia decides to enter the silk importing business. The trade is notoriously biased against women, and she fears that her company will suffer if her interest in it is known. She therefore hires Phil as her general manager, but sets up the company so that Phil appears to the outside world as the owner. It is common in this trade for silk importers to sell to large customers on credit, but Sylvia instructs Phil never to extend more than $50,000 of credit to any customer without Sylvia's approval. One day, in order to close an important deal, Phil agrees, without consulting Sylvia, to extend $150,000 of credit to one customer. Although Phil acted without actual or apparent authority, Sylvia, the company's true owner and Phil's undisclosed principal, is bound. "An undisclosed principal who entrusts an agent with the management of his business is subject to liability to third persons with whom the agent enters into transactions usual in such businesses and on the principal's account, although contrary to the directions of the principal."[87] ◄◄◄

c. Policy-Based Limitations to the Rule

This rule of inherent agency power has two policy-based limitations. The rule does not apply if either: (i) the third party knows that the agent is acting without authority; or (ii) the agent is not acting in the principal's interest. If the third party knows of the lack of authority, then the third party is not innocent, which renders inapposite a key aspect of the rule's rationale.[88] If the agent acts on the agent's own behalf, the conduct is not part of the enterprise from which the principal stands to benefit, which renders inapposite another key aspect of the rule's rationale. Remember, however, that apparent authority might exist.

§2.6.3 R.3d's Approach

R.3d expressly declines to use the concept of inherent agency power,[89] but states a black letter rule for undisclosed principals that produces essentially the same results: "An undisclosed principal may not rely on instructions

87. R.2d, §195.

88. Recall from Section 2.6.1 that inherent agency power functions to allocate the risk between two relatively blameless parties.

89. R.3d, §2.06, comment b.

given an agent that qualify or reduce the agent's authority to less than the authority a third party would reasonably believe the agent to have under the same circumstances if the principal had been disclosed."[90]

§2.7 RATIFICATION

§2.7.1 The Role, Meaning, and Effect of Ratification

Ratification occurs when a principal affirms a previously unauthorized act. Ratification validates the original unauthorized act and produces the same legal consequences as if the original act had been authorized.[91] If, for instance, a party ratifies a contract, the ratification binds both that party and the other party to the contract.

Example

Toklas is a janitor in a large residential apartment complex. She has neither actual nor apparent authority to act for the owner of the complex in renting apartments. She also lacks inherent agency power. Nonetheless, she shows apartment 101B to Alice and agrees to rent the apartment to her on a six-month lease. Later, when Alice telephones the rental office to check on her move-in date, she speaks to the actual owner. The owner says, "Well, you know Toklas had no business renting that apartment to you. She's just the janitor. But we'll go ahead." The owner has ratified Toklas's previously unauthorized actions, and Alice and the owner are both bound to the lease. ◄◄◄

Ratification typically concerns "the making or breaking of a contract,"[92] although both R.2d and R.3d contemplate the ratification of torts.[93]

In theory, *as between the principal and the third party*, ratification matters only when no other attribution rule applies. If an actor has actual, apparent, or inherent authority, or if estoppel applies, the third party has no need to show that the principal retroactively validated the act. In practice, however, "[r]atification often serves the function of clarifying situations of ambiguous or

---

90. R.3d, §2.06(2).

91. R.3d, §4.01(1) states: "Ratification is the affirmance of a prior act done by another, whereby the act is given effect as if done by an agent acting with actual authority."

92. R.2d, §84, comment *a*.

93. There are indeed a *few* cases that cite ratification as the reason for holding one party liable for another's tort. Most of those cases seem to involve the ratification of a course of conduct that happened to include a tort, rather than a purposeful embracing of the tort and its attendant liability. Some of the cases involve facts that support a "scope of employment"/*respondeat superior* determination (Section 3.2.5) as much as a holding of ratification.

uncertain authority,"[94] and in litigation, parties often argue ratification in the alternative. In addition—*as between the principal and the agent*—"[r]atification . . . exonerates the agent against claims otherwise available to the principal on the basis that the agent's unauthorized action has caused loss to the principal,"[95] except where the principal has ratified to "cut his losses."

Example

Acting beyond his authority, Edmund sells and delivers to Lucy goods belonging to Peter. Peter decides to go through with the contract, even though he might have made a better deal elsewhere. Edmund is not liable to Peter for acting without authority, even if Peter could prove with requisite specificity the availability and value of the "better deal." ◄◄◄

Example

Acting beyond his authority, Edmund sells and delivers to Lucy goods belonging to Peter. Lucy then resells the goods to an innocent third party and fails to pay Peter. Peter files suit against Lucy for the contract price, in essence ratifying the sale. Edmund remains liable to Peter for any damages resulting from the unauthorized sale. ◄◄◄

§2.7.2 Mechanics of Ratification

For ratification to occur, certain preconditions must exist and the purported principal must embrace the previously unauthorized act ("affirmance").

a. Preconditions

Ratification can occur only in the context of certain preconditions:

- There must have been some transaction or event involving an unauthorized act.
  - — Typically, someone ("the purported agent") will have purported—either expressly or impliedly—to act on behalf of another (the "purported principal") in some transaction with a third party.
  - — Under the R.3d, ratification can apply as well to the unauthorized act of an agent for an undisclosed principal.[96]

94. R.3d, §4.01, comment *b*.
95. R.3d, Chapter 4, Introductory Note.
96. R.3d, §4.03, comment *b*.

- At the time of the unauthorized act, the purported principal must have existed and must have had capacity to originally authorize the act.
- At the time of the attempted ratification:
  — the purported principal must have knowledge of all material facts; and
  — the third party must not have indicated—either to the purported agent or to the purported principal—an intention to withdraw from the transaction (i.e., the transaction must still be available to ratify).

b. Affirmance—the Act (or Inaction) of Ratification

If the necessary preconditions exist, a purported principal ratifies by either:

- making a manifestation that, viewed objectively, indicates a choice to treat the unauthorized act as if it had been authorized; or
- engaging in conduct that is justifiable only if the purported principal had made such a choice.

In the simplest of situations, a purported principal affirms just by stating a choice.

Example

Having read that car dealers generally make better deals for male customers than for female customers, Sally hires Ralph to purchase a used car on her behalf. She specifically instructs him, however, not to buy any foreign-made car. Purporting to act on Sally's behalf, Ralph makes a great deal on a used BMW. When Sally hears of the deal, she says, "Okay, for a deal like that I don't have to 'buy American.' I'll take the car." Sally has ratified the deal. ◄◄◄

Affirmance occurs when the manifestation occurs. The manifestation need not reach the third party to be effective.[97]

A purported principal can also affirm through inaction—that is, by failing to repudiate the act "under such circumstances that, according to the ordinary experience and habits of men, one would naturally be expected to speak if he did not consent."[98] Such failure to repudiate creates a situation resembling agency by estoppel.

97. This rule parallels the rule governing an agent's consent to act on behalf of a principal. See Section 1.4.2. In that case also, the manifestation is viewed objectively and need not reach the other relevant party to be effective (Section 1.4.3).
98. R.2d, §94, comment *a*. In gender-neutral and less ornate language, R.3d, comment *d* states that a "person may ratify the act through conduct justifiable only on the assumption that the person consents to be bound by the act's legal consequences."

Example

Acting without either authority or power to bind the owner of an apartment complex, Toklas, the janitor, offers a resident manager job to Felix. The landlord learns of the offer and also hears that Felix is planning to quit his current job so he can become resident manager. The landlord says nothing to Felix, and Felix quits his current job. By this inaction, the landlord has ratified Toklas's offer. ◄◄◄

A purported principal can also ratify by accepting or retaining benefits while knowing that the benefits result from an unauthorized act. If the purported principal accepts benefits *without* the requisite knowledge, the third party may have an action in restitution or *quantum meruit*. Ratification is usually preferable for the third party, however, because ratification entitles the third party to the full benefit of the bargain. Restitution or *quantum meruit*, in contrast, entitles the third party only to the value of the benefit actually conferred.

Example

Toklas, the self-aggrandizing janitor, offers to rent an apartment to Mike for a year at $50 per month off the regular monthly rent if Mike agrees to keep the grass well mowed. During his first month as a tenant, Mike mows the grass four times. If the landlord knew of the unauthorized offer, the landlord has ratified the agreement by accepting the services. Mike may therefore hold the landlord to the full bargain (i.e., to a lease and a rent reduction for a year). If, however, the landlord did not know of the offer, Mike has a right only to restitution or *quantum meruit* (i.e., only to be paid for the fair value of the mowing work he has already done).[99] ◄◄◄

Restatement on Point — Principal Must Have Existed When Act to Be Affirmed Occurred — R.3d §4.01, Ill. 1

A, acting on behalf of P Corporation, which is not yet incorporated, enters into an oral employment contract for a term of 18 months with B. Once formed, P Corporation adopts the contract 13 months after *A* made the contract with B. The applicable Statute of Frauds requires that contracts not to be performed within one year of their making, including contracts of employment, be evidenced by a writing signed by the party to be charged.

99. If a third party has fully performed an unauthorized contract, the difference may well be immaterial. In theory, the measure of recovery will be different — benefit of the bargain versus value of services conferred — but in practice, courts often use the contract price to measure the benefit.

B's contract is enforceable notwithstanding the Statute of Frauds because P Corporation's adoption does not relate back to the time of the original contract.[100]

c. The "All-or-Nothing" Rule

Ratification occurs on an "all-or-nothing" basis. If a purported principal attempts to ratify only part of a single transaction, then either the entire transaction is ratified or there is no ratification at all.

Example

Acting without authority, Rebecca purports to sell Vladi's car to Michael for $500. Rebecca also purports to extend a 90-day warranty on the car. Vladi cannot ratify the sale without also ratifying the warranty. ◀◀◀

If a purported principal makes a "piecemeal" affirmance, whether ratification has occurred depends essentially on whether the purported principal has manifested:

- an intent to ratify and has sought to impose some exclusions or qualifications (in which case the entire transaction has been ratified and the sought-after exclusions and qualifications are ineffective); or
- an intent to be bound only if the exclusions or qualifications are part of the transaction (in which case there is no ratification and neither the purported principal nor the third party is bound, unless the third party manifests consent to the conditions).[101]

§2.7.3 Principal's Ignorance or Knowledge of Material Facts: Whose Burden of Proof?

According to the R.2d, "If, at the time of affirmance, the purported principal is ignorant of material facts involved in the original transaction, and is unaware of his ignorance, he can thereafter avoid the effect of the affirmance."[102] However, many courts and the R.3d treat the purported

100. As stated in the Reporter's Notes to R.3d §4.04, this illustration is based on *McArthur v. Times Printing Co.*, 51 N.W. 216, 217 (Minn. 1892).
101. This fact determination resembles the determination made under §2–207(1) of the Uniform Commercial Code. That "battle of the forms" provision distinguishes between "a definite . . . expression of acceptance . . . which . . . states terms additional to or different from those offered" and an expression in which "acceptance is . . . made conditional on assent to the additional or different terms."
102. R.2d, §91(1).

principal's knowledge of material information as a precondition to ratification. "A person is not bound by a ratification made without knowledge of material facts involved in the original act when the person was unaware of such lack of knowledge."[103] The difference is more than semantic; it determines the burden of proof.

a. Materiality Defined

R.2d defines *material facts* as those that "so affect the existence and extent of the obligations involved in the transaction that knowledge of them is essential to an intelligent election to become a party to the transaction."[104] R.2d then confines this seemingly broad concept by specifically excluding knowledge:

- of the legal effect of ratification; and
- about the value of the transaction or the transaction's desirability, other than knowledge of important representations made by the agent or third party as they entered into the transaction.

R.3d uses a much briefer formulation, albeit one that is somewhat vaguer. The black letter refers to "material facts *involved in the original act*,"[105] and a comment to the black letter explains that "[t]he point of materiality . . . is the relevance of the fact to the principal's consent to have legal relations affected by the agent's act."[106]

The difference between the two Restatements could have substantial practical implications, depending on how a court interprets R.3d's language.

Example

Acting beyond her authority, *A* purports to bind P to a contract to sell frozen orange juice to T. Thinking the contract an excellent one for P, *A* immediately communicates with P, who affirms the contract. However, unbeknownst to P or *A* when they made the contract, a pest infestation in South America has eliminated a major source of frozen orange juice, which portends a significant rise in the market price for orange juice. The contract is therefore a very bad one for P. That information is certainly relevant to the principal's decision to embrace the deal, but it is also "about the value of

103. R.3d, §4.06.
104. R.2d, §91, comment *d*.
105. R.3d, §4.06.
106. R.3d, §4.06, comment *c* (stating, "[f]or definitions of materiality, see Restatement (Second), Torts, §538(2)(a); Principles of Corporate Governance: Analysis and Recommendations, §1.25").

the transaction or the transaction's desirability." Under the R.2d approach, the information is not material to the decision to ratify. Under the R.3d, the issue is less clear. ◀◀◀

b. Knowledge Requirement Not Purely Subjective

At first glance, the knowledge requirement seems straightforward. Knowledge is a state of mind. What should matter, therefore, is whether the purported principal lacks subjective knowledge of material facts, not whether the purported principal has reason to know those facts.

However, both Restatements and the case law eschew this conceptually pure approach. According to the R.3d: "A factfinder may conclude that a principal has [assumed the risk of ignorance and ratified] when the principal is shown to have had knowledge of facts that would have led a reasonable person to investigate further, but the principal ratified without further investigation."[107]

c. Principal's Ignorance Versus Third Party's Reliance

The principal's ignorance ceases to be a factor if the third party has learned of and detrimentally relied on the principal's affirmance.[108]

§2.7.4 The Third Party's Right of Avoidance

Ordinarily, a purported principal's affirmance binds not only the purported principal but also the third party. As explained previously, a third party can *preclude* ratification by giving notice of withdrawal from the transaction *before* the purported principal affirms.[109] In two situations, the third party can also *avoid* an otherwise binding affirmance.

a. Changed Circumstances (Other Than Conflicting Arrangements Made by Third Party)

The third party may avoid a ratification if, before the purported principal ratifies, circumstances change so materially that holding the third party to the contract would be unfair. Obviously, at some point the third party will have to inform the purported principal of the changed circumstances. However, it is not necessary that the third party give notice before the affirmance.

---

107. R.3d, §4.06, comment *d*.
108. R.3d, §4.08; R.2d §91, comment *b*.
109. See Section 2.7.2.

Both Restatements use the same, classic example:

Purporting to act for P but without power to bind P, *A* contracts to sell Blackacre with a house thereon to T. The next day the house burns. P's later ratification does not bind T. T may elect to be bound by the contract.[110]

b. Conflicting Arrangements

A third party can also avoid ratification if the third party:

- learns that the purported agent acted without authority;
- relies on the apparent lack of authority; and
- makes substitute, conflicting arrangements or takes some other action that will cause prejudice to the third party if the original transaction is enforced.[111]

For the necessary reliance to exist, the third party must act before learning of the purported principal's affirmance.

§2.7.5 The Term "Ratification" in Other Contexts; Contrasted with Adoption and Novation

a. Generally

In agency law, ratification is a term of art with a very specific and intricate meaning, but agency law has no monopoly on the use of the word. For example, "ratification" is often used to describe the final step in an approval process involving different sets of decision-makers at each step.

Example

Article V of the U.S. Constitution states: "The Congress, whenever two thirds of both Houses shall deem it necessary, shall propose Amendments to this Constitution, or on the Application of the Legislatures of two thirds of the several States, shall call a Convention for proposing Amendments, which, in either Case, shall be valid to all Intents and Purposes, as Part of this Constitution, when ratified by the Legislatures of three fourths of the several States, or by Conventions in three fourths thereof, as the one or the other Mode of Ratification may be proposed by the Congress; . . ." ◀◀◀

110. R.3d, §4.05, Ill. 2, which is taken almost verbatim from R.2d, §89, Ill. 1.
111. R.3d, §4.05(2); R.2d, §95, comment *b*.

b. Ratification, Adoption, and Novation

Even in the agency context, cases sometimes use "ratification" carelessly, usually by confusing and interchanging the terms *ratification*, *adoption*, and *novation*. Many of these cases involve contracts made by promoters on behalf of limited liability companies, corporations, or other entities not in existence when the contract is made. To the extent that the three terms have separate meanings, those meanings are as follows.

(1) **Ratification.** Ratification is the retroactive approval of a previously unauthorized act. Subject to the conditions and exceptions discussed in this section, ratification binds both the purported principal and the third party to the original undertaking and discharges the purported agent from any liability on that undertaking.

(2) ***Adoption.*** Adoption occurs when:

- a purported agent has purported to bind a purported principal to an agreement while lacking the power to do so;
- the purported principal cannot ratify the purported agent's unauthorized act, typically because, at the time of the act, the purported principal either did not exist or lacked capacity to authorize the act;
- the original agreement made by the purported agent and the third party expressly or impliedly empowers the purported principal to choose to receive the benefits and assume the obligations of the agreement; and
- the purported principal manifests—either expressly or through a course of conduct—its desire to receive the benefits and assume the obligations of the agreement.

Like ratification, adoption binds both the principal and the third party to the original agreement. *Unlike* ratification, adoption does not relate back in time to the unauthorized act. So, if for any reason the starting date of the relationship between the adopting principal and the third party is important, that date is the date of the adoption, not the date of the unauthorized act. Moreover, adoption does not release the purported agent from any liability it may have to the third party on account of the original agreement, unless the original agreement provides that the principal's adoption will indeed release the agent.

(3) **Novation** is a new, independent agreement between the principal and the third party. Novations arise from the same circumstances that give rise to adoptions, and it is often the original, unauthorized contract that causes the purported principal and the third party to consider doing business with each other. The terms of the novation may be and often are identical to the terms of the prior, unauthorized agreement.

Nonetheless, a novation reflects an entirely separate process of contract formation. Once formed, the novation contract completely displaces the original, unauthorized contract and relieves the purported agent from any liability it may have had to the third party on account of that prior contract.

Whether the new arrangement is an adoption (which does not release the purported agent) or a novation (which does) is a question of the parties' intent.

Example

Sebastian decides to go into business with a 1950s-style hamburger joint. He plans to organize the business as a limited liability company under the name Charlotte's Place, LLC. He signs a lease for the restaurant, however, before actually forming the limited liability company. In signing the lease, he purports to act as president of Charlotte's Place, LLC and neglects to inform the lessor that Charlotte's Place, LLC, has not yet come into existence. ◀◀◀

Since a nonexistent limited liability company cannot authorize anyone to do anything, Sebastian's act in signing the lease is unauthorized and does not bind the LLC. As of that moment, Sebastian, not the LLC, is liable to the lessor on the lease.[112]

When Sebastian does form the LLC, the LLC may decide to take responsibility for the lease. However, the LLC cannot by itself take Sebastian off the hook. Ratification would release Sebastian, but ratification is not possible: At the time of the lease signing, the LLC did not exist, so one of the necessary preconditions to ratification is absent. The LLC can adopt the lease, but that adoption will not release Sebastian. If the LLC later defaults, he will still be liable.

If the lessor agrees, the LLC and the lessor can make a novation. A new contractual relationship between the lessor and the LLC will replace the original lease, the LLC will be bound, and Sebastian will no longer be liable.

§2.8 CHAINS OF AUTHORITY

§2.8.1 Multilevel Relationships

For the most part, the Examples used in this chapter so far have been "flat." The principals act through a single agent, and agents draw their authority

112. See Section 4.2.2.

directly from manifestations made by the principal. Third parties claim apparent authority from manifestations made directly by a principal.

Real-life relationships tend to be more complex. Agency law handles such complexity in characteristic fashion. It establishes categories, labels the categories, and attaches consequences to the categories. In matters of contract and communication, the key labels are *superior agents*, *subordinate agents*,[113] and *subagents*.

§2.8.2 Superior and Subordinate Agents

a. The Categories

A principal can use one of its agents to select, direct, manage, supervise, and discharge other agents of the principal. Using "superior agents" to deal with "subordinate agents" is merely a specific instance of a principal acting through its agents. The principal uses one (or more) of its agents to manifest its desires to the principal's other agents.

This concatenated, hierarchical structure is commonplace. Only the smallest of organizations can operate without the "top dog" delegating some responsibility to superior and subordinate agents. Moreover, the delegation often works through several levels (in military terms, the "chain of command"), with agents being simultaneously superior agents *vis-à-vis* those "below" them, and subordinate agents *vis-à-vis* those "above" them. Superior agents and subordinate agents are "co-agents" of the principal. A subordinate agent is never the agent of a superior agent.

Example

Marcia is the manager of an airport office of a rental car company, hired by and appointed to the position by a regional vice president of the company, acting within his actual authority. As part of her job, Marcia hires, supervises, and, when necessary, fires the people who staff that office. Those people are agents of the rental car company, not of Marcia, even though: (i) it was Marcia who told each of them, "You're hired"; and (ii) the company itself has never made any direct manifestation to any of them. ◄◄◄

113. Neither the R.2d nor the case law provides any names for these important links in the chain of agency authority. For the first edition of this book, the author coined the terms "intermediary" and "subordinate." R.3d uses the terms "superior and subordinate co-agents" §1.04(9). and this edition follows that usage.

Example

Seeking to increase business, Marcia retains the services of Abitatruth, Inc., an advertising agency. Acting on behalf of the rental car company, Marcia authorizes the agency to spend $10,000 to rent advertising space around the airport on the company's behalf. The agency assigns the work of renting the advertising space to Alan, one of its employees. Alan has the power to bind the rental car company, even though: (i) Marcia has never made any manifestation to Alan; and (ii) Marcia does not even know that Alan exists. ◀◀◀

Each of these Examples involves a "concatenation" of responsibility. That is, in each situation a *chain* of relationships or events makes the rental car company the principal and gives the person at the bottom of the chain the power to bind. Thus, a person can be an agent without ever having met or communicated directly with the principal.

For instance, in the first Example (Marcia hires the staff), the employees are agents of the rental car company because another agent of the company (Marcia), acting within her actual authority, has made manifestations (attributable to the company) that the company (as principal) desires the employees to act on the company's behalf and subject to the company's control. See Figures 2-3 and 2-4.

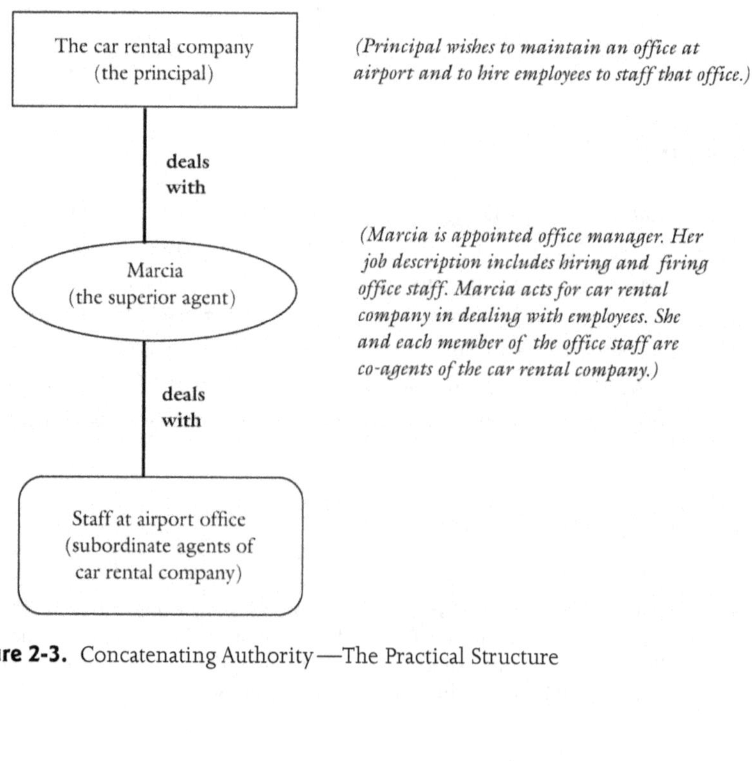

Figure 2-3. Concatenating Authority—The Practical Structure

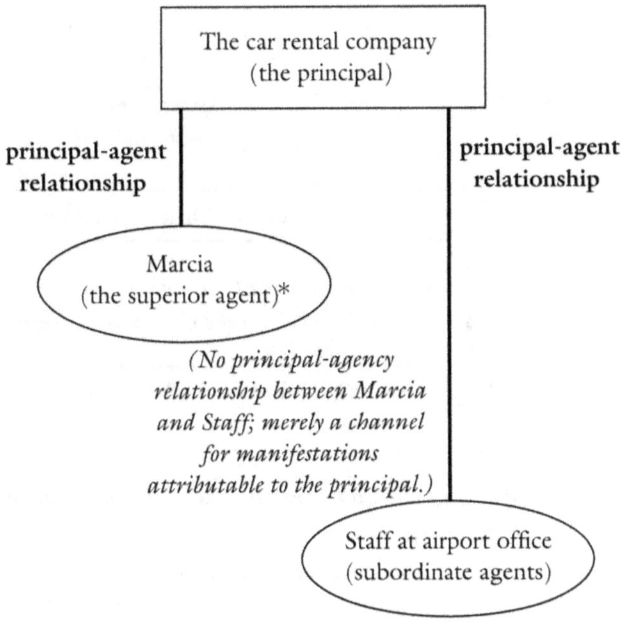

*Note that, if Marcia "reports" to the regional vice president who appointed her, Marcia is a subordinate agent vis-à-vis that vice president.

Figure 2-4. Concatenating Authority—The Agency Structure

Example

Marcia's actual authority to run the airport office might derive as follows: The rental company's regional vice president appointed Marcia to the position and generally described to her the duties and authority of the position. The regional vice president obtained the actual authority to make such manifestations on behalf of the company when the Executive Vice President for Leasing Operations appointed him to the regional vice president position. The Executive Vice President, in turn, obtained her actual authority to manifest the company's choice of regional vice presidents (and to manifest the company's wishes as to the duties and authority of those vice presidents) when the Chief Executive Officer (CEO) appointed her as Executive Vice President and outlined the duties and authority of that position. The company made the necessary manifestations to appoint and authorize the CEO when the company's board of directors elected the CEO.[114] See Figure 2-5. ◄◄◄

114. As to the conduct of a corporation's day-to-day affairs, the board of directors has the ultimate authority and power. See, e.g., Revised Model Business Corporation Act, §8.01(b) ("All corporate powers shall be exercised by or under the authority of, and the business and affairs of the corporation managed under the direction of, its board of directors. . . .").

Board of Directors

manifests the Company's consent and establishes actual authority in

the Chief Executive Officer [a superior agent]

who, acting within his actual authority as an agent of the Company, did an act attributable to the Company, namely — appointing

the Executive Vice President for Leasing [a subordinate agent and simultaneously a superior agent]

who, acting within her actual authority as an agent of the Company, did an act attributable to the Company, namely — appointing

the Regional Vice President [a subordinate agent and simulaneously a superior agent]

who, acting within his actual authority as an agent of the Company, did an act attributable to the Company, namely — appointing

Marcia, the manager of the airport office [a subordinate agent and simultaneously a superior agent]

Figure 2-5. The Rental Car Company's Chain of Command

Most often, superior and subordinate agents are part of the same organization, but the concepts apply as well when the one agent is part of the organization comprising the principal and the other is not.

Example

International Diversified Operations, Inc. ("IDO") does not have its own sales force but instead relies on independent agents who work on commission and have specified authority to accept purchase orders on IDO's behalf. IDO appoints Asif, one of IDO's employees, as national sales director, with authority to issue instructions to the independent agents. Asif is a superior agent, and the independent agents are subordinate agents. ◀◀◀

Regardless of whether superior and subordinate agents are part of the same organization, and no matter how much authority and discretion a superior agent has, the superior agent acts on behalf of the principal and not on the agent's own account. So long as a superior agent acts with actual authority, apparent authority, or inherent agency power, the superior agent's manifestations—whether to the subordinate agents or to third parties—are attributable to the principal.

b. A Subordinate Agent's Power to Bind the Principal

A subordinate agent binds its principal under the same rules applicable to "plain" agents. The key questions are therefore the same; namely, did the subordinate agent act with actual authority, apparent authority, inherent agency power, under circumstances giving rise to estoppel? Answering these questions involves looking at the conduct attributable to the principal, including any manifestations made by superior agents within the scope of their actual authority, apparent authority, or inherent agency power.

Example

Marcia, the manager of the rental car company's airport office, has engaged Abitatruth, an ad agency, to develop advertising for the rental car company. Marcia brings along Sara, one of her assistants, to a series of conferences with Abitatruth. During these conferences Marcia repeatedly seeks Sara's opinion as to choices posed by the ad agency and occasionally defers to Sara's judgment. Later, when the ad agency cannot get in touch with Marcia, it asks Sara to approve the content of several advertising posters. Although Marcia has stated privately to Sara that Marcia plans to approve all posters, Sara tells the ad agency, "Go ahead." ◀◀◀

This approval binds the rental car company. Although Marcia's private statements to Sara preclude a claim based on actual authority, Sara did have apparent authority. Apparent authority presupposes a manifestation *of the rental car company*, which Marcia's conduct supplies. Consulting with and relying on subordinates—even in the presence of others—was certainly within Marcia's actual authority. That conduct is therefore, by attribution, the conduct of the rental car company. Coupled with the ad agency's resulting reasonable belief in Sara's authority, this attributed manifestation gave Sara apparent authority to approve the posters on the rental car company's behalf.

c. Superior Agent's Limited Responsibility for the Misconduct of Subordinate Agents

All agents owe a duty of care to their principal,[115] and superior agents must exercise care in selecting, directing, managing, supervising, and discharging subordinate agents. If a superior agent fails to do so and that breach of duty

115. See Section 4.1.4.

proximately causes injury to the principal, the superior agent is liable to the principal for resulting damages.

Example

Marcia hires Henry to drive the courtesy van that takes passengers between the airport and the car rental office. Marcia carelessly fails to check Henry's references and driving record. The references are false, and the record includes several drunk-driving convictions. One day Henry drives the van while drunk and causes an accident. Under the doctrine of *respondeat superior*, the car rental company is liable for any damage Henry caused to others.[116] Marcia is liable to the car rental company for its obligations to others, plus any damage to the company's courtesy van. She breached her duty of care in selecting and supervising a subordinate agent. ◀◀◀

A superior agent is not, however, the guarantor of the subordinate agent's performance.

Example

Same situation, except Henry's references are okay, his driving record is clean, and Marcia uses reasonable care in hiring and supervising Henry. The car rental company remains liable to others for harm caused by Henry's drunken driving, but Marcia is not liable to the car rental company. ◀◀◀

§2.8.3 Subagents

a. The Category

When a principal engages an agent to perform a task, the principal has in effect delegated the task to the agent. If the agent, acting with authority, in turn delegates part or all of that task to an agent of its own, then the second agent becomes a subagent of the original principal.

Restatement on Point

P retains *A*, a real estate broker, to sell Blackacre. P knows that *A* employs salespeople to show property to prospective purchasers and to state the terms on which the property is for sale. The salespeople are *A*'s employees, not P's employees. The salespeople are also P's subagents.[117] ◀◀◀

116. See Section 3.2.
117. This Example is taken verbatim from R.3d, §1.04, Ill. 4.

b. The Agent's Authority to Further Delegate

In theory, an agent has no authority to delegate its tasks to its own agents. However, a principal can authorize its agent to delegate, and, when the agent is a limited liability company, corporation, or other legal entity, some authority to delegate is inescapably implied. Legal "persons" can act only through the endeavors of natural persons.

The general rules for creating actual authority apply to determine whether an agent has authority to re-delegate to its own agents.[118] Consistent with those rules, implied actual authority to delegate exists when: (i) the delegation relates merely to the mechanical aspects of the agent's tasks; (ii) the agent is a limited liability company, partnership, corporation, or other organization; or (iii) it is customary for agents in similar situations to delegate. The principal can of course override these implications with an express manifestation, but where the agent is an organization some delegation is inevitable.

Example

Sylvia, a rock singer, retains David, a well-known agent, to arrange on her behalf the facilities and amenities to be made available to Sylvia on an upcoming tour. David has several assistants, and they normally handle such "logistical details." Sylvia, however, says, "I want your personal touch on this. Don't let anyone else work on it." David has no actual authority to delegate the work. ◄◄◄

Example

Sylvia, a rock singer, retains Pauline's Representation, Inc. ("Pauline's"), to arrange bookings. Pauline's is a limited liability company, with the necessary right to delegate the task. Sylvia, however, imposes a restriction, saying, "Make sure whoever works on my account has been with you for at least five years." ◄◄◄

c. A Subagent's Power to Bind the Principal

The R.2d and R.3d differ in their approach to this issue. The R.2d approach is more elaborate and more precise. Assuming that an agent has the authority to delegate tasks to a subagent, under the R.2d, determining the scope

118. Recall that if the delegation is to another agent of the principal (rather than to an agent of the agent), subagency is not involved. Instead, the "redelegator" is a superior agent, delegating to a subordinate agent.

of a subagent's power to bind the principal in contract involves a two-stage analysis:

1. What is the scope of the agent's power to bind the principal?
2. Of that scope, what has the agent authorized the subagent to perform?[119]

Example

The car rental company (acting via Marcia) gives Abitatruth actual authority to spend up to $10,000 in renting advertising space [stage 1]. Moe is a junior vice president of Abitatruth, with actual authority (from Abitatruth) to make leasing commitments of $1,000 or less [stage 2]. Moe has neither apparent authority nor inherent agency power to exceed the $1,000 limit while acting for Abitatruth [stage 2]. Moe purports to commit the car rental company to space Alpha for $800 and to space Beta for $1,250. ◂ ◂ ◂

In each instance, Moe has acted as an agent for Abitatruth and subagent for the car rental company. The commitment on space Alpha binds the car rental company, because the commitment was within Abitatruth's authority *vis-à-vis* the company [stage 1] and within Moe's authority *vis-à-vis* Abitatruth [stage 2]. The commitment on space Beta does not bind the car rental company, because that commitment exceeded Moe's authority *vis-à-vis* Abitatruth [stage 2]. In sum, to bind the principal under the R.2d, a subagent's act must be both within the subagent's power to bind the agent and the agent's power to bind the principal.

The R.3d approach has the virtue of simplicity:

> As between a principal and third parties, it is immaterial that an action was taken by a subagent as opposed to an agent directly appointed by the principal. In this respect, subagency is governed by a principle of transparency that looks from the subagent to the principal and through the appointing agent. As to third parties, an action taken by a subagent carries the legal consequences for the principal that would follow were the action instead taken by the appointing agent.[120]

Unfortunately, this approach also has the defect of indeterminacy. Surely not every act of a subagent binds the principal, especially not acts that would not bind the agent.

d. Agent as the Guarantor of the Subagent's Performance

When an agent delegates all or part of its responsibilities to a subagent, the agent remains "on the hook" to the principal. Delegation does not relieve

---

119. R.2d, §5, comment *d*.
120. R.3d, §3.15, comment *d*.

the agent of its responsibilities. If the subagent's performance satisfies the obligations the agent owes to the principal, then the agent, acting through the subagent, has performed its responsibilities as agent. If, however, the subagent's performance fails to satisfy the agent's obligations, then the agent is directly responsible to the principal.[121]

§2.8.4 Distinguishing Subordinate Agents from Subagents

The concepts of subordinate agent and subagent both presuppose a hierarchy with:

- the principal at the top,
- the subordinate agent or subagent at the bottom, and
- an intermediary (either a superior agent or an agent) in between.

Nonetheless, the two concepts reflect very different relationships with very different legal consequences. It is therefore important to distinguish one relationship from the other.

The crucial point of distinction is the manifestation that the principal makes to the intermediary. Does that manifestation, reasonably interpreted, lead the intermediary to believe that:

- the principal wishes the intermediary to retain or supervise *another agent of the principal*
  - in which case the intermediary is to be a superior agent, the other agent is to be a subordinate agent, and both the superior and subordinate agents are to be co-agents of the principal;

or

- the principal wishes to retain the intermediary *as the principal's agent* and recognizes that the agent may delegate some or all of its responsibility to another person
  - in which case that other person is an agent of the agent and simultaneously a subagent of the principal?

121. The rule stated here closely parallels a rule of contract law: When an obligor delegates its performance obligations to another, that delegation does not by itself discharge the obligor's duties to the obligee. *See, e.g.*, *Fed. Ins. Co. v. Winters*, 354 S.W.3d 287, 295 (Tenn. 2011) ("The delegation of performance . . . does not relieve the contractor from the duties implicit in the original contract.").

Example

A landlord retains a management company to manage 150 separate apartment buildings owned by the landlord. The landlord wants a resident manager in each building and expects these caretakers to be employees of the management company. The managers will be agents of the management company and subagents of the landlord. ◀ ◀ ◀

Superior and subordinate agents are usually part of the same company, as in the Examples in Section 2.8.2 involving Marcia and the car rental company. However, that circumstance is *not* an element of the superior/subordinate agent analysis.

Example

The management company's contract with the landlord has significantly increased the company's obligations, and the company needs interim help recruiting and supervising resident managers. On an interim basis, the management company retains Carolyn, an experienced real estate attorney, to interview applicants for caretaker positions, and gives her authority to hire applicants she considers appropriate. The management company also retains Carolyn to supervise the applicants she hires. Like her, the caretakers she hires will be agents of the management company.[122] When she supervises, she will be acting as a superior agent *vis-à-vis* subordinate agents. ◀ ◀ ◀

Problem 1

Captain Miles Standish loved the fair damsel Priscilla, but Standish's intense shyness prevented him from speaking to her. One day Standish lamented the situation to his friend John Alden, and Alden offered to speak to Priscilla and, on Standish's behalf, invite her to an upcoming community dance. Standish responded, stroking his beard reflectively, "I dunno. That might be a good idea." Alden took that comment as assent and rode off to see Priscilla. However, Standish did not intend to consent. Right after Alden rode off, Standish wrote in his diary, "Told Alden that I would think about his offer. Have done so and will reject it as soon as I next see him."

Before Standish saw Alden again, Alden saw Priscilla. Alden explained Standish's great love, and—purporting to act on Standish's behalf—invited Priscilla to accompany Standish to the dance. Priscilla accepted. Later, Standish saw Alden and told him not to talk to Priscilla. Alden told Standish, "Too late, fellow; you're going to the dance."

---

122. Unlike Carolyn, the resident managers will probably also be servants of the management company. See Section 3.2.4. However, that distinction is immaterial here.

Assume that, as a matter of contract law, contracts to attend dances are valid and enforceable. Is Standish bound? ◀ ◀ ◀

Explanation

Standish is bound only if Alden had actual authority to extend the invitation.[123] The creation of actual authority requires: (i) a manifestation by the principal; (ii) the agent's reasonable interpretation of that manifestation as a request that the agent acts for the principal; and (iii) the agent's manifestation of consent to act. The first and last certainly occurred. Standish's comment ("That might be a good idea") suffices as a manifestation. Alden's action reflects his consent. The question of the agent's interpretation, however, is more difficult. Although Standish's subjective intent is irrelevant, Standish's response was objectively ambiguous. Especially given what Alden knew of Standish's shyness, it was probably unreasonable for Alden to consider himself authorized without having first sought clarification. Therefore, no actual authority existed, and Standish is not bound on the contract. ◀ ◀ ◀

Problem 2

A tenant rents her apartment on a month-to-month tenancy, with each term beginning on the first of the month. Under local law, the tenant can terminate the tenancy by giving a full calendar month's notice. For example, for the tenancy to end on March 31, the tenant must give notice before March 1. A resident manager, whom the landlord has authorized to receive notices from tenants, manages the building. On December 28, the tenant gives proper notice to the resident manager, stating that the tenant will vacate by January 31. Unfortunately, the resident manager fails to pass the notice on to the landlord until January 3. Will the tenancy end on January 31? ◀ ◀ ◀

Explanation

Yes. When an agent has actual authority to receive a notice, receipt of that notice is attributable to the principal. The agent's failure to communicate the information to the principal may be a breach of the agent's duty to the principal[124] but has no effect on the attribution rule. ◀ ◀ ◀

---

123. Since there is no indication of Priscilla's being aware of any manifestation by Standish, there can be no apparent authority. Since Alden is not a general agent, there can be no inherent power. Since Priscilla has not changed position to her detriment, there can be no estoppel. (The facts do not indicate that she has bought a new dress or rejected other invitations.)
124. See Sections 4.1.4 and 4.1.5.

Problem 3

A gay man, well known as a gay rights advocate, seeks to buy a house for sale in a fashionable neighborhood, but fears that the owner, a well-known opponent of gay rights, will refuse to sell to him. The would-be buyer therefore secretly authorizes a friend to negotiate and consummate the purchase, ostensibly in the friend's name. It never occurs to the seller that the ostensible purchaser might be a front, and the seller asks no questions to that effect. The friend of course makes no comment on the subject. At closing the seller learns that the gay man is the undisclosed principal. Is the seller obliged to go through with the sale? ◀ ◀ ◀

Explanation

EXPLANATION

Yes. Although both the agent and the undisclosed principal had reason to know that the third party would have refused to deal with the principal, there was no affirmative misrepresentation.[125] ◀ ◀ ◀

Problem 4

Mr. and Ms. Yup, high-power corporate lawyers, mesh their schedules and arrange a week's vacation hiking in the Andes Mountains. To babysit their offspring ("Little Yup") and to housesit their house, the Yups hire a babysitter ("Babysitter"). The Yups provide the babysitter, among other information, the name, office phone number, and office address of Little Yup's pediatrician. They also leave a health insurance card that indicates a health insurance account number for Little Yup. Unfortunately, while the Yups are away, Little Yup becomes seriously ill. The babysitter takes Little Yup to the hospital, where expensive medical procedures enable Little Yup to recover. In order to have the hospital provide the services, Babysitter shows the health insurance card and signs a contract with the hospital. Queried about the child's parents, Babysitter responds, "They're backpacking in the Andes. I am babysitting for their child for this week." Babysitter signs the

---

125. This Example assumes the transaction is not subject to a law prohibiting discrimination on account of sexual orientation.

hospitalization contract: "I.M. Babysitter, for Mr. and Ms. Yup." Are Mr. and Ms. Yup bound on that contract? ◀ ◀ ◀

Explanation

The Yups are bound, certainly on actual authority and perhaps on apparent authority as well. Merely by entrusting the child to Babysitter for a week and leaving the country, the Yups manifested consent to have Babysitter arrange for necessary medical care, and Babysitter certainly believed her or himself authorized to do so. By providing Babysitter the name of the pediatrician and the health insurance card, the Yups made an additional manifestation and buttressed the reasonableness of Babysitter's belief. The Yups did not specifically mention hospitalization and did not specifically authorize Babysitter to sign hospital contracts on their behalf, but Babysitter certainly had implied actual authority to arrange hospitalization in an emergency and to sign all reasonably necessary documents for that purpose.

The argument for apparent authority is also strong. The hospital must be able to point to some manifestation of the Yups that, reasonably interpreted, led the hospital to believe that Babysitter was authorized to bind the Yups. The hospital can identify three manifestations: the Yups' entrusting of their child to Babysitter; the Babysitter's possession of the insurance card; the Babysitter's statement about her responsibilities. The first manifestation arguably establishes apparent authority by position, although babysitters do not customarily commit parents to large hospital bills. The possession of the insurance card made it more reasonable for the hospital to believe that the parents had given Babysitter authority to arrange for medical services. It is the third manifestation—Babysitter's statement—that is perhaps the strongest point. Had that statement been made directly by the Yups, there would have been no question of Babysitter's apparent authority. When Babysitter accurately described her authority, she was acting within her actual authority. As a consequence, her statement had the same effect as if the Yups had made it themselves. ◀ ◀ ◀

Problem 5

Pickwick owns an antique store called Pickwick's that occupies the first three floors of a four-story brownstone. Pickwick lives on the fourth floor, has security cameras throughout the first three floors, and has a rather lackadaisical attitude toward maintaining personal surveillance over the store premises. He customarily leaves the store door unlocked even when he is upstairs having lunch or taking a nap. A large sign just inside the store entrance advises: "For assistance, pull on cord to ring bell."

One day, two newlyweds enter the store and are promptly approached by a respectable-looking lady who identifies herself as "Mrs. Pickwick."

With Mrs. Pickwick's assistance, the newlyweds examine several large antiques and decide to purchase two of them. The newlyweds give Mrs. Pickwick $200 in cash as a down payment and arrange for a delivery day. Mrs. Pickwick takes from a roll-top desk a sheet of letterhead for "Pickwick & Company" and writes out and signs a receipt.

"Mrs. Pickwick" is in fact an imposter. Is Mr. Pickwick bound to the purported contract? If not, is Mr. Pickwick obliged to make good the $200? ◀ ◀ ◀

Explanation

EXPLANATION

Although the imposter lacked actual and apparent authority,[126] Mr. Pickwick is probably liable via estoppel at least for the $200. The newlyweds "changed their position because of their belief that the transaction was entered into . . . for" Mr. Pickwick, and Mr. Pickwick "carelessly caused such belief" through his lackadaisical attitude toward security.[127] At minimum, the newlyweds are entitled to their reliance damages and perhaps to their expectation interest as well. ◀ ◀ ◀

Problem 6

Henry comes to town one day looking for some land to purchase. He learns that Eleanor has a parcel of lakefront property that she wishes to sell. Henry meets Eleanor, explains that he is "in town acting for a group of investors who are looking for lakefront in this area," and goes with Eleanor to inspect the property. Henry appears impressed, but says to Eleanor, "I'm just the gofer. I'll have to check with the folks in charge." The next day Henry comes back and tells Eleanor that he is authorized to pay her $70,000 for the property. Eleanor thinks the price is a fair one, and together they go to a local stationery store and buy a legal form titled "Contract for the Sale of Land." They fill in all the blanks, Eleanor signs as seller, and Henry signs as "agent for the Aquitaine LLC, Buyer." As completed and signed, the contract indicates that, on behalf of Aquitaine LLC, Henry has put $100 down and that the limited liability company will deliver the rest of the purchase price within 30 days.

Two weeks after the contract is signed, Eleanor sees Henry walking down a street in town. Walking with Henry is a man whom Henry introduces as Richard, the managing member of Aquitaine LLC. (This man is indeed Richard, and Richard is indeed managing member of Aquitaine.)

---

126. No manifestation attributable to Mr. Pickwick, the principal.

127. R.2d, §8B(1)(a), discussed in Section 2.6. See also R.3d, Ch. 2, Topic 4, Introduction.

After casual remarks about the weather, Eleanor asks, "Does Henry do a lot of work for your company, Richard?" Richard responds, "We've used him on a number of occasions. He's quite a go-getter."

Thirty days pass after the signing of the contract, and Eleanor receives no payment. When she contacts Aquitaine LLC, the company denies that Henry was authorized to act on its behalf. The company (acting through an agent with actual authority) truthfully states that: (i) the company never made any manifestation to Henry regarding Eleanor's parcel, and (ii) Henry never had any ongoing responsibilities with Aquitaine but instead occasionally received specific assignments. Aquitaine denies any responsibility for the Eleanor–Henry transaction and flatly refuses to pay.

With Henry being nowhere to be found, Eleanor brings suit on the contract against Aquitaine LLC. Assume that the "equal dignities" rule does *not* apply in the jurisdiction. Assume also that Richard's comments to Eleanor are attributable to Aquitaine. What results in Eleanor's suit? ◀◀◀

EXPLANATION

Explanation

Eleanor will lose. She will be unable to attribute Henry's actions to Aquitaine.

Since Aquitaine never made any manifestation to Henry regarding Eleanor's parcel, actual authority did not exist. Since Henry's role with Aquitaine never involved any "continuity of service," he was never a general agent. Consequently, he had no inherent agency power to enter into contracts on Aquitaine's behalf. The doctrines of apparent authority and estoppel are Eleanor's only hope, and that hope is forlorn.

The problem with apparent authority is one of timing: The apparent principal's manifestation came too late. To establish apparent authority, Eleanor must show some conduct attributable to Aquitaine that *as of the moment of contract formation* caused her to reasonably believe that Henry had authority. Until just prior to the execution of the form contract, Eleanor did not even know who the supposed principal was. Even when Henry disclosed Aquitaine's identity, Eleanor's inference that Henry had authority was based solely on Henry's remarks, not on any conduct of Aquitaine.

In some circumstances, an apparent principal's silence in the face of an apparent agent's known conduct will suffice as a manifestation. However, in this case there is no indication whatsoever that at the time of contract formation Aquitaine LLC was aware of Henry's claim of agency status.

The conversation between Eleanor and Richard cannot salvage the situation for Eleanor. Even if Eleanor reasonably interpreted Richard's comments to mean that Henry had authority, there remains the problem of timing. Even under the Restatement view, the claimant must link the manifestation to a reasonable belief that existed *as of the moment of the relevant act*. A post hoc manifestation cannot justify an ante hoc belief. By the time Eleanor spoke with Richard, Eleanor had already executed the contract.

The Eleanor–Richard conversation will be likewise unavailing for a claim of estoppel. Even assuming that Richard's casual remark "intentionally or carelessly" caused Eleanor to believe that Henry had acted with authority,[128] that belief did not cause any relevant harm. Eleanor had already signed the contract. Unless she can show that she suffered some additional prejudice subsequent to her conversation with Richard (e.g., turning down another potential buyer), she cannot establish estoppel.[129] ◄ ◄ ◄

Problem 7

A small real estate company is planning to rent office space to an entrepreneur who needs "a place to hang my hat, pick up my mail, and get telephone calls." The real estate company's premises are small and its phone system very basic. The entrepreneur's calls will come through the main switchboard without a dedicated line, and her desk will be located in the same open space used by employees of the company. How can the real estate company minimize the chances that it will be held responsible for its tenant's dealings with third parties? ◄ ◄ ◄

Explanation

Perhaps the most important safeguard is to expend the time and effort necessary to check into the *bona fides* of the would-be tenant. Problems will arise only if the entrepreneur cheats her customers or suppliers.

As for the agency law analysis, apparent authority is the key concept. Under that concept, the main risks would come from: (i) ambiguous manifestations by the real estate company; and (ii) reasonable misinterpretations by third parties. Due to the limitations of the phone system and the office setup, certain manifestations are inherent in the proposed arrangement. The key, therefore, is to preclude reasonable confusion. The safest approach is to make sure that an appropriate clarification accompanies each potentially confusing manifestation. For example, when the receptionist receives a call for the entrepreneur, the receptionist should use a greeting that indicates that the real estate company does not employ the entrepreneur. As for the office setup, a sign on the office entrance should indicate the entrepreneur's independent, unassociated status. ◄ ◄ ◄

---

128. R.2d, §8B(1)(a), discussed at Section 2.6.

129. To assert that Richard's comments caused ratification is too much of a stretch. Ratification requires a manifestation of affirmance, and the purported principal's manifestation must relate specifically to the unauthorized act being ratified.

Problem 8

For several years, a local band has played mostly for free at various local venues, seeking thereby to gain the experience and exposure and "break through" to paying opportunities. For the past two years, the band has relied on Oliver, its unpaid manager, to arrange its bookings.

Over the past several months, due to the band's increasing popularity, Oliver has been able to arrange modest fees for each performance. As is customary in the locality, payment is made immediately after each performance.

Last week, success created problems, as Oliver insisted on a percentage of future fees, the band told him no, he objected, and at 10 P.M. the band "fired" him. The next morning, at 10 A.M., Oliver went to a bar at which the band had previously played several times for free, as arranged by Oliver. On this occasion, Oliver: (i) purported still to be the band's manager; (ii) persuaded the bar to pay a performance fee of $500; (iii) insisted on collecting $100 in advance; (iv) succeeded with that insistence, due to the band's increasing popularity; (v) pocketed the money; and (vi) never told the band anything. Is the band obligated to perform? If the band does not perform, is the band obligated to "return" the $100 to the bar? ◄◄◄

Explanation

As a matter of agency law and lingering apparent authority, the band probably is bound to the contract made by Oliver purportedly on its behalf. If so, (i) contract law determines the bar's remedy if the band breaches its obligation; and (ii) at minimum, the bar will have a claim for restitution of the $100 advance payment. If the band is not obligated to perform, the band is not liable for the $100.

Obviously, Oliver's actual authority ended when the band fired him. However, his apparent authority lingered as to the bar, which had previously dealt with the band through Oliver. By performing in the past as arranged by Oliver, the band manifested to the bar that Oliver was authorized to act on its behalf. Because the bar neither knew nor had reason to know of the split between Oliver and the band, that manifestation supports a claim of lingering apparent authority.

Oliver's pocketing of the money is irrelevant to the claim; apparent authority applies to a faithless or even fraudulent apparent agent. However, the band might argue that both the fee and the requirement of an advance payment triggered a duty of inquiry.

The first of those arguments is make-weight. Except in unusual circumstances, the authority to arrange for free performances certainly suggests the authority to arrange for compensated performances.

The advance payment requires a more complex assessment. Although advance payments are not customary, the bar evidently considered it reasonable in these circumstances to make an advance payment. Why, then, would it be unreasonable for the bar to believe that the band had authorized its manager to collect the advance payment?

If Oliver had lingering apparent authority, the band is obligated on the contract. However, if Oliver lacked apparent authority, the band is neither bound to the contract nor obligated for the $100. No apparent authority means no imputation to the band of Oliver's receipt of the money.[130] ◀◀◀

Problem 9

Jeffrey is a buyer's broker in the recycled newspaper business. On behalf of various newsprint manufacturers, he locates and purchases recycled newspapers. Each time Jeffrey makes a purchase, he is acting on behalf of a particular customer. He nonetheless makes each purchase in his own name.

For the past five years, one of Jeffrey's customers has been Amalgamated Newsprint. During that time Jeffrey has made about four purchases per year for Amalgamated. On each occasion Jeffrey and Amalgamated have followed the same procedure: Amalgamated places an order with Jeffrey, stating a quantity and a maximum price. When Jeffrey finds the necessary newspapers, he purchases them in his own name and informs Amalgamated of the delivery date and price. Amalgamated then wires funds to Jeffrey, and Jeffrey pays the vendor. A commission structure rewards Jeffrey for bringing in an order below the maximum allowed price. Jeffrey understands that he is not authorized to make any purchases for Amalgamated without first having an order in hand.

Nonetheless, after five years Jeffrey has begun to anticipate Amalgamated's needs. Last week he saw a great purchase opportunity and, expecting an order from Amalgamated, he agreed to make the purchase. Although, as always, Jeffrey made the purchase in his own name, he noted the purchase on his books as "for Amalgamated." If Jeffrey is unable to pay for the purchase, can the vendor enforce the contract against Amalgamated? ◀◀◀

Explanation

EXPLANATION

Probably not. Since Jeffrey lacked the right to purchase for Amalgamated without first having an order and since Amalgamated was an undisclosed principal, neither actual nor apparent authority apply. Also, since there is no

130. The facts do not support a claim for agency by estoppel. There are no facts to suggest that the band had reason to suspect that Oliver would respond to his firing by acting dishonestly, and the short time between the firing and Oliver's dishonesty negates any suggestion that the band was dilatory in informing the past customers of the change in Oliver's status. Also, although Oliver had been a general agent, his inherent authority ended when the band terminated the agency relationship.

evidence that Amalgamated knew of Jeffrey's conduct in this instance or was careless, there can be no estoppel.

The vendor's only hope is inherent agency power. The vendor must: (i) label Jeffrey as Amalgamated's general agent; (ii) delineate Jeffrey's agency function as acquiring newspaper for Amalgamated on an ongoing basis; and (iii) characterize the purchase contract as "usual or necessary" to Jeffrey's authorized activities.[131]

The vendor will likely fail in all three respects, because it will fail in the first. Jeffrey is not a general agent. He is not "authorized to conduct a series of transactions involving a continuity of service."[132] To the contrary, he receives and needs separate authorization for each individual transaction. As a result, Jeffrey has no "ongoing" authorized responsibilities and the unauthorized purchase was not "usual or necessary" to any authorized activity. ◀◀◀

Problem 10

Jeffrey makes the unauthorized purchase described in Problem 9, but in doing so tells the vendor that the purchase is being made on behalf of Amalgamated. Jeffrey then calls Amalgamated and reports his "great find." Amalgamated shocks Jeffrey by saying, "Nothing doing. No order with us, no deal from us."

Jeffrey immediately contacts the vendor, seeking a brief delay on delivery. "I bought this for a customer," he explains, "and I didn't exactly have their okay in advance. They're balking a bit. I've got to make nice with them." Jeffrey then calls Amalgamated again, apologizes profusely, and extols the benefits of this bargain. After a 45-minute conversation, Amalgamated relents and says, "All right. We'll take it."

Jeffrey immediately calls the vendor back and says, "No problem. We're fine." The vendor responds, "I'm fine anyhow. As soon as I learned that you were a go-between and had no authority, I went looking for another buyer. Just two minutes ago I sold the goods to somebody else."

Can Amalgamated enforce the original agreement against the vendor? ◀◀◀

Explanation

EXPLANATION

No. Amalgamated did eventually affirm Jeffrey's unauthorized act, and ordinarily that affirmance would effect a ratification and bind both the vendor

131. R.2d, §194 (inherent agency power of general agent of undisclosed principal), discussed in Section 2.6.2.
132. R.2d, §3(1) (general agent defined), discussed at Section 2.6.2.

and Amalgamated to the contract. In this instance, however, the vendor can avoid the ratification. In reliance on Jeffrey's lack of authority, the vendor changed its position and bound itself to another buyer. The fact that Amalgamated ratified before that change in position took place is irrelevant. What matters is that the vendor changed position before learning of the ratification.[133] ◀◀◀

Problem 11

January 1, 2017	Elvira enters into an oral contract with three entrepreneurs who are founding a community theater. The contract calls for Elvira to begin work managing the theater on March 1, 2017, and to work in that capacity for one year. All parties understand that the entrepreneurs plan to form a limited liability company to own the business and that the limited liability company will take over Elvira's contract.
March 1, 2017	Elvira begins work as manager.
May 1, 2017	The entrepreneurs form Community Theatre, Inc ("CTI"), a member-managed limited liability company. They then appoint Roberta as chief executive officer and formally (albeit orally) agree to have CTI "take over the management contract with Elvira."
May 2, 2017	Acting on behalf of CTI, Roberta informs Elvira of CTI's formation, Roberta's appointment as CEO, and the members' decision to take over Elvira's contract. Roberta says, "As of now, your management contract is with CTI."
May 31, 2017	Elvira receives her monthly salary check, this time drawn on a CTI checking account.
June 30, 2017	Elvira receives her monthly salary check, drawn on a CTI checking account.
July 10, 2017	Roberta terminates Elvira as manager.

Elvira subsequently sues CTI for breach of contract, asserting that under the contract CTI was obligated to continue her employment through

133. This Problem concerns "conflicting arrangements" rather than "changed circumstances." See Section 2.7.4.

February 29, 2018. CTI defends in part invoking the statute of frauds, noting that the original agreement contemplated performance that would extend more than one year beyond the making of the contract.

Elvira responds that: (i) the original agreement with the three entrepreneurs may have been within the statute, but she is not suing them; (ii) when CTI "took over" the contract, the contract called for less than a year of performance; and therefore (iii) the statute of frauds does not apply to CTI's obligations.

CTI rejoins that: (i) by "taking over" the contract, CTI ratified the original agreement; (ii) ratification relates back to the time of the action being ratified; and therefore (iii) CTI's ratification results in a contract that is within the statute of frauds.

Who is right? ◀ ◀ ◀

Explanation

Elvira. A party can ratify a prior act only if the party existed at the time of the act. A limited liability company can therefore never ratify an act taken on its behalf before the company came into existence. ◀ ◀ ◀

Problem 12

The board of directors of Rollerskating, Inc. (Rollerskating) adopts a resolution authorizing the CEO "to appoint such officers, managers, and employees of the corporation as the CEO deems appropriate, and to prescribe their respective duties, subject only to the numerical limits established by the board of directors from time to time." Aware of the resolution, Rollerskating's CEO appoints Rachael to be its purchasing agent. The CEO provides Rachael with a four-page memo outlining the internal approvals necessary before Rachael may place an order. For instance, orders costing less than $50,000 can be approved by the CEO; orders costing less than $25,000 may be approved by any vice president; orders costing less than $5,000 may be approved by any department manager. Rachael receives a request from a vice president to order a Model 5400 Wodget from Charlotte Equipment Corporation ("Charlotte Equipment") at a price of $15,000, and she places the order. Does the order bind Rollerskating? ◀ ◀ ◀

Explanation

Yes. In placing the order, she is acting with the reasonable belief that she is authorized to do so. Her belief is based on manifestations from a superior agent (her appointment to the position of purchasing; the memo of internal procedures). Those manifestations are within the superior agent's actual authority and are therefore attributable to the principal. In short, Rachael has actual authority. ◄◄◄

Problem 13

Over the next three months, Rachael places several more orders with Charlotte Equipment Company, each properly requested by a Rollerskating vice president and each costing between $10,000 and $24,000. In due course, Charlotte Equipment delivers the equipment and bills Rollerskating. The bills come to the Rollerskating comptroller, whom the CEO has made responsible for reviewing and approving for payment all invoices over $10,000. The comptroller reviews the invoices, notes that each order was properly authorized and has been fulfilled, okays the payment, and signs and sends to Charlotte Equipment a payment for the invoiced amount.

Subsequently, Rachael is promoted out of the purchasing department and is replaced by Herman. Rachael's last responsibility as purchasing agent is to brief Herman on his new responsibilities. Rachael does so, directing Herman's attention to the CEO's memo on internal approvals. Herman reads the memo but promptly forgets its provisions.

The next day Herman receives a rush request to order another Model 5400 Wodget from Charlotte Equipment Company at a price of $15,000. The request comes from a department manager, not a vice president, but Herman places the order anyway. Does Herman's order bind Rollerskating? ◄◄◄

Explanation

After having read the CEO's memo, Herman lacked actual authority to place the order. He could not *reasonably* have believed himself authorized. He did, however, have apparent authority. Rollerskating is therefore bound.

The apparent authority arises from manifestations attributable to Rollerskating, Herman's principal. Those manifestations were: (i) Herman's position as Rollerskating's purchasing agent; and (ii) Rollerskating's conduct on past orders placed with Charlotte Equipment by a Rollerskating purchasing agent. On each prior occasion, Rollerskating's comptroller approved and sent payments. The comptroller was acting within her actual authority, so her actions are attributable to Rollerskating. The sequence of events—order from a purchasing agent followed by payment without protest—presumably led Charlotte Equipment to believe that Rollerskating purchasing agents have authority to place such orders. In light of the past events, that belief was certainly reasonable.

Herman may also have had inherent agency power. He was a general agent, acting in his principal's interest. Ordering the Model 5400 could be seen as an act usual or necessary to serving Herman's authorized purpose.[134] ◄◄◄

Problem 14

A large corporation is facing a large number of product liability suits venued around the country but involving the same product. For efficiency's sake, the corporation hires a large firm of experienced and expensive lawyers ("Big Firm") to serve as national coordinating counsel to the corporation. In that capacity, Big Firm acts on the corporation's behalf to: (i) retain local counsel to represent the corporation in the various lawsuits; (ii) facilitate and coordinate the exchange of information and work product among the various local counsel; and (iii) to supervise the work of the local counsel.

Big Firm uses due care in carrying out its duties. Unfortunately, however, local counsel in one case commits discovery abuses that result in a $50,000 sanction being assessed against the corporation. Is Big Firm liable to the corporation for some or all of this amount? ◄◄◄

Explanation

EXPLANATION

No, because local counsel is a subordinate agent of the corporation and not a subagent of Big Firm. Distinguishing between a subordinate agent and a subagent involves focusing on the manifestations of the principal. In this instance, the principal (the corporation) told the intermediary (Big Firm) to "retain local counsel to represent the corporation"; that is, to retain counsel to act as agents of the corporation. Therefore, Big Firm and local counsel are co-agents of the corporation, and Big Firm is a supervisory agent *vis-à-vis* local counsel. In that capacity, Big Firm is not the

134. In one respect, this explanation is unrealistically "flat." The third party, Charlotte Equipment, has no mind in which to form or harbor beliefs and therefore cannot *directly* believe anything about Herman's authority. The relevant beliefs are those of Charlotte Equipment's agents, which are attributable to their principal according to agency law. Whether those attributed beliefs are reasonable depends in part on what Charlotte Equipment knows or has reason to know. Since Charlotte Equipment cannot *directly* know anything, what it knows or has reason to know likewise depends on the attribution rules of agency law.

guarantor of local counsel's conduct and would be liable for local counsel's mistakes only if Big Firm had breached its duty of care in supervising local counsel. ◀ ◀ ◀

Problem 15

The ________ Law School Exam Conflict and Make-Up Policy, printed in the Student Handbook, states in part:

> Students will take exams at the time and place announced in the exam schedule unless:
>
> 1. A student is prevented from taking the exams because of his or her illness or illness or death in the student's immediate family;
> 2. A student has two exams scheduled on the same day;
> 3. A student has three exams scheduled within a period of three calendar days;
> 4. A student has two exams scheduled to begin within 23 hours of each other;
> 5. A student has exceptional circumstances that, in the discretion of the dean of students, justify a rescheduling. Exceptional circumstances must relate to personal situations, not to a burdensome examination schedule.
>
> No makeup exam will be given more than one week after the end of the regular exam period, except when such a delay is necessitated by illness or other exceptional circumstances.
>
> No student shall take any exam before the regularly scheduled time for the exam.

On account of a serious illness in the immediate family, a student requests permission to reschedule an exam. Due to the student's long-standing and significant employment responsibilities, the only practical time for the makeup exam is three days before the regularly scheduled time. The dean of students grants the request, and the student buys two nonrefundable airline tickets. The dean is aware that the student will be purchasing airline tickets but not that the tickets will be nonrefundable.

Subsequently, the professor whose exam is involved learns that an unidentified student will take a makeup in advance of the rest of the class. The professor objects and asserts that an advance makeup violates the policy quoted above. Has the action of the dean of students bound the law school to allow the advance makeup? ◀ ◀ ◀

Explanation

The dean can bind the law school through some form of agency power (actual authority, apparent authority, inherent agency power) or through estoppel. In this matter, none of these attribution rules apply and the college is not bound.

For actual authority to exist, some manifestation of the principal must cause the agent to reasonably believe the agent has the right to bind the principal. The most salient manifestation given by the facts is the Student Handbook. That handbook expressly precludes the scheduling of advance makeups. The dean's discretion, mentioned in item 5, relates to adequate cause for a makeup and does not override the subsequent, express prohibition on advance makeups. The dean could not reasonably believe that he or she has the right to schedule advance makeups.

For similar reasons, apparent authority will not help the student. For apparent authority to exist, some manifestation of the principal must cause the third party (here, the student) to reasonably believe the agent has the right to bind the principal. Arguably, at least, the dean's position constitutes a manifestation, as does the handbook's reference to the dean as the person who authorizes makeups. However, those who rely on the appearance of authority have a duty of reasonable diligence. For a law student, that duty encompasses knowing the contents of the Student Handbook. Therefore, the student could not *reasonably* believe that the dean has the authority to violate the policy.

Inherent authority also will not help the student, even though the dean is a general agent (i.e., authorized "to conduct a series of transactions involving a continuity of service"). In some circumstances a general agent has the inherent power to bind its principal even through an unauthorized act. However, the power does not exist when the third party has reason to know that the act is unauthorized.

Estoppel is likewise unavailing. The student may have believed the dean to be authorized to permit an advance makeup, but, given the clear statement in the Student Handbook, the law school cannot be said to have "intentionally or carelessly caused such belief."[135] Moreover, through the Student Handbook, the law school had taken "reasonable steps to notify [the student] of the facts."[136]

---

135. R.2d, §8B(1)(a), discussed in Section 2.5.
136. R.2d, §8B(1)(b), discussed in Section 2.5.

CHAPTER 3

Binding the Principal in Tort

§3.1 OVERVIEW

In a modern economy, most principals work through agents, and most tortious conduct is committed by agents.

EXAMPLE

Example

A delivery company uses appropriate care in selecting, training, and scheduling its drivers. On the way to make a delivery, one of the company's drivers drives negligently and injures a third party. The driver's conduct is directly tortious, but the company's is not. ◀◀◀

EXAMPLE

Example

The owner of an office building hires a real estate broker to sell the building. The broker finds a prospective buyer and, in extolling the building's virtues, purposely misrepresents several material matters. The owner is unaware of the misrepresentations and certainly has not authorized them. The broker's conduct is fraudulent, but the building owner's is not. ◀◀◀

In the two circumstances just described, and in many others, the principal will be responsible for the agent's tort. Agency law contains rules for attributing an agent's tort to its principal, even though the principal has not itself engaged in any wrongful conduct.[1]

These attribution rules divide roughly into two categories, according to the nature of the agent's conduct and the nature of the third party's injury. If an agent's physical conduct causes physical harm to a third party's person or property, then the concepts discussed in Chapter 2 are largely irrelevant, and the applicable doctrine is *respondeat superior*. This rule of inherent agency power applies only to a subcategory of agents known for centuries as "servants" and relabeled by the R.3d as "employees."[2] A principal is generally not responsible for the physical torts of its non-servant (or "nonemployee") agents.[3]

In contrast, if the agent's misconduct consists solely of words and the third party suffers harm only to its emotions, reputation, or pocketbook, the servant/non-servant (or, in R.3d terminology, employee *vel non*) distinction is rarely relevant. *Respondeat superior* is largely inapposite,[4] and attribution occurs according to the same rules of actual authority, apparent authority, and inherent agency power that apply to contractual matters.

§3.2 *RESPONDEAT SUPERIOR*

§3.2.1 The Rule Defined

Respondeat superior is a venerable doctrine that imposes strict, vicarious liability on a principal when:

- an agent's tort—typically negligence[5]—has caused physical injury to a person or property;
- the tortfeasor agent meets the criteria to be considered a "servant" (or, under the R.3d, "employee") of the principal; and
- the tortious conduct occurred within the servant's/employee's "scope of employment."[6]

---

1. If a principal does engage in wrongful conduct, direct liability results. For a discussion of the direct duties of principals to third parties, see Section 4.4.
2. R.3d, §2.04, comment *a*.
3. Liability may exist when the work involved is inherently dangerous.
4. *Respondeat superior* is relevant in certain borderline areas, such as malicious prosecution and intentional interference with business relations. See Section 3.4.4.
5. Most *respondeat superior* cases involve claims that the tortfeasor employee (or servant) has been negligent, but the doctrine also applies to intentional torts involving physical harm. See Section 3.2.7.
6. The injured party may also assert claims of direct responsibility against the principal. See Section 4.4. In any event, the tortfeasor agent will be directly liable. See Section 4.2.3.

When triggered, *respondeat superior* automatically renders the principal (referred to as "the master" or, per the R.3d, "employer") liable for the servant/employee's misconduct regardless of whether the master/employer: (i) authorized the misconduct; (ii) forbade the misconduct; or (iii) even used all reasonable means to prevent the misconduct.

The scope of *respondeat superior* thus depends on the definition and application of two key concepts: *servant (employee) status* and *scope of employment*. The more expansively each is defined, the broader the scope of the rule. As a result, disputes between an injured third party and an alleged master/employer typically involve battles over characterization. Was the tortfeasor a servant/employee? Was the tortious conduct within the scope of employment?

§3.2.2 The Nomenclature Question

Agency law is in transition concerning a crucial aspect of *respondeat superior* terminology. The R.2d and most cases use "master-servant," while the R.3d uses "employer-employee." A few cases use both.

Case in Point — *Dias v. Brigham Medical Associates, Inc.*

"Broadly speaking, *respondeat superior* is the proposition that an employer, or master, should be held vicariously liable for the torts of its employee, or servant, committed within the scope of employment."[7] ◄◄◄

Case in Point — *Butera & Andrews v. IBM, Corp.*

In the same string citation,[8] the court quotes one case stating that "[i]t is not enough that an employee's job provides an 'opportunity' to commit an intentional tort"[9] and another case (holding that "[t]he mere existence of [a] master and servant relationship is not enough to impose liability on the master.").[10] ◄◄◄

7. *Dias v. Brigham Med. Assoc.'s, Inc.*, 780 N.E. 2d 447, 449 (Mass. 2002).
8. *Butera v. IBM, Corp.*, 456 F. Supp. 2d 104, 112 (D.D.C. 2006).
9. *Haddon v. United States*, 68 F.3d 1420, 1424 (D.C. Cir. 1995).
10. *Keys v. Wash. Metro. Area Transit Auth.*, 408 F. Supp. 2d 1, 4 (D.D.C. 2005).

As the following definitions show, the difference is a matter of semantics, not substance.

R.2d, §220(1)	A servant is a person employed to perform services in the affairs of another and who with respect to the physical conduct in the performance of the services is subject to the other's control or right to control.
R.3, §7.07(3)(a)	[A]n employee is an agent whose principal controls or has the right to control the manner and means of the agent's performance of work. . . .[11] In 2015, the ALI published the Restatement of the Law of Employment ("R-EL"). That Restatement addresses a few topics covered by agency law, see, e.g., R-EL §8.01 ("Employee Duty of Loyalty to the Employer"), and defines "employee" consistently with both the R.3d and R.2d R-EL §1.01(a) (stating that "an individual renders services as an employee of an employer if: (1) the individual acts, at least in part, to serve the interests of the employer; (2) the employer consents to receive the individual's services; and (3) the employer controls the manner and means by which the individual renders services, or the employer otherwise effectively prevents the individual from rendering those services as an independent businessperson").

The R.3d rejects the older terminology because: "The connotation that household service is the prototype for employment is dated, as is its suggestion that an employer has an all-pervasive right of control over most dimensions of the employee's life."[11]

This assessment is correct. In the agency law sense, the term *servant* has nothing to do with servile status, menial tasks, or connection to a household. R.2d servants are everywhere in modern society: A maid who works full time in one household will be a servant, but so too are the top executives in any large corporation. Neither the exercise of responsibility nor the possession of professional skills suffices to negate servant status.[12] A master plumber employed by a plumbing contractor is likely a servant, as is the skilled staff physician employed by a hospital. The modern employee is, in R.2d parlance, a servant, and the modern employer is a master.

11. R.3d, Introduction.

12. However, in some circumstances an alleged servant's skills can argue against servant status, especially when the alleged master lacks the necessary expertise to effectively exercise control.

Unfortunately, "employer" and "employee" are not perfect replacements as agency law terms of art, because the terms have a well-established ordinary (or "lay") meaning. The resulting connotation is that the agency law meaning corresponds to the ordinary meaning, and that connotation is inaccurate. While all employees in the lay sense may well be employees in the R.3d sense, not all R.3d employees are necessarily employees in the lay sense.

Most importantly, an organization can be a "servant" of another organization, and that characterization is crucial for attributing to the second organization torts ascribed to the first organization.[13] Using "employee" as an agency law term of art can distract from this analysis, because the lay meaning of the word conjures up the image of an individual, not an organization. The same has not been true of the word "servant," because for at least a century agency law has applied that term of art far beyond its lay meaning. Ironically, it is the dissonance between the lay and technical meanings of "servant" that makes the word a better term of art in the context of what might be called "organizational *respondeat superior*."[14]

More generally, the overlap between lay and technical meanings may cause some people (especially but not exclusively law students) to assume that, because a person is an employee in the ordinary, lay sense of the word, the person can be treated as an employee in the R.3d sense *without need for any supporting analysis*. That would be a serious mistake.

Nonetheless, future cases will likely follow R.3d usage, because the ALI's latest pronouncements are always influential and the overwhelming majority of *respondeat superior* cases will involve tortfeasors who are, in fact, individuals. This book will generally follow the R.3d, while occasionally using the old and the new terminology in tandem.

§3.2.3 The Rule's Rationale

The doctrine of *respondeat superior* rests on three rationales: enterprise liability, risk avoidance, and risk spreading. It sometimes seems, however, that the doctrine's real purpose is to "find the deep pocket."

---

13. Ascribing a tort to the first organization also involves agency law analysis, typically *respondeat superior*. For a detailed discussion of "organizational *respondeat superior*," see Section 3.5. That section also discusses a theory under which employees of the first organization can be treated directly as employees of the second organization.
14. For further discussion, see Section 3.5.

a. Enterprise Liability

As explained in more detail in Chapter 2, this rationale attempts to link risks to benefits and hold accountable for risk-creating activities the enterprise that stands to benefit from those activities.[15] As explained in detail below, in the *respondeat superior* context:

- an "employee" (or, in the older nomenclature, a servant) is subject to its employer's (or "master's") detailed control as to means as well as ends and is thus integrally connected to the employer's (or "master's") enterprise; and
- an employee's (or servant's) scope of employment comprises those activities that are fairly considered part of the employer's (or master's) enterprise.

b. Risk Spreading

According to this rationale, the employer/master should strictly and vicariously bear the risk of its employees'/servants' misconduct because the employer/master can: (i) anticipate the risks inherent in its enterprise; (ii) spread the risk through insurance; (iii) take into account the cost of insurance in setting the price for its goods or services; and (iv) thereby spread the risk among those who benefit from the goods or services.

c. Risk Avoidance

According to this rationale, *respondeat superior* serves to protect society from dangerous occurrences. Since the existence of employee/servant status means that the employer/master has the right to control the employee/servant's physical performance, the employer/master is well positioned to prevent the employee/servant from engaging in careless or otherwise improper conduct. Imposing strict liability creates a strong incentive for the employer/master to use its position of control to achieve "risk avoidance."

Viewed from this perspective, the rule may seem overbroad. If we are looking to encourage "safety-producing" conduct by employers, why impose liability even if the employer has taken reasonable care in selecting, training, and supervising its servants? Why, that is, have strict liability? Why not impose liability only when the master has failed to properly select, train, or supervise?[16]

---

15. See Section 2.6.1 (Discussing Enterprise Liability as a Rationale for Inherent Agency Power).

16. An employer/master (or other principal) can be directly liable on this basis. See Section 4.4.1.

In part, the answer is that both the *enterprise liability* and *risk spreading* rationales support a broad approach. Expediency is also involved. A narrowly tailored rule would present significant problems of proof, and those problems of proof would make a narrowly tailored rule ineffective. The difficulty of proving direct negligence on the part of the master warrants a rule of vicarious, strict liability.[17]

d. The Deep Pocket Theory

The overwhelming majority of employees have fewer resources than do their employer. It may be tempting to look to this economic reality and characterize the doctrine of *respondeat superior* as a mere guise for reaching nonnegligent defendants with convenient deep pockets.

Indeed, a few cases have expressly sought to justify *respondeat superior* as a mechanism for assuring victim compensation, and the rule does owe its practical importance to the deep pockets of masters.

Case in Point — *Harbury v. Hayden*

"Many states and D.C. apply the scope-of-employment test very expansively, in part because doing so usually allows an injured tort plaintiff a chance to recover from a deep-pocket employer rather than a judgment-proof employee."[18] ◄◄◄

Restatement on Point

In addition to other rationales, "Respondeat superior also reflects the likelihood that an employer will be more likely to satisfy a judgment."[19] ◄◄◄

However, as discussed above, the doctrine has independent theoretical justification.

---

17. In this regard, this rationale for *respondeat superior* parallels one of the rationales for strict product liability. See, e.g., *Phipps v. General Motors Corp.*, 363 A.2d 955, 958 (Md. 1976) (strict liability warranted in part due to the difficulty of proving producer negligence).
18. *Harbury v. Hayden*, 522 F.3d 413, 422 n.4 (D.C. Cir. 2008) (dicta; plaintiff's claim dismissed on other grounds).
19. R.3d, §2.04, cmt. b.

§3.2.4 Employee/Servant Status

a. Employee (Servant) Further Defined: A Factor Analysis

Like many legal questions, the issue of employee status is a *vel non* ("or not") question.[20] The alleged tortfeasor either fits within the category or does not. Like most legal issues, this one applies to a wide range of possible facts. At the far ends of the range, the determination is (by hypothesis) clear-cut.

Example

Dennis works as a baker's assistant in Marcia's bakery. Marcia provides all the necessary equipment, sets Dennis's hours, assigns his particular tasks, supervises his performance, and pays Dennis an hourly wage. Dennis is Marcia's employee, and Marcia is the employer. ◀ ◀ ◀

Example

Marcia, the baker, hires Joe, a carpenter, to remodel the front of the bakery. Marcia provides a detailed plan for the remodeling and agrees that Joe will work on a "time and materials" basis. That is, Joe will charge her for the materials he uses, plus an hourly fee for the time he spends working. Joe agrees that Marcia can end the job at any time for any reason. Despite Marcia's right to terminate, Joe is an independent contractor (in the language of the R.2d and many cases), not Marcia's employee (in the language of the R.3d). Carpentry is a skilled occupation, and Marcia lacks the expertise to control the details of the work. Moreover, Joe supplies his own tools, the work is not part of Marcia's regular business, and Joe is engaged in a distinct occupation. ◀ ◀ ◀

Both Restatements include a set of factors for making the employee/servant *vel non* determination. A comment to R.3d provides the following list, which is drawn essentially verbatim from a black letter list in R.2d. Brackets are the author's, indicating which way each factor "cuts." [E] means that establishing the factor cuts in favor of employee status. [N-E] means that establishing the factor cuts against that status.

1. The extent of control that the agent and the principal have agreed the principal may exercise over details of the work [E];

20. The R.2d uses the term "independent contractor" to describe the "or not" category. The R.3d rejects that usage as confusing, noting that the R.2d applies the phrase both to describe nonagent service providers (independent contractors *simpliciter*) and nonservant agents (independent contractor agents). R.3d, §1.01, comment c.

2. whether the agent is engaged in a distinct occupation or business [N-E];
3. whether the type of work done by the agent is customarily done under a principal's direction [E] or without supervision [N-E];
4. the skill required in the agent's occupation [N-E if great skill required; E if unskilled work];[21]
5. whether the agent [N-E] or the principal [E] supplies the tools and other instrumentalities required for the work and the place in which to perform it;
6. the length of time during which the agent is engaged by a principal [the longer the time, the more E];
7. whether the agent is paid by the job [N-E] or by the time worked [E];[22]
8. whether the agent's work is part of the principal's regular business [E];
9. whether the principal and the agent believe that they are creating an employment relationship [E]; and
10. whether the principal is or is not in business [E, although here "business" means any ongoing enterprise that deals in the commercial world, including nonprofit enterprises].[23]

As with any "factor" analysis, these criteria are rarely outcome determinative. They merely delineate the lines of argument. As a result, as the Ninth Circuit has stated, "Drawing the line between 'employee' and 'independent contractor' is a difficult task, with significant consequences for workers and businesses, that has long vexed courts and lawmakers across the country."[24]

---

21. Modern circumstances have weakened the power of this factor. At least through the pre-industrial era, a person who possessed special vocational skills was likely to be outside any effective or nuanced supervision by the principal, who typically lacked sufficient knowledge to have any detailed insight into the work. Also, artisans and, even more so, professionals tended to work for themselves—that is, to have "a distinct occupation or business." In the modern world, in contrast, principals that are organizations often employ skilled individuals who, on the principal's behalf, can exercise the necessary skill and judgment to effectively supervise even a "professional." But see *Renaissance Med. Found. v. Lugo*, No. 23-0607, 2025 WL 1478694, at *9 (Tex. May 23, 2025) (discussing a statute prohibiting an organization from interfering with a physician employee's "independent medical judgment"; assuming that the organization might interfere without considering the possibility that the organization might act through the actions of another physician employee).

22. In this context, "time worked" includes both wages (paid according to the hours worked) and salary (paid according to "payroll periods" without accounting for hours actually worked).

23. R.3d, §7.07, comment f, relying on R.2d, §220(2). Numbering not present in original.

24. *Olson v. California*, 104 F.4th 66, 71 (9th Cir.), cert. denied, 145 S. Ct. 382, 220 L. Ed. 2d 145 (2024).

Example

Big Scale Construction, LLC ("BSC") employs a doctor full-time to attend to on-the-job injuries suffered by BSC employees while on remote locations. BSC pays the doctor a regular salary, which is reported to the IRS on a W-2 form (the form used for "employees" as that term is understood in tax law). BSC also provides the doctor lodging and meals while she is stationed at remote locations and requires that she stay on-site 24/7, except for approved "days away."

The doctor is responsible for supplying her own "black bag" [factor 5] and her occupation requires great skill [factor 4]. In addition, BSC does not interfere with her exercise of medical judgment [factor 1].

Nonetheless, she is an "employee" for *respondeat superior* purposes. Almost all the factors so indicate:

1. the extent of control that the agent and the principal have agreed the principal may exercise over details of the work—*BSC does not interfere with the doctor's medical judgment, but does determine where she goes to work and requires her to be on-site and away from home for long periods of time*
2. whether the agent is engaged in a distinct occupation or business—*she is not; her work is part of BSC's business*
3. whether the type of work done by the agent is customarily done under a principal's direction or without supervision—*many doctors now work as parts of large organizations, although the principal purpose of most such organizations is the delivery of health-care services*
4. the skill required in the agent's occupation—*this one factor "cuts the other way"*
5. whether the agent or the principal supplies the tools and other instrumentalities required for the work and the place in which to perform it—*she supplies her black bag, but BCS "supplies" the place in which to perform her work (the various remote locations)*
6. the length of time during which the agent is engaged by a principal—*this is long-term engagement*
7. whether the agent is paid by the job or by the time worked—*she is paid by salary; i.e., by time worked*
8. whether the agent's work is part of the principal's regular business—*it is, albeit in an ancillary way*
9. whether the principal and the agent believe that they are creating an employment relationship—*the only relevant fact (the W-2) suggests that they do*
10. whether the principal is or is not in business—*BCS is in business* ◄◄◄

No single factor is determinative, and the language of an agreement will not prevail over the reality of the relationship. The right to terminate is not by itself dispositive. It carries weight only to the extent that it creates the practical ability to control the agent's performance. Similarly, formal independence will be discounted if the master's right to fire results in practical control.[25]

The R-EL provides a useful perspective for "close call" situations. "An individual renders services as an independent businessperson and not as an employee when the individual in his or her own interest exercises entrepreneurial control over important business decisions, including whether to hire and where to assign assistants, whether to purchase and where to deploy equipment, and whether and when to provide service to other customers."[26]

Case in Point—*Search v. Uber Techs., Inc.*

Plaintiff was knifed by an Uber driver, sued Uber, and asserted *inter alia* a *respondeat superior* claim. Uber moved to dismiss the claim on the pleadings, asserting that the driver was not an Uber employee.

The court described Uber's relationship with its driver per the allegations in the Complaint:

> Uber is a car service that provides drivers to customers on demand through a cell phone application, or "app,". . . . Uber[] . . . dictates the fares charged in each jurisdiction in which it operates, collects the appropriate payment from each passenger, and then passes on to its drivers 75–80 percent of the fares collected while keeping the remaining portion for itself. Uber drivers do not collect any form of payment directly from consumers; rather, they receive payment for their work . . . via weekly direct deposit. . . .
>
> Uber controls the rate of refusal of ride requests, the timeliness of the drivers' responses to requests, the display on vehicles of its logo, the frequency with which drivers may contact passengers, the drivers' interactions with passengers (including how they accept tips and collect fares), and the quality of drivers via its rating system.

The court denied the motion to dismiss because, "taking these allegations as true, a reasonable factfinder could conclude that Uber exercised control over [the driver] in a manner evincing an employer-employee relationship."[27]

---

25. See R.3d, §7.07, comment f (stating that "the extent of control that the principal has exercised in practice over the details of the agent's work" is "relevant" to the analysis).

26. R-EL §1.01(b).

27. *Search v. Uber Techs., Inc.*, 128 F. Supp. 3d 222, 226–27, 233 (D.D.C. 2015) (citations to Complaint omitted). The court also rejected Uber's assertion that, even assuming employee status, the knife attack, being an intentional tort, was outside the scope of employment. "Plaintiff has alleged facts suggesting that the dispute giving rise to [the] attack grew out of an encounter related to Uber's business. . . . This is sufficient to survive a 12(b)(6) motion." *Id.* at 234. For a discussion of scope of employment and intentional torts, see Section 3.2.7.

Example

A pizza shop contracts with a driver to provide home delivery. A written agreement between the shop and the driver:

- labels the driver an "independent contractor";
- permits the pizza shop to terminate the contract at any time without cause;
- requires the driver to provide his own car, car insurance, and uniform;
- requires the driver to know the streets of the delivery area and to choose his own route on each delivery;
- provides for payment by delivery, not by the hour;
- permits the driver to have other jobs; and
- provides that each Friday the pizza shop will communicate to the driver a proposed schedule for the following week and requires that the driver notify the pizza shop within 24 hours if the driver has any objections to the schedule.

The driver, however, has no other employment. Moreover, it is well known that drivers who do not regularly accept the proposed weekly schedule are terminated.

One evening, while making a delivery for the pizza shop, the driver has an auto accident. The other driver sues the pizza shop, successfully invoking *respondeat superior*. Despite the driver's formal freedom of action and the contract's label of "independent contractor," the pizza shop's right to terminate at any time gave the shop effective control of the driver's performance. Given the driver's dependence on the job, the driver was likely to obey any "suggestions" the shop happened to make and to accept each proposed work schedule. Given the unskilled nature of the work, the shop had whatever expertise was necessary to actually make suggestions or give orders. Moreover, the driver has no distinct occupation and the work is an integral part of the pizza shop's business. ◄ ◄ ◄

b. *Respondeat Superior* and Volunteers

Almost all *respondeat superior* cases deal with tortfeasors who are paid in some way, but the doctrine can apply to unpaid volunteers. Many recent volunteer cases involve sexual misconduct.[28]

28. In addition to the "employee" *vel non* question, these cases raise the difficult "scope of employment" issues discussed in Section 3.2.7.

CASE IN POINT

Case in Point—*Doe v. Boys Clubs of Greater Dallas, Inc.*

An individual who volunteered due to community-service requirement of court-imposed sentence for driving under the influence had the status of an employee for purposes of *respondeat superior* when the employer had the right to direct the volunteer's duties, had an interest in the work to be accomplished, accepted direct or indirect benefit from the work, and had the right to fire or replace the volunteer.[29] ◄◄◄

Applying *respondeat superior* makes sense when the employer is an enterprise of some sort (e.g., a nonprofit organization), but is questionable as a matter of policy when the alleged "employee" is merely a friend or relative of the alleged employer and is merely helping with some household or home improvement task. *Respondeat superior* is a theory of enterprise liability that seeks to encourage risk avoidance by the enterprise. In the "help with a chore" situation, there is no enterprise involved.

In any event, the R.2d expressly contemplates the "help with a chore" situation, although the stated rationale has little to do with the policies underlying the *respondeat superior* doctrine:

> One who volunteers services without an agreement for or expectation of reward may be a servant of the one accepting such services. . . . Consideration is not necessary to create the relation of principal and agent, and it is not necessary in the case of master and servant.

RESTATEMENT ON POINT

Restatement on Point

"*A*, a social guest at P's house, not skilled in repairing, volunteers to assist P in the repair of P's house. During the execution of such repair, *A* negligently drops a board upon a person passing upon the street. *A* may be found to be a servant of P."[30]

c. The Relationship of Employee Status to Agent Status

The R.3d treats "employee" as an integral part of agency law and a subcategory of agent status. The R.2d does the same with "servant." In theory,

---

29. 868 S.W.2d 942, 949–50 (Tex. App. 1994), *aff'd*, 907 S.W.2d 472 (Tex. 1995). However, the sexual misconduct was outside the "scope of employment." *Id.* at 950.
30. R.2d, §225, comment *a* and Ill. 1.

therefore, any *respondeat superior* case should begin with a threshold question: Is the alleged tortfeasor an agent of the person sought to be held accountable via *respondeat superior?*

In practice, however, cases litigating employee/servant status rarely, if ever, consider the agent *vel non* issue. Instead, they proceed directly to the subcategory; that is, employee *vel non*.

History may explain the omission. The law of master-servant predates the modern law of agency. At some point, the former was subsumed (more or less freestanding) into the latter. Moreover, *respondeat superior* has to do with the employer's right of control and the employee's integration into the master's enterprise. There are circumstances in which the elements of servant status exist but without it being clear that the alleged employee was asked or manifested assent to act as the alleged employer's fiduciary. In those circumstances, it makes sense to apply *respondeat superior* without regard to the agent *vel non* analysis. As Oliver Wendell Holmes explained, "The life of law has not been logic; it has been experience."[31]

d. The Impact of Employee/Servant Status on Other Areas of Law

Agency law's employee/servant concept helps set the scope for a wide range of statutes designed to regulate or tax the modern employment relationship. In areas ranging from civil rights to payroll taxes, these statutes typically cover "employees" but neglect to define the term. Courts must therefore develop a definition, and many have turned to the agency notion of servant. Some decisions make explicit reference to the law of agency; others use its concepts without attribution.

The agency law concepts have influenced the reach of statutes in the following areas, among others:

- discrimination in employment
- unemployment compensation
- workers' compensation
- Social Security
- payroll taxes

31. Oliver Wendell Holmes, *The Common Law* (1881) at 5.

Case in Point — *Clackamas Gastroenterology Assocs., P.C. v. Wells*

"[W]hen Congress has used the term 'employee' without defining it, we have concluded that Congress intended to describe the conventional master-servant relationship as understood by common-law agency doctrine."[32] ◀◀◀

Case in Point — *CBS Corp. v. F.C.C.*

In the aftermath of the infamous "wardrobe malfunction" during a Superbowl halftime show,[33] the FCC fined CBS, asserting *inter alia respondeat superior*. The Third Circuit disagreed: "Jackson and Timberlake were independent contractors, who are outside the scope of *respondeat superior*, rather than employees as the FCC found." ◀◀◀

e. Employee/Servant and the "Gig" Economy

Beginning in approximately 2009, economists and other commentators began referring to "the gig economy." According to the Internal Revenue Service (in 2025): "The gig economy—also called sharing economy or access economy—is activity where people earn income providing on-demand work, services or goods. Often, it's through a digital platform like an app or website."[34]

Uber and Lyft are probably the most well-known examples. Using a digital platform, each company matches persons seeking a taxi-like ride ("customers") and drivers willing to provide the rides. In addition to providing the matching function, the company bills and collects from the

32. *Clackamas Gastroenterology Assocs., P.C. v. Wells*, 123 S. Ct. 1673, 1678 (2003) (quoting *Nationwide Mut. Ins. Co. v. Darden*, 503 U.S. 318, 322–23 (1992); internal quotation marks omitted).
33. *CBS Corp. v. F.C.C.*, 535 F.3d 167, 189 (3d Cir. 2008) *cert. granted*, judgment vacated, 129 S. Ct. 2176, 173 L. Ed. 2d 1153 (U.S. 2009).
34. Internal Revenue Service, Gig Economy Tax Center, What is the Gig Economy?, https://www.irs.gov/businesses/gig-economy-tax-center, last retrieved 5/7/25.

customer and remits part of the collected amount to the driver who provides the ride.[35]

Employee/independent contractor issues arise at the very core of a gig relationship if the relationship involves providing services. For example, if an Uber or Lyft driver is an *employee*, then *respondeat superior* applies if the driver is involved in an accident while "on the job." More importantly (as a practical matter), if an Uber or Lyft driver is an employee, the company must provide the driver the panoply of rights and benefits prescribed by state law for all employees. In the latter context, the resulting costs will be very, very large.

Uber and Lyft set and enforce standards of conduct for their respective drivers, provide backup auto liability insurance for the drivers, and control the platform that makes the driver' work possible. And some courts have found Uber or Lyft drivers to be employees.[36]

However, the traditional common law analysis suggests that the drivers are independent contractors rather than employees. Most saliently, each driver:

- provides the key equipment necessary to the task (the vehicle);
- determines when to work; and
- while working, decides which tasks to undertake (i.e., whether to go after a ride opportunity communicated by the company).

In some states, the legislature has weighed in. California, for example, adopted a complex classification system that "appl[ied] one test to determine the classification of Uber drivers [result: employees] and a different test to determine the classification of dogwalkers who provide services through Wag!, the 'Uber for dogs.' [result: independent contractors]"[37]

Although California's classification system survived an equal protection attack,[38] California's voters adopted Proposition 22, under which "a

---

35. The Internal Revenue Services has provided the following, non-exhaustive list of gig arrangements:

> "Drive a car for booked rides or deliveries; Rent out property or part of it; Run errands or complete tasks;. . . . Provide creative or professional services; Provide other temporary, on-demand or freelance work." Internal Revenue Service, Gig Economy Tax Center, What is Gig Work?, https://www.irs.gov/businesses/gig-economy-tax-center, last retrieved 5/7/25.

36. See above, Case in Point—Search v. Uber Techs., Inc.
37. *Olson v. California*, 104 F.4th 66, 71 (9th Cir.) (2024). The Ninth Circuit described the California legislation as "an effort to address what [the California legislature] perceived as a systemic problem of misclassification—that is, businesses improperly characterizing their workers as independent contractors to avoid fiscal responsibilities owed to employees." Id.
38. *Olson v. California*, 104 F.4th 66 (9th Cir.) (2024).

driver for an app-based transportation or delivery company, such as Uber Technologies, Inc. (Uber), Lyft, Inc. (Lyft), or DoorDash, Inc., is an independent contractor and not an employee of the company as long as several conditions are met."[39]

The bottom line: in the gig economy, the employee/independent-contractor issue is a question of common law, except in jurisdictions that have legislated on the issue. In such jurisdictions, the issue may turn on circumstances irrelevant to the common law analysis.

§3.2.5 Scope of Employment

a. The Rationale and Reach of the Concept

Scope of employment is the other main *respondeat superior* battleground. Even if the tortfeasor is an employee, vicarious liability results only if the tort occurred within the scope of employment.[40] This restriction fits the rationale of the rule. *Respondeat superior* is a doctrine of enterprise liability, and the "scope of employment" element seeks to confine the master's liability to risks arising from the enterprise.[41]

b. The R.2d Sets Four Preconditions to Finding a Person's Conduct Within the Scope of Employment

> (a) it is of the kind he is employed[42] to perform;
> (b) it occurs substantially within the authorized time and space limits;
> (c) it is actuated, at least in part, by a purpose to serve the master; and
> (d) if force is intentionally used by the servant against another, the use of force is not unexpectable by the master.[43]

---

39. *Castellanos v. State of California*, 16 Cal. 5th 588, 595–96, 552 P.3d 406, 410 (2024) (rejecting a claim under the California constitution against the statutes enacted by Proposition 22).

40. An employer may nonetheless face direct liability. For example, if a resident manager rapes an apartment tenant, that conduct is probably outside the scope of employment. See Section 3.2.7 (Discussing *Respondeat Superior* and Intentional Torts). However, if the manager had an extensive criminal record involving violence toward women and the landlord overlooked that record, the landlord may be directly liable on a claim of negligent hiring or for failure to provide safe premises. See Sections 4.4.1–4.4.2.

41. The restriction also fits the R.2d's view of *respondeat superior* as a type of inherent authority. Seen from this perspective, the "scope of employment" element seeks to confine the master's liability to risks that inhere in the employee's assigned tasks.

42. Under the R.3d and the R-L, and in ordinary parlance, the word "employment" describes a business relationship that agency law classifies as master-servant. In contrast, the R.2d uses "employment" as a term of art, to mean a principal's engagement of an agent to accomplish some task or provide some service. Thus, in R.2d terms, a principal can "employ" a nonservant agent.

43. R.2d, §228(1). A few jurisdictions omit the "actuated in part" element when considering intentional torts. See Section 3.2.7.

The R.3d is less formulaic:

> An employee acts within the scope of employment when performing work assigned by the employer or engaging in a course of conduct subject to the employer's control. An employee's act is not within the scope of employment when it occurs within an independent course of conduct not intended by the employee to serve any purpose of the employer.[44]

Note particularly that R.3d has revised the R.2d's third condition—substituting "an independent course of conduct not intended by the employee to serve any purpose of the employer" for "actuated, at least in part, by a purpose to serve the master." This issue is relevant when an employee commits a tort of negligence while deviating from the tasks of his or her employment[45] and also when *respondeat superior* is invoked to hold the employer liable for intentional torts.[46]

As to the R.2d's second condition—"substantially within the authorized time and space limits"—the R.3d rejects it entirely as antiquated:

> This formulation does not naturally encompass the working circumstances of many managerial and professional employees and others whose work is not so readily cabined by temporal or spatial limitations. Many employees in contemporary workforces interact on an employer's behalf with third parties although the employee is neither situated on the employer's premises nor continuously or exclusively engaged in performing assigned work.[47]

The concept of "authorized place and time" may still be helpful to courts in interpreting old-fashioned situations, while the R.3d's more open-ended language can help courts deal with contemporary situations—for example, employees who telecommute or use cell phones to mix personal and business activities.

Example

Early one morning, Dennis, a baker's assistant and full-time employee, is at his job kneading dough in the bakery. He notices that a stray cat has wandered in and is about to jump on a counter that is covered with freshly baked cookies. Dennis scoops the cat up and gently tosses it out the door into the alley. Unfortunately, the cat lands atop a crate packed with cut glass that belongs to the china shop next door. The crate falls over and the glass

44. R.3d, §7.07(2).
45. See Section 3.2.6.
46. See Section 3.2.7.
47. R.3d, §7.07, comment b.

breaks. Dennis has acted within the scope of his employment. He was doing the kind of work he was employed to perform, in his usual (and therefore authorized) place and during the usual (and therefore authorized) time. He acted to serve his master's interests.[48] ◀◀◀

Example

After work one day Dennis stops by a bookstore, looking for a book on baking techniques. He wishes to improve his own skills so that he can do a better job at the bakery. While browsing through the aisles he trips over a step stool and bumps another customer. This accident was not within the scope of his employment. Although he was "actuated, at least in part, by a purpose to serve the master," he was not doing the type of work for which he was hired. Moreover, he was outside the authorized time and far from his authorized place of work. ◀◀◀

c. Factor Analysis

The R.2d lists 10 factors to be considered in determining whether a servant's conduct is within the scope of employment:

> (a) whether or not the act is one commonly done by such servants;
> (b) the time, place, and purpose of the act;
> (c) the previous relations between the master and the servant;
> (d) the extent to which the business of the master is apportioned between different servants;
> (e) whether or not the act is outside the enterprise of the master or, if within the enterprise, has not been entrusted to any servant;
> (f) whether or not the master has reason to expect that such an act will be done;
> (g) the similarity in quality of the act done to the act authorized;
> (h) whether or not the instrumentality by which the harm is done has been furnished by the master to the servant;
> (i) the extent of departure from the normal method of accomplishing an authorized result; and
> (j) whether or not the act is seriously criminal.[49]

"[T]he formulation of the scope-of-employment doctrine in [the R.3d] differs from its counterparts in Restatement Second, Agency §§228 and 229

48. As for R.2d, §228(1)(d) (intentionally use force "against another"), using force against a cat is not, in R.2d terms, using force "against another." Although this Example involves an employee acting within the scope of his employment, for *respondeat superior* to apply, the china shop must also demonstrate that Dennis's act was tortious.
49. R.2d, §229(2).

because it is phrased in more general terms."[50] However, courts like detailed guidance, and the R.2d factors are likely to remain influential.

As those factors indicate, scope of employment is not limited to the servant's proper or authorized conduct. To be within the scope of employment, "conduct must be of the same general nature as that [actually] authorized, or incidental to the conduct authorized."[51] However, the notion of "incidental" goes a long way. It is inevitable that employees will on occasion transgress and that some of the misconduct will occur on the periphery of the employee's authorized work. An act can therefore be within the scope of employment even though: (i) the employer has expressly forbidden the act; (ii) the act is tortious;[52] or (iii) the act constitutes a minor crime. (On these points, the R.3d is in accord.)

Example

Renee is a regional sales manager. She spends most of her work time at her company's office. The company has a policy that forbids employees from making or receiving work-related phone calls while driving. However, one evening, while driving home from work, Renee decides to telephone one of "her" sales reps. Making the phone call distracts her from her driving, and she negligently causes an accident. At the time of the accident, she was within the scope of her employment. Although she was not "substantially within the authorized time and space limits," R.2d, §228(1)(b), she was both "performing work assigned by the employer [and] engaging in a course of conduct subject to the employer's control." R.3d, §7.07(2). ◄◄◄

d. The Relationship of the Scope of the Employer's Control to the Scope of Employment

Whether the "principal controls or has the right to control the manner and means of the agent's performance of work" determines whether an agent is an employee,[53] but an employee's scope of employment can extend beyond the range of the principal's effective control. That is, the principal must have a certain amount of control over the agent's physical performance in order for employee status to exist, but that control will not necessarily extend to every aspect of the employee's tasks. It is therefore possible for a servant's

50. R.3d, §7.07, comment *b*.
51. R.2d, §229(1).
52. If tortious acts were necessarily outside the scope of employment, *respondeat superior* would never impose vicarious liability. The doctrine operates to attribute the servant's tort to the master.
53. R.3d, §7.07(3)(a).

scope of employment to include areas in which the master does not exercise control.[54]

Example

Marcia, a baker, employs Sarah, an expert wedding cake designer. Marcia pays Sarah a weekly salary and provides the location and all necessary equipment and materials for Sarah's efforts. Marcia determines Sarah's working hours and working conditions and assigns Sarah particular cake orders to fill. In short, Sarah is Marcia's employee. Nonetheless, Marcia and Sarah both expect Sarah to use her own judgment, discretion, and expertise in designing, baking, and constructing wedding cakes. Marcia does not supervise Sarah's work.

On one occasion, Sarah leaves a small metal wire inside an apparently edible portion of a cake, and a customer is injured. Sarah's negligence is within the scope of her employment. Even though the negligence occurred outside the master's zone of control, the conduct was nonetheless "of the same general nature as that [actually] authorized, or incidental to the conduct authorized."[55] ◀◀◀

§3.2.6 Scope of Employment and an Employee's "Peregrinations"[56]

a. Travel as Part of Work Distinguished from Commuting; "Special Errand" Exception

As the R.3d explains: "In general, travel required to perform work, such as travel from an employer's office to a job site or from one job site to another, is within the scope of an employee's employment, while traveling to and from work is not."[57] While commuting may be a precondition to the employee performing his or her tasks, the commute itself is not normally part of those tasks.

---

54. R.3d, §7.07, comment *b* (stating that "although an employer's ability to exercise control is an important element in justifying *respondeat superior*, the range of an employer's effective control is not the limit that *respondeat superior* imposes on the circumstances under which an employer is subject to liability"). See also *Renaissance Med. Found. v. Lugo*, No. 23-0607, 2025 WL 1478694, at *6 (Tex. May 23, 2025) ("[W]e have rejected a task-by-task assessment of control as an unworkable paradigm [for vicarious liability] that conceivably could result in an individual shifting between employee and independent contractor status countless times in a given work day.") (citation and internal quotation marks omitted).

55. R.2d, §229(1).

56. R.3d, §7.07, cmt. *e* uses this term.

57. R.3d, §7.07, comment 3.

In R.2d terms:

- the commute may seem to be "actuated, at least in part, by a purpose to serve the master"[58]
  Jeeze, why else would I get out of bed before daybreak and spend an hour in traffic?
- but, in fact, the commuter's purpose is merely to position herself to be able to serve the master
  that is, merely to get to work
- in sum, the commuting is:
  — neither "the kind [of task the commuter] is employed to perform"[59]
  — nor does "it occur[] substantially within the authorized time and space limits"[60]

However, if an employee undertakes an errand at the employer's request, the entire trip is part of the scope of employment, even if the employee does the errand while traveling to or from work.

Example

As the company's receptionist is leaving work at the end of the day, the office manager asks him to "drop off this bottle of Scotch" at the house of one of the company's major customers. The receptionist agrees, delivers the Scotch without incident, and is driving straight home from the customer's house when an accident occurs. The drive home (and the accident) are within the receptionist's scope of employment.[61] ◄ ◄ ◄

A few cases hold that an employee is within the scope of employment while driving home from a work-related social event if: (i) attendance at the event was required or otherwise part of the employee's job; (ii) the employee became intoxicated at the social event and remained so while driving home; and (iii) the employee caused an accident while driving home intoxicated.

b. Tangential Acts: Frolic and Detour

Even when the scope of employment includes travel on the employer's behalf, "[a]n employee's act is not within the scope of employment when it occurs within an independent course of conduct not intended by the

58. R.2d, §228(1)(c).
59. R.2d, §228(1)(a).
60. R.2d, §228(1)(b).
61. This Example is based on *Trejo v. Maciel*, 48 Cal. Rptr. 765 (Cal. Ct. App. 1966).

employee to serve any purpose of the employer."[62] However, a mere "incidental deviation from [the] performance of assigned work" remains within the scope of employment,[63] even when the deviation is exclusively to serve the employee's own purposes. In contrast, a substantial deviation puts the employee outside the scope of employment.

Agency law has a pair of labels to distinguish small-scale deviations from substantial ones. During a mere "detour," the employee remains within scope of employment (and consequently *respondeat superior* still applies). Not so when the employee is on a "frolic" of his or her own. The labels date from 1834 and the famous case of *Joel v. Morrison*.[64]

Example

Nick and Nora drive a delivery van for Asta Delivery Company. During their lunch break, they take the company truck and drive across town to the opera house to buy tickets to *La Boheme* for their own use. Buying opera tickets is not incidental to making deliveries. During this trip, Nick and Nora are not acting within the scope of their employment. They are on a frolic of their own. ◄◄◄

Example

On their way to make a delivery for Asta, Nick and Nora realize that they are hungry and that the city's best deli is just two blocks off their direct route. They are entitled to a full lunch break but know that the customer is anxiously awaiting delivery. They decide just to get something "to go" at the deli. On their brief trip to the deli, they remain within the scope of their employment. Although they are temporarily on business of their own, they remain "actuated, at least in part, by a purpose to serve the master." In traditional terms, they are merely on a "detour." ◄◄◄

Frolic and *detour* are powerful labels. They determine whether *respondeat superior* applies. Unfortunately, neither the cases nor the commentators provide coherent, specific guidance for determining when which label applies. One famous case requires the conduct to be at least "incidental" to the servant's duties.[65] But how to determine whether a detour is incidental enough to avoid being a frolic? One prominent commentator has suggested, "A temporary deviation from one's work can be incidental to one's

---

62. R.3d, §7.07(2). See also R.2d, §228(1)(c) (for conduct to be within the scope of employment, the servant must be "actuated, at least in part, by a purpose to serve the master").
63. R.3d, §7.07, Ill. 14.
64. *Joel v. Morrison*, England, Nisi Prius (Exchequer), 6 Car. & P. 501, 172 Eng. Rep. 1338 (1834).
65. *Fiocco v. Carver*, 137 N.E. 309, 311 (N.Y. 1922).

task; a temporary abandonment cannot be."[66] But how does one distinguish between a deviation and a temporary abandonment?

There are no simple answers to these questions. The cases sometimes refer to the distinction being "a matter of degree," or to the determination necessarily being made on a "case-by-case basis." Such expressions are really a code for "we know the difference when we see it (maybe), but we cannot articulate any rule to allow lawyers (or law students) to easily predict outcomes."

In the face of this uncertainty, those seeking to predict outcomes should read a range of "frolic or detour" cases, try to develop a sense of their "flavor," and keep in mind the following themes:

- Employees predictably engage in small-scale deviations from single-minded concentration on the master's interests. Ordinary, expectable deviations are likely to be considered mere detours. "De minimis departures from assigned routes are not 'frolics.'"[67]
- Deviations that pose risks of harm of a type significantly different from the types inherent in the servant's task are more likely to be considered frolics.[68]
- If the employee's deviating conduct occurs far outside the "time and space" authorized by the employer, the deviation is more likely to be a frolic.
- Cases decided under workers' compensation statutes often tilt in favor of classifying activity as within the scope of employment. This tilt reflects a policy judgment and typically traces to specific statutory language.

c. Ending the Frolic

Frolics rarely last forever. At some point, the employee "reenters employment"[69] and *respondeat superior* again applies. Reentry has certainly occurred once the employee is fully back in the employer's service—that is, once the servant is:

- again actuated at least in part (or in some jurisdictions, predominantly) by a desire to serve the master's interest;
- again within the authorized space and time limits; and

66. J. Hynes, *Teacher's Manual to Agency and Partnership: Cases, Materials, Problems* 3rd ed. (1989) 41.
67. R.3d, §7.07, comment *e*.
68. *Respondeat superior* is a doctrine of inherent agency power, and this theme is consistent with that doctrine's rationale; that is, imposing liability on the principal only for risks inherent in the enterprise. See Section 3.2.3.
69. R.3d, §7.07, comment *e*. See also R.2d, §237, comment *a* (reenter the employment).

- actually taking (or has taken) some action in the master's interests not necessitated by the frolic itself.

Example

After purchasing their opera tickets, Nick and Nora get back into the Asta delivery van, drive to their next delivery stop, and begin unloading packages. One of the packages falls and lands on the toe of a passerby. Assuming that Nick and Nora have been negligent, *respondeat superior* will apply. Nick and Nora's frolic has ended, and they have reentered employment. ◄◄◄

The analysis is murkier, however, if a servant negligently causes harm while merely "on the way back" to employment. Indeed, the law here is as difficult to pin down as the law distinguishing frolic from detour. The following themes provide some guidance:

- An employee has not reentered the scope of employment merely by deciding to return to serving the employer's interest.
- An employee does not necessarily have to return to the point the frolic began in order to reenter the scope of employment.
- Views differ as to how complete the employee's return must be for reentry to occur.
  — According to the R.2d, the employee must be at least "reasonably near the authorized space and time limits" for reentry to occur.[70]
  — In some jurisdictions, merely starting back toward a place where servant duties are to be performed suffices to reenter the scope of employment.
  — In other jurisdictions, the employee must have actually returned to the authorized "time and space."
  — The R.3d rule is vague: "When a frolic consists of a physical journey away from the workplace or a material departure from an assigned route of travel, an employee reenters employment when the employee has taken action consistent with once again resuming work."[71]

Example

Nick and Nora's trip to the opera house has taken them a half-hour off their regular delivery route. After purchasing their tickets, they get back into the Asta delivery van and head for their next stop. As they are pulling away from the curb, they negligently hit another car. In some jurisdictions, *respondeat superior* will apply, because the employees have started back to their

70. R.2d, §237.
71. R.3d, §7.07, comment *e*.

authorized work location (i.e., the next delivery stop). In other jurisdictions, the distance between that location and the accident site will preclude a finding of reentry into employment. ◀ ◀ ◀

d. Personal/Business Multitasking: On-Site Frolics and Negligent Self-Distraction

The frolic label most often applies to employees whose personal agenda takes them away physically from a location appropriate to their business task. However, in the modern world of mobile phones, computers, and tablets, an employee can be on a frolic while still at his or her desk.

Restatement on Point

P Insurance Co. furnishes telephones to its office staff with the direction that they may be used only when necessary to an employee's work. *A*, a claims processor, uses the telephone P Insurance Co. provides to make statements defamatory of T, a personal enemy of *A*'s. The recipients of *A*'s defamatory statements are unrelated to P Insurance Co.'s business. P Insurance Co. is not subject to liability to T. *A*'s conduct in defaming *T* was not within the scope of *A*'s employment. *A* acted only for *A*'s own purposes.[72] ◀ ◀ ◀

In contrast, if an employee undertakes personal matters simultaneously with business tasks, the business task remains within the scope of employment. Indeed, the employee's self-distraction may constitute negligence in performing the business task.

Example

Leighton is a housing inspector whose job requires him to drive from inspection site to inspection site. One afternoon, while en route from one site to another, Leighton uses his personal mobile phone to make a personal call. During the call, Leighton negligently collides with another car. The collision is within the scope of Leighton's employment. ◀ ◀ ◀

§3.2.7 Intentional Torts

a. Scope of Vicarious Liability

Although most *respondeat superior* cases involve torts of negligence, the doctrine's rationale and reach also extend to some intentional torts. When an

72. R.3d, §7.07, Ill. 10.

employee, acting within the scope of employment, commits an intentional tort causing physical harm, the employer is vicariously liable. The intentional nature of the tort does not preclude vicarious liability, and even an expressly forbidden or criminal act can be within the scope of employment.

Overly aggressive barroom employees provide prime examples.

Example

A bar owner instructs a bouncer never to use a particular chokehold in restraining obstreperous customers. One night the bouncer overreacts to an especially troublesome patron and uses the hold. The patron subsequently files a civil suit against the bar owner asserting *respondeat superior* for the bouncer's intentional tort of battery. The patron also complains to the police, and the bouncer is charged with and later convicted of misdemeanor assault.

The bouncer's conduct fits within the general guidelines of R.2d, §228(1)[73] and therefore was within the bouncer's scope of employment. The use of a forbidden tactic does not militate otherwise; unauthorized conduct can be within the scope of employment. Likewise, it does not matter that the bouncer's conduct was criminal. "The master can reasonably anticipate that servants may commit minor crimes in the prosecution of the business."[74] ◀◀◀

b. The Purpose Test

In most cases asserting *respondeat superior* for an intentional tort, employee status is clear and scope of employment is therefore the crucial issue. On that issue, under the R.2d and the overwhelming majority of cases, the pivotal inquiry is whether:

- the employee;
- in engaging in the conduct that constituted the intentional tort;
- was motivated at least in part by a desire to serve the master.[75]

The R.2d also focuses attention on "the similarity in quality of the act done to the act authorized."[76]

---

73. Quoted at note 29. Restraining patrons is the kind of work a bouncer is "employed to perform." The bouncer's purpose was to serve the bar owner (by quieting a disruption), and the actions occurred when and where they were supposed to. A bouncer's use of force should come as no surprise to a bar owner.

74. R.2d, §231, comment *a*.

75. R.2d, §228(1)(c), discussed in Section 3.2.5, makes this an entrance criterion to scope of employment.

76. R.2d, §229(2)(g). For further discussion of this issue, see the discussion *infra* in this section about the "scope of employment and seriously criminal behavior."

The R.3d uses a different formulation—namely, whether the tortious act "occurs within an independent course of conduct not intended by the employee to serve any purpose of the employer."[77] The newer formulation is intended to clarify rather than revise the older one.

Example

An employee of a finance company is lawfully using "self help" to repossess a car. When the owner happens to come home and see the repossession in progress, he loudly voices his objections and places himself in the path of the car to block its departure. The employee stops the car, gets out, knocks the owner to the ground, reenters the car, and drives away.

Assuming that the employee is liable for the tort of battery, the finance company is liable in *respondeat superior*. Although the employee's conduct may well have been forbidden by the finance company, the tort occurred as the employee was trying to effect the repossession. The assault-via-vehicle was not "a departure from [but rather merely] an escalation of conduct involved in performing assigned work."[78] ◄◄◄

Example

Throughout a lengthy bus ride, a passenger is noisy and disruptive. After the bus arrives at the terminal and the passenger has disembarked and begun walking away, the bus driver grabs the passenger and punches him. The bus company is not vicariously liable.[79] Since the trip is over and the passenger's misbehavior no longer affects the master's interest, the "servant" (bus driver) could not be actuated by a desire to serve the "master" (the bus company). By the time the tort occurs, the employee has embarked on "an independent course of conduct not intended by the employee to serve any purpose of the employer."[80] ◄◄◄

The "purpose rule" has always been pliable.[81] "Judge Learned Hand concluded that a drunken boatswain who routed the plaintiff out of his bunk with a blow, saying, 'Get up, you big son of a bitch, and turn to,' and then continued to fight, might have thought he was acting in the interest of the ship."[82] One court even found the necessary "purpose to serve the master" when a police trainee, practicing his quick draw inside the police

---

77. R.3d, §7.07(2).

78. R.3d, §7.07, comment i.

79. If the bus company owns the terminal, it may be directly liable for failing to provide safe premises to business invitees.

80. R.3d, §7.07(2).

81. See R.3d §7.07, cmt. b, Reporter's Notes (citing the second edition of this book).

82. *Ira S. Bushey & Sons, Inc. v. United States*, 398 F.2d 167, 170 (2d Cir. 1968) (citing *Nelson v. American-West African Line*, 86 F.2d 730 (2d Cir. 1936), *cert. denied*, 300 U.S. 665 (1937)).

station, accidentally shot a fellow officer. The court held that the trainee was trying to improve his firearms techniques, to the benefit of his employer.[83]

CASE IN POINT

Case in Point — *Hass v. Wentzlaff*

In *Hass v. Wentzlaff*, the South Dakota Supreme Court transmuted "*intent* to serve" into "beneficial *effect*" — even if incidental.

An insurance agent stole funds from monies a customer had on account with an insurance company. The customer sued the insurance company, asserting *respondeat superior*. As to a series of initial thefts, the South Dakota Supreme Court held that the agent "was not serving [the insurance company] when he committed the thefts." However, the agent:

> eventually began withdrawing amounts that resulted in surrender charges and interest adjustments [against the customer]. In fact, [the company] received over $36,000 in penalty fees or surrender charges due to the withdrawals . . . which could be considered a benefit for the company. Therefore, . . . it becomes more likely that [the agent's] purpose, at least in part, was to further the insurance companies' business.[84]

c. The Incidental/Foreseeable Test

A few more or less recent cases have abandoned the purpose test and have asked instead "whether [the] conduct [constituting the intentional tort] should fairly have been foreseen from the nature of the employment and the duties relating to it,"[85] or "whether the risk [of such conduct] was one that may fairly be regarded as typical of, or broadly incidental to, the enterprise undertaken by the employer."[86]

In the most well reasoned of these "incidental/foreseeable" cases, the courts identify some special characteristic of the employee's assigned task as facilitating or at least occasioning the abusive conduct.

CASE IN POINT

Case in Point — *Marston v. Minneapolis Clinic of Psychiatry and Neurology, Ltd.*

A psychologist employed by a clinic engages in sexual relations with a patient. The patient later asserts that the psychologist's emotional control over her vitiated any apparent consent and that the psychologist's conduct

83. *Thompson v. United States*, 504 F. Supp. 1087 (D. S.D. 1980).
84. *Hass v. Wentzlaff*, 2012 S.D. 50, ¶¶ 24–25, 816 N.W.2d 96, 104.
85. *Marston v. Minneapolis Clinic of Psychiatry and Neurology, Ltd.*, 329 N.W. 2d 306, 311 (Minn. 1983).
86. *Whitson v. Oakland Unified School District*, 123 Cal. App. 3d 133, 142 (1981) (citations and internal quotations omitted).

constituted an intentional tort. She sues both the psychologist and the clinic. The clinic may well be liable vicariously, because the psychologist's conduct was both foreseeable and incidental to his job. "[S]exual relations between a psychologist and a patient is a well-known hazard and thus, to a degree, foreseeable and a risk of employment. In addition, the . . . situation would not have occurred but for [the psychologist's] employment; it was only through his relation to [the patient] as a therapist that [the psychologist] was able to commit the acts in question."[87] ◄◄◄

In *Marston*, the therapist's employment did more than create a happenstance opportunity for sexual assault. The proper performance of the therapist's assigned task involved exploring, developing, and using the patient's vulnerability for therapeutic purposes.

Unfortunately, in many other incidental/foreseeable cases the holdings are far broader and more troublesome. In one jurisdiction, for example, courts have held that:

- sexual harassment of a waitress by a coworker is arguably "foreseeable" (and therefore arguably within the scope of employment) because the restaurant had a policy prohibiting sexual harassment;[88]
- when a day-care worker sexually assaults a little child, a *respondeat superior* claim against the day-care center can survive a motion for summary judgment on the strength of a single expert affidavit stating that in the day-care industry "sexual abuse of children is a paramount concern";[89]
- an individual's alleged violations of the Uniform Trade Secrets Act while attempting to switch customers from his old employer to his new employer did *not* support a *respondeat superior* claim by the former against the latter, because:
  — although the individual's tortious conduct clearly benefited and was intended to benefit the new employer's business;

87. *Marston*, 329 N.W.2d at 311. Cf.R.2d, §229(2)(h) (referring to "whether or not the instrumentality by which the harm is done has been furnished by the master to the servant").

88. *Boykin v. Perkins Family Restaurant*, C9-01-1100, 2002 WL 4548 (Minn. App. 2002). The Minnesota Supreme Court has since walked Minnesota law back from this precipice. In *Frieler v. Carlson Mktg. Grp., Inc.*, 751 N.W.2d 558, 584 (Minn. 2008), the Court held that "[t]he fact that an employer proactively adopts such a policy is insufficient, in and of itself, to create a genuine issue of material fact regarding whether the sexual harassment committed by an employee was foreseeable." The Court noted the perverse incentives inherent in a contrary approach: "[E]mployers should be *encouraged* as a matter of public policy to implement policies to prevent and address harassment in the workplace." *Id.* (emphasis added).

89. *L.M. v. Karlson*, 646 N.W. 2d 537, 539 (Minn. App. 2002). Remember that *respondeat superior* imposes automatically liability on the employer regardless of how careful the employer has been in hiring, training, and supervising its employees.

— the scope of employment question turned on "foreseeability"; and
— the old employer failed to introduce any evidence that trade secret violations were a "well-known hazard" in the particular industry at issue.[90]

The R.3d has criticized and rejected the incidental/foreseeable test:

> [F]ormulations based on assessments of "foreseeability" are potentially confusing and may generate outcomes that are less predictable than intent-based formulations. "Foreseeability" has a well-developed meaning in connection with negligence and to use it, additionally, to define a different boundary for *respondeat superior* risks confusion. . . . [T]he possibility that the work may lead to or somehow provide the occasion for intentional misconduct that is distinct from an employee's actions in performing assigned work . . . is indeed always "foreseeable," given human frailty, but its occurrence is not a risk that an employer can effectively control and its occurrence may be related causally to employment no more than to other relationships and circumstances in an errant employee's life more generally. Moreover, a "foreseeability" formulation for imposing vicarious liability may penalize an employer who has taken reasonable precautions against employee misconduct to the extent it enables a plaintiff to demonstrate that the employer did indeed foresee the risk of misconduct.[91]

d. Scope of Employment and Seriously Criminal Behavior

The incidental/foreseeable cases often involve seriously criminal behavior, for which, given the proper facts, victims can hold the employer *directly* liable for negligence in hiring, training, or supervising the employee. The greater the foreseeable vulnerability of the victim, the more exacting is the standard of ordinary care.[92]

Nonetheless, some of the incidental/foreseeable cases have bent the concept of *respondeat superior* so far as to hold the employer liable *without fault* so as to access the deep pocket.

> In many of these cases, the plaintiffs are victims of an employee's sexual misconduct. In one case, the victims were only three and four years old. It is difficult to criticize decisions that stretch a concept to succor such victims, but [law reflected in many of the incidental/foreseeable cases] has gone beyond stretching. It has been recast in an extraordinary and fundamentally unfair way.[93]

90. *Hagen v. Burmeister & Associates, Inc.*, 633 N.W. 2d 497, 505 (Minn. 2001).
91. R.3d, §7.07, comment *b*.
92. See Section 4.4.1. In this context, "foreseeability" is an appropriate concept, because the direct claims are negligence claims.
93. Daniel S. Kleinberger, "Respondeat Superior Run Amok," 59-Nov BENCH & B. MINN. 16 (Westlaw) (November 2002) (footnote omitted).

Fortunately, in most jurisdictions and the overwhelming majority of cases, the purpose test remains key to establishing *respondeat superior* liability for intentional torts. When an employee chooses to commit a serious crime on the employer's premises and against a customer or patron of the employer, it is unlikely that the employee is seeking to serve the employer's interest.[94]

Or, in R.3d terms, the "extreme quality" of "a serious crime . . . may indicate that [the employee] has launched upon an independent course of action,"[95] which ousts the conduct from the scope of employment if the "independent course" is "not intended by the employee to serve any purpose of the employer."[96]

§3.3 LIABILITY FOR PHYSICAL HARM BEYOND *RESPONDEAT SUPERIOR*

In general, a principal is not vicariously liable for physical harm caused by the torts of a nonemployee agent (in R.2d terms, an "independent contract agent"). *Respondeat superior* controls most such cases, and it applies only to employees (servants). In a few situations, however, other rules apply, and these rules impose liability for the torts of nonemployee agents.

§3.3.1 Principal's Liability to a Third Party

If a principal owes a direct duty of care to a third party in connection with the principal's use of an agent, the principal may be liable for breach of that duty. The most noteworthy such duties involve due care in the selection, training, supervision of agents, discussed in Section 4.1.1(a). Also, if a principal relies on an agent to fulfill the principal's contract (or similar) obligations to a third party and the agent fails to perform appropriately, the

94. Moreover, under the R.2d's approach to scope of employment:

- "whether or not the act is seriously criminal" is itself a factor in making the scope of employment determination, as is "the similarity in quality of the act done to the act authorized," R.2d, §229(2)(g) and (j), and
- a serious crime is unlikely to meet the requirements that the tortious act be "of the kind [the servant] is employed to perform" and that "if force is intentionally used by the servant against another, the use of force is not unexpectable by the master." R.2d, §228(1)(a) and (d).

95. R.3d, §7.07, comment c.
96. R.3d, §7.07(2).

principal will typically be liable to the third party. Section 4.4 discusses such situations. Section 4.4.2 discusses "nondelegable duties," a term that is most often a misnomer.

§3.3.2 Selected Special Categories of *Respondeat Superior*

a. Intentional Torts of Nonemployee Agents

When a nonemployee agent commits an intentional tort and causes physical injury, the relevant law is muddy. According to some authorities, the principal is not liable unless: (i) the principal intended or authorized the result or the manner of performance;[97] or (ii) the principal owed a duty to the injured party to have the agent's task performed with due care.

Notable exceptions exist to this rule. For example, store owners often face liability when a hired guard service falsely arrests or imprisons a customer of the store. The liability comes despite the store owner's protestation that the guard service acted as an independent contractor. Some of the cases that impose liability rest on a finding of control by the store of the guard service. Others assert that the principal ratified the guard service's wrongful act (e.g., by not terminating services of the independent tortfeasor). Other cases hold the store liable for breaching its duty to protect its customers from unwarranted attack.[98] Still other cases simply hold that independent contractor status does not bar vicarious liability for an agent's *intentional* (as distinguished from negligent) torts.

b. Misrepresentation by an Agent or Apparent Agent

If: (i) a person has actual or apparent authority to make statements concerning a particular subject; (ii) the person makes a misstatement of fact concerning that subject; (iii) a third party relies on that misstatement; and (iv) the third party suffers physical harm as a result, then the actual or apparent principal is liable to the third party.[99]

---

97. In such circumstances, an employer would also be liable for the intentional tort of its employee. The employer's intent would bring the employee's act within the scope of employment.

98. Under this theory, the store is not vicariously liable for the guard service's intentional tort. Rather, the store is directly liable for having breached its duty to provide safe premises for its business invitee. See Section 4.4.2.

99. R.3d, §§7.04 (actual authority) and 7.08 (apparent authority). See also R.2d §§251(b) (actual authority) and 266 (apparent authority).

Example

Office Realty, Inc. ("Realty") is substantially remodeling an office building that it owns and wishes to allow prospective tenants to see the work in progress. Realty has hired a construction manager to supervise the remodeling work and instructs that manager to tell prospective tenants which sites within the building are safe to view. One day, the construction manager makes a mistake and sends Bill, a prospective tenant, into an unsafe stairwell. Bill is injured. Realty is liable, regardless of whether the construction manager is an employee or independent contractor. Realty's agent had actual authority to identify the safe locations, and relying on the agent's misstatement on that subject caused Bill physical harm.[100] ◀ ◀ ◀

Example

Realty tells Alice, another prospective tenant, "If you want to see how the place will look, go over to the building. It's under construction, but one of our people will tell you where it's okay to go." Alice goes over to the building and meets a security guard, who is employed by a guard service hired by Realty. Neither the guard service nor its employees have actual authority to direct prospective tenants. However, when Alice asks, "How do I get to look at some redone offices?" the guard responds by directing Alice into the unsafe stairwell. If Alice is injured as a result, she can hold Realty vicariously liable. The guard's statement was made with apparent authority because Realty's manifestations to Alice caused her to reasonably believe the guard was authorized to give directions to prospective tenants.[101] ◀ ◀ ◀

c. Negligence of Apparent Servants

In one area, the doctrine of *respondeat superior* meshes with the law of apparent authority and produces vicarious liability for those who merely appear to be masters. In the words of the R.2d:

> One who represents that another is his servant or other agent and thereby causes a third person justifiably to rely upon the care or skill of such apparent agent is subject to liability to the third person for harm caused by the lack of care or skill of the one appearing to be a servant or other agent as if he were such.[102]

---

100. Bill may also have another theory of recovery: Realty's direct liability for failure to use reasonable care to protect business invitees. See Section 4.4.2.
101. For the rules for establishing apparent authority, see Section 2.3.
102. R.2d, §267.

The R.3d states an even broader rule:

> A principal is subject to vicarious liability for a tort committed by an agent in dealing . . . with a third party on or purportedly on behalf of the principal when actions taken by the agent with apparent authority constitute the tort.[103]

Regardless of which formulation applies, the rule is important. In our modern economy, many businesses present themselves to the marketplace as economically integrated enterprises while substituting independent contractors for traditional employees.

Case in Point—*Gizzi v. Texaco, Inc.*

An oil and gas company conducts a national advertising campaign, encouraging customers to have their cars serviced at service stations carrying the company's logo. In the words of the ad campaign: "You can trust your car to the man who wears the star." Some of the service stations are, in fact, independently owned and operated. These stations are not the company's agents, let alone the company's employees. In agency parlance, the independent operators are independent contractors. ◀◀◀

One such independent contractor negligently repairs a car, and the customer suffers injury as a result. The injured customer may well have a claim against the oil and gas company. In R.2d terms, the ad campaign may have created an appearance of servant status, and the customer may indeed have "trusted" that relationship in choosing the service station. If so, the oil company will be vicariously liable.[104]

Case in Point—*Jones v. HealthSouth Treasure Valley Hosp.*

Family members of a patient who died during surgery filed medical malpractice and wrongful-death claims against the surgery center, alleging that it was vicariously liable, under a theory of apparent agency, for the negligence

103. R.3d, §7.08. According to the Reporter's Notes to R.3d, §7.07, comment *a*, section 7.07 "is a consolidated treatment of topics covered in several separate sections of Restatement Second, Agency, including §267." However, R.3d, §7.07 does not address the appearance of employee status. See also *Restatement (Second) of Torts* 429 (1965) ("One who employs an independent contractor to perform services for another which are accepted in the reasonable belief that the services are being rendered by the employer or by his servants, is subject to liability for physical harm caused by the negligence of the contractor in supplying such services, to the same extent as though the employer were supplying them himself or by his servants.").

104. *Gizzi v. Texaco, Inc.*, 437 F.2d 308 (3d Cir. 1971) (directed verdict for defendant reversed; jury question as to whether ad campaign induced reasonable reliance).

of two anesthesiologists and a cell-saver technician who attended the surgery as independent contractors. The trial court granted summary judgment for the surgery center. The state supreme court reversed and remanded, holding, *inter alia*, that a hospital could be found liable under Idaho's doctrine of apparent authority for the negligence of independent personnel assigned by the hospital to perform support services, where a patient accepting the services did so in the reasonable belief that the services were rendered on behalf of the hospital.[105] ◀ ◀ ◀

§3.4 TORTS NOT INVOLVING PHYSICAL HARM

§3.4.1 The Basic Paradigm: Closer to Contracts Than to Physical Torts

If an agent's misconduct consists solely of words and the third party suffers harm only to its emotions, reputation, or pocketbook, the agency analysis resembles the approach used in applying agency attribution rules to contractual matters. The key rules are those of actual authority, apparent authority, and inherent agency power.[106] Except for the borderline areas of malicious prosecution and intentional interference with business relations, *respondeat superior* is largely irrelevant.

§3.4.2 The Tort of Misrepresentation

a. The Attribution Rule

It is commonplace for agents negotiating or communicating on behalf of principals to make statements concerning the subject matter of a potential transaction. If an agent makes a misstatement within the scope of the agent's actual authority, apparent authority, or inherent power, the misstatement itself is attributable to the principal for contract law purposes. If the misstatement is tortious in and of itself, the principal will be vicariously liable if the agent acted with actual[107] or apparent authority.[108]

105. 206 P.3d 473 (Idaho 2009).
106. For a detailed discussion of these rules, see Chapter 2.
107. R.3d, §7.03, comment *b*.
108. R.3d, §7.08. See also R.2d, §257.

CASE IN POINT

Case in Point—*Rodi v. S. New England Sch. Of Law*

A law school graduate who could not take the bar examination because his school was unaccredited sued the school (and other defendants) for fraudulent misrepresentation. The graduate claimed that he had relied on the dean's recruitment letter, which stated that the American Bar Association's accreditation committee had voted to recommend the school for provisional accreditation and that the dean was highly confident of receiving requisite ratification. The graduate also alleged that, after negative ABA action following his enrollment, he decided not to transfer from the law school because the school's acting dean assured him that there was no cause for pessimism about accreditation. The court held that, because deans were high-ranking school employees, their misrepresentations were attributable to the law school.[109] ◀◀◀

EXAMPLE

Example

Rebecca retains Michael to sell a plot of land she owns near the river and makes his authority generally known. Michael shows the land to Samantha, who seems quite interested. She asks, "Has there ever been any trouble with flooding from the river?" Michael knows that, in fact, almost every spring the river floods at least a little and that often the water temporarily covers a quarter of Rebecca's plot. However, fearful of losing the sale, he responds, "Oh no. Not at all." Samantha agrees to buy the land and signs a purchase agreement. Planning to build a house near the river, she hires and pays an architect to do preliminary plans. She then learns the truth about the flooding and, pursuant to contract law, rescinds the purchase agreement.[110] The architect's plans are now worthless to Samantha, and she may recover their cost from Rebecca (as well as directly from Michael). Michael, Rebecca's agent, made a material misstatement with intent to deceive and thereby committed the tort of intentional misrepresentation.[111] Michael lacked the actual authority to falsely describe the flooding situation, but his false description came within his apparent authority. Samantha relied on the false statement and as a consequence suffered injury. Rebecca is therefore vicariously liable for Michael's tort. ◀◀◀

When a misrepresentation is made with apparent authority, the principal is liable even if the person making the misrepresentation "acts entirely

109. 389 F.3d 5 (1st Cir. 2004). The court invoked *respondeat superior* rather than actual or apparent authority.

110. Michael's misstatement as to the flooding is attributed to Rebecca, so Samantha can rescind for fraud in the inducement. See Section 2.4.6.

111. Michael is also liable. See Section 4.2.3.

for his [sic] own purposes, unless the [third party] has notice of this."[112] In general, "A principal who puts a servant or other agent in a position which enables the agent, while apparently acting within his authority, to commit a fraud upon third persons is subject to liability to such third persons for the fraud."[113] Moreover:

> [A] corporate employer can be held vicariously liable for an intentional act of its employee when the employee is acting within the scope of the employer's apparent authority, even if the employer did not permit or otherwise authorize the act, or it was not necessary or appropriate to serve the interest of the employer.[114]

b. Tort Attribution Contrasted with Contract Attribution

Besides saddling a principal with tort liability, as the Example above illustrates, an agent's misstatements can also give rise to contractual claims against the principal, particularly claims for breach of warranty and rescission. The tort attribution rules differ from the contract rules, however, with regard to what is being attributed and, consequently, with regard to the role of innocent misstatements.

For tort law purposes, the principal's liability is vicarious, and the attribution involves a complete tort: a material misstatement made by an agent with the requisite state of mind (e.g., intent, negligence), followed by a third party's injurious reliance. Establishing the principal's liability involves two steps: Tort law recognizes a tort as committed by the agent; agency law attributes that completed tort to the principal. Therefore, since innocent misstatements do not constitute torts, an agent's innocent misstatements do not trigger the tort attribution rules.

The process works differently with contractual claims. Unless the principal is undisclosed, no contractual claim is complete at the agent's level and no complete claim exists to be attributed.115 Instead, agency law attributes the agent's statement, and contract law then imposes liability as if the principal had itself made the statement. The principal's liability is direct ("on the contract"), even though one of the elements creating liability (the misstatement) is satisfied only by attribution. For contract law purposes, therefore, an agent's misstatement is attributed regardless of whether the misstatement

112. R.2d, §262.

113. R.2d, §261. See also R.3d, §7.08, comment *b* ("When an agent acts with apparent authority, the agent's motivation is immaterial to the legal consequences that the agent's action carries for the principal. Likewise, the fact that an agent's conduct is not in fact beneficial to the principal does not shield the principal from legal consequences.").

114. *Thompson v. Orange Lake Country Club, Inc.*, 224 F. Supp. 2d 1368, 1377 (M.D. Fla. 2002).

115. If the principal is undisclosed, the agent is a party to the contract, and the third party's claim will be valid against the agent as well as the undisclosed principal. See Section 4.2.1.

Figure 3-1. Comparison of Tort and Contract Attribution Paradigms

	Agent's Level	What Is Being Attributed	Principal's Level
Tort	Agent commits a tort of misrepresentation (which necessarily involves a non-innocent misstatement).	Agent's tort	Vicarious Liability for the attributed tort of Agent
Contract	Agent makes a statement which may be a misstatement, which in turn may be innocent.	Agent's (mis) statement	Direct Liability (if provided by applicable substantive law), in part due to the attributed (mis)statement of Agent

was innocent, negligent, reckless, or intentional. Indeed, the attribution occurs essentially as if the statement were accurate.[116] For a graphic explanation, see Figure 3-1.

Often, the same situation supports both contract and tort claims. Whether the third party prefers one claim over another often depends on issues outside of agency law, such as which remedy is the most desirable or whether the statute of limitations has run on one claim but not on the other.

§3.4.3 Defamation

A principal is liable for an agent's defamation if the agent acted with actual or apparent authority in making the defamatory statement. It is not necessary that the agent be actually or apparently authorized to commit defamation, but rather that the agent be actually or apparently authorized to make the statement. For apparent authority to be relevant, the agent must have appeared authorized to "those hearing or reading the statement."[117]

116. Assume, for example, that a principal authorizes an agent to sell the principal's car and to describe the car's characteristics to prospective purchasers. The agent says to a third party, "This car will get at least 25 miles per gallon on the highway," and in reliance the third party agrees to buy the car. Agency law attributes the mpg statement to the principal, and under contract law the statement creates a warranty that binds the principal. If the statement happens to be true, contract law gives the buyer no claim against the principal. If the statement happens to be false, contract law will provide the buyer several remedies (e.g., rejection, revocation of acceptance, action for damages for breach of warranty). The distinction drawn in the text parallels a distinction between contract law and tort law. Under contract law, innocent misstatements by or attributed to a party can be actionable. Under tort law, they are not.
117. R.2d, §247.

Example

A credit bureau authorizes its employees to report information contained in the bureau's database to subscribers. A bureau employee receives a call from a subscriber who is seeking information about James Hobbs. The employee consults the database and reports, "Two convictions for larceny, and 12 bounced checks." In fact, the database is completely wrong, and, up to this moment, Mr. Hobbs's reputation has been unblemished. The credit bureau is liable for defamation. The employee had actual authority to make the report that turned out to be defamatory. ◄◄◄

Example

A newspaper columnist has written a series of columns harshly criticizing the city's parking commissioner. The newspaper's publisher becomes concerned that the columns are getting perilously close to the "actual malice" necessary to allow a public figure to recover for defamation. The publisher therefore orders the columnist to cease writing about the commissioner. Assuming that the columnist will obey, the publisher neglects to mention the order to the paper's managing editor. The columnist disobeys the publisher's order, and another column appears that contains scurrilous statements that are clearly defamatory. The newspaper is liable to the commissioner for defamation. Although the columnist lacked actual authority to write on the subject, to the newspaper's readers the columnist appeared to be authorized.[118] ◄◄◄

The example of the columnist highlights the policy behind using apparent authority as an attribution rule for defamation. In the words of the R.2d:

> [D]efamation is effective, in part at least, because of the personality of the one publishing it. Thus, one who appears to have authority to make statements for the employer gives to his statements the weight of the employer's reputation.[119]

§3.4.4 Malicious Prosecution and Interference with Business Relations

These torts often involve both words and actions, and in this borderline area *respondeat superior* is the chief rule.

118. The newspaper's manifestation was, of course, the running of the column.
119. R.2d, §247, comment c. See also R.3d, §7.08, comment *d* ("The effectiveness of the defamation—its credibility to those to whom it is published and its propensity to harm the person defamed—is often tied to the reputation and thus the personality of its publisher.").

Example

Todd is a salaried sales rep for the Nickel Surgical Products Company ("Nickel"). Nickel trains its sales reps to pursue business aggressively. Todd persuades Ace Hospital to stop buying its surgical drapes from Amalgamated Hospital Supply ("Amalgamated") and buy instead from Nickel. Ace's decision and subsequent purchases from Nickel breach a contract with Amalgamated. Todd has tortiously induced that breach of contract, and Nickel is vicariously liable.[120] ◀◀◀

§3.5 ATTRIBUTING TORTS IN MULTILEVEL OR OTHERWISE COMPLEX RELATIONSHIPS

§3.5.1 Borrowed Servants, Leased Employees, and Remote Masters

Respondeat superior attributes an employee's (servant's) tort to the employer/master on the grounds that the employer/master has the right to control the tortfeasor's performance. In some situations, however, it may be difficult to identify the person that controls the conduct giving rise to the tort.

a. Borrowed Servants and Leased Employees

In several circumstances, one party's employee may come under the temporary control of another party. For example:

- an equipment leasing company lends an equipment operator to a construction company;
- a surgeon conducts an operation with the assistance of nurses employed by a hospital; or
- a company "leases" an employee to another company, with:
  - the leasing company handling personnel, accounting, employee tax, and similar matters; and
  - the employee working under the direction and control of the other company.

The first and second type of situation have been around for a long time, and agency law has long used the *borrowed servant* doctrine in those contexts.[121] Leased employees are a modern-day development, increasingly widespread, and some cases have used the borrowed servant analysis to determine

120. For a discussion of the factors used to determine scope of employment, see Section 3.2.5.

121. A comment to the R.3d suggests the term "lent employees" while acknowledging "borrowed servants" as the prevalent term of art. R.3d, §7.03, comment *d* (2).

whether application to the leasing company is vicariously liable for a leased employee's on-the-job negligence.

The borrowed servant analysis is best presented by example.

Example

Hoister Crane Company ("Hoister") owns and leases out large cranes used in major construction projects. Operating such a crane requires considerable skill, so Hoister employs a staff of trained, full-time operators and assigns an operator to run each leased crane. Hoister charges its customer a single fee that includes both the use of the crane and the services of the operator.

Hoister rents a crane to General Contractor, Inc. ("General Contractor"), a construction company building a large office building. At the worksite, Hoister's operator runs the crane, but General Contractor's site supervisor tells the operator what tasks to do and when to do them. When the crane is in operation, the site supervisor uses hand signals to direct the operator. While lifting a load of steel bars, the operator negligently allows three bars to fall, injuring a passerby. Whether *respondeat superior* implicates Hoister or General Contractor depends on whether, at the time of the accident, the crane operator was General Contractor's borrowed servant. ◄◄◄

Example

Jeff Couteau, a surgeon, has operating privileges at Morgan Hospital ("the hospital") but is not a hospital employee. When he performs surgery at the hospital, he is assisted by operating room nurses who are hospital employees. During the course of an operation these nurses take orders from whatever physician is in charge.

At the end of one of Couteau's operations, a nurse neglects to make a proper sponge count and the patient is closed with one sponge still inside. In the subsequent malpractice action, the patient asserts that *respondeat superior* makes Couteau liable for the nurse's negligence. Whether this claim succeeds depends on whether, during the operation (and more particularly, at the time of the negligent sponge count), the nurse was Couteau's borrowed servant. ◄◄◄

Case in Point — *Vasquez v. United Enterprises of Sw. Florida, Inc.*

Holly Marie Vasquez was injured in an automobile accident, caused by the negligence of Gladys Dias. Dias managed two restaurants owned by Ramon Rodriguez. Rodriguez leased Dias from Fidelity United. In her claim against Fidelity, Vasquez asserted *respondeat superior*. Fidelity United conceded Dias's negligence. The jury found against Vasquez on the *respondeat superior* issue, Vasquez appealed, and the appellate court affirmed on the following rationale:

> It is a fundamental rule that the respondeat superior doctrine applies only when the alleged master has the ability and authority to direct and control the pertinent acts of the employee. . . . Absent control, there is no vicarious liability for the act of another, even for an employee. Florida courts do not use the label "employer" to impose strict liability under a theory of respondeat superior but instead look to the employer's control or right of control over the employee at the time of the negligent act. Here, Fidelity United is an employee leasing company. Its clients out source [sic] payroll and other administrative, personnel-related functions to it. Fidelity United relieves its clients of most of their administrative burdens but does not supervise employees or control their day-to-day activities.[122] ◀◀◀

The precise contours of the borrowed servant doctrine vary from jurisdiction to jurisdiction. In most jurisdictions a party invoking the rule must show that:

- the regular master (sometimes called "the general employer") assigned or allowed its servant to work for and under the supervision of another party (sometimes called "the special employer");
- at the time of the servant's tortious conduct:
  - —the special employer had the right to control in detail the performance of the servant's work; and
  - —the general employer retained no significant right of control over the servant, including the right to reassign the servant to other tasks.

The doctrine is relevant only when a servant is alleged to have committed a tort, so "the important question is not whether or not [the servant] remains the servant of the general employer as to matters generally, but whether or not, as to the act in question, [the servant] is acting in the business of and under the direction of [the general employer] or [the special employer.]"[123] The inquiry is always very fact intensive, and "[e]ven within the same jurisdiction, it may be difficult to predict whether a given set of indicia will demonstrate that a special employer has assumed the right of control."[124]

---

122. 811 So. 2d 759, 760–61 (Fla. Dist. Ct. App. 2002) (citing *Postal Telegraph & Cable Co. v. Doyle*, 123 Fla. 695, 167 So. 358 (1936) as "(observing that under [the] borrowed servant rule, one who borrows and exercises control over the servant or worker of another in effect assumes all liability for the activities of the borrowed servant or worker)") (first ellipsis added; quotation marks and other citations omitted; second ellipsis and brackets in the original).
123. R.2d, §227, comment *a*.
124. R.3d, §7.03, comment *d* (2).

Although the borrowed servant doctrine can be described as an exception to *respondeat superior*, the doctrine is better understood as an application of *respondeat superior* principles. *Respondeat superior* attributes a servant's negligence to the servant's master, and the borrowed servant doctrine redirects that attribution away from the regular master ("the general employer") to a temporary master ("the special employer"). The redirection is appropriate because the special employer has a transitory but substantial right to control the servant. Since *respondeat superior* rests on the master's right to control, vicarious liability should follow the control. When the general employer allows the special employer to control the servant's performance, the "borrowed" servant's torts should be attributed to the special employer.

As for the case of the crane operator, courts have gone both ways.[125] Some have looked to the general contractor's detailed control over the operator (e.g., the hand signals) and have found the operator to be the general contractor's borrowed servant. Other courts have held to the contrary, following a R.2d comment that "a continuation of the general employment is indicated by the fact that the general employer can properly substitute another servant at any time, that the time of the new employment is short, and that the lent servant has the skill of a specialist."[126]

As for the medical malpractice case, if the hospital lacked the right to reassign the nurse during the operation, the borrowed servant doctrine probably applies. As for leased employees, the law continues to develop.

b. Remote Masters[127]

The remote master problem typically arises when: (i) the employee of one party (the "employer") commits a tort; (ii) the employer is itself subject to substantial control or influence by another party; and (iii) the tort victim seeks to recover from that other party. The issue often arises in the context of franchise relationships or construction projects. Following are two paradigmatic examples.

---

125. *Compare DePratt v. Sergio*, 306 N.W. 2d 62 (Wis. 1981) (holding crane operator who obeyed hand signals to be a borrowed servant), *with Gulf, Colorado & Santa Fe Co. v. Harry Newton, Inc.*, 430 S.W. 2d 223 (Tex. Civ. App. 1968) (holding crane operator not to be a borrowed servant even though operator was following instructions of the special employer).

126. R.2d, §227, comment c. Presumably the operator's skill makes it less practical for the special employer to assert effective control. See Section 3.2.4 (when agent possesses special skills that principal lacks, principal is less able to exert control and less likely to be a master).

127. Unlike "borrowed servant," this phrase does not appear in the Restatements or case law. The phrase is instead the author's shorthand.

Example

A franchisor licenses a local company to run a hotel using the franchisor's name, logo, business practices, and national reservation system. The franchise agreement requires the franchisee to abide by a thick book of regulations on topics ranging from style of linen to lawn care. One winter a custodial employee of the *franchisee* carelessly shovels a sidewalk and leaves behind a thin sheet of ice. A customer of the franchisee slips and falls. The customer sues not only the franchisee but also the franchisor. ◀◀◀

Example

A construction company ("the general contractor") wins a bid to build a new apartment building. The general contractor subcontracts the electrical work to an electrical subcontractor and the plumbing work to a plumbing subcontractor.[128] Concerned about workplace safety, the general contractor has its own site supervisor regularly check on the work of all the subcontractors. An electrician, employed by the electrical subcontractor, negligently leaves some equipment lying around, and an employee of the plumbing subcontractor trips and suffers injury. The injured employee sues not only the electrical subcontractor but also the general contractor. ◀◀◀

The outcome of each of these situations depends on whether the plaintiff can find a chain of attribution that links the tortfeasor (in the above examples, the custodian and the electrician) to the distant party (the franchisor and the general contractor). Unfortunately, many of the cases in this area fail to articulate a complete analysis. For example, courts in franchise cases often: (i) note that the tortfeasor is the servant of the franchisee; (ii) determine that the franchisee is the servant of the franchisor; and (iii) on that basis alone hold the franchisor liable for the tortfeasor's misconduct. These courts neglect to explain why the franchisor is responsible for the torts of its servant's servant.

At least three different theories could apply.[129] First, the tortfeasor could be deemed the subservant of the distant party. According to the R.2d, if a master's servant engages servants of its own to conduct the master's

128. Sometimes a business that is providing services or producing a product will delegate or "subcontract" part of the work to another business. The reasons for this practice vary. The delegating party may lack the necessary in-house expertise; it may have the expertise, but its own employees may be busy on other projects; it may be able to save money by delegating work to a company that is more efficient or that pays its employees lower wages. Subcontracting is characteristic of the construction industry and increasingly prevalent in the manufacturing sector.

129. Agency case law and the R.2d offer several different views on that subject. The R.3d does not address this issue.

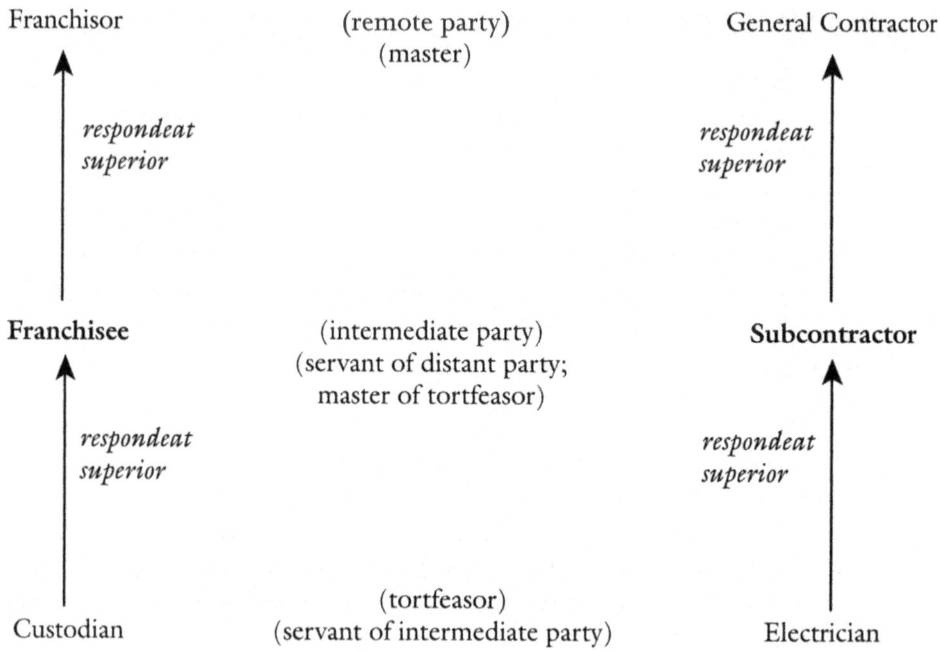

Figure 3-2. Master of Master Analysis

business, then the servant's servants are subservants of the master.[130] In that event, *respondeat superior* attributes the subservant's torts (if within the scope of employment) directly to the master.[131] Under this approach, the franchisor and the general contractor would be masters, the franchisee and the electrical contractor would be servants, and the custodian and the electrician would be subservants. See Figure 3-2.

The problem with this analysis is that, for a subservant to exist, the master must have expressly or impliedly authorized the servant to engage servants of its own to do the master's business. Moreover, the master will have the "prerogative of overriding his servant in giving directions [to] the subservant."[132] In the situations under discussion, neither of these elements is present. The remote party (i.e., the franchisor and the general contractor) does not consider the intermediate party (i.e., the franchisee and the electrical contractor) to be its servant. To the contrary, the typical franchise agreement and the typical construction subcontract each expressly disclaim any

130. R.2d, §5(2). The R.3d does not use the term "subservant" and does not consider how *respondeat superior* might apply to a remote master. See R.3d, §7.03, comment *d* (1) (stating that, "[w]hen a subagent is an employee . . . of the appointing agent, the *appointing agent* is subject to vicarious liability for torts committed by the subagent within the scope of employment" but only contemplating "the appointing agent and the principal [being] subject to vicarious liability when a subagent acts with *apparent authority* in committing a tort") (citation omitted; emphasis added).
131. R.2d, §5(2), comment *e*.
132. Id.

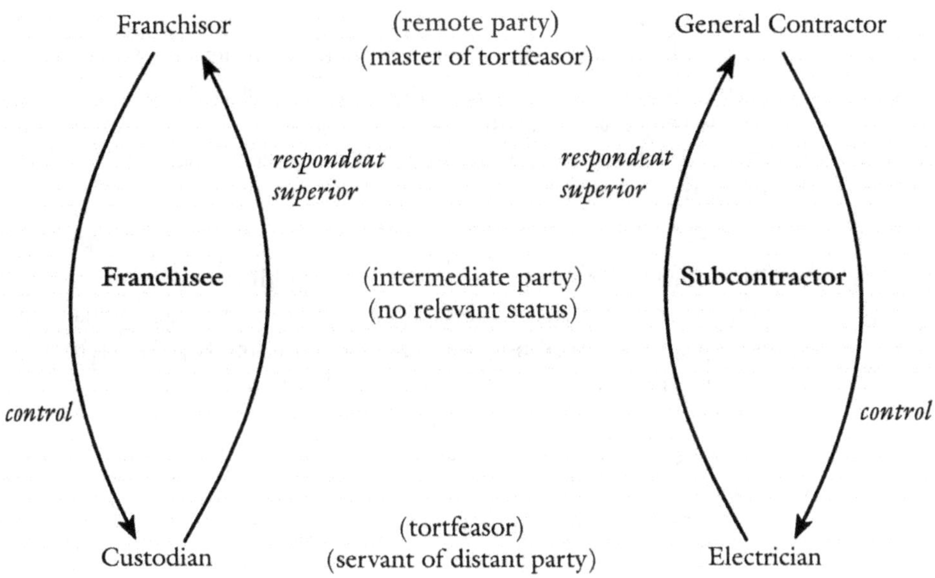

Figure 3-3. Direct Control Analysis

agency status whatsoever. It is therefore unlikely that the distant party has consented to having the intermediate party engage *subservants*. Likewise, the intermediate parties see themselves as independent contractors, especially when it comes to control of their employees. They would hardly view the distant party as having the "prerogative" to directly control their employees.

The second approach follows more closely the actual business relationships and involves two steps of attribution. Under this approach, the tortfeasor (i.e., the custodian and the electrician) is seen simply as the servant of the intermediate party (i.e., the franchisee and the electrical contractor), and the intermediate party is seen as the servant of the distant party (i.e., the franchisor and the general contractor). *Respondeat superior* then operates twice: The tortfeasor's negligence is attributed to the intermediate party, and the intermediate party's (attributed) negligence is attributed to the distant party. See Figure 3-3.

Case in Point—*Estate of Miller v. Thrifty Rent-A-Car Sys., Inc.*

A rental-car passenger died following an accident in which the rental car's brake system allegedly seized. The car had been rented from a franchisee, and the decedent's estate and family sought to hold the franchisor liable on claims of negligence, strict liability, and breach of warranty. Granting summary judgment for defendant, the court held, *inter alia*, that defendant was not vicariously liable for franchisee's provision of the allegedly defective vehicle under theories of agency or *respondeat superior*. The court reasoned, in part, that only one factor potentially weighed in favor of finding franchisee to be an employee of franchisor rather than an independent contractor—namely, whether the work was part of the regular business of the employer. The most important factor, control, weighed heavily against employee status, because the agreement between franchisor and franchisee was oriented toward "results" rather than "means."[133] ◀ ◀ ◀

The third approach is the most direct, holding that the distant party has retained or exercised a direct right to control the intermediate party's employees and is accordingly the tortfeasor's master. *Respondeat superior* therefore applies directly. See Figure 3-4. In most circumstances, there will be no express evidence of the distant party's right of control. Indeed, the typical franchise agreement and the typical construction subcontract will state to the contrary. However, the parties' conduct may belie their formal manifestations. If, for example, the general contractor's site supervisor regularly issues orders to the employees of the electrical subcontractor and those

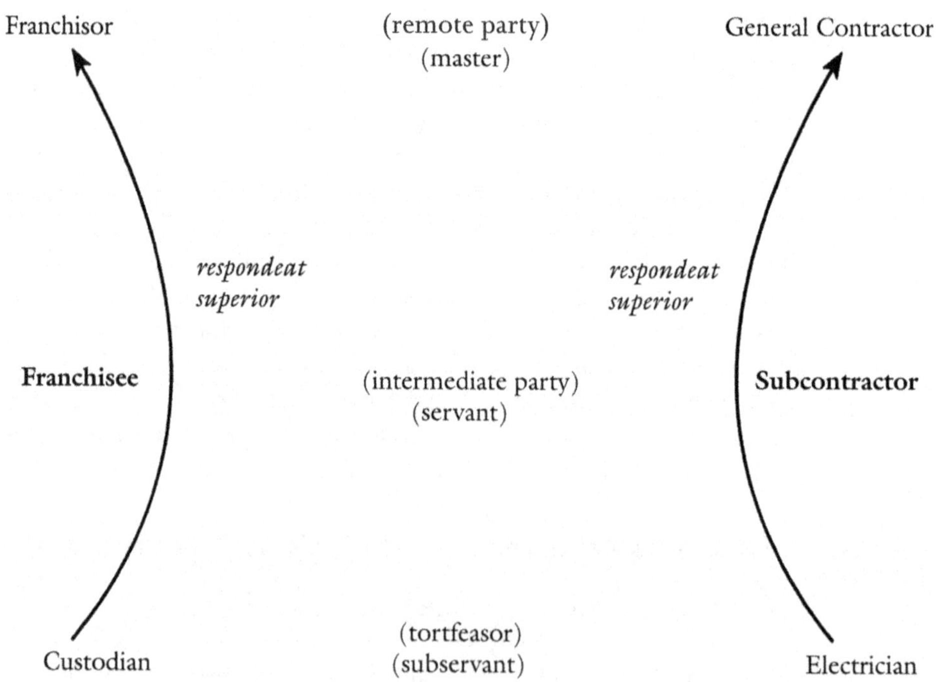

Figure 3-4. Subservant Analysis

133. 637 F. Supp. 2d 1029 (M.D. Fla. 2009).

employees obey, then the right to control is present and *respondeat superior* may well apply. Similarly, if the franchisor regularly sends out inspectors, these inspectors give orders directly to the franchisee's employees, and the employees obey, then the franchisor may well find itself at the receiving end of *respondeat superior* liability.

Problem 16

Rachael retains Jan, an experienced attorney, to represent her in a commercial dispute. Driving to a settlement conference, Jan negligently hits a pedestrian. The pedestrian sues Rachael, asserting *respondeat superior*. What result? ◀ ◀ ◀

EXPLANATION

Explanation

The pedestrian's claim will fail. For *respondeat superior* to apply, the tortfeasor must be a servant. For servant status to exist, the principal must have the right to exercise detailed control of the agent's manner of performance. A lawyer's client does not have that right. The client sets the goal and may make major strategy decisions. Tactics, however, are the lawyer's domain. ◀ ◀ ◀[134]

Problem 17

Athos buys new vinyl tile for his kitchen floor from Porthos Floor Coverings Unlimited ("Porthos"), a discount retailer of carpet, linoleum, tile, and other floor coverings. Porthos does not have any installers on staff, but tells Athos that it will arrange to have the tile installed by one of the "licensed, bonded contractors who do this sort of work for us." Porthos arranges for Michael Planchet to install Athos's tile. Planchet runs his own small contractor business and does jobs for various retailers and directly for homeowners. Porthos does not guarantee him any regular work and pays him a flat fee per square yard on each installation. (The fee does vary depending on the floor covering being installed.)

In due course, Planchet arrives at Athos's kitchen with the tile and the installment materials. Those materials include an effective but highly volatile

134. Consistent with current usage in the cases and commentary, these Explanations will sometimes refer to master-servant, sometime to employer-employee, and sometimes to both.

adhesive for securing the tiles to the subfloor. Unfortunately, Planchet fails to read or follow the instructions on the adhesive can, and a fire breaks out. Athos sues Porthos, asserting *respondeat superior*. What result? ◀ ◀ ◀

Explanation

Athos will lose. Planchet is an independent contractor, not Athos's employee.

Virtually all the factors listed in R.3d, §7.07, comment f indicate Planchet's independence. Porthos, the alleged master, has no control "over the details of the work." Planchet, the alleged servant, is skilled, "is engaged in a distinct occupation or business," and supplies his own tools. The employment is episodic, not sustained, and payment is by the job. Moreover, Porthos and Planchet do not consider themselves employer and employee.[135] ◀ ◀ ◀

Problem 18

A newspaper provides its customers home delivery through a network of "independent delivery agents." A written contract between the newspaper and each agent: (i) assigns each agent a particular route; (ii) provides the agent a percentage commission based on the subscription price of papers delivered; (iii) allows the newspaper to terminate the relationship at any time without cause; and (iv) expressly disclaims any master-servant relationship. The newspaper conducts training programs on how to make deliveries and increase sales. Although the contract does not mention these programs, the newspaper considers regular attendance to be mandatory. Each delivery agent supplies his or her own car or van to make the deliveries. Many of the routes are quite large, and many of the agents have no other gainful employment. The newspaper does not withhold Social Security taxes from the commission checks and does not pay the employer's portion of Social Security on the commission amounts.

While delivering papers one morning, one of the agents loses control of the car and crashes into a building. The building owner sues the newspaper, asserting *respondeat superior*. What result? ◀ ◀ ◀

135. Athos may have a successful contract claim, however, if he can establish that his contract with Porthos included installation. See Section 4.4.3. Porthos's reference to "contractors" probably negates an apparent servant claim. See Section 3.3.4.

Explanation

The building owner may well prevail, although several factors from the R.2d and R.3d point the other way.

The parties apparently did not consider themselves master and servant. The contract expressly disclaimed that relationship, and the principal did not withhold or pay Social Security taxes on account of the commissions.[136] The newspaper did not pay a set wage or salary,[137] and the delivery agent supplied the key instrumentality (i.e., the car).[138]

The key question, however, is the right to exercise control. The newspaper's right to terminate without cause and without advance notice suggests that, practically speaking, the newspaper had considerable control over the agents' performance. The fact that few of the agents were "engaged in a distinct occupation or business"[139] made each especially susceptible to the threat of termination. That the threat carried weight is evidenced by the required attendance policy.

Although the R.3d/R.2d factors may thus point in opposite directions, the policies underlying *respondeat superior* clearly favor a finding of servant status. Home delivery is an integral part of the newspaper's enterprise, and that enterprise should bear the costs of accidents foreseeable in that phase of the business. As for risk avoidance, the training sessions demonstrate that the newspaper can and already does influence the agents' manner of performance. Moreover, as for risk spreading, the newspaper is far better able to anticipate, calculate, and spread the cost than are the individual agents. ◀◀◀

Problem 19

This problem is derived from *Curry v. Equilon Enters., LLC.*[140] ARS, a company separate from Shell Oil Company (Shell), had hired the Plaintiff, (Curry) to manage two Shell-brand gas stations operated by ARS. Under a very detailed contract with Shell, ARS obtained gas to sell and the right to use Shell trademarks. The following facts are quoted from that case. (Some internal quotations omitted.)

> [At the relevant time and in the relevant locations] Shell no longer operated its own service stations with its own employees. Instead, Shell offered leases and operating agreements to entities that sought to run Shell's service stations.

136. R.2d, §220(2)(i); R.3d, §7.07, comment f.
137. R.2d, §220(2)(g); R.3d, §7.07, comment f.
138. R.2d, §220(2)(e); R.3d, §7.07, comment f.
139. R.2d, §220(2)(b); R.3d, §7.07, comment f.
140. *Curry v. Equilon Enters., LLC*, 23 Cal. App. 5th 289, 293–94, 233 Cal. Rptr. 3d 295, 297–98 (2018), as modified on denial of reh'g (May 18, 2018)

The leases provided that the operators/lessees (Operators) had a lease interest in the service stations' convenience stores and carwash facilities. Operators retained all the profits from the convenience stores and carwash facilities.

[ARS and Shell entered Shell's standard contracts under which ARS] operated the stations' fuel facilities for Shell in exchange for compensation from Shell. Shell owned the gasoline that was sold to customers. Shell received all the revenue from the fuel sales. Shell unilaterally set the fuel prices. Operators were required to complete daily gasoline price surveys from competing gas stations, submit that information to Shell, and then change the fuel prices as directed by Shell. Shell reimbursed Operators for the labor expenses associated with operating the fuel portion of the service station.

In addition, . . . Shell required [ARS] to perform various tasks for the purposes of maintenance, safety, accounting, and maintaining Shell's brand standards. . . . Although Shell required Operators to conduct certain tasks, [ARS] always maintained control over the daily work of [its] own employees . . .

[More particularly, as stated in the Shell-ARS agreement]:

- "[ARS] has the right to select, hire, and discharge such employees, provided, however, Operator shall remove any such employee promptly upon [Shell's] request for good cause shown."
- "[Shell] shall not select, hire, discharge, supervise or instruct any of Operator's employee."
- "[Shell], its agents, and representatives may enter any [station], at all reasonable times, to inspect the facilities, procedures, and material being used in the sale of the Motor Fuel Products or other products, to obtain samples of and conduct tests on the Motor Fuel Products, to inspect the Records, and to audit, observe, and otherwise verify [ARS's] compliance with [the Shell-ARS agreement."

Assume that Curry, while managing one of the ARS stations, was grossly negligent and foreseeably caused substantial harm a customer of the station. The customer seeks to hold not only Curry but also Shell liable. What result and why?

Explanation

EXPLANATION

The customer should lose, even though, in the court's words, "Shell, along with ARS, provided Curry a place to work and the equipment with which she performed her job." Per the court:

> Providing a portion of Curry's work location and equipment is insufficient to raise a triable issue of material fact as to Shell being Curry's employer due to the many other factors reflecting Shell is not Curry's employer.
>
> In other words, one could not reasonably conclude that Shell controlled the manner and means by which Curry accomplished her work because Shell did not supervise Curry, Shell did not have input on Curry's skills, Shell did not have control over the length of time Curry performed her job, Shell did not pay

Curry, Shell was not in the business of operating service stations, and Shell and Curry did not believe they were creating an employer-employee relationship.

Problem 20

Sandpit Gravel Company ("Sandpit") is excavating a deposit of gravel from a large open pit. Among the Sandpit employees working in the pit is a group of dump truck drivers. There are two ways to drive out of the pit: one safe but very time-consuming, the other quick and quite dangerous. Sandpit has repeatedly instructed the drivers to take the safe route and has repeatedly forbidden them to use the dangerous one. The drivers are generally happy to comply, because the company pays them by the hour. At closing time, however, the drivers have a different attitude. When the closing whistle blows, the drivers are "off the clock" and want to get themselves home as soon as possible. Nonetheless, they obey the rules and take the slow way out, until one day, when a driver in a big rush tries the fast route. The truck slides off and rolls over, crushing the leg of an OSHA inspector. The OSHA inspector sues Sandpit, alleging *respondeat superior*. What result? ◄ ◄ ◄

Explanation

Sandpit is liable. An employee's act can come within the scope of employment even though forbidden by the employer. In this case, the driver was conducting the employer's business, with an "instrumentality . . . furnished by the master";[141] the act was quite similar "in quality . . . to the act authorized";[142] "the departure from the normal method of accomplishing an authorized result"[143] was moderate; and "the master [had] reason to expect that such an act [would] be done."[144] ◄ ◄ ◄

Problem 21

A shopping mall employs its own staff of private security guards. These guards receive regular wages, wear uniforms supplied by the mall, report to the mall's director of security, and work shifts assigned by the director. The mall, through the director, has forbidden the security guards to carry guns.

One day a guard disobeys that policy and brings an unlicensed gun to work. While at work, the guard has a scuffle with an unruly patron, and the

141. R.2d, §229(2)(h).
142. R.2d, §229(2)(g).
143. *Id.* §229(2)(i).
144. *Id.* §229(2)(f). The master saw a need to repeat the prohibition, suggesting that the master considered the prohibited conduct to be at least somewhat attractive to the drivers.

gun inadvertently discharges and wounds a patron in the leg. The patron sues the mall, alleging *respondeat superior*.[145] What result? ◀ ◀ ◀

Explanation

Assuming that the patron can establish the guard's underlying tort, vicarious liability will probably exist. Dealing with unruly patrons is central to the guard's responsibilities, and as shown in Problem 20, a forbidden act can be within the scope of employment. The servant's illegal act—carrying an unlicensed weapon—will undercut the patron's claim only if that act is considered "seriously criminal" and even then only if the act is considered unforeseeable. ◀ ◀ ◀

Problem 22

A major league pitcher is having a bad day on the mound. Not only are the opposing batters doing well, but there is also a heckler in the stands who is increasingly obnoxious. Finally, distracted beyond endurance, the pitcher whirls and fires the ball straight at the heckler. This pitch is right on target, hitting the heckler on the head. The heckler sues the pitcher's employer, the ball club, asserting *respondeat superior* liability. What result? ◀ ◀ ◀

Explanation

This intentional tort may be one instance in which the incidental/foreseeable test is worse for the plaintiff than the more traditional purpose test. Beaning a spectator is hardly incidental to pitching a ball game, and there is nothing in the nature of a pitcher's task that makes the assault foreseeable. It might be established, however, that the pitcher's purpose was in part to serve the master. The heckling was distracting the pitcher and interfering with his ability to perform well for his employer. To silence the heckler therefore was to advance the master's interests. The result will thus depend on whether the court uses the purpose test and, if so, how malleable the court considers that test to be.[146] ◀ ◀ ◀

---

145. The patron would probably also assert direct claims, such as negligent hiring and failure to provide reasonably safe premises to customers. See Section 4.4.2.

146. In any event, the heckler may have a direct claim against the owner of the ballpark for failing to provide reasonably safe premises to a customer (see Section 4.4.2) and can certainly sue the pitcher for battery. See Section 4.2.3.

Problem 23

A large school district, serving tens of thousands of students and with thousands of employees, assigns a custodian to work at a high school. Subsequently, the custodian sexually assaults a student at the high school. The student sues the school district, asserting *respondeat superior*.[147] What result? ◀◀◀

Explanation

If the jurisdiction uses the purpose test, the student will inevitably lose. By no stretch of the imagination can a sexual assault be said to serve the school district's interests.

Even if the jurisdiction uses some form of the incidental/foreseeable test, the student's chances are slim. Abstractly, it may be foreseeable that an organization that has a large enough number of employees will inevitably employ some "bad apples." However, for an intentional tort to be foreseeable in the sense of *respondeat superior*, there must be something about the nature of the employee's job or the employer's enterprise that facilitates or specially occasions the harm. Unlike the psychologist-patient relationship discussed previously,[148] a custodian's role does not make the victim especially vulnerable to sexual assault. Sexual assault is not incidental to custodial work. ◀◀◀

Problem 24

Same facts as in Problem 23, except: (i) the employee is a teacher and coach of the high school debate team; (ii) the victim is a minor and a member of the debate team; (iii) the sexual activity develops in the context of one-on-one coaching by the teacher of the victim, initially at the school but eventually at the teacher's apartment; and (iv) the victim initially gives actual (but of course legally ineffective) consent to the relationship. Is the school district liable per *respondeat superior*? ◀◀◀

Explanation

Most likely not. When coaching morphs into predatory sexual behavior, the employee has embarked on "an independent course of conduct not intended by the employee to serve any purpose of the employer."[149] Moreover, the

---

147. The student would probably assert direct claims as well, such as negligent hiring and supervision and failure to provide safe premises. See Sections 4.4.1–4.4.2.
148. *See* Section 3.2.7.
149. R.3d, §7.07(2).

teacher's conduct is "seriously criminal," and there is zero "similarity in quality of the act done to the act authorized."[150]

The plaintiff would have more room to argue under the incidental/foreseeable test. If the jurisdiction misequates foreseeability with the notion of "a well-known hazard," the plaintiff might survive a summary judgment motion simply by submitting press clippings about notorious teacher-student sex scandals. ◀◀◀

Problem 25

Your adult son, though employed, has substantial limitations in intellectual functioning and ability to adapt to changes in social situations. Ordinarily, you drive him to and from work, but over the next several weeks you will be out of town for a number of days. You decide to have a particular taxicab company fill in for you, and you make the necessary arrangements through a telephone call to the company's dispatcher.

You believe the cab company employs cab drivers as well as dispatchers, and your belief comes from the company's trade name, trade dress, advertisements, signage, and published telephone numbers. This appearance plays a role in your decision to have this particular company dispatch drivers to transport your son.

In due course, you leave town and the cab company dispatches cabs to transport your son. Unfortunately, one of these cabs is involved in an accident, the driver is at fault, and your son is injured. When you seek compensation on behalf of your son from the taxicab company, you discover that the company does not in fact employ the drivers. Contrary to appearances, the drivers in those distinctively marked cabs are all independent contractors. The taxicab company denies any legal responsibility for the driver's negligence and for your son's injuries. Assuming that the drivers are indeed independent contractors, is the taxicab company correct? ◀◀◀

Explanation

No. Under the stated facts, the drivers are the apparent servants of the taxicab company. Through its "trade name, trade dress, advertisements, signage, and published telephone numbers," the taxicab company "represent[ed] that another [was] his servant," and that representation justifiably caused you to "rely upon the care or skill of such apparent agent."[151] According to R.2d, §267, therefore, the taxicab company "is subject to liability . . . for

150. R.2d, §229(2)(g) and (j).
151. R.2d, §267.

harm caused by the lack of care or skill of the one appearing to be a servant . . . as if he were such."[152] ◀ ◀ ◀

Problem 26

A hotel franchisor is concerned about apparent servant liability, but still wants its franchisees to make abundant use of the franchise name, logo, and trademarks. Consistent with that business purpose, how can the franchisor reduce its exposure to apparent servant liability? ◀ ◀ ◀

Explanation

EXPLANATION

The core of apparent servant liability is the appearance of servant status. Therefore, the simplest solution, at least in concept, would be to eliminate the appearance at its source. The legal problem would disappear if the franchisees were to remove all insignia that make their hotels appear to belong to the franchisor and that make their employees appear to be the franchisor's servants. This would be legally perfect treatment—after which the patient (i.e., the business) would unfortunately die.

A less pure but more practical solution would be to leave the insignia in place but act affirmatively to avoid the misapprehension. For example, the franchisor could require all its franchisees to prominently indicate that their hotel, although part of the national chain, is "independently owned and operated." The proclamation might appear on all significant signage, the hotel's stationery, and on all check-in and checkout documents. ◀ ◀ ◀

Problem 27

An air-conditioning manufacturer is about to ship a valuable load of equipment to a developer that is constructing a new office building. The manufacturer is, however, concerned about the developer's ability to pay for the equipment. The developer assures the manufacturer, "No problem. We've got a loan commitment from First National Bank that will cover the entire cost of construction. Why don't you call the bank's vice president for commercial loans and get that confirmed?"

The manufacturer takes the suggestion and calls the vice president. The vice president confirms that the bank has committed to a loan up to $10 million and that current cost projections total only $8.5 million. Satisfied, the manufacturer ships the equipment.

---

152. Id. This Problem is based on Daniel S. Kleinberger and Peter Knapp, "Apparent Servants and Making Appearances Matter: A Critique of Bagot v. Airport & Airline Taxi Cab Corp.," 28 WM. MITCHELL L. REV. 1527 (2002).

Unfortunately for the manufacturer, the bank had made no loan commitment. The vice president lied in return for a $5,000 bribe from the developer. The office-building project eventually folds, the manufacturer's equipment is nowhere to be found, and the developer is bankrupt. Can the manufacturer recover from the bank? ◀ ◀ ◀

Explanation

Yes. The bank's agent, its vice president for commercial loans, committed the tort of intentional misrepresentation. That tort will be attributed to the bank if the agent had actual authority, apparent authority, or inherent agency power to make the statement in question. The vice president had apparent authority by position. It is customary for bank officers to provide the type of information the vice president provided, so it was reasonable for the manufacturer to believe the vice president was speaking for the bank. The vice president's ulterior motive is immaterial. Apparent authority can exist even though the apparent agent does not intend to serve the interests of the apparent principal.[153] ◀ ◀ ◀

Problem 28

Morgan Hospital has an in-patient psychiatric ward that is run under the direction of Dr. Stanley, a board-certified psychiatrist who is a full-time employee of the hospital. Dr. Stanley has become increasingly frustrated with Medical Indemnity Company, an insurance company that provides health insurance coverage to many people in Morgan's vicinity. Medical Indemnity has been disallowing a large number of claims made by patients treated in Morgan's in-patient psychiatric ward. Dr. Stanley believes that most of these disallowances are unjustified, and he faults two psychologists who review patient claims for Medical Indemnity. Dr. Stanley's job has never involved public relations, but he decides "enough is enough." In a fit of frustration and without discussing the matter with any of Morgan's higher-ups, he fires off a letter to the local medical association, the local association of clinical psychologists, and the president of Medical Indemnity. The letter, written on Morgan Hospital letterhead and signed by Stanley as "Director, In-Patient Psychiatry Unit, Morgan Hospital," scathingly criticizes the two psychologists. Embarrassed and humiliated, the two psychologists sue both Dr. Stanley and Morgan Hospital for defamation. Assuming that Dr. Stanley's letter defamed the plaintiffs, is Morgan Hospital liable to them? ◀ ◀ ◀

---

153. See Section 2.3.5(d) (apparent agent can bind apparent principal even though apparent agent intends to take for itself the benefits of the transaction).

Explanation

Probably. An agent's defamatory statement is attributable to the principal if the agent had actual or apparent authority to make the statement. Dr. Stanley probably lacked actual authority. Nothing in his job implied the authority to speak for Morgan Hospital on matters of public concern, and Dr. Stanley did not receive any specific authorization before sending the letter. To those who received the letter, however, Dr. Stanley likely and reasonably appeared to be speaking on Morgan Hospital's behalf. Morgan arguably manifested as much when it clothed Dr. Stanley with an impressive title. Certainly, Dr. Stanley's use of the title and Morgan letterhead added weight to the comments and power to the defamation.[154] ◀ ◀ ◀

Problem 29

Ziegler Limo Leasing and Sales, Inc. ("Ziegler") sells and leases limousines and also provides limousine service on an hourly, daily, and weekly basis. Newly wealthy, Irv is considering buying a limousine from Ziegler. Selma, Ziegler's owner, says, "Tell you what, I'll let you use a limo and a driver for a week for free. It's kinda slow for us right now, and you'll get a feel for what it's like to have a limo at your beck and call. Then you can decide. Just one thing, though—if business heats up I'll have to take the limo back."

Irv happily agrees to the arrangement, and Selma assigns Jeffrey, one of her best drivers, to drive a stretch limo for Irv. Selma tells Jeffrey, "Listen. Show him our best red carpet service. That way, if he decides not to buy, he'll know we're the only place to rent from. But also—you know how new millionaires sometimes get aggressive. Remember our safe driving policy."

Two days later, Jeffrey is driving Irv to a party when a sports car cuts them off. Enraged, Irv yells to Jeffrey, "That [expletive deleted] can't do that to us. Catch him and pass him." Ziegler's operating rules require all Ziegler drivers to obey speed limits and strictly prohibit "aggressive driving." Irv is insistent, however, and Jeffrey gives in. In the rush to catch the sports car, the limo sideswipes another car. Assuming that Jeffrey has been negligent, can the driver of the other car successfully invoke *respondeat superior* against Irv? ◀ ◀ ◀

154. Note that Dr. Stanley's use of the title and Morgan letterhead are probably not manifestations attributable to Morgan but do support the reasonableness prong of the apparent authority analysis. See Section 2.3.5(c).

Explanation

Probably not. At the time of the accident, Jeffrey probably was not Irv's borrowed servant. Although Jeffrey's general employer (Ziegler) had assigned Jeffrey to work for Irv, Ziegler retained considerable control over Jeffrey's conduct. Selma had reminded Jeffrey that Ziegler's safe driving rules still applied. Moreover, Ziegler had retained the right to reassign Jeffrey at any time. When Irv successfully urged Jeffrey to speed up, Irv was merely persuading Jeffrey to violate the general employer's rules. Irv was not establishing the type of total, temporary control that establishes a special employer. ◀ ◀ ◀

Problem 30

A city hires an electrical contractor to remove above-ground electrical lines that had once served a trolley system. The contract gives the contractor total control and responsibility for the work, provided only that the contractor minimizes interference with traffic. However, the city's manager of public works worries incessantly about safety on the job. The manager repeatedly makes surprise visits to the worksites and often speaks directly to the contractor's employees. The employees report these contacts to the contractor. The contractor is fearful of losing the contract by offending the public works manager and instructs its employees to take the manager's suggestions "unless they're dangerous, expensive, or off the wall."

Midway through the project, a live line falls on a passing car. Fortunately, no one is injured, but the car is severely damaged. Assuming that the conduct of the public works manager is imputable to the city[155] and the accident resulted from the negligence of an employee of the contractor, does the car owner have a claim against the city? ◀ ◀ ◀

Explanation

Yes. The city's interference in the performance of the work demonstrates a right to control the employees of the contractor. Those employees are therefore servants of the city, and *respondeat superior* accordingly applies. ◀ ◀ ◀

155. For a discussion of this type of question, see Chapter 2.

Problem 31

When a business contracts out work, for quality control and safety reasons, the business may wish to closely supervise the contracted work. If an accident occurs, however, the injured party will point to the close supervision and seek to invoke *respondeat superior*. By acting on its concern for quality and safety, the delegating party will have risked vicarious liability. Propose a solution to this conundrum. ◀◀◀

EXPLANATION

Explanation

The Problem cannot be totally resolved, because a tension will always exist between the amount of control and the amount of risk. The key is to find ways to influence performance that stop short of actionable control. The first step, whenever possible, is to reduce the risk by avoiding mishaps. The delegating party should therefore find contractors that have good safety records and justified reputations for quality work. Second, the delegating party should limit its review of the work to inspection and suggestion. This step will, perhaps, prevent the delegating party from being deemed the master of the contractor. Third, the delegating party should avoid any direct instructions to the contractor's employees. This step will, perhaps, prevent those employees from being deemed servants of the delegating party. ◀◀◀

CHAPTER 4

Duties and Obligations of Agents and Principals to Each Other and to Third Parties

§4.1 DUTIES AND OBLIGATIONS OF THE AGENT TO THE PRINCIPAL

§4.1.1 Duty of Loyalty: Hallmark of Agent Status

a. The Opposite of an Arm's-Length Relationship

Agency is emphatically not an arm's-length relationship. In its very first line of black letter, R.3d labels the relationship a "fiduciary relationship,"[1] and the duty of loyalty is a hallmark characteristic of agent status. The principal's objectives and wishes are dominant; the agent functions essentially as a means to accomplish the principal's ends.[2] Except when the principal

1. R. 3d, §1.01 begins, "Agency is the fiduciary relationship . . . ," and R.2d, §1(1) characterizes agency as a "fiduciary relation." R.3d, §1.01, comment *e* explains: "The word 'fiduciary' appears in the black-letter definition to . . . emphasize that an agency relationship creates the agent's fiduciary obligation as a matter of law." Nonetheless, R.3d, Introduction accurately recognizes that: "The fiduciary character of the relationship does not explain all of the doctrine included within agency law. For example, the bases for the *respondeat superior* doctrine are not necessarily linked to the bases for treating agents as fiduciaries." For a further discussion of this point, see Section 3.2.4 (Relationship of Employee Status to Agent Status).

2. "As of the publication of this 6th edition, it had become commonplace to use "agency" to signal self-determination. For example:

> Agency is the sense of control that you feel in your life, your capacity to influence your own thoughts and behavior, and have faith in your ability to handle a wide range of tasks and situations.

has knowingly agreed to the contrary or when extraordinary circumstances exist,[3] the agent is obliged to prefer the principal's interests over the agent's own and to act "solely for the benefit of the principal in all matters connected with [the] agency."[4]

The duty of loyalty is so deeply ingrained into agency law that few cases address the rationale underlying the duty. Some modern commentators speak in terms of economic efficiency, and it would certainly be woefully inefficient if agent and principal had to negotiate their expectations in detail prior to the formation of each agency relationship. Having a standard set of "default" rules thus reduces transaction costs,[5] but it is unclear how efficiency is enhanced by applying the label "fiduciary" to (at least some) of the default rules. Similarly, some commentators assert that a strict regime of selflessness probably reduces the principal's monitoring costs.[6]

However, these perspectives find little voice in the case law. When judges explain the duty of loyalty, they do so with a decidedly moralistic tone. When a principal engages an agent, the principal reposes trust and confidence in that agent and the agent accepts a position of trust and confidence. To allow an agent to violate that confidence, betray that trust, and then profit from the abuse is simply unacceptable.[7]

> Your sense of agency helps you to be psychologically stable, yet flexible in the face of conflict or change. Agency is your very own power, your ability, to affect the future.

https://www.ppccfl.com/blog/take-control-of-your-life-the-concept-of-agency-and-its-four-helpers/As should be apparent, this usage of "agency" is antipathetical to the common law's usage.

3. See Section 4.1.1(d) in this section for discussion of "reshaping the duty of loyalty by consent" and "the agent's legitimate disloyalty."

4. R.2d, §387, quoted in Reporter's Notes to R.3d, §8.01, comment *a*.

5. A default rule is a rule that applies in a relationship absent a contrary agreement between or among the persons in the relationship. "Gap filler" is a synonym.

6. "Monitoring costs" are the principal's costs of keeping guard against misconduct by the agent. The stricter the rules of loyalty, the easier it will be to establish misconduct and obtain a right of recovery. The most important monitoring costs, however, relate not to recovering for misconduct but rather to preventing it. It is not clear how strict loyalty rules reduce those costs.

7. Justice Cardozo's comment in *Meinhard v. Salmon*, 164 N.E. 545, 546 (N.Y. 1928), exemplifies this tone: "Many forms of conduct permissible in a workaday world for those acting at arm's length, are forbidden to those bound by fiduciary ties. A trustee is held to something stricter than the morals of the market place. Not honesty alone, but the punctilio of an honor the most sensitive, is then the standard of behavior." *Meinhard* concerned a joint venture, but the case is often cited and Cardozo often quoted in cases concerning an agent's duty of loyalty.

b. The Restatements' Difference of Opinion

According to the R.3d, the duty of loyalty applies regardless of how grand or menial an agent's role may be and unquestionably encompasses all modern-day employees:

> As agents, all employees owe duties of loyalty to their employers. The specific implications vary with the position the employee occupies, the nature of the employer's assets to which the employee has access, and the degree of discretion that the employee's work requires. However ministerial or routinized a work assignment may be, no agent, whether or not an employee, is simply a pair of hands, legs, or eyes. All are sentient and, capable of disloyal action, all have the duty to act loyally.[8]

The R-EL states a narrower scope. According to section 8.01(a):

> Employees in a position of trust and confidence with their employer owe a fiduciary duty of loyalty to the employer in matters related to their employment. Other employees who come into possession of the employer's trade secrets owe a limited fiduciary duty of loyalty with regard to those trade secrets. In addition, employees may, depending on the nature of the employment position, owe an implied contractual duty of loyalty to the employer in matters related to their employment.

A comment to the section states: "As a general matter, the duty of loyalty stated in this section has little practical application to the employer's 'rank-and-file' employees, i.e., employees who are subject to the employer's close oversight or supervision, or who are not granted substantial discretion in carrying out their work responsibilities."

This difference between the Restatements makes little, if any, practical difference.

c. Aspects of the Duty

An agent's duty of loyalty includes a number of specific duties of selflessness, all serving to protect the principal's economic interests.

(1) **Unapproved Benefits.** Unless otherwise agreed, an agent may not benefit from its efforts on behalf of the principal. This rule applies regardless of whether the benefit is received from the principal or from a third party.

8. R.3d, §1.01, comment *e*.

Of course, in most agency relationships the principal agrees to compensate the agent for the agent's efforts, so the agent has the right to receive and retain those benefits. An agreement to allow the agent to profit may be express or implied.

(2) **Confidential Information.** An agent has a duty to safeguard the principal's confidential information and not to use that information for the agent's own benefit or the benefit of others. Confidential information includes any information that is not generally known and that either carries an economic benefit for the principal, or could, if disclosed, otherwise damage or embarrass the principal. Trade secrets, customer lists, unique business methods, and business plans are examples of confidential information.

The duty of nondisclosure and nonuse applies to any confidential information the agent acquires or develops during the course of the agency relationship. The duty applies even if the confidential information does not relate to the subject matter of the agency.

Restatement on Point

"An agent's relationship with a principal may result in the agent learning information about the principal's health, life history, and personal preferences that the agent should reasonably understand the principal expects the agent to keep confidential. An agent's duty of confidentiality extends to all such information concerning a principal even when it is not otherwise connected with the subject matter of the agency relationship."[9]

(A) **Information and Skills Distinguished.** The duty of nondisclosure does *not* apply to special skills an agent develops while performing agency tasks. That is, the agent need not refrain from utilizing the special skills outside of the agency relationship, subject to a duty not to compete (discussed below). Thus, in this context the distinction between information and skills is crucial.

Example

Ralph works as a waiter in an upscale restaurant. None of Ralph's duties involve preparing food. One day, while standing in the kitchen waiting for an order, Ralph sees and reads the restaurant's secret recipe for stuffed mushrooms. Ralph may not use the recipe or disclose it to others. Even

9. R.3d §8.05, comment c.

though his role as an agent does not involve preparing food, Ralph must keep the recipe confidential. ◀◀◀

Example

Bernice works as an assistant cook in the same restaurant. She learns all of the restaurant's special recipes and also learns how to make *pâte brisée* (a type of pastry that is standard in upscale cooking but very difficult to make well). Bernice may not use the recipes outside her job, because they are confidential information. Bernice's knowledge of how to make *pâte brisée*, however, is an expertise, not confidential information. Subject to her duty not to compete, Bernice may make *pâte brisée* wherever she likes. ◀◀◀

The duty to respect confidential information continues even after the agency ends. Confidential information belongs to the principal, and the end of the agency relationship does nothing to alter the principal's property rights in the information.[10]

(B) The Role of Employment Agreements. Each employee, as an agent, has a duty of loyalty with respect to the employer's confidential information. "An employee . . . breaches the duty of loyalty to the employer if, without the employer's consent, the employee discloses to a third party or uses for the employee's own benefit or a third party's benefit the employer's trade secrets. . . ."[11] Nonetheless, written employment agreements typically include a confidentiality provision, for one or more of the following reasons: (i) making the obligations express may increase the likelihood of employee compliance; (ii) a contract can tailor the scope of confidential information to fit an employer's particular circumstances; (iii) attorneys sometimes take the "belt and suspenders" approach to important issues; (iv) not all attorneys (or judges) are familiar with the law of agency; and (v) "we've always done it this way."

(3) No Competition. Unless otherwise agreed, the agent has a duty not to compete with the principal in any matter within the scope of the agency relationship. This noncompetition duty follows from the theme of selflessness and applies regardless of whether the agent:

- uses the principal's facilities, property, or confidential information to find or pursue an opportunity; or
- finds or pursues an opportunity "on its own time."

---

10. R.3d §8.05, comment c ("An agent's duties concerning confidential information do not end when the agency relationship terminates."); R-E §8.02(a). For further discussion of this point, see Section 5.3.5 (use of confidential information following termination of agency).
11. Restatement of Employment Law §8.03(a).

Case in Point—*Huong Que, Inc. v. Luu*

The defendants sold a company to plaintiff and agreed not to compete "as owners" and also to act as the company's managing agents. The defendants allegedly stole the company's customer list and used the list to solicit business for a competing enterprise, which they did not own. The trial court granted a temporary injunction against the defendants. The court of appeals affirmed due to the defendants' duty of loyalty as managing agents.[12] ◄◄◄

The noncompetition aspect of the duty of loyalty runs counter to a strong public policy in favor of open competition. Once the agency relationship ends, that public policy reasserts itself. As a matter of agency law, the noncompetition duty ends. The duty to respect the principal's confidential information remains, but otherwise, subject to the duty to "get out clean," agency law allows a former agent to compete with its former principal.[13]

(4) ***No Acting for Others with Conflicting Interests.*** Unless otherwise agreed, an agent may not act for anyone whose interests might conflict with the interests of the principal. The mere existence of a *dual agency* violates the duty of undivided loyalty, unless both principals consent after the agent discloses all material facts to each. Moreover, the dual agent risks specific conflicts of duty as to a myriad of individual issues. The fact that these individual conflicts may be irreconcilable does not justify the agent ignoring one duty or the other. Rather, if any such specific conflict materializes, the agent is destined to be liable to one principal, the other, or both.

Example

A real estate broker agrees to help Charlotte locate and purchase a new house. The broker knows that Rachael is interested in selling her house. The broker contacts Rachael and agrees to help sell her house to Charlotte. Since Rachael's and Charlotte's interests are in some ways conflicting, the broker has breached a duty of loyalty to both Charlotte and Rachael merely by acting for both simultaneously. ◄◄◄

---

12. *Huong Que, Inc. v. Luu*, 58 Cal. Rptr. 3d 527 (Cal. Ct. App. 2007).

13. For further discussion of this point, see Section 5.3.5 (post-termination competition and the duty to "get out clean").

Example

Same situation as above, plus Rachael wishes not to disclose to Charlotte certain information which in an arm's-length transaction it is lawful to withhold. Rachael mentions the information to the broker, but instructs the broker not to tell Charlotte. The broker's duty of obedience to Rachael compels compliance,[14] while the broker's duty to provide information to Charlotte requires disclosure.[15] ◀ ◀ ◀

If an agent arranges a transaction in violation of the dual agency rule:

- if neither principal knows about the dual agency, either principal may rescind;
- if one principal knows, the other principal may either: (i) affirm the transaction and seek damages from the agent and the knowing principal; or (ii) rescind.[16]

(5) ***Dealing with the Principal—"Adverse Party."*** An agent may not be "the adverse party" to a transaction with the principal, unless the agent is "up-front" about its role and the principal consents. In R.2d terminology, without the principal's consent, the agent may not be "the adverse party" and may not "act on his own account."[17] The R.3d states: "An agent has a duty not to deal with the principal as . . . an adverse party in a transaction connected with the agency relationship."[18]

Example

Horace wishes to go into the restaurant business and retains Elizabeth to locate a restaurant that Horace can purchase. Elizabeth happens to own a restaurant and wishes to sell it to Horace. She may do so only if she discloses her ownership to Horace and he consents. She may not hide her ownership and make the sale through a "straw man." ◀ ◀ ◀

Even if the principal does consent, the duty of loyalty continues to affect the transaction. In an arm's-length transaction, each party is obliged merely to avoid misstatements. When an agent acts as the adverse party, the agent has an affirmative duty to disclose all facts that the agent knows or should know could affect the principal's decision.

14. See Section 4.1.3.
15. See Section 4.1.5. Some states have adopted statutes or regulations governing dual agency situations in the context of real estate brokers.
16. R.3d, §§8.01, comment *d*(1) and 8.03, comment *d*.
17. Restatement §389, comment *d*.
18. R.3d, §8.03.

(6) ***Good Conduct.*** The agent's conduct can reflect on the principal, so the agent must not act in a way that brings disrepute on the principal. "Regardless of its size, power, or wealth, a principal is always vulnerable to the impact that its agents' actions may carry for its reputation."[19]

This aspect of the duty of loyalty "may extend to conduct that, although it is beyond the scope of activity encompassed by the agency relationship itself, is nonetheless closely connected to the principal or the principal's enterprise and is likely to bring the principal or the principal's enterprise into disrepute."[20]

Restatement on Point

The Reporter's Notes to R.3d §8.10 (good conduct), comment *b* includes this citation: *Murray v. Bragge* (1889) 7 N.Z.L.R. 252 (discharge justified when schoolmaster's horse seen tied up outside house of ill repute).

The Internet and social media have made this type of problem more noticeable and probably more frequent.

Example

"A . . . woman who was caught having sex in the men's room at an Iowa Hawkeye football game in Minneapolis last weekend says she'd had so much wine before kickoff that she doesn't remember walking into the restroom, the man she had sex with in a stall, or when the police opened the door. . . . [The woman], a married mother of three, has been the target of Internet jokes and prank telephone calls today. She was fired this morning from an assisted living center, where she had been an administrator."[21] ◀◀◀

The problem becomes more acute (or, at least, the outcome becomes more certain), the closer the off-the-job conduct is to the agent's on-the-job responsibilities

19. R.3d, §8.10, comment *b*.
20. R.3d, §8.10, comment *b*.
21. Update: Hawk fan says bathroom sex scandal "ruined my life," The Des Moines Register, desmoinesregister.com (Nov. 26, 2008).

Example

Metro Nashville Police Department fired an officer once the Department "[discovered a video . . . [online] and detectives identified [the officer] as the person in a Metro Nashville Police Department uniform who took part in a mock traffic stop in an OnlyFans skit when he groped the exposed breast of a woman driver."[22]

Example

Melissa Mercado, a detective in the New York Police Department, appeared in "Doin [sic] That," a lewd rap video. Mercado twerked (conspicuously) in the video while wearing scant and quite revealing clothing. Ironically, at the time Mercado worked in the Department's Special Victims Unit; her assignment was to investigate allegation of sex crimes.

The video did not identify Mercado, nor did it indicate Mercado's relationship to the NYPD. Nonetheless, the video went viral within the Department, and the Department promptly began a review of Mercado's behavior and relieved of her duties in the sex crimes department.

The NYPD "didn't immediately answer when asked if the seven-year NYPD veteran had broken any specific rules when she appeared in the . . . video."[23]

According to a retired NYPD Special Victims Division Chief, "it was particularly disturbing for a sex crimes investigator to make a video that's degrading to women." The retired chief characterized Mercado's conduct as "unbecoming a police officer" and "wrong morally" for a detective in the Special Victims Unit.[24]

d. The Agent's Legitimate Disloyalty

According to the R.2d, an agent may legitimately act against the principal's interests "in the protection of [the agent's] own interests or those of others."[25] The notion of self-protection seems straightforward. The agent may

22. Caleb Wethington and Gray News staff, "Former officer accused of participating in OnlyFans video while on duty," WKYD (published: June 14, 2024 at 10:37 a.m. CDT), https://www.wkyt.com/2024/06/14/former-officer-accused-participating-only fans-video-while-duty/, last retrieved 5/19/25.

23. Tina Moore, "Pole-dancing NYPD detective pulled from active cases in sex crimes unit: police sources," New York Post, published: March 8, 2025 at, 5:50 p.m. ET, https://nypost.com/2025/03/08/us-news/pole-dancing-nypd-detective-melissa-mercado-no-longer-on-active-cases-police-sources/, last viewed 5/20/25.

24. Quoted in Id., internal quotation marks omitted.

25. R.2d, §387, comment *b*. R.3d considers this issue only in the context of an agent's duty to safeguard the principal's confidential information. R.3d, §8.05, comment *c* states, "An agent may reveal otherwise privileged information to protect a superior interest of the agent or a third party," and provides examples of legitimate "whistle-blowing" activities.

assert its contract rights against the principal and may defend itself if the principal makes accusations of misconduct. The notion of protecting others is far vaguer. For instance, must the other party's interest be especially substantial in order to warrant the agent being disloyal? If the disloyalty will undermine one of the principal's significant interests, must the other party's interest be even more substantial?

In extreme circumstances, the answers seem clear enough.

Example

Arnold works for a real estate development company in the land acquisition department. He knows that his friend, Alice, is about to give Ralph an option to buy some land she owns. Through his work, Arnold knows that: (i) the real estate company plans to develop the area in which Alice's land is located; (ii) the value of Alice's land is therefore destined to rise sharply; and (iii) the option Alice plans to grant will allow Ralph, rather than Alice, to profit from the increase in value. Arnold may not disclose his principal's confidential information to Alice. ◄◄◄

Example

Through his work in the land acquisition department, Arnold discovers that the real estate company is engaged in a pattern of criminal fraud that, if unchecked, will cost innocent landowners thousands of dollars. Arnold may disclose the information not only to the landowners, but also to the police. ◄◄◄

Between the extremes, however, the rule is obscure. A court might consider the following factors to determine whether "the protection of . . . [the] interests of . . . others"[26] justifies an agent's act of disloyalty:

- the legitimacy of the other party's interest and the importance of that interest to the other party;
- to the extent to which the other party reasonably expects that the interest will be respected by the world in general and the principal in particular;
- the legitimacy of the principal's interest and the importance of that interest to the principal; and
- the extent to which the agent might have protected the other party's interests while using means that were either less injurious or less disloyal to the principal.

26. R.2d, §387, comment *b*.

e. Reshaping the Duty of Loyalty by Consent

Agency law allows a principal and agent wide latitude to reshape the duty of loyalty. Agreements can limit or even eliminate each of the specific duties discussed in this section. For instance, a principal can always consent to the agent's disclosure of confidential information or allow the agent to profit from agency efforts.[27]

Three qualifications do exist, however. *First*, the duty of loyalty applies to the manner in which an agent obtains agreement from the principal. The overall relationship remains a fiduciary one, so arm's-length bargaining is inappropriate.[28] When an agent seeks agreement from the principal, the agent must refrain from overreaching and must disclose to the principal all material information.

Example

A real estate broker agrees to help Charlotte locate and purchase a new house. The broker already has in mind a house owned by Rachael. Without disclosing that information, the broker asks Charlotte, "If I find a house, would you mind if I also worked with the seller to work out a deal you both can live with?" Charlotte agrees, but the broker's conflict-of-interest problem remains. Since the broker breached its duty of disclosure in obtaining Charlotte's consent, the consent is ineffective. ◄◄◄

Second, to be effective, a limitation to fiduciary duty must be clearly stated and unequivocal. Although a limitation can be implied (e.g., a waiter's right to retain tips), most limitations are stated in writing. Any ambiguity or vagueness will be strictly construed against the person who owes the fiduciary duty. If the agent (or other fiduciary) drafted the limitation, the contract rule of *contra proferentem* will also apply.[29]

---

27. Cases and practitioners sometimes use the term "waiver" to describe an agreement to limit or eliminate a particular facet of the loyalty duties, although "waiver" is most often used to describe a relinquishment of a known right, which, being extra-contractual and not separately supported by consideration, can be withdrawn absent reliance by the other party.

28. Cf. ULLCA (2013) §105(d)(3), comment (recognizing that an operating agreement can substantially limit the fiduciary duties of those who manage the limited liability company, but noting that "the operating agreement may not transform the relationship *inter se* members, managers, and the LLC into an entirely arm's length arrangement"). *Contrast* Del. Code Ann. tit. 6, § 18–1101(c) (stating that "[a] member's or manager's or other person's duties may be expanded or restricted or *eliminated* by provisions in the limited liability company agreement") (emphasis added). For a discussion of contractual limitations of fiduciary duty in the context of limited liability companies, see Section 15.4.7.

29. Black's Law Dictionary, 8th ed. (2004) ("The doctrine that, in interpreting documents, ambiguities are to be construed unfavorably to the drafter").

Third, the common law disfavors "general provisions eliminating fiduciary duties."[30] The fiduciary duty of loyalty is of the essence of an agency relationship, and the common law limits the power of a principal to contract away wholesale the protections of fiduciary duty:

> Common-law agency does not accord effect to all manifestations of assent by a principal that purports to eliminate or otherwise affect the fiduciary duties owed by an agent. . . . [T]he law, and not the parties, determines whether a particular relationship is one of agency . . . ; and the law applicable to relationships of agency . . . imposes mandatory limits on the circumstances under which an agent may be empowered to take disloyal action. These limits serve protective and cautionary purposes. Thus, an agreement that contains general or broad language purporting to release an agent in advance from the agent's general fiduciary obligation to the principal is not likely to be enforceable. This is because a broadly sweeping release of an agent's fiduciary duty may not reflect an adequately informed judgment on the part of the principal; if effective, the release would expose the principal to the risk that the agent will exploit the agent's position in ways not foreseeable by the principal at the time the principal agreed to the release. In contrast, when a principal consents to specific transactions or to specified types of conduct by the agent, the principal has a focused opportunity to assess risks that are more readily identifiable. Likewise, when a principal consents after-the-fact to action taken by an agent that would otherwise breach the agent's fiduciary duty to the principal, the principal has the opportunity to assess what the agent has done with a degree of specificity not available before the agent takes action.[31]

To a contractarian, this approach may seem paternalistic. However, both history and epistemology support the approach:

> The open-ended nature of fiduciary duty reflects the law's long-standing recognition that devious people can smell a loophole a mile away. For centuries, the law has assumed that (1) power creates opportunities for abuse, and (2) the devious creativity of those in power may outstrip the prescience of those trying, through *ex ante* contract drafting, to constrain that combination of power and creativity. For an attorney to advise a client that the attorney's drafting skills are adequate to take the place of centuries of fiduciary doctrine may be an example of chutzpah or hubris (or both).[32]

30. Reporter's Notes to R.3d, §8.06, comment *b*.
31. R.3d, §8.06, comment *b*.
32. Daniel S. Kleinberger, Two Decades of "Alternative Entities": From Tax Rationalization Through Alphabet Soup to Contract As Deity, 14 Fordham J. Corp. & Fin. L. 445, 471 n. 129 (2009) (quoting an earlier version of BISHOP & KLEINBERGER ON LIMITED LIABILITY COMPANIES: Carter G. Bishop and Daniel S. Kleinberger, LIMITED LIABILITY COMPANIES: TAX AND BUSINESS LAW (Warren Gorham & Lamont/RIA, 1994; Supp. 2007–2) ¶14.05[4][a][ii]).

§4.1.2 Duty to Act Within Authority

Although an agent may have the power to act beyond the scope of actual authority,[33] an agent does not have the *right* to do so. To the contrary, the agent has a duty to act only as authorized.[34] An agent who violates this duty is liable to the principal for any resulting damage. A parallel rule applies to nonagents who purport to be agents and thereby bind the apparent principal.

If an agent has reason to doubt the scope of authority, except in emergency situations the agent has a duty to inquire of the principal.

Example

Sally arranges for Ralph to buy a car on her behalf. She specifies, "Buy American." Ralph finds a good deal on a car assembled in the United States from components made almost exclusively overseas. Before buying the car for Sally, Ralph should check with her. ◄ ◄ ◄

Example

Biscuit is an employee of a brewery in the city of Indianapolis. During the height of the National Football League controversy, "DeflateGate," involving quarterback Tom Brady,[35] Biscuit stamped "Tom Brady Sux" on 20,000 cans of Wee Mac Scottish-style Ale, one of the brewery's most popular brews. Biscuit acted without actual authority.[36] ◄ ◄ ◄

---

33. See Sections 2.3 (Apparent Authority) and 2.6 (Inherent Agency Power).

34. The scope of that authority is determined objectively, based on the agent's reasonable interpretations of the principal's manifestations. See Section 2.2.2.

35. Per ESPN:

> At its core, Deflategate suggested that the New England Patriots used an illegal process for lowering the inflation of game footballs at the behest of quarterback Tom Brady, who preferred the grip of softer balls. The NFL thought it found proof during a surprise and unprecedented inflation check at halftime of the 2014 AFC Championship Game, a 45–7 drubbing of the Indianapolis Colts.

Dan Wetzel, "Deflategate 10 years later: Was it an actual scandal or an absurd comedy?" Yahoo Sport, January 23, 2025, https://sports.yahoo.com/deflategate-10-years-later-was-it-an-actual-scandal-or-an-absurd-comedy-160751902.html?guccounter=1&guce_referrer=aHR0cHM6Ly93d3cuZ29vZ2xlLmNvbS8&guce_referrer_sig=AQAAAIyLSSQ3evldybZkI1BsL-R4GxNJp64obUFSNXE3K_IAylx7kBO8sr4UTcRvcLoiSgx42l6kAQR3n1ZcJy4bct2y6-igJkCUtGAQduHq1pUyk6iJ26uONWi-YxeXxiDmvpTdwnJ_YRxqqfuXwcjjmPxp3lJMM-VYam-td1gAipWK, last viewed 5/20/25.

36. This Example is based on the article, Brewery employee stamps 20,000 cans of beer with "Tom Brady Sux," FoxNews.com (Aug 12, 2015).

§4.1.3 Duty to Obey Instructions

The principal always has the *power* to instruct the agent concerning the subject matter of the agency. Accordingly, an agent has a duty to obey instructions from the principal unless the instructions call for the agent to do something improper.

Example

Charlotte works for a car dealership in the used car department. He reports to the owner that he cannot sell a particular used car at the desired price because the car has too many miles on it. The owner responds, "Well, just roll back the odometer a bit." Despite being the owner's agent, Charlotte has no duty to comply. Rolling back an odometer is illegal, and Charlotte has no duty to obey instructions that call for wrongful conduct. ◀◀◀

The agent's duty to obey instructions is consistent with the agent's duty to act within authority. Instructions from the principal are manifestations from the principal, and the agent's authority comes from the agent's reasonable interpretation of the principal's manifestations. Therefore, if an agent disregards the principal's instructions, the agent is in effect acting without actual authority.

The duty to obey instructions exists even if the principal has contracted away the *right* to instruct. The agent may have a claim for breach of contract, but nonetheless is obliged either to obey the principal's instructions or resign.[37]

§4.1.4 Duty of Care

An agent has a duty to act with "due care." How much care is due depends on: (i) whether the agent is paid or unpaid (gratuitous); and (ii) any relevant agreement between the principal and agent.

For paid agents, due care is ordinary care; a standard of ordinary negligence applies. The determination of what constitutes ordinary negligence is quite similar to the determination made under the "negligence" rubric in the law of torts. Indeed, the R.3d characterizes the agent's duty of care as "derived from tort law,"[38] and the R.3d black letter reads like a tort formulation:

---

37. See Sections 4.1.3 and 4.1.6.
38. R.3d, §8.08, comment *b*.

> Subject to any agreement with the principal, an agent has a duty to the principal to act with the care, competence, and diligence normally exercised by agents in similar circumstances. Special skills or knowledge possessed by an agent are circumstances to be taken into account in determining whether the agent acted with due care and diligence.[39]

As to gratuitous agents, older cases hold that the standard of care is the same standard that applies to other gratuitous actors (e.g., gratuitous bailees)—gross negligence. In contrast, the black letter of the R.3d makes no reference to whether the agent acts gratuitously. A comment suggests that the ordinary care standard applies to gratuitous agents as well as to paid agents, but the discussion and illustrations center on professionals (i.e., lawyers) or other situations in which the principal might reasonably be expected to be relying on some special skill or knowledge possessed by the agent.[40]

a. Agreements Affecting the Standard of Care

An agreement between the principal and agent can change the level of care owed by the agent or the consequences of the agent's failure to meet the standard of care. For instance, a principal might agree (i) that a paid agent is obliged only to avoid gross negligence;[41] or (ii) not to hold the agent responsible for harm caused by ordinary negligence (an "exculpatory agreement").

Public policy limits the validity of some "care reducing" agreements. For example, ethical rules prohibit lawyers from making "an agreement prospectively limiting the lawyer's liability to a client for malpractice."[42] In some states, exculpatory provisions relating to negligence are void or subject to strict construction.

It is theoretically possible for an agent to agree to raise the general standard of care, but such agreements are rare. More common are agreements under which an agent promises to produce certain results. In that case, the agent is contractually obliged to produce the promised results and cannot excuse failure by claiming the exercise of due care.[43]

---

39. R.3d, §8.08.
40. R.3d, §8.08, comment *e*.
41. Under UPA (1997) (last amended 2013) §409(c), a partner's duty of care is "to refrain from engaging in grossly negligent or reckless conduct, willful or intentional misconduct, or a knowing violation of law." For further discussion, see Section 9.6.2.
42. Model Rules of Professional Conduct Rule 1.8(h) (1983).
43. For precisely this reason, agents (as well as independent contractors) prefer to promise "reasonable efforts" to produce specified results.

§4.1.5 Duty to Provide Information

If an agent possesses information and has reason to know that the principal may need or desire the information, the agent has a duty to provide the information to the principal. This duty underlies the attribution rule that binds a principal on account of information possessed by its agent.[44] An agent's duty of care may require the agent to acquire information for the principal.

Of course, an agent's duty to provide information pertains to the agent's principal and not to third parties.

Case in Point—*Blickman Turkus, LP v. MF Downtown Sunnyvale, LLC*

CASE IN POINT

A lessor sued the lessee's real estate agent for failing to disclose that the lessee had financial difficulties that might interfere with the lessee's ability to make the lease payments. The court rejected that assertion: "[N]o . . . authority known to us . . . supports the imposition of a duty on a lessee's agent in a commercial real estate transaction to disclose to the lessor information, acquired after execution of a lease, concerning the buyer's finances."[45] ◀◀◀

When the principal is an organization, an agent necessarily discharges this duty by providing information to a fellow agent or, in the case of a top executive providing information "up the chain," to the organization's governing body.[46]

§4.1.6 Contractual Overlay

As the previous sections have discussed, an agent has obligations to its principal as a matter of agency law. Those obligations are only part of the story, however. A contractual relationship usually overlays the agency relationship, and so an agent typically owes duties in contract as well as under agency law.[47]

Not every agency relationship has a contractual overlay. As explained in Chapter 1, an agency relationship is consensual, but not necessarily

44. See Section 2.4.

45. *Blickman Turkus, LP v. MF Downtown Sunnyvale, LLC*, 76 Cal. Rptr. 3d 325, 339 (Cal. Ct. App. 2008). Note, however, that an agent has a tort-based duty to avoid fraud and misrepresentations in dealing with a third party. See Section 4.2.3.

46. Typically a "subordinate agent" provides the information to a "superior agent." See Section 2.8.

47. Likewise, the principal may have contractual obligations to the agent. See Section 4.3.3.

contractual.[48] Typically, however, the reciprocal consents that create an agency relationship also reflect an exchange of consideration. The agent undertakes to perform some task or achieve some objective for the principal, and the principal undertakes to compensate the agent for the agent's efforts. Thus, a process of contract formation typically accompanies the process of "agency formation."[49]

Rights and duties created by contract often supplement the rights and duties existing under agency law. For example, a contract may set performance standards for the agent, and the agent will then have to satisfy those standards as well as agency law's duty of care.[50] A contract may also define or circumscribe duties arising under agency law. For example, a contract can delineate the scope of an agent's duty of care by specifying the scope of the agent's endeavors or eliminate the agency law duty of care in deference to a standard of performance stated in the contract. A contract can also limit an agent's fiduciary duties. For instance, as discussed previously, an agent has a duty not to compete with its principal, unless the principal consents.[51] A contract can embody that consent.

There are, however, certain aspects of the agency relationship that a contract cannot reach. For example, under agency law the principal always has the power to control the goals of the agency relationship and the means by which the agent pursues those goals.[52] A contract may limit a principal's rights in these matters but cannot abrogate the power. Accordingly, when a principal exercises the power of control, the agent has an agency law duty either to comply or to resign. If the principal's exercise of agency law power violates the agent's contractual rights, then the agent may pursue contract law remedies.

EXAMPLE

Example

Ralph hires Sally, a real estate broker, to sell his house. The brokerage agreement gives Sally the right to decide when to show the house. Ralph subsequently decides that he does not want the house shown on weeknights. Sally has a duty to abide by Ralph's decision or to resign. In either case, however, she can sue Ralph for breach of contract. (To recover, of course, she must prove damages.) ◀ ◀ ◀

In like fashion, the principal always retains the power, if not the right, to terminate the agency relationship.[53]

---

48. See Section 1.5.
49. As with most contracts, terms may be implied by custom and usage.
50. Section 4.1.4 discusses the agent's duty of care.
51. See Section 4.1.1.
52. If the principal also has the *right* to control the means, then the agent is likely an employee (R.3d)/servant (R.2d). See Section 3.2.4.
53. See Section 5.2.

§4.1.7 Principal's Remedies for Agent's Breach of Duty

a. Damages

If an agent's breach of duty to the principal causes damage to the principal, the principal can recover those damages from the agent. If an agent's breach of duty renders the principal liable to a third party, the agent must indemnify and hold harmless the principal from that liability.

b. Additional Remedies for Breach of the Duty of Loyalty

If the agent breaches a duty of loyalty, the principal's remedies include not only *damages* (if provable) but also *disgorgement* of any profits derived by the agent from the disloyal transaction and *rescission* of any transaction between the principal and agent if the breach infected that transaction.

Example

Mikki is selling her hobby farm to a shopping mall developer and must therefore dispose of five horses. Four of the horses are quite old, but the fifth is quite valuable. Ellen approaches Mikki and proposes to arrange the sale of the four older horses for a 5 percent commission and then buy the fifth horse for herself at a below-market price. Mikki agrees, on condition that Ellen sells to "people who will care about my horses." Ellen accepts the condition.

Within a few days Ellen reports that she has sold the horses to "some real nice folks." After those horses are shipped, Ellen collects her commission and pays for and takes the fifth horse.

Mikki later discovers that Ellen sold the four horses to a glue factory. Because Ellen gained the commission through dishonesty to her principal, the commission is subject to disgorgement. Because Ellen's disloyalty infected her purchase of the fifth horse, Mikki may rescind that transaction. ◄◄◄

Both disgorgement and rescission are considered equitable remedies, and both are available without proof of damage. Courts ordering disgorgement often do so by imposing a "constructive trust" on the agent's ill-gotten gains. A court will order disgorgement even though the remedy leaves the principal better off than the principal would have been had the agent complied with its duty of loyalty.

Example

A blockbuster adventure movie creates intense demand for a line of toys based on the movie. Williams Manufacturing, Inc. ("Williams") has the exclusive right to manufacture the toys. Although it raises its prices to take advantage of the demand and increases production, for several months

Williams has more orders than it can fill. During this time, Max, Williams's national sales manager, gives order preference to those customers willing to "make it worth my while." The gratuities range from cash to cases of wine to airline tickets. No one else at Williams is aware of what Max is doing.

By profiting without his principal's consent, Max breached his duty of loyalty. If Williams can prove that Max's conduct damaged Williams's good will, Williams can recover from Max the amount of the damage. Even without proof of damage, Williams can recover from Max the value of the gratuities. A claim for disgorgement will prevail even if Max can prove that: (i) Williams suffered no damages; and (ii) consequently, disgorgement will make Williams better off than it would be absent Max's breach of duty. Williams may also be able to recover from Max whatever salary he received during his period of dishonesty. ◀◀◀

In many jurisdictions, breach of the duty of loyalty can support a claim for punitive damages. Also, in many jurisdictions the statute of limitations incorporates some form of the "discovery" rule—that is, the clock does not start until the principal knows or has reason to know of the breach.

§4.2 DUTIES AND OBLIGATIONS OF THE AGENT TO THIRD PARTIES

§4.2.1 Obligations "On the Contract"

a. Rules for Determining Agent's Liability

Agents often make contracts on behalf of principals, and agency law provides rules for determining whether the agent is liable on such contracts.[54] The analysis turns on whether the agent's principal is disclosed.[55]

If the principal is disclosed, then the agent is not liable on the contract. The rationale for this rule is straightforward. With a disclosed principal, the third party enters into the contract knowing that the agent is merely a representative and that the principal will be the obligor. The agent is not promising any performance of its own,[56] and the third party may look only to the principal for performance.

This rule applies even if the third party bases a warranty claim on a statement made by the agent.

54. Agency law also determines whether the principal is liable. See Chapter 2.

55. Section 2.2.3 (in creation of actual authority, third-party knowledge of principal-agent relationship is irrelevant).

56. The agent is, however, implicitly promising that the principal will be obligated. If the principal is not obligated, the agent will be liable. See Section 4.2.2 (Warranty of Authority).

Example

A patron at a gambling casino approaches the roulette wheel and asks the employee operating the wheel, "Is this game honest?" The employee, believing the answer to be yes, responds, "As honest as the day is long." The patron places several bets, losing each one. Subsequently, the patron discovers that the wheel is rigged and claims breach of warranty against both the employee and the casino. The claim against the employee will fail.[57] The patron's bets were transactions between the patron and the casino, and the employee's principal was disclosed. The employee is therefore not liable on the contract—even though the employee's statement gave rise to the breach of warranty claim.[58] ◀ ◀ ◀

If the principal is only partially disclosed (or, in R.3d terms, unidentified), then the agent is almost always liable on the contract. The rationale is again one of expectations. The third party knows that the agent is acting for another. But without knowing the identity of the other (i.e., the principal), the third party must rely on the trustworthiness, creditworthiness, and *bona fides* of the agent.

Example

An attorney contacts an art dealer and contracts to buy a famous Picasso print. The attorney explains that she is acting for a client, but declines to identify the client. (The client dislikes notoriety.) The attorney is liable on the contract.[59] ◀ ◀ ◀

Expectations also explain the "auctioneer" exception to this rule. When an auctioneer sells an item for an unidentified owner, no one expects the auctioneer to "stand behind" the goods.[60]

When the principal is undisclosed, the agent is liable *a fortiori*. As far as the third party knows, the contract is with the agent and none other.

---

57. The claim against the casino will prevail, however, since the employee's statement is attributed to the casino. See Section 2.4.6 (agent's statements attributable to the principal for contract law purposes).

58. If the employee made the misstatement negligently or intentionally, the employee may be liable in tort. See Section 4.2.3. This Example derives from a scene in the movie *Casablanca*, https://share.google/z22OUSNjeBC40v5M8, last viewed 5/20/25.

59. The client is liable, too. See Sections 2.2.2, 2.2.4, and 4.2.1.

60. R.3d, §1.04, Reporter's Notes, section *b*.

Example

A power company authorizes a coal broker to buy coal for it. The broker contracts to buy the coal in its own name, without disclosing its status as agent for the power company. The broker is liable on the contract.[61] ◄◄◄

These rules on contract liability are default rules. They can be overridden by express or implied agreement between the agent and third party.

Example

A seeks to induce **T** to enter into a contract with P. **T** distrusts P and declines the transaction unless **A** guarantees **P**'s performance. **A** agrees to do so, and **T** agrees to the contract. If **P** fails to perform, **A** will be liable on the guarantee—even though **A**'s principal was fully disclosed.

b. The Importance of Signature Blocks

As a practical matter, a person signing a contract as an agent should always make that status known on the face of the document, at least by means of the signature block. Otherwise, the obligee may point to the signer's bald signature as a manifestation that the signer agreed to be party to the contract. ◄◄◄

Case in Point—*Baraby v. Swords*

The case concerned an apartment property ostensibly owned by a limited liability company,[62] an apartment lease, a fire in the apartment subject to the lease, and a plaintiff's claim that Lawrence, a member of the limited liability company was personally liable on plaintiff's claims arising from the fire. The trial court had granted summary judgment to Lawrence, but the appellate court reversed.[63] Because "[t]he rental application contained the business name 'Marcar Enterprises' but listed Lawrence's and another person's names in the address section, the court held that "Lawrence may

---

61. The power company is liable too. See Sections 2.2.2 and 2.2.6 (in creation of actual authority, third-party knowledge of principal-agent relationship is irrelevant). As for the relationship of the broker's liability to the power company's liability, see 4.2.1(c) in this section.
62. For an introduction to this type of business organization, see Chapter 13.
63. *Baraby v. Swords*, 851 NE2d 559 (Ohio App. 3d Dist. 2006).

have incurred individual liability by holding himself out as the landlord of the property."[64,65] The court further noted:

> Apparently, Lawrence executed the lease in his personal capacity, as there was no notation as to his capacity to act on behalf of a business. On the lead-based paint disclosure, Lawrence signed his name next to the phrase "Owner or agent." However, Lawrence testified that he intended to bind Swords Property. On these facts, there is a genuine issue of material fact as to whether Lawrence incurred individual liability as a landlord.[66]

c. The Agent's Liability and Available Defenses

Unless otherwise agreed, an agent's contractual liability is as a *guarantor* when the principal is undisclosed or unidentified. The agent partakes of any of the principal's defenses that arise from the transaction and can also assert any personal defenses or setoffs the agent may have *vis-à-vis* the third party. The agent may not assert defenses or setoffs that are personal to the principal (i.e., defenses arising from other interactions or relationships between the principal and the third party).

§4.2.2 Warranty of Authority

When a person purports to bind another person to a contract, the law implies a warranty of authority—that is, a promise that the purported agent actually has authority to act for the purported principal. If the purported principal is not bound, then the purported agent has breached the warranty of authority and is liable to the third party for expectation damages as well as reliance damages.

The warranty applies:

- both to true agents who act outside their authority and to mere purported agents who have no actual authority at all;
- regardless of whether the purported principal is disclosed or partially disclosed (unidentified);[67] and

64. *Id.* at 572.
65. *Id.*
66. *Id.* For further discussion of this issue in the context of limited liability companies, see BISHOP & KLEINBERGER ON LIMITED LIABILITY COMPANIES §§ 6:66–6:69 (liability of member as a party to the contract).
67. With a partially disclosed (unidentified) principal, the purported agent will be bound whether or not a contract is formed. If the principal is bound, a contract results and the agent is liable as a guarantor. See Section 4.2.1. If the principal is not bound and no contract is formed, then the agent is liable under the warranty of authority. With an undisclosed principal, the warranty does not apply because the agent is not purporting to act on behalf of another. However, the agent is bound on the contract as a party. See Section 4.2.1.

- even though the third party could have discovered the lack of authority by exercising reasonable care.

The warranty does *not* apply if:

- the purported agent disclaims having authority to bind or indicates that it doubts its own authority; or
- for some other reason, the third party knows that the purported agent lacks authority.

Example

An employee of Harris, Inc. ("Harris") purports to retain Pauline, a real estate broker, to sell two acres of land that Harris owns. The employee signs an engagement letter, purportedly on Harris's behalf, agreeing that Harris will reimburse Pauline's reasonable expenses and will pay a commission in the event Pauline finds a buyer willing and able to pay the asking price. Pauline finds such a buyer, who signs and delivers an offer letter to Pauline. Pauline takes the letter, making clear that she has no authority to accept the offer on Harris's behalf. When Pauline brings the offer to Harris, she discovers that: (i) the Harris employee acted without authority in dealing with Pauline; and (ii) Harris does not wish to sell the land. If the deal does not go through, the Harris employee will be liable to Pauline for breach of the warranty of authority. The liability will include not only Pauline's reasonable expenses but also the commission she would have earned on the sale. Pauline, in contrast, will not be liable to the disappointed buyer, since she never represented that she had authority to bind Harris. ◀◀◀

If a purported agent acts without actual authority but manages to bind its purported principal through apparent authority, inherent agency power, or estoppel,[68] the warranty of authority is not breached. The third party has received just what the purported agent promised—a binding contract with the purported principal.[69] Likewise, no breach occurs if the purported principal ratifies the contract.[70]

Example

The counter clerk in a dry cleaner promises to have your interview "power suit" ready by the next day. The clerk has made comparable promises to you

---

68. For a discussion of these attribution rules, see Sections 2.3 (Apparent Authority), 2.6 (Inherent Agency Power), and 2.5 (Estoppel).

69. The purported agent may be liable to the purported principal. See Section 4.1.2 (Duty to Act Within Authority).

70. For a discussion of ratification, see Section 2.7.

before, and the dry cleaner has always fulfilled them. Last week, however, the owner instituted a new policy, depriving employees of the authority to promise next-day service. Although the clerk lacks actual authority to bind the dry cleaner to a contract for next-day service, the clerk's apparent authority binds the principal. Therefore, there is no breach of the warranty of authority.[71] ◀◀◀

§4.2.3 Obligations in Tort

a. A Tort Is a Tort Is a Tort

Being an agent does not immunize a person from tort liability. A tortfeasor is personally liable, regardless of whether the tort was committed on the instructions from or to the benefit of a principal. A tortfeasor cannot defend itself by saying, "Well, I did what I did to serve my principal."[72]

For example, if a supermarket employee negligently drops a carton of cans on a customer's foot, the customer has a negligence claim against the employee.[73] Similarly, an agent who intentionally misstates a material fact while selling its principal's goods is personally liable for misrepresentation,[74] and, in some jurisdictions, can also be liable for aiding and abetting the principal's fraud. For aiding and abetting to apply, the agent must know of the fraudulent plan and give substantial assistance. The assistance need not involve directly fraudulent conduct.

Example

Al's Used Cars advertises for sale an automobile with interiors of "fine Corinthian leather." In response to that ad, a customer comes in and talks with Emily, a salesperson for Al's. Emily knows that the interiors are not leather and that the ad was a purposeful "come on." However, she closes the

71. If the dispute were to end up in court, you would sue on both theories, in the alternative.
72. The principal may well be liable, too. The liability may be vicarious (see Chapter 3), or direct (see Section 4.4, principal's direct duties), or both.
73. For tactical reasons the customer may decide not to assert this claim, instead relying exclusively on claims against the principal (e.g., *respondeat superior*, failure to provide reasonably safe premises to business invitees). Tactical considerations could include the small chance of collecting any substantial judgment from the employee; removing the employee as a party to allow the jury to see the matter as a David versus Goliath conflict (i.e., injured "ordinary folk" versus rich, impersonal mercantile establishment); eliminating the employee's financial incentive to justify his or her own conduct.
74. If the agent innocently passes on the principal's misrepresentations, the agent is not liable. For the tort of intentional misrepresentation, most jurisdictions require intent to deceive or at least reckless disregard of truthfulness. Some jurisdictions recognize also a claim for negligent misrepresentation.

deal without mentioning the interiors. She is liable to the buyer for knowingly assisting in her principal's fraud. ◄◄◄

In the modern world, the "tort is a tort is a tort" issue arises most often when the agent is acting as manager or other employee of a business organization. It is well settled in corporation law that a person who commits a tort while acting for the corporation is nonetheless personally liable for the tort. In the context of limited liability companies, a few courts have struggled with the idea, confused by statutory language that shields members and managers of limited liability companies from liability for the company's debts when the liability is asserted "solely" by reason of a person's status a member or manager.

Case in Point — *Allen v. Dackman*

In the words of the Maryland Supreme Court: "An LLC member is liable for torts he or she personally commits, inspires, or participates in because he or she personally committed a wrong, not 'solely' because he or she is a member of the LLC."[75]

b. Agency-Related Rights and Duties That Negate or Give Rise to Torts

Although agency status does not create tort immunity, rights created by agency status can negate the existence of a tort. For example, an agent acting within the scope of authority may exercise and benefit from its principal's privileges. Those privileges can transform otherwise tortious conduct into lawful behavior.

Example

The owner of Sherwood Forest allows no one but his guests to enter the Forest. Robin purchases the right to enter the Forest to collect certain examples of local fauna. Acting as Robin's agent, Tuck enters Sherwood Forest to collect specimens. Tuck's conduct is proper. He benefits from Robin's right to enter the land. Were Tuck entering for his own purposes, he would be committing the tort of trespass. ◄◄◄

75. *Allen v. Dackman*, 413 Md. 132, 154, 991 A2d 1216, 1229 (2010) (collecting cases).

Agency status can also give rise to duties, the breach of which will constitute torts.

Example

The owner of Sherwood Forest is leaving the country on an extended sabbatical. She hires John Little to conduct hunting expeditions into the Forest and gives him complete authority to manage the Forest premises. As a matter of tort law, Little has a duty to third persons to use care in maintaining the Forest.[76] Little's duty arises from his control of the premises, and that control comes from his authority as an agent. ◀ ◀ ◀

§4.2.4 Breach of Duty to Principal Not by Itself a Breach to Third Party

When an agent breaches a duty of care or proper performance to its principal and the principal suffers harm, the agent is liable to the principal for damages.[77] The same misconduct may also harm a third party, but an agent's breach of duty to its principal does not automatically create a damage claim for the third party.[78] Rather than simply "borrowing" the principal's breach of duty claim, the third party must characterize the agent's conduct as breaching a duty to the third party.

A third party can succeed with such a characterization if the tortfeasor's role as an agent happens to involve tasks that, *as a matter of tort law*, create an independent duty to third parties. In such circumstances, the same pattern of conduct happens to breach both a duty to the principal and, separately, a different (albeit somewhat similar) duty to the third party.[79]

Case in Point — *Baird v. Shipman*

"It is not [the agent's] contract with the principal which exposes him to, or protects him from, liability to third persons, but his common-law obligation to so use that which he controls as not to injure another. That obligation is neither increased nor diminished by his entrance upon the duties

76. How much care is due depends on the jurisdiction and, in some jurisdictions, on the status of the injured party (e.g., business invitee, trespasser).

77. The duty of care arises from the agency relationship. See Section 4.1.4. A duty of proper performance may arise from a contract between the principal and agent. See Section 4.1.6. Section 4.1.7 discusses the damage remedy.

78. The principal may well be liable to the third party, either vicariously (see Section 3.2, *Respondeat Superior*), or directly (see Section 4.4).

79. This rule is the flip side of the "tort is a tort is a tort" rule. See Section 4.2.3.

of agency; nor can its breach be excused by the plea that his principal is chargeable."[80] ◀◀◀

Case in Point—*Schur v. L.A. Weight Loss Centers, Inc.*

After a customer of a weight loss center died of liver failure, her estate sued the center in state court. The defendant removed the case to federal court asserting diversity jurisdiction and complete diversity between itself and the customer, an Illinois resident. The plaintiff then sought to add as defendants two employees of the center, both Illinois residents, and have the case remanded to state court for lack of complete diversity. The district court refused, seeing the addition of the employees as "fraudulent joinder" because "Poole and Morr, as agents of LA Weight Loss, would not be personally liable for any tort they may have performed while working within the scope of their employment." The court of appeals reversed, noting: "The district court may have confused the doctrines of vicarious (derivative) liability and individual (direct) liability. . . . [A]n agent can be individually liable even where his employer is *also* vicariously liable."[81] ◀◀◀

§4.3 DUTIES AND OBLIGATIONS OF THE PRINCIPAL TO THE AGENT

§4.3.1 Principal's Duty to Indemnify

When an agent acts on behalf of its principal, the agent may incur expenses, make payments, suffer injury, and even offend the rights of third parties. As a matter of agency law, a principal has a duty to indemnify its agent for:

- payments made or expenses incurred within the agent's actual authority;
- payments made to the principal's benefit, but without authority, if:
  - the agent acted in good faith (and unofficiously), mistakenly believing her, him, or itself to be authorized; and
  - under the principles of restitution it would be unjust not to require indemnity;[82]
- claims made by third parties on contracts entered into by the agent, with authority, and on the principal's behalf;

80. *Baird v. Shipman*, 23 N.E. 384, 384 (Ill. 1890) (per curiam).
81. *Schur v. L.A. Weight Loss Centers, Inc.*, 577 F.3d 752, 764–65 (7th Cir. 2009).
82. Note that a mistaken belief of authority does not by itself qualify the resulting loss or expense for indemnity.

- claims made by third parties for torts allegedly committed by the agent, if:
  — the agent's conduct was within the agent's actual authority; and
  — the agent was unaware that the conduct was tortious.

No duty to indemnify exists for:

- payments made or expenses incurred that are neither within the agent's actual authority nor of benefit to the principal;
- losses resulting from the agent's negligence or from acts outside the agent's actual authority; and
- losses resulting from the agent's knowing commission of a tort or illegal act.

A duty to indemnify is a duty to hold harmless; that is, to reimburse the agent for payments made, to compensate the agent for losses suffered, to protect the agent from third-party claims. Protecting against claims means: (i) paying for any liability, including reasonable settlements; and (ii) providing a reasonable defense to the claims or reimbursing the agent for the costs of defending, including reasonable attorney's fees and other costs of litigation.

To trigger the principal's duty to pay the costs of defense, the agent must give the principal reasonable notice of the claim, allow the principal to manage the defense, and cooperate with the principal in the defense. If the agent fails to notify the principal, the principal is not responsible for the costs of defense and will be responsible for the agent's liability only if the agent made a reasonable defense.

Example

Alvin, an up-and-coming rock singer, hires Dave as road manager for Alvin's new tour. On Alvin's instructions, Dave uses his own credit card to book Alvin into the fanciest suite in the fanciest hotel in each of the tour stops. Alvin has a duty to indemnify Dave for the room charges. Alvin's instructions gave Dave actual authority to incur the expenses. ◀◀◀

Example

Following a concert, Alvin directs Dave to bring back to the hotel a new amplifier that Alvin used during the concert. The amplifier actually belongs to the owner of the concert hall, and the owner subsequently sues Dave for conversion. Dave promptly notifies Alvin. Although Dave may well be liable for conversion,[83] Dave is entitled to indemnity from Alvin. Dave did not know he was committing a tort, and, as between Dave and Alvin, taking the amplifier was an authorized act. Alvin must therefore: (i) defend Dave or pay Dave's reasonable costs of defense; and (ii) cover any liability. ◄◄◄

Example

Although Dave's responsibilities only relate to the road tour, Dave has visions of getting Alvin a recording contract. Without checking with Alvin, Dave starts wining and dining various record company executives. Dave's efforts are fruitless, but he does manage to run up $12,000 in "entertainment" expenses. Alvin has no duty to indemnify Dave. Dave had no actual authority to incur the expenses, and the expenses were of no benefit to Alvin. ◄◄◄

The principal's duty to indemnify is a "default rule"—subject to change by any valid contractual arrangement between the agent and principal. A contract can expand, reduce, or merely further define the scope of the principal's duty.

§4.3.2 Principal's Duties in Tort (Physical Harm to the Agent)

a. Nonemployee (Non-servant) Agents[84]

A principal owes its nonemployee agent whatever tort law duties the principal owes to the rest of the world. In addition, a principal has a duty to warn its nonemployee agent of any risk involved in the agent's tasks if the principal knows or should know that: (i) the risk exists; and (ii) the agent is unlikely to be aware of the risk.

Example

Rachael owns and runs her own hauling service, and Charlotte hires her on commission to sell and deliver firewood. To pick up the firewood Rachael must enter Charlotte's property, and, in most jurisdictions, Charlotte will owe her a duty of reasonable care. That duty arises from Rachael's status as an entrant on land and not from her status as Charlotte's agent. ◄◄◄

83. Conversion is a strict liability tort. Therefore, Dave's innocent state of mind is irrelevant to the owner's suit.

84. For the rules that determine whether an agent is a servant (R.2d nomenclature) or employee (R.3d nomenclature), see Section 3.2.4.

Example

On Charlotte's land, the shortest route to the stacks of firewood crosses an old wooden bridge. After one of Rachael's trips to pick up firewood, Charlotte notices a hairline crack in the bridge's supporting structure. The crack is not visible from the road. Charlotte has reason to know that the bridge is dangerous and that Rachael is unlikely to be aware of the danger. Charlotte therefore has a duty to inform Rachael of the risk before she makes her next trip to the stacks of firewood. ◀◀◀

b. Employees (Servants)

Before the advent of workers' compensation statutes, the common law delineated a master's liability for work-related physical injuries suffered by its servants. The common law was complex and confusing. In theory, the master had a duty to provide reasonably safe working conditions for its servants. In reality, three doctrines combined to eviscerate that duty and tilt the law strongly toward the master.

(1) **The "fellow servant" rule.** This rule prevented servants from holding their masters vicariously liable for the tortious conduct of a "fellow servant." The R.2d defined fellow servants as "servants employed . . . in the same enterprise or household and so related in their labor that, because of proximity or otherwise, there is a special risk of harm to one of them if the other is negligent."[85] The definition (and therefore the rule) swept broadly. For instance, if a master operated several tugboats within a harbor and the negligence of a servant on one boat happened to cause injury to a servant on another, the fellow servant rule barred recovery. Since many workplace injuries resulted, at least in part, from the negligence of fellow employees, this rule left many injured servants without a remedy.

(2) **Assumption of risk.** At one time this doctrine applied generally within tort law. In the master-servant context, it barred servants from recovering for injuries arising from the ordinary dangers of their work, because servants were said to have assumed the risk of such injuries. The more dangerous the work, therefore, the less likely a servant was to recover.

(3) **Contributory negligence.** At one time this doctrine also applied generally within tort law. In the master-servant context, it barred recovery whenever an injured servant's own negligence had helped cause the injury.

---

85. R.2d, §475.

Today, workers' compensation statutes provide a no-fault compensation regime and preempt the common law.

§4.3.3 Contract-Based Duties

As explained previously, usually a contract between agent and principal overlays the agency relationship and imposes contractual duties on each party.[86] For principals, the most common contract-based duty is compensation.

Although the rules for construing a principal's contract-based duties are for the most part identical to the rules for construing the duties of any party to any contract, the concept of implied terms does require some special attention. As with contracts generally, the law can supply a term ("implied in law") and terms can be implied "in fact" from: (i) the express terms of the agreement; (ii) the parties' conduct (before or after contract formation); and (iii) other circumstances (including usages of trade). However, no implication arises solely by reason of the agency relationship or the principal's promise to pay the agent.

§4.4 DUTIES AND OBLIGATIONS OF THE PRINCIPAL TO THIRD PARTIES

§4.4.1 Agency Law Duties

a. Principal's Direct Duty to Properly Select and Use Agents

Under the rules discussed in Chapters 2 and 3, an agent's conduct can indirectly cause the principal to be liable to a third party. Agency law also imposes obligations that run directly from principals to third parties.

Most importantly, a principal has a duty to use reasonable care in choosing, informing, training, and supervising its agents. If a principal breaches this duty of care and as a foreseeable result the principal's agent injures a third party, the principal is liable. This liability "stem[s] from general doctrines of tort law"[87] and results from the principal's direct duty to the third party. The liability exists even though the most direct cause of the harm was the act or omission of the agent.

---

86. See Section 4.1.6.

87. R.3d, §7.05, comment *b*.

Example

The employee of a private snowplowing company drives one of the company's trucks to a customer's residence in order to plow snow from the driveway. Unbeknownst to the agent, the company has installed a new module to control the snowplow attached to the front of the truck. When the agent arrives at the customer's residence and attempts to lower the plow to street level, the plow lowers so quickly that it gouges a hole in the city street. The company is liable to the city for the cost of the street repair, even though the employee has not been negligent. The relevant negligence is that of the company, which failed to properly instruct and inform its agent. ◄ ◄ ◄

The fact that an agent has acted negligently does not by itself establish that the principal breached its direct duty of care.

Example

Harris Carpeting sells floor coverings and provides installation services through various nonemployee agents. It is customary for Harris to deliver the floor covering to the customer's location and for the installer to arrive separately. Harris uses only skilled installers and follows up with customers to determine their satisfaction both with the carpet and the installation. Harris therefore sees no need to incur the expense of supervising the installers.

One of Harris's regular installers is Albert, who has done installation work for 15 years and has an exemplary record. One day Albert uses a new type of adhesive to install vinyl tile and carelessly fails to read the instructions. He therefore fails to ventilate the room properly, and a fire results. Despite Albert's negligence, Harris has not breached its duty of care. In light of Albert's experience and reputation, it was reasonable to select Albert and to allow him to work without supervision.[88] ◄ ◄ ◄

b. The Nexus Requirement (Causation)

"Liability under this rule [of direct liability] also requires some nexus or causal connection between the principal's negligence in selecting or controlling an actor, the actor's employment or work, and the harm suffered by the third party."[89] This nexus requirement conceptually parallels the "scope of employment" requirement of *respondeat superior*.

---

88. As stated in the first sentence of this Example, Albert is a *nonemployee* agent. If he were an employee (servant), the analysis on the direct claim would not change, but the principal (employer/master) would be liable vicariously. See Section 3.2 (*Respondeat Superior*).
89. R.3d, §7.05, comment c.

Restatement on Point

"If the actor's tort is causally unrelated to the actor's employment by the defendant, [the principal's duty of care] does not subject the defendant to liability to a third party injured by the actor's tort although the defendant was negligent in employing or retaining the actor."[90] ◄ ◄ ◄

Example

Richard is employed as a camp counselor at a summer camp. During the summer he steals property from other counselors and from campers as well. A simple background check would have revealed that Richard has a criminal record that includes several convictions for theft. The camp's negligence in hiring Richard makes it liable to the counselors and campers for the thefts.[91] ◄ ◄ ◄

Example

Jackson, an employee of a restaurant, pleaded guilty to criminal sexual conduct with a minor and the distribution and receipt of child pornography. The restaurant had been warned multiple times that Jackson was engaging in pedophilia, but the restaurant did not report Jackson and retained him as an employee. Jackson's ex-wife sought damages from the restaurant for negligent supervision of Jackson. Barring some change in the common law, the claim should fail for lack of nexus.[92] ◄ ◄ ◄

Even if a sufficient nexus exists initially, it does not continue indefinitely, especially after the agency has ended.

Case in Point—*Phillips v. TLC Plumbing, Inc.*

"In 1999 TLC employed Cain as a plumbing service repairman. At the time Cain was hired, Condon, as owner of TLC, learned Cain was on parole and apparently had been convicted of a domestic violence and/or arson offense involving his then wife. On April 2, 2003, TLC dispatched Cain on a service

---

90. R.3d, §7.05, comment c.

91. Note that, assuming the jurisdiction uses the purpose test, *respondeat superior* will not apply. However, the campers may have a contract claim.

92. This example is based upon article, Debra Cassens Weiss, Subway pitchman's ex-wife seeks damages for failure to report 'pedophile behavior,' ABA Journal (Oct. 25, 2016).

call to Judith's residence. On April 24, TLC dispatched Cain on another service call to her residence. On or about May 21, TLC terminated Cain's employment for misuse of a company vehicle, drug and alcohol use, and apparently threatening a coworker. Cain and Judith apparently began a social relationship in April 2003 after his first service call. Their relationship seemingly evolved over time into a romantic one. On May 19, 2005, after Judith had ended their relationship and applied for a restraining order against Cain, he shot her. She died the following day and Cain was convicted of her murder." Judith's daughter sued TLC for negligent hiring and retention and lost on summary judgment. The appeals court affirmed: "[A]n employer does *not* owe a plaintiff a duty of care in a negligent hiring and retention action for an injury or other harm inflicted by a *former* employee on the plaintiff even though that employee, as in this case, initially met the plaintiff while employed by the employer. Accordingly, we agree with Defendants' assertion that because Cain's tortious act on Judith occurred *two years after* his employment with TLC was terminated, Defendants did not owe Plaintiff a duty of care at the time of Cain's tortious act and therefore cannot be held liable on a cause of action for negligent hiring and retention."[93] ◀◀◀

c. The Standard of Care and Vulnerable Customers, Patients, etc.

A standard of ordinary care requires different conduct in different circumstances. "The most important circumstances are the foreseeable likelihood that conduct will result in harm, the foreseeable severity of that harm, and the burdens imposed by precautions to eliminate or reduce the possibility of harm."[94]

More particularly, the risk of harm is greater if those at risk of harm cannot protect themselves from an agent's improper conduct:

> [I]n some settings and relationships, a person's vulnerability to harm may affect the measures that a principal may reasonably be required to take to safeguard against risks, including those posed by employees and other agents. In particular, relationships that expose young children to the risk of sexual abuse are ones in which a high degree of vulnerability may reasonably require measures of protection not necessary for persons who are older and better able to safeguard themselves. Such measures may include prohibiting unsupervised contact between a child and an employee. Likewise, persons of any age taken into custody by law-enforcement officers are vulnerable to risks of harm against which they may lack the ability to safeguard themselves.[95]

---

93. *Phillips v. TLC Plumbing, Inc.*, 91 Cal. Rptr. 3d 864, 866, 870 (Cal. App. 4 Dist. 2009).
94. R.3d, §7.05, comment *b*, citing Restatement Third, Torts: Liability for Physical Harm §41 (Proposed Final Draft No. 1, 2005).
95. R.3d, §7.05, comment *e*.

d. Relationship of Principal's Direct Duty to Principal's Vicarious Liability

The principal's liability under the direct duty of care is different from the principal's vicarious liability under the doctrine of *respondeat superior*. The two liabilities can, however, overlap. If a principal negligently selects, informs, trains, or supervises an employee and the employee negligently injures a third party while acting within the scope of employment, the principal will be liable to the third party on two counts: directly, for a breach of the duty of care, and vicariously, through the doctrine of *respondeat superior*.

Besides overlapping, the two liabilities can create a double bind for principals who hire agents to do potentially dangerous work. If the principal adopts a hands-off attitude and something goes wrong, the principal may be liable for failure to adequately supervise, train, inform, or instruct. If, in contrast, the principal seeks to avoid such a result with a hands-on approach, the law will take the principal's right of control to mean that the agent is an employee. If so, any negligence of the employee will make the principal vicariously liable.

Table 4.1 shows how the principal's direct and vicarious liability relate to each other and also how the principal's liability in tort is affected by the negligence of the principal, the negligence of the agent, and the status of the agent as employee or nonemployee. Table 4.1 assumes that conduct of the agent has caused physical injury to the person or property of a third party.

4.1 Principal's Direct and Vicarious Liability: The Roles of Negligence and Agent Status (assuming negligence is otherwise actionable under applicable tort law)

	Principal Breached Duty of Care	Principal Did Not Breach Duty of Care
Agent's Conduct ***Negligent***	Regardless of whether agent is an employee, principal liable on direct claim *if* sufficient nexus exists. Also liable vicariously *if* agent was employee acting within scope of employment.	Principal not liable on direct claim. Liable vicariously *if* agent was employee and was acting within scope of employment.
Agent's Conduct ***Not Negligent***	Principal liable on direct claim only, regardless of whether agent is employee *if* sufficient nexus exists.	Principal not liable.

§4.4.2 "Nondelegable" Duties Imposed by Other Law

Nonagency law sometimes imposes duties on account of a person's status or relationship to others. For example, in most jurisdictions the owner of a business has a duty to use reasonable care to make the premises safe for customers. Although the law sometimes calls such obligations "nondelegable duties," the term is usually a misnomer. With most such duties a person may indeed delegate the responsibility to others. For example, a store owner may appoint a store manager and leave her in charge of the premises. The mere fact of delegation breaches no duty.

A better, albeit more cumbersome, name for these duties would be "duties that may be delegated but that are not discharged merely by delegation." When a person delegates to an agent, the delegating person's relationship with the person accepting the delegation is a matter of agency law. However, neither the delegation nor the law of agency affects the original duty. Regardless of the care the principal uses in selecting, informing, training, and supervising the agent, the principal remains on the hook until and unless the agent properly performs the delegated tasks. If the agent does so, then the principal has satisfied its obligations under nonagency law. If, however, the agent does not perform properly, the principal is liable. The principal may have a claim against the agent, but that claim does not excuse the principal.

Example

Under a statute governing the leasing of residential premises, a landlord owes a tenant a duty to maintain the premises in "habitable" condition. The landlord hires a resident manager and instructs the manager "to do whatever is necessary to keep this place in good condition." The resident manager neglects the job, and a tenant sues the landlord for breach of the statutory "warranty of habitability." The landlord cannot successfully defend by blaming the resident manager, because delegating the responsibility did not discharge it.[96] ◄◄◄

§4.4.3 Duties Assumed Under Contract

In any contract the parties undertake duties to each other, and in most situations a contract obligor may delegate performance of a duty to someone else.[97]

96. The results are the same when a person delegates a duty to a nonagent. See, e.g., Restatement (Second) of Contracts §318(3) (unless otherwise agreed by the obligee, delegation does not discharge the obligor's duty to the obligee).

97. Sometimes the nature of the obligation (e.g., personal service) precludes delegation. Sometimes the contract validly prohibits delegation. In such circumstances, contract duties are genuinely "nondelegable," and the obligee need not accept the delegated performance.

When a contract obligor does delegate performance to an agent,[98] agency law relates to that delegation in the same way it relates to the delegation of duties imposed by law. The delegation does not discharge the duty. The obligor remains strictly responsible to the obligee, even if the obligor uses the greatest care in selecting, supervising, and instructing the agent.

Problem 32

In his first meeting with Friar Tuck, Robin Hood compels Tuck to carry him across a stream. Hood uses his sword as the instrument of coercion. Tuck undertakes the task, but midway across purposely drops Hood into the stream. Has Tuck breached his duty of loyalty? Would it matter if Tuck's conduct were grossly negligent rather than intentional? ◄◄◄

Explanation

Tuck has not breached his duty of loyalty, because none exists. For an agency relationship to exist, *inter alia* the agent must manifest consent to act on the principal's behalf. Tuck made no such manifestation, but merely yielded temporarily to coercion. (Moreover, even assuming consent, Tuck is most likely a nonservant service provider—in R.2d terms, an independent contractor—not an agent.) ◄◄◄

Problem 33

Traveling across country by car after the death of her husband, Alice stops at a roadside diner for lunch. The diner is in chaos. The one waitress has just quit, and Mel, the owner and cook, has a room full of increasingly irate customers. Sensing a job opportunity, Alice says to Mel, "Hey, I can wait tables. Want some help?" Mel responds, "Minimum wage. You're hired. Your shift ends at 7 P.M."

Alice works hard and extremely well. By the end of the day, she has collected $150 in tips. She is shocked when Mel says, "The tips belong to me. I didn't say nothing about you keeping the tips." Is Alice obliged to surrender the tips? ◄◄◄

98. It is possible and quite common to delegate duties to a nonagent independent contractor. See Section 6.1.2 (Distinguishing Agents from Independent Contractors).

Explanation

No. Although an agent must have the principal's consent to profit from the agency, custom may imply the necessary consent. It is certainly customary for waitresses and waiters to retain their tips unless the restaurant specifies otherwise. ◀ ◀ ◀

Problem 34

Victoria commissions Albert to get a Contracts casebook for her at the used bookstore. She specifically instructs him that she wants him to buy a book that was previously used, underlined, and annotated by someone who received at least an A- in the Contracts course. She promises to pay Albert a $5 fee if he succeeds in purchasing for her a book that meets her specifications.

Albert goes to the bookstore and initially attempts to perform his task. However, the bookstore clerk tells Albert that the bookstore has no way of knowing how well the former owner of any particular book did on any particular exam. Not wanting to lose a sale and always on the lookout for a little personal gain, the clerk suggests a little scam. The clerk will telephone Victoria and tell her that the bookstore does indeed have a book that was owned by someone who received an A in Contracts. The clerk will also tell Victoria that, since the book has such a good pedigree, the book costs $15 instead of the regular used price of $12. If Albert will back up the story, the clerk will split the extra $3 with him, fifty-fifty. Albert agrees.

The scam works. Victoria gives Albert $20 ($15 for the supposed price of the book and $5 for Albert's commission). Twelve dollars of Victoria's money goes into the bookstore's cash drawer. The clerk splits the other $3 with Albert. Albert also pockets the $5 commission.

But not for long. The scam unravels when Victoria learns that the former owner of the book flunked out of law school without ever having achieved a grade above C-. Threatened with dire consequences, the clerk spills his guts and tells Victoria the whole sordid story. Victoria rescinds her purchase. The clerk returns to Victoria the full $15 purchase price, taking $12 from the bookstore's cash drawer and the other $3 from his own pocket. Victoria then goes after Albert. She sues him not only for the return of the $5 commission, but also to disgorge the $1.50 kickback. Albert concedes the $5 and pays it back to Victoria. Albert contests the $1.50, however. He points out that he has paid the $5 and the clerk has paid the $15, so Victoria is now "whole." According to Albert, Victoria has recovered whatever damages she suffered and is now looking for a windfall. What result? ◀ ◀ ◀

Explanation

Albert must disgorge the $1.50. When an agent profits by breaching the duty of loyalty, the law imposes a constructive trust in favor of the principal. It is irrelevant that Victoria can prove no damages, and it is immaterial that disgorgement will make Victoria "more than whole" financially. It is better that the principal receive a windfall than the agent profit from a breach of fiduciary duty. ◀◀◀

Problem 35

After graduating from law school, Beth goes to work for a law firm. Several months later, an uncle contacts Beth and asks her to handle a closing on the sale of some land. Beth says, "I'd be delighted. When would you like to come down to the office?" The uncle responds, "Oh, I don't want to get your office involved. I don't really want to pay downtown lawyer fees. Why don't I just come by your house tonight?"

Beth explains that she is really obligated to work through her firm, but her uncle is insistent. Finally, Beth hits upon a solution. "Listen, uncle," she says, "You're family. Let me do this closing as family, no charge. We'll call it an introductory offer." Her uncle agrees.

Beth spends about six hours preparing for and attending the closing, and all goes well. Two weeks later, she receives at home a beautiful silver necklace, with a note from her uncle: "Dear Beth, With thanks to my favorite niece. Love, Your Uncle." The necklace is worth approximately $1,200. What should Beth do? ◀◀◀

Explanation

Beth faces a difficult situation. Presumably, she does not want to hurt her uncle's feelings, and for sentimental, aesthetic, and financial reasons she may well want to keep the necklace for herself. However, as Beth explained to her uncle, she is obliged to do her legal work through her firm. Her duty of loyalty precludes her acting in competition with her principal or from secretly benefiting from doing irregularly the type of work she is regularly employed to do. No matter how earnest her efforts to avoid a problem and how pure her motives, she cannot retain benefits made through such activity unless she has her principal's informed consent.[99]

---

99. It might be argued that Beth took an opportunity away from her principal when she undertook to do her uncle's work for free. That argument presupposes that the firm could have convinced the uncle to hire the firm. Nonetheless, Beth probably should have discussed the matter with her principal before "diverting" her uncle into the "no charge" arrangement.

That analysis dictates Beth's next steps. She must either return the necklace to her uncle or disclose the situation to the firm and seek the firm's permission to retain the necklace. ◄ ◄ ◄

Problem 36

Charlotte obtains from a video game distributor the right to place its video games in bars, restaurants, and arcades throughout a tri-state area. The right is quite valuable, because this manufacturer has several very popular video games and rations the number of games allowed in any one geographic area. Charlotte retains Eli to represent her in locating the best possible locations for the games and to negotiate with the owners and managers of those locations. Eli makes a number of recommendations, which Charlotte follows. Per their agreement, Charlotte pays Eli a fee of $500 per location selected.

The games do not produce the revenue Charlotte expected, and after about six months she looks more carefully into the locations Eli recommended. Charlotte discovers that: (i) half of the locations are owned by Interactive Display Outlets, LLC ("IDO"); (ii) during the time that Eli was advising Charlotte, Eli was also on retainer to IDO as a management consultant; (iii) many of the IDO locations are not in high-traffic areas; and (iv) Eli could easily have arranged superior, non-IDO placements that would have produced better revenues for Charlotte. What recourse does Charlotte have against Eli? ◄ ◄ ◄

Explanation

By acting for IDO, a potentially adverse party, without having Charlotte's consent, Eli breached his agent's duty of loyalty. He is liable to Charlotte for damages, that is, the present value of the additional revenues that would have been produced by the easily arranged, superior, non-IDO placements. Eli may also have to disgorge the compensation he received from Charlotte, as well as any compensation he received from IDO for having gotten Charlotte's video games into IDO locations. ◄ ◄ ◄

Problem 37

Sandy agrees to go to an auction for Ralph and bid for a particular picture. Ralph authorizes Sandy to bid up to $20,000. Both Sandy and Ralph expect the auction to end by 6 P.M. The auction runs late and Sandy must leave to pick up a child from day care. The day-care center closes at 6:30 P.M. After Sandy leaves, the picture Ralph wanted is sold for $18,000. Ralph later buys the picture from the purchaser for $20,000. He learns that the purchaser would have stopped bidding at the auction when the price hit $19,000.

Ralph then sues Sandy for $1,000—the difference between what would have been a winning bid at the auction and the price Ralph had to pay to get the painting after the auction. What is Ralph's theory of recovery? What will Sandy argue? What will Ralph respond? ◀ ◀ ◀

Explanation

EXPLANATION

Ralph will argue that: (i) Sandy was his agent; (ii) Sandy owed Ralph an agent's duty of loyalty, which Sandy breached by leaving the auction before the bidding finished (or at least before the $20,000 limit was reached on the picture); and (iii) Sandy is liable for the $1,000 of damages proximately caused by Sandy's breach of fiduciary duty.

Sandy will make two arguments. First, Sandy will argue that, by at least tacit agreement of the parties, the agency (and Sandy's fiduciary duty of loyalty) terminated at 6 P.M., when both the principal and agent expected the auction to be over. Second, Sandy will argue that even assuming the agency continued past 6 P.M., the agent's duty of loyalty yields when necessary to protect important interests of others. Preventing a child from being abandoned at a day care center should qualify as such an interest. Protecting children is certainly a legitimate social value and should outweigh some relatively minor financial harm to the principal.

Ralph will respond that Sandy had available at least two alternatives for protecting the child's interest without sacrificing the principal's. First, by anticipating the problem and disclosing it in advance to Ralph, Sandy would have allowed Ralph to make other arrangements for covering the auction. Second, when the auction appeared to be running long, Sandy could have used her cell phone to call the day care center to try to arrange for a late pickup. ◀ ◀ ◀

Problem 38

Sylvia decides to enter the silk importing business. The trade is notoriously biased against women, and she fears that her company will suffer if her interest in it is known. She therefore hires Phil as her general manager, but sets up the company so that Phil appears to the outside world as the owner. It is common in this trade for silk importers to sell to large customers on credit, but Sylvia instructs Phil never to extend more than $50,000 of credit to any customer without Sylvia's approval. One day, in order to close an important deal, Phil extends $150,000 of credit to one customer without consulting Sylvia. The customer makes only $20,000 of payments and then defaults. Assuming that Phil's judgment about the customer's creditworthiness was reasonable, does Sylvia have any claim against Phil? ◀ ◀ ◀

Explanation

Yes. Phil owes Sylvia $130,000. He breached his duty to act within his authority, and he is liable to his principal for the resulting harm. The reasonableness of Phil's judgment about the customer's creditworthiness is irrelevant. Sylvia is not claiming breach of the agent's duty of care. ◄ ◄ ◄

Problem 39

The owner of a car dealership appoints Rachael to manage the used car department. The owner promises that Rachael can have a "free hand" running the department. Rachael decides to open the department on Sundays. Although Sunday openings are not against the law, the owner considers them "inappropriate." The owner instructs Rachael to stay closed on Sunday. Must Rachael comply? ◄ ◄ ◄

Explanation

Although this instruction breaches the agreement between the owner and Rachael, Rachael has a duty either to obey or to resign. If Rachael can prove damages, she may recover for breach of contract. ◄ ◄ ◄

Problem 40

Sidney hires Sam, a private detective, to locate and deliver to Sidney a valuable statue of a bird. Sidney agrees to a fee of $200 per day, plus reasonable expenses, with a $15,000 bonus if Charlotte succeeds in finding and delivering the statue. Charlotte is on the verge of locating the statue when Sidney learns that Charlotte is carrying a gun. Charlotte is properly licensed to do so, but Sidney tells Charlotte, "I abhor violence. You may not carry that thing when you are working for me." Must Charlotte obey? Does he have any recourse against Sidney? ◄ ◄ ◄

Explanation

A principal always has the power to control the agent, so Sam must either obey or resign. Sam may nonetheless have a claim against Sidney for breach of contract. If, for example, the local custom is for detectives to carry properly licensed firearms, that custom may have implied an agreement requiring Sidney to respect Sam's discretion. If so, and if Sam could for instance prove that his lack of a gun cost him the opportunity to retrieve the statue, Sam could recover the $15,000 bonus from Sidney. ◄◄◄

Problem 41

Esther seeks to sell her business and enlists Harry to locate and help evaluate prospective buyers. With Harry's advice, Esther decides on a price of $31.5 million. She is willing to finance the sale (i.e., to receive payments in installments) but only with a down payment of at least 10 percent. Both Esther and Harry believe that buyers are more likely to succeed if they have some of their own money at risk.

Initially Harry has difficulty locating qualified buyers, but after three months he presents an offer from JoDot Enterprises ("JoDot"). JoDot offers to pay $31.5 million, with $1.5 million down. Esther accepts the offer, and the sale goes through.

Unfortunately, JoDot cannot operate the business at a profit and defaults on its obligations to Esther. Esther then learns that: (i) JoDot did not actually have the $1.5 million needed for the down payment and had to borrow $750,000 from a third party; and (ii) Harry was aware of that fact when he presented JoDot's offer to Esther. Does Esther have any recourse against Harry? ◄◄◄

Explanation

Yes. Harry breached his duty to provide information to Esther, his principal. Harry understood both the importance of the down payment and Esther's view of the subject. He therefore knew or should have known that Esther would want to know that the prospective buyers lacked a true down payment.[100]

Esther can compel Harry to disgorge any commission he earned on the deal. If she can prove causation, she can also claim damages. ◄◄◄

100. It is also possible to view Harry's conduct as a breach of his duty to obey instructions. This view assumes that Esther instructed him to bring her only offers from "qualified" buyers, that is, buyers capable of meeting the 10 percent down-payment requirement.

Problem 42

An attorney contacts an art collector, seeking to buy a famous Picasso print on behalf of a client. The attorney explains to the collector that she is acting for a client but declines to identify the client. (The client dislikes notoriety.) The attorney has actual authority to offer up to $450,000 for the print, and she persuades the collector to sell for $415,000. It is late Friday afternoon, and the attorney can have a cashier's check for the contract price by 10 A.M. Monday morning. The attorney wishes, however, to sign a binding sale agreement with the art collector, so that the collector cannot change his mind over the weekend. The attorney has $5,000 of her own money immediately available that she is willing to use as an earnest deposit. The attorney does not, however, wish to be liable on the contract itself. What should she do? ◄ ◄ ◄

Explanation

The attorney's potential problem comes from a rule of agency law. When an agent makes a contract for an identified (i.e., partially disclosed) principal, the agent is liable to the third party as a guarantor of the principal's performance—unless the agent and the third party have agreed otherwise. This rule dictates the attorney's strategy. The sale agreement must let her off the hook.

From the attorney's perspective, the ideal solution would be to include in the sale agreement an express statement that the attorney is not liable. It seems possible, however, that the collector would balk at such a term. After all, he would be committing to take the print off the market in return only for a promise to pay from a party whose creditworthiness he is unable to assess. The attorney could respond to this concern by limiting the duration of the collector's risk. The agreement could require payment by cashier's check by Monday at noon and provide that any delay in payment would entitle the collector to rescind the agreement. If the collector required further inducement, the agreement could provide for a nonrefundable "earnest money" payment of $5,000, or could offer to recast the contract as involving $5,000 payment for an option contract, with the payment to be credited to the purchase price if the unidentified principal timely exercises the option. ◄ ◄ ◄

Problem 43

Rose's Marina rents berths to various boat owners and also does boat and engine repair. The Marina does not ordinarily sell boats. Phil rents a berth at the Marina for his cabin cruiser. He happens to mention to Rose that he is thinking about selling his boat. Phil then leaves town on a two-week vacation. Three days later Rose meets Irv, who is interested in buying a cabin cruiser just like Phil's. Rose shows Phil's cruiser to Irv, and Irv immediately offers to pay $25,000 for the boat. Overcome by her enthusiastic desire to help Phil, Rose says, "Okay. He'll take it. Give me $500 earnest money." Irv does so, receiving in return a receipt from Rose: "Received from Irv, nonrefundable down payment on Phil's boat. By Rose, acting for Phil."

When Phil returns to town, he refuses to go through with the sale. Assuming that Phil is not bound,[101] does Irv have any recourse against Rose? ◄◄◄

Explanation

EXPLANATION

Yes. When Rose purported to act on Phil's behalf in selling the boat, she impliedly warranted her authority to bind Phil. In fact, she was not Phil's agent and lacked any power to bind him. She has breached her warranty of authority and is liable to Irv for both reliance and expectation damages. ◄◄◄

Problem 44

Jerry, the owner of Jerry's Gas, Service, and Repair Station, instructs Leah, one of his employees, to "pick up the blue Chevy station wagon parked in the driveway of 1346 Lincoln Avenue. The customer called and says it won't start and we should get it and fix it." Leah takes the station's tow truck and does as instructed. On the way back from the driveway, a semitrailer crosses a median strip and smashes into the station wagon. Fortunately, no one is injured, but the station wagon is totaled. Moreover, it later develops that Jerry made a mistake on the address: The customer who authorized the repair work lives at 1436 Lincoln. Is Leah liable to the owner of the station wagon? ◄◄◄

---

101. According to the rules discussed in Chapter 2, Rose had no power to bind Phil. He made no manifestation that could have *reasonably* caused her to believe that he wanted her to sell his boat. Therefore, she had no actual authority. He made only one manifestation that reached Irv—leaving the boat at the Marina. That manifestation was insufficient to cause Irv to *reasonably* believe that Rose was Phil's authorized agent. Therefore, Rose had no apparent authority. Cf. U.C.C. §2–403(2) (power of merchant who deals in goods of the kind to transfer entruster's title to a buyer in ordinary course). Inherent power is inapplicable, because Rose was not Phil's agent, much less his general agent. Estoppel will not work because Phil neither knew of nor carelessly caused Irv's misapprehension.

Explanation

Yes. Leah is liable for conversion, a strict liability tort. That she acted on her principal's instructions and without negligence is irrelevant to the question of her liability. Leah certainly has a right to be indemnified by her principal, and her principal is doubtlessly liable to the wagon's owner.[102] Nonetheless, she remains responsible for the tort she committed. ◀◀◀

Problem 45

Seller owned five acres of land on which he had built stables, corrals, fencing, and other improvements useful for raising horses. He retained Broker to sell the land on his behalf. Seller walked the property with Broker, showing Broker the various improvements and the property lines. Together they found most of the boundary markers, but could not find some. On the east side of the property, they found the northeast marker but could not find the southeast one. A line of trees seemed to confirm Seller's description of the east boundary. Moreover, Seller assured Broker, "I know where my land is and where I built. All my improvements are on my property." Broker did not independently verify the boundary lines.

When Broker showed the land to the eventual Buyers, Broker represented that all the improvements were within the property. After closing, the Buyers discovered that a corral on the east side of the property encroached several feet into the neighboring parcel. The cost for moving the improvements was $26,000. Was Broker liable to Buyers for that amount? ◀◀◀

Explanation

No. An agent is not liable for an innocent misrepresentation. The third party must show either intentional or negligent misrepresentation. There is no case here for intentional misrepresentation. Broker actually believed its own statements about the boundaries. Nor do the facts support a finding of negligent misrepresentation. Broker had no reason to doubt Seller's assurances, especially when the land's natural features (i.e., the trees) and what markers could be found seemed to support those assurances. ◀◀◀

---

102. This liability rests on *respondeat superior*. See Section 3.2.

Problem 46

In an attempt to get better bookings for his client, Dave (Alvin's road manager) threatens a booking agent with imminent bodily harm. The booking agent sues Dave for assault and for intentional infliction of emotional distress. Is Alvin obliged to indemnify Dave? ◄ ◄ ◄

Explanation

EXPLANATION

No. The suit arises from a tort knowingly committed by an agent. The principal therefore has no duty to indemnify.[103] ◄ ◄ ◄

103. Alvin may yet get involved, however, since the booking agent may have a *respondeat superior* claim. Dave's intentional tort may have been within his scope of employment. See Section 3.2.7.

CHAPTER 5

Termination of the Agency Relationship

§5.1 ENDING THE AGENCY RELATIONSHIP

An agency relationship may end in numerous ways, many of which have analogs in the law of contracts.

§5.1.1 Through the Express Will of Either the Principal or the Agent

Both the principal and the agent have the *power* to end the agency relationship at any time.[1] Either party can exercise this power simply by communicating to the other that the relationship is at an end. The principal's exercise of this power is sometimes called *revocation* (as in revocation of the agent's authority), while the agent's exercise is sometimes (though less frequently) called *renunciation*. Like other agency manifestations, communications of revocation and renunciation are judged by an objective standard.

1. As discussed previously, power is not the same as right. See Sections 1.5.1, 4.1.3, and 4.1.6. Whether a particular revocation or renunciation is "rightful" depends on the contract overlaying the agency relationship. See Section 5.2. If the principal lacks the power to terminate, no true agency exists. See Section 6.2 (Power Coupled with Interest; Authority [or Power] Given as Security).

Example

A Western town employs a sheriff to act on its behalf to "keep the peace." Despite receiving no support from the townspeople, the sheriff survives a gunfight with several outlaws. As the townspeople come out of hiding and try to congratulate the sheriff, he looks at them with disgust, takes off his badge, and throws it into the dirt. The sheriff has renounced his agency.[2] ◄◄◄

§5.1.2 Through the Expiration of a Specified Term

Principal and agent can and often do specify that the relationship will last for a particular period of time. If so, the relationship automatically terminates at the end of the specified period unless the parties agree to an extension or renewal. That agreement can be inferred from the parties' conduct.

Example

Mark retains Tonya to find a buyer for Mark's condominium. They agree that Tonya will have the exclusive agency for 90 days. They also agree that during those 90 days Tonya will have the authority to accept any cash offer of at least $90,000. On the 101st day, Tonya purports to accept a cash offer for $92,000. Tonya lacks the actual authority to accept the offer on Mark's behalf. That authority, and Tonya's role as agent, terminated at the end of 90 days. ◄◄◄

Example

Same facts, except that following the 90th day, Mark and Tonya continue to discuss the condo, and Tonya, with Mark's knowledge, continues to show the condo to prospects. The conduct of Mark and Tonya implies an agreement to extend the agency. ◄◄◄

§5.1.3 Through the Accomplishment of the Agency's Purpose

If the manifestations that create an agency indicate a specific objective, achieving that objective ends the agency. Without further manifestations from the principal, the agent has no basis for believing that either its authority or its agency continues.

---

2. This Example derives from the classic movie *High Noon*.

Example

Capitalist, Inc. hires Veronica to lobby for the passage of a bill in Congress and to negotiate on Capitalist's behalf concerning any proposed changes in the bill language. As part of her efforts, Veronica "wines and dines" congressional staff members. She sends expense reports to Capitalist, which promptly reimburses her. On October 12, the bill passes and is sent to the President. The next day, Veronica takes three staffers out to a "thank you for all your hard work" lunch. Without some additional manifestation from Capitalist, Veronica may not bill this lunch (or her time) to Capitalist. Her agency relationship with Capitalist ended when the goal of the agency was accomplished. ◀◀◀

Sometimes an agent will continue to exert effort for the principal even after accomplishing the agency task. The principal's acceptance or even acknowledgment of those efforts may manifest consent for the agency to continue or resume.

Example

Irv hires Jeff to help arrange a loan to finance Irv's acquisition of a business. Jeff arranges a loan and receives a fee from Irv. Jeff keeps in touch with the lender and some months later learns that Irv is having difficulty meeting his payments. Without first talking to Irv, Jeff contacts the lender to talk about refinancing the loan. At this point, Jeff is not acting as Irv's agent.[3] Subsequently, Jeff talks to Irv and says, "I understand from your lender that the payments are too large. I think I can work something out. Do you want me to try?" Irv replies, "Sure. Why not?" From that point, Jeff is again acting as Irv's agent. ◀◀◀

§5.1.4 By the Occurrence of an Event or Condition

Sometimes the manifestations that create an agency indicate that a particular event or condition will end the agency. If so, once the event or condition occurs, the agent can no longer reasonably believe itself authorized to act on the principal's behalf. The agency therefore terminates.

Example

Larry hires Howie to sell hot dogs at the beach, "but only until my daughter gets here from summer school." When Larry's daughter arrives, Howie's agency ends. ◀◀◀

3. Jeff may nonetheless have the apparent authority to bind Irv. See Sections 5.3.1 and 5.3.2.

The same rationale applies if the original manifestations call for the agency to end if a particular event or condition does not occur.

§5.1.5 By the Destruction of or the End of the Principal's Legal Interest in the Property

If the agent's role is predicated on some particular property and the property is no longer practically or legally available to the agent, the agency ends.

Example

Larry hires Howie to skipper Larry's yacht during the summer, including to make appropriate arrangements on Larry's behalf with harbor authorities. In June the yacht sinks. Howie's agency ends. ◀ ◀ ◀

Example

Same facts, except that the yacht does not sink. In June Larry sells the yacht. The yacht still exists, but Larry no longer has a legal interest in it. Howie's agency ends.[4] ◀ ◀ ◀

§5.1.6 By the Death, Bankruptcy, or Mental Incapacity of the Agent or Principal

Under traditional common law rules, any of these events terminates the agency relationship. However, modern statutes allow for substantial exceptions, and the R.3d, "following the lead of commercial legislation and §4(a) of the Uniform Durable Power of Attorney Act,"[5] has reformulated the common law. Section 5.3.2 discusses the R.3d's approach.

§5.1.7 By the Expiration of a Reasonable Time

Where the original manifestations set no specific term, the agency relationship expires automatically after a reasonable time has passed. What constitutes a reasonable time depends on a number of factors, including:

---

4. If the end of the agency means that Larry has breached an agreement with Howie, Howie may pursue contract remedies. See Section 5.2. Nonetheless, the agency ends.
5. R.3d, §3.06, comment d.

- the manifestation of the parties when the agency is created;
- the extent and nature of the communications between the parties after the agency is created (including indications by a party that it wishes to end the agency or that it believes the agency has ended);
- the particular objective of the agency;
- past dealings, if any, between the principal and agent; and
- the custom, if any, in the locality with regard to agency relationships of the same or similar type.

§5.2 POWER VERSUS RIGHT IN TERMINATION

As previously indicated,[6] both principal and agent always have the *power* to end a true agency relationship. Whether either has the *right* to do so depends on the content of any contract overlaying the agency relationship as well as on contract law concepts of good faith and detrimental reliance.

§5.2.1 The Role of Contract

Contractual terms can, *inter alia:*

- set a specific duration for the agency, during which neither party may rightfully end the relationship without having cause;
- provide for the agency to continue indefinitely, until ended by either party giving notice;
- define "cause" sufficient to allow one party, the other, or both to end the agency;
- and provide for the agency to continue so long as the agent meets certain performance requirements.

Regardless of its terms, a contract leaves intact the parties' *power* to end the agency relationship. If a revocation or renunciation breaches a contract between principal and agent, the non-breaching party may seek contract damages but cannot avoid the destruction of the agency. In any damage action, ordinary contract rules (e.g., assertions of prior breach, the duty to mitigate) will apply.

6. See Section 5.1.1.

Example

Marge enters into a contract calling for her to serve as Mountain Fleece, Inc.'s East Coast regional sales representative for 18 months. Despite the contract, Mountain Fleece terminates the agency a mere six months later. As a matter of agency law, Marge cannot compel Mountain Fleece to continue the relationship.[7] She can, however, sue for damages. ◀◀◀

Example

Same situation, except that Marge prematurely renounces. As a matter of agency (and contract) law, Mountain Fleece cannot compel Marge to serve. It can sue her for damages. ◀◀◀

§5.2.2 Implied Terms

For the most part, the rules on implying terms in an agency contract are identical to the rules for implying terms in any contract. A difference exists, however, with regard to terms restricting the right of the parties to terminate the relationship.

An express term can certainly restrict either party's right to terminate the agency. For example, most collective bargaining agreements expressly preclude the principal (i.e., the employer) from terminating without "just cause" an employee covered by the agreement. Courts will not, however, easily imply such a restriction. To the contrary, most agents have the right to renounce at will and most serve at the will of the principal.[8]

Courts are most likely to find an implied, contractual limit on termination when:

- the agency relationship is outside the employment context;
- the limitation is asserted by the agent, against the principal; and

---

7. However, nonagency law might provide for such compulsion. For example, a state statute might protect sales representatives against unfair termination and might authorize a court to order Marge's reinstatement.

8. In the employment context, this situation is known as *employment at will*, and the employment-at-will doctrine dates back more than a century. Many modern commentators have attacked the doctrine, and some courts have created exceptions relating, for example, to retaliatory firing of whistleblowers and to promissory estoppel. Statutory developments have also made inroads. Statutes prohibiting employment discrimination, for instance, do not directly require an employer to have "good cause" to terminate an employee but do prohibit an employer from terminating an employee for bad cause— that is, in violation of the statutory rules prohibiting discrimination. For the most part, however, the employment-at-will doctrine remains intact. See R-EL §2.01 (2013). ("Either party may terminate an employment relationship with or without cause unless the right to do so is limited by a statute, other law or public policy, or an agreement between the parties, a binding employer promise, or a binding employer policy statement.")

- either:
  - — the principal's manifestations are the source of the implication; or
  - — the agent has reasonably incurred costs in undertaking the agency and needs time to earn back those costs.

Example

A manufacturer retains a nonemployee salesperson as the manufacturer's selling agent and states, "We will supply all the widgets you can sell during the next year." Depending on other relevant circumstances, a court might imply a term under which, during that next year, the manufacturer has the right to terminate the agency only for cause. ◄◄◄

Example

A manufacturer retains a nonemployee salesperson as the manufacturer's selling agent. Nothing is said about duration, but the salesperson is required to and does buy from the manufacturer demonstration equipment costing $4,200. The manufacturer may be contractually obliged either to buy back the demonstration equipment or to let the agency exist long enough to allow the agent to recoup the $4,200 through commissions. ◄◄◄

§5.2.3 Breach of the Duty of Good Faith

A principal may not terminate an agency relationship in order to deprive the agent of a bonus or commission that would otherwise be due to the agent. However, the remedy is not reinstatement but rather the value of the bonus or commission improperly avoided.

Example

Marcia tells Teri, "Find me a bona fide buyer for my restaurant and help put the paperwork together, and I'll pay you a finder's fee of $10,000." Teri finds a prospect. As soon as Marcia learns of the prospect, she tells Teri, "Changed my mind. Think I'll wait awhile." Marcia then contacts the prospect directly and arranges the sale. Even though the agency relationship contained no express limitations on Marcia's right to terminate the relationship, Marcia will be liable to Teri for the finder's fee. Marcia terminated the relationship in bad faith.[9] ◄◄◄

9. This concept of good faith is quite different from the implied contractual covenant of good faith as explained in Sections 9.7.4 and 15.4.8.

§5.2.4 The Gratuitous Agent and Detrimental Reliance

If the agency is gratuitous, then by definition the agent's right to terminate is not limited by contract.[10] However, principles akin to promissory estoppel impose some restrictions. If a gratuitous agent: (i) makes a promise or engages in other conduct that causes the principal to refrain from making different arrangements; and (ii) the gratuitous agent had reason to know that the principal would so rely, then:

- if alternative arrangements are still possible, the agent has a duty to end the agency only after giving notice so the principal can make alternative arrangements; and
- if alternative arrangements are not possible, the agent has a duty to continue to perform the agency as promised.

Like any other agent, a gratuitous agent always has the power to renounce. However, if a gratuitous agent improperly leaves the principal in the lurch, the agent will be liable for damages.

§5.3 EFFECTS OF TERMINATION

§5.3.1 Effects on Agent's Authority and Power to Bind Principal — R.2d Approach

According to traditional common law principles, the agent's actual authority to bind the principal terminates when the agency terminates. Any inherent agency power also ends, because that power presupposes the status of general agent.

The fate of the agent's apparent authority depends on the reason the agency terminated. According to the R.2d and some older cases, if the principal has died or lacks capacity, the agent's apparent authority terminates immediately. In other circumstances, the agent's apparent authority terminates as to any particular third party only when: (i) the third party learns that the agency has ended; or (ii) in light of other information, the third party can no longer reasonably believe that the agent is authorized to act.

10. Although an agency can exist without consideration, a contract generally requires consideration to be enforceable.

Example

Melinda is a rancher. Charlotte is a horse breeder. On Monday, Melinda introduces Rebecca to Charlotte as "my agent for buying horses." On Tuesday, as Rebecca is negotiating with Charlotte, Melinda dies. Unaware of the death, Rebecca and Charlotte reach agreement on a horse purchase and Rebecca purports to bind Melinda. Under R.2d, Melinda's estate is not bound, because Melinda's death terminated Rebecca's apparent as well as actual authority.[11] ◀◀◀

Example

Same situation, but Melinda does not die. Instead, Melinda fires Rebecca for insubordination but fails to tell Charlotte. The next day, Rebecca—concealing her firing—purports to buy a horse from Charlotte on Melinda's behalf. Under R.2d, Rebecca's action binds Melinda, although the firing ended Rebecca's actual authority. Because neither death nor incapacity caused the agency relationship to end, Rebecca's apparent authority remained intact.[12] ◀◀◀

§5.3.2 Statutory Developments and the R.3d Approach

In some jurisdictions, statutes have changed the common law, providing that upon a principal's death or incapacity, the agent's actual authority continues until the agent knows of the death or incapacity and the apparent authority continues until the third party knows.[13] Other statutes allow principals to execute documents creating agency powers that survive the principal's disability or incapacity, even after the disability or incapacity becomes known.[14]

R.3d has reformulated the common law rules in this area:

> The impact of the principal's death on an agent's actual authority has the potential to create harsh consequences because the agent, unaware of the principal's death, may continue to act in good faith following it. The agent risks claims from third parties that the agent breached express or implied warranties of authority. Third parties risk the loss of transactions to which the agent committed the principal. Legislation has long mitigated the common-law result. Widespread adoption of consistent legislation of general applicability is a reliable measure of contemporary policy. The residual common-law rule

11. Rebecca is therefore liable for breach of the warranty of authority. See Section 4.2.2.
12. See Section 2.3.7 ("Lingering" Apparent Authority).
13. Uniform Durable Power of Attorney Act §4 (1979) (applicable to written powers of attorney).
14. Uniform Durable Power of Attorney Act §2 (1987).

> should reflect the policy judgments reflected in legislation such as the Uniform Commercial Code, the Uniform Durable Power of Attorney Act, and contemporary partnership statutes.[15]

Accordingly, R.3d §§3.07(2) and 3.08(1) state that:

> The death of an individual principal terminates the agent's actual authority. The termination is effective only when the agent has notice of the principal's death. The termination is also effective as against a third party with whom the agent deals when the third party has notice of the principal's death.[16]
>
> An individual principal's loss of capacity to do an act terminates the agent's actual authority to do the act. The termination is effective only when the agent has notice that the principal's loss of capacity is permanent or that the principal has been adjudicated to lack capacity. The termination is also effective as against a third party with whom the agent deals when the third party has notice that the principal's loss of capacity is permanent or that the principal has been adjudicated to lack capacity.[17]

As to apparent authority, the R.3d states: "An agent may act with apparent authority following the principal's death or loss of capacity because the basis of apparent authority is a principal's manifestation to third parties, coupled with a third party's reasonable belief that the agent acts with actual authority. Neither element requires that the principal consent or manifest assent at the time the agent takes action. When third parties do not have notice that the principal has died or lost capacity, they may reasonably believe the agent to be authorized."[18]

Example

Same facts as in the first Example in Section 5.3.1 (involving Melinda's death), except that the relevant jurisdiction follows the R.3d approach. Under that approach, and subject to any contrary provisions of applicable estate law, Melinda's estate is bound. Neither the agent (Rebecca) nor the third party (Charlotte) had notice of her death, so at the time of the transaction the agent had both actual and apparent authority. ◄ ◄ ◄

---

15. R.3d, §3.07, comment *d*.
16. R.3d, §3.07(2). R.3d, §1.04(4) defines "notice" as "A person has notice of a fact if the person knows the fact, has reason to know the fact, has received an effective notification of the fact, or should know the fact to fulfil a duty owed to another person."
17. R.3d, §3.08(1).
18. R.3d, §3.11, comment *b*.

§5.3.3 Agent's Obligation to Cease Acting for Principal

Once the agent has reason to know that the agency relationship has ended, the now former agent has a duty not to act for the principal. If the former agent violates this duty and binds the former principal, the former agent will be liable for damages.

§5.3.4 Principal's Duty to Indemnify Agent

The termination of the agency relationship does not eliminate any right of indemnity that the agent may have on account of events that occurred before the termination.

Example

As an authorized part of her lobbying for Capitalist, Inc., Veronica "wines and dines" important people. She periodically submits her bills to Capitalist for reimbursement. Capitalist one day decides that having lobbyists is not good for its image and therefore terminates its relationship with Veronica. At that time, Veronica has $1,500 of reimbursement claims submitted but as yet unpaid and $1,400 of expenses incurred but not yet submitted for reimbursement. Veronica is entitled to both the $1,500 and the $1,400. Both amounts relate to events that occurred before the termination of the agency relationship. ◀◀◀

§5.3.5 Agent's Right to Compete with Principal

While an agency relationship exists, the agent's duty of loyalty precludes competition with the principal. Unless the principal consents, the agent must refrain from engaging in any competitive activity that relates to the scope of the agency relationship.[19]

Once the agency relationship ends, however, so does the absolute barrier to competition. Public policy strongly favors free competition, and the former agent has a right to compete with its former principal. A former agent may even recruit customers from the former principal's clientele.[20]

The right to compete does, however, have three limitations: a prohibition against using the former principal's confidential information; the duty

19. See Section 4.1.1.

20. However, customer lists can be confidential information. If so, a former agent will breach a duty by making use of the lists to compete with the former principal.

to "get out clean"; and the obligation to abide by any valid "noncompete" agreements.

a. Prohibition Against Using the Former Principal's Confidential Information

The agent's duty not to disclose or exploit the principal's confidential information[21] clearly continues after the agency relationship ends. Disputes about the duty center around the question of just what kinds of information are protected from use.

Although in theory the same question exists during the agency relationship, at that juncture the question has far less practical import. Most alleged misuses involve some form of competition, and during the agency relationship competition is itself barred. As a result, during the relationship a claim of misuse of confidential information is often just a "tagalong" to a claim of improper competition. The question of whether allegedly misused information is truly confidential (and therefore protected) is unlikely to be crucial.

Post-termination competition, however, is not by itself improper,[22] and a claim of information misuse can therefore be crucially important in a conflict between former principal and former agent. In that context the question of what constitutes confidential information can be dispositive.

Analyzing that question can involve two different but complementary perspectives:

1. Does the information warrant protection as a trade secret? That is:
   — Has the principal expended effort and incurred expense to obtain or create the information?
   — Does the principal derive economic advantage from the information's not being generally known?
   — Has the principal used reasonable efforts to protect the confidentiality of the information?
2. Does the information consist of facts or confidential, specialized techniques (as distinguished from general expertise that an agent might develop while performing agency tasks)?

A "yes" answer to either question 1 or 2 means the information is confidential and belongs to the principal.[23]

---

21. See Section 4.1.1.
22. A valid "noncompete" agreement can make post-termination competition improper. See Section 5.3.5(c).
23. For a discussion of the distinction between confidential information and generally-applicable "know how," see Section 4.1.1(c)(1).

b. Duty to "Get Out Clean"

During the agency relationship an agent may properly contemplate post-termination competition with the principal. An agent may not, however, disregard its current loyalty obligations to further its post-termination plans. Put colloquially, the agent must "get out clean."

This part of the duty of loyalty has two major aspects. First, the agent has a duty not to begin actual competition while still an agent. Thus, during the agency relationship, an agent may not discuss with the principal's customers or potential customers the agent's post-agency venture. In addition, attempts to enlist other *key* agents of the principal may also violate the duty of loyalty. However, the agent may have discussions and even make agreements with parties *other than customers, potential customers, and key fellow agents* of the principal. For instance, the agent may properly have stationery printed, rent an office, and apply for a license.

Second, the agent may not actively deceive the principal as to the agent's reasons for terminating the agency relationship. The agent probably has no affirmative duty to provide reasons or even to respond if the principal asks, "Why are you quitting?" The agent may not, however, lie to conceal its plan to compete. Moreover, subject to its right not to reveal its plans for the future, the agent must continue to provide agency-related information to the principal[24] right up to the moment that the agency ends.

An agent who fails to "get out clean" may be liable to the former principal both for damages and for disgorgement.[25]

Example

May works as the headmaster of a private school. Frustrated by policies set by the board of trustees, she decides to start her own school. Before resigning, she discusses her plans with several of the private school's major donors and obtains commitments from them for start-up funding. She also copies the private school's mailing list of the families of current students. Her actions breach her duty of loyalty. She has the right to compete with the private school for donations, but only after she terminates her agency relationship. She never has the right to purloin her principal's mailing list.[26] ◄◄◄

24. See Section 4.1.5.
25. See Section 4.1.7 for a discussion of the principal's remedies for an agent's breach of the duty of loyalty.
26. It is immaterial whether May copies the list or commits it to memory. R.3d §8.05, Reporter's Notes, comment c.

c. Noncompetition Obligations Imposed by Contract

A contract between the principal and agent can restrain the agent from competing after the relationship ends, although the law's strong pro-competition stance causes courts to scrutinize such agreements carefully. The restraints must be reasonable with respect to the scope of activities foreclosed, the geographic area foreclosed, and the duration of the foreclosure. In some states, overbroad restraints are simply unenforceable. In most states, however, courts will "blue-pencil" overbroad "noncompetes"—carving the restraints back until they are reasonable.

Despite the judicial skepticism, contractual noncompetes are common and quite important whenever an agent is likely to develop strong relationships with the principal's customers.

Example

A wholesale tire company assigns a three-state territory to a sales representative and instructs that representative "to get to know every potential buyer in the territory. Get them to know us and like us." As the sales rep fulfills those instructions, a personal relationship between the sales rep and the tire wholesaler's customers will almost inevitably develop. It makes little sense for the tire wholesaler to pay the sales rep to develop all this "good will" if the sales rep can simply resign and take the business to a competing wholesaler. ◀◀◀

However, in some jurisdictions a statute replaces the common law rule.

Example

Cal. Bus. & Prof. Code § 16600.1(a) states, "It shall be unlawful to include a noncompete clause in an employment contract, or to require an employee to enter a noncompete agreement, that does not satisfy an exception in this chapter." There are no exceptions applicable to the typical employee-employer relationship.

Problem 47

For the past several years, Ventura Company ("Ventura") has been acting as a buying agent for Ilan Enterprises ("Ilan") in the U.S. soybean market. Ventura has had authority to make purchases up to $250,000 without prior approval from Ilan.

Recently, Ilan discovered improprieties in Ventura's conduct. Ilan wishes to terminate the relationship immediately and wants to know how to do so. Ilan is also concerned about its responsibility if Ventura continues to trade on Ilan's account even after Ilan terminates the relationship. Advise Ilan how best to proceed. ◀◀◀

EXPLANATION

Explanation

Ilan can terminate the agency simply by giving notice to Ventura. A principal always has the power to terminate an agency. In this instance Ilan also has the right to do so, since the facts reveal no express or implied agreement as to term. Ilan should make the notice in writing and use some means of transmission that allows proof of delivery. (Agency law does not require written notice. The writing and delivery precautions are to simplify proof.)

As for the possibility that Ventura will bind Ilan through post-termination trading, the termination notice will end Ventura's actual authority and inherent agency power.[27] Ilan should be concerned, however, with Ventura's lingering apparent authority. If Ilan has a list of traders and other parties with whom Ventura has dealt, Ilan should send each a brief notice, stating in effect, "Effective [date of termination], Ventura Company is no longer authorized to sell, buy, make trades, or conduct any other business for Ilan Enterprises."[28] This notice will prevent the recipients from reasonably believing that Ventura remains authorized and will thereby stop them from claiming apparent authority as to any future transactions.

Ilan must also consider the rest of the marketplace. It is possible that Ventura possesses apparent authority in the soybean market generally — even with parties who have never dealt with Ventura. Ventura may have previously and accurately described itself as having authority, and that description is attributable to Ventura's principal.[29] Moreover, the Ventura–Ilan relationship may be generally known, with that knowledge traceable to the fact that Ilan has followed through on deals made by Ventura.

Because this aspect of the Problem relates to a possible public perception, public preventive measures are necessary. Ilan should identify some trade publication or other medium of communication that reaches those who participate in the soybean market and insert in that medium the same "no longer authorized" notice just described. Ilan should also post the notice conspicuously on Ilan's website.

Besides addressing the apparent authority concerns, Ilan's private and public notices will also block attempts to claim agency by estoppel. Knowing that market participants might believe Ventura is still authorized to act for Ilan and that they "might change their position because of it," Ilan will have taken "reasonable steps to notify them of the facts."[30] ◄ ◄ ◄

---

27. See Section 5.3.1.

28. As a matter of agency law, the notice need not explain why this change has occurred; as a matter of *defamation* law, the notice *should* not explain. (Even if the explanation were accurate and even though truth is a defense to a defamation claim, why invite trouble?)

29. See Section 2.3.3 (agent has implied actual authority to accurately describe its authority to act for the principal).

30. R.2d, §8B(1)(b). See Section 2.5. Note that this Explanation does not mention that Ventura would be breaching a duty if it purported to act for Ilan after receiving a termination notice. Although that assertion is correct, see Section 5.3.3, the breach of duty is not relevant to the issue presented.

Problem 48

Roseanne gets a job at a posh new restaurant in an upscale mall where the wait staff all wear uniforms. Each uniform costs $85 dollars, and the restaurant requires Roseanne to buy four before starting work. Three days after Roseanne starts work, the restaurant manager decides that the staff is too large for the current volume of business. He fires the newest employee—Roseanne. Does Roseanne have any recourse? ◀ ◀ ◀

Explanation

The answer will probably depend on how strongly the relevant jurisdiction adheres to the employment-at-will doctrine. Roseanne will argue that, by requiring her to buy so many uniforms, the restaurant impliedly agreed not to terminate her without cause at least until she had worked long enough to make the uniform purchase an economically rational act. As a fallback, she will argue that the restaurant must buy the uniforms back from her. ◀ ◀ ◀

Problem 49

Eli is a regional sales agent for Maurice Ball Bearing, Inc. ("Maurice"). Eli and Maurice have a written agreement that: (i) grants Eli an exclusive territory in which to promote and solicit orders for Maurice products; (ii) provides that Eli has no authority to accept any order on behalf of Maurice and that all sales will be made by Maurice directly to customers; (iii) establishes a commission schedule; (iv) requires Eli to follow lawful and ethical business practices but otherwise allows him complete discretion in how he conducts his operations; and (v) allows either party to terminate the relationship without cause on seven days' notice. Under the commission schedule, Eli qualifies for a $30,000 bonus in any calendar year in which he books orders aggregating more than $3 million.

It is October. So far Eli has booked $2.8 million, and he will certainly reach the bonus level by year's end. However, Maurice has decided for its own reasons to "go direct" in Eli's region. That is, Maurice wishes to use its own employees, rather than Eli, to solicit orders. The CEO of Maurice wishes to terminate Eli immediately and asks you for legal advice. Provide it. ◀ ◀ ◀

Explanation

Maurice has the power to terminate its agent at any time and appears to have the right to do so simply on seven days' notice. However, with Eli so close to qualifying for the bonus, a precipitous termination could raise suspicions of bad faith. A principal has no right to terminate an agency merely to deprive the agent of benefits that the agent is on the verge of earning.

Even if Maurice succeeds in demonstrating a good faith reason for terminating Eli, Eli might still make trouble by claiming breach of an implied agreement. He could argue that the agreement, which offers a large bonus based on a calendar year's effort, impliedly prohibits Maurice from terminating at year's end any agent who is about to earn the bonus, unless the agent has engaged in misconduct.

If Maurice believes it essential to terminate the agency before year's end, in the long run Maurice may find it less expensive and less stressful to send with the termination notice an offer to pay the $30,000 bonus. ◀◀◀

Problem 50

May works as an agent for Broker, Inc. ("Broker"), a company that, for a commission, helps U.S. firms sell goods to foreign governments. May's responsibilities include traveling around the United States to try to persuade U.S. companies to use Broker's services. During one trip, May decides to go into business for herself. Aware (because Broker has told her) that the government of Argentina is seeking bids for major construction projects, May contacts a number of U.S. companies. She gets "in the door" as a representative of Broker, but once in she tells the companies that she will soon be providing the same services as Broker—and for a lower commission. She does not, however, close any deals for herself. At the end of the trip, May returns to Broker's home office and resigns. She explains her resignation by saying that her brother-in-law has offered her a job in the family upholstery business. May then promptly sets up her own firm, pursues the contacts she made on the last trip, and lands a number of lucrative contracts related to the Argentine project. Does Broker have any recourse against May? ◀◀◀

Explanation

Broker has a claim for disgorgement of May's profits. In two or perhaps three ways, May has breached her duty of loyalty. First, by promoting her own services in contrast to Broker's, she began to compete while still an agent. Second, she lied to her principal about her reasons for leaving. Third, her pursuit of contracts related to the Argentine project *may* have been a misuse of Broker's confidential information. Broker's information about the project certainly was of economic importance to Broker, but Broker would have to show in addition that: (i) the existence of the project was not generally known; (ii) Broker had expended effort or expense to obtain the information; and (iii) Broker used reasonable means to protect the information. ◀◀◀

Problem 51

Captain Miles Standish found himself deeply in love with "the damsel Priscilla." Unfortunately, Captain Standish was a shy fellow (except in matters of war) and could not find within himself the strength to approach Priscilla on his own behalf. He turned, instead, to his good friend John Alden. He asked Alden to visit Priscilla and express to her Standish's feelings.

Alden also loved Priscilla, but did not mention that fact to Standish. Instead, "[f]riendship prevailed over love," and Alden agreed to act on Standish's behalf. Alden went to Priscilla's house and explained his mission. Priscilla responded with the immortal words, "Why don't you speak for yourself, John?" Consistent with the principles of agency law, could he? If not, what could he have done to free himself to speak? ◀◀◀

Explanation

Alden may not speak for himself right away. He has consented to act on Standish's behalf. He is therefore Standish's agent and has a duty of loyalty that bars selfish conduct. That he is acting gratuitously affects neither his status as agent nor his duty of selflessness. While he remains Standish's agent, Alden simply cannot advance his own cause adverse to his principal's interests.

If Alden wishes to respond to Priscilla's invitation, he must first "get out clean" from his agency. To do so, he must notify Standish that he (Alden) can no longer represent Standish's interests to Priscilla. Although Alden probably has no duty to disclose that he intends to compete for Priscilla's attention, he probably does have a duty to report to Standish what Priscilla has said. That information came to Alden during his agency, and he has reason to know that his principal would consider the information important. He therefore must communicate that information to his principal.

Once has he done so, he may terminate the agency. Then he may indeed speak for himself.[31] ◀◀◀

31. It might seem at first glance that Alden may not use his knowledge of Priscilla's interest, because he gained that information during the agency. However, the information is not Standish's property; it is not confidential to Standish. Priscilla can rightfully disclose the information as she sees fit.

CHAPTER 6

Distinguishing Agency from Other Relationships

§6.1 AGENCY AND OTHER BENEFICIAL RELATIONSHIPS

§6.1.1 The Existence and Consequences of the Issue

There are myriad relationships in which one party benefits another, but not all "beneficial" relationships qualify as agency relationships. Consider, for example, the relationship between you and:

- the dry cleaner that cleans your wool sweater;
- the firefighter who carries you out of a burning building;
- the espresso café that feeds your caffeine habit;
- the law school that provides you a legal education;
- the bank that provides you a student loan; and
- the trustee who administers the trust fund established for you by your late, lamented, rich aunt.

In each of these relationships, the other party provides you benefits (goods, services, money) without becoming your agent. Likewise, an executor of an estate benefits the heirs and the conservator of a person benefits the conservatee, but neither the executor nor the conservator are agents.

6. Distinguishing Agency from Other Relationships

Agency *vel non*[1] is often a high-stakes issue because the agency label carries significant legal consequences. Indeed, disputes about the label are essentially disputes about those consequences. The consequences can follow from agency law itself or from the interaction of agency status and some other body of law.

Example

A grain elevator goes bankrupt owing money to local farmers and to the multinational company that provided the elevator a line of credit. The farmers try to establish that the elevator acted as the agent of the multinational company and not merely as a debtor. The farmers care about the "agent" label only as a means of establishing that the multinational company is liable for the debts incurred by the elevator.[2] ◀ ◀ ◀

Example

A cattle rancher delivers cattle to a cattle company, which delivers the cattle to a meatpacker. The meatpacker pays the cattle company, but the cattle company fails to pay the rancher. The rancher seeks to characterize the cattle company as the meatpacker's agent and not an independent buyer/reseller, so that agency law attribution rules will make the meatpacker liable to the rancher for the unpaid contract. ◀ ◀ ◀

Example

A manufacturer markets its products by delivering them to intermediaries who then sell them to the ultimate users at a price dictated by the manufacturer. Accused of an antitrust violation known as "resale price maintenance," the manufacturer asserts that the intermediaries are its agents and not distributors, and so the resale price maintenance rule does not apply.[3] ◀ ◀ ◀

Example

A service station operator obtains gas from an oil company and sells it to customers. The operator fails to pay for the gas and is charged with embezzlement. The prosecution asserts that the operator was the oil company's

1. This Latin phrase means "or not" and is a very useful term of art because so many points of legal analysis involve "yes/no" characterizations.
2. This Example is based on *A. Gay Jenson Farms Co. v. Cargill, Inc.*, 309 N.W.2d 285 (Minn. 1981).
3. Until 2007, resale price maintenance was *per se* illegal, and this Example is based on *United States v. Gen. Elec. Co.*, 272 U.S. 476, 480–85 (1926). In 2007, the U.S. Supreme Court rejected the *per se* rule and substituted the "rule of reason." *Leegin Creative Leather Prod., Inc. v. PSKS, Inc.*, 551 U.S. 877 (2007).

agent and therefore (i) the proceeds from the sale belonged to the oil company, minus only the operator's agreed-upon commission, and (ii) the operator had a fiduciary duty to turn the proceeds over to the oil company. The operator defends by denying an agency relationship and asserting that a *buyer's* failure to pay for goods is not criminal. ◀◀◀

§6.1.2 Distinguishing Agency from Other Similar Relationships

Disputes over the existence of an agency relationship usually relate to one of the two fundamental characteristics of an agency: the principal's right of control or the fiduciary nature of the relationship. For an agency to exist, the party receiving the benefits must have the right to control at least the goals of the relationship, and the person providing the benefits must be acting "on behalf of" the person receiving the benefits.[4] A beneficial relationship that lacks either or both of these characteristics is not an agency.

a. The Party Providing Benefits Is Not a Fiduciary and Is Not Subject to Control

The typical contract is an "arm'slength" relationship, so most ordinary contracts fit into this category. Neither party has manifested assent to act "on behalf" of the other; to the contrary, each party has entered into the contract to further its own interests. Moreover, the contract does not contemplate one party having any "power to subject the [other party] to personal liability" to third parties.[5] Both parties are subject to the obligations of the contract, but that control device is a product of the agreement between the parties.

The R.2d uses the term "independent contractor" to refer to a person who provides benefits to another under a *nonagency*, contractual relationship.[6] However, that usage is confusing because the R.2d also uses the same words to describe *agents* who are not servants: that is, "independent contractor agents."[7] The R.3d eschews the term "independent contractor" entirely and substitutes "nonagent service provider" and "nonemployee agents."[8]

A building contractor is often described as the classic example of an independent contractor (or, in R.3d terms, a nonagent service provider).

4. These characteristics are introduced in Sections 1.4.6 and 1.4.7.

5. R.2d, §12 (Agent as Holder of a Power), comment *c*. See also R.3d, §1.01, comment *c*. ("The common-law definition requires that an agent hold power, a concept that encompasses authority but is broader in scope and connotation.")

6. R.2d, §14 N, comment *b*.

7. R.2d, §14 N, comment *a*.

8. R.3d, §1.01, comment *c*.

Moreover, *most* commercial and consumer relationships involve nonagent service providers.

Example

Exhausted but exalted after completing your final exams, you decide to go to a local shopping mall for some "R & R." Contemplating the eventual consumption of alcoholic beverages, you decide to take the bus rather than drive. The bus company is a nonagent service provider. ◀ ◀ ◀

Example

When you are at the mall, you enter Sharon's Custom T-Shirts and purchase a custom-made T-shirt that says, "I Survived the Rule Against Perpetuities." Sharon's relationship to you as she prepares and sells the T-shirt is that of an independent contractor. ◀ ◀ ◀

Example

Slipping on your new T-shirt, you proceed to Don't Doubt This Thomas—Homemade Desserts, where you purchase a dish of peach cobbler, which is handed to you by Malika, the general manager of the store. Malika is an agent of the store, but the store is acting as an independent contractor when it provides you the peach cobbler. ◀ ◀ ◀

An escrow arrangement provides a more specialized example. When two parties agree that a third will hold an item of value (e.g., money, stock, a deed) until specified conditions are met and then deliver the item per the agreement, the item is considered in escrow and the third party is the escrow holder. Neither of the escrow parties has a right to control the escrow holder, who is obligated only to perform as the escrow agreement requires. The escrow holder does not act primarily for the benefit of either party to the escrow agreement, but rather acts to fulfill its own obligations. The escrow holder is therefore not an agent.

b. The Party Providing the Benefits Is Subject to Control but Is Not a Fiduciary

Under some contracts, one party may have substantial, practical control over the conduct of the other, but the relationship is still not an agency. The "on behalf of" (fiduciary) element is missing, and the control is not general.[9]

9. Some courts, seeking the liability consequences that attach to the agency label, will ignore the fiduciary element of the agency relationship and find agency based on control alone. See Section 3.2.4(c) (explaining how "servant" status is not necessarily a subcategory of "agent" status, because, in the context of *respondeat superior* claims, some courts make the servant

(1) **Distributor of goods and its supplier.** Some distribution agreements give the supplier considerable control over the distributor, regarding, for example: (i) where the distributor can resell the goods; (ii) how the distributor may advertise the goods, (iii) what kinds of after-sale service the distributor must provide, and (iv) in some instances, even the price at which the distributer may resell the goods. Nonetheless, the distributor is not the supplier's agent because the relationship's primary purpose is not to benefit the supplier. In this arm's-length transaction, each party's own interest is primary to that party. Moreover, the supplier does not have the overarching right to control the goals of the relationship.

(2) **Supplier of specially designed goods and its customer.** In some circumstances, a customer will exercise considerable control over its supplier. For example, if the customer is buying components from the supplier to incorporate into the customer's own products, the customer may (i) design the component; (ii) specify the raw materials the supplier is to use; and (iii) even insist on the right to monitor the supplier's production activities. The supplier is not the customer's agent, however, because the relationship's primary purpose is not to benefit the customer. In this arm's-length transaction, each party to the relationship seeks its own benefit, and neither party's benefit is primary to the other party.

c. The Party Providing the Benefit Is a Fiduciary but Is Not Subject to Control

(1) **Trustee of a trust and the trust beneficiary.** The trustee is obliged to act solely for the benefit of the beneficiary, but the beneficiary does not have the right to control the trustee.

(2) **Conservator and conservatee.** Appointed by a court to take care of the financial affairs or personal decisions (or both) of an incompetent person, the conservator is obliged to act in the best interests of the conservatee. The conservatee has neither the right nor power to control the conservator.

(3) **Directors of a corporation and the corporation.** Although the directors do owe duties of loyalty to the corporation, the corporation does not control the directors. To the contrary, the directors control the corporation.[10]

---

determination without first considering whether the tortfeasor is an agent of the alleged master) and Section 6.3.2 (discussing R.2d, §14 O and the *Cargill* case).

10. Some commentators describe directors as the agents of the shareholders (i.e., of the people and organizations who own stock in the corporation). Although used in this way the agency concept helps analyze certain corporate law issues, the usage does not fit with the common law definition of agency. Shareholders have the right to exercise only limited and intermittent control over the directors.

§6.2 ERSATZ AGENCY[11]

In two related circumstances, what may appear to be an agency is in fact a different, *irrevocable*, nonagency relationship. In each situation:

- one person grants another the right to bind the grantor and lacks the power (not merely the right) to revoke that grant;
- the authority to bind is granted *not* to benefit the grantor (i.e., the party who seems like a principal), but rather to benefit the grantee (i.e., the party who seems like the agent); and
- the grantee (not the grantor) is in charge.[12]

The two circumstances have traditionally gone under the names of "agency (or power) coupled with an interest" and "authority (or power) given as security." The R.3d treats the former concept as encompassed within the latter[13] and provides this black letter definition:

> A power given as security is a power to affect the legal relations of its creator that is created in the form of a manifestation of actual authority and held for the benefit of the holder or a third person. It is given to protect a legal or equitable title or to secure the performance of a duty apart from any duties owed the holder of the power by its creator that are incident to a relationship of agency. . . .[14]

Because many jurisdictions still treat the two concepts separately, and because the "coupled with an interest" concept has "a distinguished lineage,"[15] the following sections separately describe the two concepts.

Whichever concept applies, under whatever name, the salient purpose of the relationship is to protect or otherwise benefit the grantee, and the key practical consequence is irrevocability. While in a true agency the principal always has the power to revoke the agent's authority, the concepts discussed here involve irrevocable grants. "If the creator of a validly created power given as security purports to revoke the holder's authority contrary to the agreement pursuant to which the creator granted the power, specific enforcement of the holder's rights is an appropriate remedy, subject to the court's discretion in granting an equitable remedy."[16]

11. From the German, meaning "seeming proper but actually not genuine."
12. This description states the default rules. The parties may agree to provide the grantor a right of revocation.
13. R.3d, §1.04, comment f ("A power coupled with an interest is an instance of a power given as security.").
14. R.3d, §1.04(6).
15. R.3d, §3.12, comment c.
16. R.3d, §3.12, comment b.

§6.2.1 Power Coupled with an Interest

For a power to be coupled with an interest:

- the grantee's power (i.e., the authority to bind, which appears like agency authority) must relate to some particular right or other property; and
- the same transaction that establishes the grantee's power must also provide the grantee some "interest" in that particular right or other property[17]

Example

Ophelia owns 200 acres of land. To induce Hamlet to sell the land for her, she gives him an undivided one-tenth interest in the land, coupled with an irrevocable power of attorney to sell her interest at any price above $500 per acre. Hamlet's power relates to the land, and he has received that power at the same time he has received an interest in the land. The power is coupled with an interest and is irrevocable. Hamlet is not Ophelia's agent. ◄◄◄

For the power to be "coupled with an interest," the power and the interest must relate to the same aspect of the particular property. If the grantee receives an interest not in the underlying property itself, but rather in the proceeds that result from the grantee's exercise of the granted power, then a true agency results and the grantee's authority is revocable, whether or not revocation breaches an agreement between the parties.

Example

As above, Ophelia owns 200 acres of land and wishes to have Hamlet sell them for her. Instead of giving him an interest in the land, however, she sends him a letter: (i) giving him a right to 30 percent of the sale price over $300 per acre; and (ii) purporting to grant him irrevocable authority to sell the land for $300 or more per acre. Hamlet's power is not coupled with an interest. His power relates to the land, and his interest relates only to the proceeds of the sale of the land. Hamlet is Ophelia's agent, and despite the letter his authority is revocable.[18] ◄◄◄

---

17. R.3d, §3.12, comment c, notes that, under this rubric, "it is necessary that a power holder possess a proprietary interest in the 'subject matter of the agency itself.' This test also requires that the power and the proprietary interest be united in the same person."

18. "An agent's interest in being paid a commission is an ordinary incident of agency and its presence does not convert the agent's authority into a power held for the agent's benefit." R.3d, §3.12, comment b. The letter probably does obligate Ophelia to refrain from revoking. She nonetheless retains the power to revoke. See Section 5.2 (Power Versus Right in Termination).

A power coupled with an interest survives the death of the grantor.

§6.2.2 Authority (or Power) Given as Security

If:

- an obligor owes a debt or other obligation to an obligee; and
- in order to provide the obligee with security, the obligor grants the obligee a power to bind the obligor; then:
  — no agency is created;
  — the power is "given as security"; and
  — the power is irrevocable during the life of the obligor.[19]

Example

Ophelia, in Dunsinane, appoints Hamlet as her agent to sell 700 crates of oranges being stored in a warehouse in Elsinore. Hamlet informs Ophelia that $500 of storage fees must be paid or the warehouse will sell the oranges. Ophelia has no funds available, and Hamlet agrees to advance the $500. To secure her obligation to repay Hamlet, Ophelia grants him the irrevocable right to collect all payments on the oranges and to repay himself from those proceeds before sending any money to Ophelia. The relationship between Ophelia and Hamlet is no longer an agency. Instead, Hamlet possesses a power given as security, which is irrevocable except through the death of Ophelia. ◄◄◄

In the above example, the power given as security is *not* a power coupled with an interest. Hamlet has no interest in the underlying property (i.e., the oranges). Often, however, circumstances will satisfy both concepts, and a power given as security will also be a power coupled with an interest.

Example

Hamlet borrows money from Ophelia, and as collateral grants Ophelia a security interest[20] in 100 shares of stock in Birnam Forest, Inc. Hamlet also grants Ophelia his proxy to vote the stock. The proxy is "given as security" for the debt and is therefore irrevocable except by Hamlet's death. Moreover, since the same transaction that granted Ophelia the proxy also gave her a

19. Under R.3d, §3.13(2)(e), in most circumstances this type of power would also survive the obligor's death.
20. A security interest is like a mortgage on personal rather than real property.

security interest in the underlying property, the proxy is "coupled with an interest." The proxy is therefore irrevocable even if Hamlet dies.[21] ◀◀◀

Whether a stock proxy is revocable also depends on the rules contained in the statute governing the corporation whose stock is involved.[22]

§6.3 CONSTRUCTIVE AGENCY

§6.3.1 The *Cargill* Case and R.2d, §14 O

Sometimes a court construes a seemingly arm's-length arrangement into an agency relationship. The case of *A. Gay Jenson Farms v. Cargill, Inc.*[23] provides the best-known examples of such *constructive agency*.[24]

Cargill arose from the financial collapse of the Warren Grain & Seed Co. ("Warren"), a grain elevator located in rural Minnesota. Warren was in the business of buying grain from farmers and then reselling that grain on the market or directly to grain companies. Cargill, Inc., financed the operations of Warren (i.e., Cargill loaned the elevator money with which to operate) and also bought substantial amounts of grain from Warren. As Warren's debt to Cargill increased, Cargill exercised more and more control over Warren's operations.

Warren's owners diverted large amounts of the company's money to their personal ends, and Warren's business eventually collapsed. At the time of the collapse, Warren owed $2 million to farmers who had sold grain to Warren but had not been paid. Warren also owed $3.6 million to Cargill.

The farmers sought to recover their $2 million from Cargill, contending that: (i) Warren was Cargill's agent; and (ii) Cargill, as principal, was liable on any grain contracts made by its agent. The jury, the trial judge, and the Minnesota Supreme Court all agreed.

Although *Cargill* quoted and purported to apply both R.2d, §1 and R.2d, §14 O, the decision turns on the latter. Comment *a* to §14 O states in part:

> A security holder who . . . takes over the management of the debtor's business . . . and directs what contracts may or may not be made . . . becomes a principal, liable as any principal for the obligations incurred thereafter in the normal course of business by the debtor who has now become his general

---

21. By its terms the proxy will likely be automatically revoked when the underlying debt is paid.
22. E.g., West's Ann. Cal. Corp. Code §705(e); McKinney's Business Corporation Law §609(f).
23. *A. Gay Jenson Farms Co. v. Cargill, Inc.*, 309 N.W.2d 285 (Minn. 1981).
24. The term "constructive agency" is the author's.

> agent. The point at which the creditor becomes a principal is that at which he assumes de facto control over the conduct of his debtor, whatever the terms of the formal contract with his debtor may be.

The *Cargill* decision held that Cargill had indeed taken over the management of the debtor's business and had consequently become liable as a principal for Warren's debts to the farmer plaintiffs.

The R.3d contains no analog to R.2d, §14 O, and dismisses *Cargill* as "[a]n unusual example . . . contrary" to the well-established proposition that "[c]ontrol, however defined, is by itself insufficient to establish agency."[25] However, the case remains a favorite of casebook editors and provides a useful lesson in distinguishing true agency from other relationships.

§6.3.2 *Cargill*: Conceptual Confusions and Practical Concerns

The *Cargill* case is troubling both conceptually and practically. The court tries to justify its decision under R.2d, §1, as well as under §14 O, and thereby confuses constructive agency with true agency. Practically, the decision is dangerous for any creditor that eschews immediate foreclosure of a problem loan and tries instead to guide its debtor through a workout.[26]

a. Constructive Versus Genuine Agency

Cargill is confusing because it misunderstands the relationship between R.2d §§1 and 14 O. Although both sections concern agency creation, they apply to quite different situations and state different and even inconsistent rules.

For an agency to exist under R.2d, §1, the principal must manifest consent for the agent to act on the principal's behalf, and the agent must manifest consent to do so. R.2d, §15 states that "an agency relation can exist *only*" under such circumstances.[27] Yet R.2d, §14 O also establishes agency status and nowhere mentions consent. Instead, §14 O focuses exclusively on control.

---

25. R.3d, §1.01, Reporter's Notes to comment (f)(1) ("In the debtor-creditor context, most courts are reluctant to find relationships of agency on the basis of provisions in agreements that protect the creditor's interests.").

26. When a debtor has difficulty paying its major lender, the lender can typically demand immediate payment of the full amount due, foreclose on any collateral, and put the debtor out of business. However, with that approach lenders rarely recover the full amount owed. Lenders therefore often try to help the debtor work its way out of its financial difficulties. Hence the term *workout*.

27. Emphasis added. Although, as stated in Section 6.3.1, the R.3d has no analog to R.2d, §14 O, R.3d, §§1.01 and 1.02 combine to reiterate the point made by R.2d, §15.

The inconsistency exists because the R.2d uses the same label ("agency") to describe two different kinds of situations:

1. "garden-variety" situations, in which the parties act in a manner that reasonably suggests they intend to establish the consensual and fiduciary relationship of true agency; and
2. extraordinary situations, in which for policy reasons the law wishes to treat creditors and debtors *as if* they had manifested consent to the garden variety of agency.

The situations share a key consequence[28]—the principal's liability on contracts made by the agent—but the criteria that trigger the consequence are fundamentally different. For the garden-variety situation, mutual consent; for the extraordinary situation, overbearing control.[29]

The rationales underlying the rules are likewise different. With a true agent, acting within its actual authority, liability arises at least in part from consent. In the extraordinary, §14 O situation, liability arises for reasons akin to the rationale for inherent agency power. That is, liability follows control, because (i) those who exercise control have the ability to avoid harm and should therefore be liable when avoidable harm occurs and (ii) when an undertaking causes harm to others, the cost of that harm should be borne by those who stand to benefit from the undertaking, and typically it is those in control who stand to benefit.

The *Cargill* decision concerns an extraordinary situation, and the opinion becomes confusing when it seeks to apply aspects of the garden-variety rule (manifestation of consent; fiduciary relationship) as well as the extraordinary rule (exercise of control). Referring, for instance, to the *principal's* manifestation of consent, *Cargill* states, "By directing Warren to implement its recommendations, Cargill manifested consent that Warren would be its agent."[30]

This assertion seems to equate control with consent. If party *A* controls party B, then through that control *A* manifests consent that B act for *A in dealing with third parties*. Although such an inference may sometimes be reasonable, it is not necessarily so. For example, a department store may control in detail the work assignments of a custodian without consenting to the custodian placing orders with dress manufacturers.

28. In the extraordinary situation, the agency label does not produce all of the consequences that attend that label in the garden-variety situation. For example, §14 O the debtor, as agent, owes a fiduciary duty to its principal, the creditor.
29. The control is "overbearing" in the sense that the creditor "takes over the management of the debtor's business." R.2d, §14 O, comment *a*.
30. 309 N.W.2d at 291.

Equally troubling is the decision's treatment of the *agent's* manifestation of consent. In this respect, the question is whether Warren manifested consent to place Cargill's interests above its own; that is, consented that the primary purpose of the relationship was to serve Cargill rather than Warren. The *Cargill* court never mentions any direct evidence on this point. Instead, the decision states: "Cargill did not think of Warren as a operator who was free to become Cargill's competitor, but rather conceded that it believed that Warren owed a duty of loyalty to Cargill."[31]

The logic here is flawed. An agent's duty of loyalty includes the duty not to compete, but an agreement not to compete does not by itself establish either a full-fledged duty of loyalty or a fiduciary relationship. A party's agreement to defer to another party's interest in one specific area neither constitutes nor implies an agreement to defer to that other party's interest throughout the relationship. In particular, noncompete agreements occur in many arm's-length relationships.

The *Cargill* decision would have been considerably clearer if the court had simply stated, "This situation warrants constructive agency analysis. Therefore, R.2d, §14 O applies, and therefore R.2d, §1, with its garden-variety criteria for establishing true agency, is irrelevant."

b. Dangers for Workouts

In applying R.2d, §14 O, the *Cargill* court noted a number of factors that evidenced Cargill's control over Warren. The court acknowledged that many of these same factors appear in ordinary debtor-creditor transactions, but assured the banking community that ordinary delinquent loans were not destined to turn into principal-agent relationships.

To support its assurances, the court noted the following differences between the Warren-Cargill relationship and an ordinary lending situation: (i) Cargill aggressively financed Warren; (ii) Cargill "was an active participant in Warren's operations rather than simply a financier"; (iii) Cargill's relationship with Warren was "paternalistic"; and (iv) Cargill's purpose, in lending money to Warren, "was not to make money as a lender but rather to establish a source of market grain for its business."[32]

Of the four distinctions noted by the court, the first three (aggressive financing, involvement in the debtor's operations, a "paternalistic" attitude) occur in most workouts. The fourth purported distinction—that Cargill was really "in it" not for the interest but rather to obtain a supply of grain—is irrelevant under §14 O. That provision makes no reference at all to the creditor's purpose in becoming a creditor.

31. 309 N.W.2d at 292.
32. 309 N.W.2d at 292–293.

Moreover, there are many lending relationships in which the lender seeks more than interest payments. A company like GMAC, for example, lends money to General Motors car dealers in part to allow them to buy cars from GM, and lends money to the dealers' customers in order to allow them to buy GM cars from the GM dealers. Is GMAC in it just for the interest, or does GMAC have the ulterior motive of increasing the marketability of GM cars?

In sum, the *Cargill* court's attempt to distinguish the Cargill-Warren situation from normal debtor-creditor relationships is unpersuasive. For lenders considering workouts, the case is a cautionary tale.[33]

Problem 52

A homebuyer ("Would-Be") contacts a real estate broker ("Broker") and solicits her assistance in locating a suitable property. Would-Be seeks a modern, upscale house with enough land to allow the installation of a swimming pool. Over the next two months, Broker calls Would-Be frequently to discuss possible purchases, and occasionally goes with Would-Be to view properties. Eventually, Broker locates a house that Would-Be decides to purchase. As Would-Be contemplates making the purchase, Broker explains, "My fee comes from the seller. It's no big deal. That's the way we do it. So you can figure out the price you're willing to pay without worrying about a commission."

Would-Be makes the purchase and subsequently discovers that his neighbors will raise zoning law objections to any pool. He also learns that the lower portion of his land is subject to flooding during the early spring. He sues Broker for not having informed him of these problems.

Assume that:

- Broker never thought of herself as Would-Be's agent, and never intended to act on Would-Be's behalf. She saw herself as acting at "arm's length" from him.

---

33. Although any informed attorney representing lenders will think about *Cargill*, few other reported cases have taken the *Cargill* approach. Only a handful of reported decisions have discussed R.2d, §14 O. Only one affirmed recovery for the plaintiff, and another reversed summary judgment for the defendant. One case, *Buck v. Nash-Finch Co.*, 102 N.W.2d 84 (S.D. 1960), acknowledged that a major creditor had controlled substantial portions of the debtor's operations, but denied recovery because the major creditor had not controlled the particular area of operations that gave rise to the plaintiff's claim. Contrast Section 3.2.5(d) (*respondeat superior* liability attaches to servant's scope of employment not to master's zone of control). Another case held that section 14 O imposed liability only when the controlling creditor had engaged in wrongdoing. Mere control was insufficient. *Lubrizol Corp. v. Cardinal Construction Co.*, 868 F.2d 767 (5th Cir. 1989).

- Would-Be, in contrast, believed all along that Broker was "on my side, looking out for my interests."
- When Would-Be expressed serious interest in the house he eventually purchased, Broker contacted the seller and arranged to act as the seller's agent in the transaction.
- Other than her comment about the seller paying her fees, Broker never explained to Would-Be Broker's view of Broker's relationship to Would-Be. Broker never disclosed that Broker was acting as the seller's agent.
- Broker's view of the relationship is consistent with the way real estate brokers in the locality ordinarily approach similar matters.
- Broker knew that the neighbors would probably object to the building of a pool, but never mentioned anything about that problem to Would-Be.
- Broker did not know about the flooding, but could have discovered the problem through the exercise of ordinary care.
- Broker never made any representations to Would-Be concerning the pool or the flooding.
- There are no statutes or government regulations relevant to this situation.[34]

Can Would-Be recover from Broker? ◄ ◄ ◄

Explanation

Since Broker made no representations about the pool or the flooding, Would-Be can recover from Broker only if he can establish that Broker had an affirmative duty to disclose. Moreover, as to the flooding problem, Would-Be will also have to establish that Broker had a duty to inquire.

Both duties existed if Broker was acting as Would-Be's agent.[35] To establish that agency relationship, Would-Be must show: (i) some manifestation from him that, reasonably interpreted, indicated his desire to have Broker act on his behalf; and (ii) some manifestation from Broker that, reasonably interpreted, indicated Broker's "consent . . . to so act."[36] The first showing is easy: Would-Be expressly and specifically solicited Broker's assistance. As for Broker's manifestation, her two months of effort certainly suffice.

Broker's subjective view of the situation is irrelevant. What matters is the reasonableness of Would-Be's interpretation, and on that point the evidence is mixed. The local custom *as known to brokers* may weigh against

34. Many jurisdictions now have statutes or regulations governing this type of situation.
35. See Sections 4.1.5 (agent's duty to disclose information that agent knows or should know is of interest to the principal) and 4.1.4 (Duty of Care).
36. R.2d, §1.

reasonableness, but reasonableness is determined from the perspective of an ordinarily prudent person *in the position of the principal*. The facts do not indicate whether the brokers' custom is generally known and understood by ordinary homebuyers.

The payment arrangement may also weigh against reasonableness. If Broker was looking out for Would-Be's interests, why would someone else—especially the adverse party—be paying the fee? Although with the principal's consent an agent may receive compensation from a third party, arguably the circumstances were unusual enough to prompt a reasonable person to inquire.

Despite this negative evidence, Would-Be may still prevail by pointing to Broker's conduct as a whole. Would-Be sought out Broker and asked for her assistance. For two months Broker provided that assistance without once indicating her arm's-length attitude. Moreover, when—at the crucial moment—Broker pledged allegiance to the adverse party, she failed to warn or even advise Would-Be. To the contrary, she induced his continuing trust by treating the fee question as "no big deal." Taking all these circumstances together, perhaps it was reasonable for Would-Be to believe that Broker had agreed to act on his behalf.

If so, Broker was acting as Would-Be's agent and was subject to duties of disclosure and due care. Broker would therefore be liable for damages suffered by Would-Be due to Broker's failure to disclose the zoning difficulty and for her failure to discover and disclose the flooding problem.[37] ◀◀◀

Problem 53

Tim buys a new truck from a local car dealer. The dealer purchases its truck inventory from the manufacturer under a dealership agreement. That agreement: (i) states that the dealer is an independent contractor and not the agent of the manufacturer; (ii) acknowledges that the dealer, not the manufacturer, controls the management of the dealer's business; (iii) describes the six-year warranty that the manufacturer extends to customers who purchase the manufacturer's trucks through the manufacturer's network of dealers; (iv) obligates the dealer to provide service under the manufacturer's warranties at no charge to the customers; and (v) provides that the dealer will bill the manufacturer for this warranty service at specified rates. Each new truck comes with an owner's manual that describes the manufacturer's warranty and directs customers to have warranty service performed at any of the manufacturer's authorized dealers.

37. Note that, if Broker was acting as Would-Be's agent, she has a "dual agency" problem. See Section 4.1.1(c)(4) (No Acting for Others with Conflicting Interests).

Tim is quite happy with his purchase for the first week. Then a problem develops in the truck's steering. Tim immediately notifies the dealer and brings the truck in for repair. Over the next two years, the truck has a series of problems with its steering mechanism. Each time a problem occurs, Tim brings the truck back to the dealer, and the dealer attempts to fix the problem. Each time the dealer assures Tim that "this is under warranty" and there is no charge. After two years, however, Tim has had enough. He decides to sue the dealer for breach of warranty and wishes also to sue the manufacturer.

Under the jurisdiction's version of the Uniform Commercial Code, a remote buyer (such as Tim) can bring a breach of warranty claim against the remote seller (such as the manufacturer) if the remote buyer has given timely notice of the defect to the remote seller or the remote seller has knowledge of the defect.[38] Tim has told the dealer of the problems as they have occurred, so the dealer has known of the defect since one week after the sale. Tim has never informed the manufacturer, however. Under the jurisdiction's case law, it is now too late to first notify the manufacturer. May Tim nonetheless bring a warranty claim against the manufacturer? ◄◄◄

Explanation

EXPLANATION

To preserve his claim against the manufacturer, Tim must show that his notice to the dealer suffices as notice to the manufacturer. To do that, he must use the attribution rules of agency law.

The agreement between the manufacturer and dealership expressly disclaims agency status, but the parties' actual relationship belies their words, at least with regard to the manufacturer's warranty program. Through its customer warranty, the manufacturer undertook to provide services to Tim. Through its dealership agreement, the manufacturer manifested consent for the dealer to provide those services on the manufacturer's behalf and the dealer manifested consent to do so. For the purposes of providing warranty service, the dealer is indeed the manufacturer's agent.

Under this agency relationship, the dealer may have implied actual authority to receive notices of defects on the manufacturer's behalf. Implied actual authority exists as acts "which are incidental to . . . , usually accompany, . . . or are reasonably necessary to accomplish" expressly authorized acts,[39] and a customer typically invokes the manufacturer's warranty (and

38. See Uniform Commercial Code §2–318 (third-party beneficiaries of warranties) and §2–607(3)(a) (buyer must give timely notice of breach or be barred from remedy) and comment 5 (requirement of timely notice applies to remote buyer making third-party beneficiary claim).

39. R.2d, §35. See Section 2.2.4. Moreover, auto dealers customarily have a contractual duty (and therefore actual authority) to report all warranty claims to the manufacturer.

triggers the dealer's expressly authorized act) by communicating with the dealer. Notice received within an agent's actual authority (express or implied) binds the principal.

Even if the dealer is not authorized to receive notice on the manufacturer's behalf, the dealer's knowledge of the defect binds the manufacturer. The defect information certainly concerns a matter within the dealer's actual authority and is therefore attributed to the principal.[40] ◀ ◀ ◀

Problem 54

Fred Hornet ("Hornet") is a midlevel manager at Commerce Bank whose responsibilities include evaluating applicants for business loans. For the past several years, Hornet has been trying to persuade the Loan Committee (a committee of five senior managers that must approve any business loan) to take a more accommodating attitude toward loan applications from female- and minority-owned start-up businesses. The discussion has proceeded through several stages, with the key points being roughly as follows:

Hornet: Our regular evaluation criteria make it highly unlikely that we will approve loan applications from minority-owned or female-owned businesses. We put a lot of weight on whether the key people in the new business have any significant prior entrepreneurial experience. It's a matter of history that, for women and minorities, access to that type of experience has been far more difficult to obtain. It's important morally, and for the social stability of our country, that we increase the access. As a practical matter, that access depends fundamentally on being able to borrow money. The way we're going now, though, it's a vicious circle. Can't borrow the money because not enough experience. Can't get experience running a small business because can't borrow any money to get one started. This bank quite rightfully prides itself on being "a good corporate citizen." To live up to our own ideals we need to relax our emphasis on prior entrepreneurial experience.

Loan Committee: We're with you in spirit, but we also have a responsibility to our stockholders and our depositors not to be careless in

40. See Section 2.4.4. Tim might also assert that the dealer has apparent authority to receive notices for the manufacturer. This argument seems weaker than the actual authority arguments, because Tim can point to only two relevant manifestations of the principal: the appointment of the dealer as an authorized seller of the manufacturer's trucks and the direction in the owner's manual that customers have warranty work done at the manufacturer's authorized dealers. From these manifestations it is reasonable to believe that the dealer is authorized to act for the manufacturer in providing warranty service, but not necessarily that the dealer is authorized to accept pre-suit notices on the manufacturer's behalf.

lending money. We have found that a lack of "prior entrepreneurial experience" tends to increase the likelihood of a loan going bad. What can you suggest to offset the increased risk?

Hornet: First, more rigorous attention to the application process—the applicant's proposed business plan, for instance. But, more importantly, I suggest an increased commitment at the bank to keeping an eye on these businesses. If we think that trouble is developing, we'll get in and work with the people—provide them advice, make sure they're using sensible business practices. In other words, if we find out that a lack of entrepreneurial experience is beginning to cost them (and threatening their ability to pay us back), we'll temporarily roll up our sleeves and help provide them the expertise that comes with experience. I realize that this approach involves an extra commitment of resources, but I think it's worth it.

Loan Committee: What if the borrowers don't want our help?

Hornet: I think for this program to work we have to be up front with the people, and tell them when they apply what might happen if things go sour later on. Also, we have to choose to lend to people whom we think will be willing to take help. Finally, under our standard loan agreements, if push comes to shove, we have the right to take control.

The Loan Committee is just about convinced to give Hornet's approach a try. Assume that they turn to you, as the Bank's lawyer, and ask, "Are there any legal wrinkles?" Advise them by: (i) identifying and explaining any agency-related legal risks involved in Hornet's proposal;[41] and (ii) suggesting changes in the proposal that will decrease those risks without sacrificing the business objectives. ◀ ◀ ◀

Explanation

Cargill and R.2d, §14 O appear to create a Hobson's choice for the bank. Measures designed to meet the bank's business needs seem destined to increase the bank's legal risk. Moreover, the legal risks will be most substantial just when the business needs are the most intense. The bank is most likely to exert control when a borrower has fallen behind in its loan payments. At that juncture, the borrower is likely also to be falling behind in its obligations to other creditors. Exerting control will create a *Cargill* claim, and the other obligations will constitute the damages.

41. Whether a borrower could successfully assert a "lender liability" claim is not a question of agency law and is far beyond the scope of this book.

The solution to this conundrum lies in analyzing Hornet's proposal and separating, as follows, the tactical objective, the tactics proposed to achieve that objective, and the rationale that links those tactics to that objective:

- *Tactical objective:* Increase the quality of the borrower's management, especially at times of financial distress.[42]
- *Rationale:* All other things being equal, inexperienced management is likely to be less effective than experienced management. A firm, experienced hand is especially necessary when a business is trying to "work out" from under financial difficulties.
- *Tactics:* Empower the bank to be that firm, experienced hand.

This analysis indicates the source of the legal risks within Hornet's proposal and thereby suggests a way to reduce those risks. R.2d, §14 O problems arise from control, and within Hornet's proposal the only flavor of control comes from the proposed tactics. Taking the tactical objective and the rationale as given,[43] the lawyer's challenge is to find substitute tactics that lack that flavor. In other words, to find another firm, experienced hand.

For example, the loan agreement might require the borrower to designate an experienced business consultant, acceptable to the Bank, to advise the borrower on an ongoing basis, and temporarily turn over management of the business to that consultant (or some other independent business expert chosen by the Bank), if: (i) the borrower falls behind in its loan payments or gives the Bank other reasonable grounds for insecurity; and (ii) the Bank elects to require the management change. These arrangements would of course require the agreement of the specified consultant, but that agreement could be obtained in advance. The loan agreement could also provide mechanisms for choosing replacements in case the designated individual or company become unable or unwilling to serve.

In all events, it would be essential for the consultant to remain independent of the Bank. If the Bank controls the consultant, the consultant could be deemed the Bank's agent and *Cargill* could then apply. (Agency law would attribute the consultant's conduct to Bank.)

The loan agreement should therefore provide that the consultant will: (i) work for and be paid by the borrower, not the Bank; and (ii) have a duty to serve the best interests of the borrower, not the Bank. It should also provide that the Bank will have no right to control the advice given or

42. The tactical objective is intended to make possible the pursuit of another objective—increasing the bank's lending to minority- and female-owned businesses.

43. It might be possible to propose additional options for the Bank by challenging the rationale. That approach is not pursued here, however, because that kind of analysis presupposes considerable familiarity with the way businesses function.

the decisions made by the consultant. The rationale and importance of these provisions should be explained to those Bank employees who deal with the borrower, so that the Bank's conduct (through those employees) conforms to these restrictions.

This structure is admittedly more cumbersome than Hornet's proposal and certainly provides less direct control for the Bank. The structure's virtue is that it significantly reduces the Bank's legal exposure while still serving the basic tactical objective of Hornet's plan.[44] ◄ ◄ ◄

44. This approach will not work, however, if the Bank's objectives include causing the borrower to prefer the Bank's claims over the claims of other creditors. If that is an objective, *Cargill* exposure is probably appropriate. Moreover, if the borrower or its creditor invoke bankruptcy law, the preference will be voidable. 11 U.S. Code §547(b).

CHAPTER 7

Introductory Concepts in the Law of General Partnerships

§7.1 THE ROLE, STRUCTURE, AND RELATIONSHIP OF UNIFORM PARTNERSHIP ACT (1914), UNIFORM PARTNERSHIP ACT (1997), AND UNIFORM PARTNERSHIP ACT (2013)

§7.1.1 General Partnership: Creature of Contract and of Statute

A general partnership is a creature both of contract and of statute,[1] but, unlike other business organizations, a general partnership is not created by filing a public document pursuant to an "organic" statute.[2] Instead, a general partnership arises when two or more persons manifest an intention to associate as co-owners in a business for profit. Their manifestations—whether

1. U.S. law encompasses two forms of partnership: general partnerships and limited partnerships. Each of these forms has a version with a corporate-like liability shield for the owners: in the case of a general partnership, a limited liability partnership (LLP); in the case of a limited partnership, a limited liability limited partnership (LLLP). Whenever this book uses the term "partnership" by itself, the term refers to a general partnership without a liability shield. For a discussion of limited partnerships, see Chapter 12. For a discussion of LLPs and LLLPs, see Chapter 17.

2. In the modern parlance of business entity law, an "organic" statute is a statute under which a business entity is created and whose provisions govern the internal relationships ("internal affairs") of those who own and operate the business entity.

by word or conduct or both—create what is essentially a contract between or among them.[3]

Some general partnerships have detailed written partnership agreements, while many other general partnerships have no written agreement at all. Regardless, one fundamental aspect of a general partnership is the contract-based relationship among the partners.

Another, equally fundamental aspect is the statutory context in which such contracts arise and exist. In every state, a partnership statute provides that context by:

- determining whether a partnership exists;
- governing the relationship of the partnership and its partners with outsiders;
- governing—largely subject to the partnership agreement—the relationship among the partners and between the partners and the partnership; and
- determining when a partnership ceases to exist and what then happens to the partners' interests, the partnership's assets, and the partnership's liabilities.

§7.1.2 History and Prevalence of UPA (1914); Advent of RUPA (UPA (1997)); Creation of UPA (2013)

For almost all the twentieth century, UPA (1914) was the backbone of partnership law in the United States. Promulgated in 1914 by the ULC, UPA (1914) was adopted in 49 states.[4]

In 1992 the ULC adopted a new uniform partnership act, which had some initial difficulties. The ULC made changes to the act in 1993, approved the revised version in 1994, and made further revisions in 1996 and 1997. The earlier versions have mostly historical interest, and this book refers to the 1997 version—i.e., UPA (1997).[5] UPA (1997) is in many ways a major improvement over UPA (1914), although some the 1997 act's provisions have been controversial, especially those relating to fiduciary duty.[6] In any

---

3. It is not necessary that the participants intend to be partners. See Section 7.2.1.
4. Louisiana was the lone holdout. The District of Columbia, Guam, and the Virgin Islands also adopted UPA (1914). Some states adopted nonuniform provisions.
5. Almost all practitioners and commentators have thought of the act—whether in version 1992, 1994, 1996, or 1997—as the Revised Uniform Partnership Act and have referred to the act by its acronym "RUPA." The promulgation of UPA (2013) makes the adjective "revised" ambiguous, so this book refers to UPA (1997) or UPA (2013), as appropriate.
6. See Section 9.7.2.

event, UPA (1997) is far more detailed and longer than UPA (1914),[7] and any UPA (1997) neophyte must invest time to assimilate the act's architecture and understand how its many sections interrelate.

Despite its complexity, UPA (1997) gradually became the dominant general partnership statute in the United States, with only a handful of holdouts. For currency's sake, this book refers principally to UPA (2013), invoking the UPA (1997) version in addition where the Harmonization Project made an important substantive change or where discussing the 1997 version helps explicate the 2013 version. The phrases "the modern acts" or "the two modern acts" both refer to the 1997 and 2013 versions. The phrase "all three acts" refers to all three versions.

Although this book describes many statutory provisions in detail and analyzes many in depth, *no secondary source can ever replace your own careful reading of a statute*. Each time you consider a section of this book that deals with a statutory section, you should compare this book's analysis with the statute's actual language.

§7.1.3 The Role of Case Law

Case law is also extremely important in the law of partnerships, perhaps more than one might expect in a field covered by apparently comprehensive statutes. This phenomenon has several interrelated causes:

- All three acts rely on judge-made law to fill statutory gaps. For example, UPA (2013), section 119 states: "Unless displaced by particular provisions of this [act], the principles of law and equity supplement this [act]."
- UPA (1914) has some substantial gaps, and judge-made law has filled those gaps—especially gaps concerning fiduciary duty.[8] In addition, a few UPA (1914) provisions are so vague or recondite as to have necessitated judicial clarification. Both modern acts are also subject to judicial interpretation.
- UPA (1997) was drafted against the backdrop of UPA (1914)-related case law, which is therefore important to understanding many provisions of both modern acts.

---

7. The text of UPA (1997) was approximately 25 percent longer than the text of UPA (1914), but that comparison is only half of the story. Both UPA (1914) and UPA (1997) contain official Comments, but the Comments to UPA (1914) are scant while the Comments to UPA (1997) are copious. The comments to UPA (2013) are also copious.
8. See Section 9.7.2.

In all three acts, most of the provisions are "default" rules, which can be displaced by agreement.[9] Numerous cases consider the existence and effect of such agreements.

§7.1.4 Flexibility: Default Rules and Agreements Among Partners

a. *Inter Se* and Third-Party Rules

The rules of all three acts can be divided into two categories:

- those that govern the relationship among the partners (*inter se* rules)
- those that govern the relationship between the partnership (and its partners) with outsiders (third-party rules)

These categories carry an important practical distinction. *Inter se* rules are almost entirely "default" rules, applicable only in the absence of a contrary agreement among the partners. Such an agreement may be express or implied, written or oral.[10]

As a matter both of partnership and contract law, *adopting* a partnership agreement always requires unanimity. Therefore, to the extent the default rules are to be changed by the initial partnership agreement, unanimous consent is required. However, a partnership agreement can provide for its own amendment on a less-than-unanimous basis (e.g., majority vote of the partners). With such a provision in place, subsequent changes to the default rules can be accomplished with less-than-unanimous consent.

In contrast, third-party rules are mandatory rules. An agreement among the partners cannot change them.[11]

---

9. For a more detailed discussion of this point, see Section 7.1.4.

10. See UPA (2013) §102(12) (defining "partnership agreement" to mean "the agreement, whether or not referred to as a partnership agreement and whether oral, implied, in a record, or in any combination thereof, of all the partners of a partnership"). For a discussion of *inter se* rules that are not default rules, see Section 7.14(b). Courts are divided as to whether the statute of frauds applies to an undertaking within a partnership agreement that would be subject to the statute if the agreement were outside the partnership context. Most of the controversy involves undertakings that concern a person becoming a partner; for example, an oral agreement to contribute land to the partnership in return for becoming a partner, or an oral promise that a person will become a partner after performing specified services that cannot be accomplished within one year of the making of the promise. For a more detailed analysis, see UPA (2013) §102(12), cmt.

11. As a matter of contract law, a third party may agree with a partnership or a partner to waive rights created under one of the mandatory, third-party rules.

Figure 7.1. Default and Mandatory Rules

Most Rules Governing *Inter Se* Relationships	Rules Governing Relationships with Third Parties
"Default rules" can be changed by agreements among partners	"Mandatory rules" cannot be changed by agreements among partners (third-party consent is necessary)
Examples:	**Examples:**
UPA (2013) §401(b); UPA (1914) §18(a) *partners share profits equally*	UPA (2013) §301; UPA (1914) §9(1) *partner has power to bind partnership through apparently usual acts*
UPA (2013) §401(f); UPA (1914) §18(e) *partners have equal rights to manage partnership and its business*	UPA (2013) §305; UPA (1914) §13 *partner's wrongful act in the ordinary course binds the partnership*

Under all three acts, the default rules comprise a basic operating system for partners who do not want to spend the time and money to develop their own "rules of the game."[12] But partners who wish to deviate from the default structure may tailor their relationship almost entirely as they see fit. This great flexibility reflects partnership law's respect for, and dependence on, the agreement among the partners.

b. *Inter Se* Rules That Are Mandatory (Non-Variable)

The special tailoring does have some limits. Deviating too far from the default rules may negate the existence of a partnership. For example, if an agreement labels a person a partner but denies that person any share in the profits, that person would not be a partner.[13] In addition, rules dealing with partner-to-partner fiduciary duties can be shaped by agreement, but not abrogated.[14]

Under UPA (1914), limitations on the power of the partnership agreement are mostly a matter of case law.[15] The modern acts, in contrast, devote major attention to the question. For example, UPA (2013) section 105 states

12. Indeed, those who become partners by inadvertence are stuck with those rules wholesale, at least initially. (Formation of a partnership requires no special formalities, and may occur even though the participants in a business relationship are unaware that the law labels their arrangement a partnership. See Section 7.2.2.)

13. See Section 7.2.3. However, if a third party knew of the label, the person might be liable to that third party *as* if a partner. See Section 7.5 (Partnership by Estoppel).

14. See Section 9.8.1.

15. UPA (1914) does contain a few statutory limitations. For example, under UPA §31(2) the partnership simply cannot prevent a partner from wrongfully causing the dissolution of the partnership by "express will." See Sections 11.2.1 and 11.6.

that, as a general rule, "the partnership agreement governs: (1) relations among the partners as partners and between the partners and the partnership; (2) the business of the partnership and the conduct of that business; and (3) the means and conditions for amending the partnership agreement." This general rule is subject to a list of specific exceptions—most notably constraints on the partnership agreement's power to (i) reshape the fiduciary duties that partners owe each other and the partnership and (ii) limit the power of partners to "dissociate" themselves from the partnership.[16] Section 105 also states that, as to relations among the partners and the partnership, "[t]o the extent the partnership agreement does not provide for a matter described in subsection (a), this [act] governs the matter."[17]

In any event, under all three acts, partnership agreements have broad latitude. Flexibility in structuring *inter se* relationships is a prime attraction of the partnership form.

§7.2 PARTNERSHIP DESCRIBED

§7.2.1 Key Characteristics

Partnership is the label that the law applies to a particular kind of business relationship. In the words of UPA (1914), "A partnership is an association of two or more persons to carry on as co-owners a business for profit."[18] UPA (2013) provides, "the association of two or more persons to carry on as co-owners a business for profit forms a partnership, whether or not the persons intend to form a partnership."[19]

The paradigmatic partnership is:

- an unincorporated[20] business, intended to make a profit,
- that has two or more participants, who may be either individuals or entities,
- each of whom "brings something to the party," such as efforts, ideas, money, property, or some combination,

16. UPA (2013) §§105(c) and (d); 106. For a more specific discussion of these constraints, see Sections 9.8.1 (limits on agreements) and 11.8.2 (Dissociation Described).
17. UPA (2013) §105(b).
18. UPA §6(1).
19. UPA (2013) §202(a). As discussed in Chapter 12, the law also recognizes a different type of partnership—a "limited partnership." When used alone, "partnership" most often refers to a general partnership.
20. A business that complies with the formalities necessary to become a corporation, limited liability company, or limited partnership cannot be a general partnership, even if in every other respect the business matches the key characteristics of a partnership.

- each of whom co-owns the business (not the assets of the business),[21]
- each of whom has a right (subject to the partnership agreement) to co-manage the business, and
- each of whom has a right to share in the profits of the business (if any).

Partnerships appear in a wide variety of forms and engage in a wide variety of businesses. Some partnerships have only two partners; others have hundreds.[22] Some partnerships are based on complicated partnership agreements. Others arise from a handshake or a course of conduct. Many small retail establishments are partnerships, as are many businesses that own real estate. At one time, lawyers wishing to combine their efforts and share profits had no choice but to form partnerships.[23]

Creating a general partnership involves no special formalities. There are no magic words that must be said or documents that need be signed or filed. If a business structure has the essential characteristics of a partnership and has not followed the formalities necessary to be a limited partnership, corporation, or limited liability company (LLC), then the business *is* a general partnership.

§7.2.2 The Consent Characteristic

All versions of the general partnership acts refer to a partnership as "an association."[24] That term connotes voluntariness, and the law has always considered a partnership to be a consensual relationship. For a partnership to exist, there must be a business relationship whose participants manifest an intention to have the kind of arrangement that the law calls a partnership.[25] The participants must agree to that arrangement, either expressly or by their conduct.

It is not necessary, however, that the participants intend or agree to the *legal label* of partnership. A partnership can exist even though the participants have no idea that the legal label applies to them. Indeed, a partnership can

21. See Sections 7.4.3 and 8.7.
22. Partnerships with large numbers of partners are not typical. Unless the partnership is a limited liability partnership ("LLP") (see Section 17.2), partners are personally liable for the debts of the partnership. See Section 7.3. Regardless of LLP status, the partnership is liable for the misconduct of its partners. See Chapter 10. The larger the number of partners, the greater is this risk of vicarious liability. Also, UPA (1914) partnerships are susceptible to dissolution (which requires the business of the partnership to be "wound up"), and increasing the number of partners increases the problems inherent in that susceptibility. See Chapter 11.
23. See Section 7.3.2 (restrictions on business forms available to professionals).
24. UPA §6(1); UPA (1997) §202(a); UPA (2013) §202(a).
25. Because a partnership is essentially a contractual relationship, the "intent" at issue is objective rather than subjective.

exist among participants who have expressly disclaimed the partnership label.[26]

Example

Sid has fallen on hard times. He receives the following letter from his brother, Jules:

Dear Sid,

I am sorry to hear that you've lost your job. Things are very tight here; otherwise, I'd be happy to send you some money to tide you over.

I do have another idea, though. You know that land I own up by the lake? I think it would make a good resort, if I could just get some cabins built on it. If you'd be willing to move up there with your family and build the cabins, I would pay for all the materials, and for food and necessities for you and your family. I couldn't afford to pay you any wages, but once we got the resort up and running I'd give you half of the profits for the first five years.

Let me know how you feel about this.

/s/Jules ◄◄◄

Sid's letter may be the blueprint of a partnership.

Example

Caesar lends money to Julio, who personally owns a company that produces and markets cheese. The loan agreement provides that, until the money is repaid, Caesar (i) will receive a share of the company's profits in lieu of interest, (ii) may have the marketing rights for 50 percent of the company's output, and (iii) may have his own accountant check the company's finances weekly and approve any payments to be made by the company in excess of $10,000. The loan agreement also expressly states that Caesar and Julio are not partners in the cheese company but rather are creditor and debtor. Nonetheless, a court may find that a partnership exists.[27] ◄◄◄

When making such a finding, courts sometimes use the label "de facto partnership"; but however labeled, partnerships that arise inadvertently are likely to be problematic. The parties will have created a legal relationship without having thought about, much less worked through, key business issues. At least initially, statutory default rules will govern their relationship,[28] but those rules may fail to match the deal the parties would have

---

26. UPA (2013) makes this point explicitly. See §202(a), quoted in Section 7.2.1.

27. The parties' self-description is not necessarily useless. The parties' label can be influential in "close call" situations. See Section 7.4.3.

28. As explained in Section 7.1.4, the partners can displace the default rules, but they can do so only by agreement.

made for themselves. In any event, the applicability of those rules will come as quite a surprise.

When a partnership arises despite an express disclaimer, there is another unpleasant consequence. Disputing the disclaimer is worthwhile only when money is at stake, so in these situations the label "partner" is invariably costly. For instance, in the Example above concerning the cheese company, if Caesar is determined a partner of Julio, then Caesar will be personally liable for the cheese company's debts.[29]

§7.2.3 The Profit-Sharing Prerequisite

For participants in a business to be partners, they must have the right to share in the business's profits. It is not necessary that the business actually makes a profit, and profit sharing is not irrefutable evidence of partner status.[30] However, the right to share whatever profits exist is a necessary precondition to being a partner. In logical terms, a right to share profits is necessary but not sufficient to establish partner status.[31]

Example

Carolyn opens an art supply store in a building she rents from Sylvia. As part of her rent, Carolyn pays Sylvia 30 percent of Carolyn's monthly revenues. No matter what other indicia of partnership are present, Carolyn and Sylvia cannot be partners. They do not share profits. ◀ ◀ ◀

Since sharing in revenues does not satisfy the profit-sharing prerequisite, it is important to understand the difference between profit sharing and revenue sharing. Roughly speaking:

- A business's revenue (or proceeds, or receipts, or gross income) consists of all the money the business takes in.
- A business's profit equals the amount of its revenue, less the amount of expenses the business has incurred in generating that revenue.

29. See Sections 7.3 and 7.4 (contesting and establishing the existence of partnerships). Since the participants do not consider themselves partners, they will not obtain the liability protection of an LLP. See Section 17.2.

30. See Sections 7.4.3 and 7.4.4, which discuss other business relationships that may involve profit sharing.

31. For a decision that misunderstands this fundamental point, see *Schaffer v. Haler*, No. A22-1393, 2023 WL 2467902, at *6 (Minn. Ct. App. Mar. 13, 2023) (holding that, although the jury had determined that the parties had formed a general partnership, the court could nonetheless find that the parties had agreed not to share profits). The author was an expert witness in this matter.

Example

The Acme Widget Company manufactures and sells widgets. In 2015, the Company

- sold 50,000 widgets, for which it received $500,000;
- spent, in order to make and sell the widgets:
  — $100,000 on materials;
  — $150,000 on salaries, wages, and sales commissions;
  — $20,000 in energy costs;
  — $30,000 in legal fees;
  — for total expenses of $300,000.

Thus, in 2015, the Company had $500,000 of revenue (or gross receipts), but only $200,000 of profits ($500,000 minus $300,000 of expenses equals $200,000).[32] ◀◀◀

Sharing in revenues tends to produce a different, narrower approach toward a business than having a share of profits. A person with a revenue share naturally focuses on the business generating as much revenue possible. Such a person may have little direct concern for the costs of providing goods or services. In contrast, for someone who shares profits, sales (and revenues) are only part of the equation; a profit will exist only if the whole business is functioning well and costs are controlled.

Example

Sylvia is a partner in the Acme Widget Company with a right to 10 percent of the profits. Phil is a salesperson for the Company, with a 5 percent commission on all revenue collected from the sales he makes. Phil has a customer who is willing to buy 5,000 widgets if Acme can ship within two weeks. Acme can make that deadline only by paying its workers substantial amounts of overtime pay. For Phil the main concern is booking the order and seeing that Acme meets the shipping deadline. Sylvia, in contrast, wants to know how much the extra overtime costs will add to the cost of manufacturing. ◀◀◀

The profit-share prerequisite thus fits well with two other key partnership characteristics: co-management and co-ownership. Those who share profits tend to view their economic fate as linked with the fate of the enterprise as a whole. As a consequence, they will wish to involve themselves in

32. For simplicity's sake, the Example lists only a few of the costs an actual company would incur. The concepts being illustrated would apply as well in a realistically complicated situation.

controlling the enterprise and will tend to see the enterprise as belonging in part to them.

§7.2.4 The Role of Loss Sharing

Express agreements to share losses certainly intensify the co-management and co-ownership inclinations just discussed,[33] and in all jurisdictions such agreements are very strong evidence of a partnership. In some jurisdictions, an express agreement to share losses is actually a prerequisite to a finding of partnership.

The majority rule, however, is to the contrary. None of the three acts mentions loss sharing as a prerequisite. Instead, the acts treat loss sharing as a consequence of partnership status.[34]

Case in Point—*Kopka v. Yockey*

"This [was] an action by appellee against appellant and one Frederick Lau to recover damages for personal injuries. It is averred in the complaint that, at the time appellee received the injuries complained of, defendants were jointly engaged in cleaning a certain public ditch; that appellee was in the employ of defendants, and was assisting them in the work of cleaning the said ditch; and that his said injuries were caused by the negligent acts of [Lau], who at the time was directing the work." The claim against the appellant rested on a claim that Lau and appellant were partners. The appellant contended that no partnership could exist, because the appellant and Lau never agreed to share losses. The court rejected that assertion: "It is not the law, as contended by appellant, that a contract creating a partnership must specifically provide that the parties thereto shall share the losses. Where, as in the case at bar, it is stipulated in the agreement that the parties are to share the profits, and nothing is said as to losses, it follows as a legal consequence that they must share the losses."[35] ◀◀◀

§7.2.5 A Meaning for "Co-Ownership"

Co-ownership is a key characteristic of a partnership, but the concept can be quite confusing. The confusion exists because:

---

33. Section 7.2.3.

34. UPA §18(a); UPA (1997) §401(b), UPA (2013) §401(a) (unless otherwise agreed, losses to be shared in the same proportion as profits are shared). See Section 8.3.1.

35. *Kopka v. Yockey*, 131 N.E. 828, 829 (Ind. Ct. App. 1921).

- none of the three acts define the term;
- the concept has a different meaning depending on whether it is used to:
  — help determine whether a partnership exists (i.e., as an entrance criterion to partner status); or
  — describe certain legal rights that follow from partner status; and
- a colloquial sense of the term reflects the now-outmoded notion that a partnership is an aggregate of its partners and not a legal entity separate from them.[36]

To understand co-ownership as an entrance criterion to partnership status,[37] consider two entrepreneurs who go into business together. They agree (as partners do) that they will jointly control whatever property the business uses ("the assets"). That is, they will decide together which assets to select; what use to make of those assets; and whether, when, and for what price to dispose of the use and control of those assets. They also agree that they will share the economic benefit (or detriment) that eventuates from their control, use, and disposition of those assets (i.e., they will share profits and losses).

In a lay sense, the two entrepreneurs co-own the assets of the business.[38] By their agreement they have arranged to share the two predominant characteristics of property ownership: the right to control use and disposition, and the right to benefit (or suffer) economically from the exercise of that right of control. Such functional co-ownership is characteristic of a partnership.[39] (Legal ownership of a partnership's assets is quite another matter, especially under UPA [1997] and UPA [2013].)

§7.2.6 Partnership Types and Joint Ventures

a. Partnership Types: The Default Paradigms

Each of the three acts contemplates three basic types of partnership, categorized according to when the partnership rightfully comes to an end.[40]

---

36. See Section 7.2.7.
37. For a discussion of the co-ownership "consequences" of partnership, see Chapter 8.
38. UPA (1914) reflects this lay construct in its approach to partnership property and the management rights of partners. See Section 8.7.2.
39. See Section 8.7.
40. Recall from Section 2.1.4 the difference between *power* and *right*. Under UPA (1914), each partner always has the *power* to call an end to the partnership. See Section 11.2.1. The situation is different under UPA (2013). See Sections 11.10 and 11.11.

- *Partnership at will.* Each partner has the right to cause the partnership to come to an end, at any time and without having to state or have "cause."[41]
- *Partnership for a term.* The partnership comes to an end at the end of the time period specified in the partners' agreement.
- *Partnership for a particular undertaking.* The partnership comes to an end when the particular task or goal specified in the partners' agreement has been accomplished.

CASE IN POINT

Case in Point—*Mack v. Mack*

Facts: Two brothers orally agreed to form a partnership, and through a series of oral agreements carried on the business, the goal of which was to continue operating their parents' farm after the parents were too old to do so. After the partnership successfully leased the property and later executed a contract for deed (at a very favorable price), one brother chose to withdraw from and end the partnership, asserting that the partnership was at will. The other brother contended that the partnership was for a particular undertaking—that of taking care of their aging parents (who were still living), which meant that neither brother had the *right* to terminate the partnership while the parents remained alive.[42] ◀◀◀

As explained in Section 11.2.1(c), these paradigms are default rules. A partnership agreement may establish rules delineating the circumstances for rightful dissolution without having to specify a definite term or undertaking.

b. Joint Ventures

The term *joint venture* provides more confusion than enlightenment. Under the law of most states, a joint venture is distinguished from a partnership by having a narrower scope than a partnership formed to conduct an ongoing business. But that distinction makes little sense; all three acts recognize limited-scope partnerships as partnerships for a particular undertaking. Moreover, under the law of most states, joint ventures are analogized to partnerships and therefore governed by partnership law.

---

41. A partner's fiduciary duty may limit this right. See Section 11.7.1.
42. *Mack v. Mack*, 613 N.W.2d 64 (S.D. 2000) (affirming the trial court's finding that the partnership was at will).

§7.2.7 Entity or Aggregate? (And Why Care?)

The question of "entity versus aggregate" has long vexed the law of partnerships. Is a partnership a separate legal person, with a legal identity distinct from its partners? Or is a partnership merely an aggregation of its partners, with no separate legal identity of its own?

a. The Schizoid Approach of UPA (1914)

The problem inheres in UPA (1914). When the act was being drafted, reasonable minds differed on the issue. As the drafting project began, the principal drafter favored the entity approach. He died, however, in the middle of the project, and his replacement favored the aggregate view.

UPA (1914) as promulgated includes both approaches. Some provisions reflect an entity concept. UPA (1914) §9(1), for example, begins: "Every partner is an agent of the partnership." Other provisions reflect the aggregate notion. For instance, UPA (1914) §29 characterizes partnership dissolution as "the change in the relation of the partners caused by any partner ceasing to be associated in the carrying on . . . of the business." Still other provisions combine the two approaches, such as UPA (1914) §25, which uses a construct that sounds in property law ("tenancy in partnership") to express partner management rights and to provide that partners have no right to use partnership assets for personal purposes.[43]

Understanding that UPA (1914) embodies two discordant themes helps make sense of some of that statute's provisions. The themes can also have an impact in determining how nonpartnership law treats partners and partnerships.

Case in Point—*State v. Pielsticker*

CASE IN POINT

A state statute prohibited banks from making loans to their own directors. A bank made a loan to a partnership in which one of the bank's directors was a partner. A court held that the bank had not violated the statute, since the partnership was an entity separate from its partners.[44] ◄ ◄ ◄

43. For example, UPA (1914) §25 (partners have no individual rights in property owned by the partnership, but do have collective rights to use and possess the partnership's property for partnership purposes).

44. *State v. Pielsticker*, 225 N.W. 51 (Neb. 1929). *Compare People v. Knapp*, 99 N.E. 841 (N.Y. 1912) (reaching the opposite conclusion in an essentially identical situation, because the court considered the partnership to be a mere aggregation of individuals).

b. The Simple Answer in the Modern Acts

For the most part, matters are far simpler under the modern acts. UPA (1997) cut the Gordian knot: "A partnership is an entity distinct from its partners."[45] The dissociation of a partner from the partnership does not necessarily cause dissolution of the partnership, and UPA (1997) eliminated entirely the notion of "tenancy in partnership."[46] The Harmonization Project made no substantive change in this area.[47]

§7.3 THE HALLMARK CONSEQUENCE OF AN ORDINARY GENERAL PARTNERSHIP: PARTNERS' PERSONAL LIABILITY FOR THE PARTNERSHIP'S DEBTS

Until the very end of the twentieth century, the most important consequence of general partner status had been simply this: *All partners are personally liable for all debts and other obligations of the partnership*. The liability is automatic, strict, and arises solely due to a person's status as a partner. As a result, the liability applies to each partner regardless of whether the partner participates in, approves, or even knows of the conduct that gives rise to the partnership obligation.

In the modern commercial world, this situation is remarkable and—for partners and potential partners—harrowing. Being a partner is tantamount to giving a personal guarantee to everyone with a claim or potential claim against the business.

Today, partners can avoid this risk by causing their general partnership to be a limited liability partnership (LLP). LLP status severs the automatic connection between partner status and liability for the partnership's debts, and partners in a "full shield" LLP are no more liable for the partnership's debt than shareholders in a corporation are liable for the corporation's debts.[48]

However, it is still necessary to understand the liability rules for ordinary general partnerships. For one thing, even under the two modern acts many of the statutory default rules reflect the assumption that the partners are liable for the partnership's debts. For another, many, many general partnerships are not LLPs. (Regulatory barriers may exist, or the partners may

45. UPA (1997) §201(a). This approach also allowed UPA (1997) to simplify partnership law's approach to partnership property. See Section 8.7.
46. Some aggregate aspects remain "under the surface" in the modern acts. See Daniel S. Kleinberger, "The Closely Held Business through the Entity-Aggregate Prism," 40 Wake Forest L. Rev. 827, 841–842 (2005).
47. UPA (2013) §§201, 401(i), 603(a).
48. Section 17.2 explains limited liability partnerships.

simply not know that LLP status is available, or not understand the dangers of eschewing that status or the business owners may not realize that they have formed a partnership.)[49]

§7.3.1 Exhaustion, Joint and Several Liability, *Inter Se* Loss Sharing

The rule of personal liability has three separate areas of complexity: an exhaustion rule, the question of joint and several liability, and the issue of how partners' liability to third parties relates to partners' obligations to share losses among themselves.

a. Exhaustion Rule

In some UPA (1914) jurisdictions, as a matter of case law a creditor of the partnership may not pursue individual partners without first exhausting the assets of the partnership. In jurisdictions with either of the modern acts, the exhaustion rule applies per the statute.[50]

b. Joint Liability and Joint and Several Liability

In most UPA (1914) jurisdictions, partners are jointly and severally liable for certain kinds of partnership obligations and jointly liable for others. Under UPA (1914) §15, partners are jointly and severally liable for partnership debts arising from partner misconduct, and merely jointly liable for all other partnership debts.[51]

The distinctions between the two types of liability relate not to the extent of each partner's personal responsibility, but rather to the steps a creditor must take to pursue the partners. Under both forms of liability, each partner may be held individually responsible for the full amount of the partnership's debt.[52] When the liability is joint *and* several, the creditor may pursue any one of the partners individually. That is, the creditor does not need to include all the partners as defendants in the same lawsuit. Moreover, the creditor may release its claim against one of the partners

49. See Section 7.3.2.
50. UPA (1997) §307(d); UPA (2013) §306(a).
51. For a discussion of how a partner's misconduct could give rise to a partnership debt, see Sections 10.5 and 10.6. For a discussion of other ways in which partners can bind their partnership to third parties, see Sections 10.2–10.4. In addition, a partnership can be bound through the conduct of its agents.
52. Of course, the creditor cannot collect more than the amount owed. That amount will be reduced to judgment. Once the creditor has collected the full judgment amount, the judgment is satisfied.

without undermining its claim against the others. In contrast, when the liability is joint *but not* several, the creditor must sue all of the partners in order to sue any of them. Likewise, if the liability is merely joint, the creditor's release of any partner releases all of them.

Under the modern acts, the rule is simpler. In an ordinary general partnership, "all partners are liable jointly and severally for all obligations of the partnership."[53]

c. Relationship of Partners' Liability to Third Parties and Partners' *Inter Se* Loss Sharing

As discussed in Chapter 8, partners characteristically share losses among themselves. Their *inter se* loss sharing has, however, absolutely no effect on a third party's claim against any particular partner.

Example

Under their partnership agreement, Larry, Moe, and Curley agree to share losses 60/20/20. Shemp has a $100,000 claim against the partnership on which each partner is jointly and severally liable. Shemp sues only Larry, seeking to recover the entire amount. Larry cannot defend by saying, "At most, my liability is $60,000 (i.e., 60 percent)."[54] ◄◄◄

§7.3.2 Why Risk It?

Why would anyone form a general partnership instead of a corporation or an LLC? Forming a corporation or LLC is a simple matter, and the resulting entity shields its owners from the debts of the business.[55] Why would anyone take the risk of partnership?

That question has had a five-part answer: (i) tax advantages, (ii) greater flexibility in structuring the "deal" among the participants, (iii) legal restrictions on the business forms available to professionals, (iv) inadvertence, (v) poor or no legal advice. The first answer was once of great

---

53. UPA (1997) §306(a); UPA (2013) §306(a). Under all three acts, a new partner's personal liability does not extend to a partnership obligation incurred before the person became a partner. UPA §17; UPA (1997) §306(b); UPA (2013) §304(b). The question of when a partnership obligation is actually incurred is complex and a matter of case law. For a detailed discussion, see UPA (2013) §306(b) and (c), cmts.

54. Larry will, however, be entitled to indemnity from the partnership. See Sections 8.9 (Partner's Right to Indemnity) and 8.3.1 (loss sharing applied when third party has collected from one partner and the partnership has failed to indemnify).

55. Of course, even with a corporation or LLC, owners of start-up businesses often have to give personal guarantees to important creditors (e.g., banks, major suppliers). However, such particularized guarantees cause far less exposure than does the simple fact of partner status.

importance, but its day has passed. The second and third are for the most part mere vestiges of past practices. The fourth and fifth have the greatest lasting significance.

a. Tax Advantages

For decades, tax advantages were a substantial reason for organizing a business as a partnership rather than a corporation. Most corporations are taxable entities and therefore face *double taxation* when distributing profits. The standard corporation can pay dividends to its shareholders (i.e., distribute profits to its owners) only in *after-tax* dollars. In essence, the corporation must first pay corporate income tax on its corporate profits before distributing any of those profits as dividends. The shareholders must in turn pay income tax on the dividends.[56]

A partnership, in contrast, is a "pass through" entity. Tax law treats the partnership's profits as allocated among (i.e., passed through to) the partners. The partnership pays no tax; only the partners do. Partners thus face only a single level of taxation. Losses also pass through. When a partnership loses money, the partners obtain tax deductions for use on their own income taxes.

For some businesses, the tax advantages of a partnership were substantial enough to warrant the risks of personal liability—especially so when the risks were either small or insurable.[57] The advent of limited liability companies and LLPs eliminated this reason for forming an ordinary general partnership.[58]

b. Greater Flexibility in Structuring the Deal

As discussed previously,[59] partners have almost unlimited flexibility in structuring their relationship with each other. With this flexibility, they may predetermine the various aspects of their deal. For example, they may agree in advance which partners will work in the business and how much, if any, extra remuneration those partners will receive for doing so. Or, in contrast, they may agree on a flexible mechanism for allocating profits. They may subject specified business decisions to the veto of each partner or give complete management authority to one or more managing partners.

56. The so-called S Corporation can avoid double-taxation, but faces limitations on who can own stock and how the stockholders can structure their *inter se* financial relationship. See Section 13.1.3.
57. For a detailed discussion of the advantages of partnership tax status, see Section 13.1.2.
58. For a discussion of limited liability companies, see Chapters 13 through 16. For a discussion of LLPs, see Section 17.2.
59. Section 7.1.4.

At one time, the corporate form did not allow comparable flexibility (and limited liability companies did not yet exist). Some courts invalidated predetermined corporate deals as attempts to "sterilize" the corporation's directors, who under traditional corporate norms are supposed to exercise independent judgment in managing corporate affairs.

Modern court decisions and modern corporate statutes have changed matters, however. In almost all jurisdictions, shareholders in a closely held corporation (i.e., a corporation with few owners) can do just as much predetermination as the partners in a partnership. Even in jurisdictions whose corporate statutes are antiquated, the limited liability company exists. Thus, it is no longer necessary to risk personal liability in order to fit the legal form to the business deal.

c. Restrictions on Business Forms Available to Professionals

At one time, states prohibited professionals from practicing in corporate form. Professional status was seen as carrying a special responsibility, so the corporate liability shield was inappropriate for a professional practice. According to this view, professionals were properly saddled with the all-encompassing, vicarious liability of a partner. Professionals who wished to practice together and co-own their practice had only one organizational choice—a partnership.

Today, in contrast, almost every state permits professionals to practice in entities that shield their owners from partner-like vicarious liability. These entities include professional corporations, professional associations, professional limited liability companies, and professional limited liability partnerships. Consequently, most professionals who today choose the partnership form do so for reasons other than necessity.

d. Inadvertence

Since creating a partnership requires no special formalities, partnerships can arise inadvertently.[60] Indeed, partnership is the "default" organizational status. If:

- a court determines that two or more persons in fact co-own a business and have agreed to share profits, and
- those persons have not formally chosen to form some other type of business entity, then

60. See Section 7.2.2.

the law classifies the business as a partnership and treats the owners of the business as partners.

CASE IN POINT

Case in Point — *In re KeyTronics*

Three individuals decided to begin a venture (an innovative payment system for car washes) together, in which a single person was the ostensible "lead" manager. They (subjectively) intended to form a corporation but never did. They carried on their venture until one of the individuals sued to dissolve what the individual alleged to be a partnership. The court agreed and ordered the winding up of the partnership and an accounting.[61] ◄◄◄

Thus, many partners assume the harrowing risk of personal liability without understanding that they are doing so.

e. Bad or No Legal Advice

Some persons knowingly become partners without appreciating the liability risk that accompanies partner status. These persons have either not sought legal advice or have received bad advice.

§7.3.3 Why Study It?

Twenty years ago, most "business associations" courses allocated little time to general partnerships, which for the reasons just described were seen as a minor and dangerous form of business organization. The advent of limited liability partnerships (LLPs) and limited liability companies (LLCs) has changed matters substantially. An LLP can be a very useful way to organize a business, and an LLP is a general partnership plus a liability shield. Also, as discussed in Chapter 13, partnership concepts have substantially shaped LLC law, and most LLC statutes include key provisions modeled on the law of general partnerships.

61. *In re KeyTronics*, 744 N.W.2d 425 (Neb. 2008). The consequences could have been much worse, if the business had been insolvent and its creditors sought to hold the co-owners liable as partners. For a discussion of partnership dissolution and winding up, see Chapter 11. For a discussion of the accounting remedy, see Section 9.9.

§7.4 CONTESTING AND ESTABLISHING THE EXISTENCE OF A PARTNERSHIP

§7.4.1 Why a Contest?

Some of the most important partnership cases involve disputes over whether a particular business relationship constitutes a partnership. These disputes usually relate to one of two major attributes of partnership status: the fact that partners are personally liable for the debts of the partnership or the fact that partners share profits with each other.

The liability attribute interests creditors seeking a "deep pocket." If the party who owes a debt cannot pay, the creditor may seek a more solvent business associate of the debtor and try to characterize that business association as a partnership.

Example

A manufacturing plant defaults on its obligation to buy power from a power company. Another creditor of the plant has exerted some control over the plant's business and has received a share of the plant's profits. The power company claims that the other creditor is in fact a partner in the plant's operations and as such is personally liable for the plant's debt. Note that, because the participants do not consider themselves partners, they will not think to obtain the liability protection of an LLP. LLP status is not available retroactively.[62] ◄◄◄

The profit-sharing attribute interests those seeking a bigger piece of a business's pie. If a person who participates in a business can establish partner status, that person stakes a potentially valuable claim. As a partner, the person is entitled to a share not only of profits made in the future but also of any profits distributed in the past (i.e., while the individual was in fact a partner although not recognized as such).

Example

Bob owns and operates a tree farm. He induces Ted to work on the farm as manager, and Ted holds that position for six years. Ted then claims that Bob had promised him a 50/50 partnership after three years. During years four through six, Bob took $200,000 in profit out of the business. A court sides with Ted and orders Bob to pay Ted $100,000 in back profits. (After

62. See Sections 17.2.2 and 17.2.5.

that payment, Bob's profit from years four through six will be reduced to $100,000, so the two partners will have profited equally.)[63] ◀◀◀

Occasionally it is the *inter se* loss-sharing attribute that is attractive.

Case in Point—*Stanford Carr Dev. Corp. v. Unity House Inc.*

CASE IN POINT

A real estate developer sued one of its lenders, alleging that a partnership existed between the parties and the lender was liable as a partner for a share of the project's losses. The first proposal for an agreement between the developer and the lender provided the lender with an "equity participation" that would have resulted in "50 percent participation of project profits" for the lender. The final version entitled the lender instead to a $1.5 million "release fee" on the loan (arguably in lieu of the earlier "equity participation"). The court determined that no partnership could have existed because the relationship lacked the prerequisite attribute of profit sharing.[64] ◀◀◀

§7.4.2 The Pivotal Question: The Character of the Profit Sharing

Since no one can be a partner without a right to share in profits, disputes about the existence of a partnership inevitably focus on the characterization issue. All three acts treat profit sharing as strongly indicative of a partnership, while recognizing that profit sharing sometimes means something else. For example, UPA (2013) §202(c)(3) provides:

> (3) A person who receives a share of the profits of a business is presumed to be a partner in the business, unless the profits were received in payment:
>
> (A) of a debt by installments or otherwise;
>
> (B) for services as an independent contractor or of wages or other compensation to an employee;
>
> (C) of rent;
>
> (D) of an annuity or other retirement or health benefit to a beneficiary, representative, or designee of a deceased or retired partner;

63. This Example is based on *Schaefer v. Bork*, 413 N.W.2d 873 (Minn. Ct. App. 1987).
64. *Stanford Carr Dev. Corp. v. Unity House Inc.*, 141 P.3d 459 (Haw. 2006).

> (E) of interest or other charge on a loan, even if the amount of payment varies with the profits of the business, including a direct or indirect present or future ownership of the collateral, or rights to income, proceeds, or increase in value derived from the collateral; or
>
> (F) for the sale of the goodwill of a business or other property by installments or otherwise.[65]

UPA (1997) §203(3) is essentially identical, and UPA (1914) contains a very similar list of protected categories.[66]

Thus, all three statutes conduce toward one basic structure of analysis:

- The party asserting the existence of a partnership must establish that each participant in the alleged partnership had a right to share in profits.
- The parties will joust over how to characterize the profit sharing. For example, did the profit share reflect the remuneration of a co-owner (a partner) or the payment on a debt, or rent, etc.?
- If the profit share does not fit into one of the "protected categories,"[67] under both modern acts the arrangement is presumed to be a partnership. UPA (1914) refers to "prima facie evidence."[68]

The partnership *vel non* determination is a question of fact, unless of course the evidence is so one-sided that a reasonable fact finder could reach only one conclusion.

---

65. UPA (2013) §202(c)(3).

66. UPA §7(4). Under UPA (1914), profit sharing is prima facie evidence of a partnership. The official Comment to UPA (1997) §202 characterizes the difference between *prima facie* evidence and a presumption as merely "a more contemporary construction." However, unlike a presumption, *prima facie* evidence does not shift the burden of proof. *Prima facie* evidence means that a party has submitted enough evidence to satisfy the burden of proof, but, as the fact finder considers all the evidence, the burden of persuasion remains on the party seeking to establish partnership status. A presumption means that the party *contesting* partnership status has the burden of persuasion.

67. UPA (2013) §202(c)(3)(E), cmt.

68. UPA (1914) §7(4). A comment to UPA (2013) §202(c) explains the difference as follows:

> UPA (1997) recast [sharing profits] as creating a rebuttable presumption of partnership rather merely constituting prima facie evidence. "*Prima facie*" means that the party with the burden of proof has adduced sufficient evidence to carry that burden, subject to the finder of fact's view of any contrary evidence. The burden of persuasion is unchanged. In contrast, "rebuttable presumption" switches the burden of persuasion.

§7.4.3 Factors in the Contest of Characterization

There is, unfortunately, no bright-line test for resolving disputes over the characterization of profit sharing. It is, however, possible to identify five factors that tend to influence courts.

a. Control

Co-management is a key characteristic of a partnership. The more an alleged partner participates in management decisions or exercises control over the business, the more likely is a finding of partnership.

The control factor can be especially problematic for creditors who receive profits "[a]s interest on a loan."[69] Many loan agreements permit the creditor a voice in or even control over management decisions if the debtor has trouble making payments. A creditor who takes a profit share and then exercises such rights faces substantial risks if the debtor's business fails. Other creditors will use the exercise of control to characterize the profit sharing as a partner's remuneration. Since in an ordinary general partnership all partners are liable for the partnership's debts, this characterization will make the profit-sharing creditor liable *on the other creditor's claims* against the debtor.

Control is a less useful factor when the alleged partner provides the business full-time services, rather than money or credit. Many key employees exercise substantial discretion in the conduct of their employer's business. Some key employees even have contract rights that oblige the employer to respect that discretion. Control can therefore be equivocal when trying to distinguish between profits received as a partner and payments received "for services as an independent contractor or of wages or other compensation to an employee."[70]

b. Agreements to Share Losses

As previously explained,[71] an express agreement to share losses is strong evidence of a partnership. Such agreements rarely, if ever, exist in the arrangements between creditor and debtor, employer and employee, or in any of the other relationships that, according to UPA (2013) §202(c) and UPA §7(4), involve profit sharing but not partnership.

69. UPA §7(4)(d). In the modern acts, the comparable language is "in payment . . . of a debt by installments or otherwise." UPA (2013) §202(c)(3)(A); UPA (1997) §202(c)(3).
70. UPA (2013) §202(c)(3)(B). UPA §7(4)(b) refers to profits received "[a]s wages of an employee."
71. See Section 7.2.4.

Business participants can and sometimes do share losses without having an express agreement to do so. That course of conduct usually implies a loss-sharing agreement and is by itself strong evidence of a partnership.

c. Contributions of Property to the Business

If a party has contributed property to the business, that contribution favors the partnership characterization. As discussed more fully in Chapter 8, partners often "buy into" a partnership by transferring to the partnership assets such as land, goods, intellectual property, or money.[72] The transfer is in return for a share of profits, plus management rights and the right, upon dissolution of the partnership, to a return of the value of the asset (but not the asset itself) measured as of the date of contribution.

A contribution of property is not a prerequisite to a finding of partnership, and many partners bring only their talents, skills, and labor.[73] However, a genuine contribution of property does "cut against" each of the nonpartnership "protected categories" under UPA (2013) §202(c) and UPA §7(4).

Property transfers do occur in some of those relationships, but the transfers are of a different nature. For example, a landlord transfers to a tenant the property right to occupy and use the leased premises, but (i) the transfer is only temporary, (ii) the landlord has a right to regain the same property and not just its value, and (iii) the return of the property ordinarily occurs at a time certain or upon specified notice, not merely when the partnership happens to come to an end. Similarly, a lender transfers to a borrower the right to use and dispose of the loaned funds, but the timing of the repayment ordinarily does not depend solely on the ending of the partnership. Even if a loan is due when the partnership ends, as explained in Chapter 11 the lender's rights are superior to the partners' rights to a return of capital.

d. The Extent to Which the Profit Share Constitutes the Recipient's Only Payout from the Business

If a profit recipient receives no other payout from the business, that fact favors the partnership characterization. If, in contrast, the profit share is just a bit of "icing" on top of some other payments, courts are more inclined toward one of the protected categories.

Example

EXAMPLE

Sylvia manages the widget factory of the Acme Widget Company. She receives no salary. Her only compensation is a 20 percent share of profits.

72. See Sections 8.1 and 8.5.
73. See Section 8.6.

She can "draw" a certain amount each month against her profit share, but, if at the end of the year her draws have exceeded her share, she must repay the excess. Phil, the national sales manager of the company, receives a salary of $50,000 per year, plus 1 percent of the Company's profit as an incentive. A court is far more likely to find Sylvia to be a partner than Phil. All her remuneration comes in the form of profits. For Phil, the profit share is small, and is a mere add-on to his salary. ◀ ◀ ◀

e. The Parties' Own Characterization of Their Relationship

Although the parties' own labels are never dispositive, in close situations some courts look to how the participants in a business relationship have characterized their relationship. This factor is probably more influential when the characterization dispute involves only the participants and especially when the business associates have held themselves out to others as partners. When someone outside the relationship (e.g., a creditor seeking to find a deep pocket) challenges the participants' self-labeling, courts are more likely to see the label as self-serving.

Case in Point — *VIDIVIXI, LLC v. Grattan*

This case turned in part on the nature of the business relationship between two individuals. The plaintiff asserted that the individuals had been partners, and the defendant vigorously disagreed. Even though the plaintiff had originally alleged an independent contractor relationship, the court found that a partnership had been formed:

> Regardless of the specific division of labor, the VIDIVIXI furniture was the result of a collaboration between Bradley and Grattan, and they held themselves out as a de facto partnership. For example, in April 2014, Bradley and Grattan signed a contract to display five of their VIDIVIXI pieces in the "Good Colony" showroom. The contract identified Bradley and Grattan as "Co–Owner[s]" of VIDIVIXI . . . [other examples omitted]. In retrospect, both Bradley and Grattan have described their relationship as a "collaboration" and a "partnership."[74]

§7.4.4 Handling the Factors (a Mode of Analysis)

Legal analysis involving factors is always difficult. Which factor is the most important? What if one factor points strongly in one direction while two other factors point weakly in the other? Unfortunately, no simple, mechanical

74. *VIDIVIXI, LLC v. Grattan*, 155 F. Supp. 3d 476, 478 (S.D.N.Y. 2016).

paradigm exists for ordering the characterization factors. However, you may find the following perspective helpful.

All disputes about the character of profit sharing are either/or disputes. The parties do not contest the general paradigm of a partnership, but instead struggle over whether a particular person is a partner or merely a participant in one of the protected categories of UPA (2013) §202(c)(3) or UPA §7(4). In one case, for example, the alleged partner will be either a partner or a wage earner receiving profits as wages. In another case, the alleged partner will be either a partner, or a lender receiving profits as interest.

To decide these either/or questions, courts can look to the factors discussed in Section 7.4.3. If all the factors point in the same direction, the analysis is simple and the answer is clear. The analysis gets complicated only when the factors point in opposite directions.

You can handle that complexity by thinking of each either/or choice as involving a multilayered continuum. Each layer reflects one of the five characterization factors. At one end of the continuum sits the "ideal type"[75] of a partner. At that end, at each layer of the continuum, the facts indicate "partner." At the other end of the continuum sits the "ideal type" of the arguably applicable protected category. At that end, at each layer of the continuum, the facts indicate "wage earner," or "lender," or whatever the category may be. For example, when the characterization choice is either "partner" or "wage earner," the continuum might look like Figure 7.2.

Figure 7.2. Partner Versus Wage Earner (assumes some right to share profits)

"Partner"		**"Wage Earner"**
participates in all important decisions	*Control*	obeys instructions; has no important discretion
has expressly agreed to share losses	*Express Loss-Sharing Agreement*	has never agreed to share losses; when losses occur, payout does not change
contributed property to the business	*Contribution*	merely works in the business
all payout via profit share	*Importance of Profit Share*	profit share is only icing on the cake
called a partner	*Self-labeling*	called an employee

75. An "ideal type" possesses all the key attributes described by a concept; it epitomizes the concept even though the epitome may rarely, if ever, exist in pure form. (The concept derives from the works of the German social theorist Max Weber.)

Although in any particular case one factor (or layer) or another may predominate, courts rarely decide on the basis of one factor alone. Instead, they look at the overall picture: The more each layer of the disputed situation leans toward one end of the applicable continuum, the more likely the court is to come down on that side of the either/or fence.

The analysis is inevitably imprecise. Since the law declines to make one factor (or combination of factors) dispositive, courts are left essentially to decide whether the disputed situation "looks" more like one end of the continuum or the other.

§7.5 PARTNERSHIP BY ESTOPPEL; LIABILITY OF A PURPORTED PARTNER

It is possible for a person to have partner-like liability for an enterprise's obligations without truly being a partner. UPA (1914) labels the applicable rule "partnership by estoppel";[76] UPA (2013) uses the caption: "Liability of Purported Partner."[77]

Unfortunately, the UPA (1914) rule is byzantine, and the modern acts have made only a few changes. Under all three statutes, however, the basic concept is fairly simple and consistent with ordinary estoppel principles:

If

- a person represents itself as being a partner in an enterprise (or allows others to make the representation);

and

- a third party reasonably relies on the representation and as a result does business with the enterprise;

then

- the person who was represented as a partner is liable on the transaction as if the person were a partner, even though the person is not in fact a partner; and
- others who have either made or consented to the representation are bound by the person's acts as if they were partners with the person represented as their partner.

76. UPA (1914) §16.
77. UPA (2013) §308.

The liability aspect of this rule rests on common beliefs about a partner's responsibilities and powers. Before the advent of limited liability partnerships, partner personal liability was a well-known fact of business life. To represent oneself as a general partner (or to allow someone else to make the representation) was therefore to impliedly promise to be "good for" any debts of the enterprise just like any other partner.[78]

The "power to bind" aspect of the rule rests on a similar rationale. It is well known that partners have certain powers to bind the partnership.[79] When a person is represented to be a partner with others, third parties will naturally believe that the person can bind the partnership and, on account of each partner's personal liability, can bind those others as well. To the extent that those others consent to the representation, a partner-like power to bind should apply.

Problem 55

Ralph wants to open a riding stable but does not have enough money. He approaches Sally, who has both experience managing start-up businesses and some money to invest. They agree that (i) each will own a half-interest in the business, (ii) Ralph will run the day-to-day operations while Sally will "handle the books," (iii) all major decisions will be made jointly, (iv) Sally will invest $50,000, and (v) Ralph will get 40 percent of the profits and Sally 60 percent. Sally is concerned with the liability that comes with being a partner, so the agreement between Ralph and Sally states clearly: "This relationship shall not be deemed to be a partnership." What legal effect will that disclaimer have on claims by creditors? ◀◀◀

Explanation

The disclaimer will be useless. Sally and Ralph have created precisely the type of business relationship that the law considers to be a partnership. They co-own, they co-manage, and they share profits. In the face of a claim by a creditor, the disclaimer will be disregarded as inaccurate and self-serving. ◀◀◀

78. If the partnership is an LLP, no partner is personally liable for the partnership's debts, so no *partnership-based* liability will attach to the person making the misrepresentation. However, other common law claims might be available, e.g., misrepresentation, fraud in the inducement. See Section 4.2.3 ("a tort is a tort is a tort").

79. For a discussion of the rules that reflect this perception, see Chapter 10.

Problem 56

Mark is the treasurer of the Zenith Vending Machine Company. In that capacity he prepares all the Company's tax returns. The Company is a partnership, and each year its partnership tax returns list the partners as Allen, Betty, Charlotte, and Ralph.[80] As part of his remuneration, Mark receives a share of Zenith's profits. If he later claims that he is a partner in the company, what role will the partnership tax returns play in the dispute? ◀ ◀ ◀

Explanation

EXPLANATION

The returns will argue strongly against him, because they list the partners and do not include Mark. As the preparer of the returns, Mark evidently assented to the exclusion. This situation therefore differs from efforts to use disclaimers against third parties. ◀ ◀ ◀

Problem 57

For 10 years Paul has operated PAUL'S, an automobile salvage business. The business buys wrecked automobiles from insurance companies or at auction, and then either rebuilds them or cannibalizes them for parts. PAUL'S sells rebuilt and used parts to car dealers, service stations, and the public.

For the past three years, Eli has been working in the business with Paul. Eli has only a third-grade education but is an excellent, street-smart auto mechanic. He is active in almost all aspects of the business: bidding at auctions, buying cars from insurance companies, and fixing cars and parts. However, only Paul determines the selling price for the cars and parts that the business sells. Paul also maintains all the business's records and takes care of the business's various tax returns.

Paul first approached Eli to come to work with him when Paul learned that Eli had won $9,000 at the racetrack. Eli gave the money to Paul, who used it to buy cars at an auction. Those cars were then used in the salvage business. Paul promised Eli 50 percent of the business's profit for as long as Eli would "work as hard, sweat as much, and do as much as I do."

Ever since Eli began work at PAUL'S, the company's records have shown him as an employee. His salary has been calculated based on 50 percent of the profits, and Social Security has been withheld from his checks. The company

80. Even though partnerships do not pay income taxes (see Section 7.3.2), they must nonetheless file tax returns.

has paid Social Security and unemployment compensation taxes on account of Eli and has maintained workers' compensation coverage for him. Both the company's various tax returns and its insurance policies list Eli as an employee.

Is Eli an employee of or a partner in PAUL'S?[81] ◀ ◀ ◀

EXPLANATION

Explanation

Eli is a partner. He shares in the profits and has made a capital contribution. Although Paul has exclusive responsibility in two areas, Eli shares management authority over other areas that are crucial to the business.

The company's books and tax returns do describe Eli as an employee, but that fact does not undermine Eli's partner status. The parties' self-descriptions can give insight into their intents, but only when the parties genuinely assent to the description. There is no evidence that Eli was aware of the way he was described in the company's records, other than the withholding of Social Security from his checks. With his lack of formal education, Eli was probably unaware of what that withholding implied about his status. ◀ ◀ ◀

Problem 58

As a sole proprietor, Bill runs a dry-cleaning store called Bill's Dry-Cleaning. He is in deep financial trouble. His bank will no longer give him any credit, and is threatening to call a loan (i.e., demand immediate payment of all money owed). Bill also owes money to various trade creditors (i.e., businesses that have supplied him goods and services). Bill approaches Chris, a well-known venture capitalist, and asks her to refinance his business. Chris reviews his books and his operations and says, "Listen, you're a great dry cleaner but a lousy businessman. I'll bail you out, but we have to divide up the responsibilities a bit. If we're going to make this business work, we have to be more hard-nosed about it. First, no more credit to law professors. They're lousy risks. Second, I want to determine who gets paid when. One of the arts of staying in business is stretching out your accounts payable. So, before you pay anyone, you check with me. Also, I want some upside potential. So long as you owe me money, I want 12 percent interest on what you owe or 10 percent of the profits, whichever is higher. You pay me the 12 percent monthly, and quarterly I'll decide whether to keep the past three months' interest or take my share of the past three months' profits."

Bill accepts Chris's terms, with one condition: "We have to pay our people (i.e., the employees) on time. If we have the money, we pay them." Chris

81. This question will have great practical importance if, for example, Paul attempts to "fire" Eli or decrease Eli's remuneration.

accepts Bill's condition, pays off the bank, and provides additional working capital to the business.

The business continues to operate under the same name, and no one except Bill knows of Chris's role in the business. Bill stops extending credit to law professors. Each month, Chris reviews Bill's accounts payable and sets the priorities for payment as follows: (i) pay Chris the interest owed her, (ii) pay overdue bills from people Bill intends to buy from again, (iii) pay overdue bills from other people who are threatening suit, (iv) pay others. Chris never does take a percentage of the profit, because the 12 percent interest figure is always higher.

Bill makes all decisions about which vendors to use. He also makes all personnel decisions (e.g., hiring, firing, salaries). After a year, the business fails. Bill owes Chris $350,000; he owes creditors a total of $175,000 ($150,000 to trade creditors and $25,000 in back wages to three employees). Bill has no money.

Can these other creditors collect from Chris? Consider Chapter 6 as well as UPA (2013) in analyzing this Problem. ◄◄◄

Explanation

Two different theories hold promise for the creditors: partnership law and constructive agency under R.2d, §14 O. If the creditors can establish that Chris is Bill's partner, UPA (2013) §306(a) will make Chris liable with Bill for the partnership's debts. If the creditors successfully invoke §14 O, Chris will be liable to the creditors as Bill's principal.

Although it is unlikely that Bill and Chris thought of their relationship as a partnership, they may nonetheless have formed one. Their thoughts about the legal label are largely immaterial. What matters is the nature of the business relationship they have intentionally created.

The other creditors will contend that the business relationship fits most of the paradigmatic characteristics of a partnership. Most importantly, Chris has a right to share profits. That right, rather than the actual receipt of profits, is the fundamental prerequisite to partner status. Chris has also "brought something to the party": not only essential working capital, but also key management services. Moreover, like a paradigmatic partner, Chris has helped run the business, exercising management control over key financial issues.

She has not "contributed" any property in the partnership law sense, because she has a contractual right to be repaid her loan. But not all partners contribute property. There is no express agreement to share losses, but most jurisdictions do not require one.

In short, Bill and Chris have shared control over the business and its assets. They have linked their economic fate to each other and to the business by agreeing to share profits. They have thus arranged to "carry on as co-owners a business for profit."[82]

Chris's response will be to characterize her right to share profits as mere "interest or other charge on a loan" and therefore not probative of partner status.[83] Both the profit-sharing agreement and the circumstances leading up to that agreement support this characterization. Chris's agreement with Bill gave her the right to take either interest at a fixed rate or a profit share. This arrangement demonstrates that profits, if chosen, were to take the place of conventional interest. Chris did not seek an interest in Bill's business, but rather demanded an option on profits as a condition to making a loan.

The biggest problem with Chris's argument is the type of control she exercised. While many loan agreements give the lender extraordinary power over the debtor's affairs in the event of a default, Chris asked for, obtained, and began exercising *mundane* control *as a condition of granting the loan*. This deviation from standard lending practice may well tip the balance against Chris.

In any event, Chris has troubles under agency law. If a creditor asserts enough control over a debtor to take over the management of the debtor's business, R.2d, §14 O makes the creditor liable for the debts of the business. Mere veto power is not enough; extensive involvement is necessary.

Chris may well have asserted the necessary control and undertaken the necessary involvement. She was certainly involved in the business; she spoke specifically of "divid[ing] up the responsibilities." Moreover, she controlled some very important aspects of the business: namely, when and which accounts would be paid and what customers would be allowed to buy services on credit. Chris can, however, point to large areas of the business that she did not control: namely, all personnel matters and the selection of vendors.

With the question of control a close one, a court may be influenced by the striking similarity between Chris's situation and the situation in *Cargill*. The creditor in *Cargill* kept the Warren grain elevator in business, obtaining grain while the elevator's debts to farmers mounted. Chris kept the dry-cleaning enterprise in business and then used her control to make sure that she was paid before all creditors other than employees. In both situations, the creditor used its control to obtain a benefit at the expense of other creditors. Such an abuse of power simultaneously (i) demonstrates that the creditor did substantially interfere with the management of the debtor's business, and (ii) provides a policy reason for making the controlling creditor liable to the other creditors.

If Chris is liable under Restatement §14 O, the extent of that liability depends on whether the court follows *Cargill* or *Nash-Finch*.[84] *Cargill* follows

82. UPA (2013) §202(a) (definition of partnership).
83. UPA (2013) §202(c)(3)(E).
84. See Section 6.3.2 n.32.

§14 O faithfully and makes the creditor-principal liable for all debts incurred in the business after the creditor took control. Under *Cargill*, therefore, Chris would be liable to all creditors for all amounts arising after she refinanced and took control of the business.

Under *Nash-Finch*, in contrast, the principal's liability extends only to debts arising within areas of the business controlled by the creditor. Under that approach, Chris would not be liable to the three employees. She did not control their selection, training, supervision, or payment. She did control payment to trade creditors and would be liable to them. ◄◄◄

CHAPTER 8

Financial Aspects of a Partnership (Creation and Operation)

§8.1 THE PRACTICAL BACKGROUND

Like any other business, a partnership needs two types of inputs in order to function: the working efforts of human beings ("labor") and the use of at least some property, be it as elaborate and tangible as a fleet of delivery trucks, as simple as paper on which to write out bills, or as conceptual as a trademark, copyright, or patent.[1]

A partnership typically obtains both labor and property from its partners, although not every partner necessarily provides both.[2] Of course, a partner who provides something of value to the partnership will want something in return, and all three uniform acts provide a comprehensive set of default rules that determine how and when partners receive a return.[3] This chapter discusses how those rules apply to the creation and operation of a partnership.[4]

---

1. In this context, property is often referred to as "capital," but "capital" also has a narrower meaning: i.e., property owned by the partnership. That narrower meaning is a term of art under partnership law, as explained below.
2. In some partnerships, for example, one partner provides all the property, while the other partner provides only labor. See Section 8.6.
3. As explained in Section 7.1.4, default rules apply except to the extent the partners have agreed otherwise. For a discussion of the history of the three uniform general partnerships acts and an explanation of this book's approach to them, see Section 7.1.2.
4. UPA (2013) §401 contains most of the default rules relevant to this chapter. In UPA (1914), §18 is the main section. When a partnership comes to an end, other financial aspects surface and other statutory provisions become relevant. Chapter 11 discusses those aspects and provisions in detail.

Partnerships can and often do obtain inputs from outsiders (i.e., from nonpartners). A partnership can, for example:

- rent office space from a landlord;
- borrow money from a bank; and
- obtain services from employees, nonemployee agents, and independent contractors.

The remuneration rules for these relationships come from contract law and, in particular, the contract defining the relationship between the partnership and the outsider.[5]

§8.2 THE PARTNER'S BASIC RETURN AND PARTNERSHIP LAW'S BASIC PREMISE

Absent a contrary agreement, a partner's financial return has two main components: (i) a right to an equal allocation and eventual distribution of the profits of the partnership, if any; and (ii) a right, when the partnership ends, to receive the value of any property whose ownership the partner transferred to the partnership. Partnership law refers to any such transfer as a "contribution" or "contribution of capital," and the contribution is valued as of the moment of contribution. Absent a contrary agreement, a partner has no right to remuneration based on the amount of labor expended (e.g., no wages or salary) or on the amount of capital contributed (e.g., no interest).[6]

In this area, the key premise of partnership law is that—unless the partners manifest otherwise—the partners consider what each partner brings to the table as roughly comparable to what each other partner brings. Put another way: The premise is that if the partners do not assume equality of interests, they will manifest their contrary views through an agreement—whether formal or informal, express or implied—that will displace the default rule.

5. Whether the partners are personally liable on such contracts is a question of partnership law. See Section 7.3 and Chapter 17.

6. See UPA (2013) §401(j), UPA (1914) §18(f) (no right to remuneration for labor provided to the partnership); UPA (1997) §401(g), UPA (1914) §18(d) (stating circumstances under which a partner is entitled to interest, omitting from those circumstances interest on contributions, and thereby implying no right to ongoing remuneration for capital contributed to the partnership). For the rules applicable once a partnership has dissolved, see Chapter 11.

A partner may also have other financial arrangements with the partnership. For example, a partner may rent property to the partnership or lend the partnership money. But such arrangements result from particular agreements between the partner and the partnership. They do not inhere in partner status.

A partner also has the right to be indemnified against expenses and liabilities incurred in the service of the partnership.[7]

§8.3 RULES FOR ALLOCATING PROFITS AND LOSSES

§8.3.1 The Size of the Share (Percentages)

a. Profits

All three acts have a simple default rule on the size of each partner's profit share. Absent a contrary agreement, each partner is allocated an equal share.[8] The rule applies regardless of how much property individual partners have contributed to the partnership, and regardless of how much individual partners work for the partnership.

Example

Larry, Moe, and Curley form a partnership to manufacture and sell whoopee cushions. To get the business started, Larry and Curley each contribute $10,000. They each work in the factory 60 hours per week. Moe, in contrast, contributes $0 and works 20 hours per week, in his words, "closing big deals." The partners have no agreement, either express or implied, regarding profit sharing. Despite the differing contributions and efforts, the partners share profits equally (i.e., one-third each). Absent a contrary agreement, the default rule applies. ◀◀◀

b. Losses

Absent a contrary agreement, partners share losses in the same percentage as they share profits. UPA (1914) §18(a) states: "Each partner . . . must contribute towards the losses . . . sustained by the partnership according to his share in the profits." UPA (2013) §401(a) states: "Each partner . . . is

7. See Section 8.9.

8. UPA (2013) §401(a); UPA (1997); §401(b); UPA (1914) §18(a). When a partnership actually distributes profits to partners is a different issue. See Section 8.3.2.

chargeable with a share of the partnership losses in proportion to the partner's share of the distributions."

If there is no *inter se* agreement addressing profits or losses, then—because the default rule on profits provides for equal profit sharing—the partners will share losses equally. If a partnership agreement establishes profit-sharing percentages but neglects to address loss sharing, the loss-sharing percentages will mirror the profit-sharing percentages.

Example

Larry, Moe, and Curley form a whoopee cushion partnership. The partnership agreement gives Moe a 60 percent share of profits and Larry and Curley each a 20 percent share. The agreement does not mention losses. If the partnership suffers losses, the partners will share the losses 60/20/20. Because the default rule applies, the loss shares match the profit shares. ◄◄◄

c. No Impact on Third-Party Claims

Loss-sharing arrangements *among* partners do not affect the personal liability of each partner to creditors for the debts of the partnership. If the partnership is a limited liability partnership (LLP), the partners are not by their status liable for the partnership's obligations.[9] If the partnership is not an LLP, each partner is either jointly liable or jointly and severally liable for each partnership debt regardless of the *inter se* situation.[10]

Inter se arrangements *do*, however, affect what happens when a creditor succeeds in collecting a partnership debt from an individual partner. If the partnership lacks the funds to indemnify that partner,[11] then the *inter se* arrangements will determine how much each of the other partners must compensate the partner who took the hit.

Example

The Larry-Moe-Curley partnership goes out of business. The partnership is not an LLP, and a creditor of the partnership subsequently collects $21,000 from Curley on a debt owed by the partnership. The partnership has no

9. See Section 17.2.

10. Statutory rules governing relationships with outsiders cannot be changed by agreements among partners. See Section 7.3.1 (relationship between partners' liability to third parties and partners' *inter se* loss sharing). Under the modern uniform acts, liability is always joint and several. Under UPA (1914), some liabilities are joint and others are joint and several. See Section 7.3.1. In an LLP, the rules on loss sharing are changed somewhat to protect the liability shield. See Section 17.2.7.

11. See Section 8.9.

funds to reimburse Curley. The partners had agreed to share losses equally. Curley has a right to collect $7,000 each from Larry and Moe. ◀◀◀

§8.3.2 Timing

a. Determining When Profits (and Losses) Are Allocated

None of the uniform acts specify how often profits and losses are allocated among the partners. However, tax law requires an annual allocation. Although a partnership pays no tax, it must annually provide each partner a "K-1" form, indicating each partner's share of profits or losses from the past tax year.

b. Determining When Profits Are Paid Out (Distributed)

I. Default Rules Under the Acts

As to when profits are actually distributed (i.e., paid out), the three acts each use different language to reach roughly the same result.

- UPA (1914) provides that "[e]ach partner shall be repaid his contributions . . . and share equally in the profits and surplus remaining *after* all liabilities . . . are satisfied."[12] The language suggests that a partnership must repay the value of all contributions and discharge all liabilities before it pays out any profit.
- UPA (1997) addresses the issue only through a comment which states: "Absent an agreement to the contrary, . . . a partner does not have a right to receive a current distribution of the profits credited to his account, the interim distribution of profits being a matter arising in the ordinary course of business to be decided by majority vote of the partners."[13]
- UPA (2013) states specifically that "a person has a right to a distribution before the dissolution and winding up of a partnership only if the partnership decides to make an interim distribution."[14]

12. UPA (1914) §18(a) (emphasis added).
13. UPA (1997) §401, Comment 3. An "interim distribution" is one that occurs before the winding up and termination of the partnership. For a discussion of partner management rights, see Chapter 9. For a discussion of winding up and termination, see Chapter 11.
14. UPA (2013) §405(b). The provision refers to "person" rather than "partner" to take into account the rights of transferees. See Section 8.8.

2. *In Practice*

In virtually all general partnerships the timing of interim distributions is a matter of agreement—either express or through a course of conduct—and most agreements contemplate some sort of annual distribution. Likewise, by express agreement or by custom, partners in many operating (as distinguished from investment) partnerships take "draws" throughout the year against their anticipated annual profit share. Under most such arrangements, matters are evened up at year's end. If a partner has overdrawn, the partner must repay the excess. If a partner has drawn too little, the partner may then withdraw the remainder.[15]

Annual reconciliation is not mandatory as a matter of partnership law. For example, a partnership agreement can appoint a later time for the "evening up" process or provide that overdraws simply be subtracted from the value of any contributions the partner has made to the partnership. Likewise, a partnership agreement could allow partners to leave in some or all of their profit share and have that amount treated as if the partners had contributed it back to the partnership.[16]

c. Determining When Losses Are "Shared"

None of the three acts specifies the timing of loss sharing. Typically, the partnership's books keep track of loss allocations on an annual basis, as required by tax law, and the recorded losses affect what each partner receives when the partnership comes to an end.[17]

§8.4 REMUNERATION FOR LABOR PROVIDED BY PARTNERS TO THE PARTNERSHIP

If partners spend time and effort furthering the partnership's business, what compensation do they receive? Under all three partnership acts, the default rule is simple. Absent a contrary agreement—be it express or implied—they

15. Profit draws are thus quite different from salary and wages. Salary and wages reflect a definite commitment by the partnership to pay a fixed amount, regardless of how much profit (if any) the partnership makes.

16. See Section 8.5.1 (contributions) and Section 11.5.3(b) (capital accounts). However, tax law has accounting requirements of its own (which are far beyond the scope of this book), and those requirements strongly influence partnership arrangements.

17. Section 11.5.3 explains both the recordkeeping process and the eventual effect of the allocated losses.

receive nothing beyond their share in the profits: no wages, no salary, and no extra compensation of any kind.[18]

Example

Larry, Moe, and Curley form a partnership to manufacture and sell whoopee cushions. They agree to share profits equally. To get the business started, they each contribute $5,000 to the partnership. Larry and Curley each work in the factory 60 hours per week. Moe works 20 hours per week "closing big deals." Larry and Curley contend that they should get "something extra" for working more. They are incorrect, unless they can show either an express or implied agreement. ◀◀◀

Although in concept the mechanism for determining whether a partner has a right to additional compensation is clear-cut, in practice fact disputes about alleged implied or oral agreements can be quite intense.

§8.5 REMUNERATION FOR PROPERTY PROVIDED BY PARTNERS TO THE PARTNERSHIP

§8.5.1 Contribution—the Basic and Simple Paradigm

Partners who provide property to a partnership most often do so by contributing the property—that is, by transferring ownership from the partner to the partnership. In such circumstances, the default remuneration rule is simple and the same under all three uniform acts. The partner's contribution is valued as of the date of contribution, and, when the partnership dissolves, the partner is entitled to the return of that amount of value (and not the contributed property itself). The contributed capital itself belongs to the partnership, and can be any property—real or personal, tangible or intangible—in which the contributing partner had a right to transfer an interest.

As with partners who expend labor and receive nothing for the "use" of their labor beyond their share in the profits, absent a contrary agreement partners who contribute "capital" receive nothing for the use of the capital beyond their share in the profits. Such partners receive no interest or extra compensation of any kind;[19] they receive merely the return

18. This rule has one exception. Under UPA (2013) §401(j) and UPA (1997) §401(j), each partner is entitled to "reasonable compensation for services rendered in winding up the business of the partnership." Under UPA (1914) §18(f), the exception is narrower; reasonable compensation for winding up is available only to a sole surviving partner.
19. See Section 8.2.

of the original contribution *value* when the partnership comes to an end.[20]

Example

Autumn agrees to contribute to the Seasons Partnership a parcel of land valued at $500,000, in return for a 20 percent share of partnership profits. During the next five years, rental from the land accounts for 25 percent of the Partnership's profits, and the land itself increases in value by 200 percent. The benefits from the land belong to the partnership, not Autumn, whose remuneration as a partner is the agreed-upon 20 percent share. If the Seasons Partnership were to dissolve, Autumn would have a right to a return of $500,000, no matter how valuable (or worthless) the parcel of land had become. ◀◀◀

§8.5.2 The Complexity—Additional Modes of Providing Property

Complexity can exist in this area of law and practice because two other methods exist by which a partner might provide property for the use of a partnership. The partner might:

- *furnish* property, providing the partnership only the use of the property for either the duration of the partnership or some other period of time, retaining title to the property and receiving no remuneration beyond the partner's share in the profits; or
- *lease* or *lend* the property, providing the partnership the use of the property for either the duration of the partnership or some other period of time, retaining title to the property and receiving rent, interest, or royalties as compensation.

Example

Larry, Moe, and Curley form a partnership. Larry *contributes* $10,000 in cash. Moe has a right under a lease to occupy certain business premises, and he *furnishes* those premises to the partnership at no charge; making the premises available is part of what Moe "brings to the party" in return for becoming a partner. Curley *leases* his truck to the partnership. ◀◀◀

20. See Section 11.5.3.

§8.5.3 Consequences of the Complexity — Different Rules for Property-Related Remuneration

It is important to distinguish among the three modes through which a partner might provide property to a partnership, because the remuneration consequences vary with the characterization. Under all three acts, the consequences have multiple, though related, aspects:

- What compensation, if any, does the partner receive for providing property to the partnership?
- Does the partner ever receive back the property? This question in turn implies two further issues:
  - — If the property depreciates while being used by the partnership, who bears the loss?
  - — If the property appreciates, who enjoys the gain?

The following figure describes and compares the consequences pertaining to each characterization.[21]

Figure 8.1. Modes of Providing Property — Consequences

Mode of Providing Property	Title to Property	Remuneration for Use	Property Returned to Partner?	Risk of Depreciation/ Benefit of Appreciation
contribution	transfers to partnership	none beyond partner's profit share	no	for partnership
furnishing	remains with partner	none beyond partner's profit share	yes, as part of winding up	for partner
leasing/lending[22]	remains with partner	per the lease/loan agreement	yes, per the lease/loan agreement	for partner

21. Like almost all matters *inter se* the partners, these consequences are subject to any contrary agreement between the partner and the partnership or among the partners. For example, a partner might agree to furnish a truck for the first three years of the partnership.

22. This situation implicates both ordinary contract principles (lessor-lessee) and a partner's duty of loyalty. For a discussion of the latter, see Section 9.7.

Example

A partner "furnishes" to the partnership the royalty-free use of a patent. After five years the partnership dissolves, and the partner regains full rights in the patent. In those five years, the patent has become more valuable because a major competing product has been discontinued as unsafe. The partnership has no right to share in that increased value. Absent a contrary agreement, the benefits of increasing value stay with the party who owns the property. ◀ ◀ ◀

Example

A partner leases to the partnership several new pieces of construction equipment, and the partnership agrees to pay rent of $5,000 per month. After five years, the partnership comes to an end and the lease terminates. The partner regains the right to possess, use, and dispose of the equipment. Although the equipment is now far less valuable than it was originally, the partnership is not obliged to compensate the lessor/partner for the decrease.[23] Absent a contrary agreement, and assuming no abuse of the property by the partnership, the risk of diminishing value stays on the party who owns the leased property. ◀ ◀ ◀

Example

To help the Larry-Moe-Curley partnership get started making whoopee cushions, Moe contributes equipment worth, at the time, $500,000. Moe makes no warranty on the equipment. A year later the equipment breaks down and becomes worthless. When the partnership later comes to an end, the partnership owes Moe $500,000, the value of his contribution. ◀ ◀ ◀

Example

Larry contributes to the partnership land worth $400,000. The land appreciates during the partnership's existence, and is worth $1,000,000 when the partnership comes to an end. Larry has no right to the return of the land; it belongs to the partnership. Larry does have a right to the return of the original value of his contribution, that is, $400,000. The $600,000 in appreciation belongs to the partnership.[24] ◀ ◀ ◀

---

23. Of course, if the lessor/partner has figured the lease payments rationally, those payments will have taken the depreciation into account. Nonetheless, as a formal matter the risk of depreciation stays with the owner.

24. Larry will receive some of the $600,000 as shared profits. See Section 11.5.3.

§8.5.4 Distinguishing the Modes of Providing Property

a. The UPA (1914) Approach[25]

UPA (1914) contains no rules for distinguishing the modes of providing property.[26] The rules come from the case law, which is plentiful. Whether a partner has leased, loaned, furnished, or contributed property to a partnership depends on the intent of the parties—that is, of the partner providing the property, and the partnership. Intent is a question of fact, to be determined objectively from the parties' manifestations. Express agreements provide the clearest manifestation.

In the absence of an express agreement, a court is unlikely to find a lease or a loan unless the partnership has in fact made payments that can be fairly construed as rent, interest, or royalties. As for distinguishing *contributed* property (ownership transfers to the partnership) from merely *furnished* property (partner retains ownership), the following factors indicate *contribution*:

- the use of the property in the partnership business, especially if the property is crucial or central to that business;
- the use of partnership funds in improving, maintaining, insuring, or paying taxes on the property;
- indications in the partnership's books that the property belongs to the partnership;
- nonreceipt of rent or other compensation by the partner who provided the property.

For two reasons, the listed factors do not include the partnership holding formal legal title to the property. First, only real property and a few forms of personal property (e.g., motor vehicles) even *have* record title. Second, in many states, before the enactment of UPA (1914), a partnership could not hold title to real property in the partnership's name.[27] It was therefore common for individual partners, or for partners jointly, to hold title to real estate that in a functional and equitable sense belonged to the partnership. As a result of custom and inertia, such arrangements have continued even under the modern uniform acts.

25. This section is drawn from Kleinberger & Wrigley, "Who Owns the Christmas Trees? The Disposition of Property Used by a Partnership," 39 Kansas L. Rev. 245, 256–57 (1991).
26. UPA §8(2) does provide a rule for characterizing property purchased with partnership funds. "Unless the contrary intention appears, property acquired with partnership funds is partnership property."
27. This disability reflected the aggregate approach to partnerships. See Section 7.2.7.

b. The Modern Approach

UPA (1997) changed the law on this subject, placing considerable emphasis on title. The change was consistent with the entity approach of UPA (1997) as well as with the statute's concern to clarify record title for real estate.[28] UPA (2013) made no changes to the statutory text but provided further explanatory comment:

> Section 204 states the rules *inter se the partners and partnership* for determining when property is acquired by the partnership and so becomes partnership property. . . .
>
> These rules provide three separate approaches—according to:
>
> - the name or names used in acquiring the property (formalities of acquisition);
> - when a partner's name appears as a transferee, the capacity in which the partner is acting property (formalities of acquisition); and
> - for property acquired by purchase, whether the partnership provided the consideration for the property.
>
> These approaches are complementary, not mutually exclusive.[29]

I. Formalities of Acquisition

Property is partnership property if acquired:

- "in the name of . . . the partnership"[30]
- in the name of "one or more partners" if "the instrument transferring title to the property" indicates "the person's capacity as a partner or . . . the existence of a partnership."[31]

Example

Rachael executes a deed to a parcel of land, with the transferee shown as "Eli, a partner." Eli is a partner in the Eli-Ilan Scissor Company, a general partnership under one of the modern partnership acts. Absent other evidence to the contrary, the land belongs to the partnership. ◀◀◀

28. See Section 10.4.3 (discussing statements of authority, limitation, and denial).
29. Section 204, comment (emphasis in original).
30. UPA (2013) §204(a)(1); UPA (1997), *Id.*
31. UPA (2013) §204(a)(2); UPA (1997), *Id.*

2. Assets Used to Accomplish the Acquisition

If the just-stated rule does not determine ownership, then the source of funds or credit used to acquire the property raises an ownership presumption.

- "Property is presumed to be partnership property if purchased with partnership assets."[32]
- "Property acquired . . . without use of partnership assets, is presumed to be separate property, even if used for partnership purposes."[33]

Although the modern rules work best with property with record title, they apply with equal force to all forms of property—e.g., real, personal, tangible, and intangible.[34]

§8.6 SPECIAL ISSUES WITH K-AND-L PARTNERSHIPS

§8.6.1 K-and-L Partnerships Described

A partner may "buy into" a partnership by providing or promising to provide capital, labor, or both. There is no requirement, however, that each partner provide both capital and labor. In some partnerships one partner provides all the capital (the K partner) and another partner provides all the labor (the L partner).[35] In the context of such K-and-L partnerships, courts occasionally have difficulties applying the statutory default rules on remuneration and loss sharing.

§8.6.2 Problems with Loss Sharing

The default rule on loss sharing is the same in each of the three acts,[36] and under each act, the rule applies regardless of the inputs the partners provide to "buy into" the partnership. Therefore, if a K-and-L partnership loses money, the L partner (i.e., the one who provided only labor) will receive nothing from the partnership. There will be no profits to share, and absent a contrary agreement, a partner receives no remuneration for services

32. UPA (2013) §204(c); UPA (1997), *Id.*
33. UPA (2013) §204(d); UPA (1997), *Id.*
34. See UPA (2013), §204, comment ("These rules apply to 'all property, whether real, personal, or mixed or tangible or intangible, or any right or interest therein.' ") (citing UPA (2013) 102(16) (defining "property")).
35. In the shorthand used by economists, K represents capital and L represents labor.
36. See Section 8.3.1(b).

provided the partnership outside of winding up.[37] Moreover, the L partner will have to "kick in" money so that K and L share losses according to the statutory default rules.[38]

Example

Cliff and Lilith form a partnership to run a dating service. They do not make any agreements displacing the remuneration and loss default rules. Lilith provides $250,000 in start-up money and does not work in the business. Cliff works full-time in the business, but contributes no capital. The partnership comes to an end after a year, having lost $250,000. (That is, the partnership manages to pay off all creditors, but then has nothing left over. Since the partnership began with $250,000, the partnership has suffered a $250,000 loss.)

For his year of work, Cliff has received nothing. There are no profits, and, whatever the applicable general partnership act, it bars any other form of compensation in the absence of an agreement. At first glance, Lilith appears to have lost $250,000. However, the partners have made no agreement as to loss sharing, so the statutory default rule on loss sharing is in effect, that is, Cliff and Lilith share losses as they would have shared profits; that is, equally. For Cliff's *out-of-pocket* losses to equal Lilith's, $125,000 must make its way from Cliff to Lilith. Cliff will pay $125,000 to the partnership, which will then distribute that amount to Lilith. Both Cliff and Lilith will then have lost $125,000. ◄◄◄

This result may appear harsh. After all, without loss sharing Cliff and Lilith appear each to have lost roughly comparable value. They have lost, that is, the value they provided the partnership in return for becoming partners.[39] Accordingly, if Cliff has to transfer $125,000 to Lilith, his loss of value will exceed hers.

Seeking to avoid such apparently harsh results, some courts have held that the L partner shares losses only if he or she has expressly agreed to do so. Appearances can mislead, however, and those courts have ignored the concept of "opportunity cost"[40] and consequently have misunderstood the balance of losses between K-and-L partners. In the example above, Cliff lost whatever value he could have derived from using his labor elsewhere during the partnership's year of operation. Lilith had a parallel loss—whatever

37. See Section 8.2.

38. Technically, the L partner would pay the partnership, which would then distribute the money to the K partner. See Section 11.5.3.

39. As explained in Section 8.2, the statutory default rules assume that those values are roughly comparable; that is the premise for allocating to Cliff and Lilith equal shares of the profits.

40. When a person has a choice between two mutually exclusive courses of action, the "opportunity cost" of pursuing one is the foregone opportunity to pursue the other.

income she could have derived from investing the $250,000 elsewhere for a year. In addition, without loss sharing, Lilith also lost the $250,000 itself.

Whether the statutory default rule is unfair to Cliff (or perhaps unfair to Lilith) will depend on how the value of Cliff's foregone labor opportunity compares with the value of Lilith's foregone capital opportunity. If Lilith could have earned 10 percent interest by investing her money elsewhere for a year, and if Cliff's lack of skills and odd personality mean that he could have earned no more than $20,000 in salary in some other position, then even after Cliff pays Lilith $125,000, Lilith will have suffered greater detriment than Cliff. Cliff will have lost $125,000 out of pocket, plus the foregone opportunity to earn $20,000 by working elsewhere for the year. Total detriment: $145,000. Lilith will have lost $125,000 out of pocket ($250,000 contributed, offset partially by Cliff's $125,000), plus the foregone opportunity to earn $25,000 interest on her capital. Total detriment: $150,000.

In any event, the language of each general partnership act expressly mandates loss sharing.

§8.6.3 Problems with Appreciation

Under the statutory default rules, when a partner contributes property to the partnership and that property subsequently increases in value, the partnership benefits, not the partner.[41] Eventually, when the partnership realizes the appreciation, that value either offsets business losses or adds to profits. To the extent the appreciation adds to profits, all partners share in the benefit according to their respective profit shares. The partner who originally contributed the property has no special claim on the appreciation.

Occasionally, courts dealing with K-and-L partnerships ignore or misunderstand the default rules and allocate all the appreciation to the K partner (i.e., the partner who contributed the property). They do so either by miscalculating the amount they award each partner or by returning the appreciated asset itself to the K partner.

Example

Cliff and Lilith form a partnership to raise chickens, agreeing to share profits equally. Cliff contributes a small farm worth $50,000. Four years later the partnership comes to an end. By selling all of its assets other than the farm, the partnership has enough cash to exactly pay off its debts.[42] During the

41. See Sections 8.5.1 and 8.5.3.

42. Life does not usually work out so precisely, but this premise simplifies the explanation of the point at issue.

life of the partnership, land values have increased sharply, so the partnership manages to sell the farm for $200,000. How the proceeds are divided will depend on whether the court follows the applicable partnership statute:

- *Applying the Default Rules of All Three Acts*—The partnership pays $50,000 to Cliff, returning to him the value of his contribution.[43] The remaining $150,000 represents post-contribution appreciation and is therefore profits. Cliff and Lilith each receive half.
- *Overcompensating the K Partner*—The partnership either allocates all $200,000 to Cliff or simply transfers ownership of the farm back to him. In either event, Cliff gets the benefit of all the appreciation. ◄◄◄

§8.7 PARTNER'S INTERESTS IN PARTNERSHIP PROPERTY

§8.7.1 Partner's Rights as to Partnership Property

Concerning a partner's rights as to partnership property, UPA (1914) and the two modern acts each reach the same result. However, the modern acts both differ substantially from UPA (1914) in how the rules are stated.

§8.7.2 The UPA (1914) Approach: Partner's Property Rights in the Partnership

According to UPA (1914) §24, each partner has three *property* rights in the partnership: "(1) his rights in specific partnership property, (2) his interest in the partnership, and (3) his right to participate in the management." As to the first and third rights, the "property" label borders on the bizarre; the rights relate to management prerogatives, not property interests. The key to understanding the UPA (1914) approach is therefore to disregard the label and attend instead to the specific content of the rights being described.

a. Management Prerogatives Disguised as Property Rights

A partner's "property" rights under UPA (1914) include two management prerogatives: (i) the right to use the assets of the partnership in furtherance

43. See Sections 8.5.1 and 8.5.3.

of the partnership's business (UPA (1914) §25) and (ii) the right to participate in the management of the partnership (UPA (1914) §24).[44]

The upshot is a fairly straightforward and commonsense notion. Absent a contrary agreement, each partner has the right to possess and use partnership property for the purposes of the business, but no partner has the right to use partnership property for other purposes. Unfortunately, UPA (1914) §25 states this notion in an unnecessarily intricate way. Taking an aggregate approach, the provision describes the right to use business assets for business purposes as "tenancy in partnership."[45]

b. The Partner's Interest — The Partner's Economic Rights

Under UPA (1914) §26, a partner's "interest in the partnership" consists of a right to share in the profits of the partnership and the right to receive, when the partnership ends, the value of any property contributed to the partnership.[46] Although labeling these rights "property" is not misleading, it is redundant. UPA (1914) §18(a) independently establishes that being a partner involves having a right to share in the profits of the business. Likewise, that subsection provides that "[e]ach partner shall be repaid his contributions."[47]

§8.7.3 The Modern Approach

UPA (1997) replaced the oblique approach of UPA (1914) with two straightforward pronouncements, which UPA (2013) has continued:

- "A partner is not a co-owner of partnership property and has no interest in partnership property which can be transferred, either voluntarily or involuntarily."[48]
- "A partner may use or possess partnership property only on behalf of the partnership."[49]

---

44. A partner's "right to participate in the management" under UPA §24(3) is redundant of UPA §18(e). Sections 9.1–9.4 discuss management rights in detail.
45. UPA §25 (1914) (1).
46. UPA §26 (1914) (share of profits and surplus).
47. As for a partner's right to receive back the value of its contribution, see Section 8.5.1 and Section 11.5.3 (describing how UPA (1914) §40 implements UPA (1914) §18).
48. UPA (1997 and 2013) §501.
49. UPA (2013) §401(i); UPA (1997) §401(g).

CASE IN POINT

Case in Point — *Cogar v. Lafferty*

A partnership's real property was sold at a tax sale after the partnership failed to pay its real estate taxes. The partnership was served notice of the right to redeem, but the individual partners were not individually served. One partner sought to invalidate and set aside the sale to a third-party purchaser because he, a partner, was not served with notice of the right to redeem. Noting that that partners of a general partnership are not co-owners of partnership property, the court held that the individual partners had no interest in partnership property and no right to notice of the right to redeem partnership property separate from that notice provided to the partnership.[50] ◀◀◀

§8.8 THE "PICK YOUR PARTNER" PRINCIPLE AND RESTRICTIONS ON THE TRANSFERABILITY (ASSIGNABILITY) OF PARTNERSHIP INTERESTS AND ON THE REMEDIES AVAILABLE TO CREDITORS OF PARTNERS AND TRANSFEREES

§8.8.1 A Note on Nomenclature: Transferee Versus Assignee

Consistent with the notion that a partnership reflects a contract among the partners,[51] UPA (1914):

- uses the contract label "assignment" to describe the transfer of a partner's ownership rights in a general partnership; and
- refers to the transferee accordingly as an "assignee."[52]

An early version of UPA (1997) replaced "assignment" and "assignee" with "transfer" and "transferee." That usage continued into the final version of UPA (1997) and was followed in the original Uniform Limited Liability Company Act (1996), the 2001 version of the Uniform Limited Partnership

50. *Cogar v. Lafferty*, 639 S.E.2d 835 (W. Va. 2006). Partners are co-owners of the partnership business. See Section 7.2.5. However, "business" and "property" are not synonymous. See, e.g., *Farmers State Bank & Trust Co. v. Mikesell*, 51 Ohio App. 3d 69, 70, 554 N.E.2d 900, 901 (1988) ("Although a partner may not assign his interest in particular assets of the partnership, he may assign his interest in the partnership, that is, his right to share in the partnership's profits and surplus.").
51. See Section 7.2.2.
52. UPA (1914) §27(1).

Act, and the Revised Uniform Limited Liability Company Act (2006). The Harmonization Project confirmed the usage.[53]

The language change is almost entirely a matter of style. Although "assignment" can be read as limited to voluntary transfers, case law under UPA (1914) has taken a broader view.[54] Moreover, the same limited reading could apply to UPA (1997), which defines "transfer" to "include [] an assignment, conveyance, lease, mortgage, deed, and encumbrance."[55]

In any event, UPA (2013) removes all doubt on this point, defining "transfer" to specifically include "a transfer by operation of law."[56] A comment notes that, given this definition, the act's transfer restrictions apply "for example, to transfers ordered by a family court as part of a divorce proceeding and transfers resulting from the death of a partner."[57]

§8.8.2 Transferability of a Partner's Ownership Interest Restricted — the Rationale ("Pick Your Partner" Principle)

To give meaning to the notion that a partnership is a *voluntary* association,[58] the law must allow partners collectively the untrammeled right to determine with whom to associate as copartners and with whom to share management and information rights. This untrammeled right reflects what has come to be called the "pick your partner" principle. Per a comment to UPA (2013): "One of the most fundamental characteristics of partnership law is its fidelity to the 'pick your partner' principle."[59]

The principle underlies all three acts, and each act protects the principle by substantially limiting (i) the transferability of partnership interests and (ii) the ability of a judgment creditor of a partner or partner's transferee to access the partner's rights in the partnership.

§8.8.3 Transferability of a Partner's Ownership Interest Restricted — the Rules

All three partnership acts have essentially the same set of default rules pertaining to the transferability of a partner's ownership interest. All three acts

53. For a discussion of the Harmonization Project of the Uniform Law Commission, see Introductory Notes — the ULC Harmonization Project.
54. See, e.g., *Block v. Lea*, 5 Haw. App. 266, 273–74, 688 P.2d 724, 731 (1984) (stating that, under the Hawaii version of UPA (1914) §27(1), a divorce decree would lack the power to substitute one former spouse for another as a partner in a preexisting partnership).
55. UPA (1997) §101(14).
56. UPA (2013) §102(22)(G).
57. *Id.*, comment.
58. See Section 7.2.2.
59. UPA (2013) §503, comment.

bifurcate the ownership interest into economic rights and all other rights. The other rights are sometimes called "management rights" or "governance rights," although the category also includes certain rights to information.[60]

A partner's economic rights are freely transferable. In sharp contrast, no partner can transfer (or assign) any other ownership rights to a nonpartner without the consent of all the other partners. In particular, a partner cannot effect a transfer to a nonpartner that causes the nonpartner to become a partner. In the words of UPA (1997):

> The only transferable interest of a partner in the partnership is the partner's share of the profits and losses of the partnership and the partner's right to receive distributions.[61]

Further, all three acts follow centuries of common law and restrict significantly the rights of a transferee/assignee. The statutory language has changed only slightly over the past 100 years. UPA (1914) §27(1) provided:

> A conveyance by a partner of his interest in the partnership does not of itself dissolve the partnership, nor, as against the other partners in the absence of agreement, entitle the assignee, during the continuance of the partnership, to interfere in the management or administration of the partnership business or affairs, or to require any information or account of partnership transactions, or to inspect the partnership books; but it merely entitles the assignee to receive in accordance with his contract the profits to which the assigning partner would otherwise be entitled.

UPA (2013) provides:

> A transfer, in whole or in part, of a transferable interest: (1) is permissible; (2) does not by itself cause a person's dissociation as a partner or a dissolution and winding up of the partnership business; and (3) [except for very limited rights of a decedent's estate] does not entitle the transferee to: (A) participate in the management or conduct of the partnership's business; or (B) except [for very limited financial information when the partnership dissolves], have access to records or other information concerning the partnership's business.[62]

---

60. See UPA (2013) §503, comment: "A partner's rights in a partnership are bifurcated into economic rights (the transferable interest) and governance rights (including management rights, consent rights, rights to information, rights to seek judicial intervention)."

61. UPA (1997) §502. Perhaps inadvertently, UPA (2013) does not contain the same statutory language. However, an official comment states pointedly that: "Absent a contrary provision in the partnership agreement or the consent of the partners, a 'transferable interest' is the only interest in a partnership that can be transferred to a person not already a partner." UPA (2013) §502, comment. Under both modern acts, a transferable interest encompasses solely economic rights. UPA (2013) §102(23); UPA (1997) §502.

62. UPA (2013) §502(a). UPA (1997) §503(a) used language very similar to the 1914 language:

Example

Larry wants to assign his right to receive profits in the Larry-Moe-Curley partnership to the First National Bank. The Bank wants the assignment as security for a loan it is about to make to Larry. The Bank also wants the right to exercise Larry's management rights while the loan is outstanding and if Larry defaults. The partnership agreement is silent on the subject. To assign the management rights to the Bank, Larry needs the consent of Moe and Curley. An attempted assignment of those rights without that consent will be ineffective. ◀◀◀

Case in Point—*In re Dews*

As part of a divorce settlement, Debtor executed a note in favor of his ex-wife. When he failed to make payments, she obtained a judgment against him. In satisfaction of the judgment, Debtor transferred to his ex-wife a 17 percent interest in a partnership. In the bankruptcy proceeding, Debtor sought to avoid the transaction. The court's decision turned on when the transfer was effected. In determining the date of transfer, the court held in the alternative that (i) a transfer of all rights (governance as well as economic) occurred because the partnership had consented to the assignment, and (ii) even if no consent had been given and no management rights had transferred, Debtor's right to partnership profits (e.g., economic rights) were freely assignable and occurred when the transfer was made.[63] ◀◀◀

This approach to transfer/assignment is consistent with partnership law's default approach to admitting new partners. To transfer or assign governance rights is tantamount to bringing the transferee or assignee into the partnership. Under UPA (1914) §18(g), absent a contrary agreement: "No person can become a member of a partnership without the consent of all the partners." Similarly, under UPA (1997) §401(i), "A person may become a partner only with the consent of all of the partners."[64] Under UPA (2013): "After formation of a partnership, a person becomes a partner . . . with the affirmative vote or consent of all the partners."[65]

> A transfer . . . of a partner's transferable interest in the partnership . . . is permissible [but] does not, as against the other partners or the partnership, entitle the transferee, during the continuance of the partnership, to participate in the management or conduct of the partnership business, to require access to information concerning partnership transactions, or to inspect or copy the partnership books or records.

63. *In re Dews*, 152 B.R. 982, 985 (D. Colo. 1993).

64. Essentially the same language appears in UPA (1914) §18(g) ("(g) No person can become a member of a partnership without the consent of all the partners.").

65. UPA (2013) §402(a)(3).

These default rules are subject to change by the partnership agreement. An agreement permitting the transfer of management rights may be made to apply generally or may pertain solely to a particular category of transfers. The partnership agreement can also restrict transferability, limiting partners' rights to assign even their economic interests.[66]

§8.8.4 "Pick Your Partner" and Restrictions on the Rights of a Partner's Judgment Creditors—the Charging Order

In general, a judgment creditor may enforce the judgment against all nonexempt property of the judgment debtor. A person's interest in a partnership is property, but judgment creditors seeking to reach that property face substantial barriers and limitations.

First, a judgment creditor of a partner (or a transferee) may not attach or levy on the partnership's property, because:

- Conceptually, that property belongs to the partnership and not to any individual partner.
- Under all three acts, an individual partner has no rights in partnership property.[67]
- Although under UPA (1914) individual partners are said to have rights in partnership property, those rights are for the purpose of the partnership business and are in any event inalienable without the agreement of the other partners.[68]

Second, a partner's judgment creditor has no access or right to the partner's noneconomic rights. Those rights are not transferable without the consent of the other partners. All three acts protect the "pick-your-partner" principle by

66. Other law may affect the enforceability of transfer restrictions imposed by statute as well as those imposed by agreement. See UPA (2013) §503, cmt. "Other law may affect the applicability of this section. See 11 U.S.C. §541(c)(1) (providing that, initially at least, all property of a debtor becomes part of the bankruptcy estate regardless of restrictions on transfer)"; See also UCC §§9–406, 9–408 [before 2018] (overriding specified restrictions on assignment in specified circumstances, regardless of whether state law or a contract imposes the restrictions)." In 2018, both UCC sections were amended to exclude ownership interests in partnerships, limited partnerships, and limited liability companies. UCC §§ 9–406(k), 9–408(f).

67. As explained in Section 8.7, the modern acts state this proposition more directly than does UPA (1914).

68. UPA §25(2)(c). Creditors seeking to collect a debt of the partnership can, in contrast, levy on the partnership's property. *Id.*

making a *charging order* the sole remedy for a judgment creditor of a partner or transferee.

This special remedy, first invented under English law,[69] is in the nature of a lien on a partner's *economic* rights. The charging order thus recognizes and reinforces the "off-limits" nature of management rights and channels efforts to obtain access solely to economic rights.

The charging order first functions as a type of garnishment. The creditor applies to a court for an order that, if granted, obligates the partnership to pay to the creditor any amounts that would otherwise be paid to the debtor partner as distributions.[70]

A charging order also functions as a judgment lien. "Upon a showing that distributions under a charging order will not pay the judgment debt within a reasonable time, the court may foreclose the lien and order the sale of the transferable interest."[71] In that event, the economic rights of the debtor partner are sold just like any other property subject to a judgment lien. "The purchaser at the foreclosure sale obtains only the transferable interest [and] does not thereby become a partner."[72] The other partners can use their own, separate funds to redeem the charged rights or buy them at the foreclosure sale, and partnership funds may be used, in the words of UPA (1914), with "the consent of all the partners whose interests are not so charged or sold."[73]

The same rules apply to a creditor of a non-partner (i.e., a transferee) when the creditor seeks to access the non-partner's transferable interest.

Example

The Larry-Moe-Curley partnership owns considerable property, including a modern factory and a large inventory of whoopee cushions. Moe personally owes Shemp $500,000, and that amount has been reduced to judgment. Shemp cannot levy against the factory or the inventory, since that property belongs to the partnership. Shemp can, however, obtain a charging order against Moe's economic rights in the partnership. With that order in place, Shemp will receive any distributions the partnership would otherwise make to Moe. ◄◄◄

A charging order and any foreclosure and sales relate only to the debtor partner's economic rights. Neither the creditor nor any foreclosure purchaser

69. English Partnership Act of 1890, §23(2). UPA (1914) §28 is derived from the English statute, and UPA (1997) §504 is derived from UPA (1914) §28. UPA (2013) §504 substantially modernizes the statutory language but without intending any change in meaning.
70. UPA (1914) §28(1); UPA (1997) §504(b); UPA (2013) §504(a).
71. UPA (2013) §504(c).
72. Id.
73. UPA (1914) §28(2)(b). See also UPA (1997) §504(c)(2) and (3); UPA (2013) §504(e).

obtains any rights to participate in the management of the partnership or to possess or use partnership property.

Example

Although the Larry-Moe-Curley partnership enjoys good long-term prospects, the business is not currently making any profits. Shemp wishes to collect on his judgment now and persuades a court to foreclose the charging order. The charged interest is sold at auction to Lucille, who in essence now owns whatever economic interests Moe had as a partner. However, neither the foreclosure nor the sale makes Lucille a partner or entitles her to participate in the operation and management of the business. ◀◀◀

§8.9 A PARTNER'S RIGHT TO INDEMNITY

UPA (1914) §18(b) states, as a default rule, that

> The partnership must indemnify every partner in respect of payments made and personal liabilities reasonably incurred by him in the ordinary and proper conduct of its business, or for the preservation of its business or property.

The most recent formulation appears in UPA (2013) §401(b)-(c):

> A partnership shall reimburse a partner for any payment made by the partner in the course of the partner's activities on behalf of the partnership, if the partner complied with this section [pertaining to management rights] and Section 409 [stating a partner's duty to partnership and fellow partners] in making the payment.
>
> A partnership shall indemnify and hold harmless a person with respect to any claim or demand against the person and any debt, obligation, or other liability incurred by the person by reason of the person's former or present capacity as a partner, if the claim, demand, debt, obligation, or other liability does not arise from the person's breach of this section or Section 407 [pertaining to unlawful distributions from a limited liability partnership] or 409.

However worded, this rule closely resembles an agent's right of indemnity from its principal.[74]

74. See Section 4.3.1.

Example

In the Larry, Moe, and Curley whoopee cushion partnership, all partners share in the marketing work. A potential customer comes to town to discuss the possibility of placing a large order. Moe spends $300 wining and dining the customer, but the customer decides against placing the order. The partnership must reimburse Moe. His efforts were reasonable in light of the shared marketing responsibilities, and the amount of expense was reasonable in light of the potentially large order. ◀ ◀ ◀

Example

Same situation, except the partners have agreed that Larry alone will handle marketing efforts and sales promotion.[75] Under UPA (1914), that agreement means that Moe's payments for wining and dining expenses have not been "made . . . in the ordinary and *proper* conduct of [the partnership's] business,"[76] and, therefore, he is not entitled to reimbursement. Under UPA (1997), the result is arguably the same, on the theory that the agreement puts Moe's entertaining outside the "the ordinary course of the business of the partnership."[77] Under UPA (2013), Moe likely will not be reimbursed. Given the agreement as to marketing, Moe's expenses were not a "payment made by the partner in the course of the partner's activities on behalf of the partnership."[78] ◀ ◀ ◀

Problem 59

The partnership agreement of a law firm provides a complicated formula for determining each partner's annual profit share. The formula takes into account billable hours, payments actually received on account of work billed, and work brought into the firm ("rainmaking"). At the end of one year, one partner seeks "a more egalitarian approach" and contends that the partnership statute requires partners to share profits equally. Is that partner correct? ◀ ◀ ◀

75. For the enforceability of such agreements *inter se* the partners, see Section 9.6. For the effect of such agreements on the *power* of partners to bind the partnership to third parties, see Sections 10.1–10.4.
76. UPA (1914) §18(b).
77. UPA (1997) §401(c).
78. UPA (2103) §401(b).

Explanation

No. All three uniform general partnership acts provide for equal profit shares *as a default rule*. When partners displace the default rule by agreement, the agreement governs. ◄ ◄ ◄

Problem 60

Paul and Dennis operate a basketball camp as an ordinary general partnership. Theirs is a handshake deal; they have no written agreement.

A camper who is hurt at the camp successfully sues the partnership for negligence and recovers a judgment of $250,000. The partnership has no money, and the camper collects the entire amount from Paul. Assuming that the partnership has sustained no other losses but has no money with which to reimburse Paul, how much, if anything, can Paul collect from Dennis? Can Dennis successfully argue that "the losses should lie where they fall"? ◄ ◄ ◄

Explanation

Dennis owes Paul $125,000. Absent a contrary agreement, partners share losses as they do profits—equally. Collection by a third party does not change how losses are allocated.[79] ◄ ◄ ◄

Problem 61

In 2005, Larry, Moe, and Curley became partners in an entertainment business. Their partnership agreement set a term of 10 years and stated

> Profits shall be calculated and paid on an annual basis, with the fiscal year being the calendar year. For any profit made in any fiscal year, Larry will receive 60 percent, Moe 25 percent, and Curley 15 percent. Losses will be shared as provided in the Uniform Partnership Act.

79. See Section 7.3.1(c).

Each year in the period 2005 through 2008, the partnership broke even. In 2009, the partnership lost $100,000. How should that loss be apportioned under UPA (1914)? UPA (1997)? UPA (2013)? ◄ ◄ ◄

Explanation

The loss should be apportioned 60/25/15. Under all three general partnership acts, absent a contrary agreement losses are apportioned the same way as profits.[80]

Problem 62

Rachael and Natasha go into partnership together to own a natural foods store. They each put up $5,000 and jointly select a storefront to rent. During the first year, Natasha is the "silent" partner. She does no work for the business. Rachael, in contrast, works about 50 hours per week in the store, with no vacation. At the end of the year, the partnership has made a profit of $30,000. Rachael proposes a profit split of $20,000 for herself and $10,000 for Natasha. She explains, "I put in at least 2,500 hours this year, and our lowest paid clerk got $4 per hour. I figure I'm worth at least that. Four times 2,500 is $10,000, leaving another $20,000, which we split equally." Is Natasha obliged to agree to Rachael's proposal? ◄ ◄ ◄

Explanation

No. Absent a contrary agreement, Rachael's work in the partnership business brings her no right to extra remuneration.[81] Absent a contrary agreement, the partners split profits equally.[82] ◄ ◄ ◄

80. See Section 8.3.1.
81. See Section 8.4.
82. See Section 8.3.1.

Problem 63

Joseph owns 500 acres of land on which he grows pine trees for harvest and for sale each year at Christmastime. The land is worth $500,000, and land values in the region are increasing steadily. Joseph asks Vladi to operate the Christmas tree business for him. In return for Vladi's promise to stay for five years, Joseph promises Vladi an annual salary of $10,000 plus half the profits.

Assume that (i) Vladi makes a number of changes to the land, including harvesting some trees, planting others, and putting in a few dirt roads; (ii) at all times relevant title to the land is in Joseph's name; and (iii) a court finds that the arrangement between Joseph and Vladi constitutes a partnership with a five-year term. If UPA (1914) governs, at the end of the five years, will Joseph still own the land? Does the result differ under UPA (1997) or UPA (2013)? ◄ ◄ ◄

Explanation

Under all three acts, the answer depends on whether Joseph has contributed the land to the partnership or merely furnished its use.

Under UPA (1914) case law, there are facts that point in the direction of *contribution*. The land was of central importance to the partnership, and the partnership did (through Vladi) make some improvements to the property.

However, it seems unlikely that Joseph intended to give up ownership of the land. Even under UPA (1914), a partnership can own land in its own name, and Joseph never transferred title to the partnership. More importantly, to view the land as contributed is to construe into existence an extraordinary sweetheart deal for Vladi.

The deal was sweet for Vladi even assuming that Joseph merely *furnished* the *use* of the land to the partnership. Vladi brought to the partnership only his labor, for which he received not only a salary but also half of the profits. At minimum, Joseph furnished the use of land worth $500,000 and contributed any trees that Vladi harvested from the land on behalf of the partnership. For that, Joseph received in return less than Vladi—that is, merely a 50 percent profit share.

If Joseph *contributed* the land, then the deal is even sweeter for Vladi. The land itself belongs to the partnership; any appreciation will belong to the partnership; and Vladi will have a right to half of that appreciation. That deal seems too good to be either true or intended.

Under UPA (1997) and UPA (2013), the result would be the same, with the analysis buttressed by the presumption established by section 204(d) of both acts:

> Property acquired in the name of one or more of the partners, without an indication in the instrument transferring title to the property of the person's

capacity as a partner or of the existence of a partnership and without use of partnership assets, is presumed to be separate property, even if used for partnership purposes. ◀ ◀ ◀

Problem 64

This Problem is based on a children's poem by Eugene Field:

> Wynken, Blynken, and Nod one night
> Sailed off in a wooden shoe—
> Sailed on a river of crystal light,
> Into a sea of dew.
> "Where are you going, and what do you wish?"
> The old moon asked the three.
> "We've come to fish for the herring fish
> That live in this beautiful sea;
> Nets of silver and gold have we!"
> Said Wynken,
> Blynken,
> And Nod.

Assume that Wynken, Blynken, and Nod are partners. Last year, before the partners divided profits, the "nets of silver and gold" were purchased using some of the revenues generated by the sale of herring fish. Wynken is taking her family fishing and wants to take one-third of the nets with her on the outing. Under UPA (1914), does she have the legal right to do so? ◀ ◀ ◀

Explanation

EXPLANATION

No—not without the consent of her fellow partners. The nets belong to the partnership, not to the partners. "Unless the contrary intention appears, property acquired with partnership funds is partnership property."[83] Under UPA (1914) §25(2)(a), Wynken has an equal right to possess partnership property, but only for partnership purposes. To use partnership property for personal purposes requires the consent of the other partners. ◀ ◀ ◀

Problem 65

Although the Rachael/Natasha health food store partnership is doing well enough, Natasha has fallen on hard times. One of her personal creditors is

83. UPA (1914) §8(2). The result would be the same under both modern acts.

about to sue her. To avoid that embarrassment, Natasha persuades the creditor to release the claim in return for "an assignment of all of my rights in the partnership I co-own with Rachael." The creditor then approaches Rachael and insists upon a voice in running the health food store. Is Rachael obliged to accede? ◀ ◀ ◀

Explanation

No, regardless of which act applies. Absent a contrary agreement, Natasha may transfer her economic rights in the partnership—her "transferable interest"—but cannot transfer her rights to participate in management.[84] ◀ ◀ ◀

Problem 66

Rosie, Philip, and Sylvia operate a dental supply business as partners. Rosie and Philip are the "outside salesmen," and Sylvia runs the office. Rosie and Philip both do a lot of driving, and every two years, partnership money is used to buy them each a new car. Title to the cars is in the partnership's name, and the partnership pays for the car insurance. However, the price of each car is reported as profit on Rosie's and Phil's respective K-1 forms. A judgment creditor of Rosie's tries to levy on the car she currently drives. What result under UPA (1914)? Under UPA (2013)? ◀ ◀ ◀

Explanation

Under either statute, the levy will be successful only if the car is not partnership property. A personal creditor of a partner cannot levy on partnership property.[85]

Under UPA (1914), several factors suggest that Rosie's car is partnership property. Partnership funds were used to purchase and to insure it. Title is in the partnership's name. Moreover, the car is of central use in the partnership's business.

The question is, however, ultimately one of the partners' intent, and the K-1 forms argue strongly that the car is Rosie's personal property. By treating the price of the car as profit allocated to Rosie, the K-1 form effectively

84. See Section 8.8.4.
85. UPA §25(2)(c); RUPA §504(e).

characterized the car as her personal property. It is hard to dismiss that characterization as self-serving or artificial, because (i) it was integrally connected with the way the partners structured their relationship, and (ii) it created tax liability for Rosie.[86]

Under UPA (2013), the result may be different, because section §204(a)(1) applies. That provision states: "Property is partnership property if acquired in the name of . . . the partnership." Because the car is titled in the partnership's name, it is evident that the car was acquired "in the name of the partnership." The creditor's only hope is to argue that the K-1 form reflects an agreement between the partnership and Rosie, making Rosie the car's owner despite the title being in the partnership's name. ◀◀◀

Problem 67

Suzanne and Bernard run a dance school as a partnership. The school serves children between the ages of 4 and 14. The highlight of each year is a splendiferous dance recital held at a public auditorium rented by the partnership. Suzanne takes care of the business side of operations, and Bernard has agreed that Suzanne alone has the right to sign checks and make payments for the partnership. Bernard handles the artistic side of the business.

This year, disaster threatened the school. On the night of the big recital, Bernard arrived at the auditorium and found it locked. After some frantic telephoning, he located the auditorium manager, who said that she had never received the dance school's rental check. (It had apparently been lost in the mail.) The manager refused to open the auditorium without a check in hand. Suzanne was out of town, so Bernard wrote a personal check for the rental fee. Under UPA (1997), is Bernard entitled to reimbursement from the partnership, or does his foray into the business side of the partnership disqualify the expense? What result if UPA (2013) applies? ◀◀◀

Explanation

Under UPA (1997), Bernard is entitled to reimbursement. Canceling or rescheduling the recital at the last minute could have been disastrous for the dance school's business. While Bernard's payment (his "foray") was probably not "in the *ordinary* course of the business of the partnership,"[87] the payment *was* "for the preservation of [the partnership's] business."[88]

The analysis under UPA (2013) §401(c) is less clear. Bernard is entitled to reimbursement for "any payment made by the partner in the course of the partner's activities on behalf of the partnership, if the partner complied

86. See Section 7.3.2(a) (profits allocated to a partner are taxable income for that partner).
87. UPA (1997) §401(c) (emphasis added)
88. *Id.*

with this section [401 —pertaining to management rights] and Section 409 [pertaining to a partner's duties] in making the payment."[89] Bernard would have to argue that the task allocation between Suzanne and him contains an implied exception for emergency circumstances. If that argument prevails, Bernard should have no problems under Section 409. ◀◀◀

89. UPA (2013) §401(b).

CHAPTER 9

Management Issues and Fiduciary Duties

§9.1 THE PANOPLY OF MANAGEMENT RIGHTS

Co-management is a key attribute of a partnership, and — under the default rules of all three uniform general partnership acts — each partner has a full panoply of management rights:

- the right to know what is going on in the partnership;
- the right to be involved in conducting the business, including in some circumstances the right to bind the partnership to third parties;[1]
- the right to participate in collective decision-making, with decisions made in some circumstances by "majority rule" and in other circumstances only with unanimous consent; and
- the right to veto certain other types of decisions.

§9.2 THE RIGHT TO KNOW

Under all three uniform acts, each partner has a right to obtain from the partnership and from fellow partners full and complete information concerning the partnership and its business.

1. Chapter 10 considers a partner's right and power to bind the partnership to third parties.

§9.2.1 Under UPA (1914)

Under UPA (1914), the right to information rests on four sources, with sections 19 and 20 providing the most direct authority. UPA (1914) §19 states that "every partner shall at all times have access to and may inspect and copy any of [the partnership books]." UPA (1914) §20 states: "Partners shall render on demand true and full information of all things affecting the partnership to any partner. . . ."[2]

UPA (1914) §18(e) provides authority by implication, entitling each partner to an equal right "in the management and conduct of the partnership business." A partner who lacks information cannot meaningfully manage or conduct business; therefore, for §18(e) to be meaningful, the provision must by implication encompass access to all relevant business information.

The concept of fiduciary duty also provides authority by implication. As discussed in Section 9.7, partners are mutual fiduciaries. Each partner owes fellow partners a duty of loyalty, which includes a duty of candor. If Partner *A* owes Partner B a duty of candor, by implication Partner B has a right to whatever information Partner *A* is duty bound to provide.

§9.2.2 Under UPA (1997)

a. In General

UPA (1997) provides far more detail on this issue than did UPA (1914). UPA (1997) §403 contains a comprehensive set of information access rules that recognize three categories of information: information in the partnership's books and records; information that one partner is obliged to volunteer to another; and information that one partner is entitled to demand and receive from another. The rules can be as succinctly quoted as paraphrased:

> (b) A partnership shall provide partners and their agents and attorneys access to its books and records. . . . The right of access provides the opportunity to inspect and copy books and records during ordinary business hours. A partnership may impose a reasonable charge, covering the costs of labor and material, for copies of documents furnished.
>
> (c) Each partner and the partnership shall furnish to a partner, and to the legal representative of a deceased partner or partner under legal disability:

---

2. In some situations, a partner has an affirmative duty to disclose information to a fellow partner, even without a demand. Section 9.7.5 discusses those situations.

> (1) without demand, any information concerning the partnership's business and affairs reasonably required for the proper exercise of the partner's rights and duties under the partnership agreement or this [Act]; and
>
> (2) on demand, any other information concerning the partnership's business and affairs, except to the extent the demand or the information demanded is unreasonable or otherwise improper under the circumstances.

UPA (1997) does not require a partnership to maintain any formal records,[3] recognizing that "general partnerships are often informal or even inadvertent."[4] However, the official Comment to Section 403 counsels:

> In general, a partnership should, at a minimum, keep those books and records necessary to enable the partners to determine their share of the profits and losses, as well as their rights on withdrawal. . . . The partnership must also maintain any books and records required by state or federal taxing or other governmental authorities.[5]

If books and records do exist, a partner is entitled to access under UPA (1997) §403(b) without having to demonstrate, state, or even possess a proper purpose. The Comment explains that "A partner's unlimited personal liability justifies an unqualified right of access to the partnership books and records."[6] However, nothing in the statutory text or comments qualifies this right when a partnership is an LLP.[7]

In contrast, the duty to volunteer information is confined to information related to a particular function—namely, information "reasonably required for the proper exercise of the [recipient] partner's rights and duties."[8] This phrase reaches not only to the conduct of the partnership business but also to some partner-to-partner interactions.

---

3. UPA (1997) §403(a) (referring to a partnership's "books and records, if *any*") (emphasis added).
4. UPA (1997) §403, comment 1.
5. *Id.*
6. *Id.*, comment 2. The same comment states: "An abuse of the right to inspect and copy might constitute a violation of the obligation of good faith and fair dealing for which the other partners would have a remedy." For a discussion of this obligation, see Section 9.7.4. If the information is misused in connection with a violation of a partner's duty of care or loyalty, the partnership and other partners might have a remedy for a breach of those duties. See Section 9.7.3.
7. In an LLP, no partner is liable for the partnership's debts solely by reason of being a partner. See Section 17.2.
8. UPA (1997) §403(c)(1).

Example

Rachael and Charlotte are each partners in a general partnership governed by UPA (1997), and Rachael is considering selling her transferable interest to Charlotte. While the two partners are negotiating price, Charlotte learns some business information that suggests that the partnership is about to enter a "boom" period. Because Rachael's transfer of her transferable interest is her right under UPA (1997) §503(a)(1), Charlotte's disclosure of that information is "reasonably required for the proper exercise of [Rachael's] rights . . . under . . . this [Act]." ◀ ◀ ◀

If a particular item of material information is apparent in the partnership's records, whether UPA (1997) obliges a partner to disseminate that information to fellow partners depends on how the circumstances array against the pivotal legal question—that is, whether, in the circumstances, disclosure by one partner is "reasonably required for the proper exercise of [another] partner's rights and duties."[9]

Example

A partnership governed by UPA (1997) has two partners, each of whom is regularly engaged in conducting the partnership's activities, both of whom are aware of and have regular access to all significant partnership records, and neither of whom has special responsibility for or knowledge about any particular aspect of those activities or the partnership records pertaining to any particular aspect of those activities. Most likely, neither partner is obliged to draw the other partner's attention to information apparent in the partnership's records. ◀ ◀ ◀

Example

A partnership governed by UPA (1997) has three partners. One of the three is the managing partner with day-to-day responsibility for running the partnership's business. The other two meet periodically with the managing partner, and together with that partner make "all decisions relating to any substantial change in policy." Most likely, the managing partner has a duty to draw the attention of the other partners to important information, even if that information would be apparent from a review of the partnership's records.[10] ◀ ◀ ◀

---

9. UPA (1997) §403(c)(1).

10. These Examples, and the passage that precedes them, are taken from the official comments to the Uniform Limited Partnership Act (2001), §407(b)(1). The author served as Reporter for the ULC committee that drafted that Act.

In some circumstances, another section of UPA (1997) may come into play. UPA (1997) §404(d) codifies the common law obligation of good faith and fair dealing,[11] and comment 4 states, somewhat cryptically (and without examples or illustration): "In some situations the obligation of good faith includes a disclosure component. Depending on the circumstances, a partner may have an affirmative disclosure obligation that supplements the Section 403 duty to render information."[12]

b. A Departure from Prior Law—Duty to Inform Not a Fiduciary Duty

Case law under UPA (1914) generally characterized a partner's obligation to provide information to fellow partners as a fiduciary duty. UPA (1997), in contrast, clearly states the contrary.[13] Section 404(a) provides: "The only fiduciary duties a partner owes to the partnership and the other partners are the duty of loyalty and the duty of care set forth in subsections (b) and (c)." The duty to provide information is "set forth" in §403, not subsection (b) or (c) of §404.[14]

The difference between UPA (1997) and prior law is more than a matter of labels. Courts typically take an expansive approach to construing and applying fiduciary duties. They are rarely as liberal when imposing liability under a statute. Moreover, a breach of fiduciary duty can support a claim for disgorgement[15] and, in egregious circumstances, for punitive damages.[16] In contrast, one who breaches a statutory duty typically risks only a claim for ordinary damages.

c. The Role of the Partnership Agreement

The information access provisions of UPA (1997) are "quasi-default rules"—that is, subject to change by the partnership agreement within limits specified by the act. In particular, "[t]he partnership agreement may not . . . unreasonably restrict the right of access to books and records under Section 403(b)."[17]

As with other aspects of the partnership agreement, a provision limiting information rights may be written, oral, or implied through conduct.[18]

---

11. See Section 9.7.4.
12. ULLCA (2013) has a very different view of this implied covenant. See Section 15.4.8.
13. Fiduciary duty is discussed in detail in Section 9.7.
14. UPA (2013) does not "cabin in" a partner's fiduciary duties. See Section 9.7.2(b).
15. For an explanation of disgorgement, see Section 9.7.3(a).
16. See Section 9.7.3.
17. UPA (1997), §103(b)(2). Note that this limit does not protect the access rights under UPA (1997) §403(c). The partnership agreement can also expand a partner's access rights beyond those specified in UPA (1997).
18. As for the dangers inherent in oral and implied agreements, see Section 9.8.2.

Case in Point — *Brennan v. Brennan Associates*

After the death of a partner, another partner brought an action seeking *inter alia* access to the partnership's books and records. The trial court: (i) noted that the plaintiff merely wanted to "peruse" the records with no particular information in mind; (ii) found in the history of this partnership that partners had not been permitted to "peruse" the records, but rather had to ask the bookkeeper to locate and deliver a specific record; and (iii) rejected the access claim. The Connecticut Supreme Court affirmed, treating the custom of the partnership as an implied agreement limiting the statutory right of access.[19] ◀◀◀

§9.2.3 Under UPA (2013)

UPA (2013) derives in part from UPA (1997) provision and in part from provisions developed in the 2001 version of the Uniform Limited Partnership Act. The principal differences between the 1997 and 2013 versions are as follows:

- As explained in detail in Section 9.7.2(b), UPA (2013) rejects UPA (1997)'s "cabined in" approach to partner fiduciary duty. Under UPA (2013), a partner's fiduciary and related duties "include" but are not limited to those stated in the statute. As a consequence, in some circumstances fiduciary duty will oblige a partner to disclose information to fellow partners, and a failure to disclose will occasion the panoply of remedies available for a breach of fiduciary duty.[20]
- UPA (2013) provides substantially more detail as to the information rights of former partners.[21]
- UPA (2013) contains an additional authorization for limiting access to information:

> In addition to any restriction or condition stated in its partnership agreement, a partnership, as a matter within the ordinary course of its business, may impose reasonable restrictions and conditions on access

19. *Brennan v. Brennan Associates*, 977 A.2d 107, 122–124 (Conn. 2009).
20. See Section 9.9.
21. UPA (2013) §408(e).

to and use of information to be furnished under this section, including designating information confidential and imposing nondisclosure and safeguarding obligations on the recipient.[22]

§9.3 THE RIGHT TO BE INVOLVED IN THE BUSINESS

Each partner has the right to be involved in the business: to get his, her, or its[23] hands dirty, to actually take part in the work of the partnership. This right brings no extra compensation, because under the default rules of all three acts working in the business does not increase a partner's payout.[24] The right to participate can be psychologically important, however, and working in the business can be a very effective way to keep "in the know."

All three acts establish this right to be involved in essentially the same language, according each partner "equal rights in the management and *conduct* of the [partnership] business."[25]

§9.4 THE RIGHT TO PARTICIPATE IN DECISION-MAKING: SOME DECISIONS SUBJECT TO MAJORITY VOTE OR CONSENT; OTHERS SUBJECT TO EACH PARTNER'S VETO

§9.4.1 The Basic Default Structure

a. The Basic Approach

When partners disagree, under the default rules of all three acts, subject to any contrary provision in the partnership agreement:

22. UPA (2013) §408(j). The subsection also provides that: "In a dispute concerning the reasonableness of a restriction under this subsection, the partnership has the burden of proving reasonableness." In contrast, if partner challenges a restriction stated in the partnership agreement, ordinary rules of civil procedure put the burden of proof on the partner.
23. A partner that is an organization (e.g., a limited liability company or corporation) would take part through its agents.
24. UPA (2013) §401(j); UPA (1997) §401(h); UPA (1914) §18(f). See Sections 8.2 and 8.4.
25. UPA (2013) §401(h); UPA (1997) §401(f); UPA (1914) §18(e) (emphasis added). UPA §25(2)(a) buttresses the point with its concept of co-tenancy in partnership: Each partner has, as a property right, "an equal right with his partners to possess specific property for partnership purposes." As previously explained, under the modern acts, management rights do not masquerade as property rights. See Section 8.7.3.

- the partners resolve the disagreement by some form of collective decision-making: typically via consent (written, oral, or implied in fact) or a vote;[26]
- each partner has equal decision-making power; thus voting or consent is *per capita*, regardless of how much: (i) each partner has contributed to the partnership; and (ii) each partner works in the partnership's business;[27] and
- some disputes are resolved by majority consent or vote, while other actions require unanimity (thus according each partner a veto right).[28]

b. Determining What Vote Is Required — UPA (1914)

Three provisions in UPA (1914) comprise the default rules for determining the consent or vote required for resolving disagreements among the partners. UPA (1914) §§9(3) and 18(g) list particular matters requiring unanimous consent. Section 18(h) provides a general rule for disagreements not covered by UPA §§9(3) or 18(g).

---

26. UPA (2013) §401(k); UPA (1997) §401(j); UPA (1914) §18(h). "Vote" implies a more formal procedure than "consent." For example, THE MERRIAM WEBSTER DICTIONARY (3d ed. 1974) defines "consent" as "to give assent or approval" and "vote" as "a usually formal expression of opinion or will in response to a proposed decision." See *York v. Mathis*, 68 A. 746, 750 (Me. 1907) ("It is not necessary that [consent] should be created by a formal vote passed at a formal meeting or proved by a formal record. It may be inferred from the situation and conduct of the parties."). UPA (1914) uses "consent" solely. See, e.g., UPA (1914) §§18(j) ("No person can become a member of a partnership without the consent of all the partners."); 25(2)(a) ("A partner, subject to the provisions of this act and to any agreement between the partners, has an equal right with his partners to possess specific partnership property for partnership purposes; but he has no right to possess such property for any other purpose without the consent of his partners."); 41(3) (Liability continues "[w]hen any partner retires or dies and the business of the dissolved partnership is continued . . . , with the consent of the retired partners or the representative of the deceased partner."). In UPA (1997), usage is inconsistent. Sometimes the act refers to "consent," sometimes to "vote," and sometimes simply to "majority." See, e.g., UPA (1997) §§401 (i) ("A person may become a partner only with the consent of all of the partners."); 401(j) ("An act outside the ordinary course of business of a partnership and an amendment to the partnership agreement may be undertaken only with the consent of all of the partners."); 1001(b) ("The terms and conditions on which a partnership becomes a limited liability partnership must be approved by the vote necessary to amend the partnership agreement. . . ."); and 401(j) ("A difference arising as to a matter in the ordinary course of business of a partnership may be decided by a majority of the partners."). UPA (2013) refers to "vote or consent." See, e.g., UPA (2013) §§402(b)(3) (providing for a person to become a partner "with the affirmative vote or consent of all the partners"); 601(4) (providing that in specified circumstances a person may be "expelled as a partner by the affirmative vote or consent of all the other partners").
27. UPA (2013) §401(h); UPA (1997) §401(f) and (j); UPA (1914) §18(e) and (h).
28. UPA (2013) §401(k); UPA (1997) §401(j); UPA (1914) §§18(h) and 9(3).

1. Particular Matters Requiring Unanimous Approval

Under UPA (1914) §9(3), unless a partnership agreement provides otherwise, the following actions require unanimous approval:

- assigning the partnership's property in trust to creditors or in return for the assignee's promise to pay the partnership's debts;
- disposing of the good will of the business;
- doing any other act which would make it impossible to carry on the partnership's ordinary business;
- confessing a judgment against the partnership;
- submitting a claim by or against the partnership to arbitration.

UPA (1914) §18(g) adds another matter: "No person can become a member of a partnership without the consent of all the partners."

2. The General Rule of UPA §18(h)

For matters not covered by UPA (1914) §§9(3) or 18(g), the general rule of §18(h) appears simple enough:

> Any difference arising as to ordinary matters connected with the partnership business may be decided by a majority of the partners; but no act in contravention of any agreement between the partners may be done rightfully without the consent of all the partners.

Example

Rachael, Charlotte, and Carolyn form a partnership to raise chickens and eventually have a disagreement about where to buy their chicken feed. Rachael wants to buy from Eli's Feed and Stock. Both Charlotte and Carolyn prefer Rebecca's Ranching Necessities. The partnership agreement is silent. On this ordinary matter, covered by neither UPA (1914) §9(3) nor §18(g), Charlotte and Carolyn will prevail. Each partner has one vote, UPA (1914) §18(e), and a majority vote controls, UPA (1914) §18(h). ◄◄◄

Example

The Rachael-Charlotte-Carolyn partnership buys chicken feed from Rebecca's Ranching Necessities. Later a dispute develops over the quality of the feed. Rebecca proposes submitting the dispute to binding arbitration. Charlotte and Carolyn think arbitration is a good idea, but Rachael objects. Rachael's objection means that none of the partners has the right to commit the partnership to the arbitration. Under UPA (1914) §9(3), unanimity is necessary unless the partnership agreement provides otherwise.[29] ◀◀◀

3. The Problem of the Omitted Category

The rule of UPA (1914) §18(h) is problematic, because its language omits a category of conduct: matters that are not "ordinary" (i.e., that are highly unusual or significant) but that do not involve "an act in contravention" of a partnership agreement. See Figure 9.1.

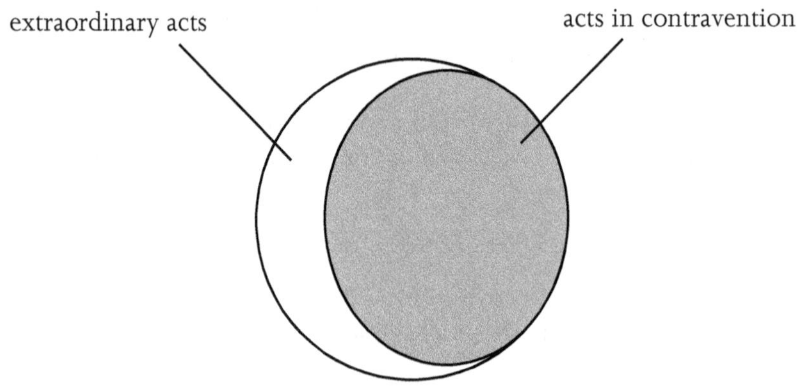

Figure 9.1. How the Set of "Extraordinary" Matters Extends Beyond the Set of "Acts in Contravention"

Example

For five years the Rachael-Charlotte-Carolyn partnership profitably raises and sells chickens. Then Rachael and Charlotte decide the partnership should "branch out" into raising cattle, which involves significantly different equipment, feed, skills, and contacts than chicken farming and would require the partnership to invest a substantial amount of money in purchasing equipment and stock. Carolyn objects to the change, but nothing in the partnership agreement limits the scope of the partnership's business. The decision on expansion is not "ordinary," but neither would expansion contravene an express provision of the partners' agreement. ◀◀◀

The case law under UPA (1914) resolves this conundrum by generally holding that extraordinary changes require unanimous consent. Some cases hold that a decision to depart substantially from past practices actually does contravene an agreement, because the past practices imply an agreement

29. As for the *power* to commit the partnership to binding arbitration, see Sections 10.3.6 and 10.4.1.

among the partners. Other cases pay less homage to the language of §18(h), recognize the omitted category, and establish a rule for it. Noting that a partnership is a *voluntary* association, and that each partner is *personally* liable for debts arising from the partnership's operations, these cases hold as a matter of policy that each partner must consent to any fundamental change in a partnership or its operations.[30]

c. Determining What Vote Is Required — the Modern Acts

Under the modern acts, the rule is simpler. The list of decisions specifically requiring unanimous consent has been winnowed down to two items: the admission of a partner and amendment of the partnership agreement.[31] The "omitted category" has been expressly included as requiring unanimous consent:

> A difference arising as to a matter in the ordinary course of business of a partnership may be decided by a majority of the partners. An act outside the ordinary course of business of a partnership and an amendment to the partnership agreement may be undertaken only with the affirmative vote or consent of all the partners.[32]

d. The Boundary Between "Ordinary" and "Extraordinary"

The precise boundary between "ordinary" and "extraordinary" is easier to find in a diagram than in actual cases or other real-life situations. A few generalizations are possible, however, and they are equally applicable under all three acts. Substantial changes to the nature of the partnership's business are likely to require unanimous consent. So too are decisions to increase substantially the size of the business, where that increase requires a significant increase in the liability exposure or investment risk of each partner. Changes in the standards for admitting new partners or expelling old ones probably also require unanimity.[33]

Example

Robert, Martin, and John have a partnership that invests in real estate. Each partner contributed $500,000 to get the business going, and for the five

30. These cases generally predate the advent of the limited liability partnership.
31. UPA (2013) §301 (1) and (2); UPA (1997) §401(i) and (j). Section 301 of the modern acts, which provide the analog to UPA (1914) §9, contains nothing of section 9(3). Under UPA (1914), amending the partnership agreement also requires unanimous consent, although UPA (1914) does not state so particularly. The rule follows from general principles of contract law and the notion that the partnership agreement is an agreement "of the partners." For further discussion of the partnership agreement, see Section 7.1.4.
32. UPA (2013) §401(k). UPA (1997) §401(j) is identical except that it refers only to consent and not also to voting.
33. For a discussion of partner expulsion, see Sections 9.7.5(c), 9.7.5(d)(1), and Chapter 11, Problem 99.

years of its existence the partnership has invested in properties averaging approximately $1,000,000 each in value. The partnership agreement does not mention any limit on the size of any single investment. Robert and Martin wish to have the partnership buy a large apartment building that has just come on the market. To buy the building, the partnership will have to assume a $12 million mortgage. Although the purchase would not contravene any express provision of the partnership agreement, it would fundamentally change the nature of the partnership business and significantly increase each partner's exposure to personal liability. Most likely, Robert and Martin need John's consent to rightfully make this extraordinary decision. ◀◀◀

§9.4.2 The Special Problem of Management Deadlock

What happens when the partners are in disagreement, a majority vote is necessary to resolve the disagreement, but no majority is possible?

Example

Alice and Ariel have a partnership that operates a grocery store. They have for several years purchased bread from National Bakery. Alice decides that the bread is inferior and the price too high. She wants to find a new supplier. Ariel thinks that both the bread and the price are fine. This is certainly an "ordinary" matter, but neither partner can muster a majority vote. ◀◀◀

This problem arises most often in two-person partnerships. The cases hold that the partner proposing the change loses; that is, the status quo prevails. As one authority put it, "[I]f the partners are equally divided, those who forbid a change must have their way."[34] This rule is consistent with all three acts; each requires at least a majority to take action in the event of a dispute. How the rule works in practice, however, can depend on how the partners (and eventually sometimes a court) conceptualize the matter in dispute.

Example

Alice and Ariel are meeting to discuss Alice's opposition to buying bread from National Bakery. Ariel says, "What's at issue is your idea that we discontinue using National. I vote no. There's no majority, so you lose." Alice says, "Oh no. You don't understand. What's at issue is where we buy bread this week. You're proposing National. I vote no. There's no majority,

34. Ernest H. Scamell, Lindley on the Law of Partnership (15th ed.), at 477 (1984), quoted in *Summers v. Dooley*, 481 P.2d 318, 321 (Idaho 1971).

so you lose. And there will be no majority until you agree on another supplier." ◀ ◀ ◀

If the deadlock concerns a substantial matter, the partners might resolve the problem by dissolving the partnership.[35]

§9.5 AGREEMENTS THAT CHANGE MANAGEMENT RIGHTS

§9.5.1 Importance and Ubiquity

One of the great advantages of the partnership form is its flexibility, and almost every partnership with a formal partnership agreement varies the management rules in some way. Moreover, the course of conduct among partners can imply agreements about management rights.

The following is a nonexclusive list of important areas in which partners often vary the default management rules provided by the relevant partnership act:[36]

- delegating to one partner or a committee of partners some or all decisions on the conduct of the business;
- changing the "one partner/one vote" rule (e.g., weighting each partner's rights to vote or consent in proportion to the capital contributed to the partnership, or allocating more votes to partners who work full-time in the business);
- changing the unanimous consent requirements (e.g., allowing the admission of new partners on a two-thirds vote of the current partners, or by approval of a management committee);
- requiring supermajority votes for important decisions (e.g., major financial commitments);
- creating a right to expel partners;
- requiring partners to seek approval before making certain kinds of commitments on behalf of the partnership; and
- delegating to a management or executive committee the right to bind the partnership to any significant obligations.

---

35. The mechanics depend on whether the partnership is "at will" and also on which partnership act applies. See Chapter 11.

36. Partners may also by agreement alter the other default rules, such as the rules on profit sharing or no remuneration for labor. See generally Chapter 8.

Example

The partnership agreement of Sachs & Harris, a 100-partner law firm, provides for the annual election of a five-partner "Management Committee" and includes the following provision:

> *Admission of New Partners:* The Management Committee shall in its sole discretion determine whether to admit any new member to the partnership. A vote of four of the five members of that Committee is necessary to admit a new partner. ◀◀◀

Agreements among partners can go quite far in changing the management structure of a partnership, even to the extent of removing the unanimous consent requirement for amending the partnership agreement.

Example

The partnership agreement of Sachs & Harris contains the following provision:

> *Amendments:* This Partnership Agreement may be amended only upon a majority vote of the members of the Management Committee followed by a two-thirds majority vote of all Partners. ◀◀◀

§9.5.2 Limits on *Inter Se* Agreements That Restructure Management

a. Under UPA (1914)

Under UPA (1914), agreements that restructure management face three constraints. First, although agreements can waive certain fiduciary duties and define others, no agreement among partners can remove totally the fiduciary obligations that partners owe each other.[37] Second, the more fundamental the obligation involved, the more likely it will be subject to judicial scrutiny. For example, a court will examine carefully any agreed-upon restrictions on a partner's right to information.[38] A restriction is most likely to be upheld if it: (i) has some important justification; (ii) is not overbroad; and (iii) does not leave the partners who lack access vulnerable to oppression.

---

37. Section 9.7 discusses partners' fiduciary duty, and Section 9.8 focuses on agreements that waive, limit, or define fiduciary duty.
38. See Section 9.2 (partner's right of access to information) and Section 9.7.5 (full disclosure).

Dicta in *McCallum v. Asbury*, a 1964 Oregon case, suggested that a partner may have the *nonwaivable* right to veto any fundamental changes in the partnership agreement which would substantially prejudice the partner's interests.[39] Later cases suggest to the contrary, however, at least where the partners are sophisticated,[40] and no subsequent case has followed the McCallum dicta.[41]

b. Under the Modern Acts

Both UPA (2013) and UPA (1997) collect in one place all the statutory limits on the power of the partnership agreement. UPA (2013) §105(c) lists 17 restrictions. The one directly relevant here appears in subsection (c)(4). A partnership agreement may not "unreasonably restrict the [information-related] duties and rights under section 408."[42]

UPA (1997) states a roughly equivalent limitation in its section 103(b). Both acts also limit the power of the partnership agreement to curtail fiduciary duties and the obligation of good faith and fair dealing.[43] Those duties and that obligation therefore overhang every partnership agreement subject to either of the modern acts.

---

§9.6 MANAGEMENT DUTIES

§9.6.1 Duty to Furnish Services

a. Does and Should a Duty Exist?

As previously discussed,[44] absent a contrary agreement each partner has a right to participate in partnership affairs. Is there also a duty to participate?

39. *McCallum v. Asbury*, 393 P.2d 774 (Or. 1964).
40. E.g., *Bailey v. Fish & Neave*, 868 N.E.2d 956 (N.Y. 2007).
41. The statement in the text reflects a Westlaw search the author conducted on May 24, 2025.
42. The paragraph also states, however, that "the partnership agreement may impose reasonable restrictions on the availability and use of information obtained under that section and may define appropriate remedies, including liquidated damages, for a breach of any reasonable restriction on use." *Id.* A partner's information rights are discussed in Section 9.2.2.
43. See UPA (2013) §105(c); UPA (1997) §103(b). UPA (2013) also contains two companion sections to its section 105. See UPA (2013) §§106 (effect of partnership agreement on partnership and person becoming partner); 107 (effect of partnership agreement on third parties and relationship to records effective on behalf of partnership). Fiduciary duty is discussed in Section 9.8. The statutory codification on the obligation of good faith and fair dealing is discussed in Section 9.7.4. The relationship between these concepts and the partnership agreement is discussed in Section 9.8.
44. See Section 9.3.

Is each partner obligated to furnish labor, services, or some other form of effort to the partnership business?

Some, mostly older cases suggest that such a duty exists. However, none of the three acts contain any support for the notion, and the case law authority may reflect an antiquated notion of the typical partnership. Perhaps at one time it made sense to imply a duty to provide services, because with only rare exceptions partnerships consisted exclusively of active partners. For a partner to decline to serve, therefore, defeated the reasonable expectations of the copartners.

Today, that inference makes far less sense. Although partnerships with exclusively active partners probably still predominate, passive partners are by no means rare—especially with the advent of LLPs.

Of course, a partnership agreement may expressly establish duties to participate, and such duties may also be implied by circumstances, including partner conduct in the formation or operation of the partnership.[45] But no duty should be presumed solely on account of partner status.

b. Remedies for Breach of the Duty

A partner who breaches a duty to provide services may be held liable for the cost of hiring someone else to perform the services, the reasonable value of the services withheld, or other damage. If the withheld services are crucial to the business, the copartners may obtain a court order bringing the partnership to an end.[46] In that case, the breaching partner would probably be liable for damages caused by the partnership's premature demise.

§9.6.2 Duty of Care

Under all three acts, each partner *qua* partner is an agent of the partnership, and under agency law the agent owes the principal a duty of care.[47] Partnership law is similar, but the standard is lower. UPA (1997) §404, comment 3, explains that "[t]he standard of care imposed by RUPA is that of gross negligence, which is the standard generally recognized by the courts" under UPA (1914).[48]

---

45. For example, it seems reasonable to expect services from a partner who has contributed neither money nor other property to the partnership.

46. See Section 11.7.

47. See Section 4.1.4.

48. UPA (2013) §409(c) provides: "The duty of care of a partner in the conduct or winding up of the partnership business is to refrain from engaging in grossly negligent or reckless conduct, willful or intentional misconduct, or a knowing violation of law." UPA (1997) §404(c) is essentially the same.

Several points are worth noting with regard to this standard:

- Gross negligence is a less demanding standard than that applicable to paid agents,[49] perhaps on the assumption that partners, who are simultaneously agents and principals, are better positioned than an ordinary principal to watch out, supervise, and, when necessary, intervene.
- A partner's misconduct may suffice to inculpate the partner and the partnership, without breaching the partner's duty to the partnership. Negligence suffices for tort liability and, under the attribution rules of all three acts, for the vicarious liability of the partnership.
- Under both modern acts, absent a contrary provision in the partnership agreement, a partner's negligence might inculpate both the partner and the partnership, while the partnership might still have the obligation to indemnify the partner.[50]

The partnership agreement may change the duty of care, but (at least under the modern acts) may not "unreasonably reduce" it.[51]

§9.7 PARTNER'S FIDUCIARY DUTY OF LOYALTY

§9.7.1 The Beauty, Ubiquity, Influence, and Vagueness of Cardozo's Language

Partners owe each other a fiduciary duty of loyalty, and the touchstone of analysis in this area is a beautiful passage in Justice Cardozo's opinion in *Meinhard v. Salmon*:[52]

> Joint adventurers, like copartners, owe to one another, while the enterprise continues, the duty of the finest loyalty. Many forms of conduct permissible in a workaday world for those acting at arm's length are forbidden to those bound by fiduciary ties. A trustee is held to something stricter than the morals of the marketplace. Not honesty alone, but the punctilio of an honor the most sensitive, is then the standard of behavior.

49. See Section 4.1.4.
50. See Section 8.9.
51. UPA (2013) §105(d)(3)(c); UPA (1997) §103(b)(4).
52. 164 N.E. 545 (N.Y. 1928).

Although *Meinhard v. Salmon* involved a joint venture rather than a partnership, Cardozo's words are equally applicable to partnerships.[53] Indeed, those words are probably the most often quoted passage in all of partnership law. They instruct courts to approach partner selfishness with a critical eye.

Beyond that general instruction, however, Cardozo's words are quite vague. It is one thing to say in general, "be your brother's keeper," but how does the principle apply when, for instance, your brother wants to watch the opera, you want to watch the football game, and your house has only one TV and no TiVo, DVR, or VCR?[54] What does "the punctilio of an honor the most sensitive" mean when the two partners in an at-will partnership are discussing a change in profit shares because one partner believes she is bringing in most of the business?[55]

The law of partner loyalty can be divided into two categories, and in one of those categories some pretty specific rules augment and define Cardozo's "punctilio." The first category consists of issues relating to the conduct or interests of the partnership's business. In that category, partner selfishness is not allowed unless the other partners consent. The second category consists of issues relating to differences of interests between or among partners. In that category the rules are less stringent and less clear. Section 9.7.3 discusses "partner versus partnership" issues, and Section 9.7.4 discusses "partner versus partner" issues. Section 9.8 examines the extent to which partner agreements can change, waive, or eliminate partner fiduciary duties. Section 9.7.2 provides an overview of the differences and similarities among the three acts in this fundamentally important area of partnership law.

§9.7.2 The Uniform Acts and the Fiduciary Duty of Loyalty

a. UPA (1997) Codifies and "Cabins In" the Duty

During the 10 years the ULC spent drafting, debating, and adopting UPA (1997), no issue generated more controversy than that act's treatment of the fiduciary duty of loyalty. In form, UPA (1997) differs from UPA (1914) in at least seven ways:

- While under UPA (1914) the duty of loyalty is mostly a matter of case law, UPA (1997) codifies the subject.

53. As explained in Section 7.2.6, in most jurisdictions the law of joint ventures is essentially identical to the law of partnerships.

54. Obviously, this example predates the prevalence of mobile phones and the widespread phenomenon of streaming.

55. Recall from Section 7.2.6 that in an at-will partnership any partner has the right to call an end to the partnership at any time. That right will have an inevitable impact on negotiations between partners.

- While under UPA (1914) the duty of loyalty is an open-ended category, the formulation in UPA (1997) purports to be exclusive and exhaustive—that is, UPA (1997) confines ("cabins in") the duty of loyalty to those rules stated in the act.
- While UPA (1914) §21(1) expresses the scope of a partner's loyalty duty by referring generally to "any transaction connected with the formation, conduct, or liquidation of the partnership," UPA (1997):
  — expressly encompasses self-dealing[56] and competition;[57]
  — provides that dissolution ends the restriction on competition;[58] and
  — entirely excludes formation activities from the duty of loyalty.[59]
- While cases under UPA (1914) generally consider a partner's duty of loyalty to include the duty to volunteer information, UPA (1997) ousts disclosure duties from the realm of fiduciary duty.[60]
- While UPA (1914) nowhere mentions any general duty of good faith,[61] UPA (1997) §404(d) provides: "A partner shall discharge the duties to the partnership and the other partners under this [Act] or under the partnership agreement and exercise any rights consistently with the obligation of good faith and fair dealing."
- While UPA (1914) is silent as to a partner's right to act in his, her, or its own self-interest, UPA (1997) §404(e) states: "A partner does not violate a duty or obligation under this [Act] or under the partnership agreement merely because the partner's conduct furthers the partner's own interest."[62]
- While UPA (1914) is silent on the extent to which the partnership agreement can alter or eliminate fiduciary duties, UPA (1997) §103(b) expressly prohibits elimination and provides standards for evaluating attempted alterations.

Of all the differences, the most controversial is embodied in UPA (1997) §404(a)-(b). Subsection (a) provides that "The *only* fiduciary duties

56. UPA (1997) §404(b)(2).
57. UPA (1997) §404(b)(3).
58. UPA (1997) §404(b)(3) (requiring a partner to "refrain from competing . . . before the dissolution of the partnership").
59. All three paragraphs of subsection (b) refer to the "conduct" or the "conduct and winding up" of the partnership business. In contrast with UPA §21, UPA (1997) §404(b) never uses the word "formation."
60. See Section 9.2.2.
61. UPA (1914) §3(1) uses the concept of "bad faith" to define "knowledge."
62. The modern uniform limited partnership act replicates this provision, ULPA (2001) (Last Amended 2013), §305(c) (limited partners) and 408(e) (general partners). ULLCA (2006), however, did not. A comment explains: "As a proposition of contract law, the language is axiomatic and therefore unnecessary. In the context of fiduciary duty, the language is at best incomplete, at worst wrong, and in any event confusing." *Id.* §409(e), cmt.

a partner owes to the partnership and the other partners are the duty of loyalty and the duty of care set forth in subsections (b) and (c)." Subsection (b), which introduces three specific prongs of the duty of loyalty, begins with the phrase "A partner's duty of loyalty to the partnership and the other partners is *limited* to the following . . . " (emphasis added).

b. The ULC Goes "Back to the Future" and Un-Cabins Fiduciary Duty

Fiduciary duty originated as an equitable concept, and courts have always taken a flexible, expansive approach to defining the obligations of a fiduciary. Critics of UPA (1997)'s "cabining in" approach have argued that the words "only" and "limited" cripple, or at least hamstring, a court's ability to deal with ingenuously structured improprieties. Defenders of the UPA (1997) approach have responded that subsection (b) properly defines a partner's fiduciary duties and that the obligation of good faith and fair dealing exists to capture and control other improperly opportunistic behavior. Critics rejoined that cabining in fiduciary duty "puts inordinate pressure on the concept of 'good faith and fair dealing.' "[63] As stated at the 2006 annual meeting of the ULC:

> [W]e are already seeing pressure in the courts on the duty of good faith and fair dealing. When you say there are no other fiduciary duties and courts for hundreds of years have looked to fiduciary duties as a policing mechanism that they can develop, if you say you can't have fiduciary duties, they will go to good faith. And, in fact, I had a conversation with . . . [t]he judge of North Carolina's business court [who] said, if you stop us on fiduciary duty, we will just go to good faith."[64]

The same year (1997) in which the ULC finished revising its then new general partnership act, the Conference began a project to revise the uniform limited partnership act. That project culminated in ULPA (2001), which followed UPA (1997)'s cabin-in approach.[65] However, in 2004 the ULC began a project to redraft the uniform limited liability company act, and that project categorically rejected cabining in fiduciary duties.[66] In 2011 and 2013, as part of the Harmonization Project, the ULC conformed UPA and ULPA to ULLCA (2006) approach.

63. Daniel S. Kleinberger, Carter G. Bishop, The Next Generation: The Revised Uniform Limited Liability Company Act, 62 Bus. Law. 515, 523 (2007). ULLCA (2013) follows ULLCA (2006) on this point.

64. *Id.* at n.49 (quoting the remarks of the author of this book, who was serving as co-reporter for the ULC committee drafting ULLCA (2006)).

65. See Section 12.3.3.

66. See Section 15.4.8.

> The 2011 and 2013 Harmonization amendments made one major substantive change; they "un-cabined" fiduciary duty. UPA (1997) §404 had deviated substantially from UPA (1914) by purporting to codify all fiduciary duties owed by partners. This approach had a number of problems. Most notably, the exhaustive list of fiduciary duties left no room for the fiduciary duty owed by partners to each other, *i.e.*, "the punctilio of an honor the most sensitive". *Meinhard v. Salmon*, 164 N.E. 545, 546 (N.Y. 1928). Although UPA (1997) §404(b) purported to state "[a] partner's duty of loyalty to the partnership *and the other partners*" (emphasis added), the three listed duties each protected the partnership and not the partners. "Un-cabining" harmonized this act to ULLCA (2006). . . . [67]

§9.7.3 Partner Versus Partnership Duty of Loyalty

In matters relating to partnership affairs, subject to the "cabin in" issue, all three acts have very similar views of a partner's duty of loyalty: In general, a partner may not profit at the expense—either direct or indirect—of the partnership. In particular, without the consent of fellow partners,[68] a partner is prohibited from:

- competing with the partnership;
- taking business opportunities from which the partnership might have benefited or that the partnership might have needed;
- using partnership property for personal gain;
- engaging in conflict-of-interest transactions.

Under UPA (1914), these restrictions begin with partnership formation and continue until the partnership terminates. Under UPA (1997 and 2013), the noncompetition restriction ends when the partnership dissolves. The other restrictions remain until the partnership terminates.[69]

a. Noncompetition

Both modern acts expressly require each partner "to refrain from competing with the partnership in the conduct of the partnership business before the dissolution of the partnership."[70] UPA (1914) §21(1) contains very broad language that includes a noncompete requirement:

---

67. UPA (2013) § 409, cmt.

68. See Section 9.7.3.

69. Under all three acts, dissolution does not terminate a partnership. Instead, the partnership enters a period of "winding up" and terminates only when winding up is complete. See Sections 11.10.1.

70. UPA (2013) §409(b)(3); UPA (1997) §409b)(3).

> Every partner must account to the partnership for any benefit, and hold as trustee for it any profits derived by him without the consent of the other partners from any transaction connected with the formation, conduct, or liquidation of the partnership. . . .[71]

To engage in a competing business is to engage in "transaction[s] connected with the . . . conduct . . . of the partnership."[72] The "account/trustee" language in section 21 means that a partner who violates the non-compete rule must disgorge to the partnership any profits made through the violation.

Example

Michael is a partner in a company that provides business consulting services throughout the United States. While on a skiing vacation in Colorado, Michael meets Dorothy, who seeks some business advice. Michael at first declines, explaining, "I'm on vacation." He suggests that Dorothy use the services of another partner and offers to call his office and arrange matters. Dorothy, however, insists on Michael's services and offers to pay double his usual charges. Michael finally agrees. He takes a day out of his vacation, provides Dorothy the advice she needs, and pockets a large fee. The fee belongs to the partnership, even though: (i) Michael did the work "on his own time"; (ii) Michael tried to steer Dorothy to another partner; and (iii) Dorothy insisted on Michael performing the services and rejected Michael's suggestion that she consult with another partner. None of those facts are relevant under any of the three uniform acts. The work Michael did was precisely the type of work the partnership does, and Michael's dealings with Dorothy therefore constituted a "transaction connected with the . . . conduct . . . of the partnership." UPA (1914) §21. For Michael to retain the fee would be to set himself as a competitor to the partnership at least on this occasion and to take for himself "a partnership opportunity." UPA (2013) §409(b)(1).

---

71. The phrase "hold as trustee" appears also in the two modern acts, but caution is required in understanding the phrase:

> The phrase "hold as trustee" dates back to UPA (1914) §21 and reflects the availability of disgorgement remedies, such as a constructive trust. In contrast to an actual trustee, a person subject to this duty does not: (i) face the special obstacles to consent characteristic of trust law; or (ii) enjoy protection for decisions taken in reliance on the governing instrument and other sources of information.

UPA (2013) §409(b)(1), comment.

72. In some circumstances, the competition might relate to formation or liquidation of the partnership.

Under generally applicable principles of fiduciary duty, a constructive trust will arise if Michael seeks to retain the fee.[73] ◄ ◄ ◄

b. Taking Business Opportunities

A partner's duty of loyalty also prevents a partner from taking business opportunities from the partnership, unless the copartners consent either generally through the partnership agreement or as to a particular transaction. In the latter event, the partner seeking to exploit the opportunity must disclose all material information related to the opportunity and the partner's history with and intentions toward the opportunity.

Protected opportunities include not only those from which the partnership might have profited, but also those that the partnership might have needed. The business opportunity duty somewhat overlaps the noncompetition duty: To compete with the partnership is to seek and take opportunities (i.e., customers) from which the partnership might have benefited. But the opportunity rule also has independent scope.

Example

Alice, a partner in a biotechnology partnership, knows that the partnership is looking to rent new office and laboratory space. She happens to know of a building, in the ideal location, suitable to house the firm's special equipment. She learns that the owner is willing either to lease or to sell. Alice decides that the building would make a fine personal investment, so she buys it for herself. She leases the building to a company that does not compete with the partnership, and later she resells the building at a profit. She must account to the biotechnology partnership for whatever profit she made on the building. Although Alice did not engage in directly competitive activity, the building could have been a fruitful opportunity for the partnership. Under UPA §21, Alice must therefore "hold as trustee . . . any profits derived . . . from [this] transaction connected with the . . . conduct . . . of the partnership." Under UPA (2013) and UPA (1997) §404(b)(1), the result is the same and the language more direct: Alice must "account to the partnership and hold as trustee for it any property, profit, or benefit . . . derived from a use by the partner of partnership property, including the appropriation of a partnership opportunity." ◄ ◄ ◄

Like other aspects of the duty of loyalty, the opportunity rule can be waived by copartners' informed consent. The consent is ineffective unless, when making the decision, the consenting partners have all material

73. See Section 4.1.7 (constructive trust and disgorgement as remedies for an agent's breach of the duty of loyalty).

information concerning the opportunity and the history with and intentions toward the opportunity of the partner seeking consent.

Unless the partnership agreement provides otherwise, such consent must be unanimous.[74] However, a partner may be able to avoid the unanimity requirement by presenting the opportunity to the partnership and having the partnership vote on taking the opportunity for itself. Arguably such a decision is an ordinary matter, and a majority vote will control.[75] If the majority rejects the opportunity and a partner then proceeds individually, the partnership will have a difficult time persuading a court to order disgorgement.

c. Using Partnership Property for Personal Gain

All three uniform acts prohibit a partner from using partnership property for personal purposes without copartner consent,[76] and each requires a partner to disgorge any gain obtained from any personal use of partnership property, unless the other partners have consented.[77]

Example

Alex is a partner in a landscaping company that works exclusively on commercial projects. On weekends, without the permission of his copartners, Alex uses company equipment to do landscaping at private homes. Although Alex's weekend activities neither compete with the partnership nor usurp a partnership opportunity, he must disgorge his profits to the partnership. They result from his use of partnership property. ◀ ◀ ◀

This rule is subject to a *de minimis* requirement. For example, a partner in a law firm who occasionally uses the firm's telephones to talk with a stockbroker will not have to disgorge profits made from stock trading.

d. Conflict of Interest

A partner has a conflict of interest when the partner causes or allows the partnership to do business with:

- the partner him-, her-, or itself;
- a closely related member of the partner's family; or
- an organization in which the partner has a material financial interest.

---

74. See Section 9.8.
75. UPA (2013) §401(k); UPA (1997) §401(j); UPA (1914) §18(h). See Section 9.5.1.
76. UPA (2013) §401(i); and UPA (1997) §401(g); UPA (1914) §25(2)(a).
77. UPA (2013) §409(b)(1)(b); and UPA (1997) §404(b)(1); UPA (1914) §21(1).

Example

Alice is a partner in a biotechnology partnership that is looking to rent new laboratory space. Alice happens to own a building, in the ideal location, suitable to house the firm's special equipment. If Alice leases or sells the building to the partnership, she will be "on both sides of the deal." She has a conflict of interest. ◀ ◀ ◀

Transactions like the one just described are often called *self-dealing*.

A partner also has a conflict of interest when acting on behalf of a party whose interests are adverse to the partnership.

Example

A partnership is considering the purchase of one of two warehouses. Acting without the knowledge of his copartners, John, one of the partners, advises May, the owner of one of the warehouses, how to present the merits of her warehouse in a way most likely to impress the partnership. John has breached his duty of loyalty. ◀ ◀ ◀

Both modern acts specifically prohibit conflicts of interest and self-dealing. Each partner must "refrain from dealing with the partnership in the conduct or winding up of the partnership business as or on behalf of a party having an interest adverse to the partnership."[78] The broad "account/trustee" language of UPA (1914) §21(1) establishes the same prohibition under that statute.

e. Remedies

A partner who breaches the fiduciary duty of loyalty must disgorge all profits gained through the disloyal act. It is not necessary for the partnership to prove damages in order to obtain disgorgement. However, if the partnership can prove damages, the partnership may also bring a damage action. In a self-dealing situation, the partnership may rescind any executory portion of a contract tainted with partner conflict of interest.[79]

§9.7.4 Obligation of Good Faith and Fair Dealing

Unlike UPA (1914), UPA (1997) includes among the duties of partners an express obligation of good faith and fair dealing. "A partner shall discharge the duties to the partnership and the other partners under this [Act] or

78. UPA (2013) §409(b)(2); UPA (1997) §404(b)(2).

79. For the procedures to be followed in bringing both damage actions and claims for equitable relief, see Section 9.9.

under the partnership agreement and exercise any rights consistently with the obligation of good faith and fair dealing."[80] The obligation is *not* a fiduciary duty, and the obligation's meaning has been controversial since UPA (1997) first codified and then commented on the obligation.

The Harmonization Project gave particular attention to the implied obligation, and Section 15.4.8 explains the results, which apply equally to the uniform general partnership, limited partnership, and limited liability company acts.

§9.7.5 Differences of Interest Between and Among Partners

a. Fiduciary Duty and a Partner's Legitimate Self-Interest

According to Cardozo, partners may not use tactics appropriate to "arm's-length" transactions in their *inter se* dealings. But even if partners are never fully at arm's length, they are nonetheless occasionally on opposite sides of the negotiating table. In such circumstances, self-interest is inherent and inevitable. It therefore cannot be *per se* evil.

UPA cases recognize this reality, and UPA (1997) §404(e) makes the point explicitly: "A partner does not violate a duty or obligation under this [Act] or under the partnership agreement merely because the partner's conduct furthers the partner's own interest." UPA (2013) §409(e) is identical, except for substituting "solely" for "merely."

It may seem difficult to harmonize self-interest with fiduciary duty, and indeed comment 1 to UPA (1997) §404 states: "Arguably, the term 'fiduciary' is inappropriate when used to describe the duties of a partner because a partner may legitimately pursue self-interest." The comment to the 2013 version takes a different approach, differentiating between a partner's responsibilities as a co-manager and rights under the partnership agreement:

> A partner in a general partnership has at least two different roles: (i) as a party to the partnership agreement, with rights and obligations under that agreement; and (ii) as co-manager of the enterprise. This provision pertains to the first role. A partner's exercise of rights under the partnership agreement is subject to the obligation of good faith and fair dealing, Subsection (d), but a partner does not breach that contractual obligation "solely because the partner's conduct furthers the partner's own interest." In contrast, this provision is ineffective with regard to a partner's duties as co-manager. For example, a partner's liability under section 409(b)(3) (prohibiting competition) is not "solely because the partner's conduct furthers the partner's own interest." Rather, the

80. UPA (1997) §404(d).

> liability results from the breach of a specific obligation, i.e., the codified aspect of the duty of loyalty that prohibits competition.[81]

In the *inter se* context, only excessive self-interest is wrongful, and questions about excess fall generally into two main categories:

- Partner-to-partner transactions (when partners engage each other in partnership-related financial transactions), including:
  - —formation of the partnership (under UPA [1914] but not UPA [1997] or UPA [2013];
  - —renegotiation of profit shares, particularly in an at-will partnership; and
  - —sale or purchase of a current partner's interest in the partnership.
- Partners' exercise of discretion *vis-à-vis* copartners, including:
  - —exercise of a right created by the partnership agreement to expel a partner "without cause";[82] and
  - —rightfully calling an end to a partnership, when the end disadvantages one partner and advantages another.[83]

On any such occasion, one partner's interests will inevitably be adverse to another's. For example, if several partners seek to buy out one of their copartners, that copartner will want as high a buyout price as possible. The would-be buyers, naturally enough, will want a low price. Similarly, when one partner wishes a higher profit share, any gain must come at the expense of some other partner or partners.

The issues raised by no-cause expulsion and ending an at-will partnership are more complicated. In each situation, the acting partner or partners apparently have absolute discretion. The law appears to entitle them to act for any reason they choose—even if their actions benefit them to the prejudice of copartners.

---

81. ULLCA (2013) §409(e), cmt.

82. Partnership agreements often authorize a specified majority of partners (or, in some agreements, a specified majority of a management committee) to expel a partner without having to state or possess "cause." Under such agreements, if the required majority decides that a partner should be out, the partner is out. There is no obligation to prove that the partner did anything wrong. See the more detailed discussion in this section and in Chapter 11, Problem 99.

83. Under UPA (1914) default rules, this situation exists only in an at-will partnership. See Section 11.2.1. A comparable situation exists, however, when one partner wrongfully dissolves a term partnership. Under UPA §38(2)(b), the other partners then have the right to preserve the partnership assets and carry on the business until the end of the original term—but only if all the remaining partners agree. Section 11.4.2. Under UPA (1997), the situation exists always in an at-will partnership, UPA (1997) §801(1), and often in a partnership for a definite term or particular undertaking. UPA (1997) §801(2)(i). Section 11.9.3.

b. How the Three Acts Approach the Issue

The three uniform partnership acts differ in how they approach partner-to-partner duties, although the practical results are likely to be similar regardless of which statute applies. UPA (1914) §21 pertains only to a partner's duty to the partnership, so under UPA (1914) rules in this area come exclusively from case law—including Cardozo's famous opinion in *Meinhard v. Salmon*.

Under UPA (1997), the situation is more complex. Like UPA (1914) §21, UPA (1997)'s duty of loyalty provision, §404, seems to run only to the benefit of the partnership:

- subsection (b)(1)—"to account to the partnership and hold as trustee for it . . .";
- subsection (b)(2)—"to refrain from dealing with the partnership . . . as or on behalf of a party having an interest adverse to the partnership";
- subsection (b)(3)—"to refrain from competing with the partnership. . . ."

What complicates matters is that, unlike UPA (1914), UPA (1997) insists that its statutory treatment of the duty of loyalty is exhaustive.[84] As a result, any partner-to-partner duties under UPA (1997) must have some other, nonfiduciary source.

UPA (1997) §403 is one such source, detailing each "partner's rights and duties with respect to information."[85] UPA (1997) §404(d), the statutory obligation of good faith and fair dealing, might be another.

As explained in Section 9.7.2, ULLCA (2006) "un-cabined" fiduciary duty, enabling courts to police partner-to-partner transactions under the traditional rubric of fiduciary duty. As a result of the Harmonization Project, UPA (2013) follows ULLCA (2006).

c. The Practical Consequences—Likely Similar Results

Although case law in this area under UPA (1997) is scant, neither the statutory text nor the comments indicate any intention to depart from prior law. It is therefore likely that courts will use UPA (1997) §§403 and 404(d) to produce substantive rules consistent with case law under UPA (1914).[86] And, as noted above, ULLCA (2006) reopened this area of law to the case law of fiduciary duty, and the Harmonization Project adopted the ULLCA

84. UPA (1997) §404(b) begins with the phrase, "A partner's duty of loyalty to the partnership and the other partners is *limited* to the following." (Emphasis added.)
85. See Section 9.2.2.
86. Remedies may be a different matter. See the discussion in Section 9.7.5(c)(4).

(2006) approach. It is likely therefore that under all three acts partners will have similar duties in partner-to-partner dealings. When partners' interests are potentially or actually adverse, a partner is obliged to: (i) provide full disclosure (which is a well-defined concept); and (ii) engage in "fair dealing" (which is not).

I. Full Disclosure in Partner-to-Partner Transactions

A partner selling a partnership interest to a fellow partner, or buying a partnership interest from a fellow partner, has an affirmative duty to disclose any material information that:

- relates to the value of the partnership interest or the partnership itself; and
- could not be learned by examining the partnership books.

The partner who possesses the information must volunteer it. "You didn't ask" is no excuse.[87]

Example

Charlotte and Todd are partners in a real estate investment partnership. The partnership has a term of 10 years, but after 5 years Charlotte wants to get her money out. Todd offers to buy her out and names what appears to be a reasonable price. Charlotte does not know, however, that Todd has received a very good offer on one of the partnership's parcels. Todd does not volunteer the information, and Charlotte accepts Todd's offer. Charlotte has a claim against Todd. Under UPA (1914), Todd breached his fiduciary duty by failing to disclose information relating to the value of the partnership that could not be learned by reviewing the partnership's books.

As to UPA (1997), the analysis must pick its way through the relevant statutory provisions, but the result is the same. The sale involves the transfer of Charlotte's transferable interest and therefore involves Charlotte's exercise of a right under UPA (1997) §503(a)(1).[88] Todd has therefore violated UPA (1997) §403(c)(1) by failing to furnish, without demand, "information concerning the partnership's business and affairs reasonably required for the proper exercise of [Charlotte's] rights . . . under . . . this [Act]." Under UPA (2013), both analyses apply. ◄◄◄

87. The partner's obligation differs substantially from the situation of a party to an arm's-length transaction. In an arm's-length transaction, a party may not misrepresent information, but—absent some special relationship—the party has no duty to volunteer. Partnership is a special (i.e., fiduciary) relationship.

88. See Section 8.8.3.

2. Fair Dealing

The vague concept of "fair dealing" has two aspects: process and substance. The process aspect concerns the manner in which partners deal with each other. The substance aspect concerns the fairness of the outcome of partner-to-partner dealings.

A. Process As a matter of *process*, partners are obliged to deal with each other in a candid, noncoercive manner. They have, as just discussed, a duty of full disclosure. They must also avoid exacting agreements through threats or other forms of intimidation. Conduct that in an arm's-length relationship would *not* amount to actionable duress or procedural unconscionability may nonetheless suffice to invalidate a transaction between partners.

B. Substance As a matter of *substance*, the cases speak of a partner's obligation to provide a "fair price" in partner-to-partner transactions. However, almost without exception "unfair price" cases are also "nondisclosure" cases. That is, the partner who agreed to the bad deal did so in the absence of material information that the other partner possessed and failed to disclose. It seems unlikely that a court would use "unfair price" to overturn a partner-to-partner deal if the partner who benefited from the deal made full disclosure and avoided abusive negotiating tactics.

In deference to freedom of contract, a partner who complies with the process aspect of "fair dealing" in a partner-to-partner transaction should not have to worry about the substantive aspect. Any *post hoc* attack on the fairness of the outcome should be rejected as "buyers' (or sellers') remorse" or "20/20 hindsight."

3. When Partners Exercise Discretion vis-à-vis Copartners

The process aspect of "fair dealing" has little relevance to a partner's right to dissolve a partnership. To cause the end of the partnership, a partner must manifest *express will*.[89] This manifestation typically involves giving notice to fellow partners, but there is no fiduciary duty to consult with them before making the decision or to hear them out if they object to ending the partnership.

Process fair dealing likewise has little relevance when a partner is expelled under a partnership agreement. Those doing the expelling must comply with any process requirements stated in the agreement, but fiduciary duty does not impose additional requirements. Unless the partnership agreement so provides, fair dealing does not mean "due process," a warning, an opportunity to be heard, or even a statement of reasons.

---

89. UPA §31(1)(b); UPA (1997) §801(1) and (2)(i); UPA (2013) §801(1).

Substance fair dealing has slightly greater impact in controlling partners' exercise of discretion. Partners may not end a partnership or effect an expulsion for the malicious purpose of depriving a fellow partner of benefits, if:

- the fellow partner had a right to expect the benefits;
- the benefits would have naturally accrued to the fellow partner absent the exercise of discretion; and
- the exercise of discretion transfers the benefits to the partner or partners exercising the discretion.

Succeeding with a claim based on this substantive aspect of fair dealing is not easy. The claimant partner must show conduct amounting to expropriation or unjust enrichment.[90]

4. Remedies

Under UPA (1914) and UPA (2013), a court has available the full panoply of remedies for breach of the duty of loyalty: damages, disgorgement (constructive trust), and rescission. Under UPA (1997), in contrast, the analysis is more complex and the remedies perhaps somewhat limited. As explained earlier in this section, under UPA (1997) partner-to-partner duties come not from the duty of loyalty but rather from UPA (1997) §§403 and 404(d). Neither of these provisions expresses a fiduciary duty.

As a result, punitive damages will likely be unavailable, and courts will have to combine common law concepts such as fraudulent nondisclosure and fraud in the inducement in order to set aside tainted transactions. Concepts of unjust enrichment may empower a court to order disgorgement.

§9.8 THE IMPACT OF AGREEMENTS ON PARTNER FIDUCIARY DUTY

§9.8.1 Limits on Agreements

Like other facets of partners' *inter se* relationships, partner fiduciary duties are subject to contrary agreement. However, fiduciary duties are not merely default rules. Although so-called contractarian scholars have argued

90. For further discussion of this vague and rarely satisfied standard, see Sections 11.2.1(d) and 11.2.1(e). Depending on the language of the partnership agreement, the implied obligation of good faith and fair dealing may offer some protection.

vehemently to the contrary,[91] "freedom of contract" is not identical to "freedom from fiduciary duty," especially within general partnerships.[92] Accordingly, in most states there are limits on a partnership agreement's power over fiduciary duty.[93]

Under all three acts, some duties can be completely waived and *a fortiori* may also be changed or limited. For example, the duties under UPA §21(1) (1914) all give way with "the consent of the other partners." Likewise, under UPA (1997) §103(b)(3)(ii) "all of the partners or a number or percentage specified in the partnership agreement may authorize or ratify, after full disclosure of all material facts, a specific act or transaction that otherwise would violate the duty of loyalty." In addition, under UPA (1997) §103(b)(3)(i) "the partnership agreement may identify specific types or categories of activities that do not violate the duty of loyalty, if not manifestly unreasonable." In no event, however, may a UPA (1997) partnership agreement "eliminate" the duty of loyalty or the obligation of good faith and fair dealing.[94]

UPA (2013) goes further, including all the provisions just listed as in UPA (1997) and adding: "If not manifestly unreasonable, the partnership agreement may: alter or eliminate the aspects of the duty of loyalty stated in Section 409(b) . . . [and] alter or eliminate any other fiduciary duty."[95] As noted in a comment to UPA (2013): "[A] properly drafted partnership agreement may substantially alter and even eliminate fiduciary duties."[96] However, as that comment further notes:

> Two important limitations exist. First, arrangements subject to this subsection may not be "manifestly unreasonable." Second, the partnership agreement may not transform the relationship inter se partners and the partnership into an entirely arm's length arrangement. For example, displacement of fiduciary duties is effective only to the extent that the displacement is stated clearly and with particularity. This rule is fundamental in the jurisprudence of fiduciary duty [and the partnership agreement may not eliminate the rule].[97]

---

91. For a discussion of this debate in the context of LLCs, see Section 15.4.7.
92. See UPA (2013) §105(d)(3), cmt. "This act rejects the ultra-contractarian notion that fiduciary duty within a business organization is merely a set of default rules and seeks instead to balance the virtues of 'freedom of contract' against the dangers that inescapably exist when some persons have power over the interests of others."
93. As explained in Section 15.4.7, Delaware law is the most hospitable to restrictions on fiduciary duty.
94. UPA (1997) §103(b)(3) and (5).
95. UPA (2013) §105(3)(A) and (D). Section 409(b) codified the three principal aspects of the duty of loyalty: no taking a partnership opportunity; no acting as or for a party adverse to the partnership; and no competition with the partnership.
96. UPA (2013) §105(d)(3), cmt.
97. *Id.*

Under case law, a UPA (1914) partnership agreement is likewise powerless to eliminate the duty of loyalty, but under both UPA (1914) and UPA (1997) it is difficult to determine exactly when a substantial limitation amounts to an elimination. Note, for example, that UPA (1997) §103(b)(3)(ii) does not require that the authorization or ratification be by *disinterested* partners. An interested partner that participates in the authorization or ratification process is subject to the obligation of good faith and fair dealing, but UPA (1997) §404(e) provides that a "partner does not violate a duty or obligation under this [Act] . . . merely because the partner's conduct furthers the partner's own interest."

Case in Point—*J & J Celcom v. AT & T Wireless Services Inc.*

AT&T, as majority partner of several partnerships, offered to buy out the interests of the minority partners. After the minority partners rejected AT&T's offer, AT&T then invoked the various partnership agreements and sold the partnerships' assets to AT&T-affiliated entities. The Washington Supreme Court, answering a certified question from the Ninth Circuit Court of Appeals, held that AT&T did not breach its fiduciary duty of loyalty because AT&T complied with the relevant partnership agreements, which expressly permitted the sale of partnership assets or dissolution of the partnership upon a majority vote. The court found that this discretion could be exercised to make a sale to an affiliated party, thereby interpreting the partnership agreement as effectively limiting the duty of loyalty.[98] ◀◀◀

In this area of law, as in many others, "pigs get fat and hogs get slaughtered." Attempts to waive process fair dealing in partner-to-partner transactions will likely be ineffective, as will attempts to authorize the expropriating use of discretion. In contrast, agreements that authorize partners to compete with the partnership, or permit self-dealing by a managing partner, are commonplace and ordinarily enforceable.

§9.8.2 Ambiguous, Oral, and Implied Agreements

Under all three acts, agreements or conduct purporting to waive or alter partner fiduciary duties are carefully scrutinized and strictly construed. The duties are fundamental to the character of a partnership and protect important interests that are potentially vulnerable to abuse. Ambiguity is construed against the purported alteration or waiver, not only because the person

98. *J & J Celcom v. AT & T Wireless Services Inc.*, 169 P.3d 823 (Wash. 2007).

asserting the alteration or waiver has often drafted language at issue (*contra proferentem*)[99] but also because, as a separate doctrinal matter, any waiver pertaining to a fiduciary duty must be established by clear and convincing evidence. Under UPA (1997 and 2013), the same approach is likely to be applied to attempts to "prescribe the standards by which the performance of the obligation [of good faith and fair dealing] is to be measured."[100]

None of the three acts requires agreements altering or waiving fiduciary duties to be in writing, but alleged oral agreements can produce wasteful and expensive "swearing contests." Courts can infer waivers from the conduct of the partners, but such inferences do not come easily. Insisting on clear and definitive evidence, courts are wary of making too much out of mere acquiescence to past conduct.

Example

Alice, a partner in a biotechnology partnership, knows that the partnership is looking to rent new office and laboratory space. She happens to know of a building, in the ideal location, suitable to house the firm's special equipment. She learns that the owner is willing either to lease or to sell. Alice decides that the building would make a fine personal investment, so she buys it for herself. Her partners later discover the transaction but make no objection. Two years later, when the partnership is looking for additional laboratory space, Alice again buys an opportune location for herself. This time her partners object, and under each of the three acts their objection is valid.[101] Their acquiescence to the first transaction did not waive Alice's duties as to the second transaction. ◀◀◀

§9.9 ENFORCING *INTER SE* OBLIGATIONS

a. Action for an Accounting

When one partner raises a breach of duty claim against another, the resulting dispute can be exceedingly complicated. Any situation nasty enough to produce litigation is likely to signal the end of the partnership at least if the partnership has few partners. If so, it may be impossible (or at least

99. Black's Law Dictionary (8th ed. 2004) defines the term as naming "[t]he doctrine that, in interpreting documents, ambiguities are to be construed unfavorably to the drafter."
100. UPA (1997) §103(b)(5); UPA (2013) §105(c)(6).
101. UPA (2013) §409(b)(1); UPA (1997) §404(b)(1); UPA §21.

extremely difficult) to determine the breach of duty claim without also settling accounts generally among all the partners.[102]

To keep this complexity within bounds, partnership law provides an equitable action for an accounting. The accounting sorts out the partners' various claims and rights and avoids piecemeal adjudication.

According to much UPA (1914) case law, an accounting is generally a condition precedent to bringing a claim for damages arising out of the partnership's affairs or business.[103]

Example

The whoopee cushion partnership of Larry, Moe, and Curley is governed by UPA (1914) and has fallen on hard times. Larry accuses Moe of failing to use his best efforts, as promised in the partnership agreement, to secure new clients. Curley claims Larry has taken excessive draws against profits and owes money to the partnership. Moe believes that the partnership owes him $5,000 in reimbursement for customer entertainment expenses. None of the partners can pursue their claims unless their prayer for relief includes an accounting. ◀◀◀

Case in Point—*Arnold v. Burgess*

"Generally, the only action which will lie between partners regarding partnership business is an action for an accounting. An accounting is an equitable proceeding for comprehensive investigation of transactions and adjudication of the rights of the partners. Other actions are premature until the business is wound up and accounts settled. This rule is based upon the inconvenience to the parties, the fact that equitable relief may be necessary to protect the right of the parties, and the notion that only after a balance has been struck can the relative rights of the parties be established. Dissolution alone does not change this rule. If partners are unable to settle their own affairs, an action in equity for an accounting is the appropriate, and sometimes exclusive, remedy to adjust and settle the affairs of a partnership. . . . The decree in an accounting action should provide for a final adjustment of all controverted questions before the trial court with "respect to a partnership accounting and distribution."[104] ◀◀◀

102. Sections 11.5.3–11.5.5 discuss the rules that apply to settle partner accounts when the partnership comes to an end.

103. Some exceptions do exist to UPA (1914)'s condition precedent rule, including claims between the partners that do not relate to the partnership business and claims that are so simple that no accounting is necessary.

104. *Arnold v. Burgess*, 747 P.2d 1315, 1319–1320 (Idaho App. 1987) (citations and internal quotations omitted).

UPA (1997) takes a different approach:

> (b) A partner may maintain an action against the partnership or another partner for legal or equitable relief, with or without an accounting as to partnership business, to:
>
> (1) enforce the partner's rights under the partnership agreement;
> (2) enforce the partner's rights under this [Act] . . . ; or
> (3) enforce the rights and otherwise protect the interests of the partner, including rights and interests arising independently of the partnership relationship.[105]

According to the official Comment, this change "reflects the increased willingness courts have shown to grant relief without the requirement of an accounting, in derogation of the so-called 'exclusivity rule.' "[106] UPA (2013) §410(b) is identical. "The Harmonization Project did not change the section other than to renumber it."[107]

b. Partner Standing to Sue Fellow Partner for Damage to the Partnership

To the extent a partnership is considered an entity separate from its partners,[108] it might appear that only the partnership itself (or a partner asserting a derivative claim)[109] has standing to sue a partner whose misconduct has injured the partnership. However, under UPA (1914), the aggregate concept prevails in this context; such claims are typically sorted out through an accounting.

As for UPA (1997), despite its expressed entity approach, one of the act's official comments flatly rejects derivative claims. "Since general partners are not passive investors like limited partners, RUPA does not authorize derivative actions, as does [the Revised Uniform Limited Partnership Act], section 1001."[110] The same comment asserts that under UPA (1997) §405(b), "a partner may bring a direct suit against the partnership or another partner for almost any cause of action arising out of the conduct of the partnership business."[111]

---

105. UPA (1997) §405(b) (emphasis added).
106. UPA (1997) §405, Comment 2.
107. UPA (2013) §410, cmt.
108. See Section 7.2.7.
109. A derivative claim is a claim asserted on behalf of an entity by one or more of its owners rather than under the direction of those with the regular authority to manage the entity. Before the advent of limited liability companies, the predominant example was in corporate law, where shareholders sue derivatively when they believe the directors of the corporations should but will not cause the corporation to sue. For further discussion in the context of limited liability companies, see Section 16.4.
110. UPA (1997) §405, comment 2.
111. *Id.*

However, UPA (2013) takes a less categorical view: "The statutory language does not contemplate derivative claims; thus, this act neither authorizes nor precludes such claims. . . . The case law does generally recognize the direct/derivative distinction in the context of general partnerships, and some cases permit a partner to sue derivatively. . . . [112]

Problem 68

A 30-partner law firm has a partnership agreement that delegates most management decisions to a 5-partner Executive Committee elected annually by all the partners. The partnership agreement states a formula for determining each partner's profit share and allocates to the Executive Committee the exclusive authority to apply the formula and determine the profit shares. The formula allows the Executive Committee some discretion, but depends very heavily on objective factors such as billable hours, payments received from clients, and clients brought to the firm.

A partner is dissatisfied with the profit share he received this year and wishes to see the partnership records the Executive Committee used in determining shares for all the partners. The Committee claims that this information "relates to the individual performance of the several partners and is therefore confidential." The Committee offers to show the partner only the records directly relevant to him. The partner accurately points out that the formula requires the Committee to compare the performance of all the partners. He insists on seeing all the relevant records. Who is right under UPA (1914)? Under UPA (2013)? ◄◄◄

Explanation

Under UPA (1914), the partner is right. UPA §20 provides that "[p]artners shall render on demand true and full information of all things affecting the partnership to any partner." The partner has made demand, and the records are connected to the fundamental partnership question of profit shares. Given that connection, they certainly contain "information of . . . things affecting the partnership."

The delegation of management authority to the Executive Committee makes no difference to this issue. A partner's right to information can be waived by agreement, but the agreement must be specific to be effective.[113]

---

112. UPA (2013) §410(b) (citations omitted).

113. There is a counterargument, based on the delegation of management authority to the Executive Committee. That delegation establishes a system of profit allocation that, arguably at least, requires confidentiality in order to work. When the partners agreed to the delegation of authority, they implicitly agreed to the necessary confidentiality.

The partner may also be right under UPA (2013). Section 408(b) provides categorically that:

> On reasonable notice, a partner may inspect and copy during regular business hours, at a reasonable location specified by the partnership, any record maintained by the partnership regarding the partnership's business, financial condition, and other circumstances, to the extent the information is material to the partner's rights and duties under the partnership agreement or this [act].[114]

However, the result would change if the partnership were to invoke UPA (2013) §408(j): "In addition to any restriction or condition stated in its partnership agreement, a partnership, as a matter within the ordinary course of its business, may impose reasonable restrictions and conditions on access to . . . information to be furnished under this section, . . . " ◀◀◀

Problem 69

Bernard and Suzanne form a partnership to run a dance school for children ages 4 to 14. Their partnership agreement delegates all artistic control to Bernard, and states that "all business decisions shall be decided by Suzanne in her sole discretion." The school sells ballet and tap shoes to its students, at a very healthy markup. Bernard thinks the shoes should be sold at cost. "We make our money from our teaching," he says. "We are not shopkeepers." Under UPA (2013), does Suzanne have a right to continue the markup approach, despite Bernard's objections? ◀◀◀

Explanation

Yes. Although under UPA (2013) §401(k) partners decide any "difference arising as to a matter in the ordinary course of business" by majority vote, that provision is a default rule. These partners have agreed to allocate all business decisions to Suzanne. Therefore, on matters such as the price of shoes, Bernard no longer has "equal rights in the management and conduct of the partnership business."[115]

---

114. UPA (2013) §410(b).

115. UPA (2013) §401(h). Without the partnership agreement, the partners would be deadlocked. See Section 9.4.2.

Problem 70

Larry, Moe, and Curley form a partnership to operate a whoopee cushion factory. Larry invests $100,000; Moe, $80,000; Curley, $20,000. They agree that (i) each will work full-time in the business; (ii) each will receive a salary of $20,000 (separate from whatever profits they may receive),[116] and (iii) none will withdraw their capital for at least three years. They make no other specific agreements.

At the end of the first year of operation, the partnership has a profit (after salaries) of $100,000. Larry and Moe want to distribute profits in proportion to the partners' respective contributions—50 percent to Larry, 40 percent to Moe, and 10 percent to Curley. They assert that profits are an ordinary part of partnership business and that therefore a majority vote controls. Are they correct under UPA (2013)? Under each of the other two uniform general partnership acts? ◀ ◀ ◀

Explanation

No. UPA (2013) §401(a) provides for partners to share distributions equally. The provision is a default rule,[117] and to amend the partnership agreement to change the default rule requires unanimous consent, not a mere majority vote.[118]

The result is identical under UPA (1997) §§401(b) (default rule of equal share of profit) and 103(a) (subject to exceptions not relevant here, partnership agreement controls relations *inter se* the partners), and UPA §18(a) (partners share profits equally, "subject to any agreement between them").

Problem 71

This Problem is based on a children's poem by Eugene Field:

> Wynken, Blynken, and Nod one night
> Sailed off in a wooden shoe—
> Sailed on a river of crystal light,
> Into a sea of dew.
> Where are you going, and what do you wish?"
> The old moon asked the three.

116. Even though the partnership agreement refers to "salary," tax law will consider the amount a "guaranteed payment" to be reported on each partner's K-1 form and not salary to be reported on a form W-2.

117. UPA (2013) §105(a)(1).

118. The result would be different if the partnership agreement permitted amendment by majority vote. See Section 7.1.4.

> We've come to fish for the herring fish
> That live in this beautiful sea;
> Nets of silver and gold have we!"
> Said Wynken, Blynken, and Nod.

Assume that Wynken, Blynken, and Nod are partners in a UPA (2013) partnership. Since the inception of the partnership, Wynken, Blynken, and Nod have always given the same answer to the old moon's question. If Wynken and Blynken want to have the partnership take up vegetable farming, and Nod opposes the idea, what results? ◄◄◄

Explanation

Absent a contrary agreement, UPA (2013) §§401(k) governs this type of situation. If the dispute over vegetable farming is a "difference arising as to a matter in the ordinary course of business," then the majority rules and Wynken and Blynken will prevail. If the dispute concerns "[a]n act outside the ordinary course of business" or constitutes an amendment to the partnership agreement, taking up vegetable farming will require unanimous consent and Nod will prevail.

The facts suggest that Nod will prevail. The partners' repeated answers to the old moon would support a finding that the partnership's ordinary course of business is fishing. In addition, the same facts could evidence an implied-in-fact agreement among the partners that the partnership will confine itself to fishing. In either case UPA (2013) §§401(k) would require unanimous agreement to take up vegetable farming.[119] ◄◄◄

Problem 72

Oscar is a partner in a partnership governed by UPA (2013) and formed, in the words of the partnership agreement, "for the purpose of investing in real estate." The agreement contains no other limitation on the scope of the partnership's business. In the five years since its formation, the partnership has invested exclusively in residential real estate located in either Minnesota or Iowa. While on vacation in Hawaii, Oscar comes across an attractive investment opportunity in an office building located there. Without informing his partners or obtaining their consent, Oscar uses his own money and buys the building. Two years later, while the partnership is still in existence, Oscar sells the building and makes a profit of $3 million. When the other partners learn of the transaction, they insist that Oscar share the profits with the partnership. Must he? ◄◄◄

---

119. UPA §18(h) would involve the same analysis and produce the same result.

Explanation

Probably. The profits certainly come from "investing in real estate," and so arguably involve "the appropriation of a partnership opportunity." UPA (2013) §409(b)(1)(C), Oscar's partners will therefore prevail, unless Oscar can show that the partnership's practice of investing solely in residential real estate impliedly limited the scope of the partnership business.[120] ◄ ◄ ◄

Problem 73

Same facts as Problem 72, except that:

1. Two weeks before his trip to Hawaii, Oscar attended a partnership meeting at which the partners reviewed the partnership's then-current finances.
2. During that review, it was apparent that the partnership had on hand only sufficient funds to meet operating expenses and did not have any cash available to make any further investments.
3. Before purchasing the Hawaii building, Oscar telephones you, his attorney, and asks, "Am I going to be in trouble with that partnership if I buy this building?"

What advice should you give Oscar? ◄ ◄ ◄

Explanation

Despite the partnership's current "cash poor" situation, the Hawaii building may still be a partnership opportunity. If made aware of the opportunity, the partners may choose to raise the necessary cash by, for example, selling some of the partnership's current holdings or borrowing against those holdings. Oscar's safest course therefore is to disclose the situation to his copartners and either: (i) obtain their unanimous consent for him to take the opportunity personally or (ii) obtain a vote of the partners rejecting the opportunity.

---

120. Under UPA (1914) §21, the key language would be "connected with . . . the conduct of the partnership." However, essentially the same analysis would apply, with the same result.

If Oscar can obtain unanimous consent, the first approach is better. It has the virtue of certainty. The second approach rests on the argument that: (i) a decision to take or reject a business opportunity is an ordinary matter and is therefore subject to a majority decision under UPA (2013) §§401(k); and (ii) the fact that a partner wishes to take the opportunity individually does not transform the decision into an extraordinary matter requiring unanimous consent.[121] ◀◀◀

Problem 74

Same facts as Problem 72, except that:

1. At a partnership meeting that took place three weeks before the Hawaii trip, the partners rejected by a vote of 3-2 a proposal to invest in an office building in Minneapolis.
2. One of the partners who voted against the proposal expressed the opinion that the partnership should "stick with residential real estate."

Will these new facts change the outcome of the partnership's disgorgement claim? ◀◀◀

Explanation

No. Neither the partnership's decision to reject an opportunity nor one partner's opinion on the subject generally will change the scope of matters constituting "a partnership opportunity."[122] If that scope does in fact include commercial real estate, then only an amendment to the partnership agreement can put such investments beyond the partnership's reach. ◀◀◀

Problem 75

Same facts as Problem 72 except that:

1. The office building is located in Minneapolis.
2. Oscar first discovers the building while inspecting several apartment complexes owned by the partnership and while driving in a car owned by the partnership.

---

121. Again, the analysis under UPA (1914) is parallel. See UPA (1914) §§21(1) and 18(h).
122. UPA (2013) §§404(b)(1)(C).

3. The partnership agreement limits investments to residential real estate.

Will these new facts change the outcome of the partners' disgorgement claim? ◀ ◀ ◀

Explanation

Yes. Oscar will not have to disgorge, even though, strictly speaking, he learned of the investment "in the conduct . . . of the partnership business" and through " . . . a use by the partner of partnership property."[123] He discovered the opportunity while engaged in the partnership's business and while driving the partnership's car. However, a *de minimis* exception applies to this rule. Because the connection is so insubstantial, and because the partnership agreement places the opportunity so clearly beyond the partnership's scope, the partnership has no claim. ◀ ◀ ◀

Problem 76

Same facts as Problem 72, except that:

1. Instead of making a profit of $300,000, Oscar loses $100,000.
2. The partnership agreement provides that all investment decisions will be made by majority vote.
3. The partnership agreement requires all partners to share partnership losses equally.

Under UPA (1997), can Oscar get any reimbursement from his copartners? ◀ ◀ ◀

Explanation

No. The reach of UPA (1997) §401(c), the 1997 Act's indemnification provision, is different from the reach of section 404(b)(1). Section 401(c) obligates the partnership to "reimburse a partner for payments made and indemnify a partner for liabilities incurred by the partner in the ordinary course of the business of the partnership or for the preservation of its business or property." Oscar's investment satisfies neither condition. He acted outside the "ordinary course of the business of the partnership" (i.e., without the authority of a partner vote) and did not act to preserve partnership

123. UPA (2013) §404(b)(1)(A) and (C).

"business or property." Oscar therefore must bear his losses alone, even though he might have been obliged to share his profits. ◀ ◀ ◀

Problem 77

Sweeney & Todd, a modest-sized metropolitan law firm, has been growing steadily and now has 50 partners. Plans call for adding another 40 partners over the next five years. Under the current partnership agreement all partners have one vote on all matters, including the annual election of the firm's management committee. Some of the more senior partners wish to give greater control to partners who have been with the firm at least 10 years. Under which of the three uniform general partnership acts should such an arrangement be lawful? If lawful, how might the arrangement be accomplished? ◀ ◀ ◀

Explanation

Such an arrangement would certainly lawful under each of the three acts. UPA (1997 and 2013) §401 and UPA (1914) §18 each state default rules, and each allows partners to shape their management structure virtually as they see fit. The partnership agreement could, for example, give extra votes to partners who have been with the firm at least ten years. Or, the agreement could create two separate classes of partnership interests, allocate the "senior" interests to partners who have been with the firm at least 10 years, and reserve specified management matters to partners holding senior interests.

To establish either structure, the partners would have to amend the partnership agreement. Unless the agreement provides for amendment on a less-than-unanimous basis, all the current partners will have to agree to any change. See UPA (1997) §401(j). ◀ ◀ ◀

Problem 78

In addition to its 50 partners, Sweeney & Todd has 50 associates and 125 other employees. The partnership agreement dates from when the firm had only 10 partners and requires unanimous consent for any amendment.

The firm's elected Management Committee wishes to implement a sexual harassment policy for dealing with complaints from firm employees. Upon the advice of counsel experienced in employment law, the Committee wishes to implement a policy that provides for confidential investigations of employee complaints and allows the Committee to impose discipline, either confidential or public, on any employee found to have engaged in harassing conduct. (This particular policy will not apply to partners. The Committee hopes soon to propose a policy on that subject.)

The Committee is quite concerned about confidentiality. "Leaks" can discourage employees from making complaints, ruin ongoing investigations, and subject the firm to damages for defamation. The Committee wants to make sure that only partners on the Management Committee will have access to information relating to complaints made, determinations reached, and sanctions imposed under the policy.

Are there any partnership law "wrinkles" to the Committee's concern under and UPA (1914) and UPA (1997)? ◄ ◄ ◄

Explanation

EXPLANATION

Yes. As to UPA (1914), §20 may give each partner a right to the information the Committee seeks to protect. Claims of sexual harassment are exceedingly serious, and their proper handling is essential to the welfare of the partnership. Obversely, poor handling of a complaint could imperil both the partnership and the partners.[124] The complaint information is therefore "information of . . . things affecting the partnership" and subject to disclosure to any partner on demand.

Since the partnership agreement can be amended only through unanimous consent, under UPA (1914), the simplest solution to this problem is to have each partner waive his or her right to the problematic information.

On the other hand, failure to adopt a workable policy on sexual harassment puts the partnership in legal peril. At least arguably, therefore, a partner who purports to veto or disregard a workable policy breaches the duty of loyalty not to harm the partnership.

A similar "wrinkle" exists under UPA (1997) §403. If the information is retained in the partnership's books and records, absent a contrary agreement each partner has a categorical right of access.[125] If the partnership never memorializes the information—a dangerous option under employment law—each partner still has an unbridled right of access to the extent the information is "reasonably required for the proper exercise of the partner's rights and duties under the partnership agreement or [UPA (1997)]."[126] The "loyalty" counterargument just discussed under UPA (1914) would not apply, due to UPA (1997)'s "cabined-in approach."[127] However, the partnership could repackage that argument as a breach of the implied covenant of good faith and fair dealing.[128]

124. Recall that, except in an LLP, partners are personally liable for the debts of the partnership. UPA (1914) §15. See Sections 7.3 and 17.2.
125. UPA (1997) §403(b).
126. *Id.*, §403(c)(1).
127. See Section 9.7.2.
128. See Sections 9.74 and 15.4.8.

The partnership agreement can place reasonable restrictions on access to partnership books and records and can completely eliminate the access rights granted by UPA (1997) §403.[129] However, in the stated situation the partnership agreement can be amended only with unanimous consent. Under UPA (1997), therefore, the partnership's best hope is to argue that: (i) information about these matters has not been memorialized into the partnership's books and records; (ii) because these matters are within the authority of the Management Committee and information concerning them is not "reasonably required for the proper exercise of the partner's rights and duties" and therefore not within UPA (1997) §403(c)(1); and (iii) under RUPA §403(c)(2), the partner has no right of access because—due to the importance of confidentiality—"the demand or the information demanded is unreasonable or otherwise improper under the circumstances." ◀◀◀

Problem 79

Same facts as in Problem 78, except that the partnership agreement provides: "This Agreement may be amended at any time upon the vote of 3/5 of the members of the Management Committee and the vote or written consent of a majority of all partners." Can Sweeney & Todd protect the complaint information through a nonunanimous amendment of the partnership agreement under UPA (1914)? UPA (1997)? UPA (2013)? ◀◀◀

Explanation

Yes. The analysis is the same under all three acts. As to the McCallum dicta,[130] no subsequent case has discussed the dicta favorably, let alone used the dicta as a rule of decision.[131] Moreover, even if good law, the McCallum dicta should not be problematic here. Although the duty to render information is a core fiduciary duty, the contemplated waiver is limited in scope, is well defined, and will clearly serve the partners' overall interests. ◀◀◀

---

129. UPA (1997) §103(b)(2) limits the partnership agreement's power to curtail access to books and records, but UPA (1997) §103 contains no restrictions on curtailing access to the other information covered by UPA (1997) §403.

130. See Section 9.5.2(a).

131. This assertion is based on a Westlaw search the author conducted on May 24, 2025, through all state and federal cases.

Problem 80

Xena, Gabriel, and Ares, Inc. (a corporation in which Xena is the sole stockholder) are going to form a UPA (2013) partnership, with Xena to act as the active managing partner. Xena wishes the partnership agreement to provide that it is not a breach of the duty of loyalty for her to cause the partnership to retain Ares, Inc., to furnish services to the partnership regardless of the amount Xena causes the partnership to pay for those services. As Xena's lawyer, you have advised her that the desired provision might fail the "manifestly unreasonable" standard of UPA (1997) §103(b)(3)(i). Paraphrasing J.P. Morgan, Xena exclaims, "I don't hire lawyers to tell me what I can't do. I hire them to tell me how to do what I want to do." She adds, "Find me another way." Do so. Would the analysis, outcome, or both change under UPA (2013)? ◄◄◄

Explanation

UPA (1997) §103(b)(3)(ii) may offer you that way. It states that "a number or percentage [of partners] specified in the partnership agreement may authorize or ratify, after full disclosure of all material facts, a specific act or transaction that otherwise would violate the duty of loyalty." If the partnership agreement provides for ratification of self-dealing transactions by a two-thirds majority of the partners, the votes of Xena and Ares, Inc., will suffice to ratify the partnership's contracts with Ares, Inc. UPA (1997) §103(b)(3)(ii) does *not* require that the ratifying partners be disinterested and is not subject to the manifestly unreasonable standard applicable to partnership §103(b)(3)(i). If Xena and Ares, Inc., ratify a grossly unfair fee, their votes could be attacked as a breach of the duty of care. However, UPA (1997)'s gross negligence standard is substantially more lenient than the duty of loyalty as applied to self-dealing transactions.

The analysis and outcome change materially under UPA (2013), because the language of the relevant provision, section 105(d)(1)(A), is materially different from UPA (1997) provision. Section 105(d)(1)(A) states: "The partnership agreement may . . . specify the method by which a specific act or transaction that would otherwise violate the duty of loyalty may be authorized or ratified by *one or more disinterested and independent persons* after full disclosure of all material facts. (Emphasis added.) Xena and Ares, Inc. are not disinterested. Any other restriction comes on the duty of loyalty under the not manifestly unreasonable standard of UPA (2013) §105(d)(3). ◄◄◄

CHAPTER 10

The Partner's Right and Power to Bind the Partnership

§10.1 OVERVIEW

§10.1.1 The Foundational Construct — Partner as Agent

For the most part, the rules for attributing partner conduct to the partnership reflect the rules of agency law. Justice Story, in his famous nineteenth-century treatise on partnership, wrote: "Every partner is an agent of the partnership,"[1] and the R.2d states: "[I]f, as is usual, a partner is a general agent for the other members of the group, rules with reference to his liability and to the liability of the others because of his conduct both to third persons and to the others, are determined by the rules stated herein [i.e., the rules of agency law])."[2]

§10.1.2 "Agent as Partner" Codified

All three uniform general partnership acts echo Justice Story's words[3] but spread the attribution rules among several different statutory provisions. All

1. Story on Partnership, §1 (1841), quoted in *Rhode Island Hospital Trust Co. v. Copeland*, 39 R.I. 193, 98 A. 273, 277–278 (R.I. 1916).
2. R.2d, §14A (Agent and Partner). R.3d has no comparable provision.
3. UPA §9(1) begins with those words exactly, while UPA (1997) §301(1) and UPA (2013) §301(1) substitute "Each" for "Every." The revision is solely a matter of drafting style.

three acts give special attention to misuse of funds provided to the partnership by third parties.[4]

Although UPA (1997) "retains the basic principles reflected in UPA [(1914)] Section 9(1), the 1997 act significantly changed the formulation."[5] The Harmonization Project made only one substantive change.

The following chart analyzes how UPA (1997) and UPA (1914) codify the "partner-as-agent" construct.[6] The material immediately after Table 10.1 refers to the one substantive change made by UPA (2013).

10.1 Partner as Agent

Agency Law Attribution Rule	Where Codified in UPA (1997) [key language]	Where Codified in UPA (1914) [key language]	Principal Function (i.e., what typically is attributed)	Notes
Actual authority	§301(1) first clause, "Each partner is an agent of the partnership for the purpose of its business."	§9 first clause, "Every partner is an agent of the partnership for the purpose of its business. . . ."	Contractual matters; information[7]	Neither act expressly delineates the scope of a partner's actual authority
Apparent authority	§301(1), "apparently/ ordinary course"—subject to the "no authority constraining rule" discussed in Section 10.4.2	§9 "apparently/ usual"—subject to a somewhat different "no authority constraining rule" discussed in Section 10.3.5	Contractual matters; information.[8]	Useful to think of as "statutory apparent authority"

4. History explains this special attention. At one time, professionals (e.g., lawyers and doctors) who wanted to practice in a firm had no choice other than a general partnership. See Section 7.3.2(c).
5. UPA (1997), §9, cmt. 2.
6. The chart does not include UPA (1914) §11, a little-used and recondite attribution rule for admissions made by partners. Neither UPA (1997) nor UPA (2013) contains an analog, and neither even mentions the concept in a comment.
7. Both acts contain specific provisions for attributing information possessed by a partner. See below.
8. These provisions also pertain to misrepresentations made with apparent authority.

10.1 Continued

Agency Law Attribution Rule	Where Codified in UPA (1997) [key language]	Where Codified in UPA (1914) [key language]	Principal Function (i.e., what typically is attributed)	Notes
Inherent agency power	§305(a) "a wrongful act or omission, or other actionable conduct, of a partner acting in the ordinary course of business of the partnership"	§13 "any wrongful act or omission of any partner acting in the ordinary course of the business of the partnership"	Wrongful acts causing harm	Provisions are the analog to *respondeat superior* but apply also to harms other than physical injury to persons and property
Apparent authority in the context of receiving property	§305(a) "a wrongful act or omission, or other actionable conduct, of a partner acting . . . with [apparent] authority of the partnership"[9]	§14(a) "[w]here one partner acting within the scope of his apparent authority receives money or property of a third person and misapplies it"	Misuse of property placed with the partnership	Reflects history—at one time professionals seeking to practice in a firm . . .
Actual authority and inherent agency power in the context of receiving property	§305(b) "in the course of the partnership's business or while acting with [actual] authority of the partnership, a partner receives or causes the partnership to receive money	§14(b) "[w]here the partnership in the course of its business receives money or property of a third person and the money or property so received is misapplied by any	Misuse of property placed with the partnership	. . . had no choice other than a general partnership

9. A comment states that "authority" in this subsection "is intended to include a partner's apparent, as well as actual, authority, thereby bringing within section 305(a) the situation covered in UPA section 14(a)." UPA (1997), §305(a), cmt. See Section 10.6. Redundantly to §301(a), §305(a) could also apply to a misrepresentation made with apparent authority. For how the Harmonization Project clarified section 305, see Section 10.5.1(a).

10.1 Continued

Agency Law Attribution Rule	Where Codified in UPA (1997) [key language]	Where Codified in UPA (1914) [key language]	Principal Function (i.e., what typically is attributed)	Notes
	or property of a person not a partner and the money or property is misapplied by a partner"[10]	partner while it is in the custody of the partnership"		
Special rules for attributing information possessed by partners	§102(f) "A partner's knowledge, notice, or receipt of a notification of a fact relating to the partnership is effective immediately as knowledge by, notice to, or receipt of a notification by the partnership"	§12 "Notice to any partner of any matter relating to partnership affairs, and the knowledge of the partner acting in the particular matter, acquired while a partner or then present to his mind, and the knowledge of any other partner who reasonably could and should have communicated it to the acting partner"	Information pertaining to the partnership	Neither actual nor apparent authority necessary; enterprise liability—i.e., inherent agency power; subject to the "fraud on the partnership" exception[11]

UPA (2013) made only one substantive change, pertaining to the "no authority constraining rule" discussed in Section 10.4.2.

10. The comment to UPA (1997), §305(b) indicates that in this subsection, "authority" refers to actual authority. See Section 10.6. The phrase "in the course of the partnership's business" betokens inherent agency power.
11. See Section 10.7.4.

§10.2 ACTUAL AUTHORITY—DEDUCING THE SCOPE

Partners may by agreement define the authority of each partner to bind the partnership, and partnership agreements often do so. Such definition is wise, for the statutory default rules are deficient in this area; they do not directly address the subject. It is, however, possible to infer the default scope of a partner's actual authority from the language of various statutory provisions. The scope is the same under all three statutes, although the analysis differs slightly because the relevant language differs.

The clearest exposition comes from UPA (2013) §401 and its comments. Section 401(h) and (k) provide:

> (h) Each partner has equal rights in the management and conduct of the partnership's business.
>
> . . .
>
> (k) A difference arising as to a matter in the ordinary course of business of a partnership may be decided by a majority of the partners. An act outside the ordinary course of business of a partnership and an amendment to the partnership agreement may be undertaken only with the affirmative vote or consent of all the partners.

The comment to UPA (2013) §401(h) explains (somewhat at length):

> The actual authority of a partner is a question of agency law, and depends fundamentally on the contents of the partnership agreement. If, however, the partnership agreement is silent on the issue, this subsection helps delineate that actual authority. Acting individually, a partner:
>
> - has no actual authority to commit the partnership to any matter for which this act requires the affirmative vote or consent of all partners;
> - has the actual authority to commit the partnership to usual and customary matters, unless the partner has reason to know that: (i) other partners might disagree; or (ii) for some other reason consultation with fellow partners is appropriate; and
> - has no actual authority to take unusual or non-customary actions that will have a substantial effect on the partnership.
>
> The first point follows self-evidently from the language of this act. Where this act requires unanimity, no partner could reasonably believe to the contrary (unless the partnership agreement provided otherwise).

The second point follows because:

- Subsection (h) serves as the gap-filler manifestation from the partnership to its partners and does *not* require partners to act *only* in concert or after consultation. To the contrary, subject to the partnership agreement, this subsection expressly provides that "each partner has equal rights in the management and conduct of the partnership's business."
- It would be impractical to require collective action on even the smallest of decisions.
- However, to the extent a partner has reason to know of a possible difference of opinion among the partners, subsection (k) requires a decision by at least "a majority of the partners" and by unanimous consent if the matter is "outside the ordinary course of the business."

The third point is a matter of common sense. The more serious the matter, the less likely it is that a partner has actual authority to act unilaterally. Cf. RESTATEMENT (THIRD) OF AGENCY §3.03, cmt. c (2006) (noting the unreasonableness of believing, without more facts, that an individual has "an unusual degree of unilateral authority over a matter fraught with enduring consequences for the institution" and stating that "[t]he gravity of the matter from the standpoint of the organization is relevant to whether a third party could reasonably believe that the manager has authority to proceed unilaterally").[12]

The analysis under UPA (1914) and UPA (1997) is quite similar, although earlier editions of this book also looked to the statutory provisions on statutory apparent authority and indemnification. For the analysis made in the comment above, sections 18(e) (equal rights in management) and 18(h) (how partners decide matters) provide the statutory basis under UPA (1914). For UPA (1997), sections are 401(f) (equal rights in management) and 401(j) (how partners decide matters) are the relevant ones.

UPA Case in Point—*Concklin v. Holland*

Homeowner, who co-owned the house with another individual, served illicit drugs and alcohol to an individual who subsequently died. Plaintiffs (decedent's parents) alleged partnership liability on the basis that the co-owners of the property intended to remodel and resell the property (thereby making it a profitable venture). The court of appeals affirmed dismissal on the pleadings on the claim of partnership liability. The "general rule is that each partner is a general agent of the firm but only for the purpose of carrying on the business of the partnership. Any sale by a partner to be valid, it must be in furtherance of the partnership business. Assuming *arguendo* that

12. The comment's analysis was derived from earlier editions of this book.

Will and Lewis bought the Fenwick property to resell, Will's distribution of illicit drugs and alcohol to third-party visitors would not be for the purpose or in furtherance of the partnership."[13] ◄◄◄

Example

Rachael, Charlotte, and Carolyn form a chicken farming partnership, but the partnership agreement does not specify who may commit the partnership to sell chickens. One day Carolyn overhears Charlotte discussing a sale of 500 chickens to an established customer. Before Charlotte can close the deal, Carolyn says, "I don't think we should sell to that customer. They're on the verge of bankruptcy." Charlotte has no actual authority to make the deal. She must refer the matter to a decision by the partners. ◄◄◄

Example

Charlotte does have the partners decide the matter, and he and Rachael vote in favor of continuing to sell to that customer on a "C.O.D." basis.[14] Charlotte closes the deal with the customer. The next week Carolyn learns that Charlotte proposes to sell another 1,000 chickens to the customer. She again objects. Since a partner vote has already settled the matter, Charlotte's awareness of Carolyn's objection does not by itself remove Charlotte's actual authority.[15] ◄◄◄

§10.3 STATUTORY APPARENT AUTHORITY—UPA (1914) §9

§10.3.1 UPA (1914) §9—the Paragon of Complexity

a. Statutory Apparent Authority—From 1914 to 1997 to 2013

UPA (1914) §9 is a complex and somewhat problematic provision, which in effect codifies a partner's apparent authority to bind the partnership. Fortunately, UPA (1997) §301 formulates the rule more simply and more clearly, and UPA (2013) follows the 1997 formulation.

13. *Concklin v. Holland*, 138 S.W.3d 215, 221 (Tenn. Ct. App. 2003) (citations and internal quotations omitted).

14. "C.O.D" stands for "cash on delivery" (i.e., no sales on credit).

15. These Examples address solely Charlotte's *actual* authority to bind the partnership. For apparent authority, see Sections 10.3. and 10.4.

Nonetheless, for several reasons it makes sense to begin by understanding UPA (1914) §9. First, UPA (1914) continues to be the law in more than a dozen states. Second, UPA (2013 and 1997) §301 can be best understood in historical context; UPA (1997)'s improvements make most sense when compared to UPA (1914) §9, and the former's remaining problems derive from the latter. Third, many limited liability company statutes incorporate UPA (1914) §9 language to provide power-to-bind rules for members and managers of LLCs. (These statutes were enacted before the widespread acceptance of UPA (1997).)[16]

b. UPA (1914) Analyzed

UPA §9 (1914) provides:

9. Partner Agent of Partnership as to Partnership Business

(1) Every partner is an agent of the partnership for the purpose of its business, and the act of every partner, including the execution in the partnership name of any instrument, for apparently carrying on in the usual way the business of the partnership of which he is a member binds the partnership, unless the partner so acting has in fact no authority to act for the partnership in the particular matter, and the person with whom he is dealing has knowledge of the fact that he has no such authority.

(2) An act of a partner which is not apparently for the carrying on of the business of the partnership in the usual way does not bind the partnership unless authorized by the other partners.

(3) Unless authorized by the other partners or unless they have abandoned the business, one or more but less than all the partners have no authority to:

(a) assign the partnership property in trust for creditors or on the assignee's promise to pay the debts of the partnership,

(b) dispose of the good will of the business,

(c) do any other act tat which would make it impossible to carry on the ordinary business of a partnership,

(d) confess a judgment,

(e) submit a partnership claim or liability to arbitration or reference.

(4) No act of any partner in contravention of a restriction on authority shall bind the partnership to persons having knowledge of the restriction.

16. Section 15.5 considers the power of members and managers to bind a limited liability company.

The difficulty in mastering UPA §9 (1914) comes from three sources: (i) the section states a very intricate set of rules; (ii) at key points the section uses language carelessly; and (iii) much of the case law is superficial and unenlightening.

1. Intricacy

The intricacy exists because UPA §9 (1914) contains multiple rules that run in opposite directions. The section's basic structure reflects a common but unfortunate tendency of lawyers to write rules in the mode of "two steps forward, but one step back." UPA §9 (1914) follows this "cha-cha" approach by providing two rules that establish a partner's power to bind, and three rules that confine that power:

- *the "agency law" empowering rule* (§9(1), *first clause*), which invokes (albeit ambiguously) the law of agency;
- *the "apparently/usual" empowering rule* (§9(1), *second clause*), which is partnership law's analog to apparent authority (and can be usefully labeled "statutory apparent authority");[17]
- *the "not apparently/usual" constraining rule* (§9(2)), which looks like the "flip side" of the "apparently/usual" empowering rule, but which serves to substantially undercut the "agency law" empowering rule;
- *the "no authority" constraining rule* (§9(1), *third and fourth clauses,* §9(4)), which is apparently so important that UPA (1914) states it twice; and
- *the "unanimous consent" constraining rule* (§9(3)), which is the clearest of all the five rules.

2. Careless Language

UPA §9 (1914) deals sometimes with the power to bind, sometimes with the right to bind, and sometimes with both at once, and the section never states explicitly when it is doing which. For example, the terms "authority" and "authorized" appear six times in the section, with no express indication whether they encompass apparent and inherent as well as actual authority.

3. Unenlightening Case Law

Many of the cases applying UPA §9 (1914) do so without much analysis, neglecting important nuances and focusing on individual parts of the rules out of context. It is impossible to construe UPA §9 (1914) in a way that reconciles all or even most of the cases.

---

17. This phrase first appeared in ULLCA (2006), §301(a), cmt., and has since become a useful term of art.

§10.3.2 The Agency Law Empowering Rule—Less Than First Meets the Eye

Broadly and seemingly without qualification, the first clause of UPA §9(1) (1914) states that "[e]very partner is an agent of the partnership for the purpose of its business." Although, as explained above, this language reflects a basic construct of partnership law, the language's practical effect is limited by the rest of §9. The clause is best understood as a reminder that a partner's power to bind the partnership includes the partner's actual authority.[18] Any broader reading would either overlap or undercut the more specific rules stated in the rest of the section.

§10.3.3 The "Apparently/Usual" Empowering Rule (Statutory Apparent Authority)

a. The Basic Rule

The second clause of UPA (1914) §9(1) reads in pertinent part: "the act of every partner for apparently carrying on in the usual way the business of the partnership of which he is . . . a member binds the partnership." This "apparently . . . usual" power is analogous to the agency law concept of apparent authority by position and is usefully labeled "statutory apparent authority."[19] A person seeking to use this attribution rule must that show that:

- at the time of the transaction
- it reasonably[20] appeared to the person that the partner's act was:
  - for carrying on the business of the partnership and
  - for doing so "in the usual way."[21]

The rule cannot apply when the partnership is undisclosed or partially disclosed (unidentified).

18. For the scope of this actual authority, see Section 10.2.
19. See ULLCA (2006) §301(a), comment.
20. Although the statute does not mention reasonableness, the case law does.
21. The phrase "the usual way" is ambiguous. Some cases hold that the third party must establish that the partner's act appeared usual for the particular partnership. Other cases hold that the third party must or may establish that the partner's act appeared usual for similar partnerships. As will be seen in Section 10.4.1, UPA (1997) resolved this issue by allowing a claimant to make either showing.

EXAMPLE

Example

Al, a partner in the Ventura Company, buys a computer for the partnership to use in its offices. It is quite usual for Ventura partners to make such purchases, and indeed Ventura partners have previously made such purchases from this seller. However, the seller does not know that Al is a partner in Ventura, and Al does not mention the partnership. Instead, Al signs an installment contract in his own name. The apparently/usual power will not bind the partnership,[22] because the seller cannot satisfy the "appearance" element. ◀◀◀

b. Relationship to Actual Authority

It is possible for a partner to have apparently/usual power while lacking actual authority and *vice versa*.

CASE IN POINT

Case in Point — *Herr v. Brakefield*

Two partners owned and raised cattle as part of their partnership business. One partner (Brakefield) sold 43 head of cattle to Plaintiffs and agreed to keep the cattle on the partnership's property until Plaintiffs would pick them up. Before Plaintiffs could fully do so, the other partner (Stidham) sold for slaughter the cattle still on the partnership property. Plaintiffs sued alleging conversion. Stidham defended, in part, on the basis that Brakefield had no authority (apparent or otherwise) to sell the cattle. The Washington Supreme Court held that — even though Brakefield lacked actual authority — he had apparent authority and the Plaintiffs did not have knowledge sufficient to contravene Brakefield's apparent authority.[23] ◀◀◀

c. Partnership Need Not Benefit

As with common law apparent authority, statutory apparent authority can apply even if the "agent" rather than the "principal" takes the benefits of the transaction.[24]

---

22. However, actual authority might well bind full partnership as an undisclosed principal. See Sections 10.2 (partners' actual authority) and 2.2.3 (undisclosed principal).
23. *Herr v. Brakefield*, 314 P.2d 397 (Wash. 1957).
24. While the first clause of UPA (1914) §9(1) empowers a partner to act only "for the purpose of [the partnership's] business," the "apparently/usual" rule contains no such restriction.

Example

Al is a partner in the Ventura Company. Purporting to act for the Company, Al buys a computer on credit from a computer store. Ventura partners have made such purchases from the computer store in the past. This time, however, Al does not deliver the computer to the partnership. Instead, he resells the computer to a friend and pockets the cash. The computer store may nonetheless collect from the Ventura Company. From the perspective of the computer store, Al's act in buying the computer was "for apparently carrying on in the usual way the business of the partnership." The partnership is therefore bound. ◄◄◄

This interpretation is not universally accepted, but it (i) seems compelled by the language of the statute; (ii) finds support in the case law; and (iii) comports with analogous tenets of apparent authority.[25] Moreover, the interpretation serves basic notions of efficiency and fairness. It is generally easier for members of a partnership to monitor each other than for third parties to inquire deeply into the bona fides of every partner who reasonably appears to be acting for the partnership. If a partner's dishonesty causes loss, that loss should fall on those better positioned to avoid it.

§10.3.4 The "Flip Side" Constraining Rule: Not "Apparently/Usual" and No Actual Authority

Under UPA §9(2) (1914), a partner lacks the power to bind the partnership if

- the partner is not "authorized by the other partners" (i.e., if the partner lacks actual authority);[26] and
- the partner's act "is not apparently for the carrying on of the business of the partnership in the usual way."

Example

Sara is a partner in Ventura Company. Under the partnership agreement, Sara has no authority to commit Ventura to any trades. Sara makes a purchase of soybeans in her own name from a farmer who is unaware of the partnership's existence. Under UPA (1914) §9(2), Sara's act cannot bind Ventura,

25. See Section 2.3.5(d).

26. In this context "authorized" must mean "actually authorized"; otherwise, the subsection would swallow its own tail.

because (i) the act was not "apparently/usual" and (ii) Sara lacked actual authority.[27] ◀◀◀

Although both the "apparently/usual" empowering rule of UPA (1914) §9(1) and the "not apparently/usual" constraining rule of UPA (1914) §9(2) have a common component, the constraining rule does not follow automatically from the empowering rule. The empowering rule states conditions under which a partner's act binds the partnership, but that rule does not itself foreclose other empowering conditions. UPA (1914) §9(2) performs that function. Taken together the two "apparently/usual" rules mean that:

- a partner who has actual authority binds the partnership within the scope of that authority, regardless of what appears to the third party; and
- a partner who lacks actual authority can bind the partnership *only* by satisfying the "apparently/usual" empowering rule.

§10.3.5 The "No Authority" Constraining Rule

UPA (1914) §9(4) and the last lines of §9(1) state the same rule. Regardless of the "apparently/usual" empowering rule, the partnership is not bound if: (i) the partner acts without actual authority; and (ii) at the time of the act the third party knows of the lack of authority.

Example

To finance its commodities purchases, the Ventura Company establishes a $4 million line of credit with the First National Bank. When Ventura applies for the line of credit, the Bank asks for and receives a copy of the Partnership Agreement. The Agreement specifies that the signatures of two partners are necessary to commit the partnership to borrow money. Four months later, Al approaches the Bank to arrange a loan outside the line of credit to finance the partnership's purchase of a $10,000 server for the partnership's network. A loan officer approves the loan, and Al signs the loan agreement on behalf of the partnership. The partnership is not bound. Although Al's act may appear "apparently/usual," under the Partnership Agreement he lacks the actual authority to borrow the money. Having received a copy of the

27. If, however, the partnership later accepts the benefits of the deal, the partnership will be bound to some extent. Acceptance may indicate ratification, which would bind the partnership to the deal itself. See Section 2.7.2(b). Short of ratification, acceptance may oblige the partnership to respond in *quantum meruit* for the reasonable value of benefits accepted. See Section 10.3.7.

Agreement, the Bank knows of that lack.[28] According to both §§9(1) and 9(4), therefore, the partnership is not bound.[29] ◄◄◄

Case in Point — *Bank of the West v. Early Farm Partnership*

Mother (Sheila) and son (Kevin) were the sole partners in a partnership that, based on its partnership agreement, required unanimous consent for any decisions which would have a "substantial effect upon the interest of the partnership." Kevin was also a stockholder of a corporation that sought debt financing and offered as collateral the assets of the partnership he owned with his mother. Kevin closed the deal and obtained the loan without Sheila's signature. After Kevin defaulted on the note, the lender's successor in interest sought to foreclose on the partnership's assets. The partnership defended the suit, in part, on the basis that the lender "received notification that Kevin lacked authority"—oral statements by Kevin and his attorney explaining that Sheila was a "required signatory" on any instrument relating to the partnership assets—thereby negating any claims that Kevin had authority to bind the partnership. The court of appeals affirmed summary judgment in favor of the lender's successor in interest, holding that a statement pertaining to a formality (required signatory) did not give notice that all partners had to consent to the transaction.[30] ◄◄◄

§10.3.6 The "Unanimous Consent" Constraining Rule

Under UPA (1914) §9(3), unless the other partners have abandoned the business, a partner needs either *actual* authority or unanimous consent from copartners to:

1. assign the partnership property in trust for creditors or on the assignee's promise to pay the debts of the partnership
2. dispose of the good will of the business
3. do any other act that would make it impossible to carry on the ordinary business of a partnership
4. confess a judgment
5. submit a partnership claim or liability to arbitration or reference

---

28. As for how a bank could "know" something, see Sections 2.4.4 and 2.4.8.
29. However, the partnership could be bound either through ratification or in *quantum meruit* if it accepts and retains the loan proceeds. See Section 10.3.7.
30. *Bank of the West v. Early Farm Partnership*, No. 10–1093, 2011 WL 1136247 (Iowa App. Mar. 30 2011). This opinion illustrates the rule, but the reasoning is dubious. For one thing, to parse the facts so carefully on summary judgment is unusual. For another, when a partner offers partnership assets to guarantee the debt of a different organization, the lender may have a duty to inquire. See Section 2.3.5(b) (apparent authority and the duty of inquiry).

In these specified areas, a partner who lacks the authority to bind the partnership also lacks the power to bind.

If a partner lacks actual authority, the copartners' unanimous consent can remedy the situation. If the consent precedes the partner's act, the consent creates actual authority. If the consent follows the act, the consent amounts to ratification. In either event, the partner's act becomes rightful, and can therefore bind the partnership.

§10.3.7 The Import of the Partnership's Receipt of Benefits

Under ordinary contract and agency law principles, a partnership's acceptance of benefits from a transaction can bind the partnership to that transaction under theories of ratification,[31] *quantum meruit*, or unjust enrichment.

§10.4 STATUTORY APPARENT AUTHORITY—UPA (1997) §301

§10.4.1 UPA (1914) Compared with UPA (1997) and UPA (2013)

UPA (1997) "retains the basic principles reflected in UPA Section 9(1)"[32] and also maintains that section's basic structure. With one exception (described in Section 10.4.2), UPA (2013) follows UPA (1997). Both UPA (1997) §301 and UPA (2013) §301 are considerably shorter than UPA (1914) §9. UPA (1997) §301 provides:

> SECTION 301. PARTNER AGENT OF PARTNERSHIP. Subject to the effect of a statement of partnership authority under Section 303:
>
> (1) Each partner is an agent of the partnership for the purpose of its business. An act of a partner, including the execution of an instrument in the partnership name, for apparently carrying on in the ordinary course the partnership business or business of the kind carried on by the partnershipbinds the partnership, unless the partner had no authority to act for the partnership in the particular matter and the person with whom the partner was dealing knew or had received a notification that the partner lacked authority.

31. See Section 2.7.2(b).
32. UPA (1997) §301, comment 2.

> (2) An act of a partner which is not apparently for carrying on in the ordinary course the partnership business or business of the kind carried on by the partnership binds the partnership only if the act was authorized by the other partners.

Length is not the only difference between the two provisions. UPA (1997) §301 differs from UPA (1914) §9 in six noteworthy ways. UPA (1997) §301:

1. Replaces UPA "apparently/usual" formulation of UPA (1914) with the phrase "for apparently carrying on in the ordinary course."
   - This change in wording has no effect on meaning.[33]
2. Delineates a partner's "apparently/ordinary" power by referring both to "the ordinary course [of] the partnership business" and to "business of the kind carried on by the partnership."
   - This change eliminates a problem of interpretation that existed under UPA (1914) §9(1) and broadens the scope of statutory apparent authority.
3. Eliminates as inflexible the "unanimous consent" constraining rule of UPA (1914) §9(3).
   - The biggest practical effect of this change is to remove an outdated barrier to agreements to arbitrate.[34]
4. Eliminates as redundant UPA (1914) §9(4).
   - This change has no effect on meaning.[35]
5. Modifies the "no authority" constraining rule, so that it applies not only if the third party knew that the partner lacked actual authority, but also if the third party "had received a notification that the partner lacked authority."
   - This change alters the balance of risk between partners and third parties, and is discussed further in Section 10.4.2.
6. Establishes a system of recorded statements of authority and limitations of authority, which can significantly affect both the apparently/ordinary empowering rule and the "no authority" constraining rule.

---

33. According to UPA (1997) §301, comment 2, "No substantive change is intended. . . . UPA [1914] and the case law use both terms without apparent distinction."

34. When UPA (1914) was promulgated in 1914, arbitration was disfavored. Today, arbitration is a commonplace species of "alternative dispute resolution," and it therefore "seems archaic that the submission of a partnership claim to arbitration always requires unanimous consent." UPA (1997) §301, comment 4.

35. The "unless" clause of UPA (1997) "section 301(1) fully reflects the principle embodied in UPA [(1914)] section 9(4) that the partnership is not bound by an act of a partner in contravention of a restriction on his authority known to the other party." UPA (1997) §301, comment 5.

- The system's primary impact is on the power to transfer real property and is discussed in Section 10.4.3.

§10.4.2 Modifying the "No Authority" Constraining Rule

UPA (1997) §301(1) modifies the "no authority" constraining rule, so that it applies not only if the third party knew that the partner lacked actual authority, but also if the third party "had received a notification that the partner lacked authority." Under UPA (1997) §102(d), "A person receives a notification when the notification: (1) comes to the person's attention; or (2) is duly delivered at the person's place of business or at any other place held out by the person as a place for receiving communications."[36]

As between a partnership and a third party, this change shifts somewhat the risk arising from a partner's unauthorized act.[37]

Example

In the Rachael-Charlotte-Carolyn chicken-breeding partnership, each partner has the authority to purchase chickens for the partnership. During a cash-flow crunch, however, the partners by a 2-1 vote decide not to buy any chickens during the next 30 days. The partnership sends a letter to each of its regular suppliers, stating, "For your convenience in scheduling, we are informing you that we will not be making any purchases during the next 30 days. We look forward to making further orders after this brief hiatus."

One week later, however, Carolyn finds what she considers a "golden opportunity" to purchase 500 chicks, cheap, from Gili's Golden Hens, one of the partnership's regular suppliers. Carolyn places an order on behalf of the partnership, and Gili accepts the order. The partnership's "hiatus" letter is sitting unopened on Gili's desk.

Under UPA (1914), the partnership is probably bound. Carolyn lacked actual authority, but she had apparently/usual power. At the relevant moment, Gili had no "knowledge of the fact that [Carolyn had] no such authority." UPA (1914) §9(1). Under UPA (1914) §3, a person has knowledge of a fact not only through "actual knowledge thereof but also when he [or she] has knowledge of such other facts as in the circumstances shows

36. This definition closely resembles the definition in UPA (1914) §3(2) for giving notice. The difference is in the operative provision, that is, UPA (1997) §301(1)'s "no authority constraining rule" refers to knowledge or receipt of notification, while UPA (1914) §9's "no authority constraining rule" refers only to knowledge.

37. Of course, a partner who acts without actual authority will be liable to the partnership for any resulting damages— see Section 4.1.2— and, if the partnership is not bound, will be liable to the third party for breach of the warranty of authority. See Section 4.2.2.

bad faith." Most likely, Gili's failure to promptly open her mail does not amount to "bad faith."

Under UPA (1997) §§301(1) and 102(d), in contrast, the partnership is probably *not* bound. The partnership's "hiatus" letter is a "notification" that has been "duly delivered at [Gili's] place of business." ◀◀◀

"The Harmonization Project shifted the risk a bit further."[38] Under UPA (2013) §301(1), the "no authority constraining rule" applies if "the person with which the partner was dealing *knew or had notice* that the partner lacked authority."[39]

§10.4.3 Establishing a System of Recorded Statements That Can Significantly Affect the Operation of UPA (1997) §301 and UPA (2013) §301

As one of its major innovations, UPA (1997) established a system of publicly filed statements to provide what is often termed "constructive notice."[40] The system, which is mechanically complex, "was refined in ULLCA (2006) and further refined in the Harmonization Project."[41]

In both UPA (1997) and UPA (2013), the key provision is section 303, which provides both for statements recognizing authority and statements limiting authority. As explained in a comment to UPA (2013) §303:

> This section is conceptually divided into two realms: (i) statements pertaining to the power to transfer interests in the partnership real property; and (ii) statements pertaining to other matters. In the latter realm, statements are filed only in the records of the filing office and operate only to the extent the statements are actually known and relied on by a third party.
>
> As to interests in real property, in contrast, this section: (i) requires double filing—with the filing office and in the appropriate land records; and (ii) provides for constructive knowledge of statements limiting authority. Thus, a properly filed and recorded statement can protect the partnership, and, in order for a statement pertaining to real property to be a sword in the hands of a third party, the statement must have been both filed and properly recorded, section 303(f). Experience suggests that statements of authority will most often be used in connection with transactions in real estate.[42]

38. UPA (2013) §301(1), cmt.
39. Emphasis added. The comment to UPA (2013) §301(1) questions how much difference the change makes: "[I]t is arguable that the Harmonization Project merely made explicit a rule implicit in the case law . . . .[T]he case law requires a third party to show a reasonable belief in the partner's authority. A third party who has reason to know of a partner's lack of authority will be hard pressed to make that showing."
40. UPA (2013) §303, cmt.
41. UPA (2013) §303, cmt.
42. Citations omitted.

The Harmonization Project made two noteworthy, substantive improvements to the statement of authority provision. First, while the 1997 version authorized statements of authority pertaining only to partners,[43] UPA (2013) §303(a)(3) authorizes a statement to pertain to any "person." Second, UPA (2013) §303(a)(2) provides that, "with respect to any position that exists in, or with respect to the partnership, [a statement of authority] may state the authority, or limitations on the authority, of all persons holding the position." As explained in a comment:

> This paragraph [i.e., section 303(a)(2)] permits a statement to designate authority by position (or office) rather than by specific person, thus avoiding the need to file anew whenever a new person assumes the position or the office. This type of a statement will enable partnerships to provide evidence of ongoing power to enter into transactions without having to disclose to third parties the entirety of the partnership agreement.

§10.5 BINDING THE PARTNERSHIP THROUGH A PARTNER'S WRONGFUL ACTS (UPA (1914) §13; UPA (1997 AND 2013) §305(A))

§10.5.1 The Attribution Rule

a. The Rule in the Three Acts

All three acts provide a rule for attributing certain "wrongful" acts or omissions of a partner to the partnership. UPA (1997) "Section 305(a) . . . is derived from UPA [(1914)] section 13,"[44] and the provisions state very similar rules.

UPA (2013) §305(a) differs from the 1997 version only by moving an important point of clarification from a comment to the statute itself. The text of UPA (1997) §305(a) provides: "A partnership is liable for loss or injury caused to a person, or for a penalty incurred, as a result of a wrongful act or omission, or other actionable conduct, of a partner acting in the ordinary course of business of the partnership or *with authority of the partnership*."[45] The official comment then states: "'[W]ith the authority of the partnership' . . . is intended to include a partner's apparent, as well as actual, authority."[46]

43. UPA (1997) §303(a)(2).
44. UPA (1997) §305, comment 1.
45. Emphasis added.
46. UPA (1997) §305, cmt.

In contrast, UPA (2013) §305(a) provides:

> A partnership is liable for loss or injury caused to a person, or for a penalty incurred, as a result of a wrongful act or omission, or other actionable conduct, of a partner acting in the ordinary course of business of the partnership or *with the actual or apparent authority of the partnership.*[47]

Table 10.2 details the similarities and mostly minor differences among the three acts.

10.2 A Partner's Wrongful Conduct

Provision	Nature of Partner's Conduct	Connection of Partner's Conduct to the Partnership	Resulting Liability of the Partnership	Applicable to Third-Party Claimants Only, or also to Injured Partners
UPA (1914) §13	"Any wrongful act or omission"	"In the ordinary course of the business of the partnership or with the [actual] authority of his copartners"	"The partnership is liable therefore to the same extent as the partner so acting or omitting to act."	Only third-party claimants
UPA (1997 and 2013) §305(a)	"A wrongful act or omission, or other actionable conduct"	"In the ordinary course of business of the partnership or with [the actual or apparent] authority of the partnership"[48]	"Partnership is liable for loss or injury caused."	Attribution rule also available to partners

47. Emphasis added.
48. See the explanation text at n.46

b. Wrongful but Ordinary?

When a claimant invokes section 305(a) of UPA (1997) or UPA (2013), or section 13 of UPA (1914), can the partnership argue that, while the "rightful" version of the partner's conduct may be "ordinary course" or authorized, the wrongful conduct is not? Cannot the partnership say, for example, "Yes, it's normal and proper for our partners to describe our products, but it is both extraordinary and unauthorized for them to make misrepresentations when doing so"?

Although superficially attractive, this argument should fail. The proper question under all three acts is not whether the specific *wrongful* act *is* "ordinary course" or authorized, but rather whether that *type* of act, *if done rightfully, would be*. For example, the question is not whether attending a Chamber of Commerce luncheon, and then driving negligently back to the office meets the scope requirement, but rather whether attendance and nonnegligent driving would do so.[49] Similarly, the question is not whether a partner's inaccurate disparagement of a competitor's product meets the scope requirement, but rather whether an accurate criticism of the product would be "ordinary course" or authorized.

Example

Ventura Partnership trades in agricultural products. In the course of discussing a soybean trade with a customer, Al offers to sell (for the partnership) 20,000 bushels "99 percent free of vermin infestation." Al knows that the soybeans in question actually have a troublesome 8 percent infestation rate. The partnership is legally responsible for Al's misstatement. Since Al's intentional misrepresentation (a wrongful act) occurred in the ordinary course of the business of the partnership, whichever uniform act applies will attribute the misrepresentation and any resulting liability to the Ventura Partnership.[50] Ventura cannot defend by claiming that "We are an honest company, and this is the first misrepresentation any of our partners have ever made." The issue is not whether misrepresentation is "ordinary course," but rather whether product description is.[51] ◀◀◀

49. This distinction parallels rules of agency law. See Section 3.2.5(c) (tortious acts can be with the scope of employment).

50. There may be contract consequences as well. If Al's misstatement came within his apparently/usual (UPA (1914) §9(1)) or apparently/ordinary power (UPA (1997 and 2013) §301(1)), the customer may succeed with a claim either for rescission or breach of warranty.

51. See UPA (2013) §305(a), cmt (quoting the 4th edition of this book).

CASE IN POINT

Case in Point — Albeit Wrongly Decided — *Jackson v. Jackson*

In *Jackson v. Jackson*, the North Carolina Court of Appeals stated that, while "[a]dvising the initiation of a criminal prosecution is clearly within the normal range of activities for a typical law partnership, . . . taking such action maliciously and without probable cause is quite a different matter." The court held that "[i]n view of [ethics] rules, which clearly forbid any attempt by a lawyer to prosecute a person without cause, it cannot be held that malicious prosecution is within the ordinary course of business of a law partnership."[52]

The comment to UPA (2013) §305(a) criticizes *Jackson*'s reasoning: "It is difficult to identify a reasonable limit to this approach. Presumably, at least, a partner's 'plain vanilla' malpractice is within a law firm's ordinary course of business despite the ethical rules requiring lawyers to act zealously and competently."

§10.5.2 *Respondeat Superior* Compared to UPA (1914) §13 and UPA (1997 and 2013) §305(a)

UPA (1914) §13 and UPA (1997 and 2013) §305(a) each state a rule of vicarious liability, and in that general respect they resemble the agency doctrine of *respondeat superior*:[53] A first legal person (the partnership or the master/employer, as the case may be) becomes liable on account of the tortious conduct of a second person[54] (the partner or the servant/employee agent), without the claimant needing to establish that the first person is at fault or directly responsible for the claimed harm. All that a claimant need show is that:

- the second person (the partner or the servant/employee agent) incurred tort liability;
- the first and second person stand in a specified relationship to each other (partner/partnership or servant-master/employee-employer); and
- the tort is sufficiently related to the first person's enterprise ("ordinary course of" the partnership or "scope of employment").

52. 201 S.E.2d 722, 724 (N.C. App. 1974). This Case on Point is taken verbatim from UPA (2013) §305(a), cmt.
53. For a discussion of *respondeat superior*, see Section 3.2.
54. UPA §13 (1914) does not encompass no-fault torts. See Section 10.4.1.

There is one major difference, however. Under *respondeat superior*, the claimant must show that the master had the right to control the means by which the tortfeasor performed his, her, or its functions. This showing is crucial to establishing servant/employee status.[55] The partnership rules have no parallel requirement; they apply regardless of whether the tortfeasor is the most subservient junior partner or the most dictatorial managing partner.

§10.6 BINDING THE PARTNERSHIP THROUGH A PARTNER'S INVOLVEMENT IN A MISAPPLICATION OF PROPERTY OWNED BY A NON-PARTNER (UPA §14; UPA (1997 AND 2013) §§305(A) AND (B))

§10.6.1 The Attribution Rule

The attribution rules under the three uniform general partnership acts are similar in structure, although the 1997 version expands and clarifies the 1914 version, and the 2013 version clarifies the 1997 version.

The three acts take roughly similar approaches to this topic. As shown in the following list and figure, each act uses roughly the same three elements to establish attribution:

- Who received the property (i.e., partner or partnership)?
- Did the circumstances of receipt justify holding the partnership liable?
- Who misapplied or misappropriated property?

55. For a discussion of the criteria for establishing employee/servant status, see Section 3.2.4.

Figure 10.1. When Partnership Is Liable for Partner's Misapplication of Non-Partner's Property[56]

Who received the property and relevant statutory section	Circumstances of receipt justifying attribution	Who misapplied or misappropriated the property
A PARTNER		
UPA §14(a)	"Acting within the scope of his [sic] apparent authority"	The partner who received the money
UPA (1997) §305(b)	"In the course of the partnership's business or while [the partner is] acting with authority of the partnership"	A partner
UPA (1997) §305(a)	"Acting . . . with authority of the partnership"[57]	A partner[58]
UPA (2013) §305(b)	In the course of the partnership's business or while acting with actual or apparent authority of the partnership	A partner
THE PARTNERSHIP		
UPA (1914) §14(b)	"The partnership in the course of its business"	"Any partner while [the property] is in the custody of the partnership"
UPA (1997) §305(b)	"A partner . . . causes the partnership to receive . . . property"	Any partner
UPA (2013) §305(b)	"A partner . . . causes the partnership to receive . . . property"	Any partner

56. A partner's misapplication of partnership property constitutes a breach of the partner's fiduciary duty to the partnership and is treated accordingly. See Section 9.7.3. A partner's misapplication of a copartner's own, separate property is covered by other law.
57. According to UPA (1997) §305, cmt., in subsection (a) "authority of the partnership" is "intended to include a partner's apparent, as well as actual, authority, thereby bringing within section 305(a) the situation covered in UPA section 14(a)."
58. UPA (1997) §305(a) does not rely on or refer to §305(b), so the latter's reference to "property . . . misapplied by a partner" cannot be used to complete the §305(a) analysis. That is, the reference to a partner misapplication must be found in §305(a). The misapplication is "a wrongful act . . . or other actionable conduct." *Id.*

Example

Chris, an attorney in a law partnership, represents a hospital in a malpractice case. Chris arranges a settlement, and the hospital sends a check, made out to the partnership, to cover the settlement amount and Chris's fees. Chris takes the entire amount for himself.

The law partnership is liable to the hospital. The position of partner in a law firm probably creates by itself the apparent authority to receive settlement checks. If so, UPA (1914) §14(a) applies. In any event, UPA (1914) §14(b) applies because (i) receiving settlement checks is undoubtedly within "the course of [a law partnership's] business," (ii) Chris probably had actual authority and undoubtedly had "apparently/usual" power to receive the check for the partnership, so under UPA (1914) §9(1) the partnership received and had custody of the check, and (iii) Chris misapplied the check while it was "in the custody of the partnership." ◀◀◀

§10.6.2 A Core Concern of UPA (1914) §14—Defalcations by Professionals

Many of the most interesting cases under UPA §14 have involved defalcations by partners in professional partnerships, and the same is likely to be true under UPA (1997). For example, a partner in a law firm induces a grieving widower to entrust the partner with the investment of his late wife's estate. The partner then steals the funds.

For further example: A partner in an accounting firm supervises a client's accounts receivable and then embezzles funds collected from the client's customers. In each case the partnership, while perhaps sympathizing with the victim, asserts that such fund handling involved is foreign to the normal business of the partnership.

The older leading cases deny recovery against the partnership. Rationales include the following:

- The mere fact of partner status does not constitute a "holding out" that a partner is authorized to handle the funds on behalf of the partnership. Therefore, without some other manifestation of authority attributable to the partnership, no apparent authority exists. Therefore, no UPA (1914) §14(a) liability. (Nor would there have been any liability under the "apparent authority" aspect of UPA (1997) §305(a).)
- The fund handling is not within "the course of [the partnership's] business." Therefore, no UPA (1914) §14(b) . . . liability. (Nor would

there have been any liability under UPA (1997 and 2013) §305(b), because the partner was acting neither "in the course of the partnership's business [n]or with [the actual or apparent] authority of the partnership.")

- The fund handling is not "within the ordinary course of the business of the partnership" and is not "authorized by [the] copartners." Therefore, no UPA §13 liability. (Nor likewise under UPA (1997 and 2013) §305(a).)

Some of the newer cases allow recovery, or at least reverse a summary judgment in favor of the defendant partnership. Rationales include:

- Apparent authority should be determined from the perspective of the client, not the profession. It may, for instance, be unreasonable for a fellow lawyer to believe that a partner in a law firm has authority to act as an investment advisor. But the proper question is whether a *client* might reasonably have that belief.
- In modern professional practices, handling funds may indeed occur in the course of the partnership's business, especially when the client entrusts the funds to a partner in connection with advice or services that themselves clearly constitute traditional "course of business" matters.
- When professionals are involved, the need to protect the public and to hold professionals to high standards of responsibility argue for an expansive interpretation of vicarious liability provisions.

CASE IN POINT

Case in Point — *Husted v. McCloud*

Defendant partner (Edgar), acting as attorney for an estate (McCloud — the deceased mother), received money from the executor of the estate (McCloud — the son) for the purpose of making payments due from the estate to the IRS. Edgar subsequently misappropriated the funds for his own use. The trial court held "the partnership responsible to [the estate] for compensatory damages," and the Indiana Supreme Court affirmed. "Edgar was acting within the ordinary course of the partnership's business and with apparent authority since Edgar's request for and acceptance of money from [son] McCloud to pay [deceased mother] McCloud's estate tax liability was well within the work parameters of an attorney properly handling a decedent's estate. We therefore find that even though fraud and conversion of a client's funds are not part of the ordinary course of a law partnership's business, the trial court correctly found pursuant to [UPA (1914)] §14 that the partnership was responsible for partner Edgar in taking money entrusted to him and misapplying it.[59] We also find that the trial court was justified in finding that McCloud's money was in the partnership's possession when it was in Edgar's possession[60] since Edgar deviated from McCloud's plan and converted the money to his own use only after he received it in the ordinary course of the partnership's business."[61] ◀◀◀

§10.7 BINDING THE PARTNERSHIP THROUGH INFORMATION KNOWN OR RECEIVED BY A PARTNER (UPA (2013) §102(E); UPA (1914) §12)

§10.7.1 The Attribution Rules—Overview

UPA (2013) §103(e) attributes to a partnership a "partner's knowledge or notice of a fact relating to the partnership."[62] UPA (1914) §12 attributes to the partnership "notice" made to a partner and "knowledge" possessed by a partner. Comparing the two provisions is somewhat tricky, because: (i) what UPA (1914) §12 means by "notice" is not what UPA (2013) means by notice; and (ii) UPA (2013) §102(e) relies on three defined terms, while UPA (1914) §12 relies on only two. Under both Acts, the attribution rules are subject to the "fraud on the partnership" exception.

Table 10.3 provides the necessary comparison.

59. This holding could rest on either UPA (1914) §14(a) (apparent authority) or (b) (course of the partnership business). Under UPA (1997), §305(a) would apply to a claim of apparent authority.
60. This holding rests on UPA §14(b). Under UPA (2013) §§305(b) would apply. UPA (1997) analysis would be more complicated. See Section 10.5.1(a).
61. *Husted v. McCloud*, 450 N.E.2d 491, 494 (Ind. 1983).
62. UPA (1997) §102(f) attributes to a partnership a "partner's knowledge, notice, or receipt of a notification of a fact relating to the partnership." The Harmonization Act removes "receipt of a notification" as surplusage. The following analysis of the relevant UPA (2013) provisions applies generally to the relevant UPA (1997) provisions.

10.3 Attributing a Partner's Information

Type/ Source of Information	UPA (1914)	UPA (2013)
Knowledge	"A person has 'knowledge' of a fact . . . not only when he has actual knowledge thereof, but also when he has knowledge of such other facts as in the circumstances shows bad faith." UPA §3(1).[63]	"A person knows a fact if the person: (1) has actual knowledge of it; or (2) is deemed to know it under subsection (d)(1) [providing constructive knowledge of specified public filings] or law other than this [act]. . . ." UPA (2013) §§103(a).
Receipt of information	"A person has 'notice' of a fact . . . when the person who claims the benefit of the notice: (a) States the fact to such person, or (b) Delivers through the mail, or by other means of communication, a written statement of the fact to such person or to a proper person at his [i.e., such person's] place of business or residence." UPA §3(2).	"[A] person notifies another person of a fact by taking steps reasonably required to inform the other person in ordinary course, whether or not those steps cause the other person to know the fact." UPA (2013) §103(c).
Reason to know	No provision	"A person has notice of a fact if the person: (1) has reason to know the fact from all the facts known to the person at the time in question; or (2) is deemed to have notice of the fact under subsection (d)(2) [providing constructive notice of specified public filings]" UPA (2013) §103(b).

As with agency law, the relevant substantive law determines the significance of any attributed information.

63. The phrase "shows bad faith" probably means "shows intentional, bad faith ignorance of the fact."

§10.7.2 Attributing Knowledge

UPA (1914)'s approach to attributing a partner's knowledge to the partnership is more nuanced (and therefore more complex) than the UPA (2013) approach. According to UPA (1914) §12, the attribution rule varies depending on whether the partner with knowledge is "acting in the particular matter":

> . . . the knowledge of the partner acting in the particular matter, acquired while a partner or then present to his mind, and the knowledge of any other partner who reasonably could and should have communicated it to the acting partner, operate as . . . knowledge of the partnership, except in the case of a fraud on the partnership committed by or with the consent of that partner.

If a UPA (1914) partner *is* acting in the matter, subject to an exception for fraud,[64] the partner's knowledge inescapably binds the partnership. UPA (1914) §12 attributes both (i) knowledge "acquired while a partner" and (ii) knowledge acquired earlier if at the time of the action the acting partner still retains the knowledge.[65]

The knowledge of a UPA (1914) partner *not* acting in a particular matter binds the partnership only if the partner "reasonably could and should have communicated it to the acting partner." The Official Comment to §12 explains the rationale:

> It seems clear that . . . the partnership should be charged [with the nonacting partner's knowledge] only when the partner having "knowledge" had reason to believe that the fact related to a matter which had some possibility of being the subject of partnership business and then only if he was so situated that he could communicate it to the partner acting in the particular matter before such partner give[s] binding effect to his act.[66]

The rule under UPA (2013) is simpler and makes no distinction between a partner who acts in the matter and one who does not, and therefore imposes greater risks on the partnership than does UPA (1914). Subject to the same fraud exception as exists under UPA (1914), under UPA (1997)

---

64. See Section 10.7.5.
65. *Id.* The precise language is: "acquired while a partner or then present to his mind."
66. The rationale here parallels the rationale for attributing to a principal an agent's knowledge concerning a matter within the agent's actual authority, while not attributing an apparent agent's knowledge concerning a matter within the apparent agent's apparent authority. In the former situation, the agent has a duty to communicate the information to the principal. In the latter, the apparent agent has no such duty. See Sections 2.4 (attribution rules for information) and 4.1.5 (duty of agent to provide information to principal).

a "partner's knowledge . . . of a fact relating to the partnership is effective immediately as knowledge by . . . the partnership."[67]

Under both UPA (1914) and UPA (2013), attribution of a partner's knowledge occurs regardless of whether the partner shares the knowledge with fellow partners.

Example

Vladi is the managing partner of the Waterville Ski Company, a general partnership that owns and operates several ski slopes. The company has an important contract with Michael, its principal ski instructor, which requires Michael to give four weeks' notice to terminate the contract. Michael attempts to give notice by sending a letter to Vladi's home address, although Vladi does not normally do business from that address. If the letter is delivered to Vladi's home, the notice is effective under UPA (1914). Under UPA (1914) §3(2)(b), Vladi, as partner, "has 'notice' of [the contents of the letter] . . . when the person who claims the benefit of the notice [i.e., Michael] . . . [d]elivers through the mail . . . a written statement of the fact to [Vladi] at his . . . residence." Under UPA (1914) §12, notice to Vladi is notice to the partnership.

The result is different under UPA (2013) §103(c). Under that provision, the question is whether Michael has "tak[en] steps reasonably required to inform the other person in ordinary course." If so, Michael has "notified" Vladi, and Vladi therefore has knowledge of the fact of the notice and its contents "whether or not those steps [have] cause[d] [Vladi] to know the fact." Under UPA (2013) §103(f), Vladi's knowledge is attributed to the partnership. ◄◄◄

§10.7.3 Attributing Information a Partner Has Reason to Know

UPA (2013) handles this category of information by using the defined term "notice," defining the term to include information that a partner "has reason to know from all of the facts known to the [partner] at the time in question,"[68] and providing that a "partner's . . . notice . . . of a fact relating to the partnership is effective immediately as . . . notice to . . . the partnership."[69] UPA (1914) has no comparable provisions. The closest UPA (1914) comes is to attribute a partner's knowledge to the partnership and to define

67. UPA (2013) §103(f).
68. UPA (2013) §103(b)(1).
69. UPA (2013) §103(e).

knowledge to include situations in which a person "has knowledge of such other facts as in the circumstances shows [the person's ignorance to be in] bad faith."[70]

§10.7.4 The "Partner Fraud on the Partnership" Exception

The attribution rules of UPA (2013) §103(e) and UPA (1914) §12 do not apply "in the case of a fraud on the partnership committed by or with the consent of [the] partner" whose knowledge or receipt of notice is to be attributed. In this context the concept of "fraud" probably includes a breach of the partner's duty of loyalty (sometimes called "equitable fraud"). Fraud blocks the attribution even if the third party was ignorant of the fraud, and has no reason to know of it.

Example

Seeking to preclude the Ventura Company from additional borrowing against its line of credit, the First Regional Bank delivers a written "no more borrowing" notice to Al, a partner. For some time, Al has been borrowing from the line of credit in the partnership's name but for his own personal benefit. Neither the Bank nor the partnership is aware of Al's misconduct. Because Al is committing "a fraud on the partnership," notice to him is not notice to the partnership. ◄◄◄

§10.8 EFFECT OF THE PARTNERSHIP AGREEMENT ON QUESTIONS OF POWER TO BIND

In some circumstances, partners' *inter se* management agreements can increase a third party's ability to hold the partnership liable. In other, more restricted circumstances, an *inter se* agreement can undercut a third-party claim.

a. Increasing the Third Party's Ability to Hold the Partnership Liable

If a partnership agreement gives a partner the right to act for the partnership on particular matters, then the partner has actual authority within that specified scope. A partner who acts with actual authority binds the partnership as a matter of agency law. There is no need to rely on any of the special partnership law rules for binding the partnership to third parties.

70. UPA (1914) §3(1).

b. Undercutting a Third Party's Claim

Just as a partnership agreement can convey actual authority, so too can an agreement negate that authority. If a partner who lacks actual authority has purported to bind the partnership to a third party, the partnership is not bound:

- under UPA (1914) §9(1), if the third party "has knowledge of the fact that [the partner] has no such authority;
- under UPA (2013) §301(1), if third party knows "knew or has received a notification that the partner lacked authority"; and
- under UPA (2013) §301(1), if the third party "knew or had notice that the partner lacked authority."[71]

Problem 81

In the aftermath of a bitter divorce, Ronald goes into partnership with Robert in a donut shop. Ronald wishes to hide his income from his ex-wife, so he and Robert agree that Ronald will be a very "silent" partner. Ronald will provide 60 percent of the capital and will share in all major decisions. Robert will handle all transactions with third parties. He will appear to third parties as the sole owner of the business. Accordingly, after consultation with Ronald, Robert signs a long-term lease for a building in which the donut shop will operate.

The business eventually fails, and only afterward does the lessor discover the relationship between Robert and Ronald. If UPA (2013) applies, can the lessor hold the partnership liable on the lease? Under UPA (1914)? ◀ ◀ ◀

Explanation

EXPLANATION

Yes, under either act. The arrangement between the partners gave Robert actual authority to sign the lease on behalf of the partnership. The fact that the partnership was undisclosed is therefore immaterial. ◀ ◀ ◀

---

71. Thus, in this limited respect, UPA (1997) §401(k) is inaccurate when it states: "This section does not affect the obligations of a partnership to other persons under section 301." UPA (2013) contains no comparable provision.

Problem 82

The Ventura Company partnership agreement gives wide-ranging authority to Beatrice, the partnership's managing partner. However, all decisions to initiate or settle litigation must be approved by a majority vote of the partners. On two occasions during the past five years, Beatrice has recommended to the partners that the partnership arbitrate a dispute, and on each occasion the partners approved.

Ventura has a dispute with Central California Soybean ("CCS") concerning a particular trade. No suit has been filed, but litigation seems inevitable. Aware that Ventura has arbitrated disputes in the past, CCS proposes arbitration. Beatrice agrees, this time without consulting the other partners. In determining whether Ventura is bound to arbitrate the dispute, does it matter which of the three acts applies? ◄◄◄

Explanation

Yes. Under UPA (1914), Ventura is not bound. Under the modern acts, the partnership might well be.

Under UPA (1914) §9(3)(e), part of UPA's "unanimous consent" constraining rule, no partner has the power to "[s]ubmit a partnership claim or liability to arbitration" unless either all the partners consent or the partner agreeing to arbitration has actual authority to do so. In this instance, the other partners have not consented, and under the partnership agreement Beatrice lacks actual authority to agree to arbitration on her own. The partnership's past practices conform with and confirm this interpretation of the partnership agreement. To obtain actual authority, Beatrice needs the consent of a majority of her partners.[72]

In contrast, neither of the modern acts has a "unanimous consent" constraining rule, and UPA (1997) §301, comment 4 states that "it seems archaic that the submission of a partnership claim to arbitration always requires unanimous consent." Because CCS is "[a]ware that Ventura has arbitrated disputes in the past," Beatrice's act is probably within her "apparently/ordinary" power. If so, the partnership is bound to arbitrate. The result would be same under UPA (2013) §301. ◄◄◄

Problem 83

Two brothers, Caleb and Adam, operate a farm as an ordinary general partnership, known as AdCal Farming Company. The two brothers are well respected. Their partnership is well known in the community, as is the fact

72. CCS may well have believed that Beatrice's agreement to arbitrate was apparently/usual. However, since UPA (1914) §9(3) applies, the apparently/usual question is immaterial.

that each partner regularly makes equipment purchases for the partnership business.

One day, Caleb goes to the local Ford dealer and buys a $55,000 Ford pickup truck on credit, signing the purchase agreement "AdCal Farming Company, by Caleb, general partner." In fact, the truck has nothing to do with the partnership business. Caleb has decided to give up farming and go "on the road." The truck is for his personal use. Under UPA (2013), may the Ford dealer hold *Adam* liable on the purchase agreement? ◄◄◄

Explanation

Yes. Adam is liable under UPA (2013) §§306(a) because the partnership is liable under UPA (2013) §§301(1). Caleb's truck purchase was "for *apparently* carrying on in the ordinary course of the partnership business."[73] The dealer knew Caleb to be a partner and saw nothing unusual in an individual AdCal partner committing the partnership to an equipment purchase. To the contrary, the partnership had a reputation for doing business this way. Moreover, Caleb asserted that he was acting for the partnership, and nothing in Caleb's reputation gave the dealer any reason to doubt that assertion.[74] ◄◄◄

Problem 84

Hiview Company is a UPA (1914) partnership that operates a drive-in movie theater. Rachael, its managing partner, purports to sell the land where the theater is located to a development company. The partnership agreement authorizes the managing partner to "make all management decisions in the ordinary course of the business." Has Rachael's action bound the partnership? Would the analysis change under UPA (1997) or UPA (2013)? ◄◄◄

Explanation

For three reasons, under UPA (1914), Rachael has not bound the partnership. Her "ordinary course" actual authority does not extend to the extraordinary decision to sell the crucial assets of the business. Her doing so could not have appeared "apparently/usual" to the buyer. Her doing so runs afoul of UPA (1914) §9(3)(c) (partner lacks power to do "any . . . act which would make it impossible to carry on the ordinary business of a partnership," unless partner has actual authority or all partners agree).

73. Emphasis added.
74. The same analysis applies under UPA (1997).

The analysis is the same under the two modern acts, except that neither contains an analog to UPA §9(3)(c). ◄◄◄

Problem 85

Illegitimus, Non, and Carborundum have formed a UPA (2013) partnership as a "handshake deal" and gave explicit thought to only two issues. First, they agreed that the sole purpose of the partnership would be to function as a locator of "spot" grapes for the makers of wine. Second, they agreed that they would share equally all profits from the partnership.

Locators of spot grapes play an important part in the production of nonvintage wines.[75] From time to time vineyards producing nonvintage wine find themselves short of a particular type of grape that they want to add to a mixture of other grapes. Locators of spot grapes are in the business of knowing which vineyards have a need for which types of grapes, and which vineyards have a surplus of that type of grape. Based on this knowledge they act to get surplus grapes to the vineyards that need them.

The overwhelming majority of locators act only as agents, never taking a position in grapes. This means that when they have a customer who needs a particular type of grape, they locate a supply of those grapes in another vineyard. Then, acting merely as the agent of the customer who needs the grapes, they arrange for the sale of grapes from the vineyard with the surplus to the vineyard with the need. In this conventional approach, the locator never takes title to the grapes, and never commits itself to pay for the grapes.

The partnership carries on its business at variance with this typical pattern. On occasion, it will buy and take title to surplus grapes held by a vineyard, speculating that it (i.e., the partnership) can find another vineyard to which it can resell the grapes. Although with this approach the partnership faces greater risk than it would if it followed the conventional pattern, the potential rewards are greater. Where it takes a position and then resells the grapes, the partnership charges a markup that exceeds the amount of commission the partnership would have received for simply acting as a locator agent.

When Illegitimus, Non, and Carborundum began the partnership, they needed start-up capital. Illegitimus contributed $30,000. Non and

75. The practices described in this problem are figments of the author's imagination. Any correspondence to actual commercial practices is entirely coincidental.

Carborundum each contributed $10,000. Each year the partners have fully drawn out all profits. They have never withdrawn any capital.

Last spring, Non and Carborundum became concerned about some of the deals that Illegitimus had made. At a regularly scheduled partnership meeting, they voted to prohibit Illegitimus from making any further purchases of grapes on behalf of the partnership. They expressly allowed him to continue arranging deals of the more conventional sort; that is, where the partnership would act only as an agent. Illegitimus objected to and voted against the limitation.

Soon after the meeting, Illegitimus took a buying tour out into the countryside and visited Schekainery Vineyard. The owner of the vineyard, Sally Schekainery, knew generally of the partnership and of Illegitimus's status as a partner. She had no particular knowledge about the partnership or about its business practices, and had never done business with the partnership before. During the visit, Illegitimus learned that the Schekainery Vineyard had several tons of surplus of a particular variety of red grape. Illegitimus believed, and reasonably so at the time, that several regular clients of the partnership would soon need this grape. Over dinner he began to negotiate with Sally for a price, and eventually Illegitimus and Sally agreed to a price of $5,000 per ton for eight tons, to be delivered within the next 30 days. The next morning Sally wrote a memorandum expressing the deal, and Illegitimus signed on behalf of the partnership.

As it turned out, several of the clients whom Illegitimus had in mind did not need that particular variety of grape. Moreover, throughout the entire valley, vineyards that needed to purchase the grapes were able to purchase easily at a price significantly below the price Illegitimus had committed to pay. When Non and Carborundum learned what Illegitimus had done, they wrote to Sally: (i) explaining that Illegitimus had no authority to act for the partnership in this matter; and (ii) stating that the partnership had no interest in purchasing the grapes. As evidence of Illegitimus's lack of authority, they enclosed a certified copy of the minutes of the meeting at which Non and Carborundum voted to "defrock" Illegitimus of his authority to enter into this particular type of transaction.

Sally consulted an attorney, who advised her to warn the partnership that: (i) she intended to hold them to the contract; and (ii) if they did not take delivery as agreed, she would mitigate her damages by selling the grapes elsewhere and would then file suit against the partnership for any difference between the mitigation price and the contract price. Hearing no response from the partnership, she proceeded as she had indicated. The difference amounted to $20,000. Sally sued the partnership. What result? ◀ ◀ ◀

Explanation

The partnership will be liable if either: (i) Illegitimus's act was "apparently/ordinary" or (ii) Illegitimus had actual authority to make the deal.

Sally's apparently/ordinary claim will fail. She cannot show that Illegitimus's act appeared for "carrying on in the ordinary course the partnership business or business of the kind carried on by the partnership." UPA (2013) §301(1). As to businesses "of the kind carried on by the partnership," industry practices suggest that Illegitimus's act should have appeared quite unusual. As to reasonable appearances and the ordinary course of *this* partnership's business, Sally has no evidence to offer. She knew nothing in particular about this partnership. She could only suppose that its commercial practices resembled those of similar partnerships.

Sally will probably fare better with her actual authority claim. Illegitimus certainly had authority to make comparable deals when the partnership began, and it is unlikely that a mere majority vote of the partners could have ended that authority. Defrocking a partner seems an extraordinary act, requiring unanimous consent. The partners' 2-1 vote did not suffice.[76]

The partnership could, however, advance a less aggressive interpretation of the 2-1 vote that, ironically, could give Sally difficulty. The partnership could argue that (i) the vote and the discussion that preceded it informed Illegitimus that his partners would differ with him anytime he contemplated making a purchase of spot grapes; (ii) Illegitimus therefore knew that any grape purchase he might contemplate would involve a "difference arising as to a matter in the ordinary course of business of [the] partnership," to be decided in each particular instance by majority vote, UPA (2013) §401(k); and (iii) as with any such difference, knowledge of the difference eliminated the acting partner's authority pending resolution "by a majority of the partners." *Id.*

If this latter interpretation prevails, the partnership will not be liable. ◀◀◀

Problem 86

Suppose that immediately after the 2-1 vote, Non and Carborundum executed and properly filed a statement of partnership authority in the appropriate filing office stating that Illegitimus lacked the authority to purchase any grapes on behalf of the partnership. Would this fact change the result? ◀◀◀

76. The facts about capital contributions are red herrings. In the default mode, capital contributions have no impact on partner voting power. Absent a contrary agreement, each partner has a single vote. See Section 9.5.1.

Explanation

No. Grapes are personal property, and the only statement authority that can provide constructive notice is a statement regarding real property.[77]

Problem 87

Since graduating from law school five years ago, Able, Baker, and Charlene have practiced law in a partnership that is not an LLP. The partners "cover" for each other during vacations, and the partnership has in place a system for avoiding conflicts of interests. Otherwise, however, each partner is responsible for his or her own files. Three years ago, attorney Able filed a consumer fraud lawsuit in state district court against Defendant, Inc. Consumer fraud was one of Able's principal areas of practice, but in this instance the claims were frivolous. Able had signed the complaint without having made any investigation into the facts.

Neither Baker nor Charlene had any involvement in the case. Indeed, Baker was not even aware that the case had been filed. The court eventually dismissed the lawsuit and, citing Rule 11 of the state Rules of Civil Procedure, ordered Able to pay Defendant, Inc., the $47,000 in attorney's fees that Defendant, Inc., had incurred in defending the lawsuit. The court specifically found that Able had violated Rule 11 by "failing to make a 'reasonable inquiry' into the facts before filing a complaint that was neither 'well grounded in fact' nor 'warranted by existing law or a good faith argument for the extension, modification, or reversal of existing law.'" The court of appeals affirmed the award against Able. Under UPA (1914), can Defendant, Inc., hold Baker and Charlene personally liable for the Rule 11 award? Under UPA (2013)? ◀ ◀ ◀

77. See Section 10.4.3. For a statement regarding real property to be effective as constructive notice, the statement must also be filed in the appropriate land title records.

EXPLANATION

Explanation

Baker and Charlene are liable jointly and severally under UPA (1914) §15(a), because the partnership is liable for the award under UPA (1914) §13.[78]

To establish the partnership's liability under UPA (1914) §13, Defendant, Inc., must show that: (i) it suffered harm from a partner's wrongful act or omission; and (ii) the conduct occurred either in the ordinary course of the partnership's business or with the authority of the other partners. Able was a partner, and filing a frivolous lawsuit is clearly a wrongful act. Defendant will therefore have no trouble on the first element of UPA (1914) §13. As to the second element, Defendant can actually meet both requirements of the either/or test. The business of the partnership ordinarily included the filing of lawsuits. Therefore, when Able filed the frivolous claim, he was "acting in the ordinary course of business of the partnership." Able was also acting with actual authority. UPA (1914) §18(e) gives all partners "equal rights in the . . . conduct of the partnership business." The partners augmented this statutory authority by granting each partner autonomous authority over his or her own files. It is not clear from the facts whether the partners agreed to this grant expressly, but the way they conducted their business certainly implied an agreement.

The fact that Baker and Charlene had no part in this misconduct is irrelevant to Defendant, Inc.'s claim. UPA (1914) §13 states a rule of vicarious liability, and UPA (1914) §15 states a rule of liability by status.

The analysis and results are the same under UPA (2013). Only the citations differ.[79] ◀ ◀ ◀

Problem 88

Mrs. Rouse recently lost her husband. He left a small estate, mostly in cash. The widow is an elderly lady who throughout her life left business affairs to her husband. She confides to her lawyer, Mr. Pollard, that she does not know how best to invest the funds.

Mr. Pollard has been a lawyer for 20 years and for the past 15 years has served as the Rouse family lawyer. For the past 16 years, he has been a partner in the law firm of What, Me, and Worry. The firm is organized as a general partnership. Mr. Pollard tells Mrs. Rouse, "My dear lady, I would be delighted to handle your investment decisions for you. Place yourself in my

78. This liability may be subject to an exhaustion requirement. See Section 7.3.1 (some jurisdictions require third parties to exhaust partnership assets before asserting UPA (1914) §15 claims against individual partners).

79. UPA (1914) §15(a) → UPA (2013) §306(a); UPA (1914) §13 → UPA (2013) §305(a); UPA (1914) §18(e) → UPA (2013) §401(h).

hands. Entrust your funds to our firm. We have quite a bit of experience in such matters."

Mrs. Rouse agrees to "put the money with the firm." She writes a check for almost the entirety of her assets. At Mr. Pollard's direction, she makes the check payable to him.

Unfortunately, Mr. Pollard is a crook. The law firm of What, Me, and Worry does not handle investments for clients. Indeed, law firms in general do not ordinarily serve as investment advisors. Mr. Pollard deposits Mrs. Rouse's check in his personal checking account and appropriates her money to his own use. For a few months he sends her checks drawn on his personal account purporting to represent a return on her investments. Then his financial house of cards topples, and his fraud is exposed.

Mr. Pollard goes into bankruptcy and thence into jail. Mrs. Rouse sues the law firm partnership for return of the money she entrusted to Mr. Pollard. What result under UPA (1914) and under UPA (2013)? ◀ ◀ ◀

Explanation

Whether Mrs. Rouse will prevail depends on how liberal a view the court takes of UPA (1914) §14(b) and UPA (2013) §305(b).

Neither UPA (1914) §13 nor the "actual authority" aspect of UPA (2013) §§305(a) can help Mrs. Rouse. To successfully invoke either of those provisions, she must show either that Mr. Pollard handled her funds in the ordinary course of the business of the partnership, or that he did so with actual authority. Mrs. Rouse can make neither showing. The law firm never acted as an investment advisor, and never authorized Mr. Pollard to do so.

For similar reasons Mrs. Rouse will be unsuccessful invoking UPA (1914) §14(b). For that provision to apply, the partnership must have received the money "in the course of its business." Arguably at least, the *partnership* never received the money at all.[80] In any event, "the course of its business" did not include investing clients' funds.

Mrs. Rouse may fare better under UPA (1914) §14(a) and UPA (2013) §§305(b). She can certainly show that Mr. Pollard, a partner, misapplied her money. It is only doubtful whether she can show that Mr. Pollard received the money within the scope of his apparent authority.

Under the older case law, Mrs. Rouse would likely lose on this point. The older cases suggest, almost as a matter of law, that no reasonable client

80. If Pollard accepted the funds with the intent to misappropriate them, he acted without actual authority, and his possession of the funds is not attributable to the partnership unless apparent authority applies.

can believe that a lawyer has the authority to handle client funds for investment purposes. More modern cases, however, treat the question as one of fact. They do not simply assume that every reasonably prudent client understands the limitations on a law firm's business.

Mrs. Rouse may therefore be able to prevail by proving that: (i) Mr. Pollard had apparent authority by position; and (ii) despite Mr. Pollard's direction that the check be made out to him personally, Mrs. Rouse was reasonable in believing that Mr. Pollard's authority extended to handling client funds for investment. Mr. Pollard's assertions about the firm's business and his own authority would not suffice as manifestations of the firm, but they could help show the reasonableness of Mrs. Rouse's belief. The long relationship of trust and confidence between Mr. Pollard, as a partner of the firm, and the Rouse family would also support Mrs. Rouse's reasonableness argument.

If Mrs. Rouse prevails on the apparent authority issue, under either UPA (1914) §14(a) or UPA (2013) §305(b), the partnership will be liable. ◀◀◀

Problem 89

For the past 15 years Lucille, Phyllis, and William have operated a fishing guide business from a piece of lakefront property in the United States near the Canadian border. They operate the business as a general partnership, share in all the work, make business decisions by consensus, and share profits equally.

The partnership rents rather than owns its lakefront location. The lease has a two-year term and renews automatically unless either party gives written notice of nonrenewal "at least 90 days but no more than 120 days in advance of the renewal date."

The lease was up for renewal last January 1. On the preceding September 15, the lessor handed a written notice of nonrenewal to William. The notice was in an envelope and the lessor did not say specifically what the envelope contained. The lessor did say, "William, this is important. Don't put it aside."

Unfortunately, William did just that. Unbeknownst to the lessor or William's partners, William was suffering a relapse into alcoholism. He lost the envelope, forgot its existence, and never mentioned it to Lucille or Phyllis. They first learned of the lessor's intention on November 15, when the lessor telephoned to discuss "transition issues." The November 15 conversation occurred too late to constitute valid notice of nonrenewal. Under UPA (1914), did the lost letter constitute valid notice to the partnership? Under UPA (2013)? ◀◀◀

Explanation

Yes, under either statute. Under UPA (1914) §3(2)(b), the lessor gave notice to William by "deliver[ing] a written statement" to William. It is irrelevant that William never read the statement. Under UPA §12 (1914), "[n]otice to any partner of any matter relating to partnership affairs . . . operate[s] as notice to . . . the partnership." It is also irrelevant that the partner never mentioned the notice to any other partner. UPA §12 (1914) contains an exception applicable "in the case of a fraud on the partnership committed by or with the consent of [the] partner" receiving notice. However, William's dereliction of duty does not constitute fraud.

The analysis is different but the results are the same under UPA (2013) §103(c). The lessor has notified William by "taking steps reasonably required to inform [William] in ordinary course." William therefore has knowledge of the fact of the notice and its contents "whether or not those steps [have] cause[d] [William] to know the fact." *Id.* Under UPA (2013) §103(f), William's knowledge is attributed to the partnership. ◄◄◄

Problem 90

Their dispute over the nonrenewal notice convinces Lucille, Phyllis, and William to buy a piece of lakefront property. After William regains sobriety, the three partners locate an apparently suitable parcel on another lake. They negotiate with the parcel's owner ("the seller") and eventually sign a contract on behalf of the partnership. During the negotiations, the seller assures all three partners that "this lake is real quiet. There's no rule against motorboats, but almost no one ever uses them here." That representation is central to the partners' decision to have the partnership buy the land.

After the contract is signed, Phyllis learns that motorboats are quite common on the lake and that during the summer months waterskiing is the dominant lake activity. The partnership seeks to rescind the contract, asserting fraud in the inducement.

In the relevant jurisdiction, a party asserting fraud in the inducement must show not only a material misstatement and reliance, but also that the reliance was reasonable. The seller contends that the partnership could not have reasonably relied on his assertions because, "Two years ago William was over here all the time, and he saw all the motorboats and the waterskiing all over the lake."

His memory prompted by the seller's contention, William acknowledges it as true. Just as truthfully, he states that (i) he visited the lake on vacation and not on partnership business and (ii) his recent bout with alcohol had previously suppressed all memory of that vacation.

Assuming that UPA (1914) applies and the seller's representations about the quiet and the lack of significant motorboat activity were false and material, what result on partnership's fraud in the inducement theory? Any difference under UPA (2013)? ◀◀◀

Explanation

If UPA (1914) applies, the partnership will lose.

The outcome turns on UPA (1914) §12 and its rule for attributing a partner's knowledge to the partnership. William was "acting in the particular matter," so the rule will attribute to the partnership any "knowledge acquired while a partner or then present to his mind." UPA (1914) §12. Although at the time of the negotiations and contract formation, William's knowledge about the motorboats was not "present to his mind," that phrase is in the disjunctive with the phrase "acquired while a partner." That is, any knowledge the acting partner acquires while a partner is attributed to the partnership, regardless of whether the acting partner happens to remember the information at the critical moment. The phrase "then present to his mind" serves only to limit attribution of information acquired before the partner became a partner. Therefore, William's dormant knowledge of the motorboat traffic is attributed to the partnership and defeats the partnership's claim of reasonable reliance.

Under UPA (2013), in contrast, the partnership might prevail. UPA (2013) §102(e) will attribute William's knowledge, if any, to the partnership, but it is arguable that at the relevant moment William had no relevant knowledge. Under UPA (2013) §102(a)(1), "knowledge" is confined to actual knowledge, and, at least according to a comment to UPA (1997), "[k]nowledge is cognitive awareness."[81] Temporary memory loss due to alcohol abuse might well negate "cognitive awareness." ◀◀◀

Problem 91

The Ventura Company ("Ventura") is a general partnership that manufactures widgets. Although Ventura has five partners, the partnership agreement provides that one of the partners, Maurice, is the managing partner and has sole authority to manage all partnership business. Ventura has a long-term contract with Rolande, Inc. ("Rolande"), under which Rolande supplies framjets to Ventura. (Ventura incorporates one framjet into each widget Ventura makes.) The Ventura–Rolande contract requires that Ventura "inform Rolande of any defect in any framjet supplied under this contract

81. UPA (1997) §102, cmt. See also Black's Law Dictionary (10th ed. 2014), Knowledge, def. 1 (defining knowledge as "[a]n awareness or understanding of a fact or circumstance; a state of mind in which a person has no substantial doubt about the existence of a fact").

within 30 days after Ventura knows of the defect, or be barred from any remedy for such defect."

One day, Alan, one of the other four partners in Ventura, happens to be walking through Ventura's factory and happens to notice that an entire pallet of Rolande framjets are defective. Alan assumes, however, that Maurice has procedures in place to check incoming products and therefore does not mention the defects to anyone.

Unfortunately, neither Maurice nor anyone else connected with Ventura notices the defect until 35 days later. In the ensuing legal struggle between Ventura and Rolande, is Ventura better off under UPA (1914) or under UPA (2013)? ◀◀◀

Explanation

Ventura is far better off under UPA (1914). Under UPA (2013) §102(e), Alan's knowledge of the defect is immediately attributable to the partnership, regardless of the fact that Alan is not involved in partnership operations. In contrast, that fact matters under UPA §12 (1914). Because Alan is not "the partner acting in the particular matter [of checking for and informing Rolande of defects]," his knowledge of the defects is attributed to the partnership only if he "reasonably could and should have communicated it to the acting partner." Obviously, Alan could have communicated his knowledge to Maurice, but it is at least arguable that Alan acted reasonably in assuming that Maurice had established appropriate inspection procedures. If Alan's assumption was reasonable, Rolande cannot satisfy the "should have communicated" requirement and Alan's knowledge of the defects did not start the clock on the 30-day notice period. ◀◀◀

CHAPTER 11

Partner Dissociation and Partnership Dissolution

§11.1 UPA (1914), UPA (1997), AND UPA (2013)

In all three uniform general partnership acts, the most elaborate provisions concern:

- partner dissociation—the separation of a partner from the partnership; and
- partnership dissolution—the point at which a partnership stops functioning as a forward-looking enterprise and begins to wind up its business.

Elaborate provisions are necessary because those two topics implicate numerous interrelated issues, including:

1. the management rights of a partner who has dissociated;
2. the management rights of the other partners after a partner has dissociated;
3. the power to bind of a partner who has dissociated;
4. the power to bind of the other partners after a partner has dissociated;
5. in an ordinary general partnership, the liability of a partner who has dissociated for the debts of the partnership incurred:
   a. before the dissociation;
   b. after the dissociation;

6. the relationship between partner dissociation and partnership dissolution;
7. the question of whether dissolution (and eventual termination) of the partnership as a legal organization (whether entity or aggregate) will result in the liquidation or the continuation of the business; and
8. the manner of winding up a dissolved partnership, including how to settle accounts with third parties and among the partners.

As to these issues, UPA (2013) made few substantive changes to UPA (1997), and enactment efforts for UPA (2013) are still in their infancy. Accordingly, this chapter focuses on UPA (1914) and UPA (1997), leaving for a subsequent edition any detailed treatment of UPA (2013)'s provisions on dissociation and dissolution.[1]

In this context, the greatest difference between UPA (1914) and UPA (1997) concerns the relationship between a partner's dissociation and the partnership's dissolution.[2] Although the *structure* of UPA (1914)'s approach can be discerned in the approach of UPA (1997), the latter has departed radically from the former's *premise*. Under UPA (1914), the dissociation of any partner necessarily causes the dissolution of the partnership. UPA (1997) rejects that premise, and the connection between dissociation and dissolution is more complicated. Consequently, while the UPA (1997) and the UPA (1914) provisions in this area have a somewhat similar architecture, UPA (1997) rules produce consequences markedly at odds with the consequences produced by the rules of UPA (1914).

It is therefore necessary to study each set of rules separately, so that each is understood as a system. The first part of this chapter deals in detail with the UPA (1914) rules, the second with the rules of UPA (1997), and the third provides a comparison.[3] The final section addresses the substantive differences between UPA (2013) and UPA (1997) and provides an example of the stylistic changes.

---

1. For a discussion of the substantive differences, see Section 11.2.2.
2. UPA (1914) does not use the term "dissociation," but the word is useful shorthand for the UPA (1914) concept of "any partner ceasing to be associated in the carrying on . . . of the business." UPA (1914) §29. UPA (1997) uses the word repeatedly without specifically defining it. See, e.g., UPA (1997) §601 (listing causes of dissociation) and comment 1.
3. Readers who are only concerned with UPA (1997) may be tempted to skip UPA (1914) materials. Certainly, the UPA (1997) materials can stand alone, but UPA (1997)—like any other statute—is best understood in light of the circumstances that gave rise to its promulgation. The UPA (1997) provisions discussed in this chapter are therefore best understood by those who also understand the UPA (1914) provisions that preceded them.

§11.2 UPA—FOUNDATIONAL NOTIONS

§11.2.1 Four Fundamental Concepts and Important Related Issues

Partnership dissolution under UPA (1914) raises complex and interrelated issues. To keep those issues straight, you must keep in mind four fundamental concepts: (i) the dissociation of any partner causes dissolution of a UPA (1914) partnership; (ii) dissolution does not end the partnership but instead puts the partnership into a period of winding up; (iii) the eventual end of a partnership is not necessarily the end of the partnership's business; and (iv) under UPA (1914), a partner always has the power (but not necessarily the right) to dissolve the partnership.

a. Dissociation Causes Dissolution

UPA (1914) has a long list of "Causes of Dissolution,"[4] but in general, dissolution "is the change in the relation of the partners caused by any partner ceasing to be associated in the carrying on . . . of the business."[5] Therefore, as a formal matter, the dissociation of any partner from the partnership automatically and unavoidably causes dissolution.[6]

Although you should read the statute carefully to familiarize yourself with all the listed causes of dissolution, you may want to note particularly the following situations:

- *Express Will Dissolution of an At-Will Partnership*—If the partners have not agreed to continue the partnership until the end of some particular term or undertaking, or have not otherwise agreed, then each partner has the power and the right to cause dissolution at any time simply by withdrawing, resigning, retiring, or otherwise making known his, her, or its *express will*.[7]

---

4. UPA (1914) §31, titled "Causes of Dissolution," lists in its six paragraphs nine different events or actions that cause dissolution. The list is actually longer, however, because UPA (1914) §31(6) incorporates another list of causes from UPA (1914) §32. The eight different causes listed in UPA (1914) §§31(1)–31(5) are all automatic and "self-actuating." If a listed event or action occurs, the partnership is dissolved. In contrast, UPA (1914) §32 lists grounds upon which "the court shall decree dissolution." A claim of dissolution under UPA (1914) §31 can nonetheless result in judicial intervention. Partners sometimes litigate over whether a dissolving event did in fact occur. They also litigate in an effort to sort out the consequences of dissolution. See Section 9.9 (action for accounting).

5. UPA (1914) §29.

6. Many partnerships and partnership agreements ignored this formal rule. See Section 11.6. That practical reality helped shape UPA (1997)'s very different approach to the dissociation-dissolution nexus.

7. UPA (1914) §31(1)(b).

- *Express Will Dissolution of a Partnership for a Term or Undertaking*—Even if the partners have agreed to a partnership for a "definite term or particular undertaking,"[8] each partner retains the *power* to cause dissolution merely by making known his, her, or its express will.[9] The resulting dissolution will be premature and wrongful, that is, "in contravention of the agreement between the partners,"[10] but it will occur nonetheless.[11]
- *Dissolution by Expelling a Partner*—An expelled partner has been dissociated, so expulsion causes dissolution. Under UPA (1914), a partnership agreement can authorize expulsion, but it cannot prevent expulsion from causing dissolution.[12]
- *Dissolution by the Death or Bankruptcy of a Partner*—Death obviously changes the deceased's relationship to fellow partners. The changes caused by bankruptcy are less permanent but often just as fundamental. Either event causes dissolution. In neither event is the dissolution wrongful.[13]
- *Expiration of a Term or Undertaking*—If the partnership agreement includes a specific term or a particular undertaking, the expiration of the term or the accomplishment of the undertaking automatically causes dissolution.[14]

b. A Partner Always Has the Power (but Not Necessarily the Right) to Dissolve a Partnership

Among the inevitable causes of dissolution is the "express will" of a partner. Under UPA (1914) §§31(1)(b) and 31(2), any partner can dissolve the partnership at any time simply by manifesting a desire to do so. For centuries the law has characterized partnership as a voluntary arrangement, and a partner's power to dissolve reflects and preserves that character.[15]

---

8. UPA (1914) §31(1)(a).
9. UPA (1914) §31(2).
10. *Id.*
11. For the distinction between wrongful and rightful dissolution, see *infra* in this section. For the consequences of the distinction, see Sections 11.4.2, 11.5.4, and 11.5.5.
12. UPA (1914) §31(1)(d) (dissolution is caused "[b]y the expulsion of any partner from the business bona fide in accordance with such a power conferred by the agreement between the partners"). For a discussion of expulsion issues under UPA (1914), see Section 11.7.2.
13. UPA (1914) §§31(4) (death) and 31(5) (bankruptcy). Bankruptcy law has much to say about the consequences of dissolution caused by a partner's bankruptcy.
14. UPA (1914) §31(1)(a). If the partnership business continues without interruption, the successor partnership is "at will." For the distinction between a partnership as a legal construct and the partnership's business as a practical reality, see Section 11.2.1(g) and (h).
15. UPA (1997) §105(b)(6) continues this approach, stating that a partnership agreement may not "vary the power to dissociate as a partner" by express will. However, the consequences of a partner's dissociation under UPA (1997) can differ significantly from the consequences under UPA (1914). See section 11.8.3.

The power cannot be eliminated by agreement. Indeed, the power exists even when its exercise will breach an agreement.[16] "[T]he express will of any partner at any time" dissolves a partnership.[17]

c. A Wrongful Dissolution Is a Dissolution That Contravenes a Partnership Agreement

Having the power to dissolve is not, however, the same as having the right to dissolve. Dissolutions that contravene a partnership agreement are "wrongful" rather than "rightful."[18] For example, a partner who withdraws "by express will" before the expiration of an agreed-upon term and the completion of an agreed-upon undertaking does so wrongfully.

Example

Five friends establish an investment club in the form of a general partnership with a term of five years. After four years, one of the friends announces that she is moving away, is quitting the club, and wants to be paid her share of the club's assets. She has dissolved the partnership, and the dissolution is wrongful.

Case in Point — *Drashner v. Sorenson*

"In January, 1951 the plaintiff, C. H. Drashner, and defendants, A. D. Sorenson and Jacob P. Deis, associated themselves as co-owners in the real estate, loan, and insurance business at Rapid City. For a consideration of $7,500 they purchased the real estate and insurance agency known as J. Schumacher Co. located in an office room on the ground floor of the Alex Johnson Hotel building. The entire purchase price was advanced for the partnership by the defendants, but at the time of trial $3,000 of that sum had been repaid to them by the partnership. . . . The agreement of the parties contemplated an association which would continue at least until the $7,500 advance of defendants had been repaid from the gross earnings of the business. Hence, it was not a partnership at will. . . ."[19]

UPA (1914) §38 dichotomizes the world of general partnerships; a partnership is either, on the one hand, for a specific term or undertaking,

16. A comparable distinction exists between wrongful and rightful terminations of agency relationships. See section 5.2.

17. UPA (1914) §31(1)(b) and (2).

18. UPA (1914) §§37, 38, and 41(5) refer to a dissolution have been caused "wrongfully" but the act nowhere uses "rightfully." However, the latter term is useful shorthand for "dissolution [being] caused . . . in contravention of the partnership agreement." *Id.* §38(1).

19. *Drashner v. Sorenson*, 75 S.D. 247, 248–50, 63 N.W.2d 255, 256–58 (1954)

or, on the other hand, at-will. Thus, the overwhelming majority of wrongful dissolution cases involve either a partnership for a term or an undertaking.

But the dichotomy is not the be all and end all. Suppose, for example, that a law firm partnership agreement provides that the partnership will continue until at least two-thirds of the partners vote to dissolve. A partner's withdrawal before any such vote would dissolve the partnership (UPA (1914) §29), but—given that the partnership agreement specifies neither a specific duration or undertaking—would the dissolution necessarily be rightful?

Courts in several states have answered no, recognizing that section 38's dichotomy, like almost all *inter se* rules of UPA (1914), is a default rule.

CASE IN POINT

Case in Point—*Osborne v. Workman*

A group of physicians form a general partnership subject to UPA (1914), and the partnership agreement provides that:

- the business of the partnership will continue indefinitely until the partnership is dissolved by the mutual consent of all partners;
- if a partner withdraws from the partnership without that consent:
  —the business of the partnership will continue uninterrupted in a successor partnership;
  —the partner will receive a specified amount in complete payment for his or her interest in the partnership; and
  —the specified amount will not include payment for the partnership's accounts receivable (A/R);[20]

A partner withdraws from the partnership. Discontented with the agreed payout amount and wanting a share of the A/R, he asserts that:

- because the partnership agreement does not provide for a definite term or undertaking, the partnership is at will; and therefore
- his dissolution is not wrongful; and therefore
- under UPA (1914) §38(1), he has the right to be paid the full value of his interest (i.e., including his share of the A/R).

The dispute goes to court, and the court emphatically disagrees with the withdrawing partner: "It is inconceivable that six doctors would form a partnership, enter into an elaborate agreement intended to promote longevity, set up a common practice, pool their equipment, records, and resources,

20. An account receivable is a payment obligation due the partnership (i.e., due but not yet received).

and intend that any one of them could end it at any time by demanding dissolution and liquidation."

As to the withdrawing partner's contention that the partnership is at will, the court again disagrees: Although "[c]ertainly any partner can withdraw at will and . . . that withdrawal is a dissolution," the dissolution is not rightful and does not occasion "the termination of the partnership [business] by liquidation." In light of the partnership agreement and the surrounding circumstances, the court "cannot agree these partners intended such a result. We think the clear intent was that dissolution by termination would occur only by mutual agreement and not by the unilateral act of a single partner."[21]

As will be discussed in detail below,[22] the wrongful/rightful distinction can significantly influence the nature of the winding-up process.

d. Wrongful Dissolution of a Partnership at Will

It might seem impossible to have a wrongful dissolution of a partnership at will. After all, the essence of an at-will partnership is that every partner has the right as well as the power to dissolve the partnership at any time. Yet a few cases have held to the contrary. These cases all involved egregious situations, in which the dissolution either made possible a substantial and unfair economic advantage for the dissolving partner or threatened significant and unfair economic disadvantage to the other partners.

The cases that have granted relief have dealt with the at-will issue in one of two ways: (i) by finding an implied agreement for a particular term or undertaking; or (ii) by holding that partners have an implied agreement not to injure each other through breach of fiduciary duty.

CASE IN POINT

Case in Point — *Vangel v. Vangel*

Three brothers formed a partnership to purchase and operate a citrus ranch. One brother was unable to furnish his share of the down payment for the ranch, so the other two brothers advanced his share. The borrower was to repay his brothers "only out of funds accumulated from the operation of the ranch or realized from its sale." The court acknowledged that the partnership agreement "does not mention the term of the partnership." It held, however, that the borrowing arrangement "seems to negate any idea of a partnership at will for it cannot be assumed that it was the intention of the

21. *Osborne v. Workman*, 273 Ark. 538, 621 S.W.2d 478 (1981). This holding is especially noteworthy because the court could have: (i) avoided the holding that the act's dichotomy is a default rule; and (ii) held instead that—whether or not the dissolution was rightful—the partnership agreement determined the payout due a withdrawing partner. See also (and to the same effect) *Congel v. Malfitano*, 31 N.Y.3d 272, 101 N.E.3d 341 (2018). The author submitted a brief as amicus curia in *Congel* in support of the partnership.

22. See Sections 11.4.2, 11.5.4, and 11.5.5.

parties that the borrower was at liberty to walk out of the partnership until the loan had been paid from either the operation or the sale of the ranch." This holding meant that the partnership was for a particular undertaking and made the dissolution premature and wrongful.[23] ◀ ◀ ◀

Case in Point — *Page v. Page*

CASE IN POINT

Two individuals formed a linen supply partnership, which after eight unprofitable years seemed about to turn the corner, as the air force had established a base in the vicinity. Just then, one of the partners dissolved the partnership. The other partner feared that his own weak financial position and lack of management experience in the business would enable the dissolving partner to pick up the business of the dissolved partnership without providing fair compensation. The California Supreme Court rejected the claim that the partnership had an implied term to continue until the losses of previous years had been recouped. It held instead that:

> If . . . it is proved that [the dissolving partner] acted in bad faith and violated his fiduciary duties by attempting to appropriate to his own use the new prosperity of the partnership without adequate compensation to his co-partner, the dissolution would be wrongful and the [dissolving partner] would be liable [under the California equivalent of UPA (1914) §38(2)(a)] (rights of partners upon wrongful dissolution) for violation of the implied agreement not to exclude the non-dissolving partner wrongfully from the partnership business opportunity.[24] ◀ ◀ ◀

e. Wrongful Versus Rightful Dissolution in the Context of Expulsion

Under UPA (1914) §31(1)(d), "the expulsion of any partner from the business bona fide in accordance with such a power conferred by the agreement between the partners" automatically dissolves the partnership. Such dissolution is ordinarily rightful, even if the agreement "confers a power"

23. *Vangel v. Vangel*, 254 P.2d 919, 921, 925 (Cal. App. 1953), *appeal (on other grounds) after remand*, 282 P.2d 967 (Cal. App. 1955), *rev'd in part and aff'd in part*, 291 P.2d 25 (Cal. 1955) *en banc*.

24. *Page v. Page*, 359 P.2d 41, 44 (Ca. 1961) (*en banc*). See also, e.g., *Arford v. Blalock*, 199 Ga. App. 434, 437–38, 405 S.E.2d 698, 702 (1991), aff'd sub nom. *Wilensky v. Blalock*, 262 Ga. 95, 414 S.E.2d 1 (1992) (quoting *Page* and stating that "Blalock [plaintiff, former partner] presented evidence from which the jury could find Arford [defendant, other former partner] wrongfully dissolved the partnership to 'freeze out' Blalock from further business opportunities with [a third party that had done business with the partnership]"); holding that the lower court did not err in denying Arford's motion for judgment notwithstanding the verdict).

to expel a partner without having, stating, or proving good cause (so-called no cause expulsion).[25]

Example

The partnership agreement among nine physicians who practice medicine together states in part:

> Expulsion: A partner will be expelled from the partnership if six of the partners vote to expel that partner. There is no requirement that the partners voting for expulsion state a reason or give the expelled partner an opportunity to be heard. The expulsion will take effect when notice of the vote is given to the expelled partner. As full compensation for his or her interest in the partnership, the expelled partner will receive an amount determined under Paragraph X of this Agreement. ◄◄◄

Although such "guillotine" provisions may at first glance seem harsh, they rest on a solid rationale. The success of a partnership often depends on the ability of the partners to work together. If, as sometimes happens, one of the partners becomes troublesome or is otherwise undermining the business, an expulsion provision allows the partnership to save the business without destroying it.[26]

The "no cause" aspect of an expulsion provision can be very important, because otherwise the partnership may have to go through the time-consuming, costly, and bitter process of proving partner misconduct. No-cause provisions help avoid litigation (what is there to litigate about?) and allow for the immediate, surgical removal of a problem partner. No-cause provisions also reflect the idea that if—for whatever reason—most of the partners decide they no longer want to work with one of their colleagues, then that decision by itself is adequate reason to separate the unwanted partner from the business.

f. The Notion of Wrongful "No-Cause" Expulsion

In a few reported cases, expelled partners have challenged their expulsion as wrongful, asserting that the expelling partners have breached a fiduciary

25. Under most no-cause provisions, the expelling partners need not even state a reason or give the expelled partner an opportunity to be heard. They just have to prove that the agreed-upon number of partners voted for expulsion.

26. To be useful, the provision must authorize the remaining partners to continue the business without causing the expelled partner to be released from personal liability on existing partnership liabilities. Obtaining a release may be very difficult, see Section 11.5.2(d), and UPA (1914) §38(1) provides as a default rule that an expelled partner may demand liquidation unless "discharged from all partnership liabilities." See Section 11.4.2(a).

duty by acting either in bad faith or without "due process." These challenges have generally failed, with the courts holding either that the plain language of the partnership agreement allows no-cause expulsion or that the expelled partner has failed to prove bad faith.

A claim for wrongful dissolution might exist if an expelled partner could prove the type of expropriating bad faith contemplated in *Page*, discussed in Section 11.7.1. *Page* involved dissolution of an at-will partnership rather than no-cause expulsion, but the situations seem analogous. The rationale that led the *Page* court to constrain a partner's seemingly absolute discretion to dissolve an at-will partnership might apply to constrain partners' seemingly absolute discretion to vote expulsion.

For very large partnerships and those with very "junior" (i.e., powerless) partners, there may be another constraint as well. If the expelled partner is a member of a protected class, he or she may be able to contest the expulsion under federal and state anti-discrimination laws. These statutes generally protect "employees," and, formally at least, partners are not employees. However, the larger the partnership and the more junior the partner, the more the situation resembles employment. Most cases raising this issue have involved large law and accounting firms and large brokerage houses, and the courts have focused primarily on the amount of management authority and responsibility enjoyed by the partner claiming employee status. So far, most decisions have gone against the plaintiff, but the courts' analysis has left the door open.[27] In a related case dealing with a professional corporation, the U.S. Supreme Court has held, according to one commentator, that "formal labels do not determine the issue. What matters is the actual governance structure of the organization."[28]

g. Dissolution Does Not End the Partnership

Dissolution is not itself the end of the partnership; it is merely the beginning of the end. Dissolution means that the partnership as a legal construct has no future, other than to finish in one way or another the work it has already begun and to settle accounts among the partners.

The finishing of business and the settling of accounts is called "the *winding up* of partnership affairs,"[29] and dissolution automatically puts the partnership into the winding-up phase. To wind up its business with outside *obligees*, the partnership must perform or otherwise satisfy the obligations.

---

27. See Daniel S. Kleinberger, "Magnificent Circularity and the Churkendoose: LLC Members and Federal Employment Law," 22 Okla. City U.L. Rev. 477 (1997), reprinted at 40 Corporate Practice Commentator 379 (1998).

28. Bishop & Kleinberger on limited Liability Companies (2025–2), § 1:48. (discussing *Clackamas Gastroenterology Assocs., P.C. v. Wells*, 123 S. Ct. 1673 (2003)).

29. UPA (1914) §30.

If, for example, dissolution occurs with a project underway for a customer, during winding up the partnership will complete the project, arrange to have someone else (including one of the partners, a successor partnership, or some other successor business) complete the project, or obtain the customer's permission to abandon the project.

For outside *obligors*, during winding up the partnership will receive performance, assign the right to receive performance, or release performance of the obligation. For example, during winding up a partnership will try to collect all of its accounts receivable (i.e., money that customers owe the partnership for products sold or services rendered). For amounts owed but not yet due, the partnership may try to collect early, offering to accept a reduced amount in return for early payment. Or, the partnership may sell to someone else (including one of the partners, a successor partnership, or some other successor business) the right to collect the debt when it comes due, or the partnership might continue winding up (at length) to collect the accounts receivable.

Winding up also involves settling accounts among the partners. If the partners have an agreement on the subject, that agreement will govern. Otherwise, the UPA (1914) default rules will control this final reckoning.

When winding up has finished, the partnership is actually and legally at an end. There are no papers to be filed or magic words to be said.[30] The end of function marks the end of existence.

h. The End of the Partnership Is Not Necessarily the End of the Partnership Business

There is a difference between the legal construct the law calls a partnership and the business that can be carried on within the partnership form. As both a theoretical and practical matter, the "partnership business" is distinct from the legal form. It is therefore possible for a particular partnership to dissolve, wind up, and terminate while the partnership business continues.

Whether the business continues depends on whether the partners have so agreed. In the default mode, UPA (1914) gives every partner the right to require liquidation,[31] but partners often relinquish this right by agreement. Such agreements can be made either before or after the dissolution. Often

---

30. In this respect, the death of a partnership resembles its creation. See Section 7.2 (no special formalities needed to create a partnership). There may, however, be some paperwork following dissolution. To protect themselves against future liabilities, partners of a dissolved UPA (1914) partnership may wish to give notice of the dissolution to third parties who have done business with the partnership and to the public generally. See Section 11.3.3.

31. In liquidation, the partnership sells off all its assets (e.g., its buildings, equipment, accounts receivable, good will) either as a whole or piecemeal. See Section 11.4.1. If a partner *wrongfully* dissolves the partnership, that partner may lose the right to compel liquidation. See Section 11.4.2.

the same agreement that forms the partnership also dictates what will happen after dissolution.

Whenever made, business continuation agreements typically provide for a successor partnership to take over from the dissolved partnership. The successor partnership may consist of some or all of the members remaining from the dissolved partnership and may also include some "new blood."

§11.2.2 Following the UPA (1914) Three-Ring Circus: Three Pathways of Post-Dissolution Concerns

Understanding what happens when a UPA (1914) partnership dissolves is a lot like watching a three-ring circus. Three different things are happening at once, and it is almost impossible to have them all in view simultaneously. It is nonetheless useful to understand that they are all occurring. Under UPA (1914), the three post-dissolution rings (or pathways) concern: (i) how the partnership is managed during winding up; (ii) what happens to the partnership business; and (iii) what happens to the partners. The following sections deal with each pathway in turn.

§11.3 MANAGEMENT ISSUES DURING WINDING UP

When a partnership dissolves, it does not immediately disappear; it lingers to wind up its affairs. Winding up can occur quickly, as when a successor partnership takes over, or may be quite lengthy, as when an extensive and complicated business is sold off in pieces. In any event, the same two basic categories of management issues exist both during winding up and before dissolution: (i) *inter se* the partners, who have the right to manage the business and make commitments on its behalf; and (ii) as between the partnership and third parties, what acts of individual partners suffice to bind the partnership.

§11.3.1 *Inter Se* Issues

a. Actual Authority to Manage the Partnership During Winding Up

UPA (1914) §37 states the default rule: "the partners who have not wrongfully dissolved the partnership . . . [have] the right to wind up the partnership affairs."[32] The section does not indicate what happens if those partners

32. When no partners survive into the winding-up period, "the legal representative of the last surviving partner, not bankrupt" may wind up. UPA (1914) §37.

disagree, but presumably UPA §18(h) applies. Under UPA §18(h) differences over "ordinary matters" are settled by majority vote, while acts "in contravention of any agreement between the partners" require unanimous consent.[33]

As explained previously,[34] UPA (1914) §18(h) fails to expressly provide a rule for matters not "in contravention" but nonetheless extraordinary. During winding up, this omitted category may cause serious problems. Some winding-up matters will be clearly ordinary—for example, deciding where to buy supplies. Others, such as deciding whether to compromise a claim or sell an important partnership asset, may be unprecedented. Some courts have solved the problem by holding that extraordinary matters can become ordinary during the winding-up process.

Example

Larry, Moe, and Curley have an at-will partnership that owns and races a single racehorse. Fed up with Moe's abuse, Curley quits. The partnership accordingly dissolves, and Moe insists on liquidation. A third party offers $100,000 for the racehorse. Larry and Curley vote yes. Moe votes no. Before dissolution, selling the partnership's key asset would have required unanimity. But in winding up, selling off assets is probably "an ordinary matter." If so, Larry and Curley's majority vote prevails. ◄◄◄

Case in Point—*Weisblatt v. Colky*

Plaintiff filed a legal malpractice claim against a law partnership and its individual attorneys for their work on several matters. Plaintiff and one of the attorney partners executed "a stipulation and mutual release agreement whereby, in consideration of mutual obligations, each party released and forever discharged the other from all claims." Later, Plaintiff argued that the release was invalid because the attorney lacked the requisite authority to bind the partnership. Plaintiff's argument was presumably based on the fact that one partner had died, and thus the partnership had dissolved. The court affirmed dismissal of Plaintiff's complaint: (i) holding in relevant part that dissolution does not entirely revoke a partner's authority, but rather partners maintain certain authority during the winding-up period; and (ii) implicitly rejecting Plaintiff's presupposition that a partner cannot sign a binding release as part of the winding-up process.[35] ◄◄◄

---

33. See Section 9.4.1.
34. See Section 9.4.1.
35. *Weisblatt v. Colky*, 637 N.E.2d 1198, 1201 (Ill. App. 1994).

UPA (1914) §37 also provides that "any partner, his legal representative or his assignee, upon cause shown, may obtain winding up by the court." The provision does not specify what constitutes cause, but courts have held that waste, fraud, and gross mismanagement justify the appointment of a receiver to wind up the partnership. Whether mere dissension among the partners justifies appointing a receiver is an open question. Even a partner who wrongfully dissolved the partnership can seek court intervention under UPA (1914) §37. Except for the provision on "winding up by the court," the rules of UPA (1914) §37 can be altered or displaced by an agreement of the partners.

b. Authority to Commit the Partnership to New Business

Dissolution deprives all partners of actual authority to transact new business. "Except so far as may be necessary to wind up partnership affairs or to complete transactions begun but not then finished, dissolution terminates all [actual] authority of any partner to act for the partnership."[36]

The precise timing of the deprivation depends on the cause of dissolution. If the act of some partner is responsible, then each partner's "new business" authority terminates upon knowledge of the dissolution.[37] When a partner's death or bankruptcy causes dissolution, each partner's "new business" authority ends upon knowledge or notice of the death or bankruptcy.[38] With all other causes, "new business" authority ends at the moment of dissolution.[39] The end of "new business" actual authority does not necessarily end the partners' power to bind the partnership as to new business.[40]

§11.3.2 The Power to Bind the Partnership After Dissolution

UPA (1914) §35 describes the post-dissolution power of a partner to bind the partnership. UPA (1914) §35(1) states empowering rules, and UPA (1914) §35(3) states constraining rules.[41] For a partner's post-dissolution act to bind the dissolved partnership, the act must: (i) qualify under one of

36. UPA (1914) §33.
37. UPA (1914) §§33(1)(b) and 34(a).
38. UPA (1914) §§33(1)(a) and 34(b).
39. UPA (1914) §33(1)(a).
40. UPA (1914) §§33(2) and 35(1)(b). See Section 11.3.2.
41. UPA (1914) §35(2) limits the personal liability of individual partners for certain post-dissolution obligations of the partnership, and UPA (1914) §35(4) makes clear that UPA §35 does not affect liability created under UPA (1914) §16 (partnership by estoppel). For an explanation of partnership by estoppel, see Section 7.5.

the rules of UPA (1914) §35(1); and (ii) not be disqualified under any of the rules of UPA (1914) §35(3).

a. The Empowering Rules of UPA (1914) §35(1)

The empowering rules of UPA (1914) §35(1) establish two categories of post-dissolution partner acts: (i) acts "appropriate for winding up partnership affairs or completing transactions unfinished at dissolution"[42] and (ii) acts that would bind the partnership if dissolution had not occurred.[43]

Under UPA (1914) §35(1)(a), acts in the former category bind the partnership, subject to the constraining rules of UPA (1914) §35(3).

Example

A partner in a dissolved auto body shop partnership orders paint so the partnership can finish work on cars already in the shop. This is an "act appropriate for . . . completing transactions unfinished at dissolution," and UPA (1914) §35(1)(a) applies; the partner acted with actual authority, thereby binding the dissolved partnership. ◄◄◄

Example

The same partner, with a view toward settling the partners' accounts with each other, hires an accountant to put a value on partnership assets. This is an "act appropriate for winding up partnership affairs," and here too UPA (1914) §35(1)(a) applies. ◄◄◄

Example

The same partner accepts a new "rush" order on a '67 Corvette and hires a "detailing" expert to do the fancy paintwork. Neither accepting the rush order nor making the new hire qualifies under UPA §35(1)(a). ◄◄◄

The rule for the second category—"transactions which would bind the partnership if dissolution had not taken place"—is considerably more complicated. The rule has two branches, depending on whether the third party extended credit to the partnership before dissolution. If yes, under UPA (1914) §35(1)(b)(I), the third party must show that: (i) absent dissolution the partner's act would have bound the partnership; and (ii) at the time of the partner's act the third party had "no knowledge or notice of the dissolution."[44]

---

42. UPA (1914) §35(1)(a).
43. UPA (1914) §35(1)(b).
44. UPA (1914) §35(1)(b)(I).

Example

A partner in a dissolved body shop partnership accepts a new, "rush" order on a '67 Corvette and hires a detailing expert to do the fancy paintwork. The expert has worked for the partnership before, always billing the partnership after completing the work.[45] No one has notified the expert that the partnership is dissolved, and she is unaware of that fact. Assuming that the partner's act of hiring the expert would have bound the partnership before dissolution, UPA (1914) §35(1)(b)(I) applies, and, even though the partner acted without actual authority, the dissolved partnership is bound. ◄◄◄

If the third party did not extend credit to the partnership before dissolution, under UPA (1997) §35(1)(b)(II) the third party must show that: (i) it knew of the partnership prior to dissolution; (ii) at the time of the partner's act it had no knowledge or notice of the dissolution; (iii) at the time of the partner's act there had been no public notice of the dissolution (through advertisement in a newspaper of general circulation in the partnership's place(s) of business); and (iv) absent dissolution the partner's act would have bound the partnership.[46]

Example

A partner in a dissolved body shop partnership accepts a new, "rush" order on a '67 Corvette, and the owner of the Corvette seeks to hold the partnership to the deal. Another partner has sent letters announcing the partnership's dissolution to all the body shop's suppliers and customers and has published the announcement in the city's main newspaper. The Corvette's owner has never been a customer before, never received a copy of the letter, never read the newspaper announcement, and was unaware of the dissolution when the first partner accepted the rush order. Even assuming the first partner's act of accepting the order would have bound the partnership before dissolution, accepting the order does not qualify under UPA (1914) §35(1)(b)(II). The owner had not extended credit to the partnership before dissolution, and "the fact of dissolution had . . . been advertised in a newspaper of general circulation in the place . . . at which the partnership business was regularly carried on."[47] ◄◄◄

Under both branches of UPA (1914) §35(1)(b), the third party must show that the partner's act would have bound the partnership absent

45. Thus, the detailing expert has "extended credit" to the partnership.
46. UPA (1914) §35(1)(b)(II).
47. UPA (1914) §35(1)(b)(II).

dissolution. To make that showing, the third party invokes the same rules that apply pre-dissolution—typically, UPA (1914) §9.[48]

b. The Constraining Rules of UPA §35(3)

UPA (1914) §35(3) contains three constraining rules. The first two are straightforward. A partner's post-dissolution act cannot bind the partnership if: (i) dissolution occurred because it was unlawful to carry on the partnership business and the partner's act is not appropriate for winding up (UPA (1914) §35(3)(a)); or (ii) the partner doing the act is bankrupt (UPA (1914) §35(3)(b)).

Example

A partner in a body shop partnership files for personal bankruptcy, causing the partnership to dissolve. The same partner then orders paint so the partnership can finish work on cars already in the shop. Although this is an "act appropriate for . . . completing transactions unfinished at dissolution," UPA (1914) §35(1)(a) does not bind the partnership. Because the acting partner is bankrupt, the partnership can invoke UPA (1914) §35(3)(b) to override UPA §35(1)(a). ◄◄◄

The third constraining rule is more important as a practical matter and decidedly more complex. The third rule determines whether a partner's *unauthorized* post-dissolution act binds the partnership.[49]

Like the empowering rule of UPA (1914) §35(1)(b), the constraining rule of UPA (1914) §35(3)(c) has two branches, depending on whether the third party extended credit to the partnership before dissolution. If yes, UPA (1914) §35(3)(c)(I) bars a third party from recovering only if the third party had "knowledge or notice of [the partner's] want of authority." If the third party had not extended credit to the partnership before dissolution, UPA (1914) §35(3)(c)(II) bars a third party from recovering if either the third party had "knowledge or notice of [the partner's] want of authority" or there has been public notice of the partner's lack of authority (through advertisement in a newspaper of general circulation in the partnership's place(s) of business).

---

48. If the partnership agreement granted actual authority to the partner for this type of transaction pre-dissolution, it should be unnecessary to invoke UPA (1914) §9—even if the same partnership agreement terminated that actual authority upon dissolution.

49. The power to bind is not the same as the actual authority to act. For a discussion of the latter, see Section 11.3.1. Lack of authority also figures in a pre-dissolution UPA constraining rule. See Section 10.2.5 (discussing the "no authority" constraining rule under UPA (1914) §9).

Example

Larry, Moe, and Curley have a partnership that owns and races a single racehorse. The partnership agreement provides that: (i) the partnership has a term of five years; (ii) after dissolution Moe will handle all discussions with third parties interested in buying the horse; and (iii) any decision to sell the horse following dissolution will be made by a majority vote of the partners. When the partnership dissolves, it places an announcement in all the major racing publications. The announcement states in part: "We are dissolving our partnership and looking for buyers for our horse. All interested parties should contact Moe."

Despite the partnership agreement, Curley starts looking for potential buyers on his own. He finds a hot prospect who has never previously done business with the partnership, has not seen the announcement in the trade papers, and is unaware that Curley is acting for a dissolved partnership. After a half-hour of hard bargaining, Curley and the prospect agree that the prospect will buy the horse for $75,000.

Despite the partnership agreement and the public announcement, the partnership is bound. Curley's act is "appropriate for winding up partnership affairs,"[50] and so qualifies under the empowering rule of UPA (1914) §35(1)(a). Curley's lack of authority does not negate this power, because under UPA (1914) §35(3)(c)(II) the prospect had "no knowledge or notice of [Curley's] want of authority" and the public notice about Moe was not in a newspaper of general circulation.[51] ◄◄◄

§11.3.3 Partner Self-Protection: The Importance of Notice

Whether a partner's post-dissolution act binds the partnership to a third party often depends on what the third party knows or has notice of. Therefore, following dissolution a partnership can limit its liability for unauthorized acts by promptly "spreading the word" both about the dissolution and about any limitations on the winding-up authority of particular partners.[52]

To spread the word effectively, the partnership should: (i) run an advertisement in "a newspaper of general circulation" published in the partnership's regular place(s) of business, stating the fact of dissolution and detailing any limitations of partner authority; and (ii) send a letter, containing the same information as the advertisement, to all third parties that

50. UPA (1914) §35(1)(a).

51. UPA (1914) §35(3)(c)(II) is the relevant constraining rule, because the third party had not extended credit to the partnership before dissolution.

52. A partner can also spread the word and would be well advised to do so if the partnership fails to act promptly.

have provided goods or services to the partnership. The advertisement will limit claims by those who have not previously extended credit to the partnership.[53] Technically, the letter need only go to those who have previously "extended credit to the partnership,"[54] but it may be difficult to determine from the partnership records which businesses have extended credit and which have acted solely on a cash basis. It is better to be over-inclusive and safe than under-inclusive and sorry.[55]

§11.4 THE FATE OF THE PARTNERSHIP BUSINESS

§11.4.1 The Fundamental Decision: Whether to Liquidate

Regardless of which uniform general partnership act applies, the most fundamental question after any dissolution is whether the partnership business will be liquidated or continued. Under all three statutes, the partnership agreement can completely answer this question.

From a business standpoint, liquidation usually produces inferior results. Unless a buyer can be found for the business as a whole, the partnership will have to sell off its assets piecemeal. Usually, a business is much more valuable as a going concern, so a piecemeal sale will produce an inferior payout. Moreover, liquidation sales are often in the nature of fire sales—everything must go within a relatively short period of time, and potential buyers know it. As a result, the seller rarely gets top dollar.

Despite the practical problems with liquidation, UPA (1914) default rules conduce toward that result. Following a rightful dissolution, absent a contrary agreement, UPA (1914) §38(1) gives every partner the right to have the assets of the partnership liquidated and the partners paid in cash.[56] In the default mode, the right to compel liquidation also exists following a wrongful dissolution unless all the partners who did not wrongfully

53. UPA (1914) §§35(1)(b)(II) and 35(3)(c)(II).

54. UPA (1914) §§35(1)(b)(I) and 35(3)(c)(I).

55. If the partnership maintains a website, the website should predominantly describe the situation. UPA (1914) provides no safe harbor based on website announcements, but an announcement can help the dissolved partnership prove that a would-be creditor knew of the dissolution.

56. In extraordinary circumstances, courts may divide the partnership's assets in-kind. In general, however, valuation problems and the prospects of "who gets what" disputes cause the law to disfavor in-kind division of assets. See Section 11.5.3

dissolve agree to carry on the business of the partnership and meet certain other statutory requirements.[57]

§11.4.2 Who Decides

Although the decision whether to liquidate or continue affects third parties, the decision itself is an *inter se* matter. Like all *inter se* matters, it is subject to the agreement of the partners. Agreement may precede or follow the dissolution.

Example

Rachael, Charlotte, and Carolyn have a partnership that operates a chicken breeding farm. There is no written partnership agreement and no commitment to continue the partnership for any particular time or undertaking. One day Carolyn decides that she is getting out of chicken farming and going to attend art school. Carolyn's friend, Randi, expresses an interest in joining the business. After discussing the matter, Rachael, Charlotte, Carolyn, and Randi agree that Randi will buy "Carolyn's share." Randi joins the business, Carolyn leaves for art school, and chicken breeding continues through the successor partnership of Rachael, Charlotte, and Randi. Carolyn's withdrawal has dissolved the old partnership, but Rachael, Charlotte, and Carolyn have each agreed not to compel liquidation. ◀◀◀

Where the partners have not agreed, the UPA (1914) default rules govern. Which particular rule applies depends on whether the dissolution was rightful or wrongful.

a. Rightful Dissolution

Following a *rightful* dissolution, liquidation is the typical default result. Under UPA (1914) §38(1), "each partner . . . , unless otherwise agreed, may have the partnership property applied to discharge its liabilities, and the surplus applied to pay *in cash* the net amount owing to the respective partners."[58] An exception exists when "dissolution is caused by expulsion of a partner, bona fide under the partnership agreement." In that event, the remaining partners can negate the expelled partner's right to force liquidation by: (i) "cashing out" the expelled partner without liquidating the

57. UPA (1914) §§38(2)(b), 38(2)(c)(II). A wrongful dissolution occurs when a partner dissolves in violation of the partnership agreement. See Section 11.2.1. In some jurisdictions, a breach of fiduciary duty can also cause a wrongful dissolution. See Section 11.7.
58. Emphasis added.

business;[59] and (ii) causing the expelled partner to be released from (not merely indemnified for) personal liability for the debts of the dissolved partnership.[60] Authority is divided as to whether the estate of a deceased partner can force liquidation. The language of UPA (1914) §38(1) implies that the estate has no such right, but language in UPA (1914) §41(3) points the other way.[61] The cases are also divided.

b. Wrongful Dissolution

Following a *wrongful* dissolution, the analysis is a bit more complicated. Under UPA (1914) §38(2), the first choice belongs to the partners who did not wrongfully dissolve:

- "The partners who have not caused the dissolution wrongfully, if they all desire to continue the business in the same name, either by themselves or jointly with others, may do so, during the agreed term for the partnership. . . ."[62]
- The remaining partners must agree unanimously and in addition must "indemnify [the wrongful dissolver] against all present or future partnership liabilities" (with the indemnity backed by a bond approved by a court) *and either* cash out the wrongful dissolver immediately[63] or promise to pay the cash-out amount at some later date and obtain a court-approved bond to secure the payment. If these criteria are met, the continuing partners "may possess the partnership property" and use it for the rest of the dissolved partnership's original term.[64]

---

59. For how the cash-out amount is calculated, see Section 11.5.4.
60. For the difficulties involved in obtaining a release, see Section 11.5.2 (effect of dissolution on the liabilities of partners). Absent a contrary agreement, each of the nonexpelled partners retains the right to compel liquidation. Ordinarily, however, the same agreement that provides for expulsion overrides UPA (1914) §38(1) generally. As a result, the nonexpelled partners lose their right to compel liquidation, and the expelled partner may lose the right to be released from partnership liabilities.
61. UPA (1914) §38(1) states only that "each *partner*" has a right to compel liquidation. The right does not extend to "persons claiming through [partners] in respect of their interests in the partnership." That latter category (persons claiming through partners) includes the estate of a deceased partner. In contrast, UPA (1914) §41(3) refers to "the business of the dissolved partnership [being] continued . . . *with the consent* of the retired partners or *the representative of the deceased partner*." (Emphasis added.)
62. UPA (1914) §38(2)(b).
63. For how the cash-out amount is calculated, see Section 11.5.5 (settling accounts among partners following wrongful dissolution).
64. UPA (1914) §38(2)(b).

If these conditions are not met, each partner—including the wrongful dissolver—has the right to demand liquidation just as if the dissolution had been rightful.[65]

§11.4.3 Continuing the Business Through a Successor Partnership (An Example)

The following Example may help you follow the various issues inherent in a decision to continue the business of a dissolved partnership through a successor partnership.

Example

Three law students, Charlotte, Paul, and Sophie, form a UPA (1914) partnership to sell used law textbooks. They place no term on the partnership, agreeing instead to continue "just as long as we all want to." The three partners rent a room in their law school, take books from fellow students on consignment, open a partnership checking account, and do a profitable business. After a year, Sophie is nearing graduation and wants to "get her money out." She dissolves the partnership.

Charlotte and Paul want to continue the bookstore business and decide to bring in Samara to take Sophie's place. To carry on the bookstore business, Charlotte, Paul, and Samara form a successor partnership. Although Sophie has the legal right to force liquidation of the dissolved partnership's business, Charlotte and Paul convince her to take a cash settlement instead. As part of the winding-up process of the dissolved partnership:

1. the dissolved partnership settles Sophie's accounts by cashing her out (that is, by paying her the settlement amount);
2. Charlotte and Paul take rights in the successor partnership as settlement of their respective accounts in the dissolved partnership;[66]
3. the dissolved partnership arranges to transfer its rights and obligations (including, for example, its lease with the law school) to the successor partnership; and

---

65. UPA (1914) §§38(2)(a)(I) (following wrongful dissolution, "Each partner who has not caused dissolution wrongfully shall have (I) all the rights specified in paragraph (1) of this section . . . ") and 38(2)(c)(I) (following wrongful dissolution, if the partnership business is not continued under §38(2)(b), wrongful dissolver has "all the rights of a partner under paragraph (1)," subject to any claims for damage on account of wrongful dissolution). As with most aspects of relations *inter se* the partners, due partnership agreement can vary those rules.

66. For a detailed discussion of settling accounts among partners, see Sections 11.5.3–11.5.5.

4. the successor partnership agrees to hold Sophie harmless from any liabilities arising from either the dissolved or successor partnership.[67]

When winding up ends, the Charlotte-Paul-Sophie partnership terminates; it no longer exists. Its business, however, continues on. With the same suppliers, the same customers, and two of the same partners, Charlotte, Paul, and Samara operate that business "at the same old stand." ◀ ◀ ◀

The following terms are useful for keeping straight the legal issues raised when the business of a UPA (1914) partnership continues despite dissolution:

- *Dissociated Partners*—Partners of the dissolved partnership who are not continuing in the business as members of the successor partnership. In the Example above, Sophie is a dissociated partner. (UPA (1914) calls such withdrawal "retirement," a term that is confusing because of its lay association with senior citizen status and warm climates.)
- *Continuing Partners*—Partners of the dissolved partnership who are continuing in the business as members of the successor partnership. In the Example above, Charlotte and Paul are continuing partners.
- *New Partners*—Partners of the successor partnership who were not members of the dissolved partnership. In the Example above, Samara is a new partner. (Not every successor partnership involves new partners.)

§11.4.4 Settling Accounts with Third Parties

The dissolution of a partnership does not abrogate obligations between the dissolved partnership and third parties. Indeed, half of the winding-up process consists of resolving those obligations.[68]

a. When the Partnership Business Is Being Liquidated

If the partnership business is being liquidated, resolving relations with third parties is theoretically quite simple. Winding up continues until the partnership has completed all performance as an obligor and received all performance as an obligee.

As a practical matter, however, such completion may be difficult and time consuming. For example, not all amounts owed the partnership can

67. This undertaking is part of the settling of accounts among the partners. See Section 11.5.4.
68. The other half consists of settling accounts among the partners. See Sections 11.5.2–11.5.5.

be collected immediately. Some obligations may not yet be due, and some obligors may be "slow pays." To the extent that prompt collection is impractical, the partnership may sell the right to collect to a third party, assign the collection right to one of the partners,[69] continue winding up (at length) solely for the purpose of collections, or simply abandon the obligation.

For obligations the dissolved partnership owes to third parties, two pathways exist. The partnership can either pay off or otherwise perform its obligations, or it can delegate the responsibility to someone else. Delegation may be especially attractive for long-term obligations, such as constructing a building. For a dissolved partnership that has long-term obligations, delegation is the only alternative to a very extended period of winding up.[70]

b. When the Partnership Business Is Being Continued

When the partnership business is being continued by a successor partnership, the theoretical structure is far more complex, although from a practical perspective the transition from the dissolved partnership to the successor partnership can be seamless. Resolving obligations owed to the dissolved partnership is usually simple enough. The dissolved partnership assigns its rights to the successor partnership.[71] Resolving obligations owed to third parties is more complicated. The dissolved partnership could in theory perform all these obligations. However, if the obligations are large relative to the assets of the business, that approach would require at least partial liquidation, which in turn would cripple the successor partnership's ability to function. Moreover, as discussed above, some obligations require drawn-out performance. Typically, therefore, the dissolved partnership resolves its obligations to third parties by delegating them to the successor partnership.

Contract law applies to these delegations. In some instances, the transfer of responsibility may require the obligee's consent.[72] In all instances, the

---

69. Such assignments typically occur as part of an agreed-upon settling of accounts among the partners.

70. Delegating an obligation does not by itself release the dissolved partnership or its partners. If the delegatee fails to perform, the obligor may proceed against those partners—even if the dissolved partnership has long since ceased to function. Moreover, if the obligation arises from a contract, the contract may purport to prohibit or restrict delegation. See Section 4.4.3 for a discussion of these issues in the agency context.

71. Complexity develops if the dissolved partnership's rights are not assignable. Certain rights to receive payments are assignable despite anything to the contrary in the contract giving rise to the rights. See UCC §§ 9–406 and 9–408 (2017). Article 9 was amended in 2018 to remove partnership and limited liability company interests from the purview of §§ 9–406 and 9–408. See also *Fairway Development Co. v. Title Ins. Co. of Minnesota*, 621 F. Supp. 120 (Ohio 1985) (holding that a successor partnership could not benefit from a title insurance policy issued to the predecessor partnership).

72. Some contracts expressly prohibit delegation without the obligee's consent, and contract law sometimes validates such provisions. See Section 4.4.3 (delegation of performance to an agent).

mere transfer of responsibility does not discharge the dissolved partnership from its obligations. As a matter of contract law, discharge occurs only if the obligee consents to a novation with the successor partnership.[73] An economically rational obligee will not agree to a novation without receiving something in return.

Example

Alex, Bernice, Carl, and Donald form a partnership to do carpentry work. To equip themselves, they borrow $10,000 from First State Bank at the then current rate of 6 percent. Two years later Alex dissolves the partnership. He is willing to let the others continue the business so long as he is released from any personal liability to the bank. Over the past two years interest rates have risen, so the going rate is now 9 percent. If Bernice, Carl, and Donald are creditworthy without Alex, then the bank may well release Alex, provided the interest rate on the loan is reset nearer to or at 9 percent. ◄◄◄

§11.4.5 Successor Liability When a Successor Partnership Continues the Business of a Dissolved Partnership

If a successor partnership continues the business of a dissolved partnership, then both contract law and partnership law make the successor partnership liable for the obligations of the dissolved partnership. The agreement transferring the business typically calls for the successor partnership to assume the obligations of the dissolved partnership, and, as a matter of contract law, creditors of the dissolved partnership can enforce the assumption agreement as intended third-party beneficiaries. Even without an assumption agreement, if the successor partnership includes any continuing partners (i.e., any members from the dissolved partnership), UPA (1914) §41 makes the successor partnership liable for the debts of the dissolved partnership as a matter of partnership law.[74]

This successor liability extends to all the partners in the successor partnership,[75] with one exception. The liability created by *partnership law* for *new partners* is limited. Under UPA (1914) §41(7), "The liability of a third person

73. See Section 2.7.5. As a matter of partnership law, delegation to the successor partnership may lead to release of dissociated partners; i.e., those partners of the dissolved partnership who are not members of the successor partnership. See Section 11.5.2.
74. UPA (1914) §41(1), (2), (3), (5), and (6). If the entity continuing the business includes no continuing partners, then the successor entity is liable for the debts of the dissolved partnership only if it has promised to assume those debts. UPA (1914) §41(4).
75. This personal liability follows from UPA (1914) §15.

becoming a partner in the partnership continuing the business, under this section, to the creditors of the dissolved partnership shall be satisfied out of partnership property only." Although the language of the statute is confusing, the phrase "a third person" refers to persons who are members of the successor partnership but were not members of the dissolved partnership. In other words, newcomers have no *personal* liability for the debts of the dissolved partnership. The entire value of their interest in the successor partnership may be consumed in paying those old debts, but those debts do not put a newcomer's personal assets at risk.[76]

UPA (1914) §41(7) expressly limits its reach to "liability . . . under this section," so a newcomer's protection relates only to liability arising from section 41. Because successor partnerships typically agree to assume the obligations of the dissolved partnership, liability typically arises not only from section 41 but also from contract law. The protections of section 41(7) do not extend to liability arising from contract law.

Example

Charlotte, Paul, and Sophie form a partnership to operate a used bookstore in the law school. When Sophie nears graduation, she dissolves the partnership. Samara joins Charlotte and Paul, and they form a successor partnership to carry on the business of the dissolved partnership. En masse the professors assign new editions, the market for used books plummets, and the bookstore goes under. The business can no longer make its lease payments to the law school. Under UPA (1914) §41(1), "creditors of the . . . dissolved partnership are also creditors of the partnership . . . continuing the business." Therefore, the law school can pursue the successor partnership for the lease payments. Under UPA (1914) §15, the law school can also pursue the successor partnership's partners.[77] If the law school bases its claims solely on UPA (1914) §41, the personal assets of Samara (the newcomer) are not at risk, due to UPA (1914) §41(7). Samara's protection under UPA (1914) §41(7) will be of no use, however, if the successor partnership contractually assumed the lease obligation of the dissolved partnership. (In any event, Charlotte, Paul, and Sophie are liable as partners of the dissolved partnership.)[78] ◄ ◄ ◄

---

76. Those assets are at risk, of course, for all other debts of the successor partnership. UPA (1914) §15. This approach mirrors UPA (1914)'s approach to persons who become partners in an existing partnership. UPA (1914) §17 ("A person admitted as a partner into an existing partnership is liable for all the obligations of the partnership arising before his admission as though he had been a partner when such obligations were incurred, except that this liability shall be satisfied only out of partnership property.").

77. In some jurisdictions, the law school will first have to exhaust partnership assets. See Section 7.3.1. If the successor partnership is an LLP, the law school will have no claim against the partners. See Section 17.2.

78. See Section 11.5.2.

§11.5 THE IMPACT OF DISSOLUTION ON THE PARTNERS

§11.5.1 Impact on Partners' Fiduciary Duties

Since dissolution does not end the partnership, dissolution does not end the partners' reciprocal fiduciary duties.[79] Indeed, these duties can take on a special importance if the partners seek to negotiate an agreement to continue the business or to buy each other out.[80]

§11.5.2 Impact on Partners' Personal Liability

Dissolution by itself does nothing to change the partners' personal liability for the debts of the dissolved partnership. In the words of UPA (1914) §36(1), "The dissolution of the partnership does not of itself discharge the existing liability of any partner." Discharge *will* occur, however, under two circumstances that may follow from dissolution.

a. Post-Dissolution Discharge by Agreement with the Creditor

UPA (1914) §36(2) states, "A partner is discharged from any existing liability upon dissolution of the partnership by an agreement to that effect between himself, the partnership creditor, and the person or partnership continuing the business. . . ." Presumably under such an agreement "the person or partnership continuing the business" will assume responsibility for the discharged partner's obligations.

UPA (1914) §36(2) also states that an agreement to discharge a member of the dissolved partnership "may be inferred from the course of dealing between the creditor having knowledge of the dissolution and the person or partnership continuing the business." The statute provides no guidance on what factors support an implied agreement. At least one case suggests, however, that a creditor risks implied discharge by acting as if the dissociated partner is no longer liable.

79. For a discussion of these duties, see Section 9.7.
80. For a more detailed discussion of this point, see Section 9.7.5.

CASE IN POINT

Case in Point—*Gjovik v. Strope*

A farmer borrowed money from a finance company and secured the debt by giving the finance company a mortgage on some farmland and a security interest in some farm equipment. The farmer subsequently sold the land and equipment (subject to the financing company's interests) to a partnership on credit. One of the partners then withdrew from the partnership, and the other continued the business. The dissociated partner assigned all his interests in the partnership to the continuing partner. From these facts the court implied an agreement by the continuing partner to assume the obligations of the dissociated partner. The court found an implied agreement by the farmer to release the dissociated partner based on the following facts: (i) the farmer learned that the dissociated partner had withdrawn from the partnership business; (ii) the continuing partner signed an agreement to assume the farmer's obligations to the finance company, but the dissociated partner did not, and apparently the farmer did not insist on the dissociated partner's signature; and (iii) when the continuing partner was unable to make a payment on the debt to the finance company, the continuing partner and the farmer agreed to sell off some farm equipment to reduce that debt. The dissociated partner was not consulted.[81] ◀◀◀

b. Discharge by Material Alteration in the Obligation

Under UPA (1914) §36(3), a creditor may inadvertently discharge UPA (1914) partners from their pre-dissolution liabilities. Discharge occurs if: (i) someone has agreed to assume the obligations of the dissolved partnership; (ii) the creditor knows of the agreement; and (iii) the creditor consents to a material change in the obligation.

Most of the cases under UPA (1914) §36(3) concern the meaning of "material alteration." Many of those cases use analogies from surety law.[82] Changes found to be material under UPA (1914) §36(3) include: extension of time to pay a debt; renewal of a promissory note; and agreement to surrender leased premises in advance of the surrender date stated in the original lease. Changes found not to be material include assignment to the creditor of accounts receivable as additional security for the debt (no change in the nature of the obligation, no possible prejudice to dissociated partner); and failure of creditor to immediately sue business to collect on overdue account (no consented-to change in the obligation).

---

81. *Gjovik v. Strope*, 401 N.W.2d 664 (Minn. 1987).

82. Absent a contrary agreement, a creditor releases a surety if the creditor and principal agree to a material change in the underlying obligation.

§11.5.3 Settling Accounts Among Partners When the Business Is Liquidated

When the business is being liquidated, settling accounts among the partners is a crucial part of winding up. An agreement among the partners can govern this *inter se* matter.

Example

Burt and Dorothy form a partnership to raise and race thoroughbred horses. The partnership has a term of five years. Burt provides all the money to buy the horses, and Dorothy contributes her considerable expertise as a trainer. Profits are split 60 percent to Dorothy, 40 percent to Burt. The partnership agreement states in part:

> **Distribution of assets following dissolution** Upon dissolution, the partnership shall pay or secure the discharge of all liabilities that it owes. Any remaining partnership property—other than horses—shall be sold and the net proceeds divided according to the partners' respective profit shares. All horses shall become the property of Burt. ◄◄◄

In the absence of an agreement, UPA (1914) §§38, 40, and 42 supply the default rules. Which particular rules apply depends on whether the business is being continued or liquidated and on whether the dissolution was wrongful or rightful.

a. Liquidation Following Rightful Dissolution

When the partnership business is to be liquidated following a rightful dissolution,[83] the UPA (1914) default rules provide a theoretically simple approach for distributing the assets of the partnership and settling accounts among the partners. Property that a partner has merely loaned or rented to the partnership returns to the partner as the partnership business comes to an end.[84] The assets that belong to the partnership are marshaled and liquidated.[85] From those assets:

- outside creditors are paid off;
- inside creditors (i.e., partners who have made loans or leased property) are paid off;

83. UPA (1914) refers to dissolution "not in contravention of the partnership agreement." UPA (1914) §38(1). The phrase "rightful dissolution" is convenient shorthand.
84. See Sections 8.5.2–8.5.4 (distinguishing property contributed to the partnership from property merely loaned, leased, or furnished).
85. UPA (1914) §38(1).

- partners are repaid their capital (i.e., the value of any property they have contributed to the partnership, plus any profits previously allocated to the partners, less any distributions previously made); and
- any remaining funds are divided, as profit, according to each partner's ordinary profit percentages and are distributed accordingly.[86]

If the partnership has insufficient funds to pay its creditors and repay capital contributions, then the partners must pay into the partnership according to their respective obligations to share losses.[87]

UPA (1914) expressly provides for the settling of accounts among partners in cash.[88] Division of assets in kind raises significant problems of valuation and so is disfavored. Partners may of course agree to settle accounts with each other through an in-kind asset distribution, but absent such an agreement, in-kind distribution is permissible only to avoid great unfairness or extraordinary waste.

Example

A partnership grew Christmas trees on land rented from one of the partners. When the partnership dissolved, growing trees not ready for harvest were a substantial partnership asset. Liquidation was impractical; to order the trees harvested and sold would have wasted the asset. Instead the court divided the growing trees between the partners. ◀ ◀ ◀

b. The Function of Partners' Capital Accounts in Dissolution

As part of the settling-up process, partners are paid the amounts owed "in respect of capital."[89] The bookkeeping devices that track the amount the partnership owes each partner "in respect of capital . . . " are called "capital accounts."[90] Property contributed to the partnership increases the contributing partner's capital account by an amount equal to the fair market value of the asset as of the time of contribution, as do profits allocated to partners from ongoing activities.[91] Distributions made to partners decrease their

---

86. §40(b). The rule that sets priorities among creditors has little practical significance. For the rule to be significant, the partnership must lack sufficient funds to pay all its creditors. In that event, however, the partnership would be insolvent, and, if the partnership files (or three of its creditors cause it to file) for bankruptcy, federal bankruptcy law would preempt the UPA (1914) rule on creditor priority.
87. UPA (1914) §§40(a)(II) and 40(d).
88. UPA (1914) §38(1).
89. UPA (1914) §40(b)(III).
90. Federal tax law contains intricate and recondite rules on partnership tax accounting, as a result of which some partnerships must use a dual approach to capital accounts. The Example in the text reflects a non-tax approach.
91. UPA (1914) §18 (a) provides the default rule on profit allocation. See Section 8.3.

respective capital accounts, as do losses allocated to partners from ongoing activities.[92] Post-contribution depreciation or appreciation of a contributed asset does not affect the contributing partner's capital account. The contribution severs the contributor's direct connection to the asset; subsequent vicissitudes in the asset's value are "for the partnership's account" (i.e., for the partnership's benefit or detriment).[93]

When the partnership dissolves and the partners settle accounts, each partner receives as a return of capital the amount in his, her, or its capital account. If the partnership has neither made nor lost money, has experienced neither depreciation nor appreciation in its assets, and has generated no saleable goodwill, then the sum of the capital accounts at dissolution will equal the net worth of the firm.

Such equality is by no means the norm, however. If, for example, the firm's assets have appreciated in value, then the net worth of the firm will exceed the sum of the partners' capital accounts. Any surplus remaining after paying creditors and discharging the capital accounts is profit—to be distributed according to the partners' respective profit shares.

In contrast, if the firm has lost money or its assets have depreciated, then at dissolution the sum of the capital accounts will exceed the firm's net worth. The loss or depreciation will have affected the firm's assets, but not the separate claims of the partners to be repaid the value of their respective contributions. The partners will have to contribute additional funds to the partnership, either to permit a full return of capital or at least to adjust the capital accounts so that losses are shared appropriately.[94]

The following Example, modeled in simplified form on *Langness v. "O" Street Carpet Shop, Inc.*,[95] illustrates how "capital accounts"[96] function under UPA (1914) §§38(1) and 40 to determine each partner's return when the partnership business is liquidated following rightful dissolution.

Example

Three individuals, *A*, *B*, and *C*, form a partnership governed by UPA (1914). They agree to share profits equally. *A* contributes $14,000. *B* contributes the vendee's interest in a real estate purchase agreement. At the time, the fair market value of the real estate is $65,000. The purchase agreement sets a price of $56,000, so the value of the contribution is $9,000. *C* makes no capital

92. UPA (1914) §18 (a) provides the default rule on loss allocation. See Section 8.3.1.
93. See Section 8.5.1.
94. UPA (1914) §40(d). Absent a contrary agreement, partners share losses in the same proportion as they share profits—i.e., equally. UPA (1914) §18(a). See Section 8.3.1.
95. *Langness v. "O" Street Carpet Shop, Inc.*, 353 N.W.2d 709 (Neb. 1984).
96. "Capital account" is a term of art in both tax accounting and ordinary (i.e., non-tax) accounting.

contribution, providing instead legal services in the drafting of the partnership agreement. At that point the capital accounts would stand as follows:

A	$14,000
B	9,000
C	0

(C's providing of legal services qualifies C for a share of the profits, but not for any credit in C's capital account.)[97]

An Interim Return of Capital: Soon after, by agreement, B receives $8,000 as a return of capital. The capital accounts would then stand at:

A	$14,000
B	1,000
C	0

Interim Capital Contributions: The partnership later purchases the property subject to the purchase agreement, and B and C each contribute $2,000 in cash to be used toward the down payment. The capital accounts would then stand at:

A	$14,000
B	3,000
C	2,000

Interim Losses: The next year the partnership suffers a $6,000 operating loss. The partners have no explicit agreement on loss sharing, so under UPA (1914) §18(a) they share losses "according to [their respective] share in the profits." The capital accounts would then stand at:

A	$12,000
B	1,000
C	0

Dissolution and Settling Up Among the Partners: Later the partnership sells the real estate, making a profit of $46,000 on the sale. The partnership then dissolves,

97. UPA (1914) §18(f). See Section 8.5.

owing $3,000 to outside creditors. The sale profits are the partnership's only asset. Under UPA (1914) §40(b)(I), the "first" $3,000 of the $46,000 goes to pay the creditors. Then, under UPA (1914) §40(b)(III), *A* and *B* receive the value of their respective capital accounts. The three partners then divide the remaining $30,000 equally, according to their original agreement on sharing profits.

Assets of the partnership	$46,000
Less payment to creditors; per §40(b)(I)	(3,000)
Available prior to return of capital	43,000
Less payout of A's capital account; per §40(b)(III)	(12,000)
Less payout of B's capital account; per §40(b)(III)	(1,000)[96] The capital claims of A and B have equal priority.
Remaining for distribution as profits; per §40(b)(IV)	30,000

Per agreement, each partner receives one-third ($10,000) of the profits. Total payout per partner:

A	$22,000 (capital account of $12,000, plus profits of $10,000)
B	11,000 (capital account of $1,000, plus profits of $10,000)
C	10,000 (no capital to return; profits of $10,000) ◄◄◄

c. Settling Accounts Following Wrongful Dissolution

If the business is being liquidated following a wrongful dissolution, the settling of accounts among the partners is the same as if the dissolution were rightful—except that the wrongfully dissolving partner's share may be decreased by the amount of damages due the other partners "for breach of the [partnership] agreement."[98]

98. UPA (1914) §§38(2)(c)(I) and (2)(a)(II). In addition, the wrongful dissolver has no right to wind up the partnership. UPA (1914) §37. See Section 11.3.1.

§11.5.4 Settling Accounts Among Partners When the Business Is Continued: Rightful Dissolution

a. Settling Accounts by Express Agreement

For the partnership business to continue after dissolution, there must be some agreement among the partners. The agreement can be made before or after dissolution, and, if the dissolution is wrongful, need not include the wrongful dissolver. But some agreement there must be; the default mode is liquidation.[99]

The agreement that provides for the continuation of the business will normally govern how the partners will settle their accounts. Indeed, any business continuation agreement should at minimum address the following five topics:

1. the transfer of the rights and obligations of the dissolved partnership to the successor partnership;
2. the conversion of the continuing partners' rights in the dissolved partnership to rights in the successor partnership;
3. the compensation of the dissociated partner for that partner's rights in the dissolved partnership;
4. the indemnification or (if possible) the release of the dissociated partner for debts of the dissolved partnership; and
5. the indemnification of the dissociated partner for debts of the successor partnership.

b. The Possibility of a Tacit Agreement to Continue the Business

If a partner rightfully dissociates from a partnership and fails to seek liquidation of the partnership business, a court may decide that the partner tacitly consented to a continuation of the business. One case found implied consent even though, throughout the period of supposed acquiescence, the dissociated partner sought to have the continuing partners buy out his interest.

Such a result is not preordained, however. For example, in another case a different court rejected the tacit consent argument even though liquidation was delayed for years following dissolution. During the delay a lawsuit was pending, challenging the partnership's ownership of important assets. The court treated the delay as a long, drawn-out wind up.

99. See Section 11.4.2 (partners' rights to compel liquidation).

c. Compensating the Dissociated Partner

A finding of tacit agreement does stave off liquidation but leaves open the question of how to compensate the dissociated partner (among other issues).[100] The same issue exists when all the partners expressly agree to continue the business but neglect the compensation issue.[101]

For these situations, UPA (1914) §42 provides a default rule, essentially treating the value of the dissociated partner's interest in the dissolved partnership as a loan to the successor partnership. Under UPA (1914) §42:

a. the value of the dissociated partner's interest in the dissolved partnership is calculated as of the date of dissolution; and

b. as compensation for the business's use of that value from the date of dissolution to the date the successor partnership cashes out the dissociated partner, the dissociated partner receives (at the dissociated partner's election) either:

i. interest on that value; or

ii. a share of the profits attributable to the successor partnership's "use of [the dissociated partner's] right in the property of the dissolved partnership."

The language of UPAUPA (1914) §42 leaves open at least seven important questions. The relevant case law is scarce, and much of the reasoning is muddy. Following are the seven troubling questions and the author's view of the answers.

1. How Long May the Successor Partnership Wait to Cash Out the Dissociated Partner?

In some circumstances, the dissociated and continuing partners may expressly or impliedly agree on a payout deadline. If not, the law must give the successor partnership some breathing room. An obligation to immediately cash out the dissociated partner could force the continuing partners to liquidate the business in order to come up with the necessary cash.[102]

---

100. In theory, a finding of tacit agreement also leaves open the question of what interests the continuing partners will have in the successor partnership. In practice, however, the conduct of the continuing partners often reflects an understanding on that point. If not, it seems reasonable to assume that the continuing partners intend their respective interests to be the same in the successor partnership as they were in the old.

101. The same issue also exists when the business of a wrongfully dissolved partnership is continued without the agreement of the wrongful dissolver. See Section 11.5.5.

102. The cases do not directly address this question, because they do not concern disputes about the timing of the cash-out. Instead, they involve disputes relating to the amount of the payment due or whether any payment was due at all.

2. Must the Successor Partnership Make Interim Payments to the Dissociated Partner Pending the Cash-Out?

The cases do not contemplate interim payments, because they all involve actions for an accounting.[103] In each of these actions, the continuing partners had disputed the cash-out amount and had made no interim payments. Nothing in the cases prejudices the continuing partners for failing to make interim payments. Nor does anything in the law prevent the partners from agreeing on interim payments.

3. When Does the Dissociated Partner Elect Between the Interest Option and the Profit-Sharing Option?

The dissociated partner may wait until an accounting reveals both the value of the partnership at dissolution and the value of the dissociated partner's interest. If the dissociated partner has to bring an accounting action to obtain the cash-out, then the dissociated partner can delay the election until the partner can determine which option will be the more lucrative. The dissociated partner's right to delay election creates an incentive for the continuing partners to cash out the dissociated partner as soon as possible.

4. May the Dissociated Partner Change the Election?

A representative of a deceased partner's estate may lack the authority to make a binding election before an accounting has revealed the value of the partnership and the value of the deceased partner's interest. Otherwise, it appears that a dissociated partner is stuck with the election once made. It does not make sense for a dissociated partner to make an election prior to cash-out unless the continuing business is making interim payments.

5. How Is the Interest Rate Determined?

There is very little authority on this point. Among the arguable positions: the legal rate for interest on judgments, the legal rate for prejudgment interest, and the amount the successor partnership would have to pay to borrow funds in an arm's-length transaction.

6. How Is the Profit Share Calculated?

The case law and commentaries indicate that the profit share equals the ratio of the value of the dissociated partner's interest in the partnership at

103. For an explanation of the action for an accounting, see Section 9.9.

dissolution to the value of the entire partnership at dissolution, regardless of the profit share enjoyed by the dissociated partner prior to dissolution.

Example

When Sophie dissolves her used bookstore partnership with Charlotte and Paul, the partnership's net worth is $10,000 and Sophie's capital account is at $5,000. Sophie agrees that the business will be continued without liquidation, but no agreement is made on compensating Sophie for her interest. If Sophie chooses the profit-sharing option, her share of the successor partnership's profits will be 50 percent ($5,000/$10,000), even though in the dissolved partnership the partners shared profits equally. ◄◄◄

7. How Long May the Business Continue Before Fully Cashing Out the Dissociated Partner?

Under the aegis of UPA (1914) §42, the successor partnership may continue the business indefinitely, subject, of course, to the power of the members of the successor partnership to dissolve that partnership. If the continuing partners do not pay the dissociated partner the cash-out amount (plus interest or profit), then the dissociated partner can sue to collect the amount due. The dissociated partner can proceed against both the partners of the dissolved partnership and against the successor partnership and its members.[104] But the dissociated partner will proceed "as an ordinary creditor"[105] and will therefore have no special rights to compel liquidation of the business of the successor partnership.

§11.5.5 Settling Accounts Among Partners When the Business Is Continued: Wrongful Dissolution

a. The Default Buyout "Package" for the Wrongful Dissolver

Following a wrongful dissolution, the partnership business may be continued either: (i) by agreement of all of the partners (typically in place before the dissociation); or (ii) under UPA (1914) §38(2)(b), by the unanimous consent of the partners who did not wrongfully dissolve. In the former instance, the partners' agreement will likely set the payout rights of the wrongful dissolver. In the latter instance, UPA (1914)

104. See Section 11.4.5.
105. UPA (1914) §42.

§38(2) provides the wrongful dissolver a buyout package consisting of three elements:

- the right (at the option of the continuing partners) either to be cashed out immediately or to be cashed out later (with the delayed payment guaranteed);
- the right to be protected against personal liability for partnership debts; and
- if the cash-out payment is not immediate, the right to compensation on account of the delay.

b. Calculating the Cash-Out Amount

When the default package applies, UPA (1914) §38(2)(c)(II) requires that "the value of [the wrongful dissolver's] interest in the partnership" be ascertained. The calculation proceeds as if the dissolution were rightful,[106] with two important exceptions:

- "in ascertaining the value of the [wrongfully dissolving] partner's interest the value of the good-will of the business shall not be considered";[107] and
- the value of the wrongful dissolver's interest is to be decreased by "any damages caused to his co-partners by the [wrongful] dissolution."[108]

c. Timing and Securing the Payment

If the wrongful dissolver has a large stake in the partnership, requiring immediate payment of the cash-out amount might interfere with or even preclude the continuation of the business. UPA (1914) therefore allows the continuing partners an option. They can either pay the wrongful dissolver immediately, or they can delay payment until the end of the original term of the dissolved partnership.[109]

If the continuing partners delay payment, they must "secure the payment by bond approved by the court."[110] That is, they must obtain a guarantee from a bonding company stating that, if the successor partnership fails to pay the cash-out amount when due, the bonding company will make payment to the wrongful dissolver. The statute does not specify whether the

106. See Section 11.5.4.
107. UPA (1914) §38(2)(c)(II).
108. *Id.*
109. For a discussion of partnership agreements that transcend the at-will/term-undertaking dichotomy, see Section 11.2.1(c).
110. UPA (1914) §38(2)(b).

bond must be for the full amount of the obligation and does not indicate whether the bond can require the wrongful dissolver to first try to collect from the members of the successor partnership. Presumably the court granting approval to a proposed bond would consider these matters.

Except for the bond, a wrongful dissolver awaiting payment has the status of "an ordinary creditor."[111] UPA §42 applies, and the wrongful dissolver appears to have no greater rights to interim payments than does any rightfully dissociated partner who becomes subject to that provision.[112]

d. Protecting the Wrongful Dissolver from Partnership Debts

UPA (1914) §38(2)(b) plainly requires that the continuing partners "indemnify [the wrongful dissolver] against all . . . future partnership liabilities." The statute's approach to current liabilities is less clear. UPA (1914) §38(2)(b) requires indemnification "against all present . . . partnership liabilities," but UPA (1914) §38(2)(c)(II) entitles the wrongful dissolver "to be released from all existing liabilities of the partnership." Neither the statute nor its official comments explain the inconsistent language. The major commentators note but do not resolve the problem.

From the perspective of the wrongful dissolver, the release approach is certainly superior. The indemnity does nothing to the underlying obligation; the obligee is still entitled to pursue the wrongful dissolver. The indemnity is therefore only as good as the solvency of the indemnitor.

From the perspective of the continuing partners, the release approach may be impractical. Generally, obligees are unwilling to release partners without receiving full payment or perhaps an increase in interest rates. After all, why should the obligee give up something—the right to pursue the wrongful dissolver—without getting something in return?

e. Rationale for Protecting the Wrongful Dissolver from Liability

It makes sense for the continuing partners to protect the wrongful dissolver against future partnership liabilities, because the wrongful dissolver will have no part in the creation of those liabilities. At most, if the cash-out payment is delayed, the wrongful dissolver will relate to the continuing business as an ordinary creditor.

The rationale for protecting the wrongful dissolver against existing liabilities is that the valuation of the dissolver's stake in the partnership takes into account those liabilities.

---

111. UPA (1914) §42.

112. See Section 11.5.4 (UPA (1914) §42 governs when rightfully dissociated partner agrees to have the partnership business continue without liquidation, but overlooks the timing issue).

Example

George, Bernard, and Shaw form a partnership with a term of five years to sell widgets. They agree to share profits equally. After three years George wrongfully dissolves the partnership. Bernard and Shaw decide to continue the business under UPA (1914) §38(2).

The value of George's interest (the cash-out amount) must therefore be ascertained. The partnership's assets, other than goodwill,[113] are as follows:

Assets	
Cash	$50,000
Accounts receivable	35,000
Orders in, but not yet billed	5,000
TOTAL	$90,000
Liabilities	
Loan due to the bank	$25,000
Accounts payable	5,000
TOTAL	$30,000

VALUE OF PARTNERSHIP: $90,000 − $30,000 = $60,000 ◄◄◄

To keep the analysis as simple as possible, assume that none of the partners has anything in his or her capital account.[114] The $60,000 value is therefore all surplus (i.e., as yet undistributed profit) to be divided equally per the original partnership agreement. George's share is $20,000. This figure is reached by *subtracting liabilities from assets* and then dividing by 3. In effect, the $20,000 figure assumes that the partnership will pay its $30,000 in liabilities, and George's cash-out amount has been decreased by his share of those liabilities. In essence, therefore, George has already "paid" his share. He should be protected against having to pay again.

§11.6 AVOIDING UPA DISSOLUTION BY AGREEMENT (A SPECIOUS IDEA)

According to the language of UPA (1914), certain events automatically and inevitably cause dissolution. Under UPA (1914) §31(4), for example,

113. Goodwill is excluded from the calculation. UPA (1914) §38(2)(c)(II). See Section 11.5.5(b).
114. For an explanation of capital accounts, see Section 11.5.3.

"Dissolution is caused . . . by the death of any partner." Under UPA (1914) §31(1)(d), the expulsion of a partner under a power conferred by the partnership agreement likewise causes dissolution. And, most fundamentally, the express will of any partner causes dissolution even when done in breach of the partnership agreement.[115]

Unlike many other provisions of UPAUPA (1914), these automatic dissolution provisions are not default rules—that is, they are not by their terms subject to contrary agreement among the partners. Nonetheless, some partnership agreements seek to avoid disruption to the partnership business by ignoring the statutory language. Typically, such agreements provide that the dissociation of a partner does not cause dissolution.

Example

The law firm of Tinkers, Evers, and Chance has a partnership agreement that provides, in part: "Neither the death, retirement, resignation, or withdrawal of any partner shall dissolve this partnership, but the partnership will buy out the dissociated partner's interest in the partnership as provided in paragraph Z of this agreement." ◀◀◀

Although there are cases upholding these agreements in disputes among the partners, such agreements are dangerous. The conflict between the language of the agreement and the language of the statute invites litigation.

Moreover, ignoring UPA (1914)'s approach to dissolution subjects the dissociated partner to an added risk of personal liability if the partnership business continues. UPA (1914) provides a panoply of protections for the dissociated partner, but all those protections revolve around the concept of dissolution:

1. UPA (1914) §§33 and 34 end the actual authority (though not the power) of the continuing partners to bind the dissolved partnership (and thereby the dissociated partner) on obligations related to new business.[116]
2. UPA (1914) §35 limits the power of the continuing partners to bind the dissolved partnership (and thereby the dissociated partner).[117]
3. UPA (1914) §36 provides, under certain circumstances, for the dissociated partner to be discharged from personal liability for debts of the dissolved partnership.[118]

115. See Section 11.2.1.
116. See Section 11.3.1.
117. See Section 11.3.2.
118. See Section 11.5.2.

4. UPA (1914) §15 imposes personal liability on the dissociated partner only for the debts of the dissolved partnership and not for the debts of any successor partnership.[119]

If dissolution does not occur, these protections are inapposite.

The answer for partners trying to avoid business disruption is to provide carefully for dissolution rather than attempt to preclude it. A well-drafted partnership agreement can ensure continuity by providing for the partnership business to be continued even as the partnership itself is wound up and terminated.[120]

§11.7 JUDICIAL DISSOLUTION

UPA (1914) §32 provides several bases for a court to "decree a dissolution." The most interesting are UPA (1914) §§31(1)(d) and (e) and 31(2). Section 32(1)(d) makes dissolution by decree of court available on "application by or for a partner" when another "partner willfully or persistently commits a breach of the partnership agreement, or otherwise so conducts himself in matters relating to the partnership business that it is not reasonably practicable to carry on the business in partnership with him." Section 32(1)(e) permits a partner to apply for judicial dissolution when "[t]he business of the partnership can only be carried on at a loss."

Section 31(2) permits a "purchaser of a partner's interest" (i.e., an assignee or a person who has purchased through a foreclosure of a charging order) to petition for dissolution "(a) [a]fter the termination of the specified term or particular undertaking, [and] (b) [a]t any time if the partnership was a partnership at will when the interest was assigned or when the charging order was issued." The rationale seems to be that a third party's right to a liquidating distribution "vests" when the third party acquires the interest (or, in the case of a charging order, acquires the equivalent of a lien on the interest).[121]

---

119. See Section 7.3 (partner's personal liability results from status as a partner in the partnership).

120. See Section 11.4.3.

121. This rationale corresponds to contract law principles pertaining to assignment. See, e.g., Restatement (Second) of Contracts §338(1) ("Discharge of an Obligor After Assignment . . . [N]otwithstanding an assignment, the assignor retains his power to discharge or modify the duty of the obligor to the extent that the obligor performs or otherwise gives value until but not after the obligor receives notification that the right has been assigned and that performance is to be rendered to the assignee").

§11.8 UPA (1997)—FOUNDATIONAL NOTIONS

§11.8.1 Four Foundational Concepts

Although UPA (1997)'s provisions on partner dissociation and partnership dissolution are as elaborate as those in UPA (1914), the approach of UPA (1997) is simpler to follow because it tilts *toward* continuity and away from dissolution. UPA (1997)'s approach rests on four major concepts:

- The dissociation of a UPA (1997) partner does *not* necessarily cause the dissolution of the partnership.
- UPA (1997) contains a "switching provision"[122]—if a partner's dissociation results in dissolution, the "switch" activates Article 8 (dissolution and winding up); if not, the "switch" activates Article 7 (buyout of dissociated partner and continuation of the partnership).
- UPA (1997) provides for statements of dissociation and dissolution, the public filing of which significantly affects power-to-bind and personal liability issues.
- Almost all of UPA (1997)'s provisions on dissociation and dissolution are subject to change by the partnership agreement, making it possible for a partnership subject to UPA (1997) to be almost as indissoluble as a limited liability company or corporation.

§11.8.2 Dissociation Described

a. Events Causing Dissociation

Under UPA (1997), partner dissociation is a pivotal term and carries forward a UPA (1914) concept—namely, that "any partner ceasing to be associated in the carrying on as distinguished from the winding up of the [partnership's] business" is an event significant both to the partner and the partnership.[123] UPA (1997) does not directly define "dissociation," but section 601 lists 10 events "upon the occurrence" of which a "partner is dissociated from a partnership." The 10 events divide roughly into four categories:[124]

---

122. UPA (1997) §603, comment 1 (describing Section 603(a)).

123. UPA (1914) §29. The significance to the partnership is that dissociation can result in dissolution. See Section 11.9.3. The connection between dissociation and dissolution reflects the aggregate view of partnership. See Sections 7.2.7 and 13.1.4 (discussing the "continuity of life" factor under the now-defunct Kintner Regulations on tax classification).

124. If subcategories are counted separately, there are 20 separate circumstances.

I. "partnership's having notice of the partner's express will to withdraw as a partner or on a later date specified by the partner";[125]

II. an event specified in the partnership agreement as causing dissociation;[126]

III. expulsion:
   A. as provided in the partnership agreement;[127]
   B. by unanimous vote of the other partners; if
      1. it is unlawful to carry on the business with the to-be-expelled partner;[128]
      2. the partner being expelled no longer has any economic stake in the business, because "there has been a transfer of all or substantially all of that partner's transferable interest in the partnership";[129] or
      3. the partner being expelled is a corporation or partnership which has lost its right to take on new business;[130]
   C. by court order, if the partner being expelled has engaged in seriously wrongful conduct;[131]

IV. the partner's ability to participate in the partnership affairs comes to an end, or the partner's economic stake in the partnership comes to an end,[132] including:
   A. the partner becoming a debtor in bankruptcy, or taking other, non-bankruptcy actions which indicate insolvency;[133]
   B. if the partner is an individual, the individual's ability to participate in partnership affairs coming to an end, either by:
      1. death; or
      2. mental incompetency, as indicated either by:
         a. "the appointment of a guardian or general conservator"; or

125. UPA (1997) §601(1). "Notice" is a defined term. See UPA (1997) §102(b), discussed in Section 10.7.1.
126. UPA (1997) §601(2).
127. UPA (1997) §601(3). "The expulsion can be with or without cause. As under existing law [i.e., UPA], the obligation of good faith under Section 404(d) does not require prior notice, specification of cause, or an opportunity to be heard." UPA (1997) §601, comment 4.
128. UPA (1997) §601(4)(i).
129. UPA (1997) §601(4)(ii). Section 503(a)(2) is not to the contrary. It provides that the transfer of a partner's transferable interest "does not *by itself* cause the partner's dissociation." (Emphasis added.)
130. UPA (1997) §601(4)(iii) and (iv).
131. UPA (1997) §601(5).
132. UPA (1997) §601(6)–(10). UPA (1997) uses this category in its definition of wrongful dissociation, UPA (1997) §602(b)(2)(i) (discussed *infra*), and in its provision on partnership dissolution, UPA (1997) §801(2)(i), discussed in section 11.11.
133. UPA (1997) §601(6).

b. "a judicial determination that the partner has otherwise become incapable of performing the partner's duties under the partnership agreement";[134]

3. if the partner is a trust or estate, its economic stake in the partnership coming to an end by the distribution (typically to the beneficiaries) of the partner's "entire transferable interest in the partnership";[135]
4. "termination of a partner who is not an individual, partnership, corporation, trust, or estate."[136]

Example

Dardale Company is a general partnership subject to UPA (1997) and has three partners: Amos, Eli, and Alan. The partnership is at-will, and the partnership agreement does not alter UPA (1997)'s provisions on dissociation. Following an intense meeting of the partners, Amos is walking home with Eli and says, "I'm tired of all this nonsense. I'm done. I quit." At that moment, Amos is dissociated. Eli has notice of Amos's "express will" (UPA (1997) §102(b)(1) defining "notice" to include knowledge), and notice to a partner is notice to the partnership. UPA (1997) §102(f).[137] Therefore, "the partnership [has] notice of [Amos's] express will to withdraw as a partner." ◄◄◄

Example

Same situation, except that Dardale Company is a partnership formed for a particular term or undertaking. Amos is dissociated, although the dissociation may be wrongful (as explained below). ◄◄◄

Example

Same situation, except that instead of quitting, Amos sells his entire transferable interest to Paul. Amos is not dissociated. However, if Alan and Eli vote to expel Amos, he will be expelled and thereby dissociated. UPA (1997) §601(4)(ii). Paul does not have a vote, because he is not a partner. UPA (1997) §§401(i) (person becomes a partner only with the consent of all the partners)[138] and 503(a)(3) (transferee has no rights in management).[139] ◄◄◄

---

134. UPA (1997) §601(7).
135. UPA (1997) §601(8) and (9).
136. UPA (1997) §601(10). Note that UPA (1997) treats partnerships and corporations differently than estates, trusts, and other nonindividual legal persons.
137. See Section 10.7.
138. See Section 8.5.
139. See Section 8.5.

b. Consequences of Dissociation — Whether or Not Dissolution Results Is Generally Dependent on Whether the Dissociation Is Wrongful or Rightful

Many of the consequences of partner dissociation depend on whether the dissociation is wrongful or rightful and on whether the dissociation results in dissolution of the partnership.[140]

c. Rightful Versus Wrongful Dissociation

UPA (1997) §602(b) expressly defines and carefully delimits "wrongful" dissociation:

A partner's dissociation is wrongful only if:

(1) it is in breach of an express provision of the partnership agreement; or

(2) in the case of a partnership for a definite term or particular undertaking, before the expiration of the term or the completion of the undertaking:

(i) the partner withdraws by express will, unless the withdrawal follows within 90 days after another partner's dissociation by death or otherwise under section 601(6) through (10) [dissociation because either the partner's ability to participate in the partnership affairs has come to an end, or the partner's economic stake in the partnership has come to an end] or wrongful dissociation under this subsection;

(ii) the partner is expelled by judicial determination under section 601(5);

(iii) the partner is dissociated by becoming a debtor in bankruptcy; or

(iv) in the case of a partner who is not an individual, trust other than a business trust, or estate, the partner is expelled or otherwise dissociated because it willfully dissolved or terminated.

Example

Dardale Company is a general partnership subject to UPA (1997) and has four partners: Amos, Eli, Alan, and Paul. The partnership is for a term of 10 years, and the partnership agreement does not alter UPA (1997)'s provisions on dissociation. Following an intense meeting of the partners, Amos

140. However, "the partner's duty of loyalty [not to compete with the partnership before dissolution] terminates" regardless of whether the dissociation was wrongful and regardless of whether dissolution has resulted. UPA (1997) §603(b)(2).

is walking home with Eli and says, "I'm tired of all this nonsense. I'm done. I quit." Amos's dissociation is wrongful, because it occurs "by express will" of a partner "before the expiration of the term" of the partnership. UPA (1997) §602(b)(2)(i). ◀◀◀

Example

As soon as Alan learns that Amos has quit, Alan announces that he is also quitting. Like Amos's dissociation, Alan's dissociation comes before the expiration of the partnership's term. However, Alan's dissociation is not wrongful, because it comes "within 90 days after another partner's . . . wrongful dissociation." UPA (1997) §602(2)(b)(i). ◀◀◀

UPA (1997) §602(b) effectively rejects cases like *Page* and *Vangel*.[141] Under UPA (1997), a dissociation is not wrongful merely because it constitutes a breach of fiduciary duty or the obligation of good faith and fair dealing. Such a breach may be separately actionable, but the consequences that attach to "wrongful dissociation" do not apply.

d. Consequences of Wrongful Dissociation

There are several consequences when a partner wrongfully dissociates:

- the wrongfully dissociated partner "is liable to the partnership and to the other partners for damages caused by the dissociation";[142]
- in a partnership for a term or undertaking, the dissociation creates the possibility of partnership dissolution, which occurs if "within 90 days after a partner's . . . wrongful dissociation . . . the express will of at least half of the remaining partners [is] to wind up the partnership business";[143]
- if the partnership continues (i.e., does not dissolve), the wrongfully dissociated partner is not entitled to any payout until the end of the original term "unless the partner establishes to the satisfaction of the court that earlier payment will not cause undue hardship to the business of the partnership";[144] and
- if the dissociation results in dissolution of the partnership, the wrongfully dissociated has no right to participate in winding up.[145]

141. See Section 11.7.1.
142. UPA (1997) §602(c).
143. UPA (1997) §801(2)(i).
144. UPA (1997) §701(h), discussed in Section 11.9.5.
145. UPA (1997) §803(a), discussed in Section 11.11.1.

Example

Amos's premature and wrongful departure from the Dardale Company causes the partnership to have to hire an employee to provide the technical expertise that Amos had been providing. Dardale's cost for this employee exceeds what Amos was receiving as a partner as remuneration for that work. The extra expense puts the partnership into a "cash poor" situation. Amos is liable in damages to the partnership to the extent of the extra expense.[146] Moreover, Amos is not entitled to any payout until the end of the original term.[147] ◄◄◄

Case in Point — *Saint Alphonsus Diversified Care, Inc. v. MRI Associates, LLP*

Various entities formed a partnership for the purpose of acquiring and providing services relating to diagnostic equipment.[148] Eventually, one partner notified the other partners that it intended to dissociate and become a partner of another business. The dissociating partner filed suit seeking a determination of the value of its interest in the partnership. The Supreme Court vacated the trial court judgment and remanded, because the trial court had found as a matter of law that Plaintiff wrongfully dissociated from the partnership. The Supreme Court determined that the provision in the partnership agreement, allegedly breached by the dissociating partner, was "not an express provision limiting the right to dissociate rightfully."[149] ◄◄◄

e. Power of Partnership Agreement over Dissociation

With only two exceptions, UPA (1997) §601 is a default rule. The partnership agreement can change or omit each of the listed causes of dissociation, except that the partnership may not eliminate a partner's power to dissociate[150] nor vary the right of a court to expel a partner.[151] As a result,

---

146. UPA (1997) §602, comment 3: "The partnership might also incur substantial expenses resulting from a partner's premature withdrawal from a term partnership, such as replacing the partner's expertise or obtaining new financing."
147. UPA (1997) §701(h). If Amos has not previously paid the partnership for the damage caused by his wrongful association, the damage amount will be offset against his payout. UPA (1997) §701(c).
148. The partnership was a limited liability partnership (LLP), but that fact is irrelevant to the issues considered here. For a discussion of LLPs, see Section 17.2.
149. *Saint Alphonsus Diversified Care, Inc. v. MRI Associates, LLP*, 224 P.3d 1068, 1078 (Idaho 2009).
150. UPA (1997) §103(b)(6).
151. UPA (1997) §103(b)(7). Despite this restriction, under federal law, a partnership agreement can probably subject expulsion matters to arbitration. See also Uniform Limited Partnership Act (2001), §110, Comment to Subsection (b)(9) (discussing a comparable provision). ("Any other interpretation would put this Act at odds with federal law. See *Southland Corp. v. Keating*, 465 U.S. 1 (1984) (holding that the Federal Arbitration Act preempts state

the partnership agreement can dramatically restrict the circumstances under which a partner may rightfully exit a UPA (1997) partnership.

In addition, as explained in comment 2 to UPA (1997) §602, because UPA (1997) §602(b) is also "merely a default rule, the partnership agreement may eliminate or expand the dissociations that are wrongful or modify the effects of wrongful dissociation."

§11.8.3 The Nexus Between Partner Dissociation and Partnership Dissolution

Under UPA (1914), the dissociation of any partner inevitably causes dissolution.[152] The situation under UPA (1997) is dramatically different. First, the statutory provisions that connect partner dissociation and partnership dissolution are merely default rules. The partnership agreement can sever the nexus completely, or to any lesser extent the partner's desire. Second, even with the default rules in place, not every dissociation causes dissolution. Dissolution follows dissociation only in two circumstances:

- in an at-will partnership, the "express will" dissociation of a partner who has not been previously dissociated through some other cause;[153] and
- in a partnership for a term or undertaking:
  - "the express will of at least half of the remaining partners to wind up the partnership business," which is
  - manifested "within 90 days after a[nother] partner's dissociation by death or otherwise under section 601(6) through (10)[154] or wrongful dissociation under section 602(b)"[155]

EXAMPLE

Example

The Sachs Company is an at-will partnership subject to UPA (1997), and its partners are Todd, Teri, Mikki, and Samantha. After Todd transfers his entire transferable interest to Jeff, the remaining partners vote

statutes that seek to invalidate agreements to arbitrate) and *Allied-Bruce Terminix Cos., Inc. v. Dobson*, 513 U.S. 265 (1995) (same).")

152. See Section 11.2.1.

153. UPA (1997) §801(1).

154. These provisions refer to dissociation that occurs either because the partner's ability to participate in partnership affairs has come to an end, or the partner's economic stake in the partnership has come to an end.

155. UPA (1997) §801(2)(i).

unanimously to expel Todd. Todd has no right to cause dissolution of The Sachs Company. ◄ ◄ ◄

Example

The Sachs Company is a partnership subject to UPA (1997) and has a term of 10 years. The company's partners are Todd, Teri, Mikki, and Samantha. Todd quits the partnership, and two weeks later Teri, Mikki, and Samantha meet to decide what to do with the partnership. Mikki and Samantha vote to dissolve, and Teri votes to continue. The partnership is dissolved. ◄ ◄ ◄

§11.8.4 The "Switching Provision" — UPA (1997) §603(a)

Different consequences follow from a partner's dissociation, depending on whether the dissociation results in dissolution of the partnership. UPA (1997) §603(a) segregates those consequences from each other by functioning as a switching provision: "If a partner's dissociation results in a dissolution and winding up of the partnership business, [Article] 8 applies; otherwise, [Article] 7 applies."

Example

The Sachs Company is a partnership subject to UPA (1997) and has a term of 10 years. The Company's partners are Todd, Jeff, Teri, Mikki, and Samantha. Todd quits the partnership, but during the next 90 days the remaining partners do not vote to dissolve the partnership. A few months later, as permitted by UPA (1997) §801(2)(ii),[156] all the remaining partners unanimously vote to dissolve the partnership. Todd wishes to be involved in winding up the partnership, but he has no right to be. Even assuming Todd's dissociation was not wrongful, UPA (1997) §803(a) is the only provision permitting a dissociated partner to participate in winding up. That provision is not available to Todd, because it is part of [Article] 8 of UPA (1997). That Article applies to Todd only if *his* "dissociation results in a dissolution and winding up of the partnership business." ◄ ◄ ◄

---

156. This provision is discussed in Section 11.11.

§11.9 DISSOCIATION THAT DOES NOT CAUSE DISSOLUTION

§11.9.1 Overview

When a partner's dissociation does not result in partnership dissolution, the partnership business continues without interruption and the partnership itself continues as the same entity that existed before the dissociation. The dissociated partner has no further role in management[157] and no further fiduciary duties.[158] A dissociated partner does, however, have a lingering power to bind the partnership and, unless the partnership is an LLP,[159] a lingering exposure to personal liability for future partnership obligations.

Unless the partnership agreement provides otherwise, the partnership must cause the dissociated partner's interest to be bought out at a price determined under a statutory formula and must indemnify the dissociated partner against all partnership liabilities. Subject to an exception derived from UPA (1914), the dissociation does not discharge the dissociated partner from liability for partnership obligations.

§11.9.2 Statement of Dissociation

As part of its system of public filings,[160] UPA (1997) provides for the filing of a statement of dissociation, "stating the name of the partnership and that the partner is dissociated from the partnership."[161] Either the dissociated partner or the partnership may file the statement.[162] If filed by the partner, the statement must be executed by that partner.[163] If filed by the partnership, the statement "must be executed by at least two partners."[164]

If properly filed, a statement of dissociation functions as a statement limiting the authority of the dissociated partner[165] and, in addition, gives constructive notice of the partner's dissociation.[166] As with statements of authority under UPA (1997) §303, statements of dissociation are to be filed

157. UPA (1997) §603(b)(1).
158. UPA (1997) §603(b)(2) and (3).
159. See Chapter 17 for a discussion of LLPs (limited liability partnerships).
160. See Section 10.4.3 for another aspect of this system.
161. UPA (1997) §704(a).
162. *Id.*
163. UPA (1997) §105(c).
164. *Id.*
165. See Section 11.9.3.
166. See Sections 11.9.3 and 11.9.4 for the operative significance of this constructive notice.

"in the office of [the Secretary of State]."[167] For a statement of dissociation to have its full effect with regard to real property owned in the name of the partnership, "a certified copy of the filed statement . . . [must be] of record in the office for recording transfers of that real property."[168]

As soon as that recording is completed, the dissociated partner loses all power to transfer real property owned in the name of the partnership.[169] With regard to any other lingering power of the dissociated partner to bind the partnership and any lingering exposure the dissociated partner may have to personal liability for future partnership obligations, "a person not a partner is deemed to have notice of the dissociation 90 days after the statement of dissociation is filed" with the appropriate filing office.[170]

§11.9.3 Dissociated Partner's Lingering Power to Bind

When a partner dissociates and the partnership does not dissolve, the dissociated partner loses any "right to participate in the management and conduct of the partnership business."[171] However, consistent with notions of apparent authority, a dissociated partner's "apparently/ordinary" power to bind the partnership lingers after the dissociation and can continue for up to two years. Under UPA (1997) §702(a), a dissociated partner's act binds the partnership if:

- before the dissociation the act would have bound the partnership under RUPA §301; and
- at the time the other party enters into the transaction:
  —less than two years has passed since the dissociation;
  —the other party does not have notice of the dissociation and reasonably believes that the dissociated partner is still a partner;
  —fewer than 90 days have passed since the filing of a statement of dissociation;[172] and
  —if the transaction involves the transfer of real property owned in the name of the partnership, "a certified copy of [a] filed statement . . . [of dissociation is not] of record in the office for recording transfers of that real property."[173]

167. UPA (1997) §105(a). The brackets indicate the ULC's recognition that in some states the central filing office is not the Secretary of State.
168. UPA (1997) §303(e).
169. UPA (1997) §704(b).
170. UPA (1997) §704(c). For a detailed explanation of how this notice curtails the power to bind and personal liability, see Sections 11.9.3 and 11.9.4, respectively.
171. UPA (1997) §603(b)(1).
172. "For the purposes of [terminating a dissociated partner's lingering power to bind the partnership], a person not a partner is deemed to have notice of the dissociation 90 days after the statement of dissociation is filed." UPA (1997) §704(c).
173. UPA (1997) §303(e), referred to by UPA (1997) §702(a)(3).

Example

The Ofek-Noam Company ("the Company") is a general partnership subject to UPA (1997) that purchases land and subdivides it for sale to home builders. The Company has three partners—Suzanne, Eli, and Gili—and for years all three have acted for the partnership in selling land to home builders. The partnership has filed a statement of authority with the Secretary of State, indicating that each partner has the authority to transfer land owned in the name of the partnership. The partnership owns a large parcel of land in Dakota County, and a certified copy of the statement of authority has been recorded with the Dakota County Registrar of Deeds.

Acting pursuant to the partnership agreement, Gili and Suzanne expel Eli from the partnership. They then execute and file a statement of dissociation with the Secretary of State and record a certified copy of the statement with the Dakota County Registrar of Deeds. Two days later, Eli purports to enter into a contract to sell some of the Dakota land to a home building firm. The Company is not bound, even if the firm could establish that Eli's act "would have bound the partnership under section 301 before [the] dissociation" of Eli.[174] "A statement of dissociation is a limitation on the authority of a dissociated partner for the purposes of section 303 . . . (e)."[175] Therefore, UPA (1997) §702(a)(3) bars the firm's claim because the firm "is deemed to have knowledge [of the limitation of Eli's authority] under section 303(e)." ◄◄◄

Example

A month after his expulsion, Eli purports to buy a new car for the Ofek-Noam Company. The Company has regularly purchased company cars from this particular dealer, and Eli has often acted for the Company. The dealer has no idea that Eli has been expelled from the partnership. Eli purchases the car on credit, takes a $1,500 "manufacturer's incentive" in cash, and takes delivery of the car. The Company is bound. Before the dissociation, Eli's act would have bound the Company under UPA (1997) §301; the dealer had neither knowledge nor notice of Eli's dissociation; the transaction does not involve real property owned in the name of the Company; and fewer than 90 days have passed since the partnership filed the statement of dissociation. ◄◄◄

---

174. UPA (1997) §702(a).
175. UPA (1997) §704(b).

Example

Same facts as the immediately prior Example, except that the transaction occurs 91 days after the filing of the statement of dissociation. The partnership is not bound. ◀ ◀ ◀

A partner's lingering power to bind has nothing to do with actual authority. If the act of a dissociated partner binds the partnership, the "dissociated partner is liable to the partnership for any damage caused to the partnership arising from [the] obligation."[176] Like the lingering power itself, this liability is consistent with agency law principles.[177]

§11.9.4 Dissociated Partner's Liability for Partnership Obligations

a. Partnership Obligations Incurred Before Dissociation

In this context, UPA (1997) continues much of the UPA (1914) approach:

> A partner's dissociation does not of itself discharge the partner's liability for a partnership obligation incurred before dissociation. . . . A dissociated partner is released from liability for a partnership obligation if a partnership creditor, with notice of the partner's dissociation but without the partner's consent, agrees to a material alteration in the nature or time of payment of a partnership obligation.[178]

b. Partnership Obligations Incurred After Dissociation — Lingering Liability

Because third parties may deal with a partnership believing that a dissociated partner is still a partner, UPA (1997) §703(b) creates a "lingering liability" rule whose structure mirrors the structure of the rule creating a lingering power to bind. Under UPA (1997) §703(b), a "partner who dissociates without resulting in a dissolution and winding up of the partnership business is liable as a partner to the other party in a [post-dissociation] transaction" if at the time the other party enters into the transaction:

- the partnership is not an LLP;
- less than two years has passed since the dissociation;

176. UPA (1997) §702(b).
177. See Section 4.1.2 (agent liable to principal for acting without authority).
178. UPA (1997) §703(a) and (d). For UPA (1914) approach, see Section 11.5.2.

- the other party does not have notice of the dissociation and reasonably believes that the dissociated partner is a still a partner;
- fewer than 90 days have passed since the filing of a statement of dissociation; and
- if the transaction involves the transfer of real property owned in the name of the partnership, "a certified copy of the filed statement . . . [is not] of record in the office for recording transfers of that real property."[179]

Example

Four months after expelling Eli from the Ofek-Noam Company, the Company sells to a home builder a lot from the Company's Dakota County parcel, giving a warranty deed. The builder has previously dealt with the Company and believes Eli to be one of the partners. Eli is liable for the partnership obligations created by the warranty deed. ◄◄◄

Example

Same situation, except that a week after being expelled Eli executes and files with the Secretary of State a statement of dissociation. He is not liable for the partnership obligations created by the warranty deed. A "person not a partner is deemed to have notice of the dissociation 90 days after the statement of dissociation is filed." UPA (1997) §704(c). As a result, Eli is protected under UPA (1997) §703(b)(3); the home builder "is . . . deemed to have had notice under Section 704(c)."[180] ◄◄◄

As part of the mandatory buyout discussed below, a dissociated partner is entitled to be indemnified "against all partnership liabilities, whether incurred before or after the dissociation," except for partnership liabilities that result from the dissociated partner's lingering power to bind.[181]

---

179. UPA (1997) §303(e), referenced in UPA (1997) §703(b)(3).

180. Eli's statement of dissociation has this effect even though not filed in the real estate records. Although the deed concerns real property, the matter at issue does not involve a question of Eli's authority to transfer real property.

181. The indemnification obligation makes sense because: (i) the buyout price presupposes the payment of all existing liabilities; and (ii) the dissociated partner should be not accountable for liabilities incurred after he, she, or it ceases to be a partner. For more discussion of the first rationale, see Section 11.5.5 (discussing the point in the context of UPA (1914) §38(2)).

§11.9.5 Buyout of the Dissociated Partner

a. Dissociated Partner's Right to a Buyout

If a partner's dissociation does not result in dissolution, UPA (1997) §701(a) provides as a default rule that the dissociated partner is entitled to be bought out: "the partnership shall cause the dissociated partner's interest in the partnership to be purchased." Unless otherwise provided in the partnership agreement, "[t]he buyout is mandatory. The 'cause to be purchased' language is intended to accommodate a purchase by the partnership, one or more of the remaining partners, or a third party."[182]

b. Determining the Buyout Price

UPA (1997) §701(b) and (c) provide the default rule for determining the buyout price:

- assume the partnership was terminated on the date of dissociation;[183]
- calculate the amount the partnership would have received for its assets on that date, both through liquidating those assets piecemeal and through a "sale of the entire business as a going concern";[184]
- using the higher of those two values, calculate the amount that would have been due the dissociated partner (taking into account all liabilities of the partnership);[185]
- subtract from that amount any "[d]amages for wrongful dissociation . . . and all other amounts owing, whether or not presently due, from the dissociated partner to the partnership";[186]
- add to that amount interest "from the date of dissociation to the date of payment."[187]

182. UPA (1997) §701, comment 2.
183. UPA (1997) §701(b).
184. UPA (1997) §701(b). "Liquidation value is not intended to mean distress sale value. Under general principles of valuation, the hypothetical selling price in either case should be the price that a willing and informed buyer would pay a willing and informed seller, with neither being under any compulsion to deal. . . . UPA (1914) §38(2)(c)(II) provides that the good will of the business not be considered in valuing a wrongfully dissociating partner's interest. The forfeiture of good will rule is implicitly rejected by UPA (1997)." RUPA §701, comment 3.
185. UPA (1997) §701(b).
186. UPA (1997) §701(c).
187. UPA (1997) §701(b).

c. Timing of and Tendering the Payment

If the partnership is for a term or undertaking and the dissociation was premature and wrongful, the partnership is presumptively entitled to defer payment:

> A partner who wrongfully dissociates before the expiration of a definite term or the completion of a particular undertaking is not entitled to payment of any portion of the buyout price until the expiration of the term or completion of the undertaking, unless the partner establishes to the satisfaction of the court that earlier payment will not cause undue hardship to the business of the partnership. A deferred payment must be adequately secured and bear interest.[188]

In all other situations, unless otherwise agreed, the partnership "shall pay, or cause to be paid, in cash" its estimate of the buyout price "120 days after a written demand for payment."[189]

The payment must be accompanied by specified financial information, "an explanation of how the estimated amount . . . was calculated," and a written notice warning that the estimate becomes final unless "within 120 days . . . the dissociated partner commences an action to determine the buyout price."[190] If the partnership is exercising its right to defer payment, it must provide the same information (including the warning) together with "a written offer to pay the amount it estimates to be the buyout price . . . stating the time of payment, the amount and type of security for payment, and the other terms and conditions of the obligation."[191]

d. Power of the Partnership Agreement

UPA (1997) §701 is entirely subject to the partnership agreement:

> The section 701 rules are merely default rules. The partners may, in the partnership agreement, fix the method or formula for determining the buyout price and all of the other terms and conditions of the buyout right. ***Indeed, the very right to a buyout itself may be modified***, although a provision providing for a complete forfeiture would probably not be enforceable.[192]

---

188. UPA (1997) §701(h). This right to "lock in" the financial interest of a partner who wrongfully dissociates parallels the right provided by UPA (1914) §38(2) with regard to a wrongful dissolver. See Section 11.5.5.
189. UPA (1997) §701(e).
190. UPA (1997) §702(g).
191. UPA (1997)) §701(f). For the mechanics of an action by a dissociated partner to determine the buyout price or contest deferral, see UPA (1997) §701(i).
192. UPA (1997) §701, comment 3 (emphasis added).

Case in Point—*Laplace v. Estate of Laplace ex rel. Laplace*

A deceased partner's heirs brought suit against the partnership's last surviving partner for a buyout of the deceased partner's interest. The partnership agreement provided for a buyout price of $100,000, but, over 45 years, this provision had been amended five times—frequently in anticipation of the death of a partner—to provide for a different price. Each amendment had a "sunset" provision restoring the agreed-upon buyout price to $100,000 if the partner did not die in the time frame originally anticipated. However, the partnership agreement had not been amended in reference to the plaintiffs' decedent. Plaintiffs sought to escape the $100,000 price, arguing that: (i) the buyout provision of UPA (1997) was not a default provision; (ii) all buyouts must be of "fair value"; (iii) in this case $100,000 did constitute "fair value"; and (iv) the provision of the partnership agreement had been modified or waived as a result of the partnership's course of conduct. The trial court dismissed the claim on summary judgment, and the appellate court affirmed.[193] ◀◀◀

§11.10 DISSOCIATION THAT CAUSES DISSOLUTION

§11.10.1 Overview

If a partner's dissociation results in dissolution, the approach of UPA (1997) is quite similar to that of UPA (1914).[194] Dissolution does not end the partnership but instead commences a period of winding up.[195] "The partnership is terminated when the winding up of its business is completed."[196] Unless the partnership agreement provides otherwise, any "partner who has not wrongfully dissociated may participate in the winding up of the partnership's business." Each partner's duty "to refrain from competing with the partnership" ends at dissolution,[197] but the other fiduciary duties and the obligation of good faith and fair dealing remain in effect.

In winding up its business, the partnership:

- may preserve the partnership business or property as a going concern for a reasonable time, prosecute and defend actions and proceedings, whether civil, criminal, or administrative, transfer the partnership's

193. *Laplace v. Estate of Laplace ex rel. Laplace*, 220 Fed. Appx. 69 (3d Cir. 2007).
194. See Sections 11.2–11.5.
195. UPA (1997) §802(a).
196. UPA (1997) §802(a).
197. UPA (1997) §803(a); UPA (1997) §404(b)(3).

property, settle disputes by mediation or arbitration, and perform other necessary acts; and

- must discharge the partnership's liabilities, settle and close the partnership's business, and marshal the assets of the partnership and distribute the net proceeds to the partners "in cash."[198]

The settling of accounts among partners is essentially the same as under UPA (1914), except that: (i) under UPA (1997), debts owed by the partnership to partners are treated the same as debts owed to third parties;[199] and (ii) UPA (1997) expressly refers to each partner having an account reflecting the partner's contributions, share of partnership profits, distributions, and share of losses,[200] and then uses that concept to describe the "Settlement of Accounts and Contributions Among Partners."[201]

In one substantive departure from UPA (1914), UPA (1997) §802(b) permits a partnership to "undo" its dissolution "[a]t any time . . . before the winding up of its business is completed." This "180" requires the waiver by "all of the partners, including any dissociating partner other than a wrongfully dissociating partner" of "the right to have the partnership's business wound up and the partnership terminated."[202] In that event "the partnership resumes carrying on its business as if dissolution had never occurred,"[203] except that "the rights of a third party . . . may not be adversely affected."[204]

§11.10.2 Partner's Power to Bind During Winding Up

Like UPA (1914), UPA (1997) specifically deals with the power of partners to bind the partnership during winding up. The approach of UPA (1997), however, is far simpler and allows for the public filing of a statement of dissolution.

UPA (1997) §804 provides that, subject to the effect of a statement of dissolution, a partnership is bound by a partner's act after dissolution that:

1. is appropriate for winding up the partnership business; or
2. would have bound the partnership under section 301 before dissolution, if the other party to the transaction did not have notice of the dissolution.

---

198. UPA (1997) §§803(c), 807(a).
199. UPA (1997) §807(a). UPA (1914) gives higher priority to obligations owed to third parties. See Section 11.4.4.
200. UPA (1997) §401(a).
201. UPA (1997) §807. The extended Example provided in Section 11.5.3(b) is thus equally useful for understanding settling accounts under UPA (1997). (That Example does not include any debts owed to partners.)
202. UPA (1997) §802(b).
203. UPA (1997) §802(b)(1).
204. UPA (1997) §802(b)(2).

In this context, the phrase "a partner's act" includes an act by the partner whose dissociation resulted in the dissolution.[205]

The filing and function of a statement of dissolution under Article 8 is roughly analogous to the filing and function of a statement of dissociation under Article 7. "After dissolution, a partner who has not wrongfully dissociated may file a statement of dissolution stating the name of the partnership and that the partnership has dissolved and is winding up its business."[206]

The effect of the filed statement varies depending on whether the transaction at issue involves the transfer of real property owned in the name of the partnership. If so, as soon as "a certified copy of the filed statement . . . is of record in the office for recording transfers of that real property,"[207] the statement has the immediate effect of "restrict[ing] the authority of all partners to real property transfers that are appropriate for winding up the business."[208]

A filed statement of dissolution also has the immediate effect of canceling all previously filed statements of partnership authority granting authority.[209]

---

205. This conclusion follows from the fact that many such partners will have the right to participate in winding up, UPA (1997) §803(a) ("a partner who has not wrongfully dissolved may participate") and from the fact that no statement of dissociation may be filed when Article 8 applies. UPA (1997) §§603(b) (switching provision) and 704 (providing for statement of dissociation).

206. UPA (1997) §805(a). The statement is not filed by the partnership and therefore does not require the signatures of two partners. UPA (1997) §105(c). In some circumstances, it would be impossible to obtain the signature of two partners who had not wrongfully dissociated, i.e., a two-person partnership for a term, where one partner wrongfully dissociates before the end of the term.

207. UPA (1997) §303(e), referenced in UPA (1997) §805(b).

208. UPA (1997) §805, comment 2. The statement has this effect because it "is a limitation on authority for the purposes of section 303(e)." UPA (1997) §805(b).

209. UPA (1997) §805(b). It is unclear whether this cancellation affects statements of authority granting a partner authority to transfer real property owned in the partnership name, if no certified copy of the statement of dissolution is filed in the office for recording transfers of that real property. Arguably, the certified copy on record in that office must lose its efficacy when the underlying filing (i.e., the filing of which it is a copy) is cancelled. However, UPA (1997) §303(d)(2) provides:

> A grant of authority to transfer real property held in the name of the partnership contained in a certified copy of a filed statement of partnership authority recorded in the office for recording transfers of that real property is conclusive in favor of a person who gives value without knowledge to the contrary, *so long as and to the extent that a certified copy of a filed statement containing a limitation on that authority is not then of record in the office for recording transfers of that real property.*

(Emphasis added.)

In addition, 90 days after filing, a statement of dissolution "operates as constructive notice conclusively limiting the apparent authority of partners to transactions that are appropriate for winding up the business."[210]

Example

The Ofek-Noam Company ("the Company") is a general partnership subject to UPA (1997) that purchases land and subdivides it for sale to home builders. The Company has three partners — Suzanne, Eli, and Gili — and for years all three have acted for the partnership in selling land to home builders. The partnership has filed a statement of authority with the Secretary of State, indicating that each partner has the authority to transfer land owned in the name of the partnership. The partnership owns a large parcel of land in Dakota County, and a certified copy of the statement of authority has been recorded with the Dakota County Registrar of Deeds.

The partnership dissolves, and Gili files a statement of dissolution with the Secretary of State and records a certified copy with the Dakota County Registrar of Deeds. Two days later, Eli purports to enter into a contract to grant another developer a five-year option on the Dakota County parcel. The Company is not bound:

- Granting a five-year option is hardly "appropriate for winding up the partnership business," so the partnership is not bound under UPA (1997) §804(1).
- Even if the developer could establish that Eli's act "would have bound the partnership under section 301 before dissolution," the partnership is not bound under UPA (1997) §804(2).[211] "A statement of dissolution cancels a filed statement of partnership authority for the purposes of section 303(d) and is a limitation on authority for the purposes of section 303(e)." Therefore, the developer cannot invoke the previously filed and recorded statement of authority and "is deemed to have knowledge" that each partner's authority to transfer real property is limited to transactions appropriate for winding up the partnership business.[212] ◄ ◄ ◄

---

210. UPA (1997) §805, comment 3. The statement has this effect because "[f]or the purposes of sections 301 and 804, a person not a partner is deemed to have notice of the dissolution and the limitation on the partners' authority as a result of the statement of dissolution 90 days after it is filed." UPA (1997) §805(c).

211. UPA (1997) §804(2). The Dakota County parcel is a major operating asset of the partnership. It is at best arguable whether a five-year option on such an asset comes within a partner's apparently/ordinary power. See Sections 10.3.3 and 10.4.1.

212. The phrase "deemed to have knowledge" comes from UPA (1997) §303(e), which applies to this situation under UPA (1997) §805(b).

Example

Same facts as in the previous Example, plus: (i) winding up The Ofek-Noam Company is a lengthy process; and (ii) six months into that process, Gili orders on behalf of the Company $5,000 worth of gifts, explaining to the vendor, "These are to promote our relationship with our long-time customers." The Company is not bound. The gifts are clearly not "appropriate for winding up the partnership business,"[213] and UPA (1997) §804(2) does not help the would-be seller because the would-be seller had "notice of the dissolution." Under UPA (1997) §805(c), "a person not a partner is deemed to have notice of the dissolution . . . 90 days after [a statement of dissolution] is filed." ◄◄◄

§11.11 OTHER CAUSES OF DISSOLUTION

Like UPA (1914), UPA (1997) provides a number of events of dissolution that are not connected to the dissociation of a partner. These events include:

- in a partnership for a term or undertaking:
  — "the expiration of the term or the completion of the undertaking";[214]
  — "the express will of all the partners to wind up the business" before the expiration or completion;[215]
- an event that the partnership agreement establishes as causing dissolution;[216]
- "on application by a partner, a judicial determination that: (i) the economic purpose of the partnership is likely to be unreasonably frustrated; (ii) another partner has engaged in conduct relating to the partnership business which makes it not reasonably practicable to carry on the business in partnership with that partner; or (iii) it is not otherwise reasonably practicable to carry on the partnership business in conformity with the partnership agreement";[217]
- "on application by a transferee of a partner's transferable interest, a judicial determination that it is equitable to wind up the partnership business: (i) after the expiration of the term or completion of the undertaking, if the partnership was for a definite term or particular undertaking at the time of the transfer or entry of the charging order that gave rise to the transfer; or (ii) at any time, if the partnership

213. UPA (1997) §805(a).
214. UPA (1997) §801(2)(iii).
215. UPA (1997) §801(2)(ii).
216. UPA (1997) §801(3).
217. UPA (1997) §801(5).

was a partnership at will at the time of the transfer or entry of the charging order that gave rise to the transfer."[218]

The grounds for judicial dissolution on application by a partner mirror the grounds for judicial expulsion under UPA (1997) §601(5) and are derived in part from UPA (1914) and in part from the Uniform Limited Partnership Act (2001). The grounds for judicial dissolution on application by a transferee come from UPA (1914) §32(2), but "[t]he requirement that the court determine that it is equitable to wind up the business is new."[219] Allowing a transferee to seek dissolution is a major exception to the general rule that transferees have no right to meddle in the management of the partnership.

Example

Larry, Moe, and Curley agree to form a partnership with a term of five years. Two years later, Moe's transferable interest becomes subject to a charging order and is eventually transferred to Shemp, a nonpartner, in a foreclosure sale.[220] Moe dissociates from the partnership, but neither Larry nor Curley wants to dissolve the partnership before the expiration of its original term.[221] They continue with their original business plan, under which they each take small salaries for the work they do, while "plowing back" all profits into the business. When the end of the five-year term approaches, Larry and Curley decide that the business is "on the cusp of a great opportunity." They believe that "with a little staying power, a little delayed gratification, we might make it big, big, big." They agree therefore to extend the partnership's term for another three years. As soon as the original five-year term expires, Shemp may go to court seeking an order dissolving the partnership despite Larry's and Curley's agreement to the contrary. Shemp's chances are greatest if Larry's and Curley's plans to "make it big, big, big" are very risky, or if the court considers the extension of the partnership term a bad faith effort to deprive Shemp of the value of his transferable interest. ◄◄◄

The partnership agreement may not vary the power of a court to order dissolution on application by either a partner or transferee.[222]

218. UPA (1997) §801(6).
219. UPA (1997) §801, comment 9. In this respect, UPA (1997) §801(6) seems to correspond with Restatement (Second) of Contracts §338(2) ("DISCHARGE OF AN OBLIGOR AFTER ASSIGNMENT. . . . So far as an assigned right is conditional on the performance of a return promise, and notwithstanding notification of the assignment, any modification of or substitution for the contract made by the assignor and obligor in good faith and in accordance with reasonable commercial standards is effective against the assignee. The assignee acquires corresponding rights under the modified or substituted contract.").
220. For a discussion of charging orders, see Section 8.8.4.
221. See Section 11.9.
222. UPA (1997) §103(b)(8).

§11.12 DISSOCIATION AND DISSOLUTION—THE THREE ACTS COMPARED

§11.12.1 UPA (1914) AND UPA (1997)

The following chart shows how UPA (1914) and UPA (1997) approach the key issues of partner dissociation and partnership dissolution. Unless marked by an asterisk (*), each provision is a default rule, subject to change by the partnership agreement.

11.1 Dissociation/Dissolution—UPA (1914) and (1997) Compared

Issue	UPA (1914)	UPA (1997)
"Dissociation" used as a statutory term of art	No	Yes*
Events of dissociation	Labeled "Causes of Dissolution" and listed in §31*	Labeled "Events Causing Partner's Dissociation" and listed in §601
Rightful and wrongful dissociation distinguished	Yes, characterized as causing "wrongful dissolution"; e.g., §§37, 38(2)	Yes, "wrongful dissociation" defined in §602(b)
Partner has power to dissociate even when wrongful effect; of partner dissociation on partnership entity/aggregate	Yes, §31(2)* Partnership inevitably dissolves, §29*	Yes, §602(a)* Dissolution not inevitable, §603(a); if no dissolution, post-dissociation partnership is the same entity that existed before dissolution*
Other causes of partnership dissolution	Yes, primarily: termination of term or undertaking, §31(1)(a), unanimous consent of partners, §31(1)(c), judicial intervention (including on behalf of assignees), §32*	Essentially the same: termination of term or undertaking, §801(2)(iii), unanimous consent of partners, §801(2)(ii), judicial intervention (including on behalf of transferees, although, UPA (1997), unlike UPA (1914), requires transferees to show that "it is equitable to wind up the partnership business"), §§801(5) and (6)*

11.1 Continued

Issue	UPA (1914)	UPA (1997)
Effect of partner dissociation on partnership business	Must be wound up, unless: (i) in rightful dissolution all partners agree to continue the business in a successor organization, §38(1); (ii) in wrongful dissolution, all partners except the wrongful dissolver agree to continue the business in a successor partnership, §38(2)(b)	None, if partnership not dissolved; must be wound up if partnership dissolved, unless by agreement some partners continue the business in a successor entity
Effect of partner dissociation on partner fiduciary duties	Duties continue through winding up	If dissociation does *not*→ dissolution, fiduciary duties of dissociated partner end, §603(b)(2) and (3); Whenever dissolution occurs, noncompete duties of all partners end, §404(b)(3); If dissociation does not → dissolution, dissociated partner has no further participation in partnership affairs, §603(b)(1)
Dissociated partner's role in management	May participate in winding up, unless dissociation caused wrongful dissolution, §37	If dissociation → dissolution, dissociated partner may participate in winding up, unless dissociation was wrongful,§803(a)
Post-dissociation power to bind of dissociated partner	Lingering power to bind, subject to the complex rules of §35, and especially §35(3)(c)*	If dissociation does *not*→ dissolution, lingering power to bind is subject to the rules of §702 and the effect of a filed statement of dissociation, §704*; if dissolution occurs later from some other cause, a filed statement of dissolution will also affect lingering power to bind, §804* If dissociation → dissolution, lingering power to bind is subject to the rules of §804 and the effect of a filed statement of dissolution, §805*

11.1 Continued

Issue	UPA (1914)	UPA (1997)
Effect of partner dissociation on dissociated partner's personal liability for predissociation obligations of the partnership	Dissolution does not discharge the liability, but discharge is possible by agreement under §36(2), or, under §36(3), if the creditor agrees to a material change in the obligation*	Dissociation does not discharge the liability, but discharge is possible under the material change rule, §703(d)*
Dissociated partner's liability for post-dissociation obligations of the partnership or the partnership business	Liable, just like other partners, for partnership obligations incurred during winding up; not liable for partnership obligations incurred by successor organization that continues the partnership business unless partnership by estoppel applies, §§16 and 35(4)*	If dissociation does *not*→ dissolution, lingering liability under §703; filing of a statement of dissociation, §704 can significantly curtail the exposure*
Ability to "lock in" the interest of a partner who has prematurely and wrongfully dissociated from a partnership for a term or undertaking	Requires unanimous consent of the remaining partners to continue the business, §38(2)(b)	Yes, unless within 90 days after the wrongful dissociation a majority of the remaining partners decide to dissolve the partnership, §801(2)(i), or, if the partnership continues, the wrongfully dissociated partner can prove that prompt payout "will not cause undue hardship to the partnership,"§701(h)
Impact of wrongful dissociation on valuation of dissociated partner's interest	Partnership valued excluding good will, §38(2)(c)(II); dissociated partner's share decreased by damages caused by wrongful dissolution, §38(2)(a)(II)	Partnership valuation includes good will, §701(b); dissociated partner's share decreased by damages caused by wrongful dissociation, §701(c)
Settling of accounts after dissolution	According to the Rules for Distribution, §40	Essentially the same as per UPA, according to Settlement of Accounts and Contributions Among Partners, §807

11.1 Continued

Issue	UPA (1914)	UPA (1997)
Presence of a "switching provision" among the rules governing dissociation and dissolution	No, because dissociation inevitably causes dissolution	Yes, under §603(a): Article 7 governs if dissociation does *not*→ dissolution; Article 8 governs if dissociation → dissolution*
Role of publicly filed statements	None	If dissociation does not→ dissolution, statement of dissociation curtails dissociated partner's lingering power to bind and lingering liability, §§702–704* If dissociation → dissolution, statement of dissolution curtails power to bind of all partners, §§804, 805*

§11.12.2 UPA (1997) AND UPA (2013)

a. Cause and Extent of Stylistic Changes

Stylistic changes account for the overwhelming majority of differences between UPA (1997) and UPA (2013). UPA (1997)'s language reflected state-of-the-art drafting in 1997, but the Harmonization Project had the advantage of: (i) drafting developments reflected in the five uniform and two model entity-related statutes that the ULC promulgated between 1997 and 2009 (when the Project began);[223] and (ii) substantial drafting insights gained through the Project itself.

As a result, the stylistic differences between UPA (1997) and UPA (2013) are generally quite substantial. For example, UPA (1997) §802(b)

223. In chronological order of promulgation: Uniform Limited Partnership Act (2001); Uniform Limited Liability Company (2006); Model Registered Agents Act (2006); Model Entity Transactions Act (2007); Uniform Unincorporated Nonprofit Association Act (2008); Uniform Statutory Trust Entity Act (2009); Uniform Business Organizations Code—Article 1 (UBOC Hub) (2011).

authorized partners to rescind the dissolution of their partnership in specified circumstances:

> (b) At any time after the dissolution of a partnership and before the winding up of its business is completed, all of the partners, including any dissociating partner other than a wrongfully dissociating partner, may waive the right to have the partnership's business wound up and the partnership terminated. In that event:
>
> (1) the partnership resumes carrying on its business as if dissolution had never occurred, and any liability incurred by the partnership or a partner after the dissolution and before the waiver is determined as if dissolution had never occurred; and
>
> (2) the rights of a third party accruing under section 804(1) or arising out of conduct in reliance on the dissolution before the third party knew or received a notification of the waiver may not be adversely affected.[224]

UPA (2013) accorded this concept its own section. Section 803 (Rescinding Dissolution) provides:

> (a) A partnership may rescind its dissolution, unless a statement of termination applicable to the partnership has become effective or [the appropriate court] has entered an order under Section 801(4) or (5) dissolving the partnership.
>
> (b) Rescinding dissolution under this section requires:
>
> (1) the affirmative vote or consent of each partner; and
>
> (2) if the partnership has delivered to the [Secretary of State] for filing a statement of dissolution and:
>
> (A) the statement has not become effective, delivery to the [Secretary of State] for filing of a statement of withdrawal under Section 115 applicable to the statement of dissolution; or
>
> (B) the statement of dissolution has become effective, delivery to the [Secretary of State] for filing of a statement of rescission stating the name of the partnership and that dissolution has been rescinded under this section.
>
> (c) If a partnership rescinds its dissolution:
>
> (1) the partnership resumes carrying on its business as if dissolution had never occurred;
>
> (2) subject to paragraph (3), any liability incurred by the partnership after the dissolution and before the rescission has become effective is determined as if dissolution had never occurred; and

224. The provision comprises 130 words.

(3) the rights of a third party arising out of conduct in reliance on the dissolution before the third party knew or had notice of the rescission may not be adversely affected.[225]

b. The Few Substantive Changes

UPA (2013) made three substantive changes to UPA (1997):

- Entity transactions—UPA (1997), Article 9 broke new ground in the law of general partnerships by providing for mergers and conversions involving general and limited partnerships.[226] UPA (2013), Article 11 authorizes mergers,[227] interest exchanges,[228] conversions,[229] and domestications[230] involving at least one general partnership.
- Providing Special Means by Which a Dissolved Limited Liability Partnership May Handle Creditor Claims
  —UPA (2013) §§807 and 808:
  - authorize a dissolved LLP to notify creditors and potential creditors of specified deadlines for asserting claims; and
  - cut off any claims not asserted by the applicable deadline.

  —UPA (2013) §809 permits a dissolved LLP to:
  - ask a court "for a determination of the amount and form of security to be provided for payment of claims that are reasonably expected to arise after the date of dissolution"[231] with regard to claims that "are contingent, have not been made

---

225. This provision comprises 219 words.
226. In a merger, one or more entities are subsumed into another entity, which may preexist the merger or be created by the merger. In a conversion, one type of entity becomes another type of entity, e.g., a general partnership might become a limited partnership.
227. The merger provisions in UPA (2013) appear in sections 1121–26 and require that at least one participant in the merger be a domestic general partnership.
228. In an interest exchange under UPA (2013), either "(1) a domestic [general] partnership may acquire all of one or more classes or series of interests of another domestic entity or a foreign entity" or "(2) all of one or more classes or series of interests of a domestic [general] partnership may be acquired by another domestic entity or a foreign entity." UPA (2013) §1131(a)(1) and (2). The interest exchange provisions appear in UPA (2013) §§1131–36.
229. In a conversion under UPA (2013), either (i) a domestic general partnership will become another type of entity, whether domestic or foreign; or (ii) another type of entity, whether domestic or foreign, will become a domestic general partnership. The conversion provisions appear at UPA (2013) §§1141–46.
230. In a domestication, either: (i) a domestic general partnership becomes a general partnership subject to the law of another jurisdiction (i.e., a foreign general partnership); or (ii) a foreign general partnership becomes a domestic general partnership. The domestication provisions appear at UPA (2013) §§1151–56. Domestications typically involve limited liability partnerships.
231. UPA (2013) §809(a).

known to the partnership, or are based on an event occurring after the date of dissolution";[232] and
    - obtain a court order limiting any such claims to the court-determined amount.
- Consequences When a Dissociation Leaves a Partnership with Only One Partner—UPA (1997) was indefinite on this point. UPA (2013) §801(6) provides that a partnership dissolves upon "the passage of 90 consecutive days during which the partnership does not have at least two partners."

Problem 92

John, Jacob, and Susan form an investment partnership with a term of five years. For the first two years everything goes fine. Then Jacob says to his partners, "I want out. I want my money out—now." Is Jacob's departure wrongful? Is the partnership dissolved? ◄◄◄

Explanation—UPA (1914)

Even though the partners (Jacob included) promised each other to maintain the partnership for five years, Jacob's "express will" causes a dissolution. Because that dissolution breaches Jacob's promise—that is, because the dissolution is in contravention of the partnership agreement—the dissolution is wrongful. UPA (1914) §31(2). ◄◄◄

Explanation—UPA (1997)

Jacob's departure is a wrongful dissociation. "A partner's dissociation is wrongful . . . if . . . in the case of a partnership for a definite term or particular undertaking, before the expiration of the term or the completion of the undertaking . . . the partner withdraws by express will." UPA (1997) §602(b)(2)(i). The partnership is not dissolved, unless within 90 days of Jacob's dissociation either John or Susan manifests the "express will" to dissolve. UPA (1997) §801(2)(i) (wrongful dissociation does not result in premature dissolution of a term partnership absent "the express will [manifested within 90 days of the dissociation] of at least half of the remaining partners to wind up the partnership business"). ◄◄◄

232. UPA (2013) §809(e).

Problem 93

John, Jacob, and Susan form a five-year investment partnership. Two years later John dies. Is the partnership dissolved? If so, was the dissolution wrongful or rightful? ◀ ◀ ◀

Explanation — UPA (1914)

The death. of a partner automatically dissolves the partnership. UPA (1914) §31(4). John's death and the resulting dissolution disappoints the expectations of Jacob and Susan but does not breach the partnership agreement or violate some other legally enforceable duty owed by John to his partners. Therefore, the dissolution is rightful. ◀ ◀ ◀

Explanation — UPA (1997)

John's death is a dissociation (UPA (1997) §601(7)(i)), but it is not wrongful. UPA (1997) §602(b). The partnership is not dissolved, unless within 90 days of Jacob's dissociation either John or Susan manifests the "express will" to dissolve. UPA (1997) §801(2)(i). ◀ ◀ ◀

Problem 94

John, Jacob, and Susan form an investment partnership with a five-year term. One of the partnership's assets is a classic car, which is in basically good shape but will require considerable mechanical work if it is to be profitably sold. Two years into the partnership John quits the partnership. He then hires a mechanic to prepare the classic car for sale. The mechanic is unaware of the partnership and is likewise unaware that John has quit the partnership. Is the partnership bound by John's act? ◀ ◀ ◀

Explanation — UPA (1914)

Most likely yes. When John quit the partnership, the partnership dissolved. UPA (1914) §31(2). If the partnership is to be wound up through liquidation, John's act is probably "an act appropriate for winding up partnership affairs." Under UPA (1914) §35(1)(a), such acts bind the dissolved partnership. Because the mechanic is unaware of the dissolution, the constraining rules of UPA (1914) §35(3)(c) cannot apply.

The answer under UPA §35(1)(a) might be different if Jacob and Susan plan to continue the partnership business under UPA (1914) §38(2)(b) and intend to wind up the affairs of the dissolved partnership by transferring them (and the dissolved partnership's assets) to a successor partnership. In that case, John's act would not be appropriate for winding-up purposes. ◀◀◀

Explanation — UPA (1997)

The partnership is not bound if the partnership is not dissolved. John's dissociation is wrongful (UPA (1997) §602(b)(2)(i)), but the partnership is not dissolved absent "the express will [manifested within 90 days of the dissociation] of at least half of the remaining partners to wind up the partnership business." UPA (1997) §801(2)(i). If the partnership does not dissolve, UPA (1997) §702 will determine John's power to bind the partnership. UPA (1997) §702(1) negates any such power, because "at the time of entering into the transaction the other party"—i.e., the mechanic—did not "reasonably believe[] that the dissociated partner was then a partner."

If John's dissociation does result in dissolution, UPA (1997) §804 will determine his power to bind the dissolved partnership. In that event, the partnership might be bound, because preparing the car for sale might well be "appropriate for winding up the partnership business." UPA (1997) §804(1).[233] ◀◀◀

Problem 95

Able and Baker have a partnership at will that buys finished cloth from mills and resells it to garment manufacturers. For the past two years the partnership has regularly bought cloth from Inventive Design Outlet, Inc. ("IDO"), using purchase orders signed by either partner. The terms of the sale have

233. UPA (1997) §804(2) would not apply, because John was not authorized to act for the partnership (UPA (1997) §803(a)), and the partnership was undisclosed. Therefore, John's act "would [not] have bound the partnership under section 301 before dissolution." See Section 10.4.1 (explaining that UPA (1997) §301 binds a partnership through a partner's actual authority and through apparently/ordinary power).

been "net 30 date of shipment," that is, payment is due 30 days after the goods are shipped.

On January 15, Baker says to Able, "This partnership is over." On that day the partnership has a few outstanding obligations to provide cloth to various manufacturers, and the partnership has sufficient cloth in stock to cover those obligations.

On January 17, Able signs and sends a purchase order to IDO for $50,000 worth of wool cloth. IDO promptly wires back its acceptance. Two days later the president of IDO telephones the partnership's offices to express appreciation for the order. Able is not in, so the president speaks to Baker. Upon hearing of the order Baker exclaims, "That order is no good. Able had no right to issue it. We dissolved this partnership two days before." The president of IDO quite accurately explains that IDO "knew nothing of any dissolution" and asserts, "That order is good. You're stuck with it."

Did Able's purchase order bind the partnership to IDO? ◄◄◄

Explanation — UPA (1914)

EXPLANATION

The partnership is bound under UPA (1914) §35(1)(b)(I).

Since the partnership was at will, Baker's January 15 statement caused a dissolution. Dissolution being caused by an act of the partner, Able lost her authority to bind the partnership for new business as soon as she knew of the dissolution—that is, immediately. UPA (1914) §§33(1)(b) and 34(a). The facts indicate that Able's order represented new business; at the time of the order, the partnership had already covered its outstanding obligations to customers. Therefore, Able was acting without authority.

Under UPA (1914) §35, however, a partner can have the power to bind a dissolved partnership even if he or she lacks the authority to do so. Since Able's order constituted new business, UPA (1914) §35(1)(b) applies.[234]

Under UPA (1914) §35(1)(b)(I), a partner's post-dissolution commitment binds the partnership if: (i) the commitment would have bound the partnership prior to dissolution; (ii) the third party had previously extended credit to the partnership; and (iii) the third party had no knowledge of the dissolution.

The given facts meet all three criteria. Able's issuing of the order was an act "for apparently carrying on in the usual way the business of the partnership," (UPA (1914) §9(1)), so the transaction would indeed have bound the partnership prior to dissolution.[235] IDO had previously extended credit

---

234. UPA (1914) §35(1)(a) is inapposite, because Able's order was not an "act appropriate for winding up partnership affairs or completing transactions unfinished at dissolution." The partnership had on hand ample cloth to finish all pre-dissolution orders.

235. See Section 10.3.

to the partnership (the "net 30" term), and, as IDO's president indicated, IDO received and accepted the order unaware of the dissolution.

None of the "de-powering" exceptions of UPA (1914) §35(3) apply. The only exception remotely connected to the facts is found in UPA (1914) §35(3)(c) (partner lacks authority and creditor had notice or knowledge of the lack of authority). Able did lack authority, but IDO was totally unaware of that fact. Able's lack of authority stemmed from the dissolution, and when IDO accepted the order, it had neither knowledge nor notice of the dissolution. ◄ ◄ ◄

Explanation — UPA (1997)

The partnership is bound. The January 15 statement dissolved the partnership (UPA (1997) §801(1)), and therefore UPA (1997) §804 controls each partner's power to bind during winding up. Although the January 17 order was not "appropriate for winding up the partnership business" (UPA (1997) §804(1)), before the dissolution the order would have been within Baker's apparently/ordinary power. IDO "did not have notice of the dissolution," so the partnership is bound under UPA (1997) §804(2). ◄ ◄ ◄

Problem 96

John, Jacob, Sara, and Susan form an investment partnership with a term of five years. John prematurely and wrongfully quits the partnership, and Susan does not want to continue the business without John's participation. Jacob and Sara do want to continue, and Susan is willing to wait for her money (assuming Jacob and Sara guarantee it and she is compensated for her wait). However, John demands liquidation. The partnership agreement does not address the situation. Can John compel liquidation? ◄ ◄ ◄

Explanation — UPA (1914)

Yes. John's departure caused a wrongful dissolution (UPA (1914) §31(2)), but Susan's desire not to participate in a successor venture costs Jacob and Sara their right to continue the partnership business under UPA (1914) §38(2)(b). That provision allows business continuation only if all the remaining partners agree. Since UPA (1914) §38(2)(b) does not apply, under UPA §§38(2)(c)(I) and 38(1) each of the partners (including John) has the right to insist on liquidation. ◄ ◄ ◄

Explanation — UPA (1997)

No. John's departure is a wrongful dissociation (UPA (1997) §602(b)(2)(i)), but the partnership is not dissolved. (UPA (1997) §801(2)(i) requiring the "express will of at least half of the remaining partners"). Suzanne has the right to dissociate herself (UPA (1997) §602(b)(2)(i) wrongful dissociation of one partner in a term partnership gives other partners the right to withdraw within 90 days), but even that withdrawal will not cause dissolution.

John does have a buyout right under UPA (1997) §701. However, under UPA (1997) §701(h) payment is not due "until the expiration of the term . . . , unless the partner establishes to the satisfaction of the court that earlier payment will not cause undue hardship to the business of the partnership."

In contrast, if Susan timely dissociates, her dissociation is not wrongful, and she is entitled to be paid "within 120 days of a written demand for payment." UPA (1997) §701(e). ◀ ◀ ◀

Problem 97 (UPA (1914) Only)

Three law students, Charlotte, Paul, and Sophie, form a partnership to operate a used bookstore at their law school. Nearing graduation, Sophie dissolves the at-will partnership. Charlotte and Paul decide, with Sophie's consent, to continue the business. They bring Samara into the business and with him form a successor partnership. The dissolved partnership assigns its lease with the law school to the successor partnership. The law school consents to the assignment but does not agree to release the dissolved partnership.

Always attentive to legal niceties, Charlotte decides that the students who consigned their used books to the old partnership should be informed that the successor partnership is taking over. On credit, she buys a $40 ad in the law school newspaper. The ad proclaims, "A Changing of the Guard," and explains the change.

Charlotte, Paul, and Samara decide that the bookstore should expand its "product line." They write to a supplier of the dissolved partnership, inform that supplier of their new arrangement, and buy on credit $500 worth of study aids for resale to the students.

1. The bookstore falls on hard times and fails to pay its rent to the law school. Whom can the law school hold liable?

2. No one pays for the study aids. Whom can the vendor hold liable?

3. No one pays for the ad in the law school paper, either. Whom can the paper hold liable? ◀ ◀ ◀

Explanation

These facially simple questions have some rather complicated answers. To keep the answers coherent, it is helpful to separate the obligors into the three groups described in Section 11.4.3:

- *The Dissociated Partner*—Sophie.
- *The Continuing Partners*—Charlotte and Paul.
- *The New Partner*—Samara. ◀ ◀ ◀

I. The Lease

All four individuals are liable.

A. Liability of Sophie (Dissociated Partner) The lease obligation is clearly a debt of the dissolved partnership. Absent a novation, even a withdrawing partner like Sophie remains liable for such debts. UPA (1914) §36(1) and §36(2).[236]

B. Liability of Charlotte and Paul (Continuing Partners) On three different grounds, Charlotte and Paul are liable on this debt. First, like Sophie, they are liable as members of the dissolved partnership. Second, under UPA (1914) §41(1), the debts of the dissolved partnership are also the debts of the successor partnership, and, per UPA (1914) §5, Charlotte and Paul are liable as members of the successor partnership. (UPA (1914) §41 does not limit their liability, because they are not new to the business.) Third, the successor partnership's assumption by contract of the dissolved partnership's obligations makes Charlotte and Paul, as members of the successor partnership, liable for this debt.

C. Liability of Samara (New Partner) Samara is also liable on the lease to the school, but only on two grounds, not three. Unlike Charlotte and Paul, Samara is not liable as a member of the dissolved partnership, but She is liable due to the operation of UPA (1914) §§41(1) and 15. However, unlike Charlotte and Paul, Samara benefits from section 41(7)'s limitation

236. There has been no material alteration in the obligation, so UPA (1914) §36(3) does not apply even if the creditor was aware that the successor partnership had assumed the responsibilities of the dissolved partnership. If the school pursues Sophie on this debt, then she will probably have an action against the successor partnership and its partners. Typically, the same agreement by which the old partners provide for the continuation of the business also obliges the successor partnership to hold harmless the withdrawing partner from any further liabilities related to the dissolved partnership.

on liability. Samara is a partner new to the business. Finally, like Charlotte and Paul, Samara is liable under contract law theory.

2. The Study Aids — Liability of Sophie (Dissociated Partner)

This debt is exclusively a debt of the successor partnership, so Sophie, who is not a member of that partnership, is not liable. UPA (1914) §35(1)(a) does not bind the dissolved partnership, because the new purchase is not "appropriate for winding up." UPA (1914) §35(1)(b) is inapposite, because the supplier had notice of the dissolution.

A. Liability of Charlotte and Paul (Continuing Partners) All three partners of the successor partnership agreed to expand the product line, so the study aids purchase binds the partnership. Under UPA (1914) §15 Charlotte and Paul are liable for the resulting debt as members of the successor partnership.

B. Liability of Samara (New Partner) Samara is personally liable for this debt as a member of the successor partnership.

3. The Newspaper Ad. Liability of Sophie (Dissociated Partner)

The question of Sophie's liability turns on whether this debt is part of the winding up of the dissolved partnership, or part of the business of the successor partnership. If the former, Sophie is liable. If the latter, she is not. (UPA (1914) §35(1)(b) will not apply because the ad itself provided the vendor notice of the dissolution.)

With the facts stated, it is impossible to characterize the debt. The person who placed the ad had authority to act for and power to bind both the dissolved partnership (UPA (1914) §§37 and 35(1)(a)), and the successor partnership (UPA §§18(e) and 9(1)). The ad's purpose was ambiguous. Was it intended to announce the demise of the dissolved partnership (hence, winding up) or to advertise the advent of the new one (hence, an act of the successor partnership)? Or both?

A. Liability of Charlotte and Paul (Continuing Partners) Charlotte and Paul are liable no matter how this debt is characterized. If it is a winding-up debt of the dissolved partnership, then the analysis is the same as for the lease. If instead the debt is directly a debt of the successor partnership, then Charlotte and Paul are liable because they are members of that successor partnership.

B. Liability of Samara (New Partner) Samara is liable no matter how this debt is characterized. If it is a winding-up debt of the dissolved partnership, then the analysis is the same as for the lease. If instead the debt is directly a debt of the successor partnership, then Samara is liable because She is a member of that successor partnership.

Problem 98

Jacob, Paul, and Leah form a partnership at will. They do not discuss how the business will be handled after dissolution. Later, Leah dissolves the partnership. She demands that the assets be liquidated so that she can have her share. Jacob and Paul object that liquidating the assets will cause everybody to lose value. Can Leah successfully insist on liquidation? What argument can Jacob and Paul make against liquidation? What additional facts could strengthen Jacob and Paul's position? ◄◄◄

Explanation — UPA (1914)

Leah can most likely compel liquidation. Since the partnership was at will, under UPA (1914) §31(1)(b) Leah's express will caused a rightful dissolution. Under UPA (1914) §38(1), absent an agreement to the contrary, following a rightful dissolution each partner has the right to compel liquidation.

Jacob and Paul might argue for an in-kind division of assets, but to succeed they will have to show something beyond the general proposition that liquidations usually do not bring best value.

With some additional facts, Jacob and Paul might also argue that the partnership had an implied term (not yet expired) or that Leah's dissolution somehow breached her duty of loyalty (e.g., by allowing her to appropriate an opportunity that otherwise the partnership would have enjoyed). Either showing would saddle Leah with the status of "wrongful dissolver." In that case, under UPA (1914) §38(2) Jacob and Paul could avoid liquidation by opting to continue the business. ◄◄◄

Explanation — UPA (1997)

Leah may successfully insist on liquidation. Under UPA (1997) §807(a), the net proceeds of winding up are to be paid to the partners "in cash."

Jacob and Paul might be able to delay the inevitable by arguing for a slow winding up in order to maximize the net proceeds. They will not, however, succeed with any claim of breach of the duty of loyalty. There is no indication that Leah is acting for any reason other than her own legitimate self-interest. According to UPA (1997) §404(e): "A partner does not violate a duty or obligation under this [Act] or under the partnership agreement merely because the partner's conduct furthers the partner's own interest." ◄◄◄

Problem 99

Last year Theodora became a partner in the law firm of Grand, Summit, and St. Clair. The firm has 150 attorneys, including 85 partners. When Theodora became a partner, she signed the partnership agreement. That agreement states in part:

> Any member may be expelled from the firm by a two-thirds majority vote of the executive committee, and the committee need not have, state, or demonstrate good cause, nor need the committee afford the member being expelled any opportunity to be heard.

On May 1 of this year, Theodora gave a speech, widely reported in the local media, on the abortion issue. The next day the president of one of the law firm's most important clients called the firm and complained vociferously to a senior partner about Theodora's speech. The president said, "Where did you guys get that crazy lady? We're not going to be able to entrust our business to a firm that gets publicly branded on this issue and can't keep its people in the office doing what they're supposed to be doing."

Although Theodora is an excellent lawyer, this is not the first complaint the firm has received about her outspoken public remarks. On May 3, the firm's nine-member executive committee meets and votes 7-2 to expel Theodora. Can Theodora establish that the expulsion was wrongful? Is the partnership dissolved? ◄◄◄

Explanation — UPA (1914)

The expulsion dissolves the partnership. Albeit against her will, Theodora is certainly "ceasing to be associated [with the other partners] in the carrying on . . . of the business." UPA (1914) §29.

The expulsion is probably not wrongful. The partnership's executive committee acted under the authority of the partnership agreement. This seems to be an expulsion "bona fide in accordance with such a power conferred by the agreement between the partners." UPA (1914) §31(1)(d).

The firm's failure to state its reasons for expulsion or to accord Theodora a hearing are not likely to change the result. By signing the partnership agreement, Theodora (like the rest of the partners) agreed to accept no-cause, "no process" expulsion.

Nor will Theodora succeed if she claims that the expulsion is wrongful because it violated the constitutional guarantee of due process. The firm is a private organization, and unlike the government, has no constitutional obligation to accord due process. For the same reason, it is likely irrelevant that the expulsion has penalized Theodora for speaking out. The First Amendment does not apply to private organizations. It is therefore not wrongful to expel a partner on account of the notoriety or even the content of his or her speech.

All is not necessarily lost for Theodora, however. Perhaps the expulsion was wrongful because it was unlawful. Was the executive committee motivated in part by the characterization of Theodora as a "crazy lady"? Would the firm have been so quick to expel a male partner? If Theodora can show that the expulsion reflected sex discrimination and that, despite her formal status as a partner, her real role was that of an employee, then she will have demonstrated not only sex discrimination but also wrongful dissolution. ◀◀◀

Explanation — UPA (1997)

EXPLANATION

The expulsion does not dissolve the partnership, even if the partnership is an at-will partnership. The expulsion itself does not cause dissolution (UPA (1997) §801), and an expelled partner cannot dissolve an at-will partnership. UPA (1997) §801(1) (in "a partnership at will, [dissolution is caused by] the partnership's having notice from a partner, *other than a partner who is dissociated under Section* 601(2) *through* (10), of that partner's express will to withdraw as a partner" (emphasis added); "expulsion pursuant to the partnership agreement" is listed in §601(3)).

As to wrongful expulsion, the analysis is the same as under UPA (1914), buttressed by UPA (1997) §404(e) ("A partner does not violate a duty or obligation under this [Act] or under the partnership agreement merely because the partner's conduct furthers the partner's own interest.") ◀◀◀

Problem 100

In 2005, four friends, Albert, Bernice, Carl, and Donald, form a partnership to do carpentry work in single-family residential construction. They make no written agreement, but after an evening-long discussion, Bernice finally says, "So that's what we're going to do. Let's do carpentry work on houses; we'll all be in it together. Share and share alike." The other three agree, and they all shake hands on the deal.

For the five years following that agreement, their partnership operates very successfully. The partners make good livings and also put a substantial amount of the partnership's revenues toward purchasing two company trucks and state-of-the-art carpentry equipment. The partnership's success impresses local banks, and the partnership obtains a line of credit with two of them. Each line of credit allows the partnership to borrow as it wishes up to a predetermined limit.

For its first five years the partnership decides by consensus which projects to bid on. In 2010, the partners have for the first time a serious disagreement about whether to bid on a particular project. The disagreement concerns a residential development called "the Eagan project." Albert objects to bidding on the Eagan project because he believes that both the profit margins and the developer's quality standards are too low. The other three partners disagree, perhaps in large part because the partnership has recently had difficulty finding work. The partners vote 3-1 to bid on the project, and the bid is successful. Albert grumbles, "I don't like this. This is not the way we've always made our decisions, and this project is not our kind of business." However, he does show up at the worksite, and for three weeks he works side by side with Bernice, Carl, and Donald.

Then, three weeks into what the partners expect to be a three-month project, Albert announces, "I've had it. I don't like this work; never did. I'm outta here. I'm going to Alaska. I've got a chance to get in on the ground floor of a new fishing business."

That evening Albert, Bernice, Carl, and Donald meet, and Bernice, Carl, and Donald declare that they intend to finish the Eagan project and "maybe keep going after that." Albert reiterates that he is leaving the project and the partnership. He adds that he wants the partnership to turn over his share of the money tied up in the partnership trucks and other equipment.

What is the status of the partnership? ◄◄◄

Explanation — UPA (1914)

It is dissolved. Albert's "express will" is clearly to dissociate himself from carrying on the partnership business. Under either UPA (1914) §§31(1)(b) (rightful dissolution of an at-will partnership) or 31(2) (wrongful dissolution), that express will causes dissolution. ◄◄◄

Explanation — UPA (1997)

The partnership is likely dissolved. Albert's "express will" has dissociated him as a partner (UPA (1997) §601(1)), the partnership is probably a partnership at-will,[237] and, as such, is dissolved by "having notice from a partner . . . of that partner's express will to withdraw as a partner." UPA (1997) §801(1). ◄◄◄

237. It is possible to argue that the partnership becomes a partnership for a particular undertaking each time the partnership agrees to take on a new project. See the Explanations to the next problem.

Problem 101

Is Albert's decision to dissociate wrongful? ◀ ◀ ◀

Explanation — UPA (1914)

Most likely not. The original, oral partnership agreement (i) did nothing to displace the act's default dichotomy of at-will/term or understanding, and (ii) specified "no definite term or particular undertaking." Therefore, under UPA (1914) §31(1)(b) Albert's express will caused a rightful dissolution.

The fact that Albert may be leaving for greener pastures does not make the dissolution wrongful. According to some cases, a partner's duty of loyalty may constrain the right to dissolve at will. But these cases all involve the dissolving partner's exploitation of assets or opportunities that belong to or are closely associated with the partnership. Those cases would not apply here. There is no apparent connection between the partnership's carpentry business and Albert's fishing prospects.

It might be possible to argue that Albert dissolved wrongfully because he contravened an implied agreement not to dissolve with a partnership project underway. Under this analysis, each decision by the partners to undertake a project would transform their partnership at-will into a partnership for that "particular undertaking."[238] Albert's dissolution would therefore be premature and wrongful. UPA (1914) §31(2). If so, Albert would lose the right to wind up the partnership, UPA (1914) §37. Beyond that, however, nothing would change. Dissolution does not end even an at-will partnership; the partnership continues until it has wound up its affairs, including ongoing projects.

Although perhaps superficially attractive, the implied agreement argument would probably fail. It is common for at-will partnerships to take on projects. The pendency of a project means a task for winding up, not that the partners have lost their respective rights to dissolve. ◀ ◀ ◀

Explanation — UPA (1997)

The analysis here mirrors UPA (1914) analysis. If the partnership was at will, Albert's dissociation was not wrongful. UPA (1997) §602(b).

As to the argument that the partnership became a partnership for a particular undertaking each time the partnership agreed to take on a new

238. Though superficially plausible, this argument would probably fail.

project, that argument would render Albert's dissociation wrongful (UPA (1997) §602(b)(2)(i)), and would deprive him of the right to participate in winding up. UPA (1997) §803(a). ◄◄◄

Problem 102

Assume that the partners had originally agreed to a partnership term of seven years. Given this change in facts, is there any way for Albert to avoid the label of "wrongful dissolver" (UPA (1914)) or "wrongfully dissociated partner" (UPA (1997))? ◄◄◄

Explanation — UPA (1914)

Probably not. Albert might be able to claim that the decision to bid on the Eagan project violated implied agreements (created through the partners' course of dealing with each other) on the type of work to be done by the partners (e.g., no low-budget, low-quality jobs) and on the decision-making process to be used by the partners (e.g., projects selected by consensus only). That argument would allow Albert to claim that the decision to bid on the Eagan project constituted a wrongful dissolution.

That argument would probably fail, however, because Albert eventually consented to the Eagan project. By showing up to work on the project, Albert at least acquiesced in the decision. That acquiescence probably satisfies the requirement of UPA (1914) §18(h) that an "act in contravention of any agreement between the partners may be done rightfully [with] the consent of all the partners." Moreover, the mere violation of the partnership agreement does not dissolve the partnership. Albert's partners did not exclude him from the partnership business; he excluded himself. ◄◄◄

Explanation — UPA (1997)

The analysis here is similar to the analysis under UPA (1914). Under UPA (1997) §401(j), Albert can argue not only that the Eagan project violated an implied agreement, but also that the project was "outside the ordinary course of business of [the] partnership."[239] ◄◄◄

239. As for judicial dissolution, UPA (1997) §801(5)(ii) and (iii) are the analogs to UPA (1914) §32(1)(d).

Problem 103

Assuming that the partnership had no specific term, can Albert force the partnership to immediately give him his share of the money tied up in the trucks and equipment? ◄◄◄

EXPLANATION

Explanation — UPA (1914) and UPA (1997)

Not at least until the Eagan project is finished. Under either statute, Albert's strongest position is to claim that the partnership is dissolved. Even assuming dissolution, the trucks and equipment are partnership property. Regardless of whether the dissolution is rightful, Albert cannot compel liquidation until, as part of winding up, the partnership has performed or otherwise discharged its obligations on the Eagan project. ◄◄◄

Problem 104

Two days after his announcement, Albert leaves for Alaska. Before leaving, he writes to all the companies that had previously sold materials to the partnership. In his letters he states, "The original partnership is dissolved. I am no longer associated with the business. I am not responsible for any of its debts." Bernice, Carl, and Donald continue to work on the Eagan project. As they continue the work, they make purchases necessary to finish the project. For example, they buy wood costing $10,000 from the Wabasco Wood Company, which happens to be a new supplier. Assuming that the partnership is not an LLP, is Albert personally liable for this debt? ◄◄◄

EXPLANATION

Explanation — UPA (1914)

Yes. This purchase is clearly an "act appropriate for . . . completing transactions unfinished at dissolution." As such, the purchase binds the dissolved partnership under UPA (1914) §35(1)(a). UPA (1914) §15 makes Albert personally liable for the partnership debt. ◄◄◄

Explanation — UPA (1997)

Yes. The purchase "is appropriate for winding up the partnership business." UPA (1997) §804(1). Albert is personally liable under UPA (1997) §306(a), although his liability is subject to the exhaustion rule of UPA (1997) §307(d). ◄◄◄

Problem 105

Bernice, Carl, and Donald also buy nails after Albert's departure. They buy from Nantucket Nail Emporium, which previously sold the partnership nails on a "net 30 date of shipment" basis (i.e., payment due within 30 days of shipment). Bernice, Carl, and Donald order and receive nails costing $600 before the Emporium receives Albert's letter, and they order and receive nails costing $1,100 after the letter arrives. Is Albert personally liable for these amounts? ◄◄◄

Explanation — UPA (1914)

Yes, under UPA §35(1)(a). The analysis is the same as for Problem 109. Albert's letter is irrelevant to the analysis under UPA (1914) §35(1)(a). Nothing in that provision concerns the third party's knowledge of the dissolution.

Albert's letter would have made a difference if the $1,100 worth of nails ordered after the letter arrived were used for new business. In that case, under UPA (1914) §35(1)(b)(I) the nail order would not have bound the dissolved partnership. ◄◄◄

Explanation — UPA (1997)

The analysis here is the same as under UPA (1914). Under UPA (1997) §804(1), notice of dissolution is irrelevant to the power of a partner to bind a dissolved partnership through "an act . . . appropriate for winding up the partnership business." ◄◄◄

Problem 106

Bernice, Carl, and Donald fare poorly on the Eagan project. Within a month after Albert leaves, the business falls behind in its payments to both banks. One bank, the First Bank, promptly sends written notice to the partnership, complaining about the delay in payments. Prior to Albert's departure, the partnership had borrowed the full $50,000 available under the First Bank line of credit. After receiving the notice, Bernice, Carl, and Donald meet with an officer of the First Bank to explain what has been happening. To help the continuing partners "get back on their feet," the bank agrees to a four-month moratorium on payments on the loan. Is Albert personally liable on the debt to the First Bank? ◄◄◄

Explanation — UPA (1914)

Possibly not. Under UPA (1914) §36(1), the dissolution by itself does not discharge him, but UPA (1914) §36(3) may. Under that latter provision, a discharge occurs if the continuing partners agree to assume the dissociated partner's liability, the creditor knows of that agreement, and the creditor agrees to a material alteration in the "nature or time of payment" of the obligation. If the continuing partners agreed to assume Albert's responsibility, and if the explanation and discussion with the Bank officer caused the Bank to know of the assumption agreement, then UPA (1914) §36(3) is probably satisfied. A four-month moratorium is probably a material change in the "time of payment." ◄◄◄

Explanation — UPA (1997)

Yes. Although UPA (1997) contains a provision analogous to UPA (1914) §36(1), that provision appears in Article 7 and applies only when a partner's dissociation does not result in dissolution. UPA (1997) §603(a). Under UPA (1997) §802(a), "a partnership continues after dissolution" and, accordingly, the partnership's obligations continue as well. The only question is whether the revised obligation is an obligation of the dissolved partnership, i.e., whether the act of Bernice, Carl, and Donald bound the partnership. The answer is yes. Since all of the funds were borrowed before Albert's departure, obtaining the moratorium was "appropriate for winding up the partnership business." UPA (1997) §804(1). Albert remains personally liable under UPA (1997) §306(a), although his liability is subject to the exhaustion rule of UPA (1997) §307(d). ◄◄◄

Problem 107

The other bank, the Second Bank, does not initially object to or even take note of the late payments. Bernice, Carl, and Donald decide to "let sleeping dogs lie."

Indeed, they decide to undertake new projects, and to fund them they actually borrow additional money under the line of credit. Before Albert's departure, the partnership had borrowed $40,000. To fund the new projects, Bernice, Carl, and Donald draw down the final $30,000 available under the original line of credit agreement. Is Albert personally liable for any of the $70,000? ◄◄◄

Explanation — UPA (1914)

Yes — for all of it. As to the first $40,000, Albert is liable under UPA (1914) §15, and UPA (1914) §36(3) will not save him. Even if the continuing partners agreed to assume Albert's liability and the $30,000 drawdown constituted a material change in the nature of the obligation, there is no basis for finding that the Second Bank knew of the assumption agreement. Indeed, the Second Bank was not even aware of the dissolution; Albert notified only "companies that had previously sold materials to the partnership."

Albert is also liable as to the $30,000 drawdown, per UPA (1914) §35(1)(b)(I). The drawdown would have bound the partnership prior to dissolution; the Second Bank had previously extended credit to the partnership; and the Second Bank had no notice or knowledge of the dissolution. ◄◄◄

Explanation — UPA (1997)

For the reasons stated in the UPA (1997) Explanation to problem 106, Albert is liable on the initial $40,000. Albert is probably also liable on the final $30,000.

As to the $30,000, the Second Bank will likely argue that: (i) when the money was borrowed, the original partnership was still winding up; (ii) the Bank had no notice of the dissolution; (iii) borrowing the money would have bound the partnership under UPA (1997) §301 before the dissolution; and therefore (iv) under UPA (1997) §804(2) the partnership is bound even though the money was used for new projects. If the partnership is bound, under UPA (1997) §306(a) Albert is liable.

Even if Bernice, Carl, and Donald were acting as members of a new partnership when they borrowed the $30,000, Albert may still be liable. By leaving in place the line of credit and not informing the Second Bank that he had quit the partnership, Albert "purports to be a partner, or consents to being represented by another as a partner, in a partnership" now actually consisting of Bernice, Carl, and Donald.[240] Albert, as "the purported partner[,] is liable to a person to whom the representation is made [i.e., the Second Bank], if that person, relying on the representation, enters into a transaction with the actual . . . partnership."[241] The pivotal question is

240. UPA (1997) §308 (Liability of Purported Partner).
241. *Id.*

whether the Second Bank allowed the $30,000 to be borrowed "relying on the representation"—that is, whether the Bank would have closed or somehow modified the line of credit if it had known of Albert's departure. ◀◀◀

Problem 108

Concerned that Bernice, Carl, and Donald will continue to undertake new projects for which he may be responsible, Albert seeks your advice on preventative measures. Advise him. ◀◀◀

Explanation—UPA (1914)

Albert must bring the fact of his departure to the knowledge of each third party that "extended credit to the partnership" prior to Albert's departure. UPA (1914) §35(1)(b)(I). For all other third parties, it will suffice to advertise "the fact of dissolution . . . in a newspaper of general circulation in the place (or in each place if more than one) at which the partnership business was regularly carried on." UPA (1914) §35(1)(b)(II). ◀◀◀

Explanation—UPA (1997)

Albert should immediately file a statement of dissolution, as provided in UPA (1914) §805. The statement's protective effect will begin 90 days after filing. UPA (1997) §805(c). There is no need to record a certified copy of the statement, because the partnership does not own any real property.

To protect himself during the 90 days following the filing, Albert should send a notification announcing the dissolution to as many potential customers, vendors, and other third parties as he can identify. Doing so will allow him to invoke UPA (1997) §804(2), which provides that, post-dissolution, no partner has the power to bind the partnership through acts not appropriate for winding up "if the other party to the transaction [has] notice of the dissolution."

Advertising the dissolution will trigger the protections of UPA (1997) §804(2) only to the extent that the advertisement comes to the attention of a third party or creates a situation in which a third party "has reason to know" that dissolution has occurred. UPA (1997) §102(b) (defining "notice of a fact"). ◀◀◀

CHAPTER 12

Limited Partnerships

§12.1 OVERVIEW

A limited partnership is an entity:

- formed under the auspices of a state statute by the filing of a specified public document with a specified public official; and
- structured under that statute to allow one or more managing owners (general partners) to run an enterprise built on money and other property contributed by those owners and one or more essentially passive owners (limited partners).

The formation of a limited partnership thus presupposes an arrangement among at least two separate persons (one limited and one general partner), and a limited partnership's activities and governance are shaped primarily by a contract among its owners (the partnership agreement). In theory, one or more would-be limited partners might seek out one or more would-be general partners, but in practice the reverse is typically the case.

§12.1.1 Limited Partnerships Distinguished from General Partnerships

Ordinary limited partnerships differ from ordinary general partnerships[1] in seven fundamental ways:

1. *Creation*—Creating a limited partnership involves special formalities: namely, the filing of a "certificate of limited partnership" with the public official or office specified in the state limited partnership act. While a limited partnership always involves a contract among its partners, a limited partnership comes into existence only upon the filing of the required document.
2. *Types of Partners*—A limited partnership has two types of partners: general partners and limited partners. Upon formation, a limited partnership must have at least one general partner and one limited partner and must have at least two partners.[2]
3. *Personal Liability*—Like the partners of an ordinary general partnership, the general partners of an ordinary limited partnership are personally liable for the partnership's debts. Limited partners are not personally liable except in extraordinary circumstances.
4. *Management*—Except as otherwise provided in the partnership agreement, both the day-to-day management of and the power to bind a limited partnership are reserved to the general partners. Limited partners have governance rights as to only a few matters,[3] and in many limited partnerships the partnership agreement restricts those rights still further.

---

1. The terms ""ordinary limited partnerships"" and ""ordinary general partnerships"" are used to distinguish these more traditional forms of organization from the shielded entities known respectively as ""limited liability limited partnerships"" (LLLPs) and ""limited liability partnerships"" (LLPs). LLLPs and LLPs are discussed in Chapter 17.
2. That is, although a person can be both a general partner and a limited partner, ULPA (2013), §109 (dual capacity), a person cannot be a limited partnership's sole general partner and sole limited partner.
3. E.g., admitting a new limited partner, Revised Uniform Limited Partnership Act ("RULPA §301(b) (consent of all partners required, unless otherwise provided in partnership agreement); Uniform Limited Partnership Act (2013) ("ULPA (2013)"), §301(b) (same); admitting a new general partner, RULPA §401 (consent of all partners required, unless otherwise provided in partnership agreement), ULPA (2013), §401(b)(3) (same); continuing the partnership following the dissociation of a general partner, RULPA, §801(4) (consent of all remaining partners); ULPA (2013), §801(3)(A) (if at least one general partner remains, continuity is subject to decision by "partners owning a majority of the rights to receive distributions as partners") and (B) (if no remaining general partner, continuity is subject to decision by "limited partners owning a majority of the rights to receive distributions as limited partners").

5. *Profit and Loss Sharing*—Except as otherwise provided in the partnership agreement, partners in a limited partnership share profits and losses essentially in proportion to their respective capital contributions.
6. *Dissolution*—Except as otherwise provided in the partnership agreement, the dissociation of a limited partner does not dissolve the partnership, and the dissociation of a general partner merely threatens the partnership with dissolution.[4]
7. *Name Requirement*—The name of a limited partnership must contain a "signifier" to indicate the enterprise's status as a limited partnership. Some limited partnership statutes require the phrase "limited partnership," while others require either that phrase or the abbreviation "LP" or "L.P."

§12.1.2 Limited Partnership Statutes

Every limited partnership is formed under and governed by some state limited partnership statute. The ULC has promulgated five versions of the Uniform Limited Partnership Act: the original Act in 1916 ("ULPA (1916)"), the Revised Uniform Limited Partnership Act in 1976 ("RULPA-1976"), the 1985 amendments to the 1976 act, with the amended act being generally referred to as the Revised Uniform Limited Partnership Act ("RULPA"), an entirely new Uniform Limited Partnership Act in 2001 ("ULPA (2001)"), and ULPA (2013), the harmonized version of ULPA (2001).[5] As of May 2025, 25 states and the District of Columbia have enacted ULPA (2001) or ULPA (2013). Most of the remaining states have RULPA still in effect. The further remainder still have ULPA (1976). Section 12.2 focuses on RULPA, and Section 12.3 discusses ULPA (2001). Section 12.4 discusses ULPA (2013).

§12.2 RULPA

§12.2.1 Not a "Stand-Alone" Statute

Although RULPA covers numerous issues peculiar to limited partnerships, the statute does not purport to be comprehensive. It does not "stand alone," but instead is "linked" to the general partnership statute: "In any case not

4. This distinction is far more substantial vis-à-vis a general partnership governed by UPA (1914) than vis-à-vis a general partnership governed by UPA (1997). See Section 11.12.
5. For an explanation of the Harmonization Project, see Introductory Note—The ULC Harmonization Project.

provided for in this [Act] the provisions of the Uniform Partnership Act govern."[6] More particularly, with regard to general partners: a "general partner of a limited partnership has the rights and powers and is subject to the restrictions of a partner in a partnership without limited partners."[7]

Example

Rachael, Charlotte, and Carolyn are the general partners in a limited partnership, organized under the law of a state that has in effect RULPA and UPA (1914). The limited partnership owns several apartment buildings, and for some time the partnership has used Joe's Maintenance for routine maintenance work. Rachael and Carolyn wish to replace Joe's with RMV Dorothy & Co., but Charlotte disagrees. RULPA provides no rules for this type of management disagreement, so UPA (1914) governs. In particular, UPA (1914) §18(h) governs this "ordinary matter"[8] unless the limited partnership agreement provides otherwise. ◄◄◄

§12.2.2 Formalities of Creating a RULPA Limited Partnership—the State of Formation, the Certificate of Limited Partnership, and the Partnership Agreement

In order to form a RULPA limited partnership, the would-be general partner[9] must select a state of formation—that is, a state under whose limited partnership statute the limited partnership will be established and governed. Under the "choice of law" rule known as the "internal affairs" doctrine, the law of the state of formation governs relations among the partners and between the partners and the limited partnership.[10]

Most limited partnerships are formed under the law of the state in which the partnership does all or most of its business, but it is not legally necessary to do so. To the contrary, a limited partnership can be properly

6. RULPA, §1105. Until the promulgation and widespread enactment of UPA (1997), this link was uniformly to UPA (1914). For its part, UPA (1914) §6(2), provides that "this act shall apply to limited partnerships except in so far as the statutes relating to such partnerships are inconsistent herewith." In states that have adopted UPA (1997) and repealed UPA (1914), the link is problematic. See Section 12.3.1–12.3.2.

7. RULPA, §403(a). Section 403(b) contains a parallel rule concerning general partner liability to the limited partnership, other partners, and third parties.

8. Under UPA, §18(h), differences as to ordinary matters are decided by majority vote, with each partner having one vote. See Section 9.4.1(b). The rule is a default rule. See Section 7.1.4.

9. For the sake of convenience, this section refers to a sole general partner, although many limited partnerships have more than one general partner.

10. For a more detailed discussion of the internal affairs doctrine, see Section 14.1.2(b) (discussing the doctrine in the context of limited liability companies).

formed "in" (i.e., under the law of) a state in which the limited partnership does no business whatsoever.[11] In such instances, the choice of the state of formation is essentially a choice of law—i.e., a choice to have that state's limited partnership act govern the partners' *inter se* relationship. In any event, if a limited partnership does business in more than one state, the partnership will necessarily do business outside its state of organization.[12]

After choosing a state of organization, the general partner must invoke that state's limited partnership statute by filing a "certificate of limited partnership" with that state's secretary of state.[13] Each general partner must sign the certificate,[14] which must contain: (i) the limited partnership's name; (ii) the name and business address of each general partner; (iii) the latest date on which the limited partnership will dissolve;[15] and (iv) the address of the office and the name and address of an agent designated to receive service of process on behalf of the limited partnership.[16]

If the certificate of limited partnership substantially complies with the limited partnership statute, filing the certificate brings the partnership into existence either immediately or at a later date specified in the certificate.[17] Once formed, a limited partnership is a legal entity, distinct from its co-owners. It is not an aggregate of its partners.[18]

A certificate of limited partnership may include information beyond the bare minimum required by statute, but most certificates do not.[19] The

11. Under RULPA, §104, a limited partnership must merely maintain an office and an agent for service of process. Service companies exist to provide both for an annual fee.

12. A limited partnership that does business in states other than its state of organization must register in each of those other states as a "foreign limited partnership." RULPA §§101(4) (defining the term) and 902 (providing for registration of foreign limited partnerships). With respect to its state of organization, a limited partnership is considered a "domestic" limited partnership. RULPA §101(7). Both the nomenclature and the registration requirement parallel those applicable to corporations and limited liability companies. See, e.g., Revised Model Business Corporation Act, §§1.40(4) (defining domestic corporation), 1.40(10) (defining foreign corporation), and 15.01 (requiring foreign corporations to obtain a certificate of authority before transacting business); Uniform Limited Liability Company Act (2006), §§102(8) (defining limited liability company), 102(7) (defining foreign limited liability company), and 809 (providing consequences for foreign limited liability company that transacts business without first registering).

13. RULPA, §201(a). Some states designate a different state office.

14. RULPA, §204(a)(1).

15. This date effectively sets the term of the partnership. Other events may dissolve the partnership before this date. See Section 12.2.7. Some RULPA states have deleted this requirement, in order to facilitate the formation of so-called family limited partnerships. See Section 12.2.7 (or see *Id.*)

16. RULPA, §201(a).

17. RULPA, §201(b).

18. Compare the mixed entity/aggregate nature of a UPA (1914) general partnership, discussed in Section 7.2.7.

19. Both ULPA (1916) and the 1976 version of RULPA required greater disclosure in the certificate. See, e.g., ULPA (1916), §§2(1)(a)(vi) (requiring disclosure of each limited partner's

certificate is a public document, and business people usually prefer to keep their business arrangements as confidential as possible.

Thus, typically the document that creates the limited partnership as a juridic entity does little to delineate the relationship of the entity's owners. For that purpose, the key document is the partnership agreement, which—like the partnership agreement of a general partnership—has the power to revise or override statutory default rules concerning relations *inter se* the partners.[20] The more sophisticated the deal, the lengthier and more detailed will be the limited partnership agreement. Nonetheless, as a formal matter, formation occurs when the certificate of limited partnership takes effect.

Case in Point—*Saulnier v. Fanaras Enterprises, Inc.*

Plaintiffs, husband and wife, agreed to form a limited partnership with Defendant. At the time, Plaintiff husband was employed by Defendant. Later, Defendant terminated Plaintiff husband's employment, and soon thereafter problems arose between Plaintiffs and Defendant with respect to the limited partnership. In the subsequent lawsuit, Plaintiffs asserted that a limited partnership was never actually formed because Defendant had failed to make the capital contributions required by the limited partnership agreement. The court disagreed, holding that Defendant's alleged breach of the limited partnership agreement was irrelevant to the question of formation *vel non*. The court explained that, because a limited partnership is a creature of statute, the parties need only to satisfy the statutory requirements to form a limited partnership. The court found that such statutory requirements were satisfied and a limited partnership had been formed.[21] ◄◄◄

---

capital contribution) and 2(1)(a)(ix) (requiring disclosure of each limited partner's profit share); RULPA (1976), §§201(a)(5) (requiring disclosure of each partner's capital contribution), and 201(a)(9) (requiring disclosure of each partner's right to receive distributions).

20. RULPA does not require a written partnership agreement, and RULPA, §101(9) defines "partnership agreement" as "any valid agreement, *written or oral*, of the partners as to the affairs of a limited partnership and the conduct of its business" (emphasis added). However, some RULPA provisions can be overridden or activated only by a written term of a partnership agreement. E.g., RULPA, §§401 ("additional general partners may be admitted as provided in writing in the partnership agreement") and 801(2) (dissolution occurs "upon the happening of events specified in writing in the partnership agreement"). As a matter of practice, limited partnerships almost invariably have written partnership agreements.

21. *Saulnier v. Fanaras Enterprises, Inc.*, 618 A.2d 841 (N.H. 1992).

§12.2.3 Personal Liability of RULPA Partners

Each general partner in an ordinary limited partnership is personally liable for the partnership's debts, just as if the partnership were an ordinary general partnership.[22]

Limited partners face no such automatic liability. Of course, a limited partner is liable for her, his, or its own torts, even if committed on behalf of the limited partnership.[23]

In addition, a limited partner may be exposed to claims from creditors of the limited partnership in the following special circumstances:

1. *Unfulfilled promise to contribute*—If a limited partner makes an enforceable promise to contribute to the limited partnership, the limited partner is liable to the partnership on that promise. If the limited partnership becomes insolvent, this liability can be invoked to benefit the limited partnership's creditors.[24]
2. *Wrongfully returned contributions*—If the limited partnership has returned all or part of a limited partner's contribution and the return violated the partnership agreement or left the partnership insolvent, then for six years afterward the limited partner is liable to the partnership for the amount of the wrongful return.[25] This liability is also available to creditors of an insolvent limited partnership.
3. *Properly returned contributions*—If: (i) the limited partnership has returned all or part of a limited partner's contribution without violating the partnership agreement and without leaving the partnership insolvent; and (ii) the limited partnership cannot pay creditors "who extended credit to the limited partnership during the period the contribution was held by the partnership," then for one year after the return the limited partner is liable to the partnership for whatever amount of the returned contribution is necessary to pay those creditors.[26]
4. *Mistaken belief in limited partner status*—If: (i) a person makes a contribution to an enterprise, believing in good faith that the contribution is made as a limited partner; (ii) either no limited partnership exists or the certificate of limited partnership erroneously identifies the person as a general partner; and (iii) when the person learns of the problem, the person either formally withdraws from the enterprise

22. RULPA, §403(b).
23. Contrast Section 4.2.3 (agent liable for tortious conduct).
24. RULPA, §502(b). For an explanation of partner contributions, see Section 8.5.1.
25. RULPA, §§608(b) (stating the general rule) and 607 (prohibiting distributions that leave the limited partnership effectively insolvent).
26. RULPA, §608(a) (stating the general rule).

or has the certificate corrected, then the person is not categorically liable as a general partner in the enterprise. However, if before the person takes corrective action a third party transacts business with the enterprise, believing in good faith that the person is a general partner, then the person is liable on that transaction as if a general partner.[27]

5. *Use of limited partner's name*—If a limited partner allows its name to be used in the name of the limited partnership and a third party extends credit to the partnership without knowing that the limited partner is not a general partner, then the limited partner is liable to that third party on the transaction as if the limited partner were a general partner.[28]
6. *Participation in control*—If: (i) a limited partner "participates in the control of the business" of the limited partnership; (ii) that conduct causes a third party to reasonably believe that the limited partner is a general partner; and (iii) with that belief the third party transacts business with the limited partnership, then the limited partner is liable to the third party as if a general partner.[29]

The last mentioned rule—known as the "control rule"—has been the most litigated of the group. Under both ULPA (1916) and ULPA (1976), it was impossible to draw any bright line or find any safe harbors for limited partner conduct. In contrast, RULPA contains a lengthy list of activities that do not constitute participating in control. The list includes both specific items (e.g., being an agent or employee of the partnership, acting as a consultant to the general partner)[30,31] and also a general provision that protects any right of control granted to the limited partners by the partnership agreement.[32]

Example

Rebecca persuades Vladi to invest $100,000 in a business. The business is supposed to be a limited partnership, with Rebecca as the general partner and Vladi as the limited partner. Vladi makes the investment, but Rebecca

27. RULPA, §304(b).
28. RULPA, §303(d). This rule does not apply if the limited partner's name is the same as a general partner's or if the limited partnership had used the name before the limited partner became a limited partner.
29. RULPA, §303(a) ("if [a] limited partner participates in the control of the business, he [or she] is liable only to persons who transact business with the limited partnership reasonably believing, based upon the limited partner's conduct, that the limited partner is a general partner").
30. RULPA, §303(b)(1).
31. RULPA, §303(b)(2).
32. RULPA, §303(b)(6)(ix).

does not immediately file a certificate of limited partnership. Subsequently, Michael sells 5,000 widgets to the business on credit, having been told by Rebecca that "Vladi has invested and is a partner." Michael believes in good faith that Vladi and Rebecca are general partners. When Vladi later learns that no certificate has been filed, he immediately confronts Rebecca and causes her to file a proper certificate of limited partnership. Vladi is nonetheless liable to Michael as a general partner on the widget transaction. (Circumstance No. 4, above (mistaken belief in limited partner status).) ◄◄◄

Example

Suzanne is the sole general partner of a limited partnership, but she relies heavily on the services of Paul, who is both a limited partner and the partnership's purchasing manager. In his capacity as purchasing manager Paul causes the partnership to buy 500,000 widgets from Rolande. The contract price is large, and it seems to Rolande that Paul has complete discretion in the matter. Rolande accordingly assumes that Paul is a general partner, although Paul signs the contract as "purchasing manager" for the limited partnership. The limited partnership has filed a certificate of limited partnership, and Paul is not listed as a general partner. No matter how reasonable Rolande's assumption, Paul is not personally liable on the widget transaction. He was acting as an employee of the partnership and is therefore within one of the safe harbors provided by RULPA. (Circumstance No. 6, above (control rule and safe harbors).)[33] ◄◄◄

Case in Point—*Alzado v. Blinder, Robinson & Co., Inc.*

In anticipation of an exhibition boxing match between Muhammed Ali and Defendant Alzado, Defendant and several others formed Combat Promotions, Inc. (CPI) to promote the match. Ali demanded a letter of credit in advance of the match in order to guarantee his participation. CPI was unable to provide the letter, but discovered Plaintiff (another corporation), which agreed to provide the letter of credit for publicity purposes. Plaintiff and CPI formed a limited partnership in which CPI was the general partner and Plaintiff was the limited partner. Defendant Alzado (one of the owners of CPI) guaranteed Plaintiff against losses. After the exhibition failed to produce the anticipated revenue, Plaintiff sued Defendant to recover its losses. Defendant filed a counterclaim alleging, in part, that Plaintiff was liable to him under another agreement because Plaintiff should be deemed a general

33. Of course, if Paul misrepresents his status, he might be liable to Rolande under other law (e.g., misrepresentation).

partner, due to its substantial role in the business. The Supreme Court held that Plaintiff had *not* exercised sufficient control to be deemed a general partner.[34] ◀◀◀

§12.2.4 Management

The default management structure of a RULPA limited partnership is easily described. The general partners manage the business, and only the general partners have the power *qua* partners to bind the partnership.[35] Because of their management role, general partners owe fiduciary duties of loyalty and care to the partnership.

Limited partners are essentially passive. Unless the partnership provides otherwise, they have no say in the ordinary operations of the partnership and no power *qua* limited partner to bind the limited partnership to third parties.

Example

Ventura, LP, is a RULPA limited partnership. Sarah is its sole general partner, and Alan is one of its limited partners. Purporting to act on behalf of Ventura, Alan signs a contract "Ventura, LP, by Alan, one of its partners." Even if the contract is well within the ordinary scope of Ventura's business, Ventura is not bound. Alan is merely a limited partner and, as such, lacks the power to bind the limited partnership.[36] ◀◀◀

Example

Same facts, except that the other party to the contract reasonably believes that Alan is a *general* partner and that belief is based on some manifestation legally attributable to Ventura. Under principles of agency law, Alan has the apparent authority to bind the limited partnership.[37] ◀◀◀

---

34. *Alzado v. Blinder, Robinson & Co., Inc.*, 752 P.2d 544 (Colo. 1988). "At the time of the bout, Alzado was a professional football player and Ali was the world heavyweight boxing champion." *Id.* 546, n.1

35. A person who is a limited partner may separately be an agent of the limited partnership (e.g., as an employee) and *in that capacity* may have the power to bind the partnership as a matter of agency law. See Chapters 2 and 3.

36. Alan will be liable for breach of agency law's warranty of authority. See Section 4.2.2.

37. See Section 2.3 (Apparent Authority).

Case in Point — *General Elec. Credit Corp. v. Stover*

A limited partnership obtained credit from Plaintiff, and Defendant (a limited partner) signed a Security Agreement along with the general partner. Later, the partnership defaulted under the agreement, and the general partner filed personal bankruptcy. Plaintiff sued Defendant, asserting Defendant had assumed personal liability by signing the agreement. Affirming judgment against Defendant, the court of appeals held that the limited partner was personally liable on the agreement. The court reasoned that the Defendant's signature must have been for purpose of binding him personally, because as a limited partner Defendant had no authority to bind the partnership.[38] ◄◄◄

Consistent with the "pick your partner" principle,[39] which is fundamental to all of partnership law, as a default rule RULPA requires the consent of all partners to the admission of any new limited or general partner.[40] Consistent with the law of contracts, any amendment of the partnership agreement requires the consent of all partners unless the agreement itself provides otherwise. In addition, limited partners have the right to information about the partnership business,[41] may have the opportunity to consent to avoid or cause dissolution,[42] and can bring derivative suits to assert partnership claims against the general partners.[43] RULPA does not, however, empower limited partners to remove a general partner, even for cause.[44]

The partnership agreement can enlarge the governance role of the limited partners. For example, some limited partnership agreements give the limited partners the right to remove the general partners. The partnership agreement can also shrink the rights of limited partners, for example by changing the quantum of consent necessary to admit new partners or setting conditions on a limited partner's access to information.

---

38. *General Elec. Credit Corp. v. Stover*, 708 S.W.2d 355 (Mo. App. 1986).
39. For a discussion of the "pick your partner" principle, see Section 8.8.
40. RULPA, §§301(b)(2) (additional limited partner may be admitted "upon the written consent of all partners") and 401 ("additional general partners may be admitted . . . with the written consent of all partners").
41. RULPA, §305.
42. See Section 12.2.7.
43. RULPA, §§1001–1004. In a derivative suit, a limited partner asserts standing to enforce the partnership's rights. Protecting the partnership's rights—whether by litigation or otherwise—is a management matter and therefore ordinarily the province of the general partners. Derivative plaintiffs typically assert, however, that the general partners cannot be trusted to protect the partnership's interests because the general partners are or will be defendants. For a more detailed discussion of derivative claims, see Section 16.4.
44. RULPA, §403(3) ("withdrawal" of a general partner occurs *inter alia* when "the general partner is removed as a general partner *in accordance with the partnership agreement*") (emphasis added).

§12.2.5 Profit and Loss Sharing

RULPA's default rules on profit and loss sharing differ both structurally and substantively from the general partnership rule. Both UPA (1914) and UPA (1997) provide simply that the partners share profits per capita (i.e., equally) and losses according to profit share.[45] UPA (2013) is essentially the same, although it refers to allocation of distributions.[46]

RULPA addresses the *allocation* of profits and losses (which is important for bookkeeping and tax purposes) separately from the sharing of actual *distributions*. However, the default rule is the same under both rubrics. Subject to the partnership agreement, profits and losses are allocated and distributions are shared in proportion to "the value . . . of the contributions made by each partner to the extent they have been received by the partnership and have not been returned."[47]

Example

Ofek, Lotem, Maor, and Noam, four cousins, are partners in Asif, LP. Ofek and Lotem are the general partners, each having contributed $10,000. Maor and Noam, the limited partners, contributed $50,000 and $40,000, respectively. Noam subsequently receives $10,000 as a partial return of her contribution. The partnership agreement provides that Ofek and Lotem will each receive $50,000 per year as a management fee but says nothing about profits, losses, and distributions. The partnership will therefore allocate profits and losses and make distributions according to the following percentages:

12.1 Allocating Profits, Losses, and Distributions Among the Four Cousins

Partner	Contributions Made and Not Yet Returned	Profit, Loss, and Distribution Allocation
Ofek	$10,000	10%
Lotem	$10,000	10%
Maor	$50,000	50%
Noam	$30,000 ($40,000-$10,000)	30% ◄◄◄

45. UPA (1914), §1 8(a); UPA (1997), §401(b). See Section 8.3.1.
46. See Section 8.3.1.
47. The same language appears in RULPA, §§503 (sharing of profits and losses) and 504 (sharing of distributions).

§12.2.6 Transfer of Partnership Interests

Like all other partnership statutes, RULPA follows the "pick your partner" rule. Unless the partnership agreement provides otherwise, no partner, whether general or limited, may transfer its governance authority to another person or substitute another person for itself as a partner without the consent of all the other partners.[48] Absent a contrary agreement, a partner may freely transfer its financial rights.[49]

§12.2.7 Partner Dissociation and Partnership Dissolution

RULPA refers to partner dissociation as "withdrawal,"[50] and a general partner in a RULPA limited partnership has the power to withdraw at any time. A general partner's withdrawal threatens but does not necessarily cause dissolution. The limited partnership can avoid dissolution if either: (i) the partnership has at least one remaining general partner, the partnership agreement allows the remaining general partners to continue the partnership, and the remaining general partners do so; or (ii) within 90 days after the withdrawal, *all* the remaining partners (limited as well as general) agree in writing to continue the partnership.[51]

If a general partner's withdrawal does result in dissolution, the consequences are comparable to the dissolution of a general partnership. If the partnership avoids dissolution, the former general partner has a right, subject to the partnership agreement, to be paid "within a reasonable time after withdrawal, the fair value of his [or her] interest in the limited partnership."[52] However, if the withdrawal breached the partnership agreement, the payout is subject to any damages caused by the breach.[53]

In this, as in almost all *inter se* matters, the partnership agreement can override the statutory default rules. For example, a limited partnership agreement can validly "freeze in" the interest of a general partner who

---

48. RULPA, §702.
49. RULPA, §702.
50. RULPA, §§602, 603. Although "withdrawal" suggests a voluntary act, *see* WITHDRAWAL, Black's Law Dictionary (12th ed. 2024); WITHDRAWAL, *id.*, RULPA uses the term to refer generally to any dissociation.
51. RULPA, §801(4). If there is no remaining general partner, then the limited partners must also consent to appoint at least one new general partner. *Id.* Influenced by tax classification developments related to limited liability companies, see Section 13.1.4(d), some RULPA states have amended their RULPA dissolution provisions to lower the quantum of consent needed to avoid dissolution following the withdrawal of a general partner.
52. RULPA, §604 (brackets in the original).
53. RULPA, §602.

withdraws in breach of the partnership agreement, eliminating the general partner's management rights and transforming the financial rights into those of a mere assignee.[54]

Whether limited partners have the power to dissociate depends on the partnership agreement—in particular on whether the partnership agreement in writing: (i) states a particular term for the partnership; (ii) authorizes limited partner withdrawal; or (iii) does both. If the partnership agreement does neither, then a limited partner can withdraw by giving at least six months' written notice to each general partner.[55] If the partnership agreement states a particular term, then a limited partner can withdraw only if allowed by the agreement. If the partnership agreement provides for limited partner withdrawal, then—regardless of whether the agreement states a particular term—a limited partner can withdraw only as provided in the agreement. In tabular form:

12.2 The Partnership Agreement and the Limited Partner's Power to Withdraw

	Limited Partnership Agreement Provides for Limited Partner Withdrawal	**Limited Partnership Agreement Does Not Provide for Limited Partner Withdrawal**
Limited Partnership Agreement Provides for Particular Term for Partnership	Limited partner can withdraw only as provided in partnership agreement	Limited partner cannot withdraw
Limited Partnership Agreement Does Not Provide for Particular Term for Partnership	Limited partner can withdraw only as provided in partnership agreement	Limited partner can withdraw on six months' written notice.

54. Under ULPA (2001), this is the default rule applicable when a general partner dissociates. ULPA (2001), §§605(a)(1) and 605(a)(5). See the discussion in Section 12.3.5. Contrast UPA (1997), §701(h) (if partner in a term general partnership dissociates prematurely, no payout until the expiration of the term unless the partner establishes that earlier payment will not cause the partnership undue hardship). See also UPA (1914), §38(2) (if a partner wrongfully dissolves a general partnership, the remaining partners may delay that partner's payout and use the resources in a successor partnership). For a discussion of UPA (1997), §701(h), see Section 11.9.5.

55. RULPA, §603. This situation seems unlikely to occur, because RULPA, §201(a)(4) requires the certificate of limited partnership to state a definite term. In light of RULPA, §603, the term will be repeated in most limited partnership agreements.

CASE IN POINT

Case in Point — *Della Ratta v. Larkin*

"This dispute among the partners of the East Park Limited Partnership ('East Park') arose in the aftermath of East Park's sole general partner issuing a substantial capital call [a demand for further contributions] in March 2002. Some of the limited partners, who believed compliance with the capital call was financially unwise, wrote to the general partner to inform him of their intention to withdraw from the partnership before the capital call became due. The general partner responded that the limited partners could not withdraw from the partnership and would be in default should they fail to comply with the capital call, the due date for which the general partner accelerated to a point in time prior to the announced effective date of the withdrawal of the pertinent limited partners." Plaintiffs filed a suit seeking a declaratory judgment that they had withdrawn properly and an injunction prohibiting the enforcement of the capital call. Affirming the prior grant of summary judgment as to this issue, the Court of Appeals determined that the Plaintiffs had properly withdrawn based on their statutory right (which was not contravened by any agreement) to withdraw from the partnership with a six-month notice to the general partner.[56] ◄◄◄

The withdrawal of a limited partner does not cause or even threaten dissolution.[57] A limited partner who withdraws does have the right to be paid out within a reasonable time, unless the partnership agreement provides otherwise.[58]

For reasons related to so-called family limited partnerships, some RULPA states have amended their version of RULPA to eliminate a limited partner's power to withdraw or to freeze in a limited partner's financial interest even after withdrawal.[59]

---

§12.3 ULPA (2001)[60]

§12.3.1 The Development of ULPA (2001)

Because RULPA is linked to UPA (1914), the ULC's promulgation of UPA (1997) raised questions about RULPA. "[UPA (1997)] differs substantially

56. *Della Ratta v. Larkin*, 856 A.2d 643, 645 (Md. 2004).
57. RULPA, §801 (stating causes of dissolution and not mentioning the withdrawal of a limited partner). The partnership agreement could make a limited partner's withdrawal a cause of dissolution. See RULPA §801(2) (allowing the partnership agreement to specify additional events that cause dissolution).
58. RULPA, §604.
59. Section 12.4 discusses family limited partnerships.
60. This section is derived from the Prefatory Notes and Official Comments to ULPA (2001), which were drafted by the author in his capacity as Reporter to the ULC Drafting Committee

from UPA (1914), and the drafters of UPA (1997) expressly declined to decide whether UPA (1997) provides a suitable base and link for the limited partnership statute."[61]

In 1997, a ULC drafting committee began considering what modifications to make to RULPA. The drafting committee quickly decided to develop a new, stand-alone statute to replace RULPA. The committee determined that linkage "has not been completely satisfactory, because the consequences of linkage are not always clear" and because "in some instances the 'not inconsistent' rules of UPA (1914) can be inappropriate for the fundamentally different relations involved in a limited partnership."[62] The committee also decided that a stand-alone act would "promote clarity and coherence in the law of limited partnerships" by recognizing that "the modern limited partnership involves fundamentally different relations than those involved in 'the small, often informal, partnership' that is '[t]he primary focus of [UPA (1997)].'"[63] In particular, a stand-alone act would "rationalize future case law, by ending the automatic link between the cases concerning partners in a general partnership and issues pertaining to general partners in a limited partnership."[64]

The drafting process took four years (during which the new Act was colloquially and temporarily referred to as the "Re-RULPA"). In August 2001, the ULC gave final approval to ULPA (2001).

§12.3.2 Basic Purpose, Assumptions, and Approach

The basic purpose, assumptions, and approach of ULPA (2001) are best summarized in the first section of the Act's Prefatory Note:

> The new Act has been drafted for a world in which limited liability partnerships and limited liability companies can meet many of the needs formerly met by limited partnerships. This Act therefore targets two types of enterprises that seem largely beyond the scope of LLPs and LLCs: (i) sophisticated, manager-entrenched commercial deals whose participants commit for the long term, and (ii) estate planning arrangements (family limited partnerships). This Act accordingly assumes that, more often than not, people utilizing it will want:
>
> - strong centralized management, strongly entrenched, and
> - passive investors with little control over or right to exit the entity.

---

for ULPA (2001). For a more detailed analysis of ULPA (2001), see Daniel S. Kleinberger, "A User's Guide to the New Uniform Limited Partnership Act," 37 Suffolk L. Rev. 583 (2004).

61. ULPA (2001), Prefatory Note, The Decision to "De-Link" and Create a Stand-Alone Act.

62. *Id.*

63. *Id.*, quoting UPA (1997), Prefatory Note.

64. ULPA (2001), Prefatory Note, The Decision to "De-Link" and Create a Stand-Alone Act.

The Act's rules, and particularly its default rules, have been designed to reflect these assumptions.[65]

§12.3.3 Overview of Major Differences Between RULPA and ULPA (2001)

There are 12 major differences between RULPA and ULPA (2001). In contrast to RULPA, ULPA (2001):

1. is a stand-alone act, as previously explained, incorporating essentially verbatim many important provisions from UPA (1997);[66]
2. provides constructive notice, 90 days after appropriate filing, of general partner dissociation and of limited partnership dissolution, termination, merger, and conversion;[67]
3. has a "perpetual duration," which means that the limited partnership continues indefinitely, without a term, unless otherwise provided in the partnership agreement and subject to dissolution by partner consent;[68]
4. expressly delineates the permissible scope and effect of the partnership agreement;[69]
5. provides a complete, corporate-like liability shield for limited partners "even if the limited partner participates in the management and control of the limited partnership";[70]
6. permits a limited partnership to be a limited liability limited partnership (LLLP), and thereby makes a complete, corporate-like liability shield available to general partners;[71]
7. gives limited partners the power but not the right to dissociate before the limited partnership's termination and allows the partnership agreement to eliminate even the power;[72]

---

65. ULPA (2001), Prefatory Note, The Act's Overall Approach. Chapters 13–16 discuss limited liability companies. Chapter 17 discusses limited liability partnerships.
66. For example, ULPA (2001) incorporates UPA (1997)'s provisions on the power of a general partner to bind the partnership. ULPA (2001), §§402 (general partner agent of limited partnership) and 403 (limited partnership liable for general partner's actionable conduct), incorporating respectively UPA (1997), §§301 and 305.
67. In this respect, ULPA (2001) follows the example of UPA (1997). See Sections 10.4.3 (UPA (1997) statements of authority), 11.10.2 (UPA (1997) statements of dissociation and statements of dissolution).
68. ULPA (2001), §§104(c) and 801 (1), (2), and (3).
69. ULPA (2001), §110.
70. ULPA (2001), §303. See Section 12.3.4.
71. ULPA (2001), §§102(9), 201(a)(4), and 404(c). Chapter 17 discusses limited liability limited partnerships.
72. ULPA (2001), §§601(a) and 601(b)(1).

8. eliminates any buyout of dissociated partners, unless the partnership agreement provides otherwise;[73]
9. eschews UPA (1914)'s open-ended approach to general partner fiduciary duties and incorporates essentially verbatim UPA (1997)'s provision on fiduciary duty and the obligation of good faith and fair dealing;[74]
10. provides for judicial expulsion of a general partner, although the partnership agreement can negate this provision;[75]
11. makes dissolution following a general partner's dissociation less likely, by replacing RULPA's unanimous consent rule with a two-pronged approach:
    a. if at least one general partner remains, no dissolution unless "within 90 days after the dissociation . . . partners owning a majority of the rights to receive distributions as partners" consent to dissolve the limited partnership;[76]
    b. if no general partner remains, dissolution occurs upon the passage of 90 days after the dissociation, unless before that deadline limited partners owning a majority of the rights to receive distributions owned by limited partners consent to continue the business and admit at least one new general partner and a new general partner is admitted;[77] and
12. authorizes a limited partnership to participate in mergers and conversions.

§12.3.4 Complete Shield for Limited Partners

ULPA (2001), §303 rejects the "control rule" of limited partner liability[78] and states:

> An obligation of a limited partnership, whether arising in contract, tort, or otherwise, is not the obligation of a limited partner. A limited partner is not personally liable, directly or indirectly, by way of contribution or otherwise, for an obligation of the limited partnership solely by reason of being a limited

73. ULPA (2001), §§602(3) (limited partners) and 605(a)(5) (general partner).
74. ULPA (2001), §408. In contrast with UPA (1997), ULPA (2001), §408(b)(3) provides that a general partner's noncompete duties continue during winding up. As part of the Harmonization Project, the ULC "un-cabined" fiduciary duty in both general and limited partnerships. For a discussion of this point, see Section 9.7.2.
75. ULPA (2001), §603(5).
76. ULPA (2001), §801(3)(A).
77. ULPA (2001), §801(3)(B).
78. See Section 12.2.3.

partner, even if the limited partner participates in the management and control of the limited partnership.

The official Comment explains: "In a world with LLPs, LLCs and, most importantly, LLLPs, the control rule has become an anachronism."

Example

Ventura, LP is an ULPA (2001) limited partnership that initially has two general partners, Maurice and Rolande. Although Maurice dissociates, the limited partnership does not dissolve. To assist Rolande on an interim basis, two limited partners, Suzanne and Alan, become deeply involved in the management of the limited partnership. Even if a third party extends credit to the limited partnership believing Alan and Suzanne to be general partners, they are not liable for Ventura's obligations.[79] ◀◀◀

As is the case with any liability shield, the limited partner's shield protects only against liability asserted "solely by reason of being" an owner of an entity.[80] As a result, the shield is irrelevant to (and therefore does not protect against) a limited partner's liability arising from: (i) wrongful personal conduct (including fraudulently describing oneself as a general partner); (ii) unfilled promises to contribute; (iii) improperly received distributions; and (iv) a mistaken belief that one is, in fact, a limited partner.[81]

§12.3.5 Freezing in the Transferable Interests of Dissociated Partners

Like UPA (1997), ULPA (2001) refers to the financial rights of a partner as the partner's "transferable interest." Under ULPA (2001), unless the partnership agreement provides otherwise, a partner who dissociates before the termination of a limited partnership becomes merely the transferee of his, her, or its own transferable interest.

79. If someone has misrepresented Alan's and Suzanne's status to the third party, the third party may have a claim for misrepresentation.
80. See Section 17.2.4 (discussing this point in the context of limited liability partnerships).
81. Compare Section 12.2.3 (personal liability of RULPA limited partners). Under ULPA (2001), use of a limited partner's name in the name of the limited partnership does not put the limited partner at risk of personal liability. ULPA (2001), §108(a).

Example

Oscar is a limited partner in an ULPA (2001) limited partnership. When Oscar dies, his transferable interest will be distributed to his heirs according to estate law. There will be no payout to his heirs; they will acquire only whatever rights Oscar had to receive distributions. They will not become limited partners. ◀◀◀

Example

Cornflakes, LP, is an ULPA (2001) limited partnership that initially has two general partners, Oscar and Felix. Oscar also owns a limited partner interest. Oscar's transferable interest as a general partner allocates to him the right to 1 percent of all distributions. His transferable interest as a limited partner allocates to him the right to 5 percent of all distributions.

Pursuant to the limited partnership agreement, Oscar is expelled as a general partner (but not as a limited partner). The limited partnership does not dissolve. Oscar continues to own the 5 percent as a limited partner (with whatever governance rights may accompany that interest). He holds his 1 percent profits interest, however, as a mere transferee. ◀◀◀

§12.3.6 The Nexus Between General Partner Dissociation and Limited Partnership Dissolution

Taking advantage of the tax classification flexibility created by the Internal Revenue Service in 1997,[82] ULPA (2001) significantly attenuates the nexus between general partner dissociation and limited partnership dissolution. ULPA (2001), §801(3) provides:

> a limited partnership is dissolved, and its activities must be wound up, . . . (3) after the dissociation of a person as a general partner:
>
> (A) if the limited partnership has at least one remaining general partner, the consent to dissolve the limited partnership given within 90 days after the dissociation by partners owning a majority of the rights to receive distributions as partners at the time the consent is to be effective; or
>
> (B) if the limited partnership does not have a remaining general partner, the passage of 90 days after the dissociation, unless before the end of the period:

82. For a detailed discussion of the IRS's revolutionary "check the box" regulations, see Section 13.1.4(d).

(i) consent to continue the activities of the limited partnership and admit at least one general partner is given by limited partners owning a majority of the rights to receive distributions as limited partners at the time the consent is to be effective; and

(ii) at least one person is admitted as a general partner in accordance with the consent; . . .

Example

Cornflakes, LP, is an ULPA (2001) limited partnership that initially has two general partners, Oscar and Felix. Felix's transferable interest as a general partner allocates to him 2 percent of all distributions. Oscar's transferable interest as a general partner allocates to him the right to 1 percent of all distributions. Oscar also owns a limited partner interest, which allocates to him the right to 5 percent of all distributions. Other limited partners in the aggregate own the right to receive 82 percent of all distributions. Nonpartner transferees in the aggregate own the right to receive 10 percent of all distributions.

Oscar dissociates from the limited partnership and hopes for dissolution. In his capacity as a *limited* partner, Oscar consents to dissolve the limited partnership. So do other limited partners owning in the aggregate 39 percent of the rights to receive distributions.

The limited partnership is not dissolved. ULPA (2001), §801(3)(A)(i) requires consent "by partners owning a majority of the rights to receive distributions *as partners*" (emphasis added). The calculation is as follows:

Felix as general partner	2%
Oscar as limited partner	5%[83] After Oscar's dissociation, he owns as a mere transferee the transferable interest (1 percent) he formerly owned as a general partner. ULPA (2001), §605(a)(5).
Other limited partners	82%
Total relevant percent (ignoring the 11% owned by nonpartner transferees)[83]	89%
Majority needed to dissolve	>44.5%
Percent consenting to dissolution	44% (Oscar as limited partner [5%] + other limited partners [39%]) ◀◀◀

83. As stated in the Example, before Oscar's dissociation 10 percent of the distribution rights were owned by nonpartner transferees. Oscar's dissociation as general partner converted the 1 percent interest he had previously held as a partner into a mere transferee interest.

§12.3.7 Dissolution by Consent of the Partners

Perhaps paradoxically, it is easier under ULPA (2001) than under RULPA to dissolve a limited partnership by consent of the partners. RULPA §801(3) requires "the written consent of all partners." In contrast, ULPA (2001), §801(2) states that the limited partnership is dissolved upon "the consent of all general partners and of limited partners owning a majority of the rights to receive distributions as limited partners at the time the consent is to be effective."

Example

XYZ is a limited partnership with three general partners, each of whom is also a limited partner, and five other limited partners. Rights to receive distributions are allocated as follows:

Partner #1 as general partner	3%
Partner #2 as general partner	2%
Partner #3 as general partner	1%
Partner #1 as limited partner	7%
Partner #2 as limited partner	3%
Partner #3 as limited partner	4%
Partner #4 as limited partner	5%
Partner #5 as limited partner	5%
Partner #6 as limited partner	5%
Partner #7 as limited partner	5%
Partner #8 as limited partner	5%
Several nonpartner transferees, in the aggregate	55%

Distribution rights owned by persons as limited partners amount to 39 percent of total distribution rights. A majority is therefore anything greater than 19.5 percent. If only partners 1, 2, 3, and 4 consent to dissolve, the limited partnership is not dissolved. Together these partners own as limited partners 19 percent of the distribution rights owned by persons as limited partners—just short of the necessary majority. For purposes of this calculation, distribution rights owned by nonpartner transferees are irrelevant. So, too, are distribution rights owned by persons as general partners. (However, dissolution under this provision requires "the consent of all general partners.")[84] ◄◄◄

84. This Example is taken verbatim from the Comment to ULPA (2001), §801, Paragraph (2).

§12.3.8 Detailed Comparison of RULPA and ULPA (2001)

The following table[85] compares some of the major characteristics of RULPA and ULPA (2001). In most instances, the rules involved are "default" rules—i.e., subject to change by the partnership agreement.

12.3 RULPA and ULPA (2001) Compared

Characteristic	RULPA	ULPA (2001)
Relationship to general partnership act	Linked, §§1105, 403; UPA (1914) §6(2)	Delinked (but many UPA (1997) provisions incorporated)
Permitted purposes	Subject to any specified exceptions, "any business that a partnership without limited partners may carry on," §106	Any lawful purpose, §104(b)
Constructive notice via publicly filed documents	Only that limited partnership exists and that designated general partners are general partners, §208	RULPA constructive notice provisions carried forward, §103(c), plus constructive notice, 90 days after appropriate filing, of: general partner dissociation and of limited partnership dissolution, termination, merger, and conversion, §103(d)
Duration	Specified in certificate of limited partnership, §201(a)(4)	Perpetual, §104(c); subject to change in partnership agreement
Use of limited partner name in entity name	Prohibited, except in unusual circumstances, §102(2)	Permitted, §108(a)
Annual report	None	Required, §210
Limited partner liability for entity debts	None unless limited partner "participates in the control of the business" and person "transact[s] business with the limited partnership reasonably	None, regardless of whether the limited partnership is a LLLP, "even if the limited partner participates in the management and control of the limited partnership," §303

85. This table appears at the end of the Prefatory Note to ULPA (2001) and is used by permission of the ULC.

12.3 Continued

Characteristic	RULPA	ULPA (2001)
	believing . . . that the limited partner is a general partner," §303(a); safe harbor lists many activities that do not constitute participating in the control of the business, §303(b)	
Limited partner duties	None specified	No fiduciary duties "solely by reason of being a limited partner," §305(a); each limited partner is obliged to "discharge duties . . . and exercise rights consistently with the obligation of good faith and fair dealing," §305(b)
Partner access to information—required records/ information	All partners have right of access; no requirement of good cause; Act does not state whether partnership agreement may limit access; §§105(b) and 305(1)	List of required information expanded slightly; Act expressly states that partner does not have to show good cause; §§304(a), 407(a); however, the partnership agreement may set reasonable restrictions on access to and use of required information, §110(b)(4), and limited partnership may impose reasonable restrictions on the use of information, §§304(g) and 407(f)
Partner access to information—other information	Limited partners have the right to obtain other relevant information "upon reasonable demand,"§305(2); general partner rights linked to general partnership act, §403	For limited partners, RULPA approach essentially carried forward, with procedures and standards for making a reasonable demand stated in greater detail, plus requirement that limited partnership supply known material information when limited partner consent sought, §304; general partner access rights made explicit, following ULLCA (1996) and UPA (1997), including obligation of limited partnership and general partners to volunteer certain information, §407; access rights provided for former partners, §§304 and 407

12.3 Continued

Characteristic	RULPA	ULPA (2001)
General partner liability for entity debts	Complete, automatic and formally inescapable, §403(b) (n.b. — in practice, most modern limited partnerships have used a general partner that has its own liability shield; e.g., a corporation or limited liability company)	LLLP status available via a simple statement in the certificate of limited partnership, §§102(9), 201(a)(4); LLLP status provides a full liability shield to all general partners, §404(c); if the limited partnership is not a LLLP, general partners are liable just as under RULPA, §404(a)
General partner duties	Linked to duties of partners in a general partnership, §403	UPA (1997) general partner duties imported, §408; general partner's noncompete duty continues during winding up, §408(b)(3)
Allocation of profits, losses, and distributions	Provides separately for sharing of profits and losses, §503, and for sharing of distributions, §504; allocates each according to contributions made and not returned	Eliminates as unnecessary the allocation rule for profits and losses; allocates distributions according to contributions made, §503 (n.b. — in the default mode, the Act's formulation produces the same result as RULPA formulation)
Partner liability for distributions	Recapture liability if distribution involved "the return of . . . contribution"; one year recapture liability if distribution rightful, §608(a); six year recapture liability if wrongful, §608(b)	Following ULLCA (1996) §§406 and 407, the Act adopts the RMBCA approach to improper distributions, §§508 and 509
Limited partner voluntary dissociation	Theoretically, limited partner may withdraw on six months' notice unless partnership agreement specifies a term for the limited partnership or withdrawal events for limited partner, §603; practically, virtually every partnership agreement specifies a term, thereby	No "right to dissociate as a limited partner before the termination of the limited partnership," §601(a); power to dissociate expressly recognized, §601(b)(1), but can be eliminated by the partnership agreement

12.3 Continued

Characteristic	RULPA	ULPA (2001)
	eliminating the right to withdraw (n.b. — due to estate planning concerns, several States have amended RULPA to prohibit limited partner withdrawal unless otherwise provided in the partnership agreement)	
Limited partner involuntary dissociation	Not addressed	Lengthy list of causes, §601(b), taken with some modification from UPA (1997)
Limited partner dissociation — payout	"Fair value . . . based upon [the partner's] right to share in distributions,"§604	No payout; person becomes transferee of its own transferable interest, §602(3)
General partner voluntary dissociation	Right exists unless otherwise provided in partnership agreement, §602; power exists regardless of partnership agreement, §602	RULPA rule carried forward, although phrased differently, §604(a); dissociation before termination of the limited partnership is defined as wrongful, §604(b)(2)
General partner involuntary dissociation	§402 lists causes	Following UPA (1997), §603 expands the list of causes, including expulsion by court order, §603(5)
General partner dissociation — payout	"Fair value . . . based upon [the partner's] right to share in distributions," §604, subject to offset for damages caused by wrongful withdrawal, §602	No payout; person becomes transferee of its own transferable interest, §605(a)(5)
Transfer of partner interest — nomenclature	"Assignment of Partnership Interest," §702	"Transfer of Partner's Transferable Interest," §702
Transfer of partner interest — substance	Economic rights fully transferable, but management rights and partner status are not transferable, §702	Same rule as RULPA, but §§701 and 702 follow UPA's more detailed and less oblique formulation

12.3 Continued

Characteristic	RULPA	ULPA (2001)
Rights of creditor of partner	Limited to charging order, §703	Essentially the same rule as RULPA (1997), but, following UPA and ULLCA (1996), the Act has a more elaborate provision that expressly extends to creditors of transferees, §703
Dissolution by partner consent	Requires unanimous written consent, §801(3)	Requires consent of "all general partners and of limited partners owning a majority of the rights to receive distributions as limited partners at the time the consent is to be effective," §801(2)
Dissolution following dissociation of a general partner	Occurs automatically unless all partners agree to continue the business and, if there is no remaining general partner, to appoint a replacement general partner, §801(4)	If at least one general partner remains, no dissolution unless "within 90 days after the dissociation . . . partners owning a majority of the rights to receive distributions as partners" consent to dissolve the limited partnership, §801(3)(A); if no general partner remains, dissolution occurs upon the passage of 90 days after the dissociation, unless before that deadline limited partners owning a majority of the rights to receive distributions owned by limited partners consent to continue the business and admit at least one new general partner and a new general partner is admitted, §801(3)(B)
Filings related to entity termination	Certificate of limited partnership to be cancelled when limited partnership dissolves and begins winding up, §203	Limited partnership may amend certificate to indicate dissolution, §803(b)(1), and may file statement of termination indicating that winding up has been completed and the limited partnership is terminated, §203
Procedures for barring claims against dissolved limited partnership	None	Following ULLCA (1996) §§807 and 808, the Act adopts the RMBCA approach providing for giving notice and barring claims, §§806 and 807

12.3 Continued

Characteristic	RULPA	ULPA (2001)
Conversions and mergers	No provision	Article 11 permits conversions to and from and mergers with any "organization," defined as "a general partnership, including a limited liability partnership; limited partnership, including a limited liability limited partnership; limited liability company; business trust; corporation; or any other entity having a governing statute . . . [including] domestic and foreign entities regardless of whether organized for profit." §1101(8)
Writing requirements	Some provisions pertain only to written understandings; see, e.g., §§401 (partnership agreement may "provide in writing for the admission of additional general partners"; such admission also permitted "with the written consent of all partners"), 502(a) (limited partner's promise to contribute "is not enforceable unless set out in a writing signed by the limited partner"), 801(2) and (3) (dissolution occurs "upon the happening of events specified in writing in the partnership agreement" and upon "written consent of all partners"), 801(4) (dissolution avoided following withdrawal of a general partner if "all partners agree in writing")	Removes virtually all writing requirements; but does require that certain information be maintained in record form, §111

§12.4 ULPA (2013)—THE HARMONIZATION AMENDMENTS[86]

ULPA (2001) substantially modernized the ULC's approach to limited partnerships, and enactments of this "pre-Harmonization" act still outnumber enactments of ULPA (2013). However, the "Harmonized" version has developed some traction of its own. Moreover, studying ULPA (2013) helps illumine certain issues under ULPA (2001).[87]

For the most part, ULPA (2013) closely follows ULPA (2001). The former makes stylistic changes to languages and renumbers various sections. According to ULPA (2013)'s official comments, only five substantive changes are noteworthy:

> The most significant substantive change is the "un-cabining" fiduciary duty; i.e., ceasing to characterize the Act's codification of fiduciary duty as exhaustive, Section 409.[88] Other substantive changes include: (i) providing a narrow exception to the rule that the amendments to the partnership agreement control the rights of persons previously dissociated as partners and of persons who had previously become transferees, Section 107(b)(2); (ii) eliminating the requirement that a domestic limited partnership designate and maintain an in-state office, Section 201; (iii) requiring that the annual report list the name of at least one general partner, Section 212(a)(4); and (iv) expressly authorizing a limited partnership to provide advancements to a person entitled to indemnification, Section 408(c).[89]

§ 12.5 FAMILY LIMITED PARTNERSHIPS

One of the major uses of limited partnerships is the so-called family limited partnership. A family limited partnership is an estate-planning vehicle whose use requires very sophisticated planning under some very abstruse IRS regulations concerning estate and gift tax. The details of that planning

86. For a discussion of the Harmonization Project, see Note on the ULC Harmonization Project at page

87. See, e.g., 15 Pa. Stat. and Cons. Stat. Ann. § 8611 et seq.(enacting Pennsylvania's version of ULPA (2013) and 8611(a) ("This chapter may be cited as the Pennsylvania Uniform Limited Partnership Act of 2016.")

88. For a discussion of the "un-cabining" issue, see Section 9.7.2.

89.

and those regulations are far beyond the scope of this chapter, but it is worthwhile to note several points that have influenced the developments in limited partnership statutes:

1. When a person makes a noncharitable gift of major value, the gift is subject to a gift tax, with the amount of tax based on the fair market value of the gift. To determine fair market value, the law tries to determine the price a hypothetical willing buyer and willing seller would agree on, with neither facing any compulsion to make a deal.
2. A major purpose of a family limited partnership is to allow wealthy members of one generation to gift property to a younger generation in a way that enables the donor to claim substantial discounts in the fair market value of the gift.
3. If a family limited partnership owns substantial assets, the would-be donors can:
   a. serve as general partners of the limited partnership, thereby keeping control of the assets during their lifetime; while
   b. gifting limited partner interests to members of younger generations; and
   c. claiming large discounts on the fair market value of the gifts because:
      i. a limited partner has no right to force distributions or dissolution (which would produce a payout via winding up and liquidation);
      ii. the general partner is not subject to removal and completely controls operations; and therefore
      iii. the hypothetical willing buyer would not pay a large amount for the limited partner interest.

From the perspective of valuation discounts, the more locked in (i.e., illiquid) a limited partner interest is, the better. And, because the IRS regulations will disregard any restrictions on liquidity created by agreement,[90] the illiquidity must be built into the default rules of the limited partnership statute.

To accommodate this perspective, a number of RULPA states have amended their version of RULPA to protect limited partnerships from

90. The rationale for disregarding what are called "applicable restrictions" is that in a family limited partnership, the family will agree to disregard the restrictions when it suits the family's purposes.

dissolution, prevent limited partners from withdrawing, and lock in a limited partner's transferable interest even if the limited partner does withdraw. ULPA (2001) has incorporated all those approaches: giving each limited partnership a perpetual term;[91] attenuating the nexus between general partner dissociation and limited partnership dissolution;[92] depriving limited partners of the right to dissociate;[93] permitting the partnership agreement to eliminate a limited partner's power to dissociate;[94] and providing that a partner who dissociates is not entitled to any payout on account of having dissociated.[95]

Problem 109

Rosebud, LP is a limited partnership with a term of 30 years. Ten years into the term, an opportunity arises to sell all the partnership's assets and make a substantial profit. All the limited partners wish to take advantage of this opportunity, but the sole general partner believes that greater returns will be available if the limited partnership continues in existence until the end of its 30-year term. Under RULPA, can the limited partners bring about the sale of the partnership's assets? Under ULPA (2001)? ◄◄◄

Explanation

No, under either statute. With exceptions not relevant here, both statutes vest management authority in the general partner. Moreover, neither statute permits the limited partners to cause the premature dissolution of the limited partnership and thereby force the general partner to sell the assets as part of winding up. Under RULPA §801(3), dissolution by partner consent requires "the written consent of all partners." ULPA (2001), §801(2) requires "the consent of all general partners and of limited partners owning a majority of the rights to receive distributions as limited partners." ◄◄◄

Problem 110

Wife is the sole general partner of a limited partnership. Husband, who is retired, assists Wife in running the business by working as the unofficial office manager of the limited partnership's principal place of business. Husband's efforts are voluntary and are not compensated. Husband owns

---

91. ULPA (2001), §104(c).
92. ULPA (2001), §801(3).
93. ULPA (2001), §§601(a) and 601(b)(1).
94. ULPA (2001), §110(b).
95. ULPA (2001), §§602(3) (limited partner) and 605(a)(5) (general partner).

a limited partner's interest in the partnership, which is reflected in the partnership agreement. The partnership agreement does not indicate that Husband has any role in managing the limited partnership.

A trade creditor of the limited partnership, knowing that Wife is a general partner and seeing that Husband performs key administrative functions, believes that Husband is also a general partner. The trade creditor maintains an "open account" with the limited partnership (i.e., delivering products without prepayment and invoicing the limited partnership for payment after delivery).

The limited partnership becomes insolvent, still owing the trade creditor substantial amounts. If the limited partnership is organized under RULPA, does the trade creditor have a valid claim against Husband? What if the limited partnership is organized under ULPA (2001)? ◀◀◀

Explanation

The trade creditor may have a valid claim under RULPA, §303(a). Husband is a limited partner who, arguably at least, has "participate[d] in the control of the business." The trade creditor has "transacted business with the limited partnership reasonably believing, based upon the limited partner's conduct, that the limited partner [was] a general partner."

However, Husband may qualify for one of the safe harbors of RULPA §303(b). Husband's best chance is to assert RULPA §303(b)(1) and claim that he was merely "being . . . an agent . . . of the limited partnership."[96]

The result is clearer under ULPA (2001) §303: "A limited partner is not personally liable, directly or indirectly, by way of contribution or otherwise, for an obligation of the limited partnership solely by reason of being a limited partner, even if the limited partner participates in the management and control of the limited partnership." ◀◀◀

Problem 111

XYZ Limited Partnership ("XYZ") is managed by a sole general partner, ABC, Inc. ("ABC"), which is itself a corporation. ABC is the general partner of several different limited partnerships and, by a resolution of its board of directors, has authorized Shapiro, its Executive Vice President, to act for ABC in all matters within the ordinary course of ABC's responsibilities as the general partner of XYZ. Shapiro is also a limited partner in XYZ.

96. It should not matter that Husband worked without pay. A gratuitous agent is just as much an agent as a paid agent. See Section 1.5.1(a).

Purporting to act on behalf of XYZ, Shapiro signs a contract for 18 months of janitorial services at the building where XYZ maintains its headquarters. Is XYZ bound by Shapiro's act? ◄◄◄

Explanation

Yes. Although under both RULPA and ULPA (2001) Shapiro *qua* limited partner lacks the power to bind XYZ, Shapiro is also the authorized agent of the XYZ's general partner. In that capacity, Shapiro has the power to bind XYZ.

Because Shapiro was acting within the actual authority conferred on him by the resolution of ABC's board of directors, Shapiro's act is deemed an act of ABC. As the sole general partner of XYZ, ABC probably has the actual authority and certainly has the apparently/usual or apparently/ordinary power to bind XYZ to a janitorial contract.[97] ◄◄◄

Problem 112

Same facts as Problem 111. Does Shapiro's substantial involvement in the management of XYZ expose him to liability for XYZ's obligations? ◄◄◄

Explanation

The answer is the same under both RULPA and ULPA (2001)—no. Under ULPA (2001), a limited partner does not risk personal liability simply by participating in control of the business. ULPA (2001), §303. As for RULPA, Shapiro's activities come within the safe harbor protection of §303(b) ("being an officer [Executive Vice President] . . . of a general partner that is a corporation"). ◄◄◄

97. If the limited partnership is governed by RULPA, per RULPA §403(a) "a general partner of a limited partnership has the rights and powers . . . of a partner in a partnership without limited partners" (i.e., UPA (1914) §9(1) applies and with it the concept of apparently/usual power). See Section 10.3.1. If the limited partnership is governed by ULPA (2001), per ULPA (2001) §402(a) a general partner has apparently/ordinary power to bind the partnership. See Section 10.4(a) (discussing this power in the context of UPA (1997) §301).

CHAPTER 13

Introductory Concepts in the History and Law of Limited Liability Companies, LLPs, and LLLPs

§13.1 THE CONTEXT

§13.1.1 The Modern Landscape for Unincorporated Business Organizations

Before 1988, the U.S. world of unincorporated business organizations had two main players:[1] ordinary general partnerships and ordinary limited partnerships.[2] Today, most general partnerships should be limited liability partnerships (LLPs), and many states have revised their limited partnership statutes to provide for limited liability limited partnerships (LLLPs). Even more fundamentally, an entirely new form of entity dominates the world of unincorporated businesses and has outpaced the corporation as the vehicle of choice for businesses whose ownership interests are not publicly traded.

The limited liability company (LLC) is a hybrid form of business entity that combines the liability shield of a corporation with the federal tax classification of a partnership. A creature of state law, each LLC is organized under an LLC statute that creates the company, gives it a legal existence separate from its owner or owners (called "members"), shields those members from

1. Some of this chapter is based on materials in Carter G. Bishop & Daniel S. Kleinberger, Bishop & Kleinberger on Limited Liability Companies (Warren, Gorham & Lamont/RIA 1994, Supp. 2025–1) ("Bishop & Kleinberger"), Chapter 1, which in turn evolved from an earlier edition of this book.
2. For the significance of the year 1988, see Section 13.1.4(b).

partner-like vicarious liability for the entity's obligations, and governs the company's structure, management, and operations (subject in most respects to the members' "operating agreement"). The essence of an LLC is the coexistence of partnership tax status with corporate-like limited liability.

§13.1.2 The Driving Force: The Tax-Shield Conundrum

The driving force behind the development and spread of the limited liability company has been the desire to solve the "the tax-shield conundrum," that is, to create an entity that:

- as a matter of non-tax, state law shields all the entity's owners from the automatic personal liability of a general partner; while
- as a matter of tax law is classified as a partnership with each owner treated as a partner.

Understanding the tax-shield conundrum requires understanding the characteristics of the corporate liability shield and the advantages of partnership tax classification.

a. Corporate Liability Shield

In a corporation, the owners (called "shareholders" or "stockholders") are not, merely on account of ownership status, liable for the obligations of the corporation. They are thus "shielded" from the automatic liability by status that comes with being a partner in an ordinary general partnership[3] or a general partner in an ordinary limited partnership.[4]

Example

Athos, Porthos, and Aramis form a corporation ("Fencing, Inc.") to teach fencing. They are its shareholders, and, as shareholders, they elect themselves to the corporation's board of directors.[5] The board elects Athos as Chief Executive Officer, Porthos as Executive Vice President, and Aramis as Chief Financial Officer. Acting through one of its duly authorized officers, the corporation then rents a building to serve as its headquarters and teaching center. Under agency law principles, the corporation is bound to

3. See Section 7.3.
4. See Section 12.2.3.
5. The board of directors is the top decision-making component of a corporation.

the lease.[6] Athos, Porthos, and Aramis, in contrast, are not. Shareholders *qua* shareholders are not personally liable for corporate obligations. ◄◄◄

Example

Same facts, except Athos, Porthos, and Aramis form an ordinary general partnership. They are each personally liable on the lease. ◄◄◄

Example

Same facts, except Athos, Porthos, and Aramis form an ordinary limited partnership, with Aramis as the sole general partner. Athos and Porthos do not involve themselves in managing the business, although they are employed as fencing instructors.[7] Aramis is personally liable on the lease; Athos and Porthos are not.

The shield does not protect a shareholder from liability resulting from the shareholder's own conduct, and the "shield" protects the shareholders, not the corporation. Nonetheless, common usage refers to "the corporate shield" or "the corporation's shield" or "the corporate liability shield."

Example

Acting as an employee of Fencing, Inc., Porthos gives fencing lessons to individual students. Distracted by personal concerns, he negligently inflicts a leg wound. The corporate shield is irrelevant to the student's tort claim against Porthos, which has nothing to do with Porthos's status as a shareholder but rather arises from his own tortious conduct. Likewise, the shield is irrelevant to the student's *respondeat superior*[8] and direct liability claims against the corporation.[9] ◄◄◄

---

6. See Section 12.2.5 (agent acting for disclosed principal).
7. See Section 12.2.3 (explaining how, under RULPA, a limited partner risks personal liability from being overly involved in the business and describing a list of safe harbors).
8. See Section 3.2 (discussing *respondeat superior*). The conduct of a person *qua* shareholder is not attributable to the corporation, but the conduct of a servant/employee (who happens to be a shareholder) may be.
9. See Section 4.4.1.

The corporate shield is not completely impermeable. When a dominant shareholder has abused the corporate form, in the interests of justice courts will "pierce the veil" and impose on the shareholder personal liability for the corporation's debts. Piercing claims are rarely successful, however, and the corporate shield is a fundamentally important advantage of the corporate form of business organization.[10]

b. Partnership Tax Classification

All business organizations are subject to the provisions of the Internal Revenue Code concerning income tax.[11] A threshold question under those provisions is whether a business organization will be classified (and therefore taxed) as a partnership or a corporation.

In most situations partnership tax status is preferable, because corporate shareholders face "double taxation" on any dividends they receive. An ordinary C corporation[12] is a taxable entity; it pays corporate income tax on any profits it earns. Dividends to shareholders are therefore made in "after-tax" dollars. Nonetheless, dividends are also taxable as received by the shareholders. Thus the profits comprising corporate dividends are taxed twice.

Partners do not suffer double taxation, because a partnership is not a taxable entity. For income tax purposes, partnerships are "pass-through" structures, with the business's profits (whether distributed or not) allocated and taxable directly to the partners. Partnership losses also "pass through" and can serve as deductions on each partner's own tax return. In contrast, the losses of an ordinary corporation stay with the entity and are useful only if the entity later enjoys a profit.

Example

In its most recent taxable year, Fencing, Inc., a C corporation, made a profit of $100,000 and would like to distribute all its profits to its shareholders. Assuming a corporate income tax rate of 25 percent, an individual tax rate of 20 percent, and that Athos, Porthos, and Aramis own the same number of shares of stock (and therefore share dividends equally), the calculations and results are:

10. See Section 16.1 for further discussion of piercing.

11. Business organizations are also subject to state tax codes, and in most matters discussed in this chapter most state income tax regimes follow the federal approach.

12. So-called because it is taxed under Subchapter C of the Internal Revenue Code.

Taxable Corporate Profit	100,000
Less Corporate Income Tax	(25,000)
Available for Distribution	75,000
Dividend to Each Shareholder	25,000
Less Individual Income Tax	(5,000)
Net to Each Shareholder	20,000
The Federal Government's "Take" (Corp. 25,000; Ind. 3 × 5,000)	**40,000**
"After Tax" Net to the Shareholders	**60,000 ◄◄◄**

Example

Same facts, including the intent to distribute all its profits to the owners, except that Athos, Porthos, and Aramis have formed a partnership.[13] The calculations and results are:

Profit	100,000
No Partnership Income Tax	(0)
Profits Available for Distribution	100,000
Profits Allocated and Distributed to Each Partner	33,333[14]
Less Individual Income Tax	(6,667)[15]
Net to Each Partner	26,666
The Federal Government's "Take" (Ind. 3 × 6,667)	**20,001**
"After Tax" Net to Partners	**79,998**[16]

13. For present purposes, it does not matter whether the partnership is a general partnership or a limited partnership.
14. Rounded, for simplicity's sake. Consistent with the pass-through nature of partnerships, it is the allocation of profits that creates tax liability for partners. So, a partner might have to pay taxes on profits not yet received.
15. Rounded.
16. One dollar is unaccounted for, due to rounding.

13.1 Comparison of Examples

	Corporation	Partnership
Federal government's "take"	40,000	20,001
Owners' "after tax" net	60,000	79,998 ◄◄◄

A partnership's "pass-through" character brings other advantages as well; the disadvantage has always been on the non-tax side, that is, personal liability. Before the invention of limited liability companies,[17] the cost of obtaining partnership tax classification was having at least one partner automatically liable for the business's debts. Put another way, entrepreneurs who wanted the full corporate shield had to pay some form of tax cost for the protection. In its simplest manifestation, that cost consisted of double taxation of a business's profits. Thus: the tax-shield conundrum.

§13.1.3 Dealing with the Conundrum — Pre-LLC

Before the advent of the LLC, entrepreneurs could resort to an ordinary limited partnership with a corporate general partner in order to achieve partnership tax status while minimizing liability risk.[18] To obtain a full corporate shield while achieving some of the advantages of partnership tax status, entrepreneurs could use an S corporation[19] or try to "zero out" the profits of a C corporation. None of these approaches were fully satisfactory.

a. Ordinary Limited Partnerships with a Corporate General Partner

Typically under this approach, a corporation would be formed for the sole purpose of serving as a limited partnership's general partner. This approach had a number of disadvantages, including: (i) complexity; (ii) a significant risk of "piercing" for the corporate general partner, unless that corporation had assets of its own (thereby diverting capital from use in the limited partnership's business); (iii) tax classification issues, unless the corporate general partner had assets of its own; (iv) difficult questions of fiduciary duty pertaining to the officers of the corporate general partner (because, as a formal matter, those officers owed duties to the corporation, but as a practical matter they were managing and typically controlling the limited

17. The advent of LLCs led to the invention of LLPs and LLLPs, discussed in Chapter 17.
18. I.e., a corporation as the general partner.
19. So-called because its owners have elected to have the corporation taxed under Subchapter S of the Internal Revenue Code.

partnership); and (v) before ULPA (2001), the "control rule," which impeded power-sharing by limited partners, even when "the deal" could be made only on that basis.[20]

b. S Corporations

An S corporation provides a full corporate liability shield with some of the benefits of pass-through tax status. Like a partnership, an S corporation generally pays no tax on its earnings, and its profits and losses are passed through and taxed directly to its shareholders.[21] However, S corporations face significant constraints that do not apply to partnerships.

1. Restrictions on Owners

For most practical purposes, all shareholders in an S corporation must be either U.S. citizens or resident aliens.[22] Subchapter S therefore rules out a long list of potential owners and investors, including corporations, investment banks, venture capital firms, and most foreign nationals. Moreover, an S corporation may not have more than 100 shareholders.

2. Restrictions on Businesses

Subchapter S also rules out a long list of business types and structures. For example, a corporation may not obtain or retain S status if it is a foreign corporation, a bank or savings and loan association, or an insurance company.

3. Restrictions on Financial Structure

An S corporation may have only one class of stock. This requirement precludes flexible allocations of profits, restricts the type of debt the corporation may issue, hampers efforts to gradually shift control of family-owned businesses, and, in general, makes passive investment very difficult to structure.[23]

---

20. For a discussion of the control rule, see Sections 12.2.3 and 12.3.4.

21. In some circumstances, an S corporation provides advantages over partnerships (and limited liability companies) with regard to employment taxes.

22. Some trusts and estates may hold S corporation stock, but the list is very limited.

23. The "one class of stock" restriction pertains to economic rights but not to governance rights.

4. Untoward Consequences for Owners

Unlike a partnership, an S corporation is not a complete pass-through entity. As a result, S corporations contain a number of traps for the unwary. For example, distributions to shareholders of appreciated property trigger a gain to the corporation and hence to the shareholders.[24]

c. C Corporations and "Zeroing Out"

A corporation that cannot elect S status, or chooses not to do so, can try to avoid double taxation by "zeroing out." To "zero out," the C corporation makes ostensibly deductible payments to shareholder-employees, thereby reducing or eliminating corporate profits. These payments can be made in a number of ways; the simplest are salaries and bonuses.

This approach is not risk free, however. The IRS may view the payments as disguised dividends, especially where: (i) the payments are excessive compared with the value of the services rendered to the corporation;[25] (ii) the payments are proportional to the shareholders' equity interests;[26] or (iii) capital is a material income-producing factor for the business and the corporation is not paying reasonable dividends.[27] Even when successful,

---

24. Appreciated property is property whose fair market value (FMV) exceeds the corporation's tax "basis" in the property. This situation can occur because the value of the property has increased since the time the corporation acquired it, or because the value of the property has decreased by an amount less than the amount of tax deductions taken by the corporation on account of the property. Suppose, for example, that Fencing, Inc., owns three antique epées, each purchased by the corporation several years ago for $1,000 (giving the corporation a tax basis of $1,000 in each epée), and each epée is now worth $2,000. If the corporation decides to distribute one epée to each of its shareholders as a dividend "in kind," and assuming (for the sake of simplicity) that the corporation has taken no deductions on account of the epées, each of the shareholders will incur $1,000 of taxable gain ($2,000 FMV minus $1,000 basis). Other "traps" include: (i) the basis of a shareholder's stock is not increased to take into account any corporate debt, thereby limiting the shareholders' ability to take advantage of passed-through losses; (ii) when a shareholder dies, the basis of the assets of the corporation is not adjusted to reflect the estate's stepped-up basis, thereby putting the estate at risk of realizing unexpected and (in an economic sense) phantom gains.

25. Unless the shareholder employees are all doing work whose fair market value just happens to be in proportion to the shareholders' stock holdings, this situation suggests that the payments are "in respect of" the ownership interests (i.e., dividends, and taxable as such) rather than in compensation for services.

26. Unless the shareholder employees are each doing work whose fair market value just happens to be in proportion to the shareholders' respective stock holdings, this situation suggests that the payments are "in respect of" the ownership interests (i.e., dividends, and taxable as such) rather than in compensation for services.

27. If assets owned by the corporation (i.e., capital) play an important role in producing revenue, the owners of the corporation would normally expect a return on (i.e., remuneration for) the investment reflected in those assets. If the corporation is not providing that return formally through appropriate dividends, it may be doing so unlawfully by disguising dividends as salary payments.

zeroing-out techniques provide none of the other advantages of pass-through tax status.

§13.1.4 Invention and Development of the LLC

a. Wyoming Starts a Revolution

Wyoming began the LLC revolution by taking seriously the IRS's "Kintner" Regulations on tax classification. Before January 1, 1997, those regulations determined how to classify unincorporated business organizations and were biased toward finding partnership status. The regulations identified four key corporate characteristics (limited liability, continuity of life, free transferability of ownership interests, centralized management) and classified an unincorporated organization as a corporation only if the organization had three or more of the corporate characteristics.

Although limited liability may seem to be the hallmark corporate characteristic, the Kintner Regulations contained no "super" factor. Each characteristic was as significant as each other.

In 1977, the Wyoming legislature sought to exploit that aspect of the Kintner Regulations in order to resolve the "tax-shield conundrum." The original Wyoming LLC Act provided for a new form of business organization, with a full, corporate-like liability shield and partnership-like characteristics as to entity management, continuity of life, and transferability of ownership interests.[28] Like a general partnership, a Wyoming LLC was managed by its owners (not centralized management). Like a limited partnership, a Wyoming LLC risked dissolution if one of its owners ceased to be an owner (no corporate-like continuity of life). As with any partnership, Wyoming LLC ownership interests were not freely transferable; absent a contrary agreement, an LLC member had the right to transfer only the economic aspect of the ownership interest (no free transferability of ownership interests).

The corporate-like liability shield was the sole characteristic pointing to corporate tax status. If the Kintner Regulations meant what they said, then a Wyoming LLC would be accorded partnership tax status.

b. IRS Response to Wyoming; Common Characteristics of Early LLCs

The IRS took more than 10 years to acknowledge the consequences of its own tax classification regulations. Revenue Procedure 88–76 classified a

28. In 2010, Wyoming adopted ULLCA (2006). Wy Laws (2010), ch. 94 (enacting Wy. Stat. §§ 17–29–102 et seq.).

Wyoming LLC as a partnership and caused legislatures around the country to consider seriously the LLC phenomenon. For the most part, Wyoming's early emulators were faithful copiers, imposing through their LLC statutes the same basic structure as ordained in the Wyoming statute. The major innovation was to establish an alternative governance template for manager-management (modeled on the limited partnership structure), while continuing to set the "default mode" as member-management.

Fidelity to the Wyoming model gave the earliest LLCs some common characteristics—at least to the extent they followed the default blueprint of their respective LLC statutes. In the default mode, an LLC:

- was managed by its members in their capacity as members
  —under the Kintner Regulations—no centralized management (like a general partnership)
- was threatened with dissolution each time a member dissociated
  —under the Kintner Regulations—no continuity of life (like a limited partnership with respect to the dissociation of any general partner)
- allowed its members to freely transfer the economic rights associated with membership, but prohibited them from transferring their membership interest in toto (or any management rights associated with membership) without the consent of all the other members
  —under the Kintner Regulations—no free transferability of interests (like both a general and limited partnership)

c. Increasing Flexibility of Form; IRS Bias Toward Manager-Managed LLCs

This characteristic picture began to lose focus in 1989 as the IRS began to loosen its approach to tax classification. In a series of public and private rulings, the IRS allowed for increasing flexibility of form, especially as to the continuity of life characteristic (i.e., the nexus between member dissociation and at least the threat of entity dissolution). This characteristic had done much to keep a "family resemblance" among LLCs because, until 1989, every LLC "blessed" by the IRS had lacked that characteristic. Beginning in 1989, the IRS began to accept both: (i) a shrinking of the categories of member dissociation that threatened dissolution; and (ii) a decrease in the quantum of member consent necessary to avoid dissolution following member dissociation. As a result, LLC organizers had a greater variety of structures from which to choose.

At the same time, however, the IRS's pronouncements on continuity of life and free transferability of interests were conducing toward a new characteristic LLC structure. Beginning with Private Letter Ruling 9210019, the IRS revealed a bias toward manager-managed LLCs.[29] In contrast to a member-managed LLC, a manager-managed LLC could achieve partnership tax status while enjoying significant protection from business disruption and significant control over member exit rights. In both official and unofficial ways, the IRS suggested that, for purposes of tax classification, LLCs were properly analogized to limited partnerships rather than to general partnerships.

In 1994, the IRS issued Revenue Procedure 95-10 and made its suggestion a matter of policy. Revenue Procedure 95-10 purported to provide guidelines for LLCs seeking advance assurance of partnership tax status under the Kintner Regulations, but in essence merely provided a series of safe harbors. Those safe harbors rested heavily on the limited partnership analogy.

d. "Check the Box" and the End to Family Resemblance

Revenue Procedure 95-10 might well have pushed LLCs into the limited partnership mold if the IRS had not subsequently decided to do away with the Kintner Regulations entirely. Effective January 1, 1997, the Treasury Department adopted a "check-the-box" tax classification regime under which, in general:[30]

- a business organization organized under a corporate or joint stock statute is taxed as a corporation;
- any other business organization:
  - □ with two of more owners is taxed as a partnership; and
  - □ with one owner is simply disregarded for income tax purposes;[31]
- unless the organization elects to be taxed as a corporation (by "checking the box").

Thus, "check the box" severed the connection between tax classification and organizational structure and invited entrepreneurs (and their attorneys) to specially tailor the structure of an LLC as each "deal" might require.[32]

---

29. Although state LLC statutes permitted manager-managed LLCs to have nonmember managers, the IRS pronouncements concerned manager-managed LLCs whose manager or managers were also members.

30. This description applies only to organizations formed under the law of one of the 50 states, the District of Columbia, or a U.S. territory. The regulations are more complicated for organizations formed under the laws of other nations and also for various special U.S. entities. The "check-the-box" regulations have no effect on the tax classification of publicly traded partnerships, which with very few exceptions are taxed as corporations.

31. The IRS treats the profits, losses, and other tax attributes of a "disregarded" entity as attributes of the person who owns the disregarded entity.

32. Although the "check-the-box" regulations were undoubtedly a response to LLCs, they apply equally to other unincorporated business organizations. As a result, "check the box" prompted changes in the law of limited partnerships, see Section 12.3, and led to the increased use of limited liability partnerships and limited liability limited partnerships. See Chapter 17.

"Check the box" also resulted in widespread changes to LLC statutes, as states moved quickly to take advantage of the newly permitted flexibility. These changes included:

- eliminating the requirement that an LLC have at least two members (like a general or limited partnership) and authorizing one-member LLCs;
- authorizing operating agreements in one-member LLCs;[33]
- allowing LLCs to have perpetual existence;
- changing the default rule on member dissociation to make dissociation more difficult, either by:
  — depriving members of the power to dissociate; or
  — freezing in the economic interest of dissociated members; and
- changing the default rule on the relationship between member dissociation and entity dissolution, either by:
  — providing that member dissociation does not even threaten dissolution; or
  — changing the quantum of consent necessary to avoid dissolution following a member's dissociation.

States did not, however, change the default rules on transferability of ownership interests.

§13.1.5 Common Elements of Contemporary LLCs; Range of Variations

a. Common Elements

Despite the great flexibility brought on by the "check-the-box" regulations, it is possible to identify some essential LLC characteristics and to describe a range of possibilities for other important attributes. Even after "check the box," every LLC:

- is organized under a state statute other than a corporation statute, which:
  — allows the LLC to exist as a legal person separate from each of its members (owners); and
  — provides rules (most of them "default" rules) for structuring, governing, and operating the entity;

33. As explained in Section 14.5.1, an LLC operating agreement functions like the partnership agreement in a general or limited partnership.

- comes into existence through the filing of a specified public document with a specified state agency:
  - —the document's name varies from state to state; however, almost without exception the name refers to either "articles of" or a "certificate of," with the object of the preposition being either "organization" or "formation";[34] but
  - —the difference in nomenclature neither reflects nor implies a difference in legal meaning;[35]
- exists as a legal entity, separate from its owners;
- need not have a specified term of existence and may instead have "perpetual" existence;
- may participate in mergers and other similar "entity" transactions;
- has a full, corporate-like liability shield to protect its owners against automatic, vicarious liability for the debts of the enterprise; and
- refers to the fundamental governing agreement among members as the "operating agreement" and gives that the agreement powers and a permissible scope parallel to those of a partnership agreement.[36]

Example — Formalities of Formation

Three individuals, Voltaire, Rousseau, and Marat, go into business with the expressed intention of forming a limited liability company under the law of State X. They draft and sign articles of organization, and Marat is given the task of actually submitting the document to the Secretary of State of State X. Unfortunately, Marat drops the document in his bath, is too embarrassed to tell Voltaire or Rousseau, and never submits the document. The business is conducted as if the papers had been submitted, accepted, and filed. In all its dealings with third parties, the business styles itself VRM, LLC. The business is not an LLC. To create an LLC requires the filing of the required document (i.e., articles or certificate depending on the nomenclature used in State X's LLC statute). ◀◀◀

---

34. For example: articles of formation; certificate of organization.

35. An official comment to ULLCA (2013) suggests a possible difference in connotation: "The original ULLCA and most other LLC statutes use 'articles of organization' rather than 'certificate of organization.' This act purposely uses the latter term to signal that the certificate: (i) merely reflects the existence of an LLC (rather than being the locus for important governance rules); and (ii) is significantly different from articles of incorporation, which have a substantially greater power to affect inter se rules for the corporate entity and its owners." ULLCA (2013) §102(1), cmt.

36. Some LLC statutes label this agreement the "limited liability company agreement." Two former statutes, since replaced by ULLCA (2006) used the term "member control agreement."

CASE IN POINT

Case in Point — *Reid v. Town of Hebron* (Significance of Separate Person)

"On May 19, 1993, the plaintiff [Reid] applied to the Commission for a [building] permit to build a single-family seasonal dwelling on the plaintiff's property. . . . On October 19, 1993 [after a public hearing], the Commission denied the plaintiff's application for a permit . . . [and the plaintiff timely appealed to the court]. A party appealing a decision of a municipal land use agency must be 'aggrieved' by the agency's decision. . . . The question of aggrievement is essentially one of standing. . . . At the hearing on September 3, 1996, evidence was proffered to show that the plaintiff transferred his interest in [the] lot . . . to M & A Investments, LLC, . . . a limited liability company, of which, [plaintiff] is a 50 percent owner. . . . The plaintiff [thereby] . . . transferred his interest in the property to another party who was not a party before the Commission and not a party to this action. Therefore, the plaintiff is not aggrieved." (Plaintiff was not the owner of the land. The LLC was.)[37] ◀ ◀ ◀

CASE IN POINT

Case in Point — *All Comp Constr. Co., LLC v. Ford* (Significance of Separate Person)

A contractor sued a subcontractor for damages, including emotional distress. The court rejected the emotional distress claim outright, stating: "[The contractor] is a limited liability company. As such, its owners are entitled to certain legal rights and protections. It is a fictional 'person' for legal purposes. [The contractor] has cited no authority which would allow it to be treated as a natural person that would be capable of experiencing emotions such as mental stress and anguish. The damages, if any, due to [the contractor] from [the subcontractor], are due to it as a fictional person, and may not be recovered by its owners. . . ."[38] ◀ ◀ ◀

UNIFORM ACT ON POINT

Uniform Act on Point — Role of the Operating Agreement:

ULLCA (2013) §102(10) defines "operating agreement" as: "the agreement, whether or not referred to as an operating agreement and whether oral, implied, in a record, or in any combination thereof, of all the members of a limited liability company, including a sole member, concerning the matters described in Section 105(a) [describing the permissible scope of an operating agreement]."

---

37. *Reid v. Town of Hebron*, No. CV 93543845, 1996 WL 634254, at *1–3 (Conn. Super. Ct. Oct. 22, 1996) (citations and internal quotations omitted).
38. *All Comp Constr. Co., LLC v. Ford*, 999 P.2d 1122, 1123 (Okla. Ct. App. 2000).

An official comment further explains:

> The definition in Paragraph 13 is very broad and recognizes a wide scope of authority for the operating agreement: "the matters described in Section 105(a)." Those matters include not only all relations inter se the members and the limited liability company but also all "activities and affairs of the company and the conduct of those activities and affairs." Section 105(a)(3). Moreover, the definition puts no limits on the form of the operating agreement. To the contrary, the definition contains the phrase "whether oral, implied, in a record, or in any combination thereof."

b. Range of Variations

Under all LLC statutes, rules pertaining to an LLC's internal structure (e.g., management rights, financial rights) are "default rules"—that is, applicable only to the extent the operating agreement does provide otherwise. The resulting flexibility is one of the great attractions of the LLC form. LLC governance structure runs the gamut from a New England town-meeting style (with decisions made through discussion and consensus among all members) to an enterprise dominated autocratically by a single managing member. Some LLCs use corporate-style governance,[39] and two state LLC statutes formerly provided that arrangement as the default structure. Most LLC statutes dichotomize governance between "member-managed" LLCs and "manager-managed" LLCs, with:

- governance in a member-managed LLC resembling governance in a general partnership; and
- governance in a manager-managed LLC resembling governance in a limited partnership.[40]

Great flexibility exists as to the rights and roles of LLC members in the LLC. To comply with IRS tax accounting requirements for partnerships, members' interests must continue to reflect a capital account and profit and loss-sharing percentages. In other respects, however, there is no paradigmatic

39. For a succinct description of "corporate-style governance," see Daniel S. Kleinberger, "Why Not Good Faith? –The Foibles of Fairness in Closely Held Corporations," 16 WILLIAM MITCHELL L. REV. 1143, 1144 (1990) ("Traditional legal theory recognizes three sharply distinct roles in corporate governance. The owners of the business, the shareholders, elect a board of directors, who function collectively to set policy for and superintend the operations of the business. The board, in turn, selects the top officers, who function as the chief administrators of the business and who manage day-to-day operations. The structure is tripartite and hierarchical."). In closely held corporations, the distinctions often blur. See *Id.*, *passim*.

40. The resemblance is not complete. For example, managers in a manager-managed LLC are not required by statute to be members, although they usually are. In contrast, the managers of a limited partnership—i.e., the general partners—are necessarily partners.

construct. In some LLCs, members are unremittingly passive—their governance rights scant and their financial rights preferred.[41] Other members have a "hands-on" role in their LLC. Depending on the operating agreement, that role ranges from intermittent to constant; responsibilities range from the most senior, supervisory of management duties to the most prosaic of day-to-day work.

Example

Hobbes, LLC is a manager-managed LLC with five members and a single manager. According to the LLC's operating agreement, the manager, who is also a member, has "full and complete authority to make all decisions concerning the operations and business of the LLC, except: (i) requiring members to make additional contributions; (ii) selling all or substantially all of the company's assets or taking or failing to take any other action that makes it impossible to carry on the company's business; (iii) dissolving the Company; and (iv) amending the operating agreement." ◀◀◀

Example

Jefferson, LLC is a member-managed LLC with five members. According to the LLC's operating agreement, "the Company will be managed exactly as if the Company was a general partnership organized under the Revised Uniform Partnership Act, and each member will have the same rights to manage and participate in the business as if she, he, or it were a partner in a general partnership organized under the Revised Uniform Partnership Act." ◀◀◀

§13.2 VARIATION AMONG LLC STATUTES; CONSEQUENCES

§13.2.1 Variations Among State LLC Statutes

The 50 states and the District of Columbia each have their own limited liability company statutes. In some ways, all LLC statutes resemble each other, for example, in the formalities involved in forming a limited liability company, the importance of the operating agreement to structuring the "deal"

41. Such members have rights that, in substance, resemble those of preferred shareholders. Preferred stock typically has some sort of preference or priority with regard to distribution rights but often lacks any voting power.

among the members, the partnership-like concept of dissolution and winding up, etc. Moreover, most provisions of an LLC statute pertain to internal affairs and, with some limitation, are merely default rules (i.e., applicable only if the company's operating agreement does not provide otherwise). In addition, all LLC statutes tend to address the same topics, even though one statute might take one approach to a particular topic while another statute might take a significantly different approach.

Still, "once you've read one LLC statute," you have **certainly not** read them all. However, a book of this size and nature cannot "cover the waterfront" and discuss 51 different statutes.[42]

The most efficient vehicle for exemplifying LLC issues is necessarily a uniform act. For several reasons, this book focuses principally on the most recent uniform act: ULLCA (2013):[43]

- Versions of ULLCA (2006) or (2013) have been adopted in 20 states and the District of Columbia. Many of the adopting states are of substantial commercial consequence, e.g., California, Florida, Illinois, New Jersey, and Pennsylvania.
- ULLCA (2013) reflects the most up-to-date, coherent, and comprehensive thinking on issues related to LLC law.
  - —The ULC promulgated its original Uniform Limited Liability Company Act in 1996.
  - —By 2004, when the ULC began drafting what became ULLCA (2006) (then known colloquially as the Re-ULLCA or RULLCA), an opportunity existed for significant improvements in the law. Many tax classification complexities had disappeared, many important non-tax issues had crystallized, and "[it was] an opportune moment to identify the best elements of the myriad 'first generation' LLC statutes and to infuse those elements into a new, 'second generation' uniform act."[44] The Re-ULLCA drafting committee benefited from excellent advice from a group of experienced advisors from the American Bar Association and observers from various backgrounds.
  - —The Harmonization Project, which began in 2009 and produced ULLCA (2013),[45] used ULLCA (2006) as its lodestone, made few policy changes, but did find opportunities to improve statutory

42. This count includes the District of Columbia.

43. The ULC's formal name for this act is ULLCA (2006) (last amended 2013).

44. ULLCA (2006), Prefatory Note (Background to this Act: Developments since the Conference Considered and Approved the Original Uniform Limited Liability Company Act (ULLCA)).

45. For an explanation of the Harmonization Project, see introductory Note on the ULC Harmonization Project.

language as to both clarity and coherence. In addition to benefiting from input from ABA advisors and various observers, ULLCA (2013) also reflects detailed review by state bar committees in Florida, Illinois, and Pennsylvania (among others).

— ULLCA (2006) contained detailed official comments useful for bringing neophytes quickly up to speed on the numerous issues addressed by the act. ULLCA (2013) has improved and extended those comments, which comprise a very useful source of information and understanding.

— ULLCA (2013) is the most current uniform limited liability company act.

One non-uniform LLC statute requires special note, and Section 13.2.2 addresses specifically the attractions, influence, and dangers of the Delaware LLC Act.

§13.2.2 Delaware Law

a. The Preeminence of Delaware Law

Although Wyoming, not Delaware, pioneered the modern limited liability company, many practitioners consider the Delaware LLC Act the statute of choice for sophisticated ventures organized as LLCs. Moreover, in many deals involving entrepreneurs or investors from more than one state, the lawyers routinely "default" to using the Delaware LLC statute rather than the LLC statute of any of the states actually involved in the deal.[46]

b. Reasons for the Preeminence[47]

1. Not the Inherent Quality of the Delaware Statute

The Delaware Limited Liability Company Act is a complex, sophisticated, and eminently flexible statute that exalts freedom of contract even to the point of permitting an operating agreement to eliminate some or all fiduciary duties. However, the act's attractiveness has little to do with its inherent qualities.

To the contrary, the act's drafting style is arcane: substantive requirements embedded in definitions, sentences in which length seems a virtue, and provisions that overlap and intertwine so as to require substantial efforts

46. See Bishop & Kleinberger on Limited Liability Companies, § 14:2 (stating that "for ventures with members or substantial business relationships in more than one state, the Delaware law seems to exert an almost gravitational pull on attorneys") (footnote omitted).

47. This section is derived from Bishop & Kleinberger on Limited Liability Companies § 14:2.

of deconstruction. As Delaware's own Supreme Court has stated, "To understand the overall structure and thrust of the Act, one must wade through provisions that are prolix, sometimes oddly organized, and do not always flow evenly."[48]

As for substance, many other states have statutes offering comparable flexibility and an essentially equal commitment to enforcing agreements made by LLC members. The Delaware act does stand out by authorizing an operating agreement to eliminate all fiduciary duties, but (i) two of Delaware's leading jurists have criticized that approach as resting on false premises and being otherwise misguided;[49] and (ii) the implied contractual covenant of good faith and fair dealing remains in place to constrain unduly opportunistic behavior.[50]

2. *The Inherent Quality of the Delaware Judiciary*

Why, then, do many non-Delaware practitioners choose Delaware when forming LLCs? The answer lies in the reputation of the Delaware judiciary. The Delaware Court of Chancery has jurisdiction over claims relating to the internal affairs of a Delaware LLC, and that court is the preeminent business court in the United States. It is comfortable with business disputes and is capable of handling esoteric and even arcane issues of law. The Delaware Supreme Court is likewise; many of its judges previously served in the Court of Chancery.

Both the Chancery Court and the Delaware Supreme Court accept and adhere to the policy of the Delaware Act "to give maximum effect to the principle of freedom of contract and to the enforceability of limited liability company agreements." Indeed, Delaware courts are conservative about contracts in general. They lean away from modernist notions that all agreements are necessarily indeterminate and toward the old-fashioned approach that a contract is a contract and that a court is not a proper forum for salving the pain from a "buyer's remorse."

c. But Don't Dabble in Delaware

Despite its ubiquitous influence,[51] the Delaware LLC Act is not safe for use by attorneys who merely "dabble in Delaware." The Act excels in flexibility

48. *Atochem N.Am., Inc. v. Jaffari*, 727 A2d 286, 291 (Del. 1999).

49. Leo E. Strine Jr. and J. Travis Laster, "The Siren Song of Unlimited Contractual Freedom," Research Handbook on Partnerships, LLCs and Alternative Forms of Business Organizations (Robert W. Hillman and Mark J. Loewenstein, eds.) (Edward Elgar Publishing, 2015).

50. For a discussion of the implied covenant, see Section 15.4.8.

51. Consider, as an example of this influence, the LLC Institute presented annually by the Limited Liability Companies, Partnerships, and Unincorporated Entities Committee of the ABA's Business Law Section. The Institute always includes a discussion of recent case

rather than guidance, and, as noted above, the drafting is byzantine, yielding meaning only after reiterative study (which must take into account statutory changes made annually).

Keeping pace with relevant Delaware LLC case law is almost a full-time job. Being a court of equity, the Court of Chancery often ladens its decision with voluminous statements of facts. Fifty-page decisions are not unusual. For some years the most important decision dealing with good faith took up 200-plus pages.

Moreover, a "Delaware LLC lawyer" must stay up -date-on more than just LLC law; Delaware LLC and limited partnership law are reciprocally precedential. Knowledge of Delaware contract law is also essential. For example, when an attorney is asked for a formal legal opinion pertaining to a Delaware limited liability company, "[i]t is . . . the responsibility of the opinion-giver to navigate Delaware common law [especially contract law] prior to rendering a Delaware LLC opinion, and to keep abreast of its shifting landscape."[52]

And sometimes—somewhat unpredictably—a "Delaware LLC lawyer" must take into account current developments in Delaware corporate law. On more than one occasion, the Court of Chancery has applied that law to resolve a dispute among members of a Delaware LLC.[53]

In short, Delaware LLC law is important and influential, but, for the *non-cognoscenti* quite dangerous.[54]

Problem 113

Under local law "a person may represent him or herself in court, but no person who is not an attorney licensed to practice in this state may represent another person." Todd Morgan has formed Todd, LLC, of which he is the sole member. Todd, LLC is the lessee on a lease with CharlotteMik, Inc., and CharlotteMik has sued Todd, LLC in state court for nonpayment of rent. May Todd Morgan, who is not an attorney, represent Todd, LLC in state court? ◄ ◄ ◄

---

developments, and that discussion allocates approximately equal time to Delaware case law and to case law from the other 49 states, the District of Columbia, and U.S. territories. For an extended discussion of Delaware influence, see Daniel S. Kleinberger, "Fezzick, Are There Rocks Ahead? Navigating the Oppression Doctrine in the Age of LLCs," 22 Florida State University Business Review 15, 54–69 (2023).

52. B.M. Gottesman & S.E. Swenson, "More Than Bargained For? Topics for Consideration in the Issuance and Acceptance of Delaware LLC Opinions," 81-FEB NY St. B.J. 20, 22 (2009) (commenting on the TriBar Opinion Committee, "Third-Party Closing Opinions: Limited Liability Companies," 61 Bus. Law. 679 (2006)).

53. For an example (and critique), see BISHOP & KLEINBERGER ON LIMITED LIABILITY COMPANIES §§ 5–131 and 5:132.

54. For further discussion, see Daniel S. Kleinberger, "Don't Dabble in Delaware," BUSINESS LAW TODAY (July 2017).

Explanation

No. An LLC and its members are separate persons. If Todd Morgan were to represent Todd, LLC, the representation would involve a "person who is not an attorney licensed to practice in this state . . . representing another person."[55] ◄ ◄ ◄

Problem 114

If Todd, LLC defaults on its lease payments, may CharlotteMik sue Todd Morgan for the amount due? ◄ ◄ ◄

Explanation

Not unless Todd Morgan has guaranteed the LLC's payment or CharlotteMik can establish grounds to "pierce the veil." An LLC member is not liable for the LLC's debts merely on account of being a member. ◄ ◄ ◄

55. In some states, either by statute or court rule, the answer would be different so long as the matter remained in "small claims" or housing court.

CHAPTER 14

Creating the LLC

§14.1 MECHANICS OF FORMATION

§14.1.1 Overview

As a matter of mechanics, the formation of a limited liability company (LLC) involves multiple components:

- one or more persons (often referred to as "organizers"):
  - —select the state LLC statute under which the limited liability company will be formed ("state of organization" or "state of formation");
  - —draft (or have drafted) the document ("articles of organization," "certificate of organization," or "certificate of formation"), the public filing of which will create the limited liability company as a legal person;
- that document is:
  - —properly drafted and signed;
  - —delivered to the public office (in most states, the state Secretary of State) specified in the LLC statute to receive the articles or certificate of organization (sometimes referred to as "delivery for filing" and sometimes as "filing");
- that office decides that the document meets the requirements of the LLC statute (almost always a merely ministerial act) and accepts the document into the public record; and

- under most LLC statutes, one or more persons—not necessarily the organizers—become the LLC's initial member or members when the LLC comes into existence.[1]

Figure 14.1 shows the sequence graphically.

Figure 14.1. Mechanics of LLC Formation—Timeline Organizers

select a state of organization
draft and sign articles (certificate) that complies with the requirements of the LLC statute of the state
deliver document to

⇩

Secretary of State
receives articles (certificate)
reviews to determine compliance with LLC statute if document complies, officially notes the compliance, and places the document on the public record (often called "filing")

⇩

as a result
*articles (or certificate) take effect**

limited liability company	**one or more persons**
comes into existence	become initial member(s)

* It is possible for the articles or certificate to have a delayed effective date.

§14.1.2 State of Formation; Choice of Law

a. Where LLCs Are Typically Formed

Most limited liability companies are formed under the law of the state in which the company does all or most of its business, but it is not legally necessary to do so. To the contrary, LLC law requires virtually no nexus between the situs of an LLC's activities and the state under whose LLC law the LLC is formed. In particular, the state of Delaware has made a business of attracting LLC formation from companies whose business has little or nothing to do with Delaware.

1. Because an LLC is a legal person separate from its members and because an LLC is created by the public filing of a document (rather than an agreement among its members), it is conceptually possible for an LLC to be formed without having any initial members. The label "shelf LLC" suggests that the memberless entity "sits on the shelf" awaiting the arrival of one or more initial members. Whether LLC statutes should allow such "shelf" LLCs has been controversial. See Section 14.3.

LLC statutes typically require only that an LLC maintain an office and an agent for service of process in the state of formation,[2] and some statutes require only a resident agent. A limited liability company that does business in more than one state inevitably does business outside its state of organization. A limited liability company that transacts business in a state other than its state of formation is required to register in that other state as a "foreign" limited liability company.[3]

b. Regardless of Where a Limited Liability Company Does Business, the Law of the Company's State of Formation Governs the Limited Liability Company's Internal Affairs

Under the "internal affairs" doctrine, the law of an LLC's state of formation governs the LLC's internal affairs, including the relationships of the members *inter se*. The doctrine is a "choice of law" rule and originated in early cases dealing with the then new phenomenon of the private corporation.[4]

Most LLC statutes codify the doctrine. For example, the South Dakota LLC statute states: "The law of this state governs [t]he internal affairs of a limited liability company."[5] Even under LLC statutes that do not codify the rule, case law produces the same result.[6]

Determining whether a matter is an "internal affair" is for the most part a straightforward task. As explained in a comment to ULLCA (2013):

> Like any other legal concept, "internal affairs" may be indeterminate at its edges. However, the concept certainly includes interpretation and enforcement of the operating agreement, relations among the members as members, relations between the limited liability company and a member as a member,

---

2. Service companies exist to provide either or both for a fee.

3. In this context, the term "foreign" does not mean "non-United States" but rather "not domestic," and a limited liability company is considered "domestic" *vis-à-vis* its state of organization. See ULLCA (2013), §§102(5) (defining "foreign limited liability company"); 902(a) (stating that "[a] foreign limited liability company may not do business in this state until it registers with the [Secretary of State] under this [article]"); 905(a) (enumerating those activities that do not constitute "transacting business" by a foreign LLC). In this regard, LLC law follows the law of other business entities. See, e.g., Rev. Model Bus. Corp. Act, §§15.01, 15.02; ULPA (2001), §§902, 903, 907.

4. For the American Law Institute's current formulation as to corporations, see Restatement (Second) of Conflict of Laws §302, cmt. a (1971) (defining "internal affairs" with reference to a corporation as "the relations *inter se* of the corporation, its shareholders, directors, officers or agents").

5. SD Stat. §47–34A-113(1). "Limited liability company" is defined to mean a domestic limited liability company, i.e., a limited liability company organized under "the law of this state." *Id.*, §47–34A-101(8). See also ULLCA (2013) §102(8) defining the term to mean "an entity formed under this [act]."

6. Ironically, even those LLC statutes that do not codify the internal affairs doctrine as to domestic LLCs do so with regard to foreign LLCs. That is, every LLC statute expressly provides that the law of the state of formation of a foreign limited liability company governs that company's internal affairs.

> relations between a manager-managed limited liability company and a manager, and relations between a manager of a manager-managed limited liability company and the members as members.[7]

c. "Internal Affairs" and the Member's Liability Shield

It is debatable whether "internal affairs" include the liability of a member as member for obligations of an LLC, because the issue certainly implicates rights of persons outside the LLC (i.e., the LLC's creditors).[8] Some LLC statutes address this issue directly, excluding the liability shield from the rubric of internal affairs but nonetheless applying the law of an LLC's statement of formation when considering the liability shield.[9] For example, ULLCA (2013) §104 states: "The law of this state governs: (1) the internal affairs of a limited liability company; and (2) the liability of a member as member and a manager as manager for a debt, obligation, or other liability of a limited liability company."

Georgia's statute makes an even broader (and lengthier) statement:

> The personal liability of a member of a limited liability company to any person or in any action or proceeding for the debts, obligations, or liabilities of the limited liability company, or for the acts or omissions of other members, managers, employees, or agents of the limited liability company, shall be governed solely and exclusively by this chapter and the laws of this state. Whenever a conflict arises between the laws of this state and the laws of any other state with regard to the liability of members of a limited liability company for the debts, obligations, and liabilities of the limited liability company or for the acts or omissions of other members, managers, employees, or agents of the limited liability company, this state's laws shall be deemed to govern in determining such liability.[10]

As a matter of legal analysis, this particular choice of law issue is important principally when a creditor of an LLC seeks to disregard the liability shield (i.e., "pierce the veil" of an LLC) and hold one or more members personally liable for the entity's debts.[11] For the most part, the legal question has no practical consequence: "The general rule is that a plaintiff's alter ego theory is governed by the law of the state in which the business at issue is organized."[12]

7. ULLCA (2013), §104(1), cmt.
8. ULLCA (2013), §104(2), cmt.
9. Such claims are typically labeled "piercing" claims. See Section 13.1.2(a).
10. Ga. Code Ann., §14–11–1107(h).
11. See Section 14.1.2(b).
12. *Rual Trade Ltd. v. Viva Trade L.L.C.*, 549 F. Supp. 2d 1067, 1077 (E.D. Wis. 2008) (quoted in ULLCA (2013) §104(2), cmt).

d. The "Internal Affairs Rule" and Legal Analysis of LLC Issues

Due to the internal affairs doctrine, the analysis of any question of LLC law must begin with specific reference to the LLC statute under which the LLC was formed. Thus, when an attorney is asked a question about an LLC matter, her or his first question should be, "What's the state of organization?"[13]

§14.1.3 Organizers

a. Nomenclature

LLC statutes differ as to how they refer to the persons who "do the paperwork" to create an LLC. Some statutes refer particularly to "organizers." For example, the Georgia LLC Act states in pertinent part: "One or more persons may act as the organizer or organizers of a limited liability company."[14]

Other statutes eschew that label and simply refer to persons acting to "form" a limited liability company. The Arizona LLC statute is an example: "One or more persons may form a limited liability company by signing and filing with the [corporation] commission an original copy of the articles of organization for the limited liability company."[15] Regardless of the statutory language, however, the term "organizer" is colloquially accepted usage.

b. Organizer(s)

1. Role

The role of the organizer is mechanically simple: cause to be drafted, signed, and submitted to the appropriate official the document whose public filing is a precondition to creating the limited liability company as a legal entity.[16] Under some LLC statutes, another requirement exists: at least one person must become a member.[17]

---

13. For a discussion of the variation among LLC statutes and this book's approach to the variation, see Section 13.2.1. The second question should be, "Is there a written operating agreement?" See Section 14.5.

14. Ga. Code Ann., §14–11–203(a). See also, e.g., Va. Code §13.1–1010 and ULLCA (2006), §102(14) (defining "organizer" as a person that acts under section 201 to form a limited liability company).

15. Ariz. Stat. §29–631(A).

16. Although the organizer must sign the document, drafting and delivery can be delegated. If the person or persons seeking to form the LLC have consulted an attorney, typically the attorney drafts the document, the organizer signs, and a paralegal or legal assistant arranges to submit the document. As noted in Section 14.1.3(b)(1), an organizer need not be a natural person. When an organization is an organizer, the organizer signs through an authorized, disclosed agent.

17. See Section 14.3.

2. Must the Organizer Be a Natural Person?

In the early days of LLCs, some statutes required that an organizer be an individual. That requirement gradually gave way, however.[18] Today, "[a]ll LLC statutes contemplate an entity acting as an organizer. Some expressly require that an individual acting as an organizer be at least eighteen years old. Others do not."[19]

3. Are Organizers Ipso Facto Members?

No. AN LLC member is a member of an LLC,[20] and the organizer's role is pre-formation. At the moment a person becomes an organizer, it is impossible for the person to be a member, because an LLC that does not yet exist cannot have members. Put another way, member status for anyone presupposes that the organizer's task is finished.

4. Must the Organizer Become a Member Upon Formation of the LLC?

No LLC statute requires that an organizer become a member when the LLC comes into existence, and many make this point expressly. For example, the Virginia statute states: "One or more persons may act as organizers of a limited liability company by signing and delivering articles of organization to the [State Corporation] Commission for filing. An organizer need not be a member of the limited liability company after formation has occurred."[21] Likewise, the Arizona statute provides: "The person or persons [who act to form the LLC] need not be members of the limited liability company at the time of formation or after formation has occurred."[22] An organizer of an LLC thus differs from the person or persons who sign and deliver the documents to form a limited partnership; the latter are necessarily general partners in the limited partnership they form.[23]

---

18. E.g., Ariz. Laws 1997, Ch. 282, §18 (amending Ariz. Rev. Stat. §29–631); Colo. Laws 2003, Ch. 352, §178 (amending Colo. Rev. Stat. §7–80–203).
19. Bishop & Kleinberger on Limited Liability Companies § 5.61 ("Practice-pointer: Even under an LLC statute that states no age requirement for organizers that are individuals, prudence requires use of only individuals who have the capacity to make a non-voidable contract.")
20. See, e.g., Del. Code Ann., tit. 6, §18–101(6) (defining "limited liability company" as "a limited liability company formed under the laws of the State of Delaware") and (11) (defining "member" as "a person who has been admitted to a limited liability company"); ULLCA (2006)§102(8) (defining "limited liability company" as "an entity formed under this [act]") and (11) (defining member as "a person that has become a member of a limited liability company"). A few statutes are careless on this conceptual point.
21. Va. Code Ann., §13.1–1010.
22. Ariz. Stat. §29–631.
23. See Section 12.2.2.

5. May an Organizer Become a Member Upon Formation of the LLC?

It is certainly permissible for an organizer to become a member once the LLC exists. No LLC statute prohibits that situation, and many expressly contemplate it. The original California statute, for example, provided: "The person or persons who execute and file the articles of organization may, but need not, be members of the limited liability company."[24]

6. What Is the Legal Relationship Between an Organizer and the LLC the Organizer Acts to Form?

In an agency law sense, there can be no legal relationship. A person cannot be an agent for a nonexistent principal.[25] In this respect, the organizer of an LLC is comparable to a person who acts to incorporate a corporation.

7. What Is the Legal Relationship Between an Organizer and the Person or Persons Who Have Agreed or Are Otherwise Destined to Become the Initial Members of the LLC?

Most LLC statutes are silent on this point. The Delaware statute is an exception, referring to "1 or more authorized persons . . . execut[ing] a certificate of formation."[26] However, the Delaware statute raises (but does not answer) the question, "authorized by whom?"

The logical answer is "authorized by the person or persons who will become the initial member or members of the limited liability company." The same characterization is appropriate under all other LLC statutes, except the few that permit an LLC to be formed without having any initial members.[27] Where the statute presupposes an initial member upon formation, the organizer must be acting to serve that person's interests.

ULLCA (2013) contains an explicit and detailed explanation of the relationship between those who form an LLC and those who become its initial members:

> (a) If a limited liability company is to have only one member upon formation, the person becomes a member as agreed by that person and the organizer of the company. That person and the organizer may be, but need not be, different persons. If different, the organizer acts on behalf of the initial member.
>
> (b) If a limited liability company is to have more than one member upon formation, those persons become members as agreed by the persons before

24. Cal. Corp. Code, §17050(a). Effective 2014, California repealed this act and substituted its version of ULLCA (2006).
25. See Section 2.7.2(a).
26. Del. Code Ann., tit. 6, §18–201(a).
27. The so-called shelf LLC is discussed in Section 14.3.

> the formation of the company. The organizer acts on behalf of the persons in forming the company and may be, but need not be, one of the persons.[28]

The word "authorized" and the phrase "acts on behalf" both signify an agency relationship, which means the organizer owes fiduciary duties to the person or persons who will become the initial member or members.[29] If the person serving as an LLC's organizer also functions as the promoter for the enterprise,[30] the person also owes duties in that capacity.

Case in Point — *Roni LLC v. Arfa*

Investors who acquired membership interest in LLCs sued the organizers/promoters of those LLCs for breach of fiduciary duties. The organizers not only promoted membership in the LLCs, they sold properties to the LLCs and allegedly failed to disclose commissions received from the sale of properties. Affirming a decision of the motion court, the appellate court likened the organizer or promoter of an LLC to a promoter of a corporation and held that (i) "the organizer of a limited liability company is a fiduciary of the investors it solicits to become members"; and (ii) "[t]he fiduciary duty includes the obligation to disclose fully any interests of the promoter that might affect the company and its members, including profits that the promoter makes from organizing the company."[31] ◀◀◀

8. One or More Organizers?

LLC statutes contemplate "one or more" organizers, but most limited liability companies are formed by a single organizer. Certainly, when the organizer is merely "doing the paperwork" on behalf of others who will become the LLC's initial members, it would be superfluous to have more than one organizer. Multiple organizers are more likely when the LLC is to have more than one initial member and those persons feel more comfortable "being on" the LLC's initial public paperwork.

---

28. ULLCA (2013) §401. ULLCA (2006), §401 is verbatim the same.

29. See Section 4.1.1.

30. "Promoter" is a term of art referring to a person who: (i) identifies a business opportunity; (ii) solicits investors who will become owners of a legal entity to be formed to house the proposed business; and (iii) sometimes makes initial arrangements for the business in anticipation of the formation of business entity.

31. *Roni LLC v. Arfa*, 74 A.D.3d 442, 444–45, 903 N.Y.S.2d 352, 355 (A.D. 1 Dept. 2010).

Example

Larry and Moe wish to form an LLC to house their new business, Whoopee-Cushions-R-Us. They consult Curley, an attorney knowledgeable about limited liability companies. Upon his advice, Larry and Moe decide *inter alia* to form their LLC under the law of their state of residence ("Home State"), where their company will do all its business. Acting on behalf of Larry and Moe, Curley drafts a certificate of organization for Whoopee-Cushions-R-Us, LLC. He signs the document as "organizer" and delivers the document to the office of the Home State Secretary of State, together with the filing fee specified by law.[32] An official in that office:

- ascertains that:
  — the certificate complies with the Home State LLC Act (including that the proposed name of the LLC is available);[33] and
  — the fee is correct; and
- files the certificate, bringing the LLC into existence.

Larry and Moe become the initial members of the LLC; Curley's role as organizer is over. ◀ ◀ ◀

Example

Same facts as the previous Example, except that Larry and Moe (acting with or without legal advice) sign the certificate as organizers and use a courier service to deliver the document and filing fee to the office of the Home State Secretary of State. Larry and Moe are the organizers of Whoopee-Cushions-R-Us, LLC. They signed the certificate in that capacity and—through an intermediary—caused the certificate to be delivered to the filing office. ◀ ◀ ◀

Example

Three large corporations agree to use an LLC to form and operate a joint venture. As the deal comes closer to closing, two of the three participants are still deciding what legal form they will use to own their respective part of the joint venture (e.g., directly as a member, through a wholly owned subsidiary that is a member). For various reasons, the parties want to have the LLC "in place" as soon as possible. They therefore form an LLC that initially has no members. Because under the relevant LLC statute admission of new

---

32. In some states, the applicable LLC statute specifies LLC-related filing fees. In other states, a statute pertaining to the filing office contains all fees for filings in that office.
33. See Section 14.1.4(c).

members is the province of the organizers, each participant may well want to serve as an organizer. ◄◄◄

§14.1.4 Articles of Organization (Certificate of Organization; Certification of Formation)

a. Nomenclature

Most LLC statutes refer to "articles of organization." A few refer instead to a "certificate" either "of formation" or "of organization." The predominant nomenclature traces back to the original Wyoming LLC Act and resonates with the nomenclature of corporate law, which predominately uses the term "articles of incorporation."[34]

The word "certificate" resonates with the law of limited partnerships,[35] is the term of art under the influential Delaware statute,[36] and was selected in the drafting process that produced ULLCA (2006) "purposely . . . to signal that: (i) the certificate merely reflects the existence of an LLC (rather than being the locus for important governance rules); and (ii) this document is significantly different from articles of *incorporation*, which have a substantially greater power to affect *inter se* rules for the corporate entity and its owners."[37]

For simplicity's sake, this book will refer generally either to "articles (or certificate) of organization" or simply "articles of organization."

b. Required Contents

LLC statutes vary as to how much information they require in the articles (or certificate) of organization, ranging from "bare bones" to fulsome. Delaware's statute exemplifies the "bare bones" approach, requiring only "[t]he name of the limited liability company" and "[t]he address of the registered office and the name and address of the registered agent for service of process."[38] The Arizona statute, section 29–632(A), illustrates the other end of the continuum:

---

34. See, e.g., Rev. Model Bus. Corp. Act, §1.40(1); Cal. Corp. Code, §154. Va. Code Ann., §13.1–603.

35. A limited partnership is formed through the signing and filing of a certificate of limited partnership. See Section 12.2.2.

36. Del. Code Ann., tit. 6, §§18–101(2) and 18–201 (using the term "certificate of formation").

37. ULLCA (2006), §102(1), cmt. (referring to "certificate of organization") (emphasis in original). ULLCA (2013) made no change. See *Id.*, §102(1) and cmt.

38. Del. Code Ann., tit. 6, §18–201(a)(1) and (2).

The articles of organization shall state:

1. The name of the limited liability company.

2. The name, street address in this state and signature of the agent for service of process required to be maintained by section 29–604.

3. The address of the company's known place of business in this state, if different from the street address of the company's statutory agent.

4. The latest date, if any, on which the limited liability company must dissolve.

5. Either of the following statements:

(a) Management of the limited liability company is vested in a manager or managers.

(b) Management of the limited liability company is reserved to the members.

6. The name and address of either of the following:

(a) If management of the limited liability company is vested in a manager or managers, each person who is a manager of the limited liability company and each member who owns a twenty per cent or greater interest in the capital or profits of the limited liability company.

(b) If management of the limited liability company is reserved to the members, each person who is a member of the limited liability company.

Most LLC statutes require the articles to state whether the LLC is member-managed or manager-managed, a characterization that has important power-to-bind implications.[39] Most statutes do not require disclosure of the identity of members or managers. Recent controversy regarding "shelf LLCs" has caused some statutes to require the articles to assert "[t]hat there is at least one member of the limited liability company."[40]

c. Name Requirement

LLC statutes require that the name of a limited liability company contain language signifying the entity's status as an LLC. Statutes typically require the name to contain either the phrase "limited liability company" or some abbreviation—for example, LLC or L.L.C.

In addition, like other business organization statutes, LLC statutes require that an LLC's name be somewhat different from other names already "on the record" in the filing office. At one time, the predominant standard (regardless of the type of entity involved) was the term "confusingly

39. See Section 15.3.

40. Colo. Rev. Stat. §7–80–204(1)(g). For a discussion of shelf LLCs, see Section 14.3.

similar,"[41] but the trend is toward "distinguishable in the records."[42] The change reflects a shift away from a consumer protection perspective—on the theory that other law adequately addresses that concern—and toward a recordkeeping perspective—that is, names must be sufficiently dissimilar to facilitate effective indexing, storage, and retrieval.

d. Optional Contents

All LLC statutes permit the articles or certificate to include additional information. Most LLC statutes leave unclear the effect of this additional information. The situation is especially complicated if the articles differ with the operating agreement.[43]

e. Notice Function

Following limited partnership law,[44] a few LLC statutes provide that an LLC's articles or certificate of organization are "constructive notice" that the organization is a limited liability company. The effect of such provisions is unclear. In a seminal case, Colorado's provision was held "ineffective to change common law agency principles, including the rules relating to the liability of an agent that transacts business for an undisclosed principal."[45]

§14.2 LIMITED LIABILITY COMPANY AS A JURIDIC PERSON

Once the articles or certificate takes effect and, if necessary, at least one person has become a member,[46] the limited liability company comes into existence as a legal person, separate from its members, with its own purpose, powers, rights, and liabilities.[47]

41. See, e.g., *Limerick Auto Body, Inc. v. Limerick Collision Center, Inc.*, 769 A.2d 1175, 1179 (Pa. Super. Ct. 2001).
42. ULLCA (2013), §112, cmt.
43. See the discussion at Section 14.5.7.
44. ULPA (2013), §103(c); ULPA (2001), §103(c).
45. ULPA (2013), §103(c), cmt, discussing *Water, Waste & Land, Inc. v. Lanham*, 955 P.2d 997, 1001, 1003 (Colo. 1998). The ULPA (2001) §103(c), cmt. is the same.
46. For a discussion of why an entity entirely separate from its owners might need to have at least one owner to come into existence, see Section 14.3.
47. For the circumstances under which members of an LLC might become liable for the LLC's liabilities, see Section 14.4.1.

§14.2.1 Permissible Purposes for an LLC

a. In General

At one time, most if not all LLC statutes required an LLC to have a business purpose, but the modern trend is to permit an LLC to have any lawful purpose. For example, ULLCA (2013) §108(b) provides that: "A limited liability company may have any lawful purpose, regardless of whether for profit." The official comment explains: "Although some LLC statutes continue to require a business purpose, this act follows the current trend and takes a more expansive approach. The phrase 'any lawful purpose, regardless of whether for profit' encompasses even charitable activities."[48]

The business purpose requirement reflects the LLC's partnership law antecedents,[49] but can raise questions when individuals seek to use the LLC to protect some of their assets from liability claims arising from noncommercial use of other assets.

Example

Several branches of the Jones family own a lake cottage and its surrounding land as tenants in common. For years the family has used the cabin for social occasions—sometimes for reunions, other times one family unit at time, sometimes simply for individual family members. For several reasons, the Jones all agree to form Jones Cabin, LLC, and contribute to that LLC their respective ownership interests in the cabin and land in return for membership in the LLC. The reasons include: (i) preventing the transfer of ownership in the cottage and land outside the family; (ii) controlling the fragmentation of ownership that will occur as the family grows; (iii) precluding an action of partition of the realty; and (iv) protecting family members from liability as owners of the land, in case someone is injured on the land. Under a "business purpose" statute, it will be plausible to attack the LLC as improperly formed. Not so under an "any lawful purpose" statute. ◀◀◀

---

48. ULLCA (2013) §108(b), cmt. The comment warns, however, that "this act does not include any comprehensive protections pertaining to charitable assets and purposes."

49. Recall that a general partnership is "an association of two or more persons to carry on as co-owners a business for profit." UPA (1914), §6(1); UPA (1997), §202(a). The ULPA (1976/1985), §106 stated that a limited partnership may carry on "any business that a partnership without limited partners might carry on" and thereby limited a limited partnership to a business purpose. The ULPA (2013) §110(b) harmonized the uniform limited partnership act with the uniform limited liability company act and thus removed the business purpose requirement: "A limited partnership may have any lawful purpose, regardless of whether for profit."

b. Tax-Exempt SMLLCs

To be "nonprofit" is not the same as being "tax exempt." To be tax exempt under federal income tax law, an organization must: (i) be organized for one or more nonprofit purposes; (ii) be classified as a corporation, comply with stringent limitations on governance, operations, and use of assets; and (iii) apply for and obtain a tax-exempt determination letter from the IRS. An LLC could obtain tax-exempt status by "checking the box" to be classified as a corporation, but, in light of the stringent restrictions, it will rarely make sense to do so.

It can, however, make sense for a tax-exempt corporation to form a nonprofit, single-member LLC ("SMLLC") to carry on one or more nonprofit projects. Using a subsidiary helps shield the organization's general assets from liability arising from special projects. A corporate subsidiary would provide the same protection, but that approach would require a separate "tax-exempt" determination letter for the subsidiary. In contrast, a single-member LLC that has not "checked the box" needs no separate determination letter. The relevant tax is the income tax, and an SMLLC is disregarded for federal income tax purposes.

Example

Low Income Housing, Inc. (LIHI), is a nonprofit corporation, tax exempt, and eligible to receive tax-deductible contributions under Internal Rev. Code §501(c). LIHI plans to build a complex of garden apartments to provide affordable housing for senior citizens on fixed incomes, and plans to finance the construction with tax-advantaged bonds. The sole recourse of the bondholders is to be the assets comprising the apartments. To insulate LIHI's assets from claims of the bondholders and any other creditors of the project, LIHI forms and becomes the sole member of Senior Housing, LLC. The limited liability company undertakes the garden apartment project, and LIHI saves the time, effort, and expense of obtaining a separate tax-exempt determination for its wholly owned subsidiary. ◄◄◄

c. Professional Firms as LLCs

States typically impose special requirements on professionals (e.g., doctors, lawyers) who wish to practice as a limited liability company. In some states, these requirements appear in a separate part of the LLC statute. Other states have a professional-firms statute applicable to LLCs, LLPs, and corporations alike.

CASE IN POINT

Case in Point—*Allstate Ins. Co. v. A&A Medical Transp. Servs., Inc.*

An insurance company asserted that it was not obligated to pay "no-fault" insurance benefits for medical services provided by clinics organized as Michigan LLCs, because:

- "a limited liability company (LLC) that provides medical, physical therapy, or occupational therapy services to the public must be organized under article 9 of the Michigan Limited Liability Company Act (MLLCA) instead of under the general provisions of the MLLCA"; and
- the clinics "were improperly organized because (1) article 9 of the MLLCA requires, among other things, that all members and managers of a company providing certain health care services 'shall be licensed or legally authorized in this state to render the same professional service'; and (2) the LLC clinic defendants could not satisfy the licensure requirements of article 9 because certain of their members lacked a professional license." ◀◀◀

In an unreported, *per curium* opinion, based on a prior unreported decision, the court of appeals rejected the insurance company's assertion. But for the precedent established in the prior case, a concurring judge would have held in favor of the insurance company, reasoning that (i) Michigan law only permitted no-fault insurance payments to entities that lawfully rendered treatment, and (ii) by not complying with article 9 of the MLLCA, the clinics were not legally authorized to render professional services in Michigan.[50]

§14.2.2 Powers of an LLC

Agency law deals comprehensively with the power of one person to bind another, but "entity law" must address the question of what powers are possessed by an entity itself. For example, may an entity buy insurance; transfer title to land; sue and be sued in its own name; make contracts? Understanding this question for LLCs requires knowing some background about the issue in the context of corporations and partnerships.

"The law of corporations has always proceeded on the fundamental assumption that corporations are creations with limited power."[51] As the U.S.

50. *Allstate Ins. Co. v. A&A Medical Transp. Servs., Inc.*, Docket Nos. 260766, 261504, 2007 WL 162477 at *1, 3–6 (Mich. App. Jan. 23, 2007) (citations omitted). The insurance company made parallel assertions with regard to clinics organized as ordinary corporations.
51. Model Business Corporation Act, §3.02, cmt.

Supreme Court explained more than 200 years ago, a corporation "is the mere creature of the [legislative] act to which it owes its existence [and] . . . it may correctly be said to be precisely what the incorporating act has made it, to derive all its powers from that act, and to be capable of exerting its faculties only in the manner which that act authorizes."[52]

Until the mid-1800s, state legislatures chartered corporations one by one, each time for a specific, narrow purpose.[53] Eventually, legislatures adopted general statutes, which permitted private individuals to organize corporations by complying with the statutory requirements. In general, the history of corporate law "in this area is largely one ensuring that corporate powers are broad enough to cover all reasonable business transactions,"[54] and today corporate statutes typically contain a lengthy and comprehensive list of particular powers.[55]

The history of partnership law is different. Neither UPA (1914) nor UPA (1997) considers the "powers" issue as a general matter.

Under the aggregate construct,[56] the notion of a partnership's power is almost an oxymoron. Indeed, when UPA (1914) was promulgated, some states did not permit a general partnership to own real property in its own name. UPA (1914) addressed that problem, but its response was specific to the questions of acquiring, owning, and transferring property.[57] Likewise, the aggregate concept raised issues about a partnership's power (or capacity) to sue and be sued in its own name, but here too partnership law (and "common name" statutes) provided a specific response.[58]

Although UPA (1997) proclaims that "[a] partnership is an entity distinct from its partners,"[59] the Act contains no general statement of the entity's powers. As for limited partnerships, before 2001 no uniform act had considered the powers issue. The 1916, 1976, and 1985 acts each contain the same language on "nature of business," but the language pertains to permitted purposes rather than powers: "A limited partnership may carry

---

52. *Head & Armory v. Providence Ins. Co.*, 6 U.S. (2 Cranch) 127, 160 (1804).
53. See Alan R. Palmiter, Corporations: Examples and Explanations 8 (Aspen 5th ed.) (2006).
54. Model Business Corporation Act, §3.02, cmt.
55. The drafters of the Model Business Corporation Act gave "serious consideration . . . to whether there was a continued need for a long list of corporate powers of whether a general provision granting every corporation power to act to the same extent as an individual might be substituted." MBCA §3.02, cmt. The decision to the contrary was "[b]ecause of the long history of these [enumerated] powers." *Id.*
56. For an explanation of the aggregate and entity construct, see Section 7.2.7.
57. UPA (1914) §§8(1), 10, and 25.
58. UPA (1914) §15 (providing for joint and several liability of partners for partnership obligations resulting from the wrongful conduct of a partner and joint liability of partners for other partnership obligations); UPA (1997), §307(a) (providing that a partnership may sue and be sued in the name of the partnership); Del. Code Ann., tit. 10, §3904 (stating that "[a]n unincorporated association of persons, including a partnership, using a common name may sue and be sued in such common name").
59. UPA (1997), §201(a).

on any business that a partnership without limited partners may carry on except [here designate prohibited activities]."[60]

In contrast, section 105 of ULPA (2001) directly addresses the powers question, stating, in pertinent part, that "[a] limited partnership has the powers to do all things necessary or convenient to carry on its activities."[61] This change in approach was occasioned by "de-linking" the limited partnership act from the general partnership act[62] but also reflects the drafters' recognition that "[a] limited partnership is a creature of statute" which "comes into existence" under the authority and requirement of the limited partnership act.[63]

Like limited partnerships, limited liability companies come into existence "under" an enabling statute, and almost all LLC statutes expressly address the powers question. Some LLC statutes eschew a corporate-like list and substitute a succinct and general statement of powers. For example, ULLCA (2013) provides: "A limited liability company has . . . the power to do all things necessary or convenient to carry on its activities and affairs."[64] The Delaware statute is in accord, although not as succinct:

> A limited liability company shall possess and may exercise all the powers and privileges granted by this chapter or by any other law or by its limited liability company agreement, together with any powers incidental thereto, including such powers and privileges as are necessary or convenient to the conduct, promotion or attainment of the business, purposes or activities of the limited liability company.[65]

Other LLC statutes ape corporate law and contain a detailed list of the powers of an LLC. For example, the original California LLC act provided the following list:

> Subject to any limitations contained in the articles of organization and to compliance with this title and any other applicable laws, a limited liability company organized under this title shall have all of the powers of a natural person in carrying out its business activities, including, without limitation, the power to:
>
> (a) Transact its business, carry on its operations, qualify to do business, and have and exercise the powers granted by this title in any state, territory,

---

60. This provision originated as §3 of the 1916 uniform act, appears unchanged in RULPA (1976), §106, and was unaffected by the 1985 amendments.
61. ULPA (2001), §105. For reasons not relevant here, the section also states a few specific powers. See *Id.*, cmt.
62. See Section 12.3.3.
63. ULPA (2001), §201, cmt.
64. ULLCA (2013) §109.
65. Del. Code Ann., tit. 6, §18–106(b).

district, possession, or dependency of the United States, and in any foreign country.

(b) Sue, be sued, complain and defend any action, arbitration, or proceeding, whether judicial, administrative, or otherwise, in its own name.

(c) Adopt, use, and at will alter a company seal; but failure to affix a seal does not affect the validity of any instrument.

(d) Make contracts and guarantees, incur liabilities, act as surety, and borrow money.

(e) Sell, lease, exchange, transfer, convey, mortgage, pledge, and otherwise dispose of all or any part of its property and assets.

(f) Purchase, take, receive, lease, or otherwise acquire, own, hold, improve, use, or otherwise deal in and with any interest in real or personal property, wherever located.

(g) Lend money to and otherwise assist its members and employees.

(h) Issue notes, bonds, and other obligations and secure any of them by mortgage or deed of trust or security interest of any or all of its assets.

(i) Purchase, take, receive, subscribe for, or otherwise acquire, own, hold, vote, use, employ, sell, mortgage, loan, pledge, or otherwise dispose of and otherwise use and deal in and with stock or other interests in and obligations of any person, or direct or indirect obligations of the United States or of any government, state, territory, governmental district, or municipality, or of any instrumentality of any of them.

(j) Invest its surplus funds, lend money from time to time in any manner which may be appropriate to enable it to carry on the operations or fulfill the purposes set forth in its articles of organization, and take and hold real property and personal property as security for the payment of funds so loaned or invested.

(k) Be a promoter, stockholder, partner, member, manager, associate, or agent of any person.

(l) Indemnify or hold harmless any person.

(m) Purchase and maintain insurance.

(n) Issue, purchase, redeem, receive, take, or otherwise acquire, own, hold, sell, lend, exchange, transfer, or otherwise dispose of, pledge, use, and otherwise deal in and with its own bonds, debentures, and other securities.

(o) Pay pensions and establish and carry out pension, profit-sharing, bonus, share purchase, option, savings, thrift, and other retirement, incentive, and benefit plans, trusts, and provisions for all or any of the current or former members, managers, officers, or employees of the limited liability company or any of its subsidiary or affiliated entities, and to indemnify and purchase and maintain insurance on behalf of any fiduciary of such plans, trusts, or provisions.

(p) Make donations, regardless of specific benefit to the limited liability company, to the public welfare or for community, civic, religious, charitable, scientific, literary, educational, or similar purposes.

(q) Make payments or donations or do any other act, not inconsistent with this title or any other applicable law, that furthers the business and affairs of the limited liability company.

(r) Pay compensation, and pay additional compensation, to any or all managers, officers, members, and employees on account of services previously rendered to the limited liability company, whether or not an agreement to pay such compensation was made before such services were rendered.

(s) Insure for its benefit the life of any of its members, managers, officers, or employees, insure the life of any member for the purpose of acquiring at his or her death the interest owned by such member, and continue such insurance after the relationship terminates.

(t) Do every other act not inconsistent with law that is appropriate to promote and attain the purposes set forth in its articles of organization.[66]

This list was preserved when California replaced its original act with the state's version of ULLCA (2006).[67]

However stated, the result is the same. In the eyes of the law, an LLC is a person with the attendant powers necessary to pursue its lawful objectives.

§14.3 SHELF LLCS—THE NECESSITY *VEL NON* OF HAVING AT LEAST ONE MEMBER UPON FORMATION

"Shelf LLC" is a colloquial term of art for "an LLC formed without having at least one member upon formation."[68] Although the concept has substantial practical advantages, it has been quite controversial. For example, the official comment to ULLCA (2006), §201 recounts that: "No topic received more attention or generated more debate in the drafting process for [the Revised Uniform Limited Liability Company Act] than the question of the 'shelf LLC.'"

Understanding the concept and the controversy involves understanding: (i) the practical advantages; (ii) the various approaches taken to the issue by LLC statutes; and (iii) the almost theological nature of the issue for some of the country's leading practitioners of LLC and partnership law.

§14.3.1 The Practical Advantages

In various situations, it can be helpful to have the LLC in existence before the precise identity of the members is determined.

66. Cal. Corp. Code §17003 (1994).

67. In the new California statute, which took effect January 1, 2013, the list appears in section 17701.05.

68. ULLCA (2006), §201, cmt.

Example

On Monday, an attorney receives a phone call from a long-time client, with whom the attorney has been discussing an LLC arrangement for several months. The client now says, "I've decided to go ahead with putting some of my assets into an LLC with some of my kids. Get the LLC organized, and I'll be in on Friday to discuss the details and tell you which kids are going to be involved." Creating the entity in anticipation of the client's detailed decisions may: (i) help the client along the decision path (by symbolizing that something concrete has been done); and (ii) avoid delay later, if the filing office has any backlog. Acceding to the client's wishes does no harm, if the attorney has properly explained to the client that merely creating the entity does not resolve many key issues that pertain to formation (e.g., the contents of the operating agreement).[69] ◀◀◀

Example

Three large corporations have been negotiating for months to shape a joint venture that will handle oil exploration on the north shore in Alaska. The key executives for each corporation have agreed on the basic structure of the LLC that will house the joint venture and on most of the "deal points" with regard to scope of the venture, investment amounts, operational control of the LLC, etc. The negotiations "have momentum"—both the lawyers and business people involved are convinced that final agreement is just a matter of time. However, two of the corporations have not yet decided how they will own their respective membership interests (e.g., directly, through a wholly owned subsidiary that is a corporation, through an SMLLC). The "closing" of the deal will involve hundreds of documents, and for various regulatory and financial reasons, timing has become quite important. Forming the LLC in advance greatly facilitates the rest of the paperwork. ◀◀◀

---

69. This Example is based on a comment by a Uniform Law Commissioner Bruce A. Coggeshall, during the floor debate on ULLCA (2006) at the 2005 Annual Meeting of the Uniform Law Commissioners:

> What often happens is, a client will call you up and say, I need to get a limited liability company formed. You have to form it right away. I am not sure who the members are going to be. It might be me. It might be my wife. It might be my kids. But I want to get the thing formed. You as the lawyer, as the organizer, sign the articles, send them to secretary of state, and then you are legally formed.
>
> But there isn't anybody who feels at that point that they're a member or that they have the obligations of a member or the obligations to a member that a member has.

§14.3.2 The Approach of LLC Statutes

LLC statutes differ in how they approach the question of shelf LLCs. Many define a limited liability company as necessarily having one or more members,[70] which might seem to prohibit a shelf LLC. But that interpretation proves too much; a single-member LLC that loses its sole member does not cease to be an LLC.[71] Also, most of these same statutes provide that an LLC is formed when the specified public official files the articles (or certificate) of organization—without reference to whether the LLC has any members at that moment. In short, on this question many LLC statutes are equivocal.[72]

A few statutes do provide a clear answer. The Virginia LLC Act, for example, expressly contemplates the shelf LLC (although not by that colloquial label). Section 13.1–1003(F)(2) provides that the articles of organization may be executed by an organizer "[i]f the limited liability company . . . has been formed without any managers or members."[73] Section 13.1–1038.1(A)(3) addresses the admission of members into "a limited liability company that has no members as of the commencement of its existence."[74]

The Colorado Act, in sharp contrast, expressly prohibits the shelf LLC. Section 7–80–204(1)(g) provides that "[t]he articles of organization shall state . . . [t]hat there is at least one member of the limited liability company."[75]

---

70. Cal. Corp. Code, §17001(t); Del. Code Ann., tit. 6, §18–101(6).

71. Under most LLC statutes, the LLC will dissolve and be required to wind up its business unless at least one new member is admitted within a specified time limit. But, as with a partnership, dissolution does not terminate the existence of the LLC. See Section 11.2.1(g) (partnership dissolution).

72. See, e.g., *Woods v. Hancock Whitney Bank*, No. CV 22–546, 2022 WL 1683425, at *2 (E.D. La. May 26, 2022) (stating that "the Louisiana Secretary of State's records reflects that Dyko has no members," without considering whether the Louisiana LLC statute permits no-member limited liability companies). In fact, La. Stat. Ann. § 12:1301(10) defines "[l]imited liability company" or "domestic limited liability company" as "an entity that is an unincorporated association having one or more members that is organized and existing under this Chapter."

The leading case is a federal district court decision, reversed on other grounds. *ConnectU LLC v. Zuckerberg*, 482 F. Supp.2d 3 (D. Mass. 2007), reversed on other grounds, 522 F.3d 82, (1st Cir. 2008). Although learned practitioners have debated whether the Delaware LLC statute permits a shelf LLC, the *ConnectU* district court held that there "simply is no requirement under Delaware law that there be members of an LLC at formation." This holding was integral to the court's decision that diversity jurisdiction did not exist, *Id.* at 27, and the Delaware LLC statute certainly supports the holding. See Del Code Ann §§ 18–201 (stating the requirements for forming a Delaware limited liability company, making no reference to having members). Case law is "sparse," *E & T Skyline Constr., LLC v. Talisman Cas. Ins. Co.*, LLC, No. 19 CIV. 8069 (AT), 2022 WL 623858, at *5 (S.D.N.Y. Mar. 2, 2022).

73. Va. Code Ann., §13.1–1003(F)(2). See also, N.C. Gen. Stat. §57C-1–20 (providing that articles of organization may be executed by an organizer or fiduciary "if no initial members of the limited liability company have been identified").

74. Va. Cod Ann., §13.1–1038.1(A)(3).

75. Colo. Rev. Stat. §7–80–204(1)(g).

ULLCA (2006) attempted to steer a middle course:

> A product of intense discussion and compromise with several ABA Advisors, ULLCA (2006) used a double filing and "embryonic certificate" approach. An organizer may deliver for filing a certificate of organization without the company having any members and the filing officer will file the certificate, but:
>
> - the certificate as delivered to the filing officer must acknowledge that situation;
> - the limited liability company is not formed until and unless the organizer timely delivers to the filing officer a notice that the company has at least one member; and
> - when the filing officer files that notice, the company is deemed formed as of the date stated in the notice.
> - if the organizer does not timely deliver the required notice, the certificate lapses and is void.[76]

An organizer who files a certificate of formation without a "no members" statement has effectively affirmed the contrary—that is, that the limited liability company will have at least one member upon formation.[77]

As part of its project on the Harmonization of Business Entity Act, the ULC abandoned this approach. ULLCA (2013) provides that: (i) a certificate of formation is effective when filed by the filing officer; but (ii) the LLC comes into existence only when the certificate is in effect and at least one person has become a member.[78]

§14.3.3 Theology, Shelf LLCs, and *Quo Vadis*?

Opposition to the idea of a shelf LLC rests on two interrelated premises: that an LLC is essentially a form of partnership and that an LLC is essentially a creature of contract. From these premises, it is simple to see that the organization should not preexist its members. How can a contract exist without parties? How can a partnership exist without partners?[79]

---

76. ULLCA (2006), §201, cmt. (citations omitted). The suggested deadline for filing the second notice is 90 days.
77. ULLCA (2006), §201, cmt., explaining the interaction between §§201(b)(3) and 207(c). This double-filing approach reflects a last-minute compromise. The official comment to §201 contains the text of the Drafting Committee's previous approach, which "provided for a 'limited shelf'—a shelf that lacked capacity to conduct any substantive activities." Id.
78. ULLCA (2013)§201(d) ("A limited liability company is formed when the company's certificate of organization becomes effective and at least one person has become a member.").
79. In contrast, a corporation can be formed without any initial shareholders. See Rev. Model Bus. Corp. Act, §§2.01 (stating that one or more persons may act as the incorporator or incorporators by delivering articles of incorporation to the Secretary of State for filing), 2.03(a) (providing that the corporate existence begins when the articles of incorporation are

This perspective hung together under the old "Kintner" tax classification regulations, which influenced LLC statutes to impose a two-member requirement.[80] Even then, however, the perspective ignored several fundamental ways in which an LLC is a "creature of statute."

1. A mere agreement among prospective members cannot bring an LLC into existence. Invocation of a statute is necessary.
2. Invoking the statute and complying with its requirements brings into existence a separate legal person—"an entity distinct from its members."[81]
3. "The 'separate entity' characteristic is fundamental to a limited liability company and is inextricably connected to . . . the liability shield."[82]
4. The liability shield is half the *raison d'être* for the LLC[83] and results from the formal invocation of the statute, not from the members' agreement.

Once the "check-the-box" regulations opened the gate (or tore down the wall) to single-member LLCs, the partnership/contract paradigm lost all claim to coherence. A contract requires at least two parties,[84] and a partnership must have at least two partners. But SMLLCs have become major players in the law and practice of business organizations, and their existence and importance irrefutably call for a paradigm shift.[85]

The SMLLC does not by itself demonstrate that shelf LLCs ought to be permitted. The SMLLC does, however, reveal that the partnership/contract paradigm is no longer a plausible reason to oppose the shelf LLC.

---

filed, unless a delayed effective date is specified), 2.05(a)(2) (providing that the incorporator or incorporators shall elect directors if none are named in the articles of incorporation).

80. For a discussion of the Kintner Regulations, see Section 13.1.4(a) and (b).

81. ULLCA (2013), §104(a). See also Del. Code Ann., tit. 6, §18–201(b).

82. ULLCA (2013), §104(a), cmt.

83. The other half is tax classification—either partnership or disregarded entity status.

84. See Restatement (Second) of Contracts, §1, cmt. c (1981) (stating that "[o]ne person may make several promises to one person or to several persons, or several persons may join in making promises to one or more persons").

85. SMLLCs are important in both (relatively) simple situations (e.g., to provide a liability shield for a business owned by an individual entrepreneur) and complex ones (e.g., to serve as a liability-deflecting wholly owned subsidiary for a nonprofit corporation, or as a "special-purpose, bankruptcy-remote entity" used to facilitate sophisticated "securitization" arrangements).

§14.4 CONSEQUENCES OF ENTITY STATUS

§14.4.1 The Liability Shield

Because a limited liability company is "an entity distinct from its member or members,"[86] its assets and obligations pertain to it and not to its members. As a result, absent extraordinary circumstances,[87] an LLC's members are not answerable *qua* members for the debts and other obligations of the LLC.[88]

LLC statutes each contain "shield language," and many statutes extend the shield to include managers. For example, ULLCA (2013) provides:

> A debt, obligation, or other liability of a limited liability company is solely the debt, obligation, or other liability of the company. A member or manager is not personally liable, directly or indirectly, by way of contribution or otherwise, for a debt, obligation, or other liability of the company solely by reason of being or acting as a member or manager.[89]

The phrase "*solely* by reason of" is crucial. The liability shield merely severs the automatic vicarious liability that would attend the status of general partner. The LLC shield provides no protection against liability that comes from some other source.

Example

A manager personally guarantees a debt of a limited liability company formed under ULLCA (2013). ULLCA (2013) §304(a) is irrelevant to the manager's liability as guarantor. (As a practical matter, the person's role as manager may cause the obligee to seek, and the manager to provide the guarantee. As a legal matter, however, the person's status as manager does not pertain to the guarantee.) ◄◄◄

86. ULLCA (2013) §108(a). See also, e.g., Del. Code Ann., tit. 6, §18–201(b).
87. See Section 16.1.
88. The obverse is true, as well. The assets and obligations of a member pertain to the member and not to the LLC. As a result, absent extraordinary circumstances, the assets of the LLC are not chargeable with the debts and other obligations of its members. See Section 14.4.2(b) (discussing the "reverse pierce" and fraudulent transfers). The term "asset partitioning" is sometimes applied to describe the separation of an entity's assets and liabilities from those of its owners.
89. ULLCA (2013), §304(a).

Example

A member purports to bind a ULLCA (2013) limited liability company while lacking any agency law power to do so. The limited liability company is not bound, but the member is liable for having breached the "warranty of authority."[90] ULLCA (2013) §304(a) does not apply. The liability is not *for* a "debt, obligation, or other liability of the limited liability company," but rather is the member's direct liability resulting because the limited liability company is *not* indebted, obligated or liable.[91] ◄◄◄

Case in Point — *People v. Pacific Landmark*

"The City of Los Angeles and the People of the State of California (collectively, the City) brought a red-light abatement action against the operators of a business and the owners of the strip mall where the business was located. The action alleged that the business was a front for prostitution and an illegal massage parlor. The trial court issued a preliminary injunction prohibiting the operation of a massage parlor or a house of prostitution. Pacific Landmark, LLC (Pacific), a limited liability company and owner of the property, and Ron Mavaddat, Pacific's manager . . . [appealed. On appeal] Mavaddat . . . contends, as manager of Pacific, that he is exempt from personal liability for any order or judgment against Pacific. . . . [W]e hold that managers of limited liability companies are not immune from personal liability if they have participated in tortious or criminal conduct while performing duties as managers."[92] ◄◄◄

The liability shield pertains only to claims by third parties and is irrelevant to claims by a limited liability company against a member or manager and *vice versa*.

Example

Narnia LLC is a member-managed LLC. Edmund, one of the members, breaches his duty of loyalty, causing damage to the LLC. For two reasons, the liability shield is irrelevant. First and foremost, Edmund's liability is not that "of a limited liability company"[93] but rather *to* the limited liability company. Second, Edmund's liability is not "solely by reason of acting as a member" but rather by reason of Edmund's breach of the duty of loyalty. ◄◄◄

---

90. See Section 4.2.2 for a discussion of this agency law doctrine.

91. These two Examples are taken essentially verbatim from the official comment to ULLCA (2006), §304(a).

92. *People v. Pacific Landmark*, 129 Cal.App.4th 1203, 1206–07 (Cal.App. 2 Dist. 2005) (citations omitted).

93. ULLCA (2013), §304(a).

§14.4.2 Other Consequences of Entity Status

There are numerous other consequences to an LLC's entity status.[94] Many can be grouped as follows.

a. Capacity to Sue and Other Matters Related to the Mechanics of Litigation

As a separate legal entity, an LLC is:

- authorized and required to sue and be sued in its own name;
- not able to be represented in court by a non-attorney member;
- subject to particular requirements relating to service of process; and
- not an agent for service of process on any of its members (including a sole member).

b. Matters Related to Property

Most courts agree that a member's contribution of property to an LLC constitutes "more than a change in the form of ownership; it is a transfer from one entity to another,"[95] which means that a contribution of property to an LLC:

- can trigger a deed tax, even if the contributor is the LLC's sole member, unless the tax statute provides otherwise;
- can entitle a real estate broker to commission for the "sale" from the member to the LLC;
- means that the former owner of property contributed to an LLC lacks standing to contest zoning activities pertaining to the property and that LLC members cannot sue to partition land contributed to (and therefore owned by) the LLC;
- puts the contributed property out of the reach of the contributor's creditors, unless a creditor can make a case of fraudulent transfer or persuade the court to do a reverse pierce, treating the LLC as if it were the member;[96]
- renders improper a *lis pendens* filed by a creditor of an LLC member against real property owned by the LLC; and

---

94. For a detailed discussion of this topic, see BISHOP & KLEINBERGER ON LIMITED LIABILITY COMPANIES §§ 5:70–5:83, on which this section is based.
95. *Hagan v. Adams Property Assocs., Inc.*, 482 S.E.2d 805, 806–07 (Va. 1997).
96. Each of these claims requires a showing of fraud or substantial injustice.

- renders inapplicable the statute of frauds to an agreement to sell an LLC membership interest, even when the LLC's only asset is land.

Case in Point — *Gebhardt Family Inv., L.L.C. v. Nations Title Ins. of NY, Inc.*

For estate planning purposes, a husband and wife formed a limited liability company, became the company's only members, and conveyed to the company real estate that they had previously owned as joint tenants. As joint tenants, they had title insurance on the property and had previously reported to the insurer a cloud on the title. After the conveyance, the insurer successfully asserted that the title insurance no longer applied. The policy excluded coverage for subsequent purchasers and the LLC had succeeded to the title by "purchase."[97] ◄◄◄

§14.5 THE OPERATING AGREEMENT

§14.5.1 Definition, Function, Power, and Scope

All LLC statutes contemplate an agreement among the members of an LLC and provide a pivotal role for that agreement; the label "operating agreement" is used by almost all LLC statutes.[98] "Like the partnership agreement in a general or limited partnership, an LLC's operating agreement serves as the foundational contract among the entity's owners."[99]

Many LLC statutes contain definitions such as the following: "'Operating agreement' means the agreement and any amendments thereto, of the members as to the affairs of a limited liability company and the conduct of its business."[100] A few statutes reserve specified matters to the articles of organization, but under all LLC acts the operating agreement has broad power and scope.

---

97. [97]*Gebhardt Family Inv., L.L.C. v. Nations Title Ins. of NY, Inc.*, 752 A.2d 1222, 1226 (Md. Ct. Spec. App. 2000).

98. The Delaware Act initially used the label "limited liability company agreement." However, in June 2002, the Delaware Legislature bowed to common usage, amending the Delaware Act to refer to "operating agreements" as well. 73 Del. Laws, Ch. 295, §1 (2002), amending Del. Code Ann., tit.6, §18–101(7).

99. ULLCA (2006), Prefatory Note, Noteworthy Provisions, The Operating Agreement. See also ULLCA (2013) §105, cmt. (Principal Provisions of the Act Concerning the Operating Agreement) (stating that "the operating agreement is pivotal to a limited liability company").

100. MD Code, Corps. & Assns., §4A-101(o).

Flexibility of structure is one the hallmarks of the LLC, and the operating agreement is the mechanism through which members can revise or displace the statutory default rules to create "a specially tailored relationship."[101] The Delaware Supreme Court has characterized the operating agreement as the "cornerstone" of a Delaware limited liability company,[102] and, assuming the members (or their lawyers) have given thought to the operating agreement, the same is true under any LLC act.

In a highly lawyered deal, the operating agreement might entirely displace the statutory default rules. The Delaware Chancery Court must have had such situations in mind when it noted that, under Delaware law, "LLC members' rights begin with and typically end with the Operating Agreement."[103]

The following is a nonexhaustive list of topics that an operating agreement might address:

- *membership*—requirements and rights for admitting members, both as to memberships obtained directly from the limited liability company and as to memberships obtained as a transferee from a current member; transferability of membership interests; conditions and consequences of member dissociation;
- *governance*—management structure; classes of membership interests; voting rights of members; number of managers; qualifications, selection procedures, and duties for managers; matters reserved for member decision;
- *finance*—amount and status of member contributions; consequences for nonperformance of a contribution promise, including the power of the limited liability company to compromise its claims; amount and timing of interim distributions; priorities in liquidating distributions; distributions in kind; and
- *dissolution*—events that trigger dissolution; ability of the limited liability company to avoid dissolution following member dissociation; authority to manage winding up; preferences in liquidating distributions.[104]

The extent to which an operating agreement can reshape or even negate fiduciary duties among members and to the limited liability company is a complicated and controversial question. Section 15.4.7 addresses that question.

---

101. Bishop & Kleinberger, ¶5.02[3][b][v].

102. *Elf Atochem N. Am., Inc. v. Jaffari*, 727 A.2d 286, 291 (Del. 1999).

103. *Walker v. Resource Dev. Co. Ltd., L.L.C.* (DE), No. CIV. A. 1843-S, 2000 WL 1336720, at *12 (Del. Ch., Aug. 29, 2000). Another Chancery Court opinion refers to the operating agreement as the LLC's "chartering agreement." *Haley v. Talcott*, 864 A.2d 86, 94 (Del. Ch. 2004).

104. This list is from Bishop & Kleinberger, ¶5.06[2][a][ii].

§14.5.2 Required upon Formation?

Few LLC statutes expressly require an LLC to have an operating agreement, but most LLC statutes define "operating agreement" so broadly that, "as soon as a limited liability company has any members, the limited liability company [necessarily] has an operating agreement."[105]

A comment to ULLCA (2006)'s definition of "operating agreement" provides a useful example:

> For example, suppose: (i) two persons orally and informally agree to join their activities in some way through the mechanism of an LLC, (ii) they form the LLC or cause it to be formed, and (iii) without further ado or agreement, they become the LLC's initial members. The LLC has an operating agreement. "[A]ll the members" have agreed on who the members are, and that agreement—no matter how informal or rudimentary—is an agreement "concerning the matters described in Section 110(a) [which delineates the broad scope of the operating agreement]."[106]

Requiring an LLC to have an operating agreement can cause mischief if the statute requires the operating agreement to be in writing.

Case in Point—*Horning v. Horning Const., LLC*

CASE IN POINT

The founder of a business transformed it into a limited liability company and, as a long-term exit strategy, agreed to have two employees become members of the LLC. When they subsequently took control of the company over the founder's objection, he sought judicial intervention. The relevant LLC statute required a written operating agreement, and no such agreement had been executed. The LLC statute allowed for court-ordered dissolution when it was not "reasonably practicable" to carry on the business of the LLC in conformity with the operating agreement, and there were ample facts to establish an oral agreement protecting the founder. However, in light of the statute's requirement for a *written* operating agreement, the court declined to apply that dissolution provision.[107] ◄◄◄

In any event, it is unwise to form a limited liability company without simultaneously arranging for an operating agreement. The simple mechanics for creating the LLC as a legal entity can be a trap for the unwary;[108] those who organize an LLC without considering an operating agreement saddle

105. ULLCA (2006), §102(13), cmt.
106. *Id.*
107. *Horning v. Horning Const., LLC*, 12 Misc.3d 402, 816 N.Y.S.2d 877 (N.Y. Sup. 2006).
108. See Section 14.1.

the members with the default provisions of the statute. Those provisions might comprise rules unexpected by the members and inappropriate for the enterprise.

§14.5.3 Operating Agreement in a Single-Member LLC?

An operating agreement is a contract, and at common law a contract necessarily has at least two parties. "It may therefore seem oxymoronic to refer to" an operating agreement in a single-member LLC.[109] However, many (perhaps most) LLC statutes do just that.

For example, under the Arizona LLC statute, operating agreement means, "[i]n the case of a limited liability company that has a single member, any written or oral statement of the member made in good faith."[110] The Oregon statute vests the "power to adopt, alter, amend or repeal an operating agreement of . . . a single member limited liability company, in the sole member of the limited liability company,"[111] and Washington law defines "limited liability company agreement" to include "any written statement of the sole member."[112]

A comment to ULLCA (2013) explains the history beyond this seemingly strange approach:

> This re-definition of "agreement" is a function of "path dependence." LLC statutes initially required an LLC to have at least two members, and almost all LLC statutes contemplated an agreement among members as an LLC's key organic document. Because LLC statutes make the operating agreement the principal way to override statutory default rules, the advent of single member LLCs made it necessary to provide that a sole member could make an operating agreement.[113]

§14.5.4 Mechanics of Adoption and Amendment

a. Adoption

An operating agreement must initially be agreed to by all persons who are members of the limited liability company at the moment at which the agreement is adopted. Some LLC statutes make this point directly. For example, the Virginia LLC act provides: "An operating agreement must initially be

109. ULLCA (2013), §102(13), cmt.
110. Ariz. Rev. Stat. Ann. §29–601 (14)(b).
111. Or. Rev. Stat. Ann. §63.431(2).
112. Wash. Rev. Code Ann. §25.15.006(7).
113. ULLCA (2013) §102(13), cmt.

agreed to by all of the members."[114] Under other statutes, the rule is implied by the definition of the term "operating agreement" as an agreement of the members and from the common law concept of "agreement."

b. Writing Requirement?

A few LLC statutes require the operating agreement to be in writing or require a writing to revise or displace specified statutory default rules.[115] However, most LLC statutes define the operating agreement as "written or oral"[116] or even as including terms implied in fact.[117]

c. Articles of Organization as Part of the Operating Agreement?

If the members of an LLC control the contents of the articles of organization and each member must consent to any change, it is possible to consider those contents to be part of the operating agreement. The broad definition of "operating agreement" invites this analysis, at least where the articles and the contents of the operating agreement do not conflict.[118]

Often, however, an LLC's articles can be amended with less than unanimous consent of the members. ULLCA (2013), for example, provides that an amendment to an LLC certificate of organization may be signed by any "person authorized by the company"[119] and does not necessarily require unanimous member consent to authorize amending the certificate.[120]

Where possible, it would be wise to have the LLC's operating agreement expressly determine whether the articles of organization comprise part of the operating agreement.

---

114. Va. Code Ann. §13.1–1023(B)(1).
115. E.g., Ga. Code Ann., §14–11–305(1) (providing that a member of a manager-managed LLC owes no duties to the LLC or to the other members solely by reason of acting in his or her capacity as a member "[e]xcept as otherwise provided in the articles of organization or a *written* operating agreement").
116. E.g., Ariz. Rev. Stat. §29–601(14).
117. E.g., ULLCA (2013) §102(13). In 2007, the Delaware statute was amended to include the concept of implied-in-fact agreements. 76 Del. Laws, Ch. 105, §1 (2007), amending Del. Code Ann., tit.6, §18–101(7).
118. For a discussion of how to resolve such conflicts, see Section 14.5.7. Under the Michigan statute, the articles are automatically part of the operating agreement. Michigan's definition of "operating agreement" states: "The term includes any provision in the articles of organization pertaining to the affairs of the limited liability company and the conduct of its business." Mich. Comp. Laws Ann. §450.4102(r).
119. ULLCA (2013) §203(a)(1).
120. See ULLCA (2013) §407. Amending the certificate requires unanimous member consent only if the amendment is an "act outside the ordinary course" of the company's activities. *Id.* §§407(b)(4) and (c)(3)(a). In contrast, §407 specifically provides that amending the operating agreement requires unanimous consent. *Id.*, §§407(b)(4)(A) and (c)(3)(B).

d. Amending the Operating Agreement — Quantum of Consent

As a default matter, amending the operating agreement requires the consent of all persons then members. This rule follows from basic contract law principles and is also stated expressly in some acts. The rule applies regardless of whether an LLC is managed directly by its members or through managers.[121]

Example

Faculty Support Services, LLC ("FSS"), is a limited liability company organized under the law of a state that requires each limited liability company's articles of organization to specify either a member-managed or manager-managed structure. FSS is manager-managed, and its operating agreement provides that "all management questions will be decided exclusively by the managers, Lynette and Melissa." Amendment of the operating agreement will nonetheless require the consent of all the members. ◀ ◀ ◀

Non-unanimous amendment is permissible, if the operating agreement itself so provides. Some statutes make this point expressly. For example, ULLCA (2013) states that the operating agreement governs "the means and conditions for amending the operating agreement."[122] It is common for operating agreements to specify a quantum of consent in terms of profit interests held by members, rather than providing that members vote *per capita*.

Example

Framers, LLC, has five members, with profit interests allocated as follows, per the operating agreement:

Ben	10%
James	30%
John	10%
Charlotte	20%
Thomas	30%

The operating agreement also provides that "this agreement may be amended by a writing signed by members who at proposed effective date of the amendment own 70 percent of the profits interests then owned by members." A writing signed by Ben, James, and Thomas will suffice to amend the

121. ULLCA (2006), §§407(b)(4)(A) and (c)(3)(B).
122. ULLCA (2013) §105(a)(4).

operating agreement, and likewise will a writing signed by all the members other than James, or all the members other than Thomas. ◀ ◀ ◀

Requiring unanimity can be problematic, but relaxing the unanimity requirement has risks as well. If unanimous consent is required, each member can in effect veto any fundamental changes in an LLC's governance and operations—no matter how advisable or even necessary the proposed changes might be. Moreover, this veto power extends to efforts to adjust even minor rules that happen to be delineated in the operating agreement. On the other hand, requiring less than unanimity carries the risk of majoritarian oppression. Requiring a supermajority reduces but does not eliminate the problem.

Example

Litigation Support Services, LLC is a member-managed limited liability company, whose operating agreement provides that the agreement can be amended by the consent of members owning 80 percent of interests in current profits owned by members. Members owning 85 percent of the interests in current profits consent to amend the operating agreement to reduce the profit percentage of the other members from an aggregate of 15 percent to an aggregate of 10 percent, with the other 5 percent being allocated among the members comprising the 85 percent majority. There is no plausible business justification for the amendment, but the amendment complies with the quantum requirement stated in the operating agreement and, at least formally speaking, is valid. ◀ ◀ ◀

Careful drafting can limit the risks of nonunanimous amendments, and sophisticated operating agreements sometimes specify several categories of amendment, each requiring a different quantum of consent (e.g., members holding a majority of profit interests owned by members; members owning a specified supermajority of profits interests; unanimous consent).

In extreme situations—such as described in the Example just above—the contractual obligation of good faith and fair dealing will apply and the perpetrators will be in breach.[123] Also, if the relevant jurisdiction recognizes member-to-member fiduciary duties, majoritarian oppression will breach those duties as well.[124]

---

123. The amendment seems designed to deprive a member of the "fruits of the bargain." For a discussion of the obligation of good faith and fair dealing, see Section 15.4.8.

124. For a discussion of member-to-member fiduciary duties, see Sections 15.4.3 and 16.4.

e. Amending the Operating Agreement — Writing Requirement

To the extent that an LLC statute requires the operating agreement to be in writing, any amendment must perforce also be in writing. Under statutes permitting oral or implied-in-fact operating agreements, it is an open question whether a written operating agreement can itself preclude oral or implied-in-fact amendments. An operating agreement is a contract, and at common law, courts have often overridden or disregarded contractual terms aimed at precluding nonwritten amendments. It is for that reason that Article 2 of the Uniform Commercial Code expressly and specifically authorizes such provisions in contracts for the sale of goods.[125]

Few, if any, LLC statutes contain language as specific as the UCC provision. However, many LLC statutes authorize an operating agreement to control the means of its amendment. For example, the Virginia LLC statute states: "If the articles of organization or the operating agreement provide for the manner by which an operating agreement may be amended, including by . . . requiring the satisfaction of conditions, an operating agreement may be amended only in that manner or as otherwise permitted by law."[126] The final phrase ("or as otherwise permitted by law") is perhaps an invitation to courts to indulge their common law antipathy. In contrast, ULLCA (2013) provides simply that "the operating agreement governs . . . the means and conditions for amending the operating agreement,"[127] and an official comment states that "Under this provision, the operating agreement can control . . . the means by which the consent [to an amendment] is manifested [including] prohibiting modifications except when consented to in writing."[128] Another section buttresses this view, stating that: "An operating agreement may specify that its amendment requires . . . the satisfaction of a condition. An amendment is ineffective if its adoption does not . . . satisfy the specified condition."[129] The comment states directly that, under the quoted language, "an operating agreement can require that any amendment be made through a writing or a record signed by each member."[130]

§14.5.5 Lacunae in the Operating Agreement

If an operating agreement does not address a particular issue, those with management authority in the LLC will likely deem the issue within their

125. The UCC §2–209(2) states: "A signed agreement which excludes modification or rescission except by a signed record may not be otherwise modified or rescinded."
126. Va. Code Ann. §13.1–1023(B)(3).
127. ULLCA, §110(a)(4).
128. *Id.*, cmt.
129. ULLCA (2013) §107(a).
130. *Id.*, cmt.

authority. In some circumstances, the results can be quite unexpected for other members.

CASE IN POINT

Case in Point—*KBL Properties LLC v. Bellin*

Two members of an LLC (constituting a majority) voted for a capital call of $225,000. Those members contributed $157,500 in the aggregate, and Bellin (the third member) contributed nothing. "Under the terms of the operating agreement, Bellin's financial interest declined to 0.00063 percent as a result of the new contributions of equity capital." Pursuant to the operating agreement, the majority members served Bellin with a notice of purchase of his interest calculated at $6.30. When Bellin would not sell, the LLC brought an action for declaratory judgment that "additional equity capital was lawfully raised, minority member's [Bellin's] financial interest was lawfully reduced, plaintiff member had lawfully exercised his buy-sell option, and that he was entitled to lawfully purchase minority member's entire membership interest in accordance with buy-sell offer." The court of chancery found that the operating agreement required unanimous consent before any mandatory capital contributions could be required and ruled the buy-sell offer to be void. The LLC appealed. The Supreme Court reversed, holding that "[the] resolution makes no change or modification to the operating agreement and, therefore, cannot be called an amendment. Thus, the operating agreement's default provision on voting applies, and this resolution could properly be approved by a vote of members holding an aggregate governance interest of at least 51 percent."[131] ◄◄◄

§14.5.6 Relationship of Operating Agreement to New Members

It would be conceptually and practically chaotic to allow persons to become members of an LLC without being bound to the operating agreement, and many LLC statutes address this issue. Delaware's approach is perhaps the most complex. ULLCA (2013)'s approach is comparatively straightforward.

131. *KBL Properties LLC v. Bellin*, 900 So.2d 1160, 1161, 1166 (Miss. 2005). The result might be different under ULLCA (2013). Under Section 407(b)(4)(A), Bellin could have argued that a capital call with such a draconian effect on his ownership was "outside the ordinary course of the activities and affairs of the company."

Under Delaware law:

> A member or manager of a limited liability company or an assignee of a limited liability company interest is bound by the limited liability company agreement whether or not the member or manager or assignee executes the limited liability company agreement. . . . A written limited liability company agreement or another written agreement or writing:
>
> a. May provide that a person shall be admitted as a member of a limited liability company, or shall become an assignee of a limited liability company interest or other rights or powers of a member to the extent assigned:
>
> 1. If such person (or a representative authorized by such person orally, in writing or by other action such as payment for a limited liability company interest) executes the limited liability company agreement or any other writing evidencing the intent of such person to become a member or assignee; or
>
> 2. Without such execution, if such person (or a representative authorized by such person orally, in writing or by other action such as payment for a limited liability company interest) complies with the conditions for becoming a member or assignee as set forth in the limited liability company agreement or any other writing; and
>
> b. Shall not be unenforceable by reason of its not having been signed by a person being admitted as a member or becoming an assignee as provided in paragraph (7)a. of this section, or by reason of its having been signed by a representative as provided in this chapter.[132]

Under ULLCA (2013), "A person that becomes a member [of a limited liability company] is deemed to assent to the operating agreement."[133]

If the relevant LLC statute is silent on this important issue, it is possible to argue that a person's assent to becoming a member amounts to assent to the operating agreement. The argument intertwines aspects of LLC law and contract law: Given the fundamental nature of an operating agreement and the chaos that would result if the operating agreement did *not* apply to all members, a reasonable person would interpret a person's manifestation of assent to becoming a member as implicit assent to the operating agreement.

There are counterarguments, however, especially if the operating agreement is not in writing and a new member claims to have assented to becoming a member while ignorant of some subsequently problematic term. In any event, careful drafting can eliminate the problem, for example, by having the operating agreement specify that no person can become a member

---

132. Del. Code Ann., tit. 6, §18–101(7) (defining "limited liability company agreement").
133. ULLCA (2013) §106(b).

without first agreeing to be a party to and bound by the operating agreement. Or, put another way, the operating agreement could provide that one of the conditions to becoming a member is to agree to (and, if the operating agreement is in writing, sign) the operating agreement.

§14.5.7 Resolving Conflicts Between Articles and Operating Agreement

Suppose that an LLC's articles of organization and operating agreement conflict. Which governs? Most LLC statutes are silent on this issue.

ULLCA (1996) was the first LLC Act to address the problem,[134] giving priority to the operating agreement in *inter se* matters and priority to the articles of organization when third-party interests are involved. However, as noted in Section 14.1.3, ULLCA (1996) has not been widely adopted.

ULLCA (2006) and (2013) both carried forward and expanded the approach of ULLCA (1996); each contemplates conflicts between the operating agreement and any "record" that has been filed by the filing officer. In the words of ULLCA (2103):

> [I]f a record that has been delivered by a limited liability company to the [Secretary of State] for filing becomes effective and conflicts with a provision of the operating agreement:
>
> (1) the agreement prevails as to members, persons dissociated as members, transferees, and managers; and
>
> (2) the record prevails as to other persons to the extent they reasonably rely on the record.[135]

This approach makes the operating agreement paramount among the members, but protects third parties that have reasonably relied on the public record.[136]

In the absence of a statutory mechanism for resolving conflicts, courts might well adopt the quoted approach as a matter of common law.[137]

---

134. ULLCA, §203(c).

135. ULLCA (2013), 107(d). ULLCA (2006) §112(d) is substantively identical. Differences are only stylistic.

136. ULLCA, §107(d), cmt.

137. See Bishop & Kleinberger on Limited Liability Companies § 5:113 (Limitation on Power: Relationship of Operating Agreement to Articles of Organization) (suggesting a mode of analysis). See also *McDonough v. McDonough*, 2015 WL 11182526, at *4 (N.H.Super. 2015) (adopting the suggested mode of analysis).

Problem 115

Standup, LLC, ("Standup"), a limited liability company organized under the law of the state of Delaware, is for all practical purposes "located" in Des Moines, Iowa. All three of its members are individual residents in Iowa, and Standup does all its business within Iowa. After fruitless attempts to collect on an invoice, Standup sues one of its customers. Which state's law applies to the dispute? ◀ ◀ ◀

Explanation

Unless the contract between Standup and its customer provides otherwise, ordinary choice of law principles make Iowa law the applicable law. Although Standup is a "Delaware" LLC, the "internal affairs" doctrine does not apply here. A dispute between a limited liability company and one of its customers is not an *internal* affair. ◀ ◀ ◀

Problem 116

Carolyn acts as the organizer of a limited liability company, formed under the law of a state whose statute has typical provisions so far as may be relevant to this question. Which of the following statements is (are) true?

1. Carolyn may be, but need not be, an initial member of the limited liability company.
2. In acting as an organizer, Carolyn does not act as an agent of the limited liability company.
3. For some purposes, the law requires at least one additional organizer.
4. Carolyn is acting on behalf of the person or persons who will become the limited liability company's initial member or members.
5. Carolyn is acting as a gratuitous agent. ◀ ◀ ◀

Explanation

1. True.
2. True—until Carolyn has completed the tasks necessary to form the limited liability company, the limited liability company does not exist. A person cannot act as agent for a nonexistent principal.[138]
3. False.

138. See Section 1.4.

4. Close call—this proposition is arguably true under most LLC statutes but problematic for those statutes that permit "shelf" LLCs.
5. Ambiguous—LLC law does not address this point. In practice, the answer varies. For example, it is quite possible for one of the initial members of an LLC to "handle the paperwork" without compensation for that task. But it is also quite common for an attorney (or an attorney's paralegal) to serve as an organizer as part of compensated legal work—typically in connection with other related tasks, such as drafting the operating agreement. ◀◀◀

Problem 117

Propane, LLC ("Propane") is a manager-managed limited liability company in the business of supplying propane to commercial and residential users. InCharge, Inc. ("InCharge"), is a member of Propane and also its sole manager. HandsOff, Inc. ("HandsOff") is the other member of Propane. Beth is the Executive Vice President of InCharge, and in that capacity directs both InCharge's efforts as manager of Propane and InCharge's other day-to-day activities.

After a propane accident at the home of one of Propane's customers, the customer sues both Propane and InCharge. Assuming that: (i) the accident was proximately and foreseeably caused by Beth's negligence; and (ii) Beth's negligence was within the scope of her employment as the Executive Vice President of InCharge, does InCharge benefit from the LLC liability shield? Does HandsOff?[139] ◀◀◀

EXPLANATION

Explanation

InCharge does not benefit. Under the doctrine of *respondeat superior*, Beth's liability is imputed to InCharge.[140] This liability is as a tortfeasor (albeit vicariously, through principles of agency law)—not by reason of InCharge's status as a manager or member of Propane.

In contrast, HandsOff does benefit from the LLC liability shield. The facts provide no nexus whatsoever between the customer's claim and HandsOff except HandsOff's status as a member of Propane. ◀◀◀

Problem 118

Todd, a physician, forms a member-managed limited liability company, Bear, LLC ("Bear") to take title to a plot of land that Todd has owned individually

139. This Example is based on *Estate of Countryman v. Farmers Coop. Ass'n*, 679 N.W.2d 598 (Iowa 2004).
140. See Section 3.2.

for 15 years. Todd contributes the land to the limited liability company in return for becoming the LLC's sole member.

Subsequently, Todd learns of a proposed zoning ordinance that would limit the permissible uses of the land. He seeks judicial intervention to fight the zoning change. May he appear *pro se?* ◀ ◀ ◀

Explanation

For several interrelated reasons, the answer is no. A non-lawyer may only represent him or herself in court, and Todd, as an individual, has no standing to object to the zoning change. That is, the land belongs to Bear, not to Todd, and, therefore, cognizable injury (if any) directly affects Bear, not Todd. A limited liability company is a legal person distinct from its members, even when the LLC has only one member. In this context, it is irrelevant that Todd's position as sole member gives him total control over Bear's activities. ◀ ◀ ◀

Problem 119

Wainright, LLC ("Wainright") has existed for five years, and since its formation has had an oral operating agreement. Gideon is admitted as a new member of Wainright without expressly agreeing to the operating agreement and later asserts that a particular provision of the operating agreement is not binding on him. The operating agreement is silent on the issue. From the perspective of the limited liability company, would the Delaware LLC Act or ULLCA (2013) be the more favorable statute? ◀ ◀ ◀

Explanation

ULLCA (2013)—it provides that "[a] person that becomes a member [of a limited liability company][141] is deemed to assent to the operating agreement and does not limit its scope to written operating agreements."[142] In contrast, the Delaware provision appears to refer to a written operating agreement: "A member or manager of a limited liability company or an assignee of a limited liability company interest is bound by the limited liability company agreement whether or not the member or manager or assignee *executes* the limited liability company agreement."[143] ◀ ◀ ◀

141. ULLCA (2013) §106(b).
142. ULLCA (2013) §102(13).
143. Del. Code Ann., tit. 6, §18–101(7). Section 14.5.4 quotes the relevant language at length.

CHAPTER 15

LLC Governance and Finance; Member Exit Rights

§15.1 FLEXIBILITY, THE MEANING OF "OWNERSHIP," AND THE RELATIONSHIP BETWEEN GOVERNANCE RIGHTS AND ECONOMIC RIGHTS

§15.1.1 Flexibility of Structure; Resulting Limits on Generalization

With regard to internal structure, the LLC is "almost ineffably flexible."[1] As a result, generalizations about LLC governance and finance are, generally speaking, less predictive than generalizations about partnerships or corporations. Although LLC statutes provide "default rules" on governance and finance,[2] these rules channel arrangements less powerfully than do default rules applicable in other mainstream business entities.

This situation stems in part from history. Ever since "check the box," flexibility of structure has been a key attraction of the LLC form.[3] In addition: (i) most LLC statutes have chosen to provide two alternate sets of

1. Daniel S. Kleinberger, "The LLC as Recombinant Entity— Revisiting Fundamental Questions through the LLC Lens," paper delivered at the 21st Century Commercial Law Forum— Seventh International Symposium 2007 (Beijing, China), published in the United States, 14 FORDHAM J. OF CORP. & FIN. L. 473 (2009).

2. See Sections 15.2 (governance) and 15.6 (finance).

3. See Section 13.1.4(d) (explaining how the IRS's "check-the-box" regulations removed constraints on LLC structure).

default rules for structuring LLC governance;[4] and (ii) the rules of partnership tax accounting undercut whatever apparent commonality an LLC statute might imply about capital structure.[5]

As a result, making an LLC the "entity of choice" for a business deal implies only weakly, if at all, a basic "menu" of arrangements from which participants will likely begin their negotiations.

§15.1.2 The Meaning of Member, Membership, and Membership Interest

This "default mode" vagueness extends to what it means to own a membership in an LLC. As a matter of nomenclature, LLC statutes differ as to whether they even use the term "membership interest" and, if so, how they define the term. For example, the original California LLC Act defined "membership interest" as "a member's rights in the limited liability company, collectively, including the member's economic interest, any right to vote or participate in management, and any right to information concerning the business and affairs of the limited liability company."[6] In contrast, the Arizona statute provides: "'Member's interest,' 'interest in a limited liability company,' or 'interest in the limited liability company' means a member's share of the profits and losses of a limited liability company and the right to receive distributions of limited liability company assets."[7]

Neither ULLCA (2013) nor the Delaware LLC Act uses "membership interest" as a defined term. And, while Delaware does define "[l]imited liability company interest," the term means only (and somewhat counterintuitively) "a member's share of the profits and losses of a limited liability company and a member's right to receive distributions of the limited liability company's assets."[8] More fundamentally, LLC statutes also differ as to

---

4. See Section 15.3.

5. Tax accounting requires separate consideration of a member's "profit interest" and "capital account." The details are far beyond the scope of this book, but they mean that:

- a person's economic stake in an LLC (or partnership) involves both concepts;
- two persons, each with, e.g., a "10% profits" interest, may have different overall economic rights (due to different capital accounts); and
- any use of LLC "units" or similar constructs is potentially confusing and often misleading (because such terms obscure the role of capital accounts and the fact that they can have a value that is not proportional to profit share).

For details, see Bishop & Kleinberger on Limited Liability Companies §§ 5:34

6. West's Ann. Cal. Corp. Code §17001(z).

7. A.R.S. §29–601(13).

8. Del. Code Ann. tit. 6, §18–101(8).

what rights are necessarily involved in being a member—that is, in being one of the entity's owners.

Extrapolating from the law of general partnerships and corporations, one might expect a straightforward answer—namely, that being an owner means having some right to share in profit distributions and some right to be involved in the organization's governance.[9] However, in this respect LLC law is far from straightforward. Probably one can state with accuracy that, under all LLC statutes, a member is a person who has been (somehow) admitted as a member of an LLC.[10] However, it is *not* accurate to state that a member necessarily has both economic and governance rights. Indeed, at least a few LLC statutes expressly provide to the contrary.

Example

ULLCA (2013) §401(d) states: "A person may become a member without: (1) acquiring a transferable interest [i.e., any economic rights]; or (2) making or being obligated to make a contribution to the limited liability company." The Comment explains the reasoning of this subsection: "To accommodate business practices and also because a limited liability company need not have a business purpose, this provision permits so-called non-economic members.[11] ◀◀◀

Example

Del. Code Ann., tit. 6, §18–301(d) provides: "Unless otherwise provided in a limited liability company agreement, a person may be admitted to a limited liability company as a member of the limited liability company without acquiring a limited liability company interest in the limited liability company." ◀◀◀

---

9. This extrapolation seems appropriate because the LLC is thought of as a hybrid between the partnership and corporate forms of organization.

10. E.g., Del. Code Ann. tit. 6 §18–101(11) (defining "member" as "a person who is admitted to a limited liability company as a member") and Ga. Code Ann. §14–11–101(16) (defining "member" as "a person who has been admitted to a limited liability company as a member"). Some people have argued that being a member is more a matter *vis-à-vis* one's fellow members (or with oneself in the case of a single-member LLC) than *vis-à-vis* the entity. See Section 16.2 ("corpufuscation"). In the context of a member's bankruptcy, this distinction is far more than theoretical. See Section 16.7.2. ULLCA (2013) §102(11) dodges this issue, at least definitionally, by defining "member" as "a person that has become a member of a limited liability company under Section 401 . . . and has not dissociated under section 601." See also ULLCA (2013) §401 (captioned "Becoming Member").

11. ULLCA (2013) §401(d)(1), cmt.

§15.1.3 Limited Generalizations About Ownership Interests in a Limited Liability Company

"Notwithstanding the foregoing" and so long as one remembers the ineffable flexibility of the LLC form, it is still possible to generalize about the typical LLC membership and the typical relationship between a member's governance rights and economic rights—keeping in mind that these generalizations are subject to variation by the operating agreement:

- When a person becomes a member through an interaction with the limited liability company (rather than as a transferee of an existing member), the person typically obtains "membership" in return for something of value the person has "brought to the party," e.g., "property transferred to, services performed for, or another benefit provided to the limited liability company or an agreement to transfer property to, perform services for, or provide another benefit to the company."[12]
- An LLC member typically has some governance rights—at minimum, rights to information about the company's activities and the right to vote on or consent to major issues; depending on the LLC's management structure, membership may include the right to participate directly in managing the company.[13] Under typical statutory default rules (i.e., subject to change by the operating agreement):
  - —Some matters typically require unanimous member consent (e.g., amending the operating agreement; according membership to a nonmember transferee of a member's economic rights).
  - —Where non-unanimous consent suffices, voting/consent power is allocated, depending on the statute:
    - ~ per capita;
    - ~ in proportion to capital contributions; or
    - ~ in proportion to profit share or distribution rights.
  - —An LLC member typically has the right to share in profit distributions. In the default mode:
- Depending on the statute, interim or "operating" distributions (i.e., distributions not connected with the dissolution and winding up of the LLC) are allocated:
    - ~ per capita; or
    - ~ in proportion to capital contributions.

12. ULLCA (2013) §402 ("Form of Contribution"). "This section is intentionally quite broad, encompassing past, present, and promised benefits," *id.*, cmt., and is easily broad enough to encompass a person's merely letting it be known that he or she is associated with the LLC.
13. See Section 15.3.1 (member management).

— When a limited liability company has dissolved and is winding up, liquidating distributions are made, to the extent the dissolved LLC's assets exceed its obligations to creditors:
  ~ first, among members who have contributed capital whose value has not already been fully returned, in proportion to the unreturned value; and
  ~ if any "surplus" remains, then among all members, in proportion to their respective right to share in profit distributions.

— To the extent the obligations of a dissolved LLC exceed the value of the LLC's assets, the losses lie where they fall. No member is required to contribute anything further to the LLC, whether to permit additional payment to LLC creditors or to equalize losses among members.[14]

§15.2 GOVERNANCE OVERVIEW

§15.2.1 Issues *Inter Se* and Issues *vis-à-vis* Third Parties

Broadly understood, LLC "governance" includes three separate but related topics:

- the internal management structure of the limited liability company;
- the duties owed by those who manage the company to the company and to the company's members; and
- the right and power of members and managers (if any) to bind a limited liability company to others.

This framework should be familiar; it has parallels in both the law of agency and the law of partnerships. However, because an LLC is fundamentally a creature of statute,[15] understanding the governance framework must begin with understanding how LLC statutes delineate governance rights, responsibilities, and powers.

All LLC statutes provide some approach to the management questions, and many apply some variant of UPA (1914) §9 to deal with the power of members or managers to bind the LLC.[16]

---

14. Unequal loss sharing may produce tax consequences, but that issue lies far beyond the scope of this book.

15. The LLC is also fundamentally a creature of contract. See Section 14.3.3.

16. When most LLC statute drafting was occurring, UPA (1997) had not yet been promulgated. UPA (1914) §9 is discussed in Section 10.3.1.

Example

Like many LLC statutes, the original Arizona LLC Act contained two distinct sections dealing respectively with "Management of limited liability company" and "Member or manager as agent." The provisions are related conceptually and practically. However, they can produce different consequences, depending on whether an issue exists *inter se* the members or between the LLC and a third party. ◄◄◄

Example

Part of the Arizona provision on "member . . . as agent" stated: "Each member is an agent of the limited liability company for the purpose of carrying on its business in the usual way."[17] Under this language, a member had the power to bind a member-managed LLC to a vendor through a transaction in what has been "the usual way"—even though, unbeknownst to the vendor, the members of the LLC have scheduled a vote to discontinue that line of business. In contrast, *vis-à-vis* the other members, the acting member would have acted improperly—contrary to the statute and thus without actual authority. Part of the provision on "Management of limited liability company" stated that "the affirmative vote, approval or consent of a majority of the members . . . is required to . . . [r]esolve any difference concerning matters connected with the business of the limited liability company."[18] ◄◄◄

§15.2.2 The "Two-Template" Paradigm

The overwhelming majority of LLC statutes:

- establish two alternative, semi-default templates: member-managed and manager-managed;
- model member management on the governance of a general partnership and manager management on the governance of a limited partnership; and
- provide for each template:
  - — *inter se* rules—mostly or entirely subject to the operating agreement[19]—which structure management rights and responsibilities *inter se* the members and managers (if any); and

17. Ariz. Rev. Stat. §29–654(A)(1) (repealed 2018).
18. Ariz. Rev. Stat. §29–681(D)(1) (repealed 2018).
19. Most LLC statutes also authorize the formation document to change these rules, but it is very unusual for a well-advised LLC to use that method. Formation documents are public: why disclose internal relationships unless doing so is required?

— "third party" rules—not subject to change by the operating agreement—that govern the power of members and managers (if any) to bind the LLC to third parties.

Two-template" statutes vary as to whether they: (i) require an LLC's formation document to choose one of the two templates; or (ii) permit the choice to be made either by the formation document or the operating agreement. Almost all "two-template" statutes establish one or the other template as the "default setting,"[20] and the default setting is predominantly member management.

Thus, under "two-template" statutes, determining the applicable governance rules for a limited liability company involves considering two layers of "default" analysis—determining:

- which default template applies; and
- to what extent the operating agreement has varied the default governance rules associated with that template.

Example

Grind the Coffee Ido, LLC ("Grind") is organized under a "two-template" statute. Grind's articles of organization state that Grind is "member managed," but its operating agreement provides that all "day-to-day" decisions are to be made by a "president" selected by the members. *Inter se* the members, no member has the right to make day-to-day decisions. ◄◄◄

Example

Espresso Omer, LLC ("Espresso") is organized under a "two-template" statute. Espresso's certificate of organization states that Espresso is "manager managed," and the statute provides that "except as otherwise stated in the operating agreement, in a manager-managed limited liability company, the managers shall be elected by the members annually." Espresso's operating agreement identifies a sole manager, Yael, "who shall serve as manager until she resigns, dies, or is removed as provided in this operating agreement." The statutory provision on annual election does not apply to Espresso and Yael. ◄◄◄

20. Minnesota is one exception. Minnesota adopted ULLCA (2006), while providing a third template: management by a board. Minnesota's original LLC act had provided for board management as the (sole) default paradigm. Adding the third template to the uniform act provided continuity for Minnesota limited liability companies organized under the original act. See Minn. Stat. § 322C.0409, subds. 1(iii) (contemplating an operating agreement selecting board management) and 4 (providing the default template for board management).

Some "two-template" statutes provide separate templates for each of the two management forms.

Example

In ULLCA (2013), the section captioned "MANAGEMENT OF LIMITED LIABILITY COMPANY" provides alternately:

> (b) In a member-managed limited liability company, the following rules apply: . . .
>
> (c) In a manager-managed limited liability company, the following rules apply: . . .

The section also identifies management rules applicable under both templates — specifically, matters requiring unanimous member consent. ◄◄◄

Other LLC statutes use cross-reference rather than duplication. These statutes provide a basic template applicable to one of the two structures and incorporate that template's rules into the other structure by reference.

Example

The original California LLC Act provided:

> [T]he business and affairs of a limited liability company shall be managed by the members subject to any provisions of the articles of organization or operating agreement restricting or enlarging the management rights and duties of any member or class of members. If management is vested in the members, each of the members shall have the same rights and be subject to all duties and obligations of managers as set forth in this title.[21] ◄◄◄

Within this latter category, the Michigan and New York statutes each provide an interesting example of a subcategory. Each of these statutes sets member-management as the default structure but provides the member-management rules with reference to manager-management (deeming the members to be acting as managers).

21. Cal. Corp. Code §17150.

Example

M.C.L.A. 450.4401 first establishes member management as the default rule:

> Unless the articles of organization state that the business of the limited liability company is to be managed by 1 or more managers, the business of the limited liability company shall be managed by the members, subject to any provision in an operating agreement restricting or enlarging the management rights and duties of any member or group of members. ◀◀◀

The section then defines member management by incorporating by reference the rules of manager-management:

If management is vested in the members, both of the following apply:

> (a) The members are considered managers for purposes of applying this act, including [the section delineating] the agency authority of managers, unless the context clearly requires otherwise.
>
> (b) The members have, and are subject to, all duties and liabilities of managers and to all limitations on liability and indemnification rights of managers.

Example

After establishing member management as the default rule for New York LLCs, McKinney's Limited Liability Company Law, §401(b) states:

> "If management of a limited liability company is vested in its members, then (i) any such member exercising such management powers or responsibilities shall be deemed to be a manager for purposes of applying the provisions of this chapter, unless the context otherwise requires, and (ii) any such member shall have and be subject to all of the duties and liabilities of a manager provided in this chapter." ◀◀◀

§15.2.3 The Corporate Governance Paradigm

a. Minnesota and North Dakota

The original Minnesota and North Dakota statutes provided a default template based on a corporate governance model,[22] using a "board of governors"

22. Minn. Stat. §322B.60; N.D. Cent. Code §10–32–67.

(like a corporate board of directors). Both statutes have since been repealed, replaced with ULLCA (2006), but each statute has retained a "board of governors" template. Under this template, the governors collectively have overall supervisory authority within the LLC while individually lacking both the right and power to act for the LLC. A governor may, however, also serve in some other capacity (e.g., Chief Executive Officer) and in that capacity have actual and perhaps apparent authority to bind the LLC.

This corporate approach is worthy of general note because:

1. corporate members of LLC joint ventures often prefer (or think they prefer) a corporate-like board structure to govern the LLC;
2. under most LLC statutes, lawyers must create a board structure through detailed provisions in the operating agreement; and
3. such provisions can leave several important issues "up in the air," including:
   — whether each person on the board owes fiduciary duty to the limited liability company or to the member that appointed the person to the board; and
   — whether any member of the board has actual authority to bind the limited liability company to third parties.

If each person on the board owes fiduciary duties only to the member that appointed the person and no person on the board has authority to bind the limited liability company to third parties, then:

- the "board" is not itself the governing body for the company; but is instead
- merely a way for the company's members to carry on *member* management through appointed representatives.

If an operating agreement refers to management by a board but leaves unclear any of the issues just discussed, serious problems can arise.

b. The "Entity Resemblance" Approach

In 2016, in *Obeid v. Hogan*, Vice Chancellor Laster of the Delaware Court of Chancery made the following holding:

> Using the contractual freedom that the LLC Act bestows, the drafters of an LLC agreement can create an LLC with bespoke governance features or design an LLC that mimics the governance features of another familiar type of entity. The choices that the drafters make have consequences. If the drafters have embraced the statutory default rule of a member-managed governance arrangement, which has strong functional and historical ties to the general partnership

> (albeit with limited liability for the members), then the parties should expect a court to draw on analogies to partnership law. If the drafters have opted for a single managing member with other generally passive, nonmanaging members, a structure closely resembling and often used as an alternative to a limited partnership, then the parties should expect a court to draw on analogies to limited partnership law. If the drafters have opted for a manager-managed entity, created a board of directors, and adopted other corporate features, then the parties to the agreement should expect a court to draw on analogies to corporate law.[23]

Several subsequent cases relied on this holding, while at least one academic criticized "the logic of Obeid" as "radically inconsistent with the cardinal rules of contract interpretation."[24]

In 2017, the Delaware legislature responded to a different aspect of Obeid,[25] but the "entity resemblance" test remains a key part of Delaware case law.

§15.3 MANAGEMENT STRUCTURES (*INTER SE* RULES)

§15.3.1 Member Management

Regardless of which LLC statute applies, member management is inherently decentralized. The members as a group hold the right to manage the business; the statute prescribes that, when management decisions are to be made, the members act collectively. As always with *inter se* matters, the statutory rules are default rules, subject to change in the operating agreement.

In this conceptual realm, variations among LLC statutes are myriad. However, in the mechanically simplest statutes the management rules closely mirror the rules for general partnerships and eschew formalities such as member meetings and proxies. Statutory complexity increases as statutes add mechanisms drawn from corporate law or practice—such as meetings (which require notice and imply that participation must be in person or through a proxy who is present).

---

23. *Obeid v. Hogan*, No. CV 11900-VCL, 2016 WL 3356851, at *6 (Del. Ch. June 10, 2016), judgment entered, (Del. Ch. Sept. 7, 2016) (footnotes omitted), aff'd on the basis of Chancery Court decision, 2019 WL 181195 (Del. Jan. 14, 2019).

24. Bishop & Kleinberger on Limited Liability Companies §5:132

25. 81 Del. Laws, c. 89, § 11 (2017), discussed *id.* § 5:133.

Example

Through 12 subsections and more than 2,400 words, the original California LLC Act provided rules for: "Meetings; time and place; presence of members; call of meetings; notice; adjournment; validity of actions; participation; quorum; validity of actions taken without meeting; proxies; record date for determining members; conduct of meetings by electronic transmissions or by electronic video screen communications."[26] ◀◀◀

Statutes differ as to the allocation of voting power among members. Contrast in the following examples the simple, per capita approach of the Georgia act with the far more elaborate approach of the original Florida statute, which: allocated votes according to profits interests; expressly contemplated the possibility of elected managing members within a *member-managed* LLC; and defined profits interests in terms of capital contributions.

Example

According to the Georgia LLC Act, subject to the articles of organization, the operating agreement, and a statutory provision listing matters requiring unanimous member consent:

> If management of the limited liability company is vested in the members, each member shall have one vote with respect to, and the affirmative vote, approval, or consent of a majority of the members shall be required to decide, any matter arising in connection with the business and affairs of the limited liability company.[27] ◀◀◀

Example

Fl. Stat. Ann. §608.422(2) provided:

In a member-managed company, unless otherwise provided in its articles of organization or operating agreement:

> (a) Management shall be vested in its members or elected managing members in proportion to the then-current percentage or other interest of members in the profits of the limited liability company owned by all of the members or elected managing members.

26. West's Ann. Cal. Corp. Code §17104. The quotation is from the section's caption. The original California statute has been repealed and replaced by California's version of ULLCA (2006). See Ca. Stats. 2012 c. 419 (SB 323).

27. Ga. Code Ann. §14–11–308(a)(1).

> (b) Except as otherwise provided . . . , the decision of a majority-in-interest of the members or elected managing members shall be controlling.

Section 608.4261 further provided that:

> If the articles of organization do not or the operating agreement does not provide for the allocation of profits and losses among members, profits and losses shall be allocated on the basis of the agreed value, as stated in the records of the limited liability company, of the contributions made by each member to the extent such contributions have been received by the limited liability company and have not been returned.[28] ◀ ◀ ◀

All LLC statutes specify some matters requiring unanimous consent. Some statutes contain a list that includes most such requirements. In other statutes, the requirements are scattered throughout the act.

Example

The Georgia statute provides a lengthy list:

> (b) Unless otherwise provided in the articles of organization or a written operating agreement, the unanimous vote or consent of the members shall be required to approve the following matters:
>
> (1) The dissolution of the limited liability company . . . ;
>
> (2) The merger of the limited liability company . . . ;
>
> (3) The sale, exchange, lease, or other transfer of all or substantially all of the assets of the limited liability company . . . ;
>
> (4) The admission of any new member of the limited liability company . . . ;
>
> (5) An amendment to the articles of organization . . . or an amendment to a written operating agreement;
>
> (6) Action . . . to reduce or eliminate an obligation to make a contribution to the capital of a limited liability company;
>
> (7) Action to approve a distribution under . . . ; or
>
> (8) Action to continue a limited liability company. . . .[29] ◀ ◀ ◀

28. In 2013, Florida repealed its original LLC act and substituted ULLCA. 2013 Fl. Laws, Chapter 2013–180. (The Florida enactment reflects the ULC's then ongoing Harmonization Project.)
29. Ga. Code. Ann. §14–11–308(b).

Example

ULLCA (2013) uses both a centralized list and separate provisions to identify matters requiring unanimous member consent. Section 407 contains a list requiring unanimous member consent to undertake "[a]n act outside the ordinary course of the activities of the company"[30] or to amend the operating agreement.[31] Individual sections require unanimity to: (i) admit a person as a member after the formation of the limited liability company;[32] (ii) approve the limited liability company's participation in a merger,[33] interest exchange,[34] conversion,[35] or domestication;[36] or (iii) cause the dissolution of the company via member consent.[37] ◄ ◄ ◄

Example

As originally enacted, the Washington LLC Act required unanimous consent to *inter alia*:

- permit a person acquiring a "limited liability company interest" to become a member;[38]
- amend the operating agreement;[39]
- "[a]uthorize a . . . member, or other person to do any act on behalf of the limited liability company that contravenes the limited liability company agreement";[40]
- compromise a member's obligation to make a contribution to the limited liability company;[41] and
- dissolve the limited liability company via member consent.[42] ◄ ◄ ◄

Obviously, where a statute requires unanimous member consent, no individual member has the right to act unilaterally. Beyond such requirements, however, LLC statutes typically do not specify when a member in a member-managed limited liability company is entitled to act unilaterally

---

30. ULLCA (2013), §407(b)(4)(A).
31. *Id.*, §407(b)(4)(B).
32. *Id.*, §401(C)(3).
33. *Id.*, §10031023(a)(1).
34. *Id.*, §1033(a)(1).
35. *Id.*, §1043(a)(1), §1007(a).
36. *Id.*, §1053(a)(1).
37. *Id.*, §701(a)(2).
38. West's RCWA §25.15.115(2)(a) and (b). In 2015, Washington repealed this statute, substituting a version of ULLCA (2006). See Wash. Laws 2015, Chapter 188,
39. *Id.*, §25.15.120(2)(a).
40. *Id.*, §25.15.120(2)(b).
41. *Id.*, §25.15.195(2).
42. *Id.*, §25.15.270(3) (written consent required).

and when a member is obliged to consult with other members before making a decision.[43] The operating agreement should address this matter.

If not, a comment to ULLCA (2013) provides a mode of analysis likely applicable to any LLC statute whose member-management template is based the management structure of a general partnership:

> In the unlikely event that two or more people form a member-managed LLC without any understanding of how to allocate management responsibility, agency law, operating in the context of the act's "gap fillers" on management responsibility, will produce the following result:
>
> A single member of a multimember, member-managed LLC:
>
> - has no actual authority to bind the LLC to any matter "outside the ordinary course of the activities of the company," section 407(b)(3); and
> - has the actual authority to bind the LLC to any matter "in the management and conduct of the company's [ordinary course of] activities and affairs," section 407(b)(2), unless the member has reason to know that other members might disagree or the member has some other reason to know that consultation with fellow members is appropriate.[44]

§15.3.2 Manager Management

a. The Typical Template

Under most LLC statutes, the manager-management template resembles a limited partnership, causing one federal judge to remark: "This animal is like a limited partnership; the principal difference is that it need have no equivalent to a general partner, that is, an owner who has unlimited personal liability for the debts of the firm."[45]

The resemblance is fundamental; in both an LLC and a limited partnership, subject to the operating agreement or partnership agreement:

- most management authority is allocated to one or more persons (manager/general partner); and
- the entity has a class of more or less passive owners (nonmanager members/limited partners).

43. The same issue exists with regard to managers of a multi-manager LLC and is discussed in that context in Section 15.3.2. The same issue also exists with general partners. See Section 9.4. As with partnerships, whether an LLC member's or manager's unilateral action has the power to bind the LLC is a separate question from the *inter se* question of "right to act."
44. ULLCA (2013) §407(b), cmt.
45. *Cosgrove v. Bartolotta*, 150 F.3d 729, 731 (7th Cir. 1998).

There are also fundamental differences. In an LLC:

- managers are not automatically liable for the entity's obligations;
- managers may be members and typically are, but there is no statutory requirement to that effect; and
- members do not risk their liability shield by being involved in management.[46]

b. Statutory Descriptions of Manager Authority

In most LLC statutes, the manager-managed template parallels many of the rules for member-management; the roles and duties of managers are described by: (i) cross-referencing the sections describing member roles and duties in a member-managed entity or *vice versa*; (ii) replicating the member-managed provisions in a manager-managed section; or (iii) stating the two sets of duties in tandem.

In addition, the typical manager-managed template: (i) provides for the selection, removal, and replacement of managers; and (ii) delineates important decisions over which members retain direct control. ULLCA (2013)'s provisions provide a useful illustration:

Example

Under ULLCA (2013) §407(c):

> In a manager-managed limited liability company, the following rules apply:
>
> (1) Except as expressly provided in this [act], any matter relating to the activities and affairs of the company is decided exclusively by the manager, or, if there is more than one manager, by a majority of the managers.
>
> (2) Each manager has equal rights in the management and conduct of the company's activities and affairs.
>
> (3) The affirmative vote or consent of all members is required to:
>
> (A) undertake an act outside the ordinary course of the company's activities and affairs; or
>
> (B) amend the operating agreement.

46. This statement also applies to limited partners in limited partnerships organized under ULPA (2001) or ULPA (2013). Under predecessor limited partnership statutes, the "control rule" applies. See Section 12.2.3.

(4) A manager may be chosen at any time by the affirmative vote or consent of a majority of the members and remains a manager until a successor has been chosen, unless the manager at an earlier time resigns, is removed, or dies, or, in the case of a manager that is not an individual, terminates. A manager may be removed at any time by the affirmative vote or consent of a majority of the members without notice or cause.

(5) A person need not be a member to be a manager, but the dissociation of a member that is also a manager removes the person as a manager. If a person that is both a manager and a member ceases to be a manager, that cessation does not by itself dissociate the person as a member.

(6) A person's ceasing to be a manager does not discharge any debt, obligation, or other liability to the limited liability company or members which the person incurred while a manager.

Although ULLCA (2013) §407(c) lists major provisions allocating governance rights to members, the list is not exhaustive. As is the situation with all LLC statutes, one must search the Act generally for other provisions relating to member governance rights in a manager-managed LLC.

Example

Under the default template for a ULLCA (2013) manager-managed LLC, the decision to allow a person to become a member is made "with the consent of all the members" and "the consent of all the members" causes dissolution. The relevant language does not appear in the act's centralized list, but rather respectively in §§401(c)(3) and 701(a)(2). ◄◄◄

N.B. Under all LLC statutes, the rules comprising the manager-managed template are default rules subject to change by the operating agreement. The actual authority of a manager is ultimately a question of agency law, with the manager as agent and the LLC as principal. The operating agreement and the statute (to the extent not displaced by the operating agreement) comprise the manifestations of the principal. "Other information may be relevant as well, such as the course of dealing within the LLC, unless the operating agreement effectively precludes consideration of that information."[47]

c. Authority for One of Several Managers to Act Unilaterally

Obviously, when a manager-managed LLC has only one manager, that manager may act unilaterally on any matter that the statute or operating

47. ULLCA (2013), §407, cmt. c.

agreement commits to the manager's discretion.[48] However, when an LLC has more than one manager, the question of authority for unilateral action is complex, and no LLC statute contains any direct answer.[49]

If an LLC has been well advised by counsel, the operating agreement will address this matter definitively. If not, the answer must be inferred—as a matter of agency law and actual authority—from any relevant language in the LLC statute and the operating agreement, as well as other circumstances that manifest the principal's (LLC's) intent. The following analysis appears in a comment in ULLCA (2013) and makes specific reference to provisions of the Act's template for manager-management. However, the analysis can likely be extrapolated to the manager-managed templates of many other LLC statutes:

> If the operating agreement states only that the LLC is manager-managed and the LLC has more than one manager, . . . [i]t is necessary to determine what actual authority any one manager has to act alone. . . .
>
> A single manager of a multi-manager LLC:
>
> - has no actual authority to commit the LLC to any matter . . . for which this act elsewhere requires unanimity;
> - has the actual authority to commit the LLC to usual and customary matters, unless the manager has reason to know that: (i) other managers might disagree; or (ii) for some other reason consultation with fellow managers is appropriate; and
> - has no actual authority to take unusual or non-customary actions that will have a substantial effect on the LLC.
>
> The first point follows self-evidently from the language of . . . provisions requiring the affirmative vote or consent of the members, which reserves specified matters to the members. Given that language, no manager could reasonably believe to the contrary (unless the operating agreement provided otherwise).
>
> The second point follows because:
>
> Subsection (c) [providing equal rights in management to all managers] serves as the gap-filler manifestation from the LLC to its managers and does

---

48. One might try to view this question from the opposite perspective; i.e., that a sole manager may act unilaterally on any matter unless either the statute or operating agreement clearly reserves the matter to the members. However, that perspective is contrary to agency law. A manager is an agent of the LLC, and the manager's actual authority extends only so far as the manager *reasonably* believes it to extend. Reasonableness includes resolving questions of authority by inquiring of the principal. See R.3d, §2.02, cmt. f.

49. The same issue exists for general partnerships (see Section 10.2) and with any limited partnership that has more than one general partner.

not require managers of a multi-manager LLC to act *only* in concert or after consultation. . . .

- It would be impractical to require collective action on even the smallest of decisions.
- However, to the extent a manager has reason to know of a possible difference of opinion among the managers, Paragraph (c)(1) requires decision by "a majority of the managers."

The third point is a matter of common sense. The more serious the matter, the less likely it is that a manager has actual authority to act unilaterally. Cf. RESTATEMENT (THIRD) OF AGENCY §3.03, cmt. c (2006) (noting the unreasonableness of believing, without more facts, that an individual has "an unusual degree of unilateral authority over a matter fraught with enduring consequences for the institution" and stating that "[t]he gravity of the matter from the standpoint of the organization is relevant to whether a third party could reasonably believe that the manager has authority to proceed unilaterally").[50]

d. The Problem of Nomenclature: What Does "Manager" Mean?

Almost all LLC statutes use "the term 'manager' to refer to those with top governance authority in a centralized management structure."[51] For example, the Delaware statute defines "manager" as "a person who is named as a manager of a limited liability company in, or designated as a manager of a limited liability company pursuant to, a limited liability company agreement or similar instrument under which the limited liability company is formed."[52] Under most two-template statutes, the terms "member-managed" and "manager-managed" are key statutory phrases; they are terms of art under almost all LLC statutes.

"This nomenclature is unfortunate, because the word 'manager' has different meanings in other contexts."[53] Sometimes the overlap is harmless.

50. ULLCA (2013) §407(c), cmt.

51. Bishop & Kleinberger, ¶7.02[1][b] (footnotes omitted). The two "corporate" model statutes (both now repealed) used the term "governor" for board members, but even they used the term "chief manager." E.g., Minn. Stat. §§322B.03, subd.24 (governors) and 322B.673, subd.2 (chief manager). See Section 15.2.3.

52. Del. Code. Ann., tit.6, §18–101(10).

53. BISHOP & KLEINBERGER ON LIMITED LIABILITY COMPANIES § 7:18. See also R.3d §3.03, cmt. *e*(3) (creation of apparent authority) (2006) ("In smaller firms, it is not unusual for the president to function as the 'general manager,' a term used in many cases involving smaller businesses and intended to describe a person with authority to bind an organization in all matters within the ordinary scope of its business.").

Example

Squid, LLC is organized under a "two-template" statute. Squid's certificate of organization states that Squid is "manager-managed," and the company's operating agreement provides for a single manager elected annually by the members. Squid's business involves owning and operating a network of "Calamari to Go" shops throughout the United States. In its employee manual, Squid refers to the employee in charge of each shop as "the shop manager." That label matches colloquial usage well. (People are generally used to asking "to speak with the manager" when a problem arises.) The label is not likely to confuse anyone into thinking that one of the shop managers is the "manager" to whom Squid's certificate of organization and operating agreement refer.[54] ◀◀◀

Other times, confusion and then litigation result.

Case in Point — *Brown v. MR Group, LLC*

A liability insurance policy covered actions by "managers" of an LLC, and the LLC sought coverage for actions allegedly taken by a person it called (and who had functioned as) a "real estate manager." The LLC was organized under a two-template statute, and its certificate of organization declared the LLC to be "manager-managed." The real estate manager was not one of the statutory managers. The court denied coverage in part on the theory that the statutory definitions were more probative than any dictionary definition of a reasonable insured's understanding of the policy term.[55] ◀◀◀

§15.3.3 Guidelines in the Midst of Ineffable Flexibility: A Checklist for Discerning an LLC's Management Structure

In a book of this nature, it is impossible to list all the ways in which LLC statutes differ (or, at the whim of a legislature, might differ) in their delineation of LLC governance structure. Likewise, space does not allow even a shorthand description of the multitudinous ways in which operating agreements have shaped the management structure of particular LLCs.

---

54. For a real-life example, see *American Anglian Envtl. Techs., LP v. Environmental Mgmt. Corp.*, 412 F3d 956, 959 (8th Cir. 2005) (deciding a dispute between a member and former member of an LLC; noting that "[b]y the Operating Agreement, day-to-day project management was the responsibility of a Project Manager appointed by EMC [one member], assisted by a deputy appointed by AAET [the other member]," but that "[w]hile EMC was the day-to-day manager of the company, the Operating Agreement establishes a Management Committee with four representatives, two each from AAET and EMC").

55. *Brown v. MR Group, LLC*, 693 NW2d 138, 142–43 (Wis. Ct. App. 2005).

However, it is possible to provide a coherent way to approach discerning the management structure of any LLC.

- Begin by identifying the relevant statute; i.e., the statute under whose authority the LLC has been created.[56]
- Read the relevant statutory language carefully, keeping in mind that statutes often address the same issue in several different places. In addition to scrutinizing any definition section and sections with captions such as "Management" or "Members," use electronic means to search the entire statute for references to "member" and "manager."
- Consider the following list of issues:[57]
    - I. What is the statutory default setting; i.e., in the absence of other arrangements made by the members, is the LLC manager-managed or member-managed?
    - II. Which document(s) can change that setting—only the articles of organization or also the operating agreement?
    - III. What does the relevant document provide; i.e., is the basic structure manager-managed or member-managed?
    - IV. Keep in mind that the statutory structures are mostly default rules, mostly subject to revision or even elimination by the operating agreement.
        - A. According to the statute, what means may be used to alter the management rules of the relevant template?
            1. Are some rules mandatory; i.e., not subject to change by either the operating agreement or articles of organization?
            2. Are some rules subject to change only in the articles?
            3. Are some rules subject to change only by a written operating agreement?
        - B. What do the operating agreement and the articles provide as to management rules and roles?
            1. Does the statute have a rule for determining the results, if these two sources of authority conflict?[58]
    - V. As to an LLC that operates under the member-managed template, under the statutory template *as modified by the operating agreement*:
        - A. Is each member expressly authorized to participate in the activities of the LLC?
        - B. Does a rule exist for determining when a member may make a decision unilaterally?

---

56. See Section 14.1.2, explaining the "internal affairs" doctrine as a choice of law concept.
57. This list does not consider issues related to the governance duties of those who manage. For those issues, see Section 15.4.
58. Most LLC statutes do not, but ULLCA (2006) and (2013) each do. See Section 14.5.7.

C. Is member decision-making contemplated to be by member "consent" or "voting" or either?
D. For what issues is member consent required by:
   1. some form of majority consent/vote?
   2. unanimous consent/vote?
E. For matters requiring majority consent/vote:
   1. Is each member's voting or consent "power" measured:
      a. per capita (by member)?
      b. per some form of economic rights?
      c. per profits interest (and if so, how defined)?
      d. per amount of capital contributed (and if so, how defined)?
   2. Are formal meetings of the members contemplated or required to make member decisions effective?
   3. Is acting by proxy expressly:
      a. authorized?
      b. prohibited?[59]
   4. Where consent/voting power is allocated according to some form of economic rights and a member has transferred some or all of the economic rights, what is the consequence to the member's consent/voting rights:
      a. none, so long as the member remains a member?
      b. diminished, to the extent the economic rights are transferred?

VI. As to an LLC that operates under the manager-managed template, under the statutory template *as modified by the operating agreement*:
A. How many managers are provided for?
B. How is/are the manager(s):
   1. selected?
   2. removed?
      a. without cause?
      b. with cause (how defined)?
   3. replaced (e.g., upon death, disability [how defined], or resignation)?
C. Does the LLC have a separate management agreement with the manager(s)?
   1. If so, how are conflicts between that agreement and the operating agreement resolved?
   2. Few LLC statutes contemplate this problem directly. An official comment to ULLCA (2006) analyzes the problem as follows:

---

59. In the absence of an express prohibition either in the statute or the operating agreement, agency law would strongly support the use of proxies except in situations in which the circumstances manifest a requirement of personal involvement.

a. If the operating agreement and a management contract conflict, the reasonable manager will know that the operating agreement controls the extent of the manager's rightful authority to act for the LLC—despite any contract claims the manager might have. See the comment section 105(a)(2) (stating that the operating agreement governs "the rights and duties under this [act] of a person in the capacity of manager").[60]

3. How is the scope of the manager(s)' authority generally delineated?
    a. obversely, how is the scope of matters reserved to the members generally delineated?
4. which, if any, matters/decisions are specifically stated as:
    a. within the manager(s)' authority?
    b. reserved to the members?

D. If the LLC has more than one manager:
1. how is authority divided among the managers?
2. does a rule exist for determining when a manager may make a decision unilaterally?
3. is manager decision-making contemplated to be by "consent" or "voting" or both?
4. are formal meetings of the managers contemplated or required to make manager decisions effective?
5. Is acting by proxy expressly:
    a. authorized?
    b. prohibited?
6. With regard to matters reserved for decision by the members, is decision-making to be by member "consent" or "voting"?
7. For what issues is member consent required by:
    a. some form of majority consent/vote?
    b. unanimous consent/vote?
8. For matters requiring majority consent/vote:
    a. Is each member's voting or consent "power" measured:
        - per capita (by member)?
        - per some form of economic rights?
            — profit interest (and if so, how defined)?
            — per amount of capital contributed (and if so, how defined)?

60. ULLCA (2013) §407(c), cmt. (citing RESTATE MENT (THIRD) OF AGENCY §8.13, cmt. b (2006) and RESTATEMENT (SECOND) OF AGENCY §432, cmt. b (1958) as stating that, when a principal's instructions to an agent contravene a contract between the principal and agent, the agent may have a breach of contract claim but has no right to act contrary to the principal's instructions). See also ULLCA (2013) §102(13), cmt.

b. Are formal meetings of the members contemplated or required to make member decisions effective?
c. Is acting by proxy expressly:
   - authorized?
   - prohibited?
d. Where consent/voting power is allocated according to some form of economic rights and a member has transferred some or all of the economic rights, what is the consequence to the member's consent/voting rights:
   - none, so long as the member remains a member?
   - diminished, to the extent the economic rights are transferred?

§15.4 FIDUCIARY DUTIES OF THOSE WHO MANAGE

§15.4.1 Overview

As in agency relationships and partnerships, management authority in LLCs comes with fiduciary duties—primarily the duties of care and loyalty. Questions as to fiduciary duties are "internal affairs" and therefore analyzed under the law of an LLC's state of organization;[61] however, regardless of the jurisdiction involved the same general issues exist:

- Who owes the duties?
  —This question is primarily a question of whether the LLC is member-managed or manager-managed. However, in a manager-managed LLC a member with enough consent/voting power to control the managers might also owe fiduciary duties.
- To whom is the duty owed?
  —This question is more complicated here than in the agency or general partnership context. The LLC is an entity separate from its owners, and in most instances those who manage the LLC owe duties directly to the entity, not to the members.
- How are the duties of care and loyalty defined?
  —Most LLC statutes contain some formulation, although the influential Delaware statute does not. Delaware courts have applied standard Delaware concepts of fiduciary duty to Delaware LLCs.

61. See Section 14.1.2.

— Two major statutory paradigms exist: one borrowing from corporate formulations, the other from the law of general partnerships.

- To what extent may an LLC's operating agreement carve back or even eliminate fiduciary duties?

§15.4.2 Who Owes the Duties?

It might seem obvious to state that "the fiduciary duties of management are owed by those with management authority," and certainly that statement is the starting point for understanding the question of "who owes the duties." Under two-template statutes, any stated fiduciary duties "switch" according to whether an LLC is member-managed or manager-managed.

Example

Under the Michigan LLC Act: "If management [of a limited liability company] is vested in the members, . . . [t]he members have, and are subject to, all duties and liabilities of managers. . . ."[62] ◄◄◄

The paradigm seems simple: in a member-managed LLC the members owe fiduciary duties; in a manager-managed LLC the managers do. There are, however, a few consequences, including a few "wrinkles."

One straightforward consequence is that, in a manager-managed LLC:

- members who are managers owe fiduciary duty *qua* managers; and
- a nonmanaging member has no fiduciary duties *qua* member.

Example

JeTodd, LLC is a manager-managed LLC with two members (Jeff and Todd) and a nonmember manager, Selma. Selma owes fiduciary duties to the LLC, but Jeff and Todd do not. Therefore, absent a contrary agreement, Selma may not compete with JeTodd, but Jeff and Todd each may. The managerial duty of loyalty includes the duty not to compete, but Jeff and Todd are not managers.[63] ◄◄◄

62. M.C.L.A. 450.4401(b).

63. This very simple Example assumes *inter alia* no use of the LLC's confidential information by a competing nonmanager member.

Case in Point—*In re South Canaan Cellular Investments, LLC*

Bankrupt LLC sued a minority member for breach of fiduciary duties. The defendant moved to dismiss for failure to state a claim because he was not a manager of the LLC and, thus, did not owe the fiduciary duties which he allegedly breached. The bankruptcy court sought to look to the operating agreement for guidance, but no operating agreement was provided. In the absence of an operating agreement, the court stated that "Delaware common law does not impose fiduciary and other related duties to members of LLCs who are neither managers nor controlling members."[64] ◀ ◀ ◀

Many LLC statutes expressly negate any fiduciary duties for nonmanaging members in a manager-managed LLC.

Example

The original Arkansas LLC statute stated: "One who is a member of a limited liability company in which management is vested in managers . . . and who is not a manager shall have no duties to the limited liability company or to the other members solely by reason of acting in the capacity of a member."[65] The current Arkansas statute, based on ULLCA (2006/2013), states the same rule albeit in different language.[66] ◀ ◀ ◀

This statutory exculpation has at least four "wrinkles" (complexities).

1. *The exculpation applies by its terms to a member's exercise of consent or voting rights within a manager-managed LLC.* That is, even though a nonmanaging member has *power* over a governance matter, the statutory exculpation prevents the application of fiduciary duties.

Example

TMS, LLC is a manager-managed LLC with three members: Teri, Mikki, and Samantha. Teri is the sole manager. The LLC owns and operates several shopping centers, and the operating agreement requires the consent of "members holding 60 percent of the interests in profits" before the LLC may acquire or build any new shopping centers. Teri proposes that the LLC build a shopping center in an area near a shopping center separately owned by Mikki. Mikki votes against the LLC building a new shopping center, because

64. *In re South Canaan Cellular Investments, LLC*, 427 B.R. 85, 102–03 (Bkrptcy. E.D. Penn. 2010).
65. A.C.A. §4–32–402(3), repealed Acts of 2021, Act 1041.
66. Ark. Code Ann. § 4–38–409(i)(1)(West)

she does not want competition with her separately owned shopping center. Mikki's self-interested vote is not a breach of fiduciary duty. ◀◀◀

Example

Same facts, except that the LLC is member-managed. Mikki's vote is burdened by fiduciary duty. ◀◀◀

2. *The statutory exculpation does not apply to liability for conduct that is wrongful regardless of a person's status as a member.*

Example

Bud, a nonmanaging member of a manager-managed LLC, learns of a potential business opportunity from confidential information provided by the LLC to its members. Knowing that the information is confidential, Bud nonetheless acts on it and takes the opportunity for himself. He is liable to the LLC for damages resulting from the breach of confidentiality. The statutory exculpation does not protect him. "A member who gains access to confidential information may be acting 'in the capacity as a member,' but a member who exploits that information for covetous purposes is not. Liability results not 'solely by reason' of the access, but rather from the act of exploitation."[67] ◀◀◀

3. *If a nonmanaging member effectively controls the manager(s), the exculpation probably will not immunize the nonmanaging member's exercise of that control.*

Case in Point — *Carson v. Lynch Multimedia Corp.*

A manager-managed LLC was governed, according to its operating agreement, by a five-person Board of Managers. The LLC's majority member was not on the Board but did appoint three of the five managers. Another member believed that the Board had badly mismanaged the company and sued both the persons on the Board and the majority member. The majority member sought dismissal on the grounds that she was a nonmanaging member and under the applicable statute owed no fiduciary duties. The court rejected that argument, holding that, if the majority of the Board were merely the "alter ego" of the nonmanaging member, the Board's fiduciary duties could be imputed to the nonmanaging member.[68] ◀◀◀

67. Bishop & Kleinberger on Limited Liability Companies § 10:10.
68. *Carson v. Lynch Multimedia Corp.*, 123 F. Supp. 2d 1254 (D. Kan. 2000).

4. *The exculpation generally does not apply to the implied contractual covenant of good faith and fair dealing.* Section 15.4.8 discusses this topic.

Wrinkles also exist with regard to member-managed LLCs, because it is possible for the operating agreement of a member-managed LLC to reserve particular management functions to only some of the members.

Example

Party LLC ("Party") is a limited liability company that organizes parties. Party was formed under a two-template LLC statute that requires the articles of organization to choose a managerial template. Party's articles state that the LLC is member-managed. Party has 15 members, who make all major decisions collectively, but Party's operating agreement provides for a three-person "management committee" to superintend Party's day-to-day activities. ◀◀◀

Given the way two-template statutes delineate fiduciary duties, it does not automatically follow that a member's fiduciary duties shrink as the member's authority shrinks. The duty of care probably does, but not necessarily the duty of loyalty. ULLCA (2013) addresses this issue by expressly empowering the operating agreement to address the issue:

> To the extent the operating agreement of a member-managed limited liability company expressly relieves a member of a responsibility that the member otherwise would have under this [act] and imposes the responsibility on one or more other members, the agreement also may eliminate or limit any fiduciary duty of the member relived of the responsibility which would have pertained to the responsibility.[69]

The same approach should be possible under LLC statutes without this specific language, given the broad powers accorded to operating agreements by all LLC statutes.[70]

§15.4.3 To Whom Are the Duties Owed?

In an agency relationship, the agent's fiduciary duties are owed to the principal, and obviously the principal has the right to sue the agent for breach of those duties. In a general partnership, each partner has the right to seek a

69. ULLCA (2013) §105(d)(2).
70. See Section 14.5.1.

remedy for harm done by another partner to the partnership—even under the "entity" approach first announced in UPA (1997).[71]

The situation with an LLC is far more complicated, as is discussed in some detail in Section 16.4. The overview is that, under the law of most states, even if the LLC statute states generally that governance duties are owed to individual members as well as to the LLC, a member may not sue directly to enforce a governance duty unless the breach of duty has *directly* harmed the member.

Example

TMS, LLC is a manager-managed LLC with three members: Teri, Mikki, and Samantha. Teri is the sole manager. Mikki and Samantha believe that Teri has mismanaged the company and thereby damaged the company's business. Although the relevant LLC statute describes the duty of care as being owed "to the company and its members," neither Mikki nor Samantha has the right to seek a remedy in their own names. They have been damaged only indirectly.[72] In such circumstances, it is meaningless (and misleading) to refer to Teri as owing a duty of care to Mikki and Samantha. For all practical purposes, Teri owes a duty of care only to TMS and not its members. ◄◄◄

The major exception to this general proposition is that, under the law of most states, members are obliged not to use managerial power to "oppress" or "unfairly prejudice" a fellow member. The concepts of "oppression" and "unfair prejudice" were developed in the law of close corporations, but courts are increasingly making use of them in analogous LLC situations. The concepts are somewhat vague, and definitions differ. At the core is a concept of unfair, almost expropriating behavior.[73]

However defined, when oppression or unfair prejudice occurs, the damage is to a member, not the LLC, and the duty runs directly from member to member as well.

---

71. UPA (1997), §405, comment 2 (stating that "a partner may bring a direct suit against . . . another partner for almost any cause of action arising out of the conduct of the partnership business" and explaining that "[s]ince general partners are not passive investors like limited partners, RUPA does not authorize derivative actions"). The comment to ULLCA (2013) §410(b) paints a murkier picture, noting that "in general . . . the cases are conflicting and somewhat confused" as to whether a partner may sue a fellow partner directly for harm the fellow partner has done to the partnership or whether the suit must be brought as a derivative action. Derivative actions are discussed in Section 16.4.

72. They therefore lack "standing" except to sue in the name and on behalf of the LLC. For a detailed discussion of this point, see Section 16.4.

73. For a comprehensive discussion of this subject, see Daniel S. Kleinberger, "Fezzick, Are There Rocks Ahead? Navigating the Oppression Doctrine in the Age of LLCs," 22 Florida State University Business Review 15 (2023).

Example

PotGold, LLC is a five-member LLC that is member-managed. Under PotGold's operating agreement: (i) any member may be expelled without cause by the consent of the other four members; and (ii) the expelled member is "bought out" under a formula based on the financial results of the preceding 24 months. PotGold is about to sell an asset for a very large profit, far out of proportion to any profits realized over the past 24 months. To grab that profit for themselves, four of the members expel the fifth. The four members have breached a duty owed directly to the fifth member. ◀◀◀

§15.4.4 The Duty of Care

Some LLC statutes set a low bar for the duty of care, requiring only that those with management authority—whether as members or managers—avoid gross negligence and intentional wrongdoing.

Example

The original Arkansas LLC Act stated:

> A member or manager shall not be liable, responsible, or accountable in damages or otherwise to the limited liability company or to the members of the limited liability company for any action taken or failure to act on behalf of the limited liability company unless the act or omission constitutes gross negligence or willful misconduct. . . .[74] ◀◀◀

The current Arkansas act, based on ULLCA (2006/2013), provides similarly:

> The duty of care of a member of a member-managed limited liability company [and the manager of a manager-managed limited liability company] in the conduct or winding up of the company's activities and affairs is to refrain from engaging in grossly negligent or reckless conduct, willful or intentional misconduct, or knowing violation of law.[75]

Other statutes borrow from a prominent corporate law formulation, requiring the exercise of ordinary care.

74. A.C.A. §4–32–402(1).
75. Ark. Code Ann. § 4–38–409(c) and (i)(1).

Example

The Georgia statute provides:

> In managing the business or affairs of a limited liability company, . . . [a] member or manager shall act in a manner he or she believes in good faith to be in the best interests of the limited liability company and with the care an ordinarily prudent person in a like position would exercise under similar circumstances.[76] ◀◀◀

This statutory "split of authority" is understandable in light of the hybrid nature of LLCs. UPA (1997), whose drafting and promulgation overlapped the early days of LLCs, codifies the general partner's duty of care as avoiding gross negligence. That point of view doubtlessly influenced some LLC statute drafters.[77] Other drafters doubtlessly were influenced by the corporate analogy.[78]

The drafters of ULLCA (2006) recognized an additional issue, namely that one standard might be appropriate in some circumstances and the other in other circumstances. The drafters' solution was to codify a hybrid standard—ordinary care "[s]ubject to the business judgment rule."[79] ULLCA (2006) chose not to define the business judgment rule,[80] and books could be (and have been) written solely exploring the meaning of that concept.

---

76. Ga. Code Ann., §14–11–305(1).

77. The UPA (1997) standard was adopted essentially verbatim into the first uniform LLC act, for example. See ULLCA §409(c) (providing that the "duty of care . . . is limited to refraining from engaging in grossly negligent or reckless conduct, intentional misconduct, or a knowing violation of law").

78. See *In re Die Fliedermaus LLC*, 323 B.R. 101, 110 (Bkrtcy. S.D.N.Y. 2005) (quoting the "ordinarily prudent person in a like position" language of the NY LLC statute, and noting: "This is the same fiduciary standard applied to corporate directors.") (quoting 16 N.Y. Jur. Business Relationships §2107; internal quotation marks omitted).

79. ULLCA (2006), §407(c).

80. A comment explains why the drafters chose to eschew a "uniform laws" definition:

> The content and force of the business judgment rule vary across jurisdictions, and therefore the meaning of this subsection may vary from jurisdiction to jurisdiction. That result is intended . . . [U]nder the law of many jurisdictions, the business judgment rule applies similarly across the range of business organizations. That is, the doctrine is sufficiently broad and conceptual so that the formality of organizational choice is less important in shaping the application of the rule than are the nature of the challenged conduct and the responsibilities and authority of the person whose conduct is being challenged. This Act seeks therefore to invoke rather than unsettle whatever may be each jurisdiction's approach to the business judgment rule.

ULLCA (2006), §407(c).

In the most general terms, the rule:

- applies when an entity (or those seeking to enforce an entity's rights)[81] challenges a decision made by those persons having top governance authority within the entity;
- presumes that those persons made the challenged decision in good faith, without any breach of the duty of loyalty, and using the requisite degree of care; and
- requires the court not to second-guess the decision—no matter how damaging it may have turned out to be—unless the complainant can rebut some aspect of the presumption of proper conduct.

The business judgment rule originated in corporate law, pertaining to directors, but recently has been used by courts considering claims against persons with top governance authority within an LLC.[82]

During the Harmonization Project, that drafting committee chose to harmonize the uniform limited liability company act with the general and limited partnership acts. Each of the latter has a "gross negligence" standard. Accordingly, ULLCA (2013) §409(c) provides: "The duty of care of a member of a member-managed limited liability company in the conduct or winding up of the company's activities and affairs is to refrain from engaging in grossly negligent or reckless conduct, willful or intentional misconduct, or knowing violation of law."[83]

§15.4.5 The Duty of Loyalty

Not all LLC statutes codify a duty of loyalty. Some states whose statutes use a corporate-like formulation of the duty of care leave the question of loyalty to case law, again paralleling their state corporate law approach. LLC statutes that address loyalty explicitly have some form of loyalty language derived either from UPA (1914) §21 or from UPA (1997) §404. ULLCA (2013) contains the most current example of the latter approach:

> The duty of loyalty . . . includes the duties:
>
> (1) to account to the company and hold as trustee for it any property, profit, or benefit derived by the member:

81. The parenthetical phrase refers to derivative claims, which are discussed in Section 16.4.
82. In 2011, as part of its project on the Harmonization of Business Entity Acts, NCCUSL eliminated the ordinary care/business judgment provision and substituted the "avoid gross negligence" standard. HULLCA, §409(c), available at http://www.uniformlaws.org/Shared/Docs/AM2011_Prestyle%20Finals/HUBOC_PreStyleFinal_Jul11.pdf.
83. The same standard applies to managers of a manager-managed limited liability company. See ULLCA (2013) §409(i)(1).

(A) in the conduct or winding up of the company's activities;
(B) from a use by the member of the company's property; or
(C) from the appropriation of a company opportunity;

(2) to refrain from dealing with the company in the conduct or winding up of the company's activities and affairs as or on behalf of a person having an interest adverse to the company; and

(3) to refrain from competing with the company in the conduct of the company's activities and affairs before the dissolution of the company.[84]

Whatever the formulation, and regardless whether statute or case law provides the rules, the core elements of the duty of loyalty are the same across jurisdictions: no usurping of a company opportunity; no self-dealing; no competition. The analysis is parallel to the analysis for agents and general partners.[85]

§15.4.6 The Duty to Provide Information

The notion that those with managerial authority have an obligation to provide information to those on whose behalf they manage:

- traces back to agency law;[86]
- is part of partnership law;[87] and
- is part of LLC law, although under some LLC statutes the duty is partially codified.

For example, ULLCA (2013) §410 includes a detailed provision on the informational rights of members, persons dissociated as members (e.g., former members), and transferees.[88] Likewise, the Delaware LLC Act has a detailed provision that closely resembles a provision in the Delaware limited partnership act:

(a) Each member of a limited liability company has the right, subject to such reasonable standards (including standards governing what information and documents are to be furnished at what time and location and at whose expense) as

84. ULLCA (2013) §409(b) (emphasis added). ULLCA (2006) §409(b) was substantively identical. The 2006 and 2013 versions "un-cabin" fiduciary duty. That is, unlike UPA (1997), neither LLC act purports to exhaustively codify fiduciary duties. For a discussion of UPA (1997)'s decision to "cabin in" fiduciary duties and the Harmonization Project reversal of that decision, see Section 9.7.2.

85. See Sections 4.1.1 (agent's duty of loyalty) and 9.7 (partner's duty of loyalty). The nuances of analysis discussed in those sections apply to LLC law as well.

86. See Section 4.1.5.

87. See Section 9.2.

88. ULLCA (2013) §410.

> may be set forth in a limited liability company agreement or otherwise established by the manager or, if there is no manager, then by the members, to obtain from the limited liability company from time to time upon reasonable demand for any purpose reasonably related to the member's interest as a member of the limited liability company:
>
> (1) True and full information regarding the status of the business and financial condition of the limited liability company;
>
> (2) Promptly after becoming available, a copy of the limited liability company's federal, state and local income tax returns for each year;
>
> (3) A current list of the name and last known business, residence or mailing address of each member and manager;
>
> (4) A copy of any written limited liability company agreement and certificate of formation and all amendments thereto, together with executed copies of any written powers of attorney pursuant to which the limited liability company agreement and any certificate and all amendments thereto have been executed;
>
> (5) True and full information regarding the amount of cash and a description and statement of the agreed value of any other property or services contributed by each member and which each member has agreed to contribute in the future, and the date on which each became a member; and
>
> (6) Other information regarding the affairs of the limited liability company as is just and reasonable.
>
> (b) Each manager shall have the right to examine all of the information described in subsection (a) of this section for a purpose reasonably related to the position of manager.
>
> (c) The manager of a limited liability company shall have the right to keep confidential from the members, for such period of time as the manager deems reasonable, any information which the manager reasonably believes to be in the nature of trade secrets or other information the disclosure of which the manager in good faith believes is not in the best interest of the limited liability company or could damage the limited liability company or its business or which the limited liability company is required by law or by agreement with a third party to keep confidential. . . .[89]

Even when a statute includes a detailed information rights provision, the courts will fill in any gaps as a matter of fiduciary duty. In particular, "many cases characterize a manager's duty to disclose as a fiduciary duty"[90] and, more generally, "some cases characterize owners' information rights as reflecting a fiduciary duty of those with management power."[91]

---

89. Del. Code Ann., tit. 6, §18–305 (limited liability companies) and §17–305 (limited partnership).

90. ULLCA (2013) §409(a), cmt.

91. *Id.*, §410, cmt. See also Restatement (Second) of Contracts §161(d) (stating that "[a] person's non-disclosure of a fact is equivalent to an assertion that the fact does not exist . . . where the other person is entitled to know the fact because of a relation of trust and confidence between them").

Example

JeTodd, LLC is a member-managed LLC with two members, Jeff and Todd. Jeff is seeking to buy Todd's interest, and the relevant LLC statute does not impose any relevant disclosure obligations on Jeff or provide any relevant information rights to Todd. Nonetheless, Jeff has a fiduciary duty to disclose material information to Todd. ◄ ◄ ◄

§15.4.7 Altering Fiduciary Duty by Agreement

As is the case with agency and partnership law, LLC law permits fiduciary duties to be delineated or modified by agreement. Delaware law is the most extreme on this point, permitting even wholesale elimination of fiduciary duties:

> To the extent that, at law or in equity, a member or manager or other person has duties (including fiduciary duties) to a limited liability company or to another member or manager or to another person that is a party to or is otherwise bound by a limited liability company agreement, the member's or manager's or other person's duties may be expanded or restricted or eliminated by provisions in the limited liability company agreement. . . .[92]

ULLCA (2013) takes a less radical, more complicated approach. Subject to a "manifestly unreasonable standard," the operating agreement may:

- "alter the duty of care, but may not authorize conduct involving bad faith, willful or intentional misconduct, or knowing violation of law";[93]
- "alter or eliminate the [core] aspects of the duty of loyalty";[94] and
- "alter or eliminate any other fiduciary duty."[95]

ULLCA (2013) derives its approach to restricting fiduciary from ULLCA (2006), and an official comment to the latter sums up the ULC's approach to an operating agreement's power over the duty of loyalty.[96] The following table is derived from that summary, revised to reflect the provisions of ULLCA (2013).

---

92. Del. Code Ann., tit. 6, §18–1101(c) (emphasis added). The subsection contains a proviso: "that the limited liability company agreement may not eliminate the implied contractual covenant of good faith and fair dealing." For a discussion of the implied covenant, see Section 15.4.8.
93. ULLCA (2013) §105(d)(3)(C).
94. ULLCA (2013) §105(d)(3)(A).
95. ULLCA (2013) §105(d)(3)(D).
96. ULLCA (2006) §110(e), cmt.

ULLCA (2013) provides various separate methods through which those with management power in a limited liability company can proceed with conduct that would otherwise violate the duty of loyalty.

15.1 ULLCA (2013) Methods for Restricting the Duty of Loyalty

Method	Statutory Authority
If not manifestly unreasonable, the operating agreement might eliminate the duty or otherwise permit the conduct, without need for further authorization or ratification.	Section 105(d)(2), (3)(A); (3)(B)
If not manifestly unreasonable, the operating agreement might establish a mechanism for authorizing or ratifying the conduct by one or more "disinterested and independent persons after full disclosure of all materials facts."	Section 105(d)(1)(A)
The conduct might be authorized or ratified by all the members after full disclosure.	Section 409(f)
In the case of self-dealing the conduct might be successfully defended as being or having been fair to the limited liability company.	Section 409(g)

In all but the most extreme circumstances, the Delaware approach and the ULLCA (2013) approach should produce the same outcome. The "manifestly unreasonable" standard does not apply under Delaware law, but in egregious situations a disputant under Delaware law can push litigation under the contractual obligation of good faith and fair dealing.

§15.4.8 The Implied Covenant of Good Faith and Fair Dealing

a. The Obligation Described[97]

1. Importance and Ubiquity of the Phrase

Over the past several decades, "good faith" has become increasingly important in the law of business organizations. The phrase appears five times in ULLCA (2013), more than 40 times in the official comments, and has

97. This section is drawn mostly verbatim from Daniel S. Kleinberger, "In the World of Alternative Entities—What Does 'Good Faith' Mean?" Business Law Today (March 2017). Used here with the author's permission.

similar importance in ULPA (2013) and UPA (2013). The phrase also has fundamental importance in the Delaware law of limited liability companies and limited partnerships and has been central in one of the most important recent developments in Delaware corporate law.[98]

2. Meaning Differs with Context

One might think, therefore, that "good faith" can be defined easily or, at least, definitively. But the term is polysemous, a chameleon whose meaning changes dramatically depending on the context. Depending on context and on jurisdiction, the term indicates a test that is either entirely subjective or has both subjective and objective aspects. In one context, the objective standard is a very lax duty of care reclassified as part of the duly of loyalty. In another context, the word "objective" has a meaning radically different from the "reasonableness" concept typically associated with an "objective" test.

3. The Salient Context for LLCs—the Implied Contractual Obligation

In the context of limited liability companies, the most important context for "good faith" is the implied contractual covenant (or obligation) of good faith and fair dealing.[99] The obligation, which is not a fiduciary duty, originated in the common law of contracts; has been codified in the Uniform Commercial Code (UCC); is variously labeled a duty, an obligation, and an implied covenant; and has in recent years developed its own, special character as applied to operating and partnership agreements.

The variation of labels imports no difference in meaning. Under the common law of contracts, the obligation of "good faith and fair dealing" is an implied and inescapable term of every agreement. Per the Restatement

---

98. See ULLCA (2013) §409(d), cmt (referring to "the corporate concept of good faith that for years bedeviled courts and attorneys trying to understand: (i) Delaware's famous corporate law exoneration provision; and (ii) that provision's exception 'for acts or omissions not in good faith' and (explaining that '[i]n' that context, good faith is an aspect of the duty of loyalty") (citing Del. Code Ann. tit. 8, §102(b)(7) (2012); In *Stone ex rel. AmSouth Bancorporation v. Ritter*, 911 A.2d 362, 369–70 (Del. 2006)). The phrase is also prominent in the law of close corporations. See, e.g., *Donahue v. Rodd Electrotype Co. of New England, Inc.*, 367 Mass. 578, 593, 328 N.E.2d 505, 515 (1975) ("[S]tockholders in the close corporation owe one another substantially the same fiduciary duty in the operation of the enterprise that partners owe to one another. In our previous decisions, we have defined the standard of duty owed by partners to one another as the utmost good faith and loyalty.") (footnotes, citations, internal quotations omitted).

99. The same is true in the context of partnerships, especially limited partnerships. Under Delaware law, on this point (and most others) LLC and limited partnership case law are reciprocally precedential. ULLCA (2013), ULPA (2013), and UPA (2013) each codify the implied obligation using identical language, accompanied by essentially identical comments. Therefore, the information provided in this section applies equally to the implied obligation in the context of partnerships.

(Second) of Contracts, §201, "Every contract imposes upon each party a duty of good faith and fair dealing in its performance and its enforcement." The official comments suggest that a complete definition is impossible—the duty "excludes a variety of types of conduct characterized as involving 'bad faith' because they violate community standards of decency, fairness, or reasonableness," but "[a] complete catalogue of types of bad faith is impossible."

This type of impossibility is a boon to litigators and a bane for transactional lawyers. "Good faith," as codified by the UCC, is little better. Under UCC, §1–201(20), "'[g]ood faith' . . . means honesty in fact and the observance of reasonable commercial standards of fair dealing." Presumably, the UCC's concept of usage of trade imparts some content to "reasonable commercial standards of fair dealing." Nevertheless (and arguably as a result), those standards assess a contract obligor's conduct from a perspective disconnected from the language of the contract. The results can be startling, as in *K.M.C. Co. v. Irving Trust Co.*, which used such standards to hold that: (i) a lender's exercise of its totally discretionary right to call a demand note was objectively unreasonable; and therefore (ii) the lender was liable for the collapse of the borrower's business.[100]

4. The Approach of the ULC and Delaware

ULLCA (2013) and Delaware law are friendlier to transactional lawyers (and their clients), although both the ULC and Delaware case law have flirted at least briefly with an objective standard divorced from the words of the parties' agreement. For example, in *Policemen's Annuity and Benefit Fund v. DV Realty Advisors LLC*, the Delaware Court of Chancery considered the implied covenant in the context of a limited partnership agreement that required the limited partners to act "in good faith" if they chose to remove the general partner but did not define good faith. The Court decided to "presume that the parties intended to adopt Delaware's common law definition of good faith as applied to contracts" and then resolved the matter in light of the UCC definition of the implied convent—including that definition's objective aspect.[101]

The Delaware Supreme Court affirmed the judgment but flatly ended the flirtation: "This Court has never held that the UCC definition of good faith applies to limited partnership agreements."[102]

---

100. *K.M.C. Co. v. Irving Trust Co.*, 757 F.2d 752 (6th Cir. 1985).
101. *Policemen's Annuity & Benefit Fund of Chicago v. DV Realty Advisors LLC*, No. CIV.A. 7204-VCN, 2012 WL 3548206, at *13 (Del. Ch. Aug. 16, 2012) (brackets in original), aff'd sub nom. *DV Realty Advisors LLC v. Policemen's Annuity & Ben. Fund of Chicago*, 75 A.3d 101 (Del. 2013).
102. *DV Realty Advisors LLC v. Policemen's Annuity & Ben. Fund of Chicago*, 75 A.3d 101, 109 (Del. 2013).

Beginning in 2013, several important Delaware decisions have moved toward greater precision, mooring both "good faith" and "fair dealing" to the words of the parties' contract:

> "Fair dealing" is not akin to the fair process component of entire fairness, i.e., whether the fiduciary acted fairly when engaging in the challenged transaction as measured by duties of loyalty and care. . . . It is rather a commitment to deal "fairly" in the sense of consistently with the terms of the parties' agreement and its purpose. Likewise, "good faith" does not envision loyalty to the contractual counterparty, but rather faithfulness to the scope, purpose, and terms of the parties' contract. Both necessarily turn on the contract itself and what the parties would have agreed upon had the issue arisen when they were bargaining originally.[103]

Because the actual words of the agreement control the application of the implied covenant:

> An implied covenant claim . . . looks to the past. It is not a free-floating duty unattached to the underlying legal documents. It does not ask what duty the law should impose on the parties given their relationship at the time of the wrong, but *rather what the parties would have agreed to themselves had they considered the issue in their original bargaining positions at the time of contracting.*[104]

At one time, the ULC appeared to do more than merely flirt with the vagueness of the common law/UCC approach. UPA (1997) §404(d) codified the implied obligation of good faith and fair dealing for the first time, and comment 4 to that section noted and argued in favor of vagueness:

> The meaning of "good faith and fair dealing" is not firmly fixed under present law. "Good faith" clearly suggests a subjective element, while "fair dealing" implies an objective component. It was decided to leave the terms undefined in the Act and allow the courts to develop their meaning based on the experience of real cases.

Having courts "develop" meaning as they go hardly makes for the rule stability that transactional lawyers seek. In 2001, the ULC adopted a new

---

103. *Gerber v. Enter. Products Holdings, LLC*, 67 A.3d 400, 418–19 (Del. 2013) (quoting *ASB Allegiance Real Estate Fund v. Scion Breckenridge Managing Member, LLC*, 50 A.3d 434, 440–42 (Del. Ch. 2012), aff'd in part, rev'd in part on other grounds, 68 A.3d 665 (Del. 2013)) (footnotes omitted) (citations omitted) (internal quotations omitted without ellipsis by *Gerber*).

104. *Gerber v. Enter. Prods. Holdings, LLC*, 67 A.3d 400, 418 (Del. 2013) (quoting *ASB Allegiance Real Estate Fund v. Scion Breckenridge Managing Member, LLC*, 50 A.3d 434, 440–42 (Del. Ch. 2012), aff'd in part, rev'd in part on other grounds, 68 A.3d 665 (Del. 2013)) (emphasis added) (footnotes omitted) (citations omitted) (internal quotations omitted without ellipsis by *Gerber*).

uniform limited partnership act with the same codifying language, but the official comment took a decidedly different approach:

> The obligation of good faith and fair dealing is *not* a fiduciary duty, does not command altruism or self-abnegation, and does not prevent a partner from acting in the partner's own self-interest. Courts should not use the obligation to change *ex post facto* the parties' or this Act's allocation of risk and power. To the contrary, in light of the nature of a limited partnership, the obligation should be used only to protect agreed-upon arrangements from conduct that is manifestly beyond what a reasonable person could have contemplated when the arrangements were made.[105]

On this point ULLCA (2006) followed ULPA (2001), and the Harmonization Project took both the statutory language and commentary further still from comment 4's embrace of indefiniteness. All three current uniform acts now expressly characterize the implied covenant as "contractual."[106] And, in their respective official comments, all three acts interweave the 2001 "non-abnegation" language with quotations from the Delaware cases quoted above.

Thus, under both Delaware law and the uniform acts, the implied covenant of good faith and fair dealing is a cautious enterprise, intended only to preserve the fruits of the bargain—as evidenced by the words of the contract—from one party's lack of prescience and the other party's desire to exploit that lack.

No contract, regardless of how tightly or precisely drafted it may be, can wholly account for every possible contingency. Even the most skilled and sophisticated parties will necessarily fail to address a future state of the world . . . because contracting is costly and human knowledge imperfect. . . .[107]

Thus, properly understood and delimited, implied covenant analysis resembles the rule for determining whether a party's contractual duties are discharged by supervening impracticably. "In order for a supervening event to discharge a duty . . . , the non-occurrence of that event must have been a 'basic assumption' on which both parties made the contract."[108] As for the implied contractual covenant, "parties occasionally have understandings or expectations that were so fundamental that they did not need to negotiate about those expectations."[109]

---

105. ULPA (2001), §305(b), cmt.

106. UPA (1997) (Last Amended 2013) §409(d); ULPA (2001) (Last Amended 2013) §§305(a), 409(d); ULLCA (2006) (Last Amended 2013) §409(d).

107. *Allen v. El Paso Pipeline GP Co., L.L.C.*, No. CIV.A. 7520-VCL, 2014 WL 2819005, at *11 (Del. Ch. June 20, 2014) (internal quotations and citations omitted).

108. Restatement (Second) of Contracts §261, cmt. b (1981).

109. *Allen v. El Paso Pipeline GP Co., L.L.C.*, No. CIV.A. 7520-VCL, 2014 WL 2819005, at *11 (Del. Ch. June 20, 2014) (internal quotations and citations omitted).

Or put another way, both doctrines identify situations or claims that—if contemplated at the time of contracting—would have been deal-breakers. Thus, "In sum, the purpose of the contractual obligation of good faith and fair dealing is to protect the arrangement the members have chosen for themselves, not to restructure that arrangement under the guise of safeguarding it."[110]

Case in Point—*PAMI-LEMB I Inc. v. EMB-NHC, LLC*

The operating agreement of a manager-managed LLC contained a buy-sell procedure for resolving disputes between the manager-member and the nonmanager member. When a serious dispute arose, the nonmanager member invoked the buy-sell provision by offering to buy the other member's interest or sell its own interest to the other member. Without breaching any specific term of the buy-sell procedure, the manager-member frustrated the procedure's purpose by: making counter offers at egregiously low prices; threatening to litigate; and announcing that it would not permit any distributions while the dispute lasted. This conduct breached the managing member's obligation of good faith and fair dealing.[111] ◀ ◀ ◀

Example

Pipeline, LLC ("Pipeline") is a manager-managed limited liability company, whose manager, Alexandria Honcho ("Honcho") owns 65 percent membership interests comprising 65 percent of member voting rights. Pipeline's operating agreement provides that: (i) Honcho can buy out the other members at any time; and (ii) the price is not subject to challenge if an independent investment bank provides an opinion that the price is "fair" to the other members (the "safe harbor").

In due course, Honcho proposes to buy out the other members at a specified price and an independent investment bank provides the necessary fairness opinion. However, in its analysis the bank does not take into account two of Pipeline's assets—namely, the value of claims the company may have against Honcho for gross mismanagement. A member challenges the buyout transaction, and Honcho asserts the safe harbor as a dispositive defense, noting that the operating agreement says nothing about how the investment bank should determine the fairness of the buyout price. Citing

---

110. ULLCA (2013) §409(d), cmt.
111. *PAMI-LEMB I Inc. v. EMB-NHC, L.L.C.*, 857 A.2d 998 (Del. Ch. 2004).

the implied contractual covenant of good faith and fair dealing, the court rejects the defense.[112]

b. May the Implied Covenant Be Delineated?[113]

May an operating agreement delineate the implied contractual obligation, perhaps identifying particular circumstances and specifying conduct as satisfying the implied obligation in those circumstances? On this question, it is worth considering both ULLCA (2013) and the Delaware law.

1. Under ULLCA (2013)

Under ULLCA (2013), the answer to the delineation question appears straightforward under the uniform act. Section 105(c)(6) states that, while an operating agreement may not "eliminate the contractual obligation of good faith and fair dealing under section 409(d)," the agreement "may prescribe the standards, if not manifestly unreasonable, by which the performance of the obligation is to be measured."[114] The official comment provides several examples, including this one:

> The operating agreement of a manager-managed LLC gives the manager "sole discretion" to make various decisions. The agreement further provides: "Whenever this agreement requires or permits a manager to make a decision that has the potential to benefit one class of members to the detriment of another class, the manager complies with section 409(d) of [this act] if the manager makes the decision with:
>
> a. the honest belief that the decision:
>
> i. serves the best interests of the LLC; or
>
> ii. at least does not injure or otherwise disserve those interests; and
>
> b. the reasonable belief that the decision breaches no member's rights under this agreement."
>
> This provision "prescribe[s] the standards by which the performance of the [section 409(d)] obligation is to be measured."[115]

---

112. This Example is a simplified version of some of the issues and facts in *Gerber v. Enter. Products Holdings, LLC*, 67 A.3d 400, 418–21 (Del. 2013), overruled on other grounds by *Winshall v. Viacom Int'l, Inc.*, 76 A.3d 808 (Del. 2013).

113. This section is drawn mostly verbatim from Daniel S. Kleinberger, "Delineating the Implied Covenant and Providing for 'Good Faith'" Business Law Today (May 2017). Used here with the author's permission.

114. This comment quotes from ULLCA (2013), text and comments, but the analysis applies equally to ULLCA (2006), sometimes informally referred to as the "RULLCA," and also to ULLCA (1996), the first uniform LLC act.

115. ULLCA (2013), §105(c)(6), cmt. (noting that *Nemec v. Shrader*, 991 A.2d 1120 (Del. 2010) "consider[ed] such a situation in the context of the right to call preferred stock and decid[ed] by a 3–2 vote that exercising the call did not breach the implied covenant of good

2. Under Delaware Law

Under Delaware law, the delineation question requires a different and more complicated analysis. The conceptual answer is "not possible," but the practical answer is "can do." Under Delaware law, the implied covenant acts as a special type of "gap filler," a process of interpolation implied by law: "An implied covenant claim . . . [asks] what the parties would have agreed to themselves had they considered the issue in their original bargaining positions at the time of contracting."[116]

The law supplies the gap-filling methodology, which no agreement has the power to change. By its nature, this approach is invariable. For instance, an operating agreement may not provide that "a manager's act in any manner pertaining to this agreement satisfies the implied covenant of good faith and fair dealing if the person asserting a breach of the implied covenant had at the time of contracting reason to know that the agreement could reasonably be interpreted to authorize the act."

However, a Delaware operating or partnership agreement can rein in the implied covenant by avoiding gaps. Consider the above example from ULLCA (2013) comments, revised as follows:

> Whenever this agreement requires or permits a manager to make a decision that has the potential to benefit one class of members to the detriment of another class, ~~the manager complies with Section 409(d) of [this act]~~the manager's decision is binding and breaches no duty to the company or its members, if the manager makes the decision with:
>
> a. the honest belief that the decision:
> i. serves the best interests of the LLC; or
> ii. at least does not injure or otherwise disserve those interests; and
> c. the reasonable belief that the decision breaches no member's rights under this agreement.

Although "[n]o contract, regardless of how tightly or precisely drafted it may be, can wholly account for every possible contingency,"[117] it is

---

faith and fair dealing"). ULLCA (2013) §409(d) provides that "A member shall discharge the duties and obligations under this [act] or under the operating agreement and exercise any rights consistently with the contractual obligation of good faith and fair dealing." Section 409(i)(3) makes the provision applicable also to managers in a manager-managed limited liability company.

116. *Gerber v. Enter. Prods. Holdings, LLC*, 67 A.3d 400, 418 (Del. 2013) (quoting *ASB Allegiance Real Estate Fund v. Scion Breckenridge Managing Member, LLC*, 50 A.3d 434, 440–42 (Del. Ch. 2012), aff'd in part, rev'd in part on other grounds, 68 A.3d 665 (Del. 2013)) (emphasis added) (footnotes omitted) (citations omitted) (internal quotations omitted without ellipsis by *Gerber*). For further explanation of this concept, see the discussion in Section 15.4.8(a).

117. *Allen v. El Paso Pipeline GP Co., L.L.C.*, No. CIV.A. 7520-VCL, 2014 WL 2819005, at *11 (Del. Ch. June 20, 2014) (internal quotations and citations omitted).

opportunistic conduct that brings Delaware's implied covenant into play. The example immediately above leaves scant, if any, room for such conduct. Thus, while under Delaware law "safe harbor" provisions cannot be upheld as "prescrib[ing] the standards . . . by which the performance of the obligation [of good faith and fair dealing] is to be measured,"[118] safe harbor provisions can render the implied covenant inapposite if carefully drafted and sensibly invoked.[119]

c. The Effect of Expressly Requiring Conduct to Be in "Good Faith"[120]

Great care is required when an operating agreement imposes an express requirement of "good faith." Left undefined, the phrase is a minefield for parties and a godsend for litigators—as exemplified in *Policemen's Annuity and Benefit Fund v. DV Realty Advisors LLC*. The case arose from a limited partnership agreement that permitted the limited partners to remove the general partner:

> "without cause by an affirmative vote or consent of the Limited Partners holding in excess of 75% of the [Limited] Partnership Interests then held by all Limited Partners; provided that consenting Limited Partners in good faith determine that such removal is necessary for the best interest of the [Limited] Partnership."[121]

The agreement did not, however, define the term.[122]

Both the Chancery Court and Delaware Supreme Court addressed the definitional omission, but each used a different approach and reached a different definitional conclusion. The Chancery Court used an *a fortiori* analysis to resolve the case without actually deciding on a definition:

> The conduct of the Limited Partners in this case does not approach the sort of unreasonable conduct that is necessarily undertaken in bad faith. A test is nevertheless required; the Limited Partners' conduct must be analyzed under some rubric. . . . The definition prescribed in [Delaware's Uniform Commercial

---

118. ULLCA (2013) §105(c)(6).

119. For example, in the author's opinion, it was not sensible to rely on a Special Approval valuation process that had ignored two assets of the company, which were arguably quite substantial. *Gerber v. Enter. Prod. Holdings, LLC*, 67 A.3d 400, 422–23 (Del. 2013) overruled on other grounds by *Winshall v.Viacom Int'l, Inc.*, 76 A.3d 808 (Del. 2013).

120. This section is drawn mostly verbatim from Daniel S. Kleinberger, "Delineating the Implied Covenant and Providing for 'Good Faith'" Business Law Today (May 2017).'

121. *Policemen's Annuity & Benefit Fund of Chicago v. DV Realty Advisors LLC*, No. CIV.A. 7204-VCN, 2012 WL 3548206, at *11 (Del. Ch. Aug. 16, 2012) (quoting Section 3.10(a)(ii) of the limited partnership agreement) (brackets in the opinion), aff'd sub nom. *DV Realty Advisors LLC v. Policemen's Annuity & Ben. Fund of Chicago*, 75 A.3d 101 (Del. 2013).

122. *Policemen's Annuity & Benefit Fund of Chicago v. DV Realty Advisors LLC*, No. CIV.A. 7204-VCN, 2012 WL 3548206, at *1213 (Del. Ch. Aug. 16, 2012), aff'd sub nom. *DV Realty Advisors LLC v. Policemen's Annuity & Ben. Fund of Chicago*, 75 A.3d 101 (Del. 2013).

> Code] §1–201(20) ["honesty in fact and the observance of reasonable commercial standards of fair dealing"] is at least as broad of a definition of good faith as that applied to contracts at common law, and . . . the Limited Partners can meet the [the broader] definition. . . . Thus, the Limited Partners necessarily satisfy Delaware's common law definition of good faith as applied to contracts, which is the definition of good faith that the Court presumes was adopted in [the limited partnership agreement].[123]

The Delaware Supreme Court flatly rejected the lower's court methodology, substituting a standard far more easily met. Relying on one of its own decisions, the Court held that the limited partners' "determination will be considered to be in good faith unless the Limited Partners went 'so far beyond the bounds of reasonable judgment that it seems essentially inexplicable on any ground other than bad faith.' "[124]

The moral of this story is clear—never use the phrase "good faith" in an operating agreement without carefully defining the term.

d. How Restrictions on Fiduciary Duty Affect the Implied Covenant of Good Faith and Fair Dealing

Restrictions on fiduciary duty affect implied covenant in two very different ways:

- Constraining fiduciary duty can put "inordinate pressure [to expand] the concept of 'good faith and fair dealing.' "[125] As explained at the ULC's 2006 Annual Meeting:

  > When you say there are no . . . fiduciary duties and courts for hundreds of years have looked to fiduciary duties as a policing mechanism that they can develop, if you say you can't have fiduciary duties, they will go to good faith. And, in fact, I had a conversation with . . . [t]he judge of North Carolina's business court [who] said, if you stop us on fiduciary duty, we will just go to good faith."[126]

- Well-written restrictions on fiduciary duty reduce the scope of the implied covenant, at least where the obligation is read narrowly (as

---

123. *Policemen's Annuity & Benefit Fund of Chicago v. DV Realty Advisors LLC*, No. CIV.A. 7204-VCN, 2012 WL 3548206, at *13 (Del. Ch. Aug. 16, 2012), aff'd sub nom. *DV Realty Advisors LLC v. Policemen's Annuity & Ben. Fund of Chicago*, 75 A.3d 101 (Del. 2013).

124. *DV Realty Advisors LLC v. Policemen's Annuity & Ben. Fund of Chicago*, 75 A.3d 101, 110 (Del. 2013) (quoting *Brinckerhoff v. Enbridge Energy Co., Inc.*, 67 A.3d 369, 373 (Del. 2013)).

125. ULLCA (2013), Prefatory Note to ULLCA (2006), Noteworthy Provisions of the 2006 Act.

126. Remarks of Co-Reporter Kleinberger at the 2006 Annual Meeting of the Uniform Law Conference, quoted in Daniel S. Kleinberger & Carter G. Bishop, "The Next Generation: The Revised Uniform Limited Liability Company Act, 62 BUS. LAW. 515, 551 n. 49 (2007).

in Delaware and under ULLCA (2013)). The implied covenant defers to express contractual provisions. Therefore, specific and clear limitations on fiduciary duty preclude application of the implied covenant within the scope of the limitations.[127]

§15.5 THE RIGHT AND POWER OF MEMBERS AND MANAGERS TO BIND A LIMITED LIABILITY COMPANY

§15.5.1 Actual Authority

As is the case with agent and principal and partner and partnership, the power of an LLC member or manager to bind an LLC encompasses both actual and apparent authority. "In general, a member's [or manager's] actual authority to act for an LLC will depend fundamentally on the operating agreement,"[128] as well as on the rules provided by whatever management template might be applicable.[129]

§15.5.2 Statutory Apparent Authority

Almost all two-template statutes provide for statutory apparent authority for members in a member-managed LLC and managers in a manager-managed LLC.[130] As explained in a comment to ULLCA (2013):

> Most LLC statutes, including the original ULLCA (1996), provide for what might be termed "statutory apparent authority" for members in a member-managed limited liability company and managers in a manager-managed limited liability company. This approach codifies the common law notion of apparent authority by position and dates back at least to the original Uniform Partnership Act. UPA (1914), §9 provided that "the act of every partner . . . for apparently carrying on in the usual way the business of the partnership . . . binds the partnership," and that formulation has been essentially followed by UPA (1997), §301, ULLCA (1996), §301, ULPA (2001), §402, and myriad state LLC statutes.[131]

The statutory power to bind switches from member to manager according to which management template the LLC has in effect, and most LLC

127. See the discussion in Section 15.4.8(b).
128. ULLCA (2013) §301(b), cmt.
129. See Section 15.3.
130. See Section 10.3 for an explanation of the term "statutory apparent authority" in the context of general partners.
131. ULLCA (2013) §301(a), cmt.

statutes also expressly negate any authority for a nonmanager member in a manager-managed LLC.

Example

For example, the Colorado LLC statute provides:

> (1) If the articles of organization provide that management of the limited liability company is vested in one or more managers:
>
> (a) A member is not an agent of the limited liability company and has no authority to bind the limited liability company solely by virtue of being a member; and
>
> (b) Each manager is an agent of the limited liability company for the purposes of its business and an act of a manager, including the execution of an instrument in the name of the limited liability company, for apparently carrying on in the ordinary course the business of the limited liability company or business of the kind carried on by the limited liability company binds the limited liability company, unless the manager had no authority to act for the limited liability company in the particular matter and the person with whom the manager was dealing had notice that the manager lacked authority.
>
> (2) If the articles of organization provide that management of the limited liability company is vested in the members, each member is an agent of the limited liability company for the purposes of its business and an act of a member, including the execution of an instrument in the name of the limited liability company, for apparently carrying on in the ordinary course the business of the limited liability company or business of the kind carried on by the limited liability company binds the limited liability company, unless the member had no authority to act for the limited liability company in the particular matter and the person with whom the member was dealing had notice that the member lacked authority.[132] ◄◄◄

Under most two-template statutes, a publicly filed document (i.e., the articles of organization, certificate of formation, etc.) must state which template applies, so in theory third parties can determine whether members of an LLC have statutory apparent authority.

§15.5.3 The ULC's New Approach: Eliminating Statutory Apparent Authority

In ULLCA (2006), the ULC broke with more than 90 years of tradition and eliminated statutory authority. That decision has not been popular, and most states that have enacted ULLCA (2006) have preserved the concept. Nonetheless, ULLCA (2013) also omits statutory apparent authority.

132. C.R.S. 7–80–405.

Although ULLCA (2013), like ULLCA (2006), provides both a member-management and manager-management template, the templates serve to structure the relations *inter se* of members and managers (if any); the templates do not, however, result in automatic apparent authority by position.

ULLCA (2013) §301(a) states: "A member is not an agent of a limited liability company solely by reason of being a member," and the Act contains no automatic, statutory apparent authority for managers. The apparent authority of members and managers is left to "other law—most especially the law of agency."[133]

Although this approach is radical, it is consistent with the underlying rationale for statutory apparent authority. As explained in the lengthy official comment to section 301(a):

> The concept [of statutory apparent authority] still makes sense both for general and limited partnerships. A third party dealing with either type of partnership can know by the formal name of the entity and by a person's status as general or limited partner whether the person has the power to bind the entity.
>
> Most LLC statutes have attempted to use the same approach but with a fundamentally important (and problematic) distinction. An LLC's status as member-managed or manager-managed determines whether members or managers have the statutory power to bind. But an LLC's status as member- or manager-managed is not apparent from the LLC's name. A third party must check the public record, which may reveal that the LLC is manager-managed, which in turn means a member as member has no power to bind the LLC. As a result, a provision that originated in 1914 as a protection for third parties can, in the LLC context, easily function as a trap for the unwary. The problem is exacerbated by the almost infinite variety of management structures permissible in and used by LLCs.
>
> The new Act cuts through this problem by simply eliminating statutory apparent authority. Codifying power to bind according to position makes sense only for organizations that have well-defined, well-known, and almost paradigmatic management structures. Because:
>
> - flexibility of management structure is a hallmark of the limited liability company; and
> - an LLC's name gives no signal as to the organization's structure,
>
> it makes no sense to:
>
> - require each LLC to publicly select between two statutorily preordained structures (i.e., manager-managed/member-managed); and then
> - link a "statutory power to bind" to each of those two structures.[134]

---

133. ULLCA (2013) §301(a), cmt.

134. ULLCA (2013) §301(a), cmt. (quoting PUBOGRAM, Vol. XXIII, no. 2 at 9–10) (internal quotation marks omitted; brackets in the original).

Under ULLCA (2013) §301(b): "A person's status as a member does not prevent or restrict law other than this [act] from imposing liability on a limited liability company because of the person's conduct." The same is true for a person's status as a manager. Indeed, either such status can be relevant to a common law authority analysis.

Example

A vendor knows that an LLC is manager-managed, but chooses to accept the signature of a person whom the vendor knows is merely a member of the LLC. Assuring the vendor that the LLC will stand by the member's commitment, the member states, "It's such a simple matter; no one will mind." The member genuinely believes the statement, and the vendor accepts the assurance. The person's status as a mere member will undermine a claim of apparent authority. R.3d §2.03, cmt. *d* (2006) (explaining the "reasonable belief" element of a claim of apparent authority, and role played by context, custom, and the supposed agent's position in an organization). Likewise, the member will have no actual authority. Absent additional facts, section 407(c)(1) ([part of the manager-management template] vesting all management authority in the managers) renders the member's belief unreasonable.[135] ◄ ◄ ◄

§15.5.4 Statements of Authority Under ULLCA (2006) and ULLCA (2013)

In part due to its rejection of statutory apparent authority, ULLCA (2006) has:

> "souped up" RUPA's statement of authority to permit an LLC to publicly file a statement of authority for a position (not merely a particular person). Statements of authority will enable LLCs to provide reliable documentation of authority to enter into transactions without having to disclose to third parties the entirety of the operating agreement.[136]

With regard to statement of authority, ULLCA (2013) closely follows ULLCA (2006), making only stylistic changes.

---

135. This Example is taken verbatim from ULLCA (2013), §301(a). On the unreasonableness of the member's belief, see R.3d §2.01, cmt. *c* (2006) (explaining the reasonable belief element of a claim of actual authority) and Section 2.2.2(e).

136. ULLCA (2006), Prefatory Note, Noteworthy Provisions of the New Act, The Power of a Member or Manager to Bind the Limited Liability Company. In both ULLCA (2006) and (2013), Section 302 contains the statement of authority provisions.

§15.5.5 The Statutory Lacuna: Power to Bind for Acts of Negligence

Although statutory apparent authority reaches torts involving misrepresentation and defamation,[137] most LLC statutes have no language to impute to the LLC torts of negligence committed by members or managers. ULLCA (1996) is an exception; it contains a provision (derived from UPA (1997) §305) captioned "Limited liability company liable for member's or manager's actionable conduct." As for ULLCA (2006), a comment specifically contemplates that "the doctrine of respondeat superior might make an LLC liable for the tortious conduct of a member."[138] The same comment appears in ULLCA (2013).[139] Under non-uniform LLC statutes, there is no guidance. This area of LLC law continues to await judicial clarification.

§15.6 CAPITAL STRUCTURE: THE ECONOMIC RIGHTS AND ROLES OF MEMBERS

§15.6.1 Overview

The phrase "capital structure" is a fancy way to label the economic rights of an entity's owners *vis-à-vis* each other and the entity. In the hybrid that is a limited liability company, the basic rules for "capital structure" derive from the law of partnerships. The situation has persisted even after "check the box," because partnership tax accounting rules still apply to any multimember LLC that is taxed as a partnership.

As a result, LLC statutes are remarkably similar in the substance of their capital structure (or "finance") provisions, although the statutory language can vary quite a bit and, of course, the operating agreement is controlling *inter se* the members. All LLC statutes:

- conceptualize a member's financial rights as separate from the member's governance rights, providing a label for the financial rights, such as:
  — "transferable interest"; or
  — confusingly — "membership interest";

137. See Sections 3.3.3, 3.4.2, and 3.4.3 (discussing how apparent authority is relevant to these torts).
138. ULLCA (2006) §301(b), cmt.
139. ULLCA (2013) §301(b), cmt.

- provide default rules for allocating distributions among members and transferees of a member's financial rights, both for operating distributions and liquidating distributions; and
- contemplate a person acquiring economic rights either:
  - —directly from the LLC by "buying into" the company and becoming a member; or
  - —acquiring economic rights from a person already a member (and either becoming a member or remaining a "mere" transferee).

§15.6.2 A Member's Contribution ("Buying In")

A person can become a member of an LLC either:

- by acquiring another person's membership and being admitted to the LLC in connection with that acquisition; or
- through a transaction with the LLC.

In the former instance, the new member does not make any payment to the LLC; any consideration passes to the seller. In the latter instance, it is usual for the person becoming a member to make a "contribution" in return for membership.

LLC statutes put almost no limits on the possible forms of contribution.

Example

The Colorado LLC Act provides that: "The contribution of a member may be in cash, property, or services rendered or a promissory note or other obligation to contribute cash or property or to perform services."[140] ◄◄◄

Example

Under ULLCA (2013):

> A contribution may consist of property transferred to, services performed for, or another benefit provided to the limited liability company or an agreement to transfer property to, perform services for, or provide another benefit to the company.[141] ◄◄◄

140. C.R.S.A. §7-80-501.
141. ULLCA (2013) §402.

What (if anything) a person contributes to the LLC in return for membership is a matter for agreement. Formally, the agreement is between the person and the LLC. In practice, especially in LLCs with few members, the agreement is reached between the new member and the existing members.

Some LLC statutes contain a statute of fraud provision applicable to promised contributions. Most LLC statutes expressly permit a person to become a member without making any contribution.

§15.6.3 A Member's "Payout" Rights (Distributions)

Most LLC statutes refer to a member's rights to share in profits, losses, and distributions. The reference to sharing profits and losses is primarily for tax purposes;[142] "distributions" refers to something of value actually transferred by an LLC to a member on account of the member's financial stake in the venture.

Example

ABC, LLC has three members, each of whom has equal rights in the company's profits, losses, and distributions. ABC's operating agreement provides that the company's sole manager decides what, if any, distributions will be made to members before dissolution. The following table shows the financial results for ABC in the years 2004 through 2007 and the effect on ABC's members. ◀ ◀ ◀

15.2 Payout Rights Over Time — A Simple Example

Year	Company's Profit/Loss (loss shown in parentheses)	Allocation to Each Member (to be accounted for on the member's own tax returns)	Distribution to Each Member (as determined, per the operating agreement, by ABC's manager)
2004	$60,000	20,000	20,000
2005	60,000	20,000	0
2006	21,000	7,000	17,000
2007	(90,000)	(30,000)	2,000

142. See Section 13.1.2(b) (explaining how an LLC's tax classification as a partnership means that its profits and losses pass through directly to its members).

Financial rights are among the most frequently negotiated parts of an LLC "deal," and therefore it is common for an LLC's operating agreement to displace the statutory default rules. The default paradigm is quite similar from statute to statute:

- The distinction between member-management and manager-management is immaterial, as is the distinction between manager members and nonmanager members in a manager-managed LLC.
- Members have no right to any "interim" distributions (i.e., distributions before dissolution and winding up).
- Distributions are made in cash, not "in kind" (i.e., in property other than cash).
- Profits, losses, and distributions (when made) are allocated either:
  —per capita; or
  —in proportion, directly or indirectly, to the value of contributions made to the LLC.[143]
- A person who acquires a member's financial rights without becoming a member of the LLC is entitled "to share in such profits and losses, to receive such distribution or distributions, and to receive such allocation of income, gain, loss, deduction, or credit or similar item to which the assignor was entitled, to the extent assigned"; i.e., a member's financial rights are transferable.[144]
- If the LLC dissolves, after all debts are paid, the surplus is distributed:
  —first "to each person owning a transferable interest that reflects contributions made by a member and not previously returned, an amount equal to the value of the unreturned contributions";[145]
  —then among the members and transferees according to the sharing ratios for distributions.

Example

XYZ, LLC is a manager-managed LLC with three members, one of whom is the company's sole manager. XYZ's operating agreement makes no changes in the financial structure provided by the relevant LLC statute but does provide that the LLC will dissolve and wind up its affairs once it has built and sold a major construction project. The relevant LLC statute allocates profits,

143. Many LLC statutes allocate distributions in proportion to the allocation of profits, which in turn are allocated per capita or in proportion to the value of contributions.

144. The quoted language is from Florida's original LLC statute, West's F.S.A. §608.432(2)(b), and is a bit more elaborate than the language found in most LLC statutes. However, the concept is universally present. (Florida has replaced its original act with ULLCA (2013). See 2013 Fl. Laws, Chapter 2013–180.

145. The quoted language is from ULLCA (2013) §707(b)(1).

losses, and distributions in proportion to "the value of contributions made and not returned."

The company was "capitalized" by a contribution of $1,000,000 from X, its managing member, and contributions of $500,000 each from Y and Z. The company did not make any distributions before dissolution. After the project was sold and creditors paid, the LLC had $10,000,000 remaining. That money is distributed as follows:

<u>$2,000,000 as return of capital</u>
$1,000,000 to X
$500,000 each to Y and Z

<u>$8,000,000 as distribution to profits, allocated in proportion to the value of capital previously contributed and not previously returned</u>
50% to X=$4,000,000
25% to Y=$2,000,000
25% to Z=$2,000,000

<u>Totals per member</u>
X: $5,000,000
Y: $2,500,000
Z: $2,500,000 ◄◄◄

§15.7 THE CONCEPT OF DISSOCIATION AND A MEMBER'S LIMITED "EXIT RIGHTS"

§15.7.1 Dissociation

In terms of susceptibility to dissolution, LLCs are at the far opposite end of the spectrum from a UPA (1914) general partnership.[146] Under all LLC statutes, an LLC has perpetual duration, unless its articles of organization or operating agreement provide otherwise, and a person's ceasing to be a member has no effect on the continuity of the entity. Therefore, to understand a person's "exit" rights as a member of an LLC, it is necessary to understand the circumstances under which a person might cease to be a member and the consequences to the person's rights when such "dissociation" occurs.

As will be seen, a member always has the power to dissociate, but under most LLC statutes dissociation does not bring anything valuable in terms

146. Under UPA (1914), the dissociation of any partner inevitably caused the partnership to dissolve, even if the dissociation was wrongful. See Section 11.2.1(a).

of "exit rights." Moreover, exit by sale—that is, selling one's interest to another member or a third party—has serious drawbacks.

LLC statutes vary with regard to how they label cessation of membership and in how they delineate the occasions for membership to end. UPA (1997) coined the term "dissociation," and many LLC statutes follow that usage. Causes of dissociation can be divided into voluntary and involuntary, with almost all statutes:

- recognizing, with regard to voluntary dissociation, that:
  - —a member always has the *power* to dissociate by expressing the intent to do so (variously called "express will," "resignation," or "withdrawal"); but
  - —the operating agreement can constrain or eliminate the *right* to dissociate (thereby making voluntary dissociation wrongful); and
- providing some grounds for involuntary dissociation, such as:
  - —death;
  - —bankruptcy;
  - —sale of all of the member's financial rights; and
  - —expulsion:
    - — by unanimous consent upon the occurrence of specified grounds; or
    - — as provided by the operating agreement.

§15.7.2 Consequences of Dissociation ("No Exit"—At Least Economically)

Dissociation ends a person's membership, which means that the person loses all governance rights in the LLC. As to the financial rights, in the early days of LLCs many statutes followed a then-prevalent tenet of limited partnership law and provided, as a default rule, that the LLC would pay the dissociating member the reasonable value of the membership's interest.

Today, the trend is to lock in the financial rights of a dissociation member (subject, of course, to a different "deal" being made in the operating agreement).

Example

EXAMPLE

ULLCA (2013), §603(a) provides:

> If a person is dissociated as a member:
>
> (1) the person's right to participate as a member in the management and conduct of the limited liability company's activities and affairs terminates;

(2) the person's duties and obligations under section 409 as a member end with regard to matters arising and events occurring after the person's dissociation; and

(3) . . . any transferable interest owned by the person in the person's capacity as a member immediately before dissociation is owned by the person solely as a transferee. ◄◄◄

§15.7.3 Exit by Sale

Under all LLC statutes, in the default mode, a member's financial rights are freely transferable. It is therefore possible for a member to "exit" an LLC by selling its interest to another member or to a nonmember. The "hitch" is that transfer to a nonmember does not entail the transfer of any governance rights, unless the other members decide to admit the transferee as a member. ULLCA (2103) states the situation quite starkly:

> [A] transfer, in whole or in part, of a transferable interest . . . does not entitle the transferee to: (A) participate in the management or conduct of the company's activities and affairs; or (B) . . . have access to records or other information concerning the company's activities [except for very limited information rights if the LLC dissolves and winds up its activities].[147]

As detailed in Section 16.6.2, mere transferees are in a very risky position, which means that a member wishing to exit by sale must:

- accept whatever price another member might be willing to pay;
- find a person willing to invest in what is usually a closely held business[148] and persuade the other members to admit that person as a member; or
- sell at a distressed price to a nonmember willing to risk the role of a mere transferee.

Problem 120

Jeff's Real Estate, LLC ("Jeff's") is a limited liability company organized under a statute that provides templates for manager-management and member-management and requires that an LLC's certificate of formation specify one

147. ULLCA (2013) §502(a)(3).

148. For several reasons, it is more difficult to find a purchaser for an ownership interest in a closely held company than in a company whose ownership interests are publicly traded. See Daniel S. Kleinberger, "Fezzick, Are There Rocks Ahead? Navigating the Oppression Doctrine in the Age of LLCs," 22 Florida State University Business Review 15, 21–25 (2023)

of the two templates. Jeff's certificate specifies manager-management. Is it lawful for Jeff's operating agreement to allocate certain day-to-day management responsibilities to a nonmanager member? ◀ ◀ ◀

Explanation

Yes. Management templates are for the most part default rules governing the relations of the members and managers (if any) *inter se*. The operating agreement can revise or even negate these default rules.[149] ◀ ◀ ◀

Problem 121

Jacob and Youngs, LLC ("Jacob and Youngs") is a five-member, member-managed LLC. Its operating agreement states that "no member shall enter into a contract with a price of more than $25,000 without either the consent of all the members or the vote of a majority of the members at a regularly scheduled meeting of the members or at a special meeting properly held to consider the matter." The operating agreement also provides that "this agreement can be amended only with the consent of all the members."

Yesterday, Kent, one of the members of Jacob and Youngs, encountered "the opportunity of a lifetime" for the LLC and purported to commit the LLC to a contract with Allegheny College with a price of $45,000. Kent signed the contract "Jacob and Youngs, a member-managed limited liability company, by Kent, in his capacity as a member."

Today, at the members' regular weekly meeting, Kent explained the situation in detail, and all the other members voted to "authorize the contract." What is the effect of that vote on the issues of:

A. Jacob and Youngs's obligation to perform the contract?
B. Kent's liability to Allegheny College with regard to the contract?
C. Kent's liability to Jacob and Youngs with regard to the contract?
D. the $25,000 limit in the operating agreement? ◀ ◀ ◀

149. The "power to bind" analysis would be more complicated, involving both statutory apparent authority of the managers and common law agency analysis for the member.

Explanation

A. The vote makes clear that Jacob and Youngs is obligated to perform the contract. According to the operating agreement, Kent lacked the right to bind Jacob and Youngs in the matter. He might, however, have had the power to do so. The facts are insufficient to decide the power-to-bind question.

The vote clarifies matters. Under agency law principles, the vote constitutes a ratification of the contract.[150]

B. The vote protects Kent from possible liability to Allegheny College. If Kent lacked both the right and power to bind Jacob and Youngs, he would have been liable to Allegheny College for breach of an agent's warranty of authority.[151] This potential liability disappeared when the members voted to ratify the contract.[152]

C. The vote protects Kent from possible liability to Jacob and Youngs. An agent is liable to the principal for damages caused when the agent acts without authority and binds the principal. This liability disappears, however, if the principal subsequently ratifies the unauthorized act.[153]

D. The vote probably has no effect on the $25,000 limit. Although a course of conduct can amend an operating agreement unless the agreement effectively provides otherwise, a single event hardly constitutes a course of conduct. The result might be different if the vote of approval had been phrased generally—for example, referring to permitting exceptions in "exigent circumstances." ◀◀◀

Problem 122

Executive Assistance, LLC is a five-member, manager-managed LLC with a single manager, Lynette, who is also a member. The LLC's business consists of providing temporary workers to perform high-level administrative functions for various clients. Melissa, a nonmanaging member, decides that she wants to open her own business, providing temporary workers to perform lower-level clerical services. Under a typical LLC statute, must she first obtain the LLC's consent? ◀◀◀

150. See Section 2.7.

151. See Section 4.2.2.

152. As a matter of agency law, he is not liable on a contract he signed on behalf of a disclosed principal. See Section 4.2.1. As a matter of LLC law, his status as a member does not make him liable for the LLC's contractual obligation. See Section 14.4.1.

153. See Sections 4.1.2 (discussing an agent's liability for acting without authority) and 2.7.1 (explaining the effect of ratification on that liability).

Explanation

The answer is no, assuming that: (i) Melissa does not use any confidential information belonging to the LLC; and (ii) the LLC's operating agreement contains no relevant restrictions. Given those assumptions, the only relevant constraint is the fiduciary duty of loyalty, with the relevant doctrine being "usurpation of a company opportunity." However, the typical LLC statute negates any fiduciary duties for nonmanaging members of a manager-managed LLC. ◀◀◀

Problem 123

Shrek and Donkey form a member-managed limited liability company, which they name Onion-Parfait Company, LLC ("OPC"), to do land development within a large swamp. They plan to: buy individual parcels of land; build a house on each purchased parcel; and then sell each parcel-with-house to a customer. The relevant LLC statute does not require a written operating agreement, and Shrek and Donkey do not have any written agreement concerning OPC. However, they do orally agree to proceed conservatively and, in particular, never to buy a parcel of land without having first arranged to have a customer committed to buy the land upon completion of a house.

One day, while traveling around the swamp for pleasure (i.e., not on OPC business), Donkey comes upon a public auction of a parcel of land zoned solely for commercial development.[154] Donkey purchases the land for himself at an excellent price, and one month later sells the land for a substantial profit. Must Donkey account to OPC for the profit? ◀◀◀

Explanation

Probably not. The facts strongly suggest that Donkey and Shrek intended their business to be limited to residential development, which argues against characterizing a commercially zoned parcel as a company opportunity. The oral agreement between Donkey and Shrek likewise suggests that OPC's agreed business methodology excludes OPC from opportunities based on purchases made "on spec"—that is, without a confirmed re-purchaser.

On the other hand, OPC could argue that: (i) commercial land development is connected closely enough with residential development as to constitute a diversification or expansion opportunity for OPC; and (ii) the oral agreement could be changed or waived by the members.[155]

154. Readers who have trouble with the notion of zoning within a fairy-tale swamp should remember that "a willing suspension of disbelief" is sometimes essential to handling law school hypotheticals.

155. As a practical matter, it would be Shrek who might want to assert this position. However, as a legal matter, the claim belongs to OPC. See Section 16.4 (derivative claims).

Donkey might respond *inter alia* that, because the land was being auctioned when he first learned of it: (i) there was no time to obtain a change in the oral agreement; and, therefore, (ii) the land purchase could not become a company opportunity.

The ultimate resolution of this matter would depend on:

- how broadly the law of OPC's state of organization applies the "company opportunity" doctrine;[156] and
- on other facts not stated in the Problem, such as OPC's financial ability to undertake "on spec" investments and the extent to which the business expertise involved in residential development overlaps the business expertise necessary for investments in commercial land. ◀◀◀

Problem 124

Roundhead, LLC ("Roundhead"), is a manager-managed limited liability company organized under an LLC statute that negates any power-to-bind of a nonmanaging member of a manager-managed LLC. Cromwell is the LLC's sole manager. Cromwell wants the LLC to rent a luxury box at the arena that houses the local professional basketball team. Busy with other matters, Cromwell asks Charles, a nonmanaging member, to reserve the box. Charles does so in his own name, using his personal credit card and expecting to be reimbursed. Is Roundhead bound? ◀◀◀

Explanation

Yes, although Charles had no power to bind Roundhead in his capacity as a member, he was acting as the agent for an undisclosed principal.[157] (As sole manager of the LLC, Cromwell certainly had the authority to establish an agency relationship between Roundhead and Charles.) ◀◀◀

Problem 125

Same facts as in Problem 124, plus the LLC statute provides that "a person who is a member of a limited liability company in which management is vested in one or more managers, and who is not a manager, shall have no

156. The duty of loyalty is an "internal affair." See Section 15.4.1.
157. See Section 2.2.3.

duties to the limited liability company or to the other members solely by reason of acting in his or her capacity as a member." After reserving the luxury box, Charles declines to sign it over to Roundhead. Does the quoted statutory language protect Charles from a claim by Roundhead? ◀ ◀ ◀

Explanation

No. Roundhead's claim is for Charles's breach of his duties as an agent[158] and not "solely by reason of acting in his or her capacity as a member." ◀ ◀ ◀

Problem 126

SansCulottes LLC ("SansCulottes"), is a limited liability company organized under a "two-template" LLC statute with a typical "statutory apparent authority" provision. Five years ago, when SansCulottes was organized, its articles of organization described it as member-managed. Until last month: (i) SansCulottes remained member-managed; and (ii) Toscin, one of its members, routinely purchased supplies for SansCulottes from Vendor. Toscin signed each purchase agreement "SansCulottes, LLC, by Toscin, one of its members."

Last month, the members of SansCulottes decided to restructure SansCulottes into a manager-managed LLC. They amended SansCulottes' articles of organization to reflect the change and then appointed Robespierre, a nonmember, as sole manager. Robespierre immediately directed Toscin to make no further purchases from Vendor on behalf of SansCulottes.

Nonetheless, last week Toscin purported to commit SansCulottes to another purchase from Vendor. Assuming that the nature of the transaction and purchase price were in line with previous transactions entered into by Toscin with Vendor on behalf of SansCulottes, may Vendor hold SansCulottes to the commitment? ◀ ◀ ◀

158. See Sections 4.1.1 (duty of loyalty) and 4.1.3 (duty to obey instructions).

EXPLANATION

Explanation

Yes. The restructuring and Robespierre's directive deprived Toscin of actual authority, and the LLC statute will negate Toscin's statutory apparent authority.[159] However, Toscin retains the power to bind SansCulottes under the agency law doctrine of "lingering apparent authority."[160] ◀ ◀ ◀

Problem 127

Which, if any, of the following statements is true *inter se* the members of a limited liability company?

A. A member's economic rights are freely transferable.
B. A member's governance rights are freely transferable.
C. Neither the governance nor economic rights of a member are freely transferable.
D. A membership's ownership rights are bifurcated into financial and governance rights.
E. In a manager-managed LLC, the power of a managing member to transfer governance rights to a nonmember is more restricted than the power of a nonmanaging member to transfer governance rights to a nonmember.

EXPLANATION

Explanation

All the listed matters are subject to change by the operating agreement, so without knowing the contents of the operating agreement, it is impossible to determine the truth or falsity of any of the statements.[161] ◀ ◀ ◀

159. Per the typical statute of this type, the negation occurs even if Vendor is unaware of the amendment to SansCulottes' articles of organization.
160. See Section 2.3.7.
161. If this Problem were revised to assume that the operating agreement contains no relevant provisions, then statements A and D would be true. Statement E might be intuitively appealing, but it is nonetheless false; following the partnership model, in the default mode LLC statutes prohibit the transfer of any governance rights to a nonmember, no matter how comparatively minor those rights might be.

Problem 128

One of the founding members of a three-person member-managed limited liability company dies, and, under the decedent's will, her interest in the limited liability company "passes in its entirety with all rights and privileges thereunto pertaining" to the widower. Assuming the operating agreement is silent both on the widower's rights in the limited liability company and on the requisites for amending the operating agreement:

A. Is the widower's consent required to amend the operating agreement?
B. How are the widower's rights to profits, losses, and distributions calculated? ◀◀◀

Explanation

EXPLANATION

A. The widower's consent is not necessary. Under all LLC statutes, absent a contrary agreement, amending the operating agreement requires the unanimous consent of the members. The widower is a mere transferee or assignee of a dissociated member; he cannot become a member without the consent of the remaining two members.

B. Under most LLC statutes, the widower is, in essence, a transferee of the decedent's economic rights. Therefore, his rights to profits, losses, and distributions are equal to whatever her rights were.[162] ◀◀◀

162. See Section 16.6.2 for a discussion of the difficult issues that arise if the members subsequently attempt to amend the operating agreement to the widower's prejudice or otherwise impair his economic rights.

CHAPTER 16

Consequences of the Churkendoose: Unique Issues of LLC Law

§16.1 THE PROPER METAPHOR: HYBRID, CHURKENDOOSE, RECOMBINANT ENTITY

In 2007, Tsinghua University in Beijing, China, convened the 21st Century Commercial Law Forum, Seventh International Symposium, around the topic "Non-Incorporated Enterprises." The keynote address discussed "Two Decades of 'Alternative Entities'" and a later-delivered paper focused on "The LLC as Recombinant Entity":

> It is conventional wisdom that U.S. "limited liability companies are a conceptual hybrid, sharing some of the characteristics of partnerships and some of corporations." A more accurate description is that an LLC combines attributes of four different types of business organizations: general partnerships, limited partnerships, corporations, and closely held corporations.
>
> From partnership law comes the "pick your partner" principle and the bifurcation of ownership interests into financial and governance rights. From corporate law comes the "liability shield"—i.e., the conceptual "non-conductor" that protects owners from automatic liability for the debts of the enterprise. From the example of general partnerships comes the notion of management by owners as owners, which has been the blueprint for the "member-managed" LLC. From the example of limited partnerships comes the centralized management structure that has been the blueprint for "manager-managed" LLCs. From the concept of the "close corporation" comes the perspective for understanding the "lock in" problem that exists when the "pick your partner" principle overlaps with "perpetual duration." To this mixture, the "check the box"

regulations have added permission for a flexibility and variability of structure unprecedented in the U.S. law of business entities.

Thus, by connotation at least, the word "hybrid" understates the multifaceted and almost plastic nature of limited liability companies. Those who invented and developed LLC statutes have done more than graft the branch of one entity to the stalk of another. They have been gene splicing, and the adjective "recombinant" is more apt than "hybrid."[1]

A competing metaphor might be "churckendoose," which, according to a children's book published in 1946, is a multisourced hybrid, "part chicken, turkey, duck, and goose."[2] But whatever the imagery, the multilateral origins of the LLC raise a set of fundamental and closely related analytic questions:

- Is the LLC of interest in its own right? Do its multisourced characteristics constitute a whole that is somehow of interest as more than the aggregate of its parts?
- or
- Are all so-called LLC issues merely "borrowed issues," to be prosaically resolved by reference to some other jurisprudence?

One LLC treatise suggests that the answers to these questions are, respectively, no, no, yes:

> [LLC] . . . statutes . . . contain little that is truly new. Almost all their provisions are derived from either partnership law or corporate law, and in some instances, the copying has been virtually verbatim.
>
> These partnership and corporate law antecedents should inform the construction of [LLC] statutes, which in turn should be interpreted in light of their origins. Statutory interpretation is essentially a search for legislative purpose, and given the largely derivative nature of [LLC] statutes, the relevant purpose may well be the purpose underlying a particular provision of partnership or corporate law. Therefore, when a court seeks to interpret or fill a gap in a particular provision of an [LLC] statute, the court should make reference to the body of law that gave rise to that particular provision. Corporate law precedent should inform the interpretation of provisions drawn from corporate law, and partnership law precedent should inform the interpretations of provisions drawn from partnership law.[3]

1. Daniel S. Kleinberger, "The LLC as Recombinant Entity—Revisiting Fundamental Questions through the LLC Lens," paper delivered at the 21st Century Commercial Law Forum—Seventh International Symposium 2007 (Beijing, China) published in the United States, 14 FORDHAM J. CORP. & FIN. L. 473 (2009).
2. Ben Ross Berenberg, THE CHURKENDOOSE (Wonder Books, 1946).
3. BISHOP & KLEINBERGER ON LIMITED LIABILITY COMPANIES § 5:8.

It is undeniable that many LLC decisions rely heavily on analogy, especially with regard to claims of "piercing the veil"[4] and claims of oppression.[5] However, it is equally true that LLC law has some unique issues of its own, which require careful analysis and should comprise a separate jurisprudence.

In particular:

- As a legal construct, the limited liability company is a "shape shifter"—sometimes treated as a legal person separate from its owners and sometimes regarded as a contract among and encompassing its members. This "dual-status" situation is more than the old "entity-aggregate" debate from the 1914 Uniform Partnership Act,[6] because:
  —according to all LLC statutes, the LLC is emphatically an entity separate from its owners; but
  —under all LLC statutes, the LLC is an *incomplete* entity—as will be seen, the "pick your partner" principle is inconsistent with the separate entity concept.

This internal inconsistency:

- is fundamental to the limited liability company both theoretically and practically; and
- gives rise to numerous issues that are:

4. The typical piercing claim seeks to disregard the legal separateness of an entity from its owners in order to hold the owners liable for the entity's debts. The picturesque label refers to putting a huge hole in the owners' liability shield, i.e., piercing the "veil" of separation. As the U.S. Supreme Court explained 100 years ago, "[a] leading purpose of [the liability shield] is to interpose a nonconductor, through which . . . it is impossible to see the men behind." *Donnell v. Herring-Hall-Marvin Safe Co.*, 208 U.S. 267, 273 (1908). The piercing doctrine originated in the corporate context and sometimes goes under the name of the "alter ego" or "instrumentality" doctrine. Piercing analysis varies from state to state in its particulars, but has an essential structure regardless of jurisdiction: (1) Piercing becomes relevant when the entity cannot pay its debts. (2) The entity's insolvency is never by itself sufficient grounds to pierce, nor is the plight *simpliciter* of the entity's creditors. (3) Piercing is warranted when the circumstances involve an abuse of the entity form by a dominant owner, where the abuse: (i) constitutes or at least approaches fraud or injustice; and (ii) involves both formal and economic disregard of the supposed separateness of entity from owner. (4) A factor test is used to assess the issues of improper dominance and disregard of separateness. Although each state has its own list of factors, the key factors always include in some form or other: (i) disregard of corporate formalities (e.g., failing to keep proper corporate records, ignoring corporate governance structures, such as meetings of directors and of shareholders); (ii) disregard of the entity's economic separateness (e.g., using entity assets for personal purposes, commingling of entity and personal funds, failing to keep separate business records for the entity); (iii) undercapitalization; and (iv) siphoning of funds out of the entity (e.g., by paying owners excessive salaries or paying dividends that leave the entity underfunded or even insolvent).

5. See Section 15.4.3.

6. See Section 7.2.7.

— LLC-specific; or if not
— are far more clearly revealed in the context of LLCs than in regard to other business organizations.

These issues include the following, which will be discussed in this chapter:

- From the contract versus entity question:
  — the supposed heresy of corpufuscation;
  — the quandary of how the LLC relates to the operating agreement;
  — the relationship of the direct/derivative distinction to claimed breaches of the operating agreement; and
  — the radicalization of contract law
- From the incomplete entity question:
  — the plight of bare naked assignee;
  — the classification of LLCs for the purpose of federal diversity jurisdiction; and
  — the effect under bankruptcy law of the bankruptcy of an LLC member.[7]

§16.2 THE SUPPOSED HERESY OF CORPUFUSCATION

"Corpufuscation" is a neologism. The term reflects the disdain expressed by some leading partnership law practitioners for what they see as the creeping corporatization of the limited liability company.[8] Such practitioners "are steeped in the practice, philosophy and law of partnerships."[9] To them, the LLC is essentially and fundamentally an *unincorporated organization*, that is, like a partnership and therefore *not* like a corporation. "They view the LLC entity mostly as a necessary evil for maintaining the liability shield," and perhaps also for obtaining perpetual duration.[10] Adding other "corporate-like" characteristics smacks of heresy, or at least of "conceptual miscegenation."[11]

The "corpufuscation" issue has influenced the question of "shelf LLCs"[12] and the question of whether an LLC should or can be a party to

7. As will be seen in Section 16.7.2, this issue also pertains to the contract versus entity question.
8. Daniel S. Kleinberger, "The Closely Held Business Through the Entity-Aggregate Prism," 40 Wake Forest L. Rev. 827, 872 (2005).
9. *Id.*
10. *Id.*
11. *Id.*
12. See Section 14.3.

the operating agreement.[13] The viewpoint is losing strength, however, in the face of practical realities, the tendencies of judges to analogize to corporate law, and cases such as *ConnectU LLC v. Zuckerberg*, which eschewed any philosophical inquiry into the "shelf" question and held, almost cavalierly, that "[t]here is no need to engage in such circumlocution; there simply is no requirement under Delaware law that there be members of an LLC at formation."[14]

§16.3 THE RELATIONSHIP OF THE LLC TO ITS OPERATING AGREEMENT

Although "the LLC comes into existence as an entity separate from its members and at least *ab initio* is a stranger to the operating agreement," as a practical matter "the member's operating agreement should govern and be enforceable by the LLC."[15]

Because the LLC is a separate juridic person, LLC statutes could certainly make the LLC *ipso facto* party to the operating agreement or at least expressly empower the LLC to become party. However, to date no LLC statute has taken either approach.

For example, ULLCA (2006 and 2013) both fudge the question; each states: "A limited liability company is bound by and may enforce the operating agreement, whether or not the company has itself manifested assent to the operating agreement."[16]

The Delaware statute is even more complex. The statute's definition of "limited liability company agreement" states the following rules: "A limited liability company is not required to execute its limited liability company agreement. A limited liability company is bound by its limited liability company agreement whether or not the limited liability company executes the limited liability company agreement."[17]

The Delaware language omits a category of situations: those in which the LLC has not executed the operating agreement but seeks to enforce it.

---

13. See Section 16.3.

14. *ConnectU LLC v. Zuckerberg*, 482 F. Supp.2d 3, 21 (D. Mass. 2007) (holding that because the LLC at issue was, in fact, formed without having a member upon formation, the LLC was "stateless" at the relevant moment for determining diversity jurisdiction and therefore complete diversity did not exist), reversed on other grounds, 522 F.3d 82 (1st Cir. 2008). For further discussion of "shelf" LLCs, i.e., limited liability companies without any members, see Section 14.3. For an explanation of diversity jurisdiction, see Section 16.7.1.

15. Daniel S. Kleinberger, "The Closely Held Business Through the Entity-Aggregate Prism," 40 Wake Forest L. Rev. 827, 869 (2005).

16. ULLCA (2013) §106(a); ULLCA (2006) §111(a).

17. Del. Code Ann. tit. 6, §18–101(7).

Example

Under the operating agreement of a Delaware LLC, a member is obligated to contribute $50,000 next Friday. When the deadline passes and the member repudiates the obligation without justification, the logical plaintiff is the LLC. The contribution was promised to the LLC, and the benefit of the promise will inure directly to the LLC, not to any of the members. However, if the LLC itself has not executed the LLC agreement, the defaulting member might plausibly contend that the LLC, as a nonparty, lacks standing to bring the claim. (On the other hand, the LLC might well have to assert standing as an intended third-party beneficiary of the operating agreement.) ◄◄◄

Example

The above situation becomes even more problematic if, before the member fails to make the promised contribution, the LLC fails without justification to make a promised distribution to the member. Suppose the member subsequently declines to make the promised contribution when due and sues the LLC for nonperformance of the distribution obligation. Does the LLC have standing to assert the contribution obligation as a set-off, other than through a third-party beneficiary claim?[18] ◄◄◄

The statutory skittishness on this issue is difficult to explain without reference to the contract-entity question. Practically, "LLC as party" makes so much sense. Conceptually, the idea is discordant:

> Although as a matter of form, an LLC cannot exist *de jure* without having filed articles of organization, as a matter of both concept and practice, the operating agreement is the foundational document. Indeed, given the expansive language most LLC statutes use to describe the operating agreement, the formation of an LLC concomitantly and inevitably brings an operating agreement into existence.[19]

Given this view of LLC formation, it is difficult for statute drafters and practitioners to think of the LLC as being a party to the operating agreement. Thinking that way is like imagining "a snake swallowing its tail."[20]

---

18. As to the merits, the member might contend that the contribution obligation, being subsequent, is a dependent promise; i.e., not due until the distribution promise is performed. The standing question is conceptually separate, however, and, moreover, prior as a matter of civil procedure. That is, if the LLC lacks standing to sue for the promised contribution, the member will have no need or occasion to raise the question of dependent promises.
19. Daniel S. Kleinberger, "The Closely Held Business Through the Entity-Aggregate Prism," 40 Wake Forest L. Rev. 827, 871 (2005) (footnotes omitted).
20. *Id.* at 872.

If the LLC were seen as fundamentally an entity, the difficulty would disappear. For example, close corporations commonly have shareholder agreements, and it is a nonissue to make the corporation itself a party. However, "everyone knows" that a corporation exists as an entity before it has shareholders. Indeed, in a formal sense, each of the corporation's initial shareholders becomes a shareholder through a transaction with the corporation. However important a shareholder agreement may be, it "is not foundational."[21]

§16.4 THE RELATIONSHIP OF THE DIRECT/DERIVATIVE DISTINCTION TO CLAIMED BREACHES OF THE OPERATING AGREEMENT

From the ordinary contract law perspective, it seems almost axiomatic—a "no-brainer"—that a party to a contract has standing to sue when the contract is breached. However, in the LLC context, the entity nature of the LLC injects a major limitation to that axiom. The limitation involves the distinction between direct and derivative claims, which, although corporate in origin, is more generally "a separate entity characteristic."[22]

To understand the relationship between, on the one hand, a member's standing to enforce the operating agreement and, on the other hand, the direct/derivative distinction, it is necessary to first understand the distinction itself.

An LLC member sues directly to remedy a damage suffered directly by the member. In contrast:

> [An LLC member] asserts a derivative claim to vindicate the rights of the [LLC]. A wrongful act has depleted or devalued [company] assets or has undercut the [company] business. The [member] has suffered harm only indirectly, as a consequence of damage done to the [limited liability company]. The wrongful conduct relates to the [member] only through the medium of the [company], by reducing the value of the [owner's membership interest]. For example, when those in control of the [company] act negligently, or waste or misappropriate company assets, it is the [LLC], not the [member], that first suffers the loss. Likewise, if a [manager of an LLC] takes for him or herself a business opportunity that properly belongs to the [LLC], it is the [LLC], not the [member], that has lost the opportunity and any attendant profits.

21. *Id.*

22. Daniel S. Kleinberger, "Direct Versus Derivative and the Law of Limited Liability Companies," 58 Baylor L. Rev. 63, 68 (2006).

> In essence, a derivative plaintiff seeks to derive standing from the injury to the [entity] and to represent the [entity]'s interests in the derivative lawsuit. In ordinary circumstances, "[w]hether or not a [entity] shall seek to enforce in the courts a cause of action for damages is, like other business questions, ordinarily a matter of internal management and is left to the discretion of [those managing the entity]."
>
> A derivative lawsuit, therefore, necessarily impugns the management of the [entity] and inevitably involves two distinct fights. One fight concerns the underlying transaction or conduct, which is alleged to have caused some harm or breached some duty to the [entity]. The other fight concerns who will control the [entity] for the limited purpose of seeking a remedy for the alleged misconduct.
>
> The typical derivative suit alleges that, with regard to the underlying transaction, [those managing the entity] have acted improperly.[23]

With the above explanation in view, it is possible to understand how a member might lack standing to sue *directly* for breach of the operating agreement. To sue directly, a person must have suffered harm directly.[24] For example, if provisions of the operating agreement express management duties of managers or managing members, a breach of those provisions will cause harm first to the LLC.

Example

Raheli, LLC is a manager-managed LLC, whose operating agreement appoints Eli as sole manager and requires him to "exercise in all efforts on behalf of the company, and in all matters pertaining to his managerial responsibilities, the care that an ordinarily prudent person would exercise in like circumstances." If Eli were to carelessly forget to maintain fire insurance on the company warehouse and a fire were to destroy 90 percent of the company's inventory, the value of the members' investment would certainly be affected. However, the injury would be first to the assets of the company; the claim would therefore be derivative. ◀ ◀ ◀

---

23. Daniel S. Kleinberger & Imanta Bergmanis, "Direct vs. Derivative, or 'What's a Lawsuit Between Friends in an "Incorporated Partnership"?' " 22 Wm. Mitchell L. Rev. 1203, 1214–15 (1996) (footnotes omitted). For a more detailed and comprehensive discussion of this Section's topic, see Daniel S. Kleinberger, "Direct Versus Derivative and the Law of Limited Liability Companies," 58 Baylor L. Rev. 63 (2006) and Daniel S. Kleinberger, "The Direct-Derivative Distinction, the Special Litigation Committee, and the Uniform Act: A Response to Professor Weidner," 77 Business Lawyer 433 (2022).

24. This "direct harm" approach is the predominant method for distinguishing between direct and derivative claims, but two others exist: the special injury approach and the duty owed approach. Also, some states have adopted an ALI approach that blurs the distinction as to closely held businesses. For a discussion and critique of the alternative approaches, see Daniel S. Kleinberger, "Direct Versus Derivative and the Law of Limited Liability Companies," 58 Baylor L. Rev. 63, 93–114 (2006) (discussing the special injury approach, the duty owed approach, and the ALI approach).

EXAMPLE

Example

Gililan, LLC is a manager-managed LLC, whose operating agreement appoints Ilan, one of its members, as sole manager. The operating agreement also creates a class of memberships ("the preferred interests") whose owners have the right to a specified distribution whenever specified financial conditions are met. On two occasions, the specified conditions are met, but Ilan declines to make the distributions. A member holding a preferred interest brings suit against the LLC and Ilan (who, as a member, is a party to the operating agreement). The claim is direct; the failure to pay the promised distribution hurts the entitled members directly, not through the medium of the LLC. ◀◀◀

Following the example of ULPA (2001),[25] both ULLCA (2006 and 2013) codify the direct harm approach to the direct/derivative distinction. ULLCA (2013) §901(b) provides: "A member maintaining a direct action under this section must plead and prove an actual or threatened injury that is not solely the result of an injury suffered or threatened to be suffered by the limited liability company." ULLCA (2006) §901 is identical. As to breaches of the operating agreement, a member's standing "to enforce the member's rights and otherwise protect the member's interests, including rights and interests under the operating agreement" is "[s]ubject to subsection (b)."[26]

CASE IN POINT

Case in Point—*El Paso Pipeline GP Co., L.L.C. v. Brinckerhoff*

As noted above, the ULC first used a limited partnership act, ULPA (2001), to codify the direct/derivative distinction and to explain how the distinction limits a partner's standing to bring a claim for breach of a partnership agreement. Delaware Supreme Court has also used the limited partnership context to note the distinction and the distinction's effect on partner standing.

In *Brinckerhoff*, a limited partner alleged a breach of the limited partnership agreement ("LPA") and argued that as a party to agreement, it had standing to sue directly. The Court rejected the argument:

> [A person's] status as a limited partner and party to the LPA [does not] enable him to litigate directly every claim arising from the LPA. Such a rule would essentially abrogate *Tooley* [a Delaware case that recognized the direct harm test for distinguishing direct and derivative claims] with respect to alternative entities merely because they are creatures of contract. Limited partnerships are governed by their partnership agreements and by the Delaware Revised Uniform Limited Partnership Act (the "DRULPA"). The partnership agreement

---

25. ULPA (2001) §1001(b).

26. ULLCA (2013) §901(a). ULLCA (2006) §901(a) has "otherwise" immediately before "protect," but is otherwise identical.

> sets forth the rights and duties owed by the partners. . . . The reality that limited partnership agreements often govern the territory that in corporate law is covered by equitable principles of fiduciary duties does not make all provisions of a limited partnership agreement enforceable by a direct claim.[27]

§16.5 THE RADICALIZATION OF CONTRACT LAW

It is axiomatic in LLC jurisprudence that the limited liability company is "a creature of contract." As if to underline this notion, ULLCA (2006)'s official Comments state the point twice, first noting that "[a] limited liability company is as much a creature of contract as of statute,"[28] and then reiterating that "[a] limited liability company is a creature of contract as well as a creature of statute."[29]

The point is also a cornerstone of Delaware law, as reflected forcefully in a 2008 letter decision from the Chancellor of the Delaware Chancery Court: "[L]imited liability companies are creatures of contract, designed to afford the maximum amount of freedom of contract, private ordering and flexibility to the parties involved. *To the extent defendants intend to argue otherwise, plaintiff need not offer a rebuttal.*"[30]

If the LLC is a creature of contract, it should follow that LLC law is at least consonant with contract law.[31] But in several ways, LLC law has ignored or overturned fundamental precepts of contract law. For example, all LLC statutes now recognize the oxymoronic notion of an operating agreement

27. *El Paso Pipeline GP Co., L.L.C. v. Brinckerhoff*, No. 103, 2016, 2016 WL 7380418 *9 (Del. Dec. 20, 2016) had created two wholly owned subsidiaries as acquisition vehicles. Applying *Tooley*, the Chancery Court had characterized the parent's claims as derivative, since the collapse of the acquisition financing first harmed the subsidiaries. The Supreme Court reversed, stating: "*Tooley* and its progeny do not, and were never intended to, subject commercial contract actions to a derivative suit requirement." Id. 179. "[A] suit by a party to a commercial contract to enforce its own contractual rights is not a derivative action under Delaware law." Id. at 182.

28. ULLCA (2006) §110, cmt. The same language appears in the Prefatory Note to ULLCA (2013), in the part captioned "Role and Inevitability of Operating Agreement."

29. ULLCA 2006) §112(d), cmt.

30. *TravelCenters of America, LLC v. Brog*, No. 3516-CC, 2008 WL 1746987 (Del. Ch. Apr. 3, 2008) (footnote and internal quotations omitted; emphasis added).

31. B.M. Gottesman & S.E. Swenson, "More Than Bargained For? Topics for Consideration in the Issuance and Acceptance of Delaware LLC Opinions," 81 N.Y. St. B.J. 20, 22 (2009) (stating that when an attorney is asked for a formal legal opinion pertaining to a Delaware limited liability company, "[i]t is . . . the responsibility of the opinion-giver to navigate Delaware common law [especially contract law] prior to rendering a Delaware LLC opinion, and to keep abreast of its shifting landscape"), quoted in Daniel S. Kleinberger, "Don't Dabble in Delaware," BUSINESS LAW TODAY (July 2017).

"among" the sole member of a single member LLC. Although this approach is in part a result of "path dependence,"[32] it also stems from trying to conceptualize a single member LLC as a contractual relationship.

The distortion of contract concepts generally is most advanced in Delaware law, where fundamental precepts of contract law are set aside under the banner of giving "maximum effect" to "freedom of contract."[33] For example, since its inception the Delaware LLC Act has repudiated contract law's traditional antipathy toward penalties. For "[r]emedies for breach of limited liability company agreement by member," the Act proclaims:

> A limited liability company agreement may provide that:
>
> (1) A member who fails to perform in accordance with, or to comply with the terms and conditions of, the limited liability company agreement shall be subject to specified *penalties* or specified consequences; and
>
> (2) At the time or upon the happening of events specified in the limited liability company agreement, a member shall be subject to specified *penalties* or specified consequences.
>
> Such specified penalties or specified consequences may include and take the form of any penalty or consequence set forth in §18–502(c) of this title [which includes, in the event of a member breaching a promise to make a contribution, "*forfeiture* of the defaulting member's limited liability company interest"].[34]

Even more fundamentally, under Section 18–1101(c) of the Delaware LLC statute, an operating agreement has the power not only to restrict but even to *eliminate* fiduciary duty:

> To the extent that, at law or in equity, a member or manager or other person has duties (*including fiduciary duties*) to a limited liability company or to another member or manager or to another person that is a party to or is otherwise bound by a limited liability company agreement, the member's or manager's or other person's duties may be expanded or restricted or *eliminated* by provisions in the limited liability company agreement. . . .[35]

32. See section 14.5.3.

33. But see Daniel S. Kleinberger, Fezzik, Are There Rocks Ahead? Navigating the Oppression Doctrine in the Age of LLCs, 22 Fla. St. U. Bus. Rev. 15, 62–67 (2023) (discussing and explaining "the minimum effect of 'maximum effect' ").

34. Del. Code Ann., tit. 6, §18–306 (emphasis added). Section 18–405 has a comparable provision applicable to managers.

35. Del. Code Ann., tit. 6, §18–1101(c). For further discussion of this issue, see Section 15.4.7. For a discussion of whether Delaware's approach toward fiduciary duty has affected the law in other jurisdictions, see Daniel S. Kleinberger, Fezzik, Are There Rocks Ahead? Navigating the Oppression Doctrine in the Age of Llcs, 22 Fla. St. U. Bus. Rev. 15, 66–68 (2023).

§16.6 THE LLC AS AN INCOMPLETE ENTITY; THE PLIGHT OF THE BARE NAKED ASSIGNEE

§16.6.1 Complete Separation of Entity and Owners: Protection for Assignees of Financial Rights

In an entity that is completely separate from its owners, the entity has no stake in the identity of its owners. A change in ownership does not imperil the continuity of the entity, and the entity statute does not restrict transferability of ownership interests. If the owners wish to restrict transferability, they may do so by contract. However, their contract-based restrictions will have to be carefully drafted and will be narrowly interpreted by courts if challenged.[36]

The modern corporation is an entity completely separate from its owners. Moreover, because stock inextricably connects financial rights to at least some governance rights, either:

- the transferee of a shareholder's financial rights will directly have some governance rights (and therefore standing as a shareholder to bring suit if the financial rights are unjustly affected by those in control of the corporation); or
- the original transferor will still be a shareholder and available (and perhaps contractually obligated) to protect the transferee's rights.

Example

The articles of incorporation of XYZ, Inc. provide for two classes of stock: ordinary, "common" stock, with distribution rights and the right to vote for directors and on major organic transactions (e.g., mergers);[37] and

36. See Daniel S. Kleinberger, "The Closely Held Business Through the Entity-Aggregate Prism," 40 Wake Forest L. Rev. 827, 863 (2005) (discussing the view of courts that such restrictions constitute restraints on alienation); see also 12 Fletcher Cyc. Corp. §5455 (stating that "[c]ourts applying common law principles have held that transfer restrictions constitute restraints on alienation and should be strictly construed") and G. Van Ingen, "Construction and application of provisions of articles, bylaws, statutes, or agreements restricting alienation or transfer of corporate stock," 2 ALR2d 745 (stating that stock transfer restrictions "are regarded with disfavor and are strictly construed").

37. A merger is an "organic" change, authorized by statute, through which two or more organizations combine into a single organization, with all of the rights and obligations of the "constituent" organizations becoming "by operation of law" those of the "surviving" organization. The surviving organization might be one of the original, constituent organizations. Or, the surviving organization might be created as part of the merger, with *all* the

nonvoting preferred stock, whose owners receive a preferential return but have no voting rights. Peter, who owns 500 shares of each class of stock, sells 100 shares of nonvoting preferred to Caspian. The corporation subsequently proposes to enter into a merger that will unjustifiably expropriate most of the value of the preferred stock. As a shareholder, Caspian has standing to seek a judicial remedy. ◄◄◄

Example

In a separate transaction, Peter borrows $50,000 from Lucy. In addition to promising to repay the amount with interest, he: (i) pledges 250 shares of his nonvoting, preferred stock to her as collateral; and (ii) assigns to her all his distributions from those shares until the loan is repaid. The loan agreement between Peter and Lucy obligates Peter to use his status as a shareholder to "at all times protect Lucy's interests under this contract." In addition, as required by the loan agreement, Peter appoints Lucy as his irrevocable proxy and "attorney in fact" to exercise his rights as a shareholder until the loan is repaid.[38] When the above-described merger is announced, Lucy can use Peter's status as a shareholder to take action to protect her economic rights. ◄◄◄

§16.6.2 Incomplete Separateness and the Risk to the Bare Naked Assignee

With an LLC, the situation is fundamentally different; the limited liability company is an entity only *incompletely* separate from its owners. Built-in statutory transfer restrictions provide a default template under which economic rights are freely transferable, but transferees do not acquire even limited governance rights, let alone become owners.

To accommodate this codified "pick your partner" approach, LLC ownership is conceptually bifurcated; a person can own financial rights without owning any governance rights. Indeed, if the original owner of the financial rights dissociates, the financial rights are completely "naked."

---

constituent organizations ceasing to exist when the merger takes effect. The "plan of merger" must *inter alia* provide for the compensation of owners of a non-surviving entity, because their ownership interests disappear when the entity ceases to exist. The compensation can be: ownership interests in the surviving entity; cash; other consideration (e.g., bonds); or some combination.

38. For a discussion of this type of "ersatz" agency, see Section 6.2.

Under LLC law, "bare naked assignees" face a substantial risk of abuse by LLC members. The term somewhat fancifully describes the situation in which:

- a person who is not a member owns financial rights as a transferee (a "naked transferee"); and
- the member to whom those rights originally pertained:
  - — has dissociated; and therefore
  - — is no longer a member; and therefore
  - — is incapable of protecting the transferee's financial rights even if the transfer contract so provided.[39]

Owning economic rights without any corresponding governance rights means:

- having no right to any say in any company decision:
  - — no matter how significant the decision is; and
  - — no matter how directly (and even exclusively) the decision might affect the financial rights;
- having no rights to information about the company, except in the unusual event of the company dissolving, and even then information access is quite limited; and
- having no standing to seek judicial intervention, either directly or on behalf of the company, because:
  - — under LLC law, "mere financial rights" do not constitute ownership; and
  - — LLC statutes expressly limit standing for judicial intervention to members.[40]

---

39. The term "bare naked assignee" was first used, albeit colloquially, during the drafting process for the Uniform Limited Partnership Act (2001). The decision to provide for perpetual duration and to attenuate the nexus between general partner dissociation and entity dissolution raised the same issues described in the text. See ULPA (2001), July 1999 Draft, §101(1) (stating that "[b]are transferable interest" means a transferable interest whose original owner is no longer a partner) and Reporter's Notes (stating that "[t]his draft gives owners of bare transferable interests very limited rights to information about the limited partnership"). See also Daniel S. Kleinberger, "The Plight of the Bare Naked Assignee," XLII SUFFOLK L. REV. 587 (2009).

40. Almost paradoxically, the Delaware LLC statute is an exception to this general statement. See Del. Code Ann., tit. 6, §18–1002 (permitting assignees to bring derivative claims).

UNIFORM ACT ON POINT

Uniform Act on Point — ULLCA (2013) §107(b)

The obligations of a limited liability company and its members to a person in the person's capacity as a transferee or a person dissociated as a member are governed by the operating agreement. . . . [A]n amendment to the operating agreement made after a person becomes a transferee or is dissociated as a member: (1) is effective with regard to any debt, obligation, or other liability of the limited liability company or its members to the person in the person's capacity as a transferee or person dissociated as a member; and (2) is not effective to the extent the amendment imposes a new debt, obligation, or other liability on the transferee or person dissociated as a member.

§16.6.3 A Problem Both Old and New

a. The Problem Has Been Around for Quite a While

The "bare naked assignee" problem is not entirely new. A handful of partnership cases address the rights of assignees of partnership interests, and these decisions all hold against the assignee.

Bauer v. Blomfield Co./Holden Joint Venture is the classic example.[41] All partners approved a commission arrangement with a third party, and the arrangement dried up all the partnership profits. An assignee of a partnership interest objected and brought suit.

The case reached the Alaska Supreme Court, where the Court majority rejected the assignee's very right to assert the claim. An assignee "was not entitled to complain about a decision made with the consent of all the partners."[42] The notion that "partners owe a duty of good faith and fair dealing to assignees of a partner's interest" was dismissed in a footnote.[43]

There was an angry dissent, which applied the law of contracts:

> It is a well-settled principle of contract law that an assignee steps into the shoes of an assignor as to the rights assigned. Today, the court summarily dismisses this principle in a footnote and leaves the assignee barefoot. . . .
>
> As interpreted by the court, the [partnership] statute now allows partners to deprive an assignee of profits to which he is entitled by law for whatever outrageous motive or reason. The court's opinion essentially leaves the assignee of a partnership interest without remedy to enforce his right.[44]

---

41. 849 P2d 1365 (Alaska 1993).
42. *Id.* at 1367.
43. *Id.* at 1367 n.2
44. *Id.* at 1367–68 (Matthews, J., dissenting).

The conflict between the *Bauer* majority and dissent is in part a theoretical battle between, on the one hand, the general law of contracts and, on the other hand, statutory provisions designed to protect the "pick your partner" principle. However, the theoretical battle has very serious practical dimensions.

> If the law categorically favors the owners, there is a serious risk of expropriation and other abuse. On the other hand, if the law grants former owners and other transferees the right to seek judicial protection, that specter can "freeze the deal" as of the moment an owner leaves the enterprise or a third party obtains an economic interest.[45]

b. The Advent of LLCs Exacerbates the Problem

For two reasons, the advent of limited liability companies has greatly exacerbated this problem. First, LLCs are far more durable than previous forms of unincorporated businesses. An assignee may be "locked in" in perpetuity. The situation was different under UPA (1914) and UPA (1997), and was arguably different under RULPA (via linkage to UPA (1914)).[46]

- UPA (1914) §32(2) permits an assignee to seek judicial dissolution of an at-will general partnership at any time and of a partnership for a term or undertaking if partnership continues in existence after the completion of the term or undertaking.
- The RULPA §201(a)(1)(4) requires the certificate of limited partnership to state "the latest date upon which the limited partnership is to dissolve." Linkage arguably makes UPA (1914) §32 applicable and permits an assignee to bring suit if a limited partnership continues past the term stated in its certificate.[47]
- UPA (1997) §801(5) and UPA (1997) §801(6) are the same as UPA (1914) §32, except the two modern acts require the court to determine whether dissolution is equitable.[48]

45. ULLCA (2013) §112(b), cmt.
46. For a discussion of "linkage," see Section 12.2.1.
47. See RULPA §1105 (providing for linkage to the general partnership statute). Because RULPA §802 addresses judicial dissolution, it is arguable that linkage does not apply. However, because the RULPA provision does not address the situation covered by UPA §32, it is also arguable that linkage does apply.
48. See also ULLCA (2006), §801(4) (permitting a dissociated member to seek dissolution on the grounds *inter alia* of oppressive conduct). The Harmonization Project deleted the provision as inconsistent with ULLCA (2013) §107(b).

The second reason is less conceptual but even more important. Before the advent of fully shielded unincorporated business organizations, partnership law was a legal backwater and the "bare naked assignee" problem was a small and rarely significant part of that backwater. With the advent of limited liability companies, the "bare naked" problem is going mainstream. "The issue of whether, in extreme and sufficiently harsh circumstances, transferees might be able to claim some type of duty or obligation to protect against expropriation, is a question awaits development in the case law."[49]

Case in Point — *Kohannim v. Katoli*[50]

In *Kohannim v. Katoli*, the court: (i) noted that the LLC's "Regulations provide[] for the distribution of 'available cash' to members quarterly provided that the available cash is not needed for a reasonable working capital reserve"; and (ii) noted that "Jacob [the defendant member] paid himself $100,000 for management services that were not performed and failed to make any profit distributions to Mike [former member and ex-spouse of the plaintiff Parvaneh] or Parvaneh [ex-spouse of Mike, who became Mike's transferee as part of their divorce proceeding] even though more than $250,000 in undistributed profit had accumulated in the company's accounts since the mortgage on the property had been paid off in February 2007"; and (iii) concluded that "more than a scintilla of evidence supports the trial court's finding that Jacob failed to make profit distributions to Parvaneh." In essence, the court upheld a finding that Jacob had breached (or caused the LLC to breach) a contractual obligation to make distributions. But the court went further: "We also agree with the trial court's conclusion that the established facts demonstrated Jacob engaged in wrongful conduct and exhibited a lack of fair dealing in the company's affairs to the prejudice of Parvaneh."[51] ◄◄◄

---

49. ULLCA (2013) §107(b), cmt.

50. *Kohannim v. Katoli*, 08–11–00155-CV, 2013 WL 3943078, at *10–11 (Tex. App. July 24, 2013).

51. The Case on Point is taken verbatim from ULLCA (2013) §107(b), cmt. (citations omitted).

§16.7 INCOMPLETE ENTITY, SHAPE-SHIFTING, AND THE OVERLAP WITH FEDERAL LAW

§16.7.1 LLCs and Federal Diversity Jurisdiction

For the federal courts to have jurisdiction over a case, the case must involve a "federal question" (i.e., a question arising from federal law), or the parties must be of diverse citizenship and the amount in controversy must meet or exceed an amount specified by statute. For the purposes of "diversity jurisdiction," diversity must be complete; that is, there must be no overlap in citizenship between parties on opposing sides of the litigation.

When an organization (such as an LLC) is a party, the federal courts must be able to assign citizenship to the organization. The citizenship of corporations is established by the federal statutes pertaining to diversity jurisdiction: "a corporation shall be deemed to be a citizen of any State by which it has been incorporated and of the State where it has its principal place of business."[52]

The diversity statutes are silent as to the citizenship of a limited liability company, and, in the early days of LLC, litigants sought to determine LLC citizenship by analogizing the LLC to a corporation. However, it soon became clear that the controlling precedent was a U.S. Supreme Court case dealing with limited partnerships.

That case, *Carden v. Arkoma Associates*, had rejected the analogical approach and looked through the limited partnership to the citizenship of its partners.[53] As a result, for diversity purposes, a limited partnership has the citizenship of each of its partners.

The same is true for an LLC and the citizenship of its members. In the words of the Eighth Circuit:

> We recognize numerous similarities exist between a corporation and an LLC, but Congress is the appropriate forum to consider and, if it desires, to apply the same "citizenship" rule for LLCs as corporations for diversity jurisdiction purposes. This issue appears resolved by Justice Antonin Scalia's analysis [for the majority] in *Carden*.[54]

Thus, for purposes of federal diversity jurisdiction, the LLC is hardly an entity at all. The practical consequences of this situation are substantial.

---

52. 28 U.S.C.A. §1332 (c)(1).
53. *Carden v. Arkoma Assocs.*, 494 U.S. 185, 195 (1990).
54. *GMAC Commercial Credit, LLC v. Dillard Dep't Stores, Inc.*, 357 F3d 827, 828 (8th Cir. 2004).

Example

Manol, LLC is a manager-managed limited liability company organized under the law of the state of Missouri. One of its members seeks to bring a derivative claim in federal court against the manager-member of the LLC. There is no diversity jurisdiction. The LLC is an indispensable party to any derivative litigation. Regardless of whether the LLC is formally aligned as a plaintiff or defendant, it will have the same citizenship as an adverse party. ◀◀◀

Case in Point—*Dixon v. DB50 2007-1 Trust*

After Defendant brought an action to foreclose on plaintiff's home, Plaintiff sued Defendant in state court. Defendant removed the action to federal court based on diversity of citizenship, contending that it was wholly owned by an LLC whose state of formation was Delaware. The court held that an LLC's state of formation is irrelevant to its citizenship for the purposes of diversity jurisdiction. Defendant had provided no information regarding the citizenship of the members of its parent. The trial court was not amused: "Although this Court is tempted to remand this action at this time, it is mindful that the Eleventh Circuit Court of Appeals has counseled that the better course is to allow Defendant an opportunity to amend its notice of removal under these circumstances. . . . Accordingly, Defendant shall have one final opportunity to cure this defect in its notice of removal."[55] ◀◀◀

§16.7.2 Bankruptcy and the LLC Member

The bankruptcy of an LLC member illumines both the "entity as contract" and the "incomplete entity" aspects of LLC law. The relevant bankruptcy law is quite intricate, but the major outlines are clear:[56]

- Bankruptcy law seeks to maximize the value of assets within the "bankruptcy estate."
- Conceptually, all "property" of a bankrupt member becomes part of the estate at least initially—including the member's normally non-transferable governance rights.

55. *Dixon v. DB50 2007-1 Trust*, No. 3:10-CV-35 (CDL), 2010 WL 5174758 at * 3 (M.D.Ga. Dec. 15, 2010) (citations omitted). Given the lack of information, it was unclear whether the defendant could cure the defect. *Id.* at *3, n.3.

56. The sections of the Bankruptcy Code of principal importance to this discussion are §§541 (dealing with property of the bankruptcy estate), 363 (dealing with the trustee's power to assume and assign contracts of the debtor), and 365 (dealing with the personal services exception to the trustee's power to assume and assign).

- As explained above, "bare naked" financial rights are more vulnerable (and therefore less valuable) than financial rights associated with governance rights.
- As a result, the trustee will seek to maximize the bankruptcy estate by claiming governance as well as financial rights.
- Federal law trumps state law where a conflict exists; therefore, the bankruptcy code overrides state law restrictions on transfer.

- If an LLC were completely an entity, the rest of the analysis would be straightforward.
  - There would be no statute-based transfer restrictions.
  - As for any contract-based restrictions, even as a matter of state law they would be unenforceable unless they provided some reasonable opportunity for the member (or the trustee, standing in the member's shoes) to sell the rights.
  - State law and bankruptcy would thus align on this issue.
- However, because the LLC is not completely an entity, the analysis is complicated, turning ultimately on whether bankruptcy law will respect the "entity as contract" construct.
  - LLC law's transfer restriction will be respected by bankruptcy law only if the member's interest in the LLC is conceptualized:
    - as an "executory contract"; and, moreover,
    - as an executory contract involving what is colloquially called "personal services."[57]
- The executory contract/personal services analysis focuses on the nature of duties the bankrupt member owes to the LLC and fellow members.
- If applicable non-bankruptcy law (in this context, essentially contract law) would consider the duties nondelegable,[58] then the trustee would have no right to make use of the bankrupt member's governance rights.[59]
- In that circumstance:
  - bankruptcy law will view the member's governance rights as contractual, rather than as part of a proprietary interest in an entity;

57. The statutory language is more elaborate. See 11 U.S.C.A. §365(c)(1)(a) (referring to "applicable law excuses a party . . . to such contract . . . [i.e., the other members of the LLC] from accepting performance from or rendering performance to an entity other than the debtor").

58. I.e., involving the exercise of substantial judgment or unusual expertise. See, e.g., Restatement (Second) of Contracts §318, cmt. c (entitled "*Non-delegable duties*" and stating that "[t]he principal exceptions [to delegable duties] relate to contracts . . . for the exercise of personal skill or discretion").

59. Depending on the contents of the operating agreement and the provision of the relevant LLC statute dealing with causes of dissociation, an analogous analysis may operate to prevent the rights from ever entering the bankruptcy estate.

— the incomplete entity aspect of LLC law will prevail; and
— the statutory transfer restrictions will work.

Case in Point—*In re Modanlo*

Chapter 11 bankruptcy trustee moved for leave to: (i) resuscitate debtor's single-member Delaware LLC, which had dissolved upon filing bankruptcy; and (ii) cause the LLC to call a meeting of shareholders of a corporation in which the LLC was the controlling shareholder. The Delaware LLC Act, Delaware tit. 6, §18–806, permits "Revocation of dissolution," but the trustee could invoke that provision only if the trustee had succeeded to the debtor's governance rights in the LLC. In ruling for the trustee, the court distinguished a single-member LLC from a multimember LLC, noting that the impetus for only allowing trustees to be assignees in the context of multimember LLCs did not and could not apply to a single-member LLC because there are no "relationships" at stake. Accordingly, the Trustee in this matter could have more than bare economic rights.[60] ◀◀◀

§16.8 THE PROTECTED SERIES

16.8.1 The Concept

The protected series is relatively new concept, located at the edge of limited liability company law, and of very restricted usefulness. The Uniform Protected Series Act (2017) ("UPSA") provides the following introduction to the concept:

> The protected series construct has the following aspects:
>
> - an identifiable 679set of assets segregated within a limited liability company ("a series limited liability company");
>   - the assets:
>   - comprise a protected series,[61] which is empowered to conduct activities in its own name;

60. *In re Modanlo*, 412 B.R. 715 (Bankr. D. Md. 2006).
61. In UPSA, "protected series" is the term of art, but other statutes simply refer to "series." See Section 16.8.3.

  - must be identified by thorough recordkeeping that distinguishes them from assets of the series limited liability company and assets of any other protected series of the company;
  - are obligated solely to persons asserting claims pertaining to activities related to the segregated assets; and
  - are not available to persons asserting claims arising from the activities of the series limited liability company or any other protected series of the company;
- one or more members of the series limited liability company may be associated with the protected series, but not necessarily; and
- distributions arising from the assets and activities go to:
  - the members associated with the protected series, if any; or
  - if the series has no associated members, the series limited liability company.

Thus, a series limited liability company contains "internal shields"—i.e., asset partitions reserving the assets of each protected series solely to creditors of that protected series. These "horizontal" shields are conceptually and practically quite different from the traditional, "vertical" shield that protects the owners of an organization from automatic, status-based liability for the organization's obligations.[62]

In addition, subject to three specific limitations "[a] protected series of a series limited liability company is a person distinct from [and yet *within*] the company."[63] Conceptually, a protected series is a person within a person.

16.8.2 A Delaware Innovation with a Limited Purpose

This notion of a "[legal] person within a separate [legal] person" entered the realm of LLCs in 1996. In that year, Delaware borrowed the series approach from the law of business trusts and authorized "series"[64] within Delaware limited liability companies.[65] In the business trust context, "series trusts" had long been a useful vehicle for investment funds. One series trust could encompass multiple investments funds, each in its respective trust series. The Securities and Exchange Commission, which regulates such funds under the Investment Company Act of 1940,[66] treats the trust and its series

62. UPSA ("2017) Prefatory Note, Part 1.
63. UPSA § 103.
64. As for why Delaware's word choice was unfortunate, see Section 16.8.3.
65. Delaware also authorized series within Delaware limited partnerships. However, instances of the latter are rare compared to incidents of the former. This Section refers exclusively to series limited liability companies, but the observations in this Section concerning Delaware series limited liability companies apply as well to series limited partnerships.
66. 15 U.S.C. §§ 80a-1–80a-64, also cited as Pub. L. 76–768.

as one person for registration purposes, which saves substantial expenses and substantially streamlines paperwork.

In 1996, "the thought [among the advocates for series limited liability companies] seemed to be a combination of 'why not?' and 'perhaps in some circumstances an LLC or LP might work marginally better than a series within a Delaware statutory trust.'"[67] The series provisions imported into Delaware LLC law had a very limited purpose—investment company work—although that statute itself contained no such limitation. However, "none of the key architects of the [Delaware] series provisions . . . [initially] . . . envisioned, let alone advocated, using series to compartmentalize the activities of operating businesses."[68]

16.8.3 A Question of Nomenclature—Series Versus Protected Series

In 1996, Delaware chose the term "series" to refer to the "person within a person" construct. This term was unfortunate and confusing, because most lawyers associated (and still associate) the term with series of bonds or series of stock. Those concepts have nothing in common with series with horizontal shields. UPSA (2017) uses the term "protected series" to avoid confusion, and this section follows that usage.

In 2019, Delaware amended its series provisions to refer to "protected series" and "registered series." What the terms mean is far beyond the scope of this book.[69]

16.8.4 Pandora's Box

Although the Delaware lawyers who drafted the series provisions neither intended nor anticipated that lawyers would use a Delaware series for operating businesses, that is precisely what occurred. Across the country, many attorneys—with more thought to marketing than to accuracy—purveyed the series construct as the best, brightest, and newest tool for a wide range of entrepreneurs. Some of the marketing also entailed persuading state legislators. As of September 17, 2017, at least 15 jurisdictions had followed Delaware and had authorized "series LLCs."[70]

67. Daniel S. Kleinberger, "Series of Unincorporated Business Entities: the Mobius Strip and Klein Bottle of Business Entity Law," BUSINESS LAW TODAY (February 2015).
68. Id.
69. For more information on the Delaware approach, see Bishop and Kleinberger on Limited Liability Companies §§ 14:27–28, 14.74.
70. UPSA, Prefatory Note, Part 1.

Because under Delaware law and the law of almost all of the copycat jurisdictions, creating a series limited liability company required no public filing, it was impossible to determine how many series limited liability companies had been formed. Likewise, no public filing was necessary to establish a series (or multiple series) within a series limited liability company. Thus, it was impossible also to determine how many series existed across the country.[71]

As of 2016, anecdotal evidence (including scuttlebutt at various meeting of the Business Law Section of the American Bar Association) suggested that use of the protected series construct was growing and that many users (and their respective attorneys) had no idea of the risks involved.[72] Most importantly, no one could reliably predict whether a court would respect the internal shields.

16.8.5 The Uniform Act—UPSA (2017)

In 2013, the Uniform Law Conference began what became a four-year project to examine the notion of "a person within a person" and to draft a uniform act to implement the notion. The drafting committee was never able to determine precisely why the concept had broad appeal:

> Although the widespread use and growing popularity of the protected series construct are undeniable, the causes are not well understood. For the most part, the legal and business relationships established through protected series can also be established with various structures involving several limited liability companies.
>
> Some situations have been identified in which protected series provide a unique benefit, but these situations involve very specialized types of arrangements and cannot account for widespread use and popularity. Some proponents note a potential convenience in some regulatory environments: With the approval of the relevant regulator, a series limited liability company makes one regulatory filing or holds a single license, and various protected series of the company function under the aegis of that filing or license.[73]

---

71. Illinois's series provisions were a notable exception, requiring a public filing to create a protected series. "As of January 1, 2017, more than 27,000 protected series were active under Illinois law." UPSA, Prefatory Note, Part 4.

72. For example, during the UPSA drafting process, one commissioner reported on a Utah series limited liability company, owned by husband and wife farmers, who had placed each of their different crops into a separate protected series.

73. USPA, Prefatory Note, Part 4. Contrary to information still widely available on the Internet, protected series do not save paperwork. To the contrary, maintaining the internal shields requires recordkeeping detailing which assets are "associated" with which protected series, which goes far beyond any paperwork in an ordinary limited liability company. See, e.g., UPSA (2017) § 301(b):

In any event, the drafting committee identified multiple problems in the then existing statutes. By far the largest problem pertained to the internal shields. Their strength was essential to the usefulness of the construct, yet that strength was entirely untested. Part 16.8.5 discusses the shield issue.

The drafting committee also considered the following questions:

- may a protected series be created without a public filing?
- will other important areas of business law accommodate the protected series?
- does/must each protected series have its own operating agreement?
  - — if not, does the operating agreement of the series limited liability company apply to protected series of that company?
- who owns property "associated" with a protected series?
  - — what "interest" does a protected series have in property associated with the series?
- how does a person make service on a protected series?
- does service on a series limited liability company effect service on all the protected series of the company?
- how do statutes requiring foreign organizations to register to do business in a state apply to foreign protected series and foreign series limited liability companies?
- who manages a protected series?
- if the same person manages more than one protected series, does the person have a built-in conflict of interest?
- may protected series do business with each other?
- for the purposes of establishing personal jurisdiction over a protected series or a series limited liability company, are the activities of one part (e.g., a protected series doing business in a state) treated as attributable to the series limited liability company? to other protected series of the series limited liability company?
- may a protect series participate in a merger with the series limited liability company, another protected series of the company, an entirely unrelated entity?

(b) An asset of a protected series of a series limited liability company is an associated asset of the protected series only if the protected series creates and maintains records that state the name of the protected series and describe the asset with sufficient specificity to permit a disinterested, reasonable individual to:

(1) identify the asset and distinguish it from any other asset of the protected series, any asset of the company, and any asset of any other protected series of the company;

(2) determine when and from what person the protected series acquired the asset or how the asset otherwise became an asset of the protected series; and

(3) if the protected series acquired the asset from the company or another protected series of the company, determine any consideration paid, the payor, and the payee.

UPSA (2017) resolved all these questions, and others as well. However, in doing so the UPSA drafting process apparently served to educate at least legislators on the complexities and potential drawbacks of the concept.[74] Since 2017 (when the ULC formally adopted USPA), the torrent of enactments has become a drip.

16.8.6 Will the Shields Hold?

a. What Would "Piercing" Look Like as Applied to Internal Shields?

Most piercing claims attack the traditional liability shield that protects an entity's owners from automatic liability for the debts of the entity.[75] While a protected series also provides this traditional "owner protection,"[76] the protected series innovation is to allow a series limited liability company to segregate its assets from the claims of creditors of the series limited liability company and any other protected series of the company.

Therefore, a piercing claim in the context of the internal shields would seek to override that segregation with regard to a protected series and make the assets associated[77] with that protected series available to satisfy judgments obtained against another protected series or the company itself.

b. No Case Law Thus No Sure Way to Tell

As of June 15, 2025, there is no case on point, or even close. No state or federal decision has considered piercing an internal shield—that is, has considered whether to allow a plaintiff with a judgment against one protected series to

74. See UPSA (2017) Prefatory Note, Part 10. Clarity and Safeguards of this Act Compared to Current Protected Series Statutes.

75. For a discussion of traditional piercing (i.e., disregarding the liability shield that protect an entity's owners from the debts of the entity), see Sections 14.1.2(c), 17.2.8, and 17.3.3.

76. UPSA § 401:

> (a) A person is not liable, directly or indirectly, by way of contribution or otherwise, for a debt, obligation, or other liability of:
>
> (1) a protected series of a series limited liability company solely by reason of being or acting as:
>
> (A) an associated member, protected-series manager, or protected-series transferee of the protected series; or
>
> (B) a member, manager, or a transferee of the company; or
>
> (2) a series limited liability company solely by reason of being or acting as an associated member, protected-series manager, or protected-series transferee of a protected series of the company.

77. "Associated" is a term of art. Associating property with a protected series is done through record keeping. UPSA § 301(b).

satisfy the judgment by levying on the assets of another protected series or the series organization itself.

For series trusts and series limited liability companies confined to investment deals, the absence makes sense. Within that confine, piercing claims do not arise, because:

- *with regard to piercing claims by "voluntary creditors"*—that is, third parties who contract with a trust series or a series trust—the contracts are written to preclude any "piercing" claims;[78] and
- *with regard to piercing claims by "involuntary creditors"*—involuntary claims against a trust series or a series trust are highly unlikely, because:
  - —the typical involuntary creditor is a tort claimant; and
  - —so long as a series trust is solely a vehicle for investment funds, neither a trust series nor a series trust is likely to face any significant tort claims.[79]

The same analysis applies to any series limited liability company, so long as the company's purpose and operations pertain to investment arrangements.

Explaining the absence of cases involving series limited liability companies housing operating companies or similar enterprises is more difficult. The two most likely venues are federal bankruptcy courts and courts in jurisdictions that have not provided for series limited liability companies (including federal courts applying the substantive law of such jurisdictions).[80]

The case that has come closest to addressing the question is *Alphonse v. Arch Bay Holdings, LLC.*[81] Initially, it appeared that the court would have to

78. E.g., investors in a fund, accountants for a fund.

79. Investment funds are not operating companies. Funds hold ownership interest in various operating business, but a fund itself has no operations or activities that could give rise to a tort claim (e.g., a factory that pollutes a waterway or that distributes dangerously defective products). No substantial tort claims means no challenges to the internal shield by tort claimants.

80. Arizona has chosen not only to eschew authorizing protected series in Arizona limited liability companies, but has also provided that the internal shields of foreign series limited liability companies are ineffective in Arizona courts under specified circumstances:

> A foreign limited liability company, its members and managers and its foreign series, if any, have no greater rights and privileges than a domestic limited liability company and its members and managers with respect to transactions in this state and relationships with persons in this state that are not managers or members. A foreign series is liable for the debts, obligations or other liabilities of the designating foreign company and of any other foreign series of that designating foreign company, arising out of transactions in this state or relationships with persons in this state and a designating foreign company is liable for such debts, obligations or other liabilities of each foreign series of that designating foreign company.

Ariz. Rev. Stat. Ann. § 29–3901(D).

81. *Alphonse v. Arch Bay Holdings, LLC*, No. CIV.A. 12–330, 2013 WL 55911, at *5–6 (ED La. Jan. 3, 2013), rev'd sub nom. *Alphonse v. Arch Bay Holdings, LLC*, 548 F. App'x 979 (5th Cir. 2013);

address a question closely related to the internal shield question—namely, whether a protected series is a juridic person separate and distinct from the series limited liability company.

The case arose out of a foreclosure, and the plaintiff alleged several counts of abusive conduct by the creditor. The plaintiff's choice of defendant raised the separate person question:

> Plaintiff filed this complaint against Arch Bay Holdings, LLC. However, AB–Series 2010B held the Note in question and initiated the action to collect the debt at issue in this case. Plaintiff claims that AB–Series 2010B is a financial instrument and not a separate juridical entity from Arch Bay Holdings, LLC.[82]

The "separate person" issue was a question of state law, and initially the case also involved a federal question.[83] For several years, leading LLC practitioners and scholars looked to *Alphonse v. Arch Bay* for a seminal opinion—which never came.

> The case had a tortuous history:
>
> - a district court decision, reversed and remanded by the Fifth Circuit;
> - on remand, another district court decision, where the court, having decided that the case presented no federal question and that diversity jurisdiction did not exist, declined to exercise supplemental jurisdiction; and
> - a Fifth Circuit decision, affirming the district court decision.[84]

It is perhaps tempting to see the absence of case law as indicating that a protected series' internal shields are not controversial. In the author's opinion, it is more likely that a sufficiently attractive case has yet to arise—e.g., internal shields used disingenuously to wall off assets from a very sympathetic claimant.

on remand *Alphonse v. Arch Bay Holdings, LLC*, No. CIV.A. 12–330, 2014 WL 6674029, at *1 (E.D. La. Nov. 24, 2014), aff'd sub nom. *Alphonse v. Arch Bay Holdings, L.L.C.*, 618 F. App'x 765 (5th Cir. 2015).

82. *Alphonse v. Arch Bay Holdings*, LLC, No. CIV.A. 12–330, 2013 WL 55911, at *4 (E.D. La. Jan. 3, 2013), rev'd sub nom. *Alphonse v. Arch Bay Holdings, L.L.C.*, 548 F. App'x 979 (5th Cir. 2013)

83. The district court therefore entertained the state law question as within its supplemental jurisdiction.

84. As of June 15, 2025, a Westlaw search found no subsequent history in state court.

16.8.7 Will Your Practice Include Protected Series?

Protected series are certainly not for "newbie" attorneys and unsophisticated clients. Even an expert LLC lawyer should avoid recommending a series limited liability company to even the most sophisticated client, unless the attorney can fully explain both the protected series construct in general and the business and legal circumstances in particular that warrant using the legal equivalent of a mobius strip or Klein bottle.[85]

Problem 129

Alphabet, LLC ("Alphabet") was a two-member, member-managed limited liability company, whose members were Alpha and Beta. The Alphabet operating agreement provided that: (i) Alpha would contribute $1,000,000 and Beta $350,000 to start up Alphabet; (ii) Alpha would contract with Alphabet to market a promising new product recently developed by Alpha, with payment and all other terms of that relationship specified in the operating agreement; and (iii) Alpha would run the day-to-day activities of Alphabet.

Alpha fulfilled its obligations under the operating agreement, but Beta never made its contribution. Over the course of several months, Alpha talked, cajoled, and remonstrated with Beta in an effort to cause Beta to comply with the operating agreement. Beta repeatedly made excuses but never made the promised contribution.

Eventually, the resulting capital shortage threatened to destroy Alphabet, taking Alpha's $1,000,000 investment "down the tubes" and also imperiling the introduction of Alpha's new product. To stave off this result, Alpha contributed another $350,000 to Alphabet.

Unfortunately, Alphabet failed despite Alpha's additional contribution; irrevocable financial damage had been done during the months of Beta's excuses. Alpha did manage to avoid harm to the marketing of its new product, but Alpha's investment loss totaled $1,350,000.

According to mainstream doctrine,[86] may Alpha sue Beta directly? If so, for what amount? ◄ ◄ ◄

85. See Daniel S. Kleinberger, "Series of Unincorporated Business Entities: the Mobius Strip and Klein Bottle of Business Entity Law," BUSINESS LAWTODAY (February 2015). A Möbius strip is a strip of paper with only one side. A Klein bottle is a closed bottle with no outside.

86. I.e., ignoring the "special injury" and "duties owed" approaches mentioned in Section 16.4.

Explanation

It is clear that Alphabet, the limited liability company, has a claim against Beta for at least $350,000 (direct damages for breach of the promise to contribute). In addition, Alphabet may have a claim for lost profits, if: (i) the jurisdiction allows a new business to claim lost profits; and (ii) Alphabet can prove the connection between Beta's breach and the company's failure and the amount of lost profits.

For Alpha to assert these claims, however, would require a derivative action. The breach first injures Alphabet—the LLC—not Alpha, the member. Beta breached an agreement to which Alpha was a party, but that does not change the fact that Alpha's injuries are indirect.

Alpha could make a "creative" claim of direct injury by asserting that Beta's breach caused Alpha to contribute (and then lose) additional capital. Under this theory, Alpha's claim would be limited to $350,000, the extra amount Alpha contributed in response to Beta's breach.[87] ◄◄◄

Problem 130

Same facts as Problem 129. Assume that the court permits Alpha to make a direct claim against Beta. May Beta effectively counterclaim that Alpha's marketing relationship with Alphabet constituted self-dealing and therefore a breach of Alpha's duty of loyalty? ◄◄◄

Explanation

For two reasons, the answer is no. First, any such claim would be a derivative claim; any harm would first affect the LLC. Second, although a member in a member-managed LLC does have a duty not to deal with the LLC, that duty can be modified or waived by agreement. The operating agreement expressly contemplated and therefore permitted Alpha to contract with Alphabet. Therefore, there was no breach of the duty of loyalty. ◄◄◄

---

87. This Problem and the theory of a direct claim are based on *Excimer Assocs., Inc. v. LCA Vision, Inc.*, 292 F3d 134, 139–140 (2d Cir. 2002) (reversing the trial court's determination that plaintiff member's claim was derivative; holding that the plaintiff stated a direct claim when it asserted that other member's failure to make a promised contribution caused plaintiff to make an additional contribution), decision after remand, *LCA-Vision, Inc. v. New York Refractive Eye Assocs., PC*, No. 98 Civ. 8387 DC, 2004 WL 213027, at *5 (SDNY Feb. 3, 2004) (concluding that no reasonable jury would sustain plaintiff's breach of contract claim, and, therefore, granting summary judgment to defendant).

Problem 131

After a member-managed limited liability company has been in existence for 10 years, its members note that 35 percent of the interests in its profits are owned by mere transferees. The members arrange to merge the LLC into another, shell limited liability company, and the plan of merger converts the interests in profits held by transferees into highly subordinated and arguably worthless debt of the surviving LLC. The merger has no independent, legitimate business purpose. Its sole function is to "shuffle the equity" to the grave prejudice of the transferees. Are the transferees better off under ULLCA (2013) or the Delaware LLC Act?[88] ◄◄◄

Explanation

This question is "too close to call."

It might appear that Delaware law is better for the transferees, because: (i) ULLCA (2013) §107(b) expressly subjects the transferees to any amendments to the operating agreement that might be made to facilitate the merger; while (ii) the Delaware LLC Act gives "assignees" standing to sue derivatively.[89]

However, the relevant claim is direct, not derivative. The merger does no damage to the LLC; the harm is solely and directly to the transferees.

The question thus becomes whether the courts of the 20+ ULLCA jurisdiction or the courts of Delaware are more likely to accord the transferees "member-like" standing to sue directly. Under ULLCA (2013), the transferees can at least cite an official comment: "The issue of whether, in extreme and sufficiently harsh circumstances, transferees might be able to claim some type of duty or obligation to protect against expropriation, awaits development in the case law."[90] On the other hand, if the limited liability company were a Delaware LLC, Delaware's Court of Chancery would have jurisdiction of the litigation, and that court is quite mindful of its role as a court of equity.[91] ◄◄◄

---

88. This Problem is derived from an Example in Bishop & Kleinberger, ¶8.06[2][e].
89. Del. Code Ann., tit. 6, §18-703(a).
90. ULLCA (2013) §107(b), cmt.
91. *Glanding v. Industrial Trust Co.*, 28 Del. Ch. 499, 511, 45 A.2d 553, 558–59 (Del. Ch. 1945) ("It cannot be said too forcefully that the general powers of the Court of Chancery refers to that complete system of equity as administered by the High Court of Chancery of Great Britain, and a proper interpretation of the constitutions of this State lead to but one conclusion; that is, that the Court of Chancery shall continue to exercise that complete system of equity jurisdiction in all respects until the Legislature of this State shall provide otherwise, as by granting the exercise of a part of that jurisdiction exclusively to some other tribunal."); see also *Nixon v. Blackwell*, 626 A.2d 1366, 1378 n.17 (Del. 1993) ("We are mindful of the elasticity inherent in equity jurisprudence and the traditional desirability in certain equity cases of measuring conduct by the 'conscience of the court' and disapproving conduct which offends or shocks that conscience.").

Problem 132

OutOfPocket, LLC ("OutOfPocket") is a manager-managed limited liability company organized under the law of the state of Illinois. OutOfPocket has five members, two of whom live in Illinois, one in Wisconsin, and two in New York City. Until last month, the sole manager of OutOfPocket was Faithless, Inc. ("Faithless"), a corporation organized under the laws of Delaware, with its principal place of business in Texas. Faithless was not and is not a member of OutOfPocket.

Last month, OutOfPocket terminated Faithless as manager, believing that Faithless had misappropriated more than $250,000 from OutOfPocket. OutOfPocket plans to sue Faithless in federal court, asserting diversity jurisdiction. The amount in controversy is more than sufficient. May OutOfPocket proceed in federal court? ◀ ◀ ◀

Explanation

Yes. Complete diversity exists. As an LLC, OutOfPocket has the citizenship of each of its members: Illinois, Wisconsin, and New York. As a corporation, Faithless has the citizenship of its state of incorporation and its principal place of business: Delaware and Texas. ◀ ◀ ◀

Problem 133

Same facts as Problem 132, but assume that OutOfPocket brings suit in federal court *before* terminating Faithless as manager. How, if at all, does the analysis change? ◀ ◀ ◀

Explanation

The analysis does not change.

For federal diversity purposes, the citizenship of each LLC *member is attributed to the LLC. The citizenship of a nonmember manager* is irrelevant. ◀ ◀ ◀

CHAPTER 17

Limited Liability Partnerships and Limited Liability Limited Partnerships

§17.1 OVERVIEW: TERMINOLOGY AND ORIGINS

§17.1.1 Terminology

a. Limited Liability Partnership (LLP)

A *limited liability partnership*:

- is a *general* partnership that has invoked the limited liability partnership provisions of its governing general partnership statute
- by filing with a specific public official a specified document (typically called "a statement of qualification" or a "registration")
- thereby becoming a limited liability [general] partnership and eliminating partially or completely the automatic personal liability of each partner for each partnership obligation.

Under some state statutes, a limited liability partnership is called a registered limited liability partnership. The term "limited liability partnership" is abbreviated *LLP* and, except in statutory provisions, the abbreviation is used far more often than the term itself.

The term "liability shield" is typically used to refer to the liability protection provided the partners of an LLP. As discussed in more detail in Section 17.2.1, almost all LLP statutes provide a "full shield" for the partners—completely eliminating a partner's liability *qua* partner for the partnership's obligations. A few LLP statutes may still provide only a "partial shield"—leaving in place some of a partner's automatic liability for partnership obligations.

b. Limited Liability Limited Partnership (LLLP)

A *limited liability limited partnership*:

- is a *limited* partnership[1] that has invoked the limited liability limited partnership provisions of its state of formation
- by identifying itself as a limited liability limited partnership either in its publicly filed certificate of limited partnership or in a separate document filed as specified by the applicable limited partnership act, which results in the limited partnership
- thereby becoming a limited liability limited partnership, a status that:
  — eliminates completely the automatic personal liability of each general partner for each partnership obligation; and
  — eliminates for limited partners the "control rule" liability risk that still exists under most limited partnership acts.[2]

The term "limited liability limited partnership" is abbreviated *LLLP* and, except in statutory provisions, the abbreviation is used far more often than the term itself. The abbreviation is usually pronounced "triple-L-P."

The term "liability shield" is used in this context too. With regard to *general* partner liability, all LLLP provisions are full-shield provisions.

§17.1.2 Origins of LLPs and LLLPs

The advent of limited liability companies had a ripple effect on the law of general and limited partnerships. Put most simply: if a limited liability company could shield its owners from automatic, vicarious liability for the enterprise's debts and still be taxed as a partnership, why not provide a comparable liability shield for general partners? Once the IRS acknowledged that its Kintner Regulations meant what they said, there was nothing in tax law to deter state legislatures from providing for both limited liability [general] partnerships—LLPs—and limited liability limited partnership—LLLPs.[3]

1. Recall that a limited partnership must have at least two partners, at least one person who is a general partner, and at least one other person that is a limited partner. See Section 12.1.1.
2. See Sections 12.2.3 and 12.3.4.
3. For a discussion of the Kintner tax classification regulations, see Sections 13.1.4(a) and (b). The "check the box" regulations, discussed in Section 13.1.4(d) removed any shadow of tax classification doubt, even for the most conservative of tax practitioners.

There remained non-tax forces of inertia, however. Most importantly, from a non-tax and historical perspective, a general partner's liability seemed inherently and inescapably the hallmark of partnership law. It took five years after the IRS's seminal ruling on LLCs for any state legislature to authorize limited liability partnerships. Moreover, the first LLP shield was decidedly inferior to an LLC or corporate shield.

Today, in contrast, the limited liability partnership is firmly established and widespread, and the limited liability limited partnership is only a few steps behind. All states authorize LLPs, and most LLP statutes now provide a shield that is essentially indistinguishable from an LLC or corporate shield. Almost 20 states have adopted either ULPA (2001) or ULPA (2103), and under either act a limited partnership can originate as or become an LLLP simply by including a one-line statement in the certificate of limited partnership.[4]

§17.2 LIMITED LIABILITY PARTNERSHIPS

§17.2.1 Origin and Development

In 1991, Texas enacted the first LLP legislation, which was targeted to help professional firms (especially firms of accountants and lawyers) and which provided a liability shield that made sense only in that context.[5] The shield was available only to general partnerships and protected only against a partner's vicarious liability[6] for:

> debts and obligations of the partnership arising from errors, omissions, negligence, incompetence, or malfeasance committed in the course of the partnership business by another partner or a representative of the partnership not working under the supervision or direction of the first partner at the time the errors, omissions, negligence, incompetence, or malfeasance occurred.[7]

4. ULPA (2013) §201(5) (requiring the certificate of limited partnership states, "(5) whether the limited partnership is a limited liability limited partnership); ULPA (2001), §201(a)(4) (same)." The provision requires those forming a limited partnership to at least consider forming an LLLP.
5. See Bishop & Kleinberger on Limited Liability Companies § 15:3.
6. Like all shields, this LLP shield offered no protection against (and, indeed, was irrelevant to) claims arising from a partner's own conduct. See Section 17.2.4.
7. 1991 Tex. Sess. Lav Serv. ch. 901 (H.B. 278), §§83–85.

The shield thus gave partners no protection whatsoever against contract-based partnership obligations. Even as to tort-based partnership obligations, the shield was ineffective if the partner invoking the shield:

1. was directly involved in the specific activity in which the errors, omissions, negligence, incompetence, or malfeasance were committed by the other partner or representative; or
2. had notice or knowledge of the errors, omissions, negligence, incompetence, or malfeasance by the other partner or representative at the time of occurrence.[8]

In addition, the efficacy of the shield was conditioned *inter alia* on the partnership carrying specified amounts of malpractice insurance.

In 1992 and 1993, a few states followed Texas's example, and in 1993 Texas clarified and refined its statute. The next major development occurred elsewhere, however.

In 1994, first Minnesota, then New York enacted "full shield" LLP provisions—enabling partners in a general partnership to have the same liability protection available to LLC members and corporate shareholders.[9]

Prior to 1996, LLP provisions were all based on UPA (1914). UPA (1997) was just beginning to gain acceptance, and, moreover, as originally promulgated in 1994, the revised act had no LLP provisions. In 1996, the ULC amended the 1994 version to provide for "full shield" LLPs,[10] and since that time most states have taken the "full shield" approach.

§17.2.2 Essential Characteristics

Most LLP provisions now appear in a state's enactment of UPA (1997), so most LLP statutes have nearly identical provisions.[11] Under UPA (1997):

1. An ordinary general partnership becomes an LLP by first obtaining the requisite quantum of consent from its partners and then filing a "statement of qualification" with a specified public official.[12]

---

8. 1991 Tex. Sess. Lav Serv. ch. 901 (H.B. 278), §§83–85. Note that these exceptions can, but do not necessarily, involve any directly culpable conduct by the partner. It is possible, for example, for an individual to be "directly involved in the specific activity in which . . . negligence" occurs without the individual being negligent. Likewise, an individual can have "knowledge or notice" of a coworker's negligence without the individual being negligent.
9. 1994 Minn. Sess. Law Serv. ch. 539, §12, amending Minn. Stat. Ann. §323.14(2); 1994 NY Laws ch. 576, §8, amending N.Y. Partnership Law §26.
10. UPA (2013)—Quick Chronology.
11. The following analysis would also apply to a state that has enacted UPA (2013).
12. UPA (1997) §1001(b) and (c).

2. Unless the partnership agreement provides otherwise, the quantum of partner consent necessary to approve becoming an LLP is the same quantum of consent as is necessary to approve an amendment to the partnership agreement "except, in the case of a partnership agreement that expressly considers obligations to contribute to the partnership, [the LLP approval quantum is] the vote necessary to amend those provisions."[13]
3. The statement of qualification "must be executed by at least two partners,"[14] must be accompanied by whatever filing fee is required by statute,[15] and must contain: "(1) the name of the partnership; (2) the street address of the partnership's chief executive office and, if different, the street address of an office in this State [i.e., the State under whose law the general partnership is becoming an LLP], if any; (3) if the partnership does not have an office in this State, the name and street address of the partnership's agent for service of process; (4) a statement that the partnership elects to be a limited liability partnership; and (5) a deferred effective date, if any."[16]
4. An LLP's name must include specified designators—that is, phrases or abbreviations that reflect the partnership's status as a limited liability partnership. "The name of a limited liability partnership must end with 'Registered Limited Liability Partnership,' 'Limited Liability Partnership,' 'R.L.L.P.,' 'L.L.P.,' 'RLLP,' or 'LLP.' "[17]
5. An LLP must file an annual report with the same public official who receives the statement of qualification. The annual report contains minimal information; its function is merely to keep current the public record.[18]

---

13. UPA (1997) §1001(b) (as to why this provision makes special reference to contribution obligations). See Section 17.2.7.
14. UPA (1997) §105(c).
15. Most LLP statutes require a small filing fee—typically less than $200—which must be paid when the general partnership first becomes an LLP and each time the LLP files an annual report or (under non-uniform statutes) renews its registration. A few states, however, impose significantly higher filing fees. Delaware, for example, imposes a fee of $200 per partner, subject to an annual limit of $120,000, for both the initial statement of qualification and each subsequent annual report. Del. Code Ann. tit. 6, §15–1207(a)(3). This fee will be a substantial expense for any LLP with numerous partners, such as a large accounting firm.
16. UPA (1997) §1001(c)(1)–(5).
17. UPA (1997) §1002. This provision does not directly require that an LLP use its special designator when transacting business. Failure to do so, however, may result in personal liability for the person acting on behalf of the LLP on the agency law theory that the person is not acting for a fully (or correctly) disclosed principal. See Bishop & Kleinberger on Limited Liability Companies §§ 6:85–6:89 (discussing the issue in the context of limited liability companies).
18. UPA (1997) §1003(a) requires the annual report to state the LLP's name; the street address of the LLP's chief executive office and, if different, the street address of an instate office, if any; and, if the LLP does not have an in-state office, the name and street address of the LLP's agent for service of process. Failure to file the annual report can result in revocation of an LLP's statement of qualification, which in turn ends the partnership's status as an LLP

6. When a statement of qualification takes effect, a full liability shield arises. "An obligation of a partnership incurred while the partnership is a limited liability partnership, whether arising in contract, tort, or otherwise, is solely the obligation of the partnership. A partner is not personally liable, directly or indirectly, by way of contribution or otherwise, for such an obligation solely by reason of being or so acting as a partner."[19]

Example

For several years, Locke, Hobbes, and Calvin have been operating a business as an ordinary general partnership governed by UPA (1997). They have no formal partnership agreement and have not previously agreed how to go about changing their *inter se* relationship. On March 1 of this year, Hobbes suggests that the partnership become an LLP. Calvin agrees, but Locke wants to "think it over for a few days." At that point the partnership cannot become an LLP. Under UPA (1997) §1001(a), the decision to become an LLP requires the same consent as is required for amending the partnership agreement. This partnership has no agreement as to amending the partnership agreement, so UPA (1997) §401(j) applies and requires unanimous consent. ◀◀◀

§17.2.3 Important Non-Uniform Provisions

Some states that have adopted UPA (1997) have nonuniform provisions explicitly stating that the liability shield does not protect a partner from liability for the partner's own misconduct or from liability for the misconduct of a person directly supervised by the partner. The former exception is unnecessary because an LLP shield by its terms addresses only a partner's liability *qua* partner for obligations *of the partnership*.[20] The latter exception is significant, however, because it goes beyond holding a partner liable for the partner's

---

and removes the liability shield. UPA (1997) §1003(c) and (d). However, revocation does not occur automatically. A specified public official must take action—giving the LLP "at least 60 days' written notice of intent to revoke the statement [of qualification]." UPA (1997) §1003(c). Even after revocation, a general partnership can retroactively regain its LLP status (and retroactively reestablish the LLP shield) by properly applying for "reinstatement" of the revoked statement of qualification. UPA (1997) §1003(e) and (f). Reinstatement nullifies the effect of revocation *ab initio* ("as if the revocation had never occurred"). UPA (1997) §1003(f). Subsection (f) does not expressly preserve the rights of third parties who may have relied on the revocation, but principles of estoppel will likely provide that protection.

19. UPA (1997) §306(c). As to why this provision makes special reference to contribution obligations, see Section 17.2.7.

20. See Section 17.2.5.

own misconduct. The "supervisee" exception appears not only to preserve a partner's liability *qua* partner for a partnership obligation resulting from a supervisee's misconduct but also to do so without even requiring the claimant to prove that the partner's supervision was negligent or otherwise deficient.

As to LLP provisions based not at all on UPA (1997), the principal variations are that:

- under a few statutes, the shield protects a partner only as to partnership obligations resulting from the malpractice or similar tort committed by a person other than the partner (leaving the partner liable *qua* partner for partnership obligations arising in any other way, including through contract);[21]
- many statutes expressly provide that the shield does not protect a partner from liability for the partner's own misconduct or from liability for the misconduct of a person directly supervised by the partner;[22]
- some statutes require each LLP to maintain specified levels of liability insurance;
- a few states require an LLP to renew its registration annually.

All these provisions are footprints from the early days of LLPs.[23]

§17.2.4 No Protection for the Partnership and No Effect on Partner's Own Misconduct

What is true for the LLC and corporate shields is equally true for the LLP shield. The LLP shield protects the partners, not the partnership; indeed, the entire point of the shield is to prevent the partnership's obligations from being automatically imputed to the partners. Also, the LLP shield does not protect against liability resulting from a partner's own conduct.

Example

Fencing, LLP is a UPA (1997) limited liability partnership, and Porthos is one of its partners. One day, while conducting the partnership's ordinary business and giving a fencing lesson to an individual student, Porthos becomes distracted by personal concerns. As a result, he negligently inflicts

21. Some of these statutes limit the shield protection to partnership obligations resulting from malpractice and other torts. Others provide protection against partnership obligations arising from all malpractice claims, regardless of whether the claim sounds in tort or contract.
22. These provisions have the same problems as noted for such provisions grafted onto uniform act LLP provisions.
23. See Section 17.2.1.

a leg wound on the student. The LLP shield is irrelevant to the student's tort claim against Porthos. The claim arises from Porthos's own misconduct and does not seek to impose on Porthos a partner's liability for an obligation of the partnership. Likewise, the shield is irrelevant to the student's UPA (1997) §305(a) claim against the partnership.[24] ◀◀◀

§17.2.5 Effects of LLP Status on the Partnership and of Dissolution on LLP Status

a. Becoming or Ceasing to Be an LLP

A limited liability partnership is a general partnership with an LLP shield. Donning or doffing the shield has considerable importance for the general partnership's partners but does not remake the underlying business organization. Whether that underlying organization is viewed as an aggregate or an entity:[25]

- the organization's becoming an LLP does not create a new partnership, and
- the organization's ceasing to be an LLP does not dissolve or terminate the existing partnership.[26]

b. Partnership Dissolution

Partnership dissolution has no effect on the partnership's LLP status. UPA (1997) makes this point explicitly,[27] but the same rule applies even under LLP provisions that lack comparable language. By definition, dissolution does not end a partnership,[28] so dissolution could affect the LLP only if statutory language were to so provide. No partnership statute contains any such language.

The situation is different, however, when a dissolved LLP winds up its business by transferring its assets, obligations, and operations to a successor general partnership. As explained in Chapter 11, for most purposes the

24. See Section 10.5.1.
25. On the entity/aggregate distinction, see Section 7.2.7.
26. As to an LLP formed under UPA (1997), see UPA (1997) §§201(b) and 1003(d) and UPA (1997) to RUPA §201.
27. UPA (1997) §1001(e). The comment expands on the point: "[L]imited liability partnership status remains even though a partnership may be dissolved, wound up, and terminated. Even after the termination of the partnership, the former partners of a terminated partnership would not be personally liable for partnership obligations incurred while the partnership was a limited liability partnership."
28. See Section 11.2.1(g).

transition can be and often is seamless.[29] However, the successor partnership is not the same organization as the dissolved partnership, which means that the successor partnership it *not* an LLP unless either: (i) the successor partnership itself files to become an LLP; or (ii) the LLP statute automatically transfers the dissolved partnership's LLP status to the successor partnership. Few, if any, LLP statutes provide for automatic transfer, and the transition to a successor partnership often occurs without the partners paying much attention or even recognizing that a transition is occurring. As a result, especially in UPA (1914), gaps in the shield seem likely.

Example

Jay, Alfred, and Proofrock are partners in a general partnership governed by the law of a state that has grafted LLP provisions onto UPA (1914). The partnership has filed the necessary document to be an LLP. On April 1, Jay decides to leave the partnership, and he, Alfred, and Proofrock informally agree that: (i) the business will continue without interruption; and (ii) Jay will be bought out at a specified price, payable in specified installments. No one thinks to do any paperwork other than a simple letter memorializing the buy-out arrangement. On May 5, a customer slips and falls while on the business's premises. On May 15, Alfred and Proofrock file the necessary document for their partnership to be an LLP. On May 20, a second customer slips and falls while on the business's premises. As to the tort claim of the first fallen customer, the partnership is not an LLP unless the LLP statute automatically transfers the LLP status of a dissolved partnership to a successor partnership. As to the second fallen customer, the partnership is an LLP regardless of whether the statute contains an automatic transfer provision. ◄◄◄

§17.2.6 When Partnership Obligations Are Incurred

Under UPA (1997 and 2013) §306(c), both apply the LLP shield to protect partners from vicarious liability for partnership obligations "incurred while the partnership is a limited liability partnership." If a general partnership is an LLP throughout its existence, the question of when a partnership obligation is "incurred" never arises in this context.[30] If the question does arise, the answer can be quite complex.

The "when incurred" language originated in UPA (1914) §17, which states the liability of a "person admitted as a partner into an existing partnership" for partnership obligations "incurred" before the partner's admission.

29. See Sections 11.4.3 and 11.4.4(b).
30. The question may be relevant to statute of limitation issues.

UPA (1997 and 2013) each replicate that approach in their respective sections 306(b).

None of the three acts provide statutory guidance on how to approach the "when incurred" question in regard to the LLP shield, but the comments to UPA (2013) §306(b) and (c) provide a careful analysis of when an obligation is incurred. The analysis begins in the comment to section 306(b):

> With regard to when a partnership incurs a debt, obligation, or other liability, the case law is scant and concerns only contractual and similar obligations. The leading case . . . holds that: (i) obligations on a loan, whether for interest or principal, are incurred when the loan is made, not when each particular payment is due; and (ii) obligations for lease payments are incurred when each rental payment is due, not when the lease is made. . . . As to when a partnership incurs a tort liability, the answer might be found by analogy to statute of limitation rules, another area of law concerned with when claims arise.

The analysis then shifts to the comment in section 306(c), in particular the part that addresses this question at length.[31] The subsection (c) analysis begins by differentiating the "when incurred" question under subsection (c) from the question under subsection (b):

> It could well be argued that "incurred" under subsection (c) has the same meaning as "incurred" under subsection (b). However, the argument should yield if the subsections' different contexts raise different issues of policy. . . .

The comment then asserts that one aspect of the analysis under subsection (b) is appropriate for the purposes of subsection (c):

> The case law [under subsection (b)] concerning contractual obligations (incurred when the contract is made) applies appropriately in the context of the LLP shield. However, the lease case law is problematic. If an obligation is incurred each time rent is due, subsection(c) is a trap for the unwary landlord.

Example

Ordinary general partnership enters into a lease with a commercial landlord. Knowing that each partner is automatically liable for the partnership's debt, the landlord does not obtain personal guarantees. Subsequently, the partnership becomes an LLP. If future rent payments are incurred when due, and not as of when the lease was made, the landlord loses a very important part of the bargain. ◄◄◄

31. UPA (2013) §306(c), The Temporal Nexus—When Claim Incurred.

Thus, for the purposes of subsection (c), lease obligations should be treated as contractual obligations, incurred when the contract is made.

The comment then addresses the "when incurred" question as applied to a partnership's tort obligations:

> Courts must look to when the conduct causing the injury takes place and not to when actual injury occurs. Otherwise, a partnership could: (i) engage in wrongful conduct that does not cause immediate injury; (ii) come to realize that the conduct has occurred; (iii) subsequently file a statement of qualification; (iv) thereby become an LLP; and (v) thereby eliminate the vicarious liability of its partners for all harm subsequently arising from the misconduct. . . .
>
> In general, courts should determine the "incurred" question under subsection (c) so that the LLP shield protects the partners of an LLP to the same extent that the corporate and LLC shields protect corporate shareholders and LLC members. From that perspective, LLP status obtained after a partnership commits a wrongful act should provide no greater protection for the partners than a sole proprietor obtains by forming an LLC after committing a wrongful act – i.e., none.

§17.2.7 The Contribution Conundrum

In an ordinary general partnership, partners share losses *inter se*, and both UPA (1914) and UPA (1997) require partners to contribute to the partnership so as to effectuate that loss sharing.[32] Many partnership agreements also establish contribution obligations among the partners, sometimes merely replicating and sometimes varying the statutory default rules.

In the context of an LLP, however, contribution is problematic. A partner's obligation to contribute to the benefit of a fellow partner translates, as a practical matter, into a liability to a creditor of the LLP.

Example

Fencing, LLP is a limited liability partnership governed by UPA (1997), and Porthos is one of its partners. He and his copartners, Aramis and Athos, share profits and losses equally. One day, while conducting the partnership's ordinary business and giving a fencing lesson to an individual student, Porthos

32. UPA (1914) §18 states: "Each partner . . . must contribute toward the losses . . . sustained by the partnership according to his state in the profits." See also UPA (1997) §40(a)(II) (a dissolved partnership's assets include the partners' respective contribution obligations). UPA (1997) §807(b) provides that, following a partnership's dissolution: "A partner shall contribute to the partnership an amount equal to any excess of the charges over the credits in the partner's account. . . ." This aspect of UPA (2013) may require revision and is currently under study by the Joint Editorial Board on Uniform Unincorporated Organization Acts ("JEBUUOA"). (The author of this book serves as Research Director for the JEBUUOA.)

becomes distracted by personal concerns. As a result, he negligently inflicts a serious leg wound on the student. The student successfully sues both Porthos and the partnership for $90,000. The partnership has no funds to pay the judgment, and—because the partnership is an LLP—the partners are not, merely on account of partner status, responsible for the partnership's obligation to the student.

Porthos, however, is directly liable for his own negligence. Porthos also has a claim against the partnership for $90,000 in indemnification.[33] If the partnership cannot meet that indemnification obligation, Porthos has suffered a loss in the conduct of the partnership business. If Aramis and Athos are obliged to contribute to the partnership so as to equalize the loss among the three partners, that obligation effectively defeats the purpose of the LLP liability shield. Assuming for the sake of simplicity that there are no other losses to be shared among the partners, Aramis and Athos will each have to contribute $30,000 to the partnership, and the resulting $60,000 will in theory be available to Porthos but in practice will be garnered by the student as a judgment creditor of Porthos, the partnership, or both.[34] ◄◄◄

UPA (1997) pays considerable attention to this issue, and sections 306(c), 807(b), 807(c), and 1001(b) each specifically refer to a partner's contribution obligations. Section 1001(b) links the consent necessary to become an LLP to the consent necessary to amend any partnership agreement provisions pertaining to contribution.[35] Section 807(b) and (c) each make a partner's contribution obligations subject to Section 306(c), which shields an LLP's partner from liability *qua* partner for a partnership obligation, whether a claim is asserted "directly or indirectly, by way of contribution or otherwise." Section 306(c) even overrides contribution obligations that the partners may have chosen to state in their partnership agreement before the partnership became an LLP.

As a result of these provisions:

- The loss-sharing provisions of UPA (1997) remain intact *as to capital losses suffered by the partners;*
- The contribution provisions of UPA (1997) will never create a hole in the LLP shield; and

---

33. "In case of partner misconduct, section 401(c) sets forth a partnership's obligation to indemnify the culpable partner where the partner's liability was incurred in the ordinary course of the partnership's business." UPA (1997) §306, comment 3. See Section 8.4.

34. UPA (1997) §807(f) provides: "An assignee for the benefit of creditors of a partnership or a partner, or a person appointed by a court to represent creditors of a partnership or a partner, may enforce a partner's obligation to contribute to the partnership."

35. The link is a default rule. If the partnership agreement contains no provision pertaining to contribution, or if the partnership agreement does not provide an amendment mechanism specific to the agreement's provisions on contribution, §1001(b) links to the consent mechanism generally applicable for amending the partnership agreement.

- a partnership agreement's provisions on contribution will jeopardize the shield only if adopted or reaffirmed after the general partnership becomes an LLP.

§17.2.8 Piercing the Veil

Although only a few LLP statutes specifically contemplate the doctrine of "piercing the veil," piercing will nonetheless be part of the law applicable to LLPs. Piercing is, after all, an equitable doctrine that originated and exists in the corporate realm as "exclusively a case law phenomenon."[36] That case law has already helped establish the piercing doctrine as part of the law of limited liability companies,[37] and there is every reason to expect the same phenomenon with LLPs.[38]

§17.3 LIMITED LIABILITY LIMITED PARTNERSHIPS

§17.3.1 Origins and Current Availability

Like LLPs, LLLPs began in Texas. In 1993, Texas amended its general and limited partnership statutes to permit a limited partnership to invoke the LLP provisions of the general partnership statute and thereby become a registered limited liability limited partnership.[39] Several other states promptly followed Texas, and over the next decade the following pattern developed:

1. Several states expressly permitted a limited partnership to invoke the LLP provisions of the state's general partnership statue.[40]

36. Bishop & Kleinberger on Limited Liability Companies §§ 6:37–6:64
37. See Section 16.1.
38. Bishop & Kleinberger on Limited Liability Companies §§ 6:37–6:64. See *Hayes v. Mingo Props. LLP*, 2025-Ohio-378, ¶ 22 ("This court, . . . is unable to locate any supporting authority where this concept [of piercing the LLP veil] has been applied to limited liability partnerships. Assuming, without deciding, that the veil of an LLP can be pierced, we find that Hayes's complaint failed to set forth sufficient facts that would provide a legitimate basis to pierce the Partnership's veil.")

The case for piercing is, if anything, stronger for most LLPs than for corporations and limited liability companies, because, unlike corporate and LLC statutes, LLP statutes other than UPA (2013) lack any provisions imposing liability either on owners or managers for distributions that left the entity insolvent or that were otherwise improper.
39. Bishop & Kleinberger on Limited Liability Companies, §15.01[4] at 15–18.
40. Most such statues refer to "limited liability limited partnerships" but a few lump both general and limited partnership under the term "limited liability partnership." See, e.g., Ariz. Rev. Stat. §29–308(C), Ga. Code §14–8–2(6.1). For simplicity's sake, this book uses the term "limited liability limited partnership" and the abbreviation "LLLP." 17.

2. A few states provided for LLLPs directly, solely through language in the limited partnership statute.
3. A few states expressly precluded a limited partnership from being an LLLP.
4. Most state partnership statutes did not expressly address the issue.

As to the first and second categories, by 2002 more than 15 states had authorized the existence of limited liability limited partnerships, although at least initially in a few of these states the LLP shield protected only general and not limited partners.[41]

As to the fourth category, despite the statutory silence, it is possible to argue "based on the language of the UPA, RUPA, and RULPA" that a limited partnership may invoke the LLP provisions of its state's general partnership act, at least to provide a liability shield for the limited partnership's general partners.[42]

In 2001, the ULC promulgated its new Uniform Limited Partnership Act and sought to bring clarity, simplicity, and uniformity to this issue. ULPA (2001):

- defines a limited liability limited partnership simply as "a limited partnership whose certificate of limited partnership states that the limited partnership is a limited liability limited partnership";[43]
- requires the certificate of limited partnership of each limited partnership to state "whether the limited partnership is a limited liability limited partnership";[44]
- uses essentially verbatim the language of RUPA's *LLP* shield to establish a full corporate and LLC-like *LLLP* shield;[45]
- eliminates the "control rule" and provides a full corporate and LLC-like liability shield for all limited partners regardless of whether the limited partnership is an LLLP.[46]

As of this writing, almost 20 states and the District of Columbia have adopted either ULPA (2001) or ULPA (2013).

---

41. See Bishop & Kleinberger on Limited Liability Companies, §15.03[3][b] at 15–73 to 15–74. As explained in section
12.2.3, in an ordinary limited partnership a limited partner's regular liability shield is subject to the "control rule," which in some circumstances exposes a limited partner to personal liability for a limited partnership obligation. If an LLLP shield applies to a limited partner, the shield overrides and renders moot the control rule.
42. See Bishop & Kleinberger on Limited Liability Companies, §15.03[2] at 15–70 for a detailed explanation.
43. ULPA (2001) §102(9).
44. ULPA (2001) §201(a)(4).
45. ULPA (2001) §404(c).
46. ULPA (2001) §303.

§17.3.2 Name Requirements

Like the name of an LLP, the name of an LLLP must include specified phrases or abbreviations so as to designate the limited partnership's special status. The designator requirements vary depending on whether the relevant statute refers to limited liability limited partnerships or, instead, treats an LLLP as merely a subset of LLPs. ULPA (2001) provides:

> The name of a limited partnership that is not a limited liability limited partnership must contain the phrase "limited partnership" or the abbreviation "L.P." or "LP" and may not contain the phrase "limited liability limited partnership" or the abbreviation "LLLP" or "L.L.L.P." The name of a limited liability limited partnership must contain the phrase "limited liability limited partnership" or the abbreviation "LLLP" or "L.L.L.P." and must not contain the abbreviation "L.P." or "L.P."[47]

§17.3.3 Piercing and Dividend Recapture

An LLLP provides a full, corporate and LLC-like liability shield. There is no reason why this shield should be immune from the equitable doctrine of piercing the veil.[48]

As to distribution recapture, most current LLLP provisions rest either on ULPA (2001) or the RULPA, each of which provides for the recapture of wrongfully made distributions.[49] The shield is inapposite to a partner's recapture liability, because the liability is not asserted "solely" on account of partner status. In this respect, LLLPs are less protective than LLPs, which typically do not provide for distribution recapture.[50]

Problem 134

Fezzik, Vincini, and Buttercup are partners in an ordinary general partnership governed by UPA (1997). Fezzik is a very wealthy individual, while Buttercup has only modest means and Vincini is nearly judgment proof. The partnership agreement: (i) names Fezzik as "managing partner"; (ii)

---

47. ULPA (2001) §108(b) and (c). ULPA (2013) §108 is identical.

48. For an explanation of this point in the context of LLPs, see Section 17.2.8. For a discussion of the factors courts use in determining piercing claims, see Section 13.5.7.

49. See Section 12.2.3. ULPA (2001) §§508 and 509 take a more corporate-like approach but nonetheless retain some recapture exposure.

50. The Harmonization Project, seeing no rational basis for the distinction, has sought to end it. See UPA (1997) (Last Amended 2013) §407 ("Liability for Improper Distributions in a Limited Liability Partnership").

authorizes him to make all decisions on behalf of the partnership that pertain to "ordinary operations and activities"; (iii) allocates profits 65 percent to Fezzik, 20 percent to Buttercup, and 15 percent to Vincini; (iv) requires unanimous consent of the partners to amend the partnership agreement; and (v) does not mention the idea of a limited liability partnership. Does Fezzik have the authority, either as managing partner under the partnership agreement or as the owner of a majority of the profits interests, to cause the partnership to become an LLP? ◄ ◄ ◄

Explanation

No. Under UPA (1997) §1001(b), unless the partnership agreement provides otherwise, the decision to file a statement of qualification requires the same quantum of consent as an amendment to the partnership agreement. This partnership agreement does not address becoming an LLP but does require unanimous consent for an amendment. Fezzik's role as managing partner and his ownership of 65 percent of the profits interests are both irrelevant. ◄ ◄ ◄

Problem 135

Same facts as Problem 134, plus the following: Fezzik suggests to Buttercup and Vincini that the partnership become an LLP. Buttercup readily agrees, but Vincini refuses. Vincini says to Fezzik, "You're going to have to make it worth my while to get my agreement. The shield doesn't much matter to me. They can't get blood from a stone. But you, Mr. Moneybags, you've got a lot to lose. If you want my agreement, you'll have to transfer me 5 percent of the profits." Does Fezzik have any claim against Vincini? ◄ ◄ ◄

Explanation

Possibly. Fezzik might succeed with a claim that Vincini has breached the obligation of good faith and fair dealing stated in UPA (1997) §404(d). Fezzik would characterize Vincini as withholding consent solely for the purpose of extorting a transfer from Fezzik. Vincini would invoke UPA (1997) §404(e) and argue that he is *entitled* to engage in "conduct [that] further [his] own interests." Fezzik would respond that:

1. UPA (1997) §404(e) in its entirety provides that "A partner does not violate a duty or obligation under this [Act] or the partnership agreement *merely* because the partner's conduct furthers the partner's own interest" (emphasis added);

2. more is involved here than mere self-interest;
3. LLP status could in no way prejudice Vincini, and Vincini was not protecting any legitimate self-interest by refusing his consent; and
4. Vincini was, in fact, using his veto power and Fezzik's concern about personal liability to coerce Fezzik. ◀ ◀ ◀

Index

Index

www.ingramcontent.com/pod-product-compliance
Lightning Source LLC
LaVergne TN
LVHW082001200926
848481LV00010B/2783

* 9 7 9 8 8 9 2 0 7 9 4 6 4 *